Ultra Wideband

edited by

Boris Lembrikov

Ultra Wideband

Edited by Boris Lembrikov

Republished by InTech

Janeza Trdine 9, 51000 Rijeka, Croatia

Publishing Process Manager Iva Lipovic

Technical Editor Goran Bajac

Cover Designer Martina Sirotic

Additional hard copies can be obtained from orders@intechopen.com

Ultra Wideband, Edited by Boris Lembrikov
p. cm.
ISBN 978-953-307-139-8

For EU product safety concerns:
IN TECH d.o.o., Prolaz Marije Krucifikse Kozulić 3, 51000 Rijeka, Croatia,
info@intechopen.com or visit our website at intechopen.com.

Meet the editor

Boris I. Lembrikov is a senior lecturer at the Faculty of Electronics, Electrical and Communication Engineering of the Holon Institute of Technology (HIT), Holon, Israel. B. I. Lembrikov received his Ph.D. in Nonlinear Optics at the Technion – Israel Institute of Technology in 1996. Since then he was an invited researcher at the Haifa University, at the Max Planck Institute High Magnetic Field Laboratory at Grenoble, France, at the Technion, Haifa, Israel. Dr. B. I. Lembrikov is an author of the book \Electrodynamics of Magnetoactive Media\, a number of chapters in scientific books, a large number of papers in international peer reviewed journals and reports delivered at the international scientific conferences. He actively participated in a number of research projects concerning optics of nanoparticles, optical communications, UWB communications. The main research fields of interest of Dr. B. I. Lembrikov are nonlinear optics, optical and UWB communications, nanostructures, quantum dot lasers.

Contents

Preface

Ultra wideband (UWB) radar systems were first developed as a military tool due to their enhanced capability to penetrate through obstacles and ultra high precision ranging at the centimeter level. Recently, UWB technology has been focused on consumer electronics and communications. The UWB technology development was enhanced in 2002 due to the Federal Communication Commission (FCC) definition of a spectral mask allowing operation of UWB radios at the noise floor over a huge bandwidth up to 7.5 GHz. According to the FCC decision, the unlicensed frequency band between 3.1 and 10.6 GHz is reserved for indoor UWB wireless communication systems. UWB technology is used in wireless communications, networking, radar, wireless personal area networks (WPAN), imaging, positioning systems, etc. UWB systems are characterized by low power, low cost, very high data rates, precise positioning capability and low interference. The UWB also improves a channel capacity due to its large bandwidth. UWB systems have a low power spectral density (PSD) and consequently can coexist with cellular systems, wireless local area networks (WLAN) and global positioning systems (GPS). Unfortunately, the UWB communication transmission distances are limited due to the FCC constraints on allowed emission levels. Recently a novel approach based on the UWB radio-over- optical fiber (UROOF) technology has been proposed combining the advantages of the fiber optic communications and UWB technology. UROOF technology increases the transmission distance up to several hundred meters.

The objective of this book, consisting of 19 chapters, is to review the state-of-the-art and novel trends in UWB technology. The book can be divided into three parts.

The first part of the book, consisting of Chapters 1-7, is related to the fundamentals of UWB communications and operation performance of UWB systems.

In Chapter 1 the background of UWB, basic UWB characteristics, advantages and benefits of UWB communications, architecture of typical UWB transceiver are discussed.

In Chapter 2 the influence of UWB interference on different types of receivers operating in microcells is investigated.

In Chapter 3 the UWB frequency multiplexing techniques implementations based on printed circuit board technologies are presented.

In Chapter 4 a novel approach for the evaluation of the UWB system performance including an additive white Gaussian noise channel is proposed.

In Chapter 5 the analog optical link for UWB signal transmission is analyzed in detail, and it is shown that the quantum dot devices can improve its performance.

In Chapter 6 the performance of UWB localization technologies is investigated. A methodology for autonomous end-to-end navigation of mobile wireless robots for automated construction applications is presented.

In Chapter 7 the UWB pulse propagation through different kinds of lossy, dispersive and layered media is discussed.

The second part of the book, consisting of Chapters 8-14, concerns the design and implementation of different UWB elements, such as UWB oscillators, transceivers and passive components.

In Chapter 8 the UWB pulse generators architectures are presented and compared. Design issues are discussed.

In Chapter 9 the analysis and design of integrated oscillator circuits for UWB applications are presented.

In Chapter 10 the UWB CMOS low noise amplifiers design and implementation are described.

In Chapter 11 the analysis of microstrip and coplanar waveguide (CPW) UWB circuits such as transitions, filters, directional couplers and antennas is presented.

In Chapter 12 the implementation and analysis of the impulse radio (IR) UWB filter bank based receiver are presented.

In Chapter 13 the design, fabrication and measurement of the key passive components such as antennas, filters, shaping networks, inverters, power combiners and splitters for UWB communications are presented.

In Chapter 14 the UWB radar system and the corresponding algorithms for the detection and localization of trapped people are developed. Finally, in the third part of the book, consisting of Chapters 15-19, development of novel microstrip UWB antennas is reviewed.

In Chapter 15 the printed UWB monopole antennas, slot antennas, notched band antennas are proposed and thoroughly investigated.

In Chapter 16 an overview of UWB antennas is presented and singularities of UWB antennas are discussed.

In Chapter 17 the concept and design of a novel planar super wideband (SWB) are reported.

In Chapter 18 a novel electrically, physically and functionally small UWB antenna is proposed.

In Chapter 19 a small compact T slots UWB antenna is presented.

We believe that this book will attract the interest of engineers and researchers occupied in the field of UWB communications and improve their knowledge of the contemporary technologies and future perspectives.

August 2010,

Editor

Boris Lembrikov
Holon Institute of Technology (HIT),
P.O. Box 305, 58102, 52 Golomb Str., Holon
Israel

Ultra wideband preliminaries

M A Matin
North South University
Bangladesh

1. Introduction

"Ultra-wideband technology holds great promise for a vast array of new applications that have the potential to provide significant benefits for public safety, businesses and consumers in a variety of applications such as radar imaging of objects buried under the ground or behind walls and short-range, high-speed data transmission" [FCC,2002]

This quote focuses the level of importance of UWB technology as its applications are various. The FCC outlined possible applications of this technology such as imaging systems, ground penetrating radar (GPR) systems, wall-imaging systems, through-wall imaging systems, medical systems, surveillance systems, vehicular radar systems and communications and measurements systems. The spectrum allocation for UWB is in the range from 1.99 GHz- 10.6 GHz, 3.1 GHz- 10.6 GHz, or below 960 MHz depending on the particular application [FCC,2002]. The global interest in this technology is huge especially in communications environment due to the potential delivery of ultra high speed data transmission, coexistence with existing electrical systems (due to the extremely low power spectrum density) with low power consumption using a low cost one-chip implementation. There are many advantages and benefits of UWB systems as shown in Table 1 over narrowband technologies. Therefore, with the approval of FCC regulations for UWB, several universities and companies have jumped into the realm of UWB research [Nokia, 2006].

Advantage	Benefit
Coexistence with current narrowband and wideband radio services	Avoids expensive licensing fees
Huge data rate	High bandwidth can support real-time high definition video streaming
Low transmit power	Provides low probability of detection and intercept.
Resistance to jamming	Reliable to hostile environments
High performance in multipath channel	Delivers higher signal strengths in adverse conditions
Simple transceiver architecture	Enables ultra-low power, smaller form factor at a reduced cost

Table 1. Advantages and benefits of UWB communication

UWB offers many advantages over narrowband technology where certain applications are involved. Improved channel capacity is one of the major advantages of UWB. The channel is the RF spectrum within which information is transferred. Shannon's capacity limit equation shows capacity increasing as a function of BW (bandwidth) faster than as a function of SNR (signal to noise ratio).

$$C = BW * \log_2(1 + SNR) \tag{1}$$

C = Channel Capacity (bits/sec)
BW = Channel Bandwidth (Hz)
SNR= Signal to noise ratio.

SNR = P/ (BW*N_0)
P = Received Signal Power (watts)
N_0= Noise Power Spectral Density (watts/Hz)

The above Shannon's equation shows that increasing channel capacity requires a linear increase in bandwidth while similar channel capacity increases would require exponential increases in power. This is why, UWB technology is capable of transmitting very high data rates using very low power. It is important to notice that UWB can provide dramatic channel capacity only at limited range which is shown in Fig. 1. This is due mainly to the low power levels mandated by the FCC for legal UWB operation. UWB technology is most useful in short-range (less than 10 meters) high speed applications. Longer-range flexibility is better served by WLAN applications such as 802.11a, whose narrowband radio might occupy a BW of 20 MHz with a transmit power level of 100 mW. The power mask, as defined for UWB by the FCC, allows up to –41.3 dBm/MHz (75 nW). From Fig. 2, it is observed that the emitted signal power can't interfere with current signals even at short propagation distances since it appears as noise.

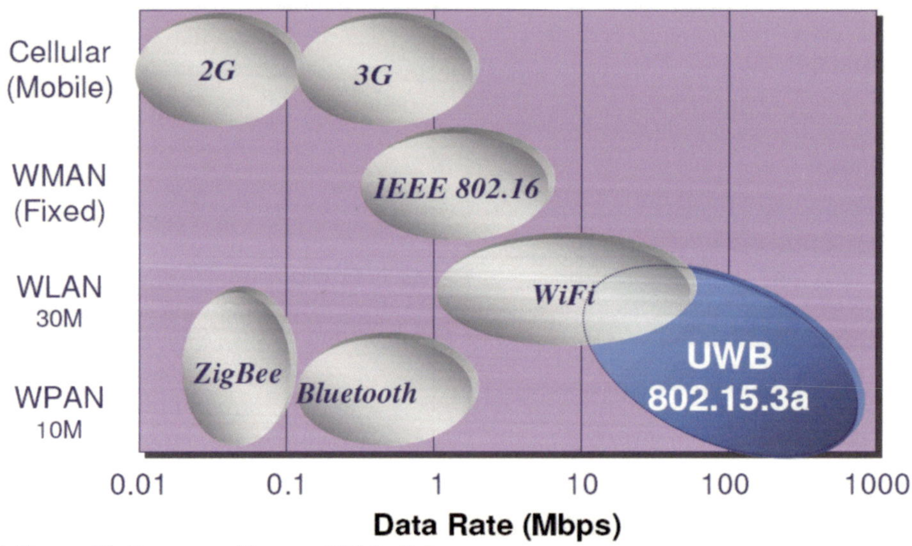

Fig. 1. Range Vs Data rate [Source WiMedia]

Fig. 3 and Fig. 4 show the typical "narrowband" and "UWB" transceiver. UWB radios can provide lower cost architectures than narrow band radios. Narrow band architectures use high quality oscillators and tuned circuits to modulate and de-modulate information. UWB transmitters, however, can directly modulate a base-band signal eliminating components and reducing requirements on tuned circuitry. On the other hand, UWB receivers may require more complex architectures and may take advantage of digital signal processing techniques. Reducing the need for high quality passively based circuits and implementing sophisticated digital signal processing techniques through integration with the low cost CMOS processes will enable radio solutions that scale in cost/performance with digital technology [Intel,2002].

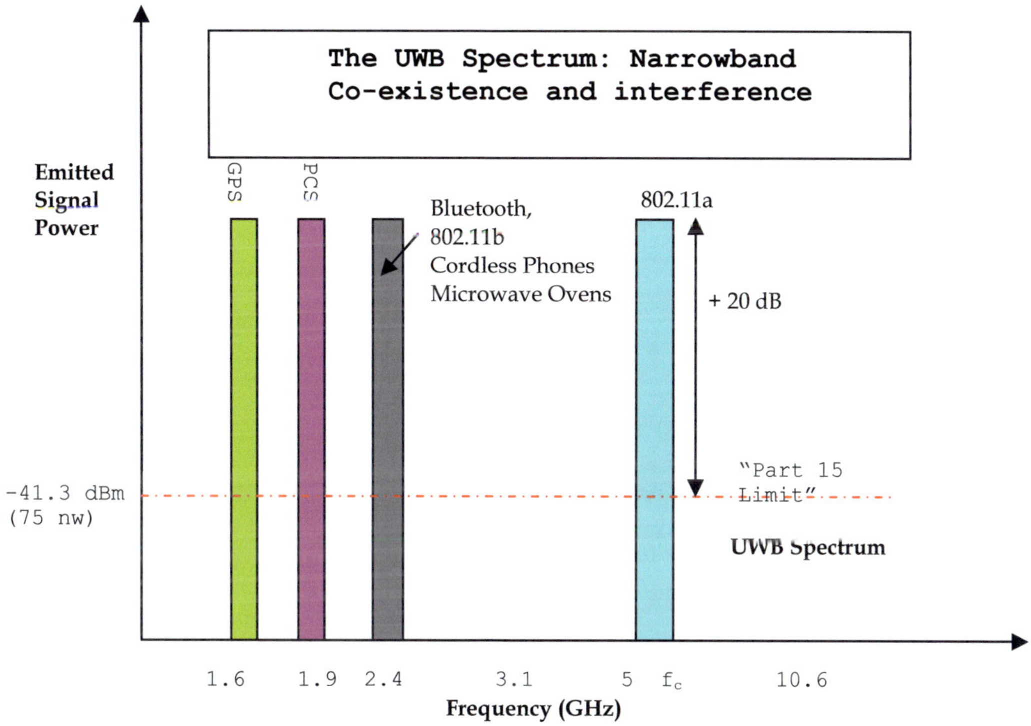

Fig. 2. Emitted signal power vs. Frequency

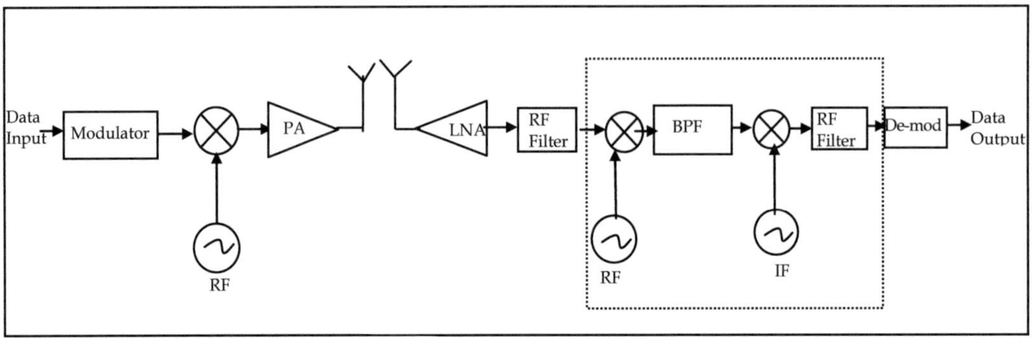

Fig. 3. Typical "narrowband" Transceiver Architecture

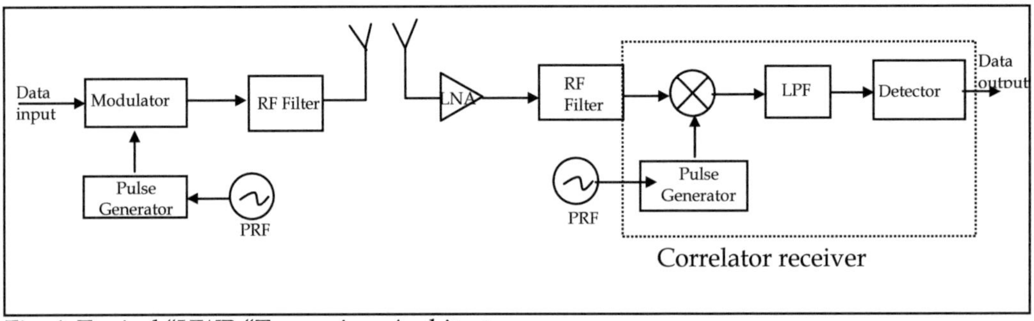

Fig. 4. Typical "UWB "Transceiver Architecture

Another key advantage of UWB is its robustness to fading and interference. Fading can be caused when random multipath reflections are received out of phase causing a reduction in the amplitude of the original signal. The wideband nature of UWB reduces the effect of random time varying amplitude fluctuations. Short pulses prevent destructive interference from multipath that can cause fade margin in link budgets. However, another important advantage with UWB technology is that multipath components can be resolved and used to actually improve signal reception. UWB also promises more robust rejection to co-channel interference and narrowband jammers showing a greater ability to overlay spectrum presently used by narrowband solutions.

2. Background of UWB

The history of interest in UWB dates back to the 1960´s. Terms used for the concept were "nonsinusoidal," "baseband," "impulse radio," and "carrier free signals." The origin of this technology stems from work in time-domain-electromagnetics in the early 1960s which describes the transient behaviour of certain classes of microwave networks by examining their characteristic, i.e. their impulse response [Multispectral solution Inc.,2001].

Time-domain electromagnetics would have probably remained a mathematical and laboratory curiosity, however, had it not occurred that these techniques could also be applied to the measurement of wide-band radiating antenna [Ross,1968]. However, unlike a microwave circuit such as microstrip filter, in which the response to an impulsive voltage excitation could be measured in circuit, the impulse excitation of an antenna results in the generation of an electromagnetic field that must be detected and measured remotely. The time-domain sampling oscilloscope, with an external wide-band antenna and amplifier, was used to perform this remote measurement. It became immediately obvious that one can now have the rudiments for the construction of an impulse radar or communications system [Bennet et al., 1978].

The term "UWB" was not adopted until approximately 1989. Prior to this Harmuth conducted revolutionary work in the late 1960´s [Harmuth,1968; 1984; 1979; 1977 ;1972, 1977; 1981; Harmuth et al., 1983]. In the early 1970s, hardware likes the avalanche transistor and tunnel diode detectors were constructed in attempts to detect these very short duration signals, which enabled real system development. The arrival of the sampling oscilloscope further aided in system development. During the 1970´s, evolution and research into UWB often focused towards radar systems, which needed to be enhanced with better resolution [Black,1992; Hussain, 1996; 1998; Immoreev et al.,1995]. This demand required wider bandwidth. At this time extensive research was conducted in the former Soviet Union by researchers like Astanin, and in China as well [Astanin et al., 1992]. Taylor has published some material based on research in the United States from this period [Taylor, 1995]. In 1978, Bennett and Ross wrote a summary of time-domain electromagnetics [Bennett et al., 1978]. At about this time, efforts using carrier-free radio for communication purposes were started. During the last decade, the military has begun to support initiatives for developing commercial applications. These commercial applications, and the evolution of increasingly faster digital circuits, have led to the development of inexpensive hardware. The possibility of producing low cost units, and unlicensed use, has recently boosted the interest in UWB.

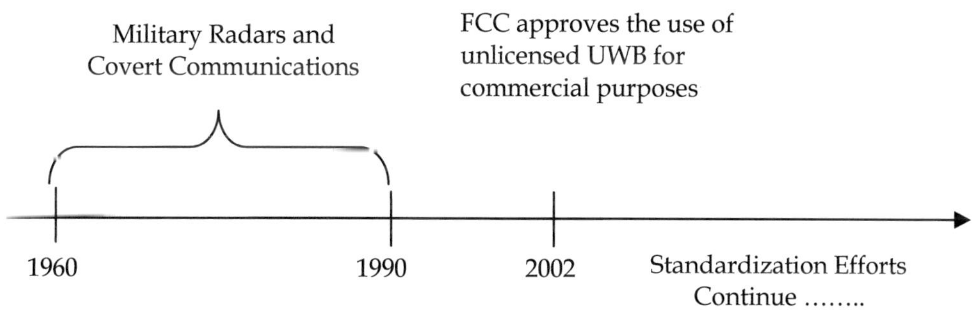

Fig. 5. UWB trend

3. UWB Characteristics

3.1 Introduction

UWB technology has been mainly used for radar-based applications [Taylor, 1995] due to wideband nature of the signal resulting in very accurate timing information. Additionally, due to recent developments, UWB technology has also been of considerable interest in communication demanding low probability of intercept (LPI) and detection (LPD), multipath immunity, high data throughput, precision ranging and localization.

Multipath propagation is one of the most significant obstacles when radio frequency (RF) techniques are used indoors. Since UWB waveforms are of such short time duration, they are relatively immune to multipath degradation effects as observed in mobile and in-building environments. Thus, UWB has gained recent attention and has been identified as a possible solution to a wide range of RF problems. For example, in communication systems, UWB pulses can be used to provide extremely high data rate performance in multi-user network applications. Additionally, UWB applications can co-exist with narrowband services over the same [[Multispectral solution Inc.,2001]

3.2 Definition of UWB Technology

UWB signals can be defined as signals having a fractional bandwidth of at least 25% of the center frequency or those occupying 1.5 GHz or more of the spectrum. Fractional bandwidth B_f is defined as:-

$$B_f = 2\frac{f_h - f_l}{f_h + f_l} \tag{2}$$

Where, B_f = Fractional bandwidth (Hertz)

f_h = The highest -10 dB frequency point of the signal spectrum

f_l = The lowest -10 dB frequency point of the signal spectrum

UWB is a wireless technology for transmitting digital data over a wide spectrum with very low power and has the ability to carry huge amounts of data over short distances at very low power. In addition, UWB has the ability to carry signals through doors and other obstacles. Instead of traditional carrier wave modulation, UWB transmitters broadcast digital pulses that are precisely timed on a signal spread across a wide spectrum. The transmitter and receiver must be synchronized to send and receive pulses with accuracies approaching picoseconds. The basic concept is to develop, transmit and receive an extremely short duration burst of RF energy, typically a few tens of picoseconds to a few nanoseconds in duration. The UWB advantage rests in its ability to spread the signal energy across a wide bandwidth.

4. UWB spectrum issues

There are many organizations and government entities around the world that set rules and recommendations for UWB usage. The structure of international radio-communication regulatory bodies can be grouped into international, regional, and national levels. At the regional level, the Asia-Pacific Telecommunity (APT) is an international body that sets recommendations and guidelines of telecommunications in the Asia-Pacific region. The European Conference of Postal & Telecommunications Administrations (CEPT) has created a task group under the Electronic Communications Committee (ECC) to draft a proposal regarding the use of UWB for Europe. At the national level, the USA was the first country to legalize UWB for commercial use. In the UK, the regulatory body, called the Office of Communications (Ofcom), opened a consultation on UWB matters in January 2005. All the regulatory bodies set rules for protection of existing radio devices and keep UWB out of their frequency range.

4.1 FCC Regulation

The Federal Communications Commission (FCC) has the power to regulate the emission limit of Ultra-Wideband (UWB) transmissions. Due to the wideband nature of UWB emissions, it could potentially interfere with other licensed bands in the frequency domain if left unregulated. It's a fine line that the FCC must walk in order to satisfy the need for more efficient methods of utilizing the available spectrum, as represented by UWB, while not causing undue interference to those currently occupying the spectrum, as represented by those users owning licenses to certain frequency bands. In general, the FCC is interested in making the most of the available spectrum as well as trying to foster competition among different technologies. The first FCC report has come on 14th Feb., 2002. They placed restriction on the allowed UWB emission spectrums. For ground penetrating radar (GPR) they required that emissions be below 960 MHz and for UWB vehicular radar, the FCC restricted the -10dB bandwidth to 22-29 GHz. There are a number of key points to the related emission regulations (US 47 CFR Part 15(f)). To avoid inadvertent jamming of existing systems such as GPS satellite signals, the lowest band edge for UWB for communication is set at 3.1 GHz, with the highest at 10.6 GHz. Within this operational band, emission must be below –43 dBm/MHz EIRP- a limit the FCC has stated to be conservative, which is shown in Fig. 6.

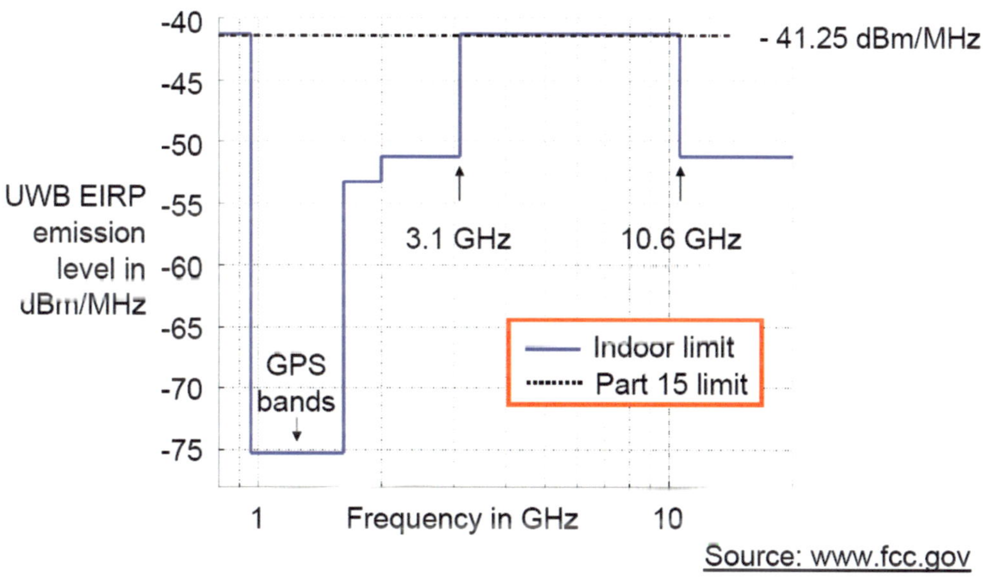

Fig. 6. UWB EIPR Emission level vs. Frequency

Following Part 15 of the FCC rules for radiated emission of unlicensed intentional radiators (such as garage door openers, cordless telephones, wireless microphones, etc., which depend on intended radio signals to perform their jobs) and unlicensed unintentional radiators (devices such as computers and TV receivers, all of which may generate radio signals as part of their operation, but aren't intended to transmit them), is divided into two classes A and B depending on the environment. Class A explains the limits related to digital devices that are marketed for use in commercial and industrial environments. The more restrictive class B explains the limits related to devices used in residential environments, as well as, commercial and industrial environments. These emissions are defined in terms of microvolts per meter (uV/m), representing the electric field strength of the radiator as

$$P = \frac{E_o^2 4\pi R^2}{\eta} \tag{3}$$

Where, E_0 = Electric field strength (V/m)

R = Radius of the sphere (meters)

η = Characteristic impedance of vacuum (377 Ω)

The FCC Part 15.209 rules limit the emissions for intentional radiators to 500 uV/m measured at a distance of 3 meters in a 1MHz bandwidth for frequencies greater than 960 MHz. This corresponds to an emitted power spectral density of -41.3 dBm/MHz. Levels for class A and B under part 15 are given in Table 2.

Class	Limits (mV/m)
A	300@ 10 m
B	500@ 3 m

Table 2. Electric field strength under part 15

4.2 Interference problem and Ofcom (Office of Communication) regulation

There are many factors which affect how UWB impacts other "narrowband" systems, including spatial separation between devices, channel propagation losses, modulation techniques, the UWB Pulse Repetition Frequency (PRF), and the "narrowband" receiver antenna gain in the direction of the UWB transmitter [Intel,2001]. For example, a UWB system that sends impulses at a constant rate (PRF) with no modulation causes spikes in the frequency domain that are separated by the PRF. Adding either amplitude modulation or time dithering (i.e., slightly changing the time the impulses are transmitted) results in spreading the spectrum of the UWB emission to look more flat. As a result, the interference caused by a UWB transmitter can be viewed as a wideband interferer, and it has the effect of raising the noise floor of a "narrowband" receiver.

There are three main points to consider when looking at wideband interference [Intel, 2001] . First, if UWB complies with the Part 15 power spectral density requirements, its emissions are no worse than other devices regulated by this same standard, including computers and other electronic devices. Second, interference studies need to consider "typical usage scenarios" for the interaction between UWB and other devices. Third, FCC restrictions are only a beginning. Further coordination through standards participation may be necessary to come up with coexistence methods for operational scenarios that are important for the industry. For example, if UWB is to be used as Personal Area Network (PAN) technology in close proximity to an 802.11a Local Area Network (LAN), then the UWB system must be designed in such a manner as to peacefully coexist with the LAN. This can be achieved through industry involvement and standards participation, as well as, by careful design. As over the designated UWB band, the existing wireless LAN operating (5.15-5.35) GHz and (5.725-5.825) GHz band, causes significant interference with UWB operations. Office of Communication, UK (Ofcom) consultants have considered the impact of regulation of UWB PAN applications under the alternative regulatory scenarios [Ofcom, 2005] – out of the 3 to 10 GHz frequency band, and UWB PAN transmissions is restricted to a lower band (3-5 GHz) and an upper band (6-10 GHz).

5. UWB signal

More popular used UWB signals are the Gaussian pulse, Gaussian doublet, Gaussian monopulse (derivative of Gaussian), Mexican hat (2nd derivative of Gaussian), Morlet (modulated Gaussian), Rayleigh, Laplacian, prolate spherical wave functions and Hermite families of waveforms [Allen et al.,2004]. The design of these signals for emission control is important. The pulse length, rise time of the leading edge of the pulse, and the pass-band of radiating antenna determine signal bandwidth and spectral shape, while the pulse shape determines its centre frequency. Gating, pulse repetition rate, modulation and selection of dithering code are other factors that determine overall waveform shape.

6. Technology basics and how it works?

UWB wireless technologies spread a signal over an incredibly wide bandwidth like spread-spectrum and orthogonal frequency-division multiplexing (OFDM) at very low power. This offers the following four benefits:-

First, due to broadband characteristics, ultra-wideband wireless technologies are better in applications that experience multipath propagation problems because the wider the bandwidth, the better the resistance to reflections and related propagation problems.

Second, with wideband wireless, many signals can be placed on top of one another, creating a form of multiplexing.

Third, wideband techniques produce signals that seldom interfere with other signals in the same spectrum due to their low power which makes them appear more like noise than as interfering signals.

Fourth, communication is secure because it's so hard to detect (low probability of intercept) and recover.

Some initial concern was raised about potential electromagnetic-interference problems generated by UWB. But most experts now agree it's not a problem. Impulse UWB is generally called time modulated or TM-UWB. This uses extremely short pulses (less than one nanosecond) with a variable pulse-to-pulse interval ie. pulse position modulation (PPM). The interval variation is measured to produce information flow across the link, including the required information plus a channel code. A single bit of information may be spread over multiple pulse pairs and coherently added in the receiver. Since TM-UWB is based on accurate timing, it is well suited to both communications and distance determination.

In direct-sequence (DS) UWB, the data to be transmitted is modulated with a signature waveform. The Gaussian pulse is first modified using unique chips which are defined as signature waveform. Modulation is either phase-shift keying (PSK) or PPM. DS-UWB transmitters are super simple and use very low power, but the receiver and its complex correlation recovery circuits are somewhat more of a challenge.

The basic transmitted CDMA waveform of user *k* is given by

$$x_k(t) = \sum_{j=0}^{N-1} C_j^k w(t - jT_c) \tag{4}$$

Where, *w (t)* represents the transmitted monocycle and C_j^k denotes jth spreading chip of the pseudo-random noise (PN) Sequence. *N* is the number of pulses of the PN sequences to be used for each user.
The transmission signal format is shown in Fig. 7. The encoded data of each user are considered as a data symbol, which is multiplied by the transmitted CDMA code.

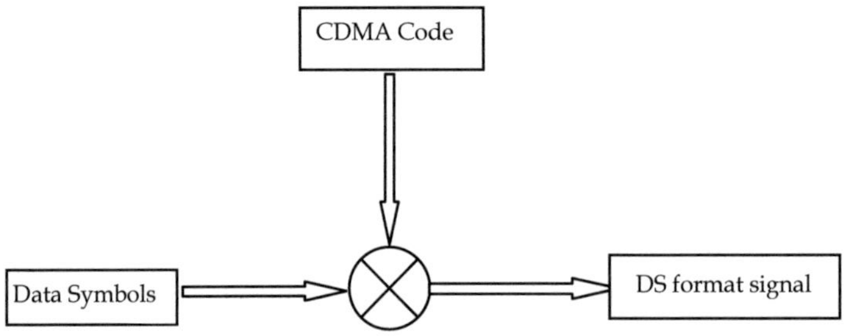

Fig. 7. Transmission signal format

Let, T_f be the symbol period and T_c be the chip period such that $T_f = NT_c$. Hence, a typical DS format of the *k*th impulse radio transmitter output signal is given by

$$S_k(t) = \sqrt{p_k} \sum_m d_m^k \, x_k(t - mT_f) \tag{5}$$

Where d_m^k represents the data symbols and p_k is the transmitted power corresponding to the *k*th user. It is important to note that even an ideal channel and antenna system modify the shape of the transmitted monocycle *w(t)* to $w_{rec}(t)$ at the output of the receiving antenna, where $w_{rec}(t)$ is the derivatives of a Gaussian function.
MB-OFDM divides the UWB spectrum into multiple 528-MHz wide bands, each 528MHz band comprises 128 carriers modulated using QPSK on OFDM tones [Batra et al., 2004]. The composite signal occupies the 528MHz band for approximately 300ns before switching to another band and is used in group of three. The group in lower band ranging from 3.168 to 4.952 GHz, make up the initial spectrum to be used, mainly because it's relatively easy these days to make all-CMOS radio ICs in this space. The centre frequencies for these three 528-MHz bands are shown in Fig. 8.The main difference between MB-OFDM and a traditional

OFDM system is that the data transmission is not done continually on all sub-bands. Instead, it is time-multiplexed between the different sub-bands.

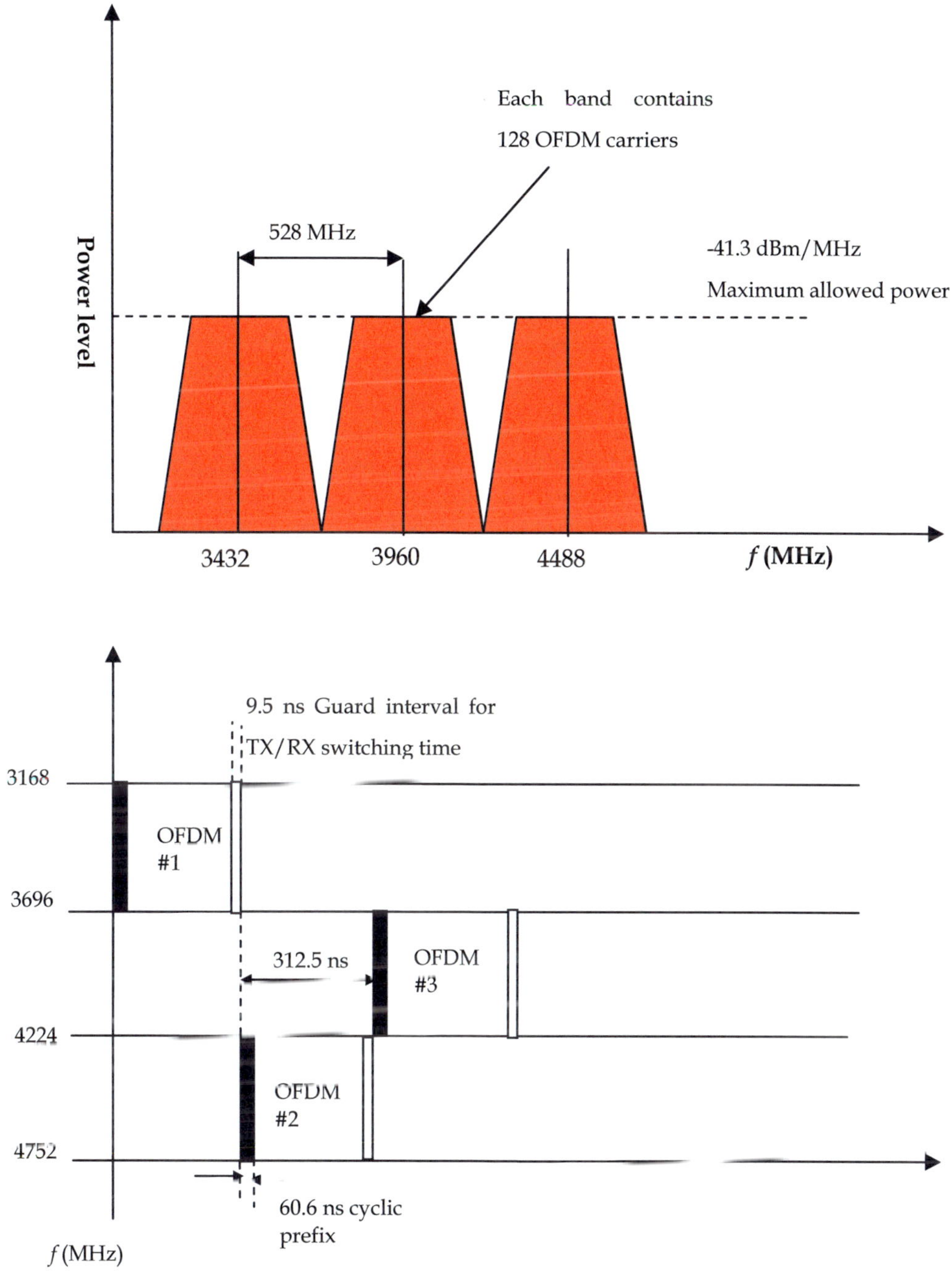

Fig. 8. MB-OFDM system [Batra et al., 2004]

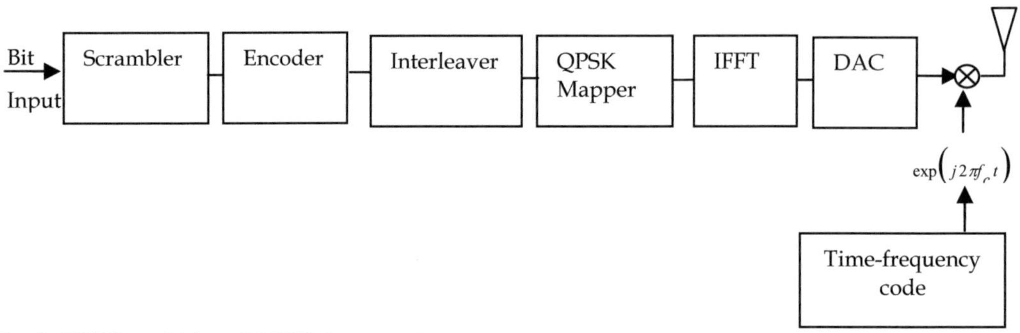

Fig. 9. UWB multi-band OFDM transmitter

The MB-OFDM radio uses the standard coding, scrambling, and inverse fast Fourier transform (IFFT) to generate the signal to be transmitted. Fig. 9 shows UWB multi-band OFDM transmit architecture which is very similar to that of a conventional wireless OFDM system, except time-frequency code. The time-frequency codes are used not only to provide frequency diversity in the system, but also to provide multiple access. At the receiver, an FFT recovers the original signal. Consequently, digital signal processing lies at the heart of an MB-OFDM UWB radio. Nonetheless, a 128-point FFT isn't that complex and can be implemented with logic in a small space these days. The resulting radio can achieve a data rate of up to 480 Mbits/s at about 2 to 3 m and up to 110 Mbits/s at 10 m. The data rate dependent modulation parameters are listed in Table 3, which summarizes the technical parameters of UWB multi-band OFDM systems. For some reason, though, the industry hasn't adopted these techniques as standards. In fact, most companies already have abandoned the impulse approach and are diving head-on into DS-CDMA and MB-OFDM. These two will form the foundation for most of the coming UWB products.

Data Rate =640Mbps*Coding Rate/Spreading

Info. Data Rate (Mbps)	Modulation/ Constellation	FFT Size	Coding Rate (K=7)	Spreading rate
53.3	OFDM/QPSK	128	1/3	4
55	OFDM/QPSK	128	11/32	4
80	OFDM/QPSK	128	1/2	4
106.7	OFDM/QPSK	128	1/3	2
110	OFDM/QPSK	128	11/32	2
160	OFDM/QPSK	128	1/2	2
200	OFDM/QPSK	128	5/8	2
320	OFDM/QPSK	128	1/2	1
400	OFDM/QPSK	128	5/8	1
480	OFDM/QPSK	128	3/4	1

Table 3. Data rate dependent parameters [Batra et al., 2004]

6. UWB applications

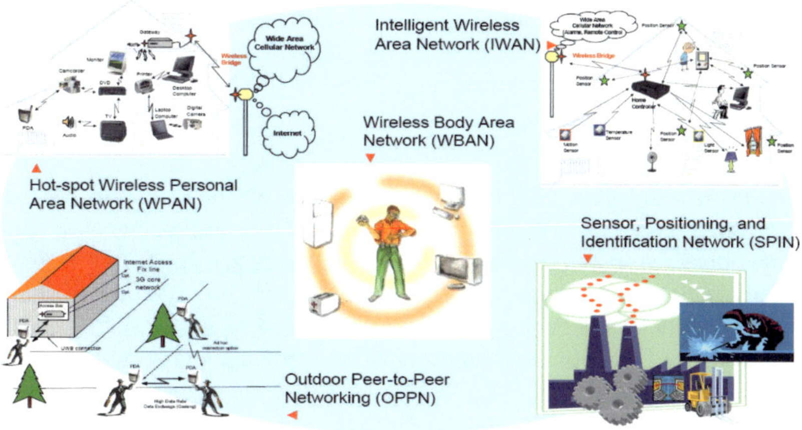

Fig. 10. Potential application scenarios [Oppermann, 2004]

The potential UWB applications scenario is shown in Fig. 10. As UWB allows high date rate throughput with low power consumption for distances of less than 10 meters, it is applicable to the digital home requirements. The digital home requirements are:

- High speed data transfer for multimedia content
- Short range wireless connectivity for transfer data to other devices
- Low power consumption due to limited battery capacity
- Low complexity and cost due to market pricing pressures

Fig. 11. UWB indoor communications [Manteuffel,2004]

For examples, the user will be able to stream video content from a PC or consumer electronics device- such as camcorder, DVD player or personal video recorder to a flat screen HDTV (high-definition television) display without the use of any wires, which is

shown in Fig. 11. Another model is the ability to view photos from the user's digital still camera on a larger display. Removing all wires to the printer, scanner, mass storage devices, and video cameras located in the home office is another possible scenario.
Due to high data rate, UWB can be used as an alternative to other wireless technologies, such as Bluetooth and WiFi, for Personal Area Network (PAN) applications.

6.1 UWB vs. Wi-Fi WLAN

UWB and Wi-Fi are seen as complementary technologies for the most part because Wi-Fi is a wireless local area network (WLAN) while UWB is a wireless personal area network (WPAN). The only area in which there is an overlap between these two technologies is in wireless video applications. Currently, Wi-Fi is not an effective method to distribute video applications wirelessly because the peak transfer rate of 54 Mbps is much too slow for video applications. UWB is a superior technology in video applications because peak transfer rates are in excess of 100 Mbps.

6.2 UWB vs. Bluetooth

Bluetooth data rates could reach 12 Mbps. This is only a fraction of UWB rates which can reach 480 Mbps. Bluetooth is sufficient for applications like mobile phones and ear phones but not sufficient for transfers of fast data and video between home appliance because of its high power consumption and poor data rates.

7. Challeges of UWB

There are several challenges that need to be considered and must be overcome to ensure the success of this technology in the wireless communication market such as multi-access code design, multiple access interference (MAI) cancellation, narrowband interference (NBI) detection and cancellation, synchronization of the receiver to extremely narrow pulses, accurate modeling of UWB channels, low-power transceiver design, RF component design and UWB tailored network design.

8. References

FCC (2002)."FCC News, Web page, New public safety application and broadband internet access among uses envisioned by FCC authorization of Ultra Wideband technology, Announcement of Commission Action."

Nokia (2006). "UWB (Ultra-wideband) Program," *http://research.nokia.com/research/programs/uwb/.*

Intel (2002)."Ultra-wideband/a Disruptive RF Technology?," in *Intel Corporation 2002.*

Multispectral Solutions Inc. (2001). "A Brief History of Ultra Wideband," *Article Source: http: //www.multispectral.com/ history.html*

G. F. Ross (1996). "A time domain criterion for the design of wideband radiating elements," *IEEE Trans. Antennas and Propagation,* vol. AP-16, pp. 355.

C. L. Bennett and G. F. Ross (1978). "Time-domain electromagnetics and its applications," *Proc. IEEE,* vol. 66, pp. 299-318.

H. F. Harmuth (1968). "A Generalized Concept of Frequency and Some Applications," *IEEE Transactions on Information Theory*, vol. IT-14,no.3, pp. 375-382.

H. F. Harmuth (1984). *Antennas and Wave Guides for Nonsinusoidal Waves*: New York: Academic Press.

H. F. Harmuth (1979). "Comments of Some Physical constraints on the Use of 'Carrier-Free' Waveforms in Radio -wave Transmission," *Proceedings of the IEEE*, vol. 67, no.6, pp. 890-891.

H. F. Harmuth (1977). *Frequently Raised Objections, Electromagnetic Waves with general time variation, Excerpt, Sequency Theory-Foundation and Applications*: New York: Academic Press.

H. F. Harmuth (1972). *Historical background and Motivation for the Use of Nonsinusoidal Functions*: New York: Academic Press.

H. F. Harmuth (1977). "Interference Caused by additional radio channels using nonsinusoidal carriers," *Second Symposium and Technical Exhibition on Electromagnetic Compatibility*, June 28-30.

H. F. Harmuth(1981). *Nonsinusoidal Waves for Radar and Radio Communications*: New York: Academic Press.

H.F. Harmuth and S. Ding-Rong (1983). "Antennas for Nonsinusoidal Waves. I. Radiators," *IEEE Transactions on Electromagnetic Compatibility*, vol. Emc- 25, no.1, pp. 13-24.

D. L. Black (1992). "An overview of Impulse Radar Phenomenon," *IEEE AES Systems Magazine*, pp. 6-11.

M. G. M. Hussain (1996). "An Overview of the Principles of Ultra-wideband impulse Radar," *CIE International Conference of Radar*, pp. 24-28.

M. G. M. Hussain(1998). "Ultra-Wideband Impulse Radar-An overview of the Principles," *IEEE Aerospace and Electronics Systems Magazine*, vol. 13, pp. 9-14.

I. Immoreev and B. Vovshin (1995). "Features of Ultra wideband Radar Projecting," *IEEE international Radar Conference*, pp. 720-725.

L. Y. Astanin and A. A. Kostylev (1997) "Ultra Wideband Signals -A New Step In Radar Development," *IEEE AES Systems Magazine*, pp. 12-15.

J. D. Taylor (1995). *Introduction to Ultra -Wideband Radar Systems*: Boca Raton, Fl.: CRC Press.

C. Leonard Bennett and G. F. Ross(1978). "Time-Domain electromagnetics and Its Applications," *Proceedings of the IEEE*, vol. 66, no.3, pp. 299-318.

Intel (2001)."Ultra-wideband Technology for short- or Medium- Range Wireless Communications," *ftp://download.intel.com/technology/itj/q22001/pdf/art_4.pdf*.

Ofcom (2005) "Ofcom consultation document on a position to adopt in Europe on Ultra - wideband devices,".

B Allen, A Ghorishi, and M. Ghavami (2004). "A Review of Pulse Design for Impulse Radio," *IEE Ultra wideband workshop*.

A. Batra, J. Balakrishnan, G. R. Aiello, J. R. Foerster, and A. Dabak (2004). "Design of a Multiband OFDM system for Realistic UWB Channel Environments," *IEEE Trans. on Microwave theory and Tech.*, vol. 52 No. 9, pp. 2123-2138.

I. Oppermann (2004). "An overview of UWB activities within PULSERS," *Presented in Ultra-Wideband in Singapore 2004 Seminar,*.

D. Manteuffel, J. Kunish, W. Simon, and M. Geissler (2004). "Characterization of UWB antennas by their spatio-temporal transfer function based on FDTD simulations," *presented at the Proc. EUROEM Conf. Magdeburg, Germany*, Jul. 12-16.

2

Impact of ultra wide band (UWB) on highways microcells downlink of UMTS, GSM-1800 and GSM-900 systems

Bazil Taha Ahmed* and Miguel Calvo Ramón**
*Universidad Autonoma de Madrid, **Universidad Politecnica de Madrid
SPAIN

1. Introduction

The Federal Communications Commission (FCC) agreed in February 2002 to allocate 7.5 GHz of spectrum for unlicensed use of ultra-wideband (UWB) devices for communication applications in the 3.1–10.6 GHz frequency band. The move represented a victory in a long hard-fought battle that dated back decades. With its origins in the 1960s, when it was called time-domain electromagnetics, UWB came to be known for the operation of sending and receiving extremely short bursts of RF energy. With its outstanding ability for applications that require precision distance or positioning measurements, as well as high-speed wireless connectivity, the largest spectrum allocation ever granted by the FCC is unique because it overlaps other services in the same frequency of operation. Previous spectrum allocations for unlicensed use, such as the Unlicensed National Information Infrastructure (UNII) band have opened up bandwidth dedicated to unlicensed devices based on the assumption that "operation is subject to the following two conditions: This device may not cause harmful interference (harmful interference is defined as the interference that seriously degrades, obstructs or repeatedly interrupts a radio communication service), and this device must accept any interference received, including those interferences that may cause undesired operation. This means that devices using unlicensed spectrum must be designed to coexist in an uncontrolled environment. Devices using UWB spectrum operate according to similar rules, but they are subject to more stringent requirements, because UWB spectrum underlays other existing licensed and unlicensed spectrum allocations. In order to optimize spectrum use and reduce interference to existing services, the FCC's regulations are very conservative and require very low emitted power.
UWB has a number of advantages which make it attractive for consumer communications applications. In particular, UWB systems

- Have potentially low complexity and low cost;
- Have noise-like signal characteristics;
- Are resistant to severe multipath and jamming;
- Have very good time domain resolution.

The spectrum for the Universal Mobile Telecommunications System (UMTS), which support voice and data services, lies between 1900 MHz to 2025 MHz and 2110 MHz to 2200 MHz.

For the mobile satellite service a separated sub-band in the UMTS spectrum is reserved (uplink 1980 MHz to 2010 MHz, downlink 2170 MHz to 2200 MHz). The remaining spectrum for terrestrial use is divided between two modes of operation. In the FDD (Frequency Division Duplex) mode there are two paired frequency bands, for the uplink (1920 MHz to 1980 MHz) and for the downlink (2110 MHz to 2170 MHz). In the TDD (Time division duplex) operation mode, the uplink and downlink are implemented by using different timeslots on the same carrier. In his case there is no need for a paired spectrum and the remaining unpaired spectrum can be used.

To serve users in rural zone highways and nearby buildings, cigar-shaped microcells are used. They are produced by two directive antennas in a mast with a height of 5 to 10 m. located in the base station.

DCS-1800 is a Digital Communications System based on GSM, working on a radio frequency of 1800 MHz. Also known as GSM-1800, this digital network operates in Europe and Asia Pacific. The DCS-1800 band provides for a DCS uplink in the range 1710-1785 MHz, a DCS downlink in the range 1805-1880 MHz.

The GSM 900 band provides for a GSM uplink in the range 890-915 MHz, and a GSM downlink in the range 935-960 MHz. The GSM 900 band is used in all countries (more than 168 across the globe) in which GSM networks are found, except for the United States. In (Hamalainen et al., 2002) the coexistence of the UWB system with GSM900, UMTS/WCDMA, and GPS has been studied. The bit error rate (BER) of the above mentioned systems for different pulse length has been given. In (Hamalainen et al., 2004) the coexistence of the UWB system with IEEE802.11a and UMTS in a Modified Saleh-Valenzuela Channel has been studied. The bit error rate (BER) of the UWB system, for different types of modulation (Direct Sequence and Time Hopping), has been presented. In (Guiliano et al., 2003) the interference between the UMTS and the UWB system, for different UWB activity factors, has been investigated. They concluded that, the UWB allowable interference limit is in the order of -100 dBm. This limit is well below the interference due to UWB transmitter at a distance of about 1 m. In (Ahmed et al., 2007), the Impact of Ultra Wide Band (UWB) on macrocell downlink of CDMA-PCS system has been investigated. In (Ahmed et al., 2008), the Impact of Ultra-Wideband (UWB) on macrocell downlink of UMTS and CDMA-450 systems has been studied.

The aim of this chapter is to present the effect of UWB signal on UMTS and GSM microcell downlink performances. The rest of the chapter is organized as follows. In Section 2, the methodology for studying the effect of the UWB interference on the UMTS microcell downlink performance is presented. Section 3 presents the methodology for studying the effect of the UWB interference on the GSM microcells downlink performance. In Section 4 several results are given. Finally, Section 5 addresses the conclusions.

2. Methodology for Studying the Effect of UWB Interference on UMTS microcells downlink

The highway UMTS microcell downlink power budget used in this section adopts the approach given in (Holma & Toskala, 2002). The parameters used in the calculations are shown in Table 1.

A	Maximum link transmit power	dBm	33
B	Transmitter gains	dB	18
C	Transmitter local losses	dB	1
D	Transmitter EIRP	dB	A+B-C
E	Receiver noise figure	dB	6
F	Thermal noise density	dBm/Hz	
G	Noise power	dBm	E+F*log10(4x10^6)
H	Load value	0.5 to 1	
I	Noise rise	dB	-10*log10(1-H)
J	Interference power	dBm	10*log10(10^((G+I)/10) -10^(G/10))
K	Noise and interference	dBm	10*log10(10^(G/10)+10^(J/10))
L	Number of users = Noise rise	dB	
M	Processing gain (G_p)	dB	
N	$(E_b/N_o)_{req}$	dB	
O	Indoor loss	dB	10 dB
P	Maximum path loss	dB	D-L-K+M-N
Q	Log normal fade margin	dB	6 dB
R	Path-loss	dB	P-Q

Table 1. UMTS microcell downlink power budget

To account for UWB, an extra source of interference is added linearly to the UMTS interference. The power of this interference is calculated by assuming that the UWB source is located at different distances from the UMTS mobile receiver. Therefore, the interference power generated by a UWB device, I_{UWB}, is given (in dBm) by:

$$I_{UWB} - P_{UWB} - L_{UWB}(d) + G_{UMTS} \quad (1)$$

where

- P_{UWB} is the UWB EIRP in dBm in the UMTS band.
- $L_{UWB}(d)$ is the path-loss between the UWB device and the UMTS receiver, which varies with the separation distance d in m, and
- G_{UMTS} is the UMTS receiver antenna gain.

Given that UWB devices are typically low power short range devices, then the line-of-sight path-loss model is often the most appropriate. In this case the UWB signal propagation loss in dB is calculated as:

$$L_{UWB}(d) \approx 39 + 20\log_{10}(d) + L_{extra} \tag{2}$$

where L_{extra} is the extra loss due to other propagation effects like shadowing.

The effect of the UWB interference reduces the microcell range and/or the microcell normalized capacity. The UMTS normalized capacity is the ratio between the UMTS capacity without UWB interference to its capacity with UWB interference. The normalized microcell capacity C_n is given as:

$$C_n = \left(\frac{I_{UMTS}}{I_{UMTS} + I_{UWB}} \right) \tag{3}$$

The calculation is carried for a range of values of d and for different UMTS service types.
To calculate the UMTS microcell propagation loss L_p we have used the two-slope propagation model) as given by:

$$L_p(dB) \approx L_b + 10 + 20\log_{10}\left(\frac{r}{R_b}\right) \quad r \le R_b \tag{4}$$

$$L_p(dB) \approx L_b + 10 + 40\log_{10}\left(\frac{r}{R_b}\right) \quad r > R_b \tag{5}$$

where r is the distance between the base station and the mobile at the point of observation, L_b is the propagation loss at the breaking point R_b and L_b and R_b are given by (Tsai & Chang, 1996):

$$L_b(dB) = \left| 10\log_{10}\left[\left(\frac{\lambda^2}{8\pi h_b h_m} \right)^2 \right] \right| \tag{6}$$

$$R_b \approx \frac{4h_b h_m}{\lambda} \tag{7}$$

where

- h_b is the base station antenna height = 7.5 m,
- h_m is the mobile antenna height = 1.5 m,
- λ is the wavelength.

In the two-slope propagation model, the exponent of the propagation loss distance dependent factor is assumed to be 2 till the break point R_b (equation 4) and then it converts to 4 (equation 5).

3. Methodology for Studying the Effect of UWB Interference on GSM microcells downlink

The highway GSM microcell downlink budget used in this section also adopts the approach given in (Holma & Toskala, 2002). The elements to the calculation are shown in Table 2.

A	Maximum link transmit power	dBm	30
B	Transmitter gains	dB	18
C	Transmitter local losses	dB	2
D	Transmitter EIRP	dB	A+B-C = 46 dBm
E	Receiver noise figure	dB	9
F	SNR_{req}	dB	10
G	Receiver sensitivity	dBm	-174+53+E+F = -102 dBm
H	Indoor loss	dB	10 dB
I	Maximum path loss	dB	D-G-H = 138 dB
J	Log normal fade margin	dB	6 dB
K	Compensated Path-loss	dB	I-J = 132 dB

Table 2. GSM microcell downlink budget

The effect of the UWB interference is to reduce the GSM microcell range.
The UWB signal propagation loss in dB at the GSM-1800 band is calculated as:

$$L_{UWB}(d) \approx 37.8 + 20\log_{10}(d) + L_{extra} \tag{8}$$

At the GSM-900 band the UWB propagation loss in dB is calculated as:

$$L_{UWB}(d) \approx 32 + 20\log_{10}(d) + L_{extra} \tag{9}$$

To calculate the GSM microcell range we also use the two-slope propagation model

4. Results

In the analysis we assume that the UWB data rate is higher than the UMTS chip rate. We assume that the UMTS mobile is in a building, located near the highway microcell and thus served by this microcell. We will study the effects of the UWB transmitters on the UMTS handset assuming three different cases:

- Line of sight case, without shadowing (L_{extra} = 0 dB).
- Line of sight case, with shadowing (L_{extra} = 5 dB).
- UWB transmitter is shadowed by a person (L_{extra} = 10 dB).

In Fig. 1 the UWB interference power on the UMTS downlink (i.e. the interference seen at the UMTS mobile) is plotted for the three cases mentioned above, assuming voice service and a P_{UWB} of -60 dBm/MHz within the UMTS bandwidth of 5 MHz.

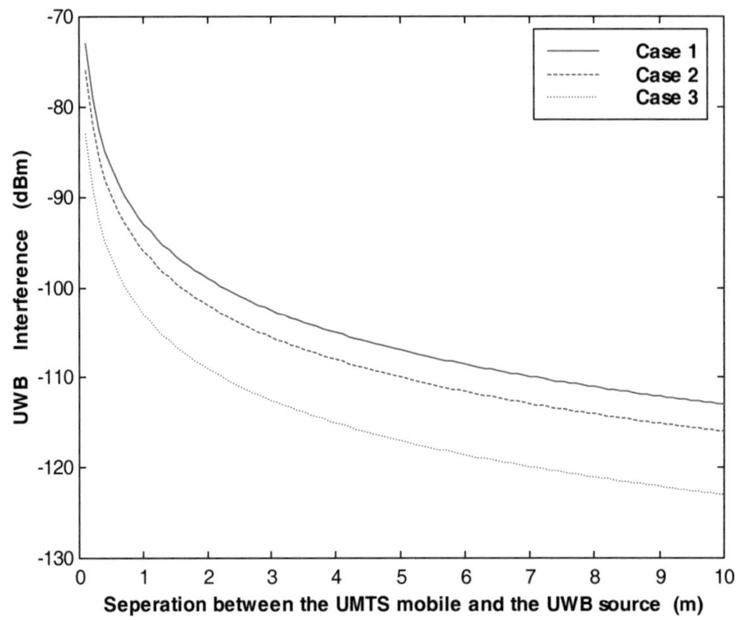

Fig. 1. UWB interference as a function of the separation between the UWB transmitter and the UMTS mobile (voice service and P_{UWB} = -60 dBm/MHz).

We study the case of voice service (G_p = 25 dB, E_b/N_o = 6 dB) assuming an UMTS total interference of -83 dBm (19 dB noise rise). In this case, the downlink microcell range is calculated to be 1.18 km. Fig. 2 shows the downlink microcell range as a function of the separation between the UMTS mobile and the UWB transmitter. It can be noticed that the UWB signal creates a high interference (which reflects a microcell range reduction) when the separation is less than 0.5 m. For larger separation, the interference is lower and, at a distance higher than 2 m, the effect of the interference is quasi null.

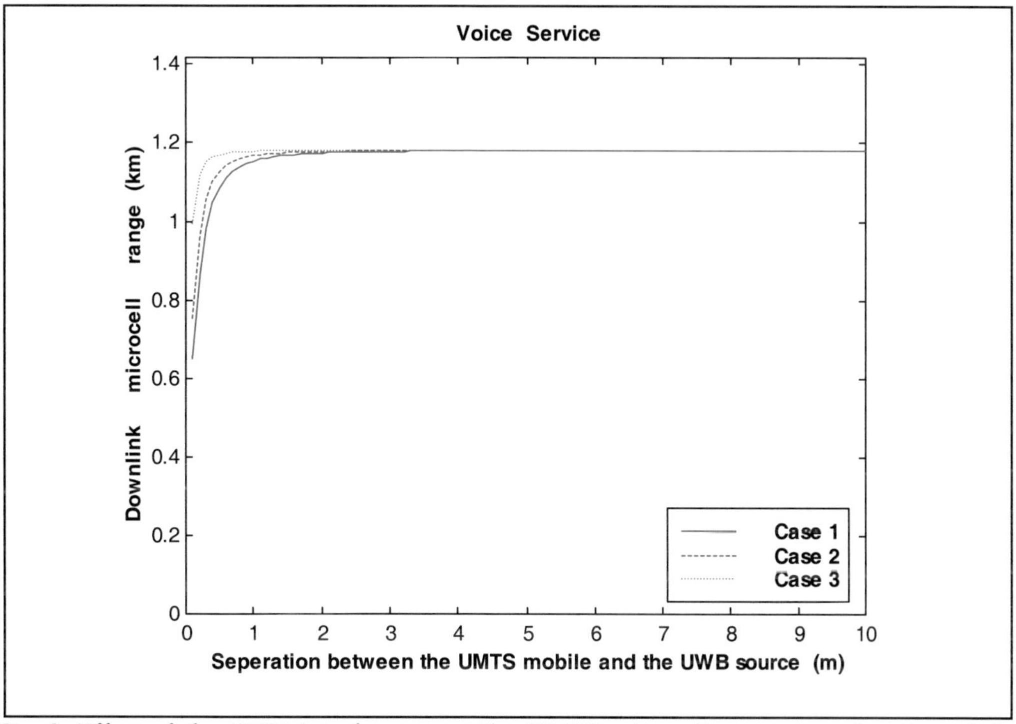

Fig. 2. Effect of the UWB interference on the UMTS microcell range as a function of the separation between the UWB transmitter and the UMTS mobile (P_{UWB} = -60 dBm/MHz).

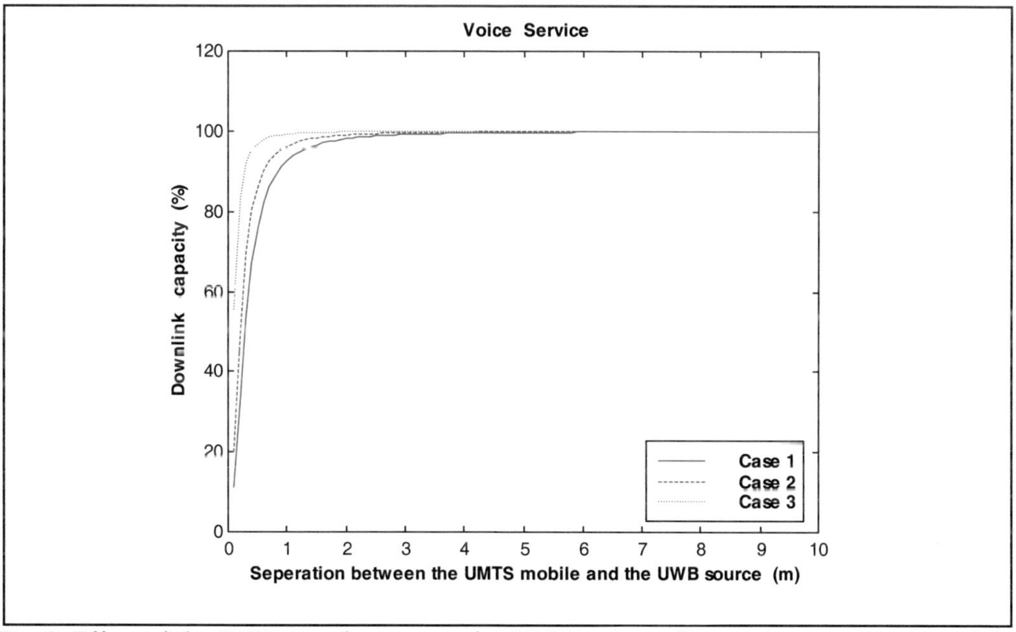

Fig. 3. Effect of the UWB interference on the UMTS microcell capacity as a function of the separation between the UWB transmitter and the UMTS mobile (P_{UWB} = -60 dBm/MHz).

Fig. 3 shows the downlink microcell normalized capacity as a function of the separation between the UMTS mobile and the UWB transmitter. It can be noticed that the microcell capacity reduction is high when the separation is lower than 0.5 m. For larger separation, the capacity reduction is lower and, at a distance higher than 3 m, the capacity reduction is negligible.

Next we study the case of a data service (G_p = 14.25 dB, E_b/N_o = 4.25 dB) assuming an UWB power density of -60 dBm/MHz and an UMTS total interference of -92 dBm (10 dB noise rise). In this case, the downlink microcell range is calculated to be 1.98 km. Fig. 4 shows the downlink microcell range as a function of the separation between the UMTS mobile and the UWB transmitter. It can be noticed that the UWB signal creates a high interference (which reflects as a microcell range reduction) when the separation is less than 1 m. For larger separations, the interference is lower. At a distance higher than 6 m, the effect of the interference is negligible.

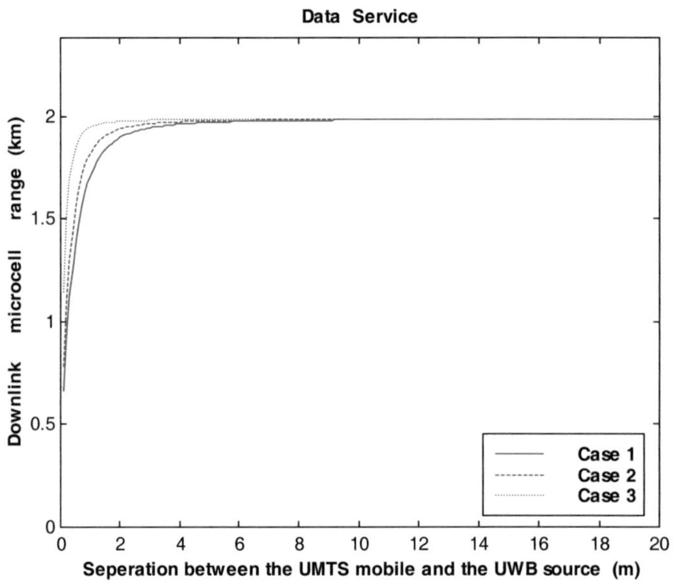

Fig. 4. Effect of the UWB interference on the UMTS microcell range as a function of the separation between the UWB transmitter and the UMTS mobile (P_{UWB} = -60 dBm/MHz).

Fig. 5 shows the downlink microcell normalized capacity as a function of the separation between the UMTS mobile and the UWB transmitter. It can be noticed that the microcell capacity reduction is high when the separation is less than 2 m. For larger separation, the reduction is lower and for a distance higher than 9 m, the capacity reduction is very small.

Let us now study the data service case assuming a P_{UWB} of -80 dBm/MHz. Fig. 6 shows the downlink microcell range as a function of the separation between the UMTS mobile and the UWB transmitter. It can be noticed that the UWB signal creates a high interference (which reflects a microcell range reduction) when the separation is less than 0.1 m. For larger separation, the interference is reduced and for distances higher than 0.45 m, the effect of the interference is quasi null.

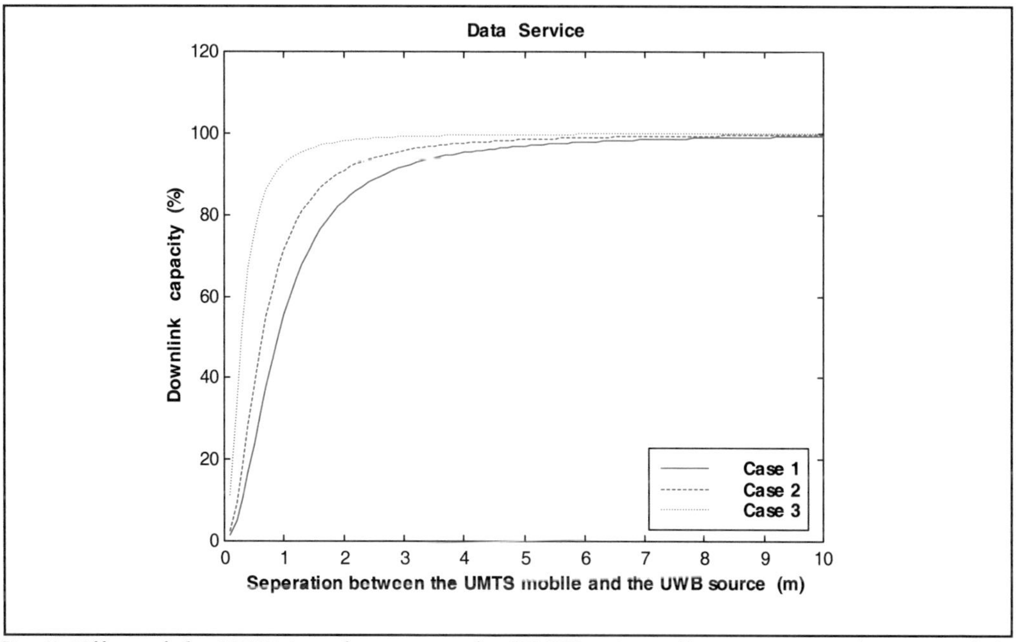

Fig. 5. Effect of the UWB interference on the UMTS microcell capacity as a function of the separation between the UWB transmitter and the UMTS mobile (P_{UWB} = -60 dBm/MHz).

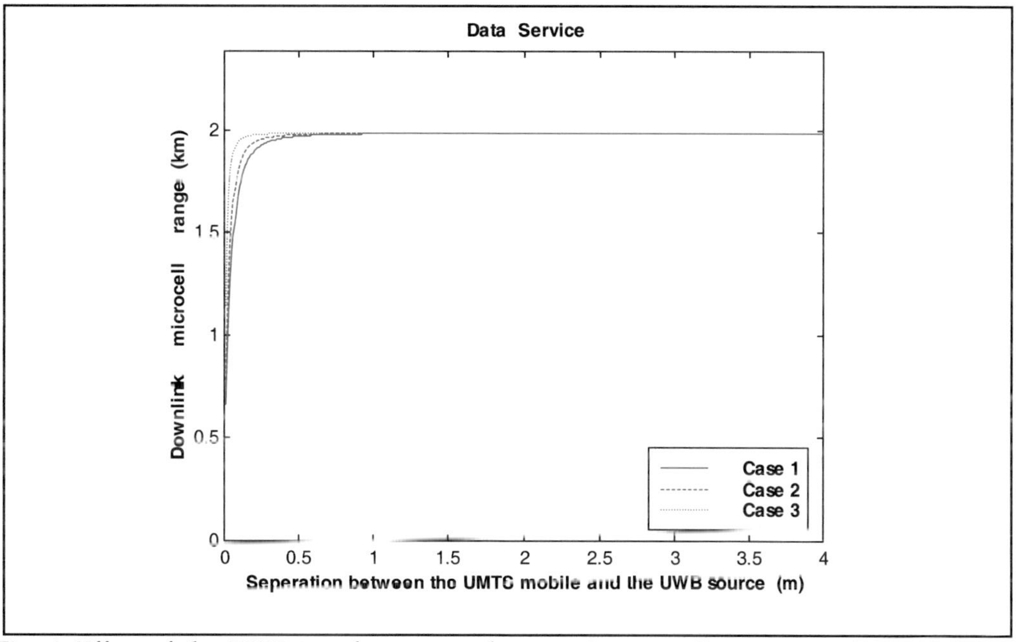

Fig. 6. Effect of the UWB interference on the UMTS microcell range as a function of the separation between the UWB transmitter and the UMTS mobile (P_{UWB} = -80 dBm/MHz).

Fig. 7 shows the downlink microcell normalized capacity as a function of the separation between the UMTS mobile and the UWB transmitter. It can be observed that the microcell capacity reduction is high when the separation is less than 0.2 m. For larger separation, the reduction is lower. At a distance higher than 0.9 m, the capacity reduction is negligible.

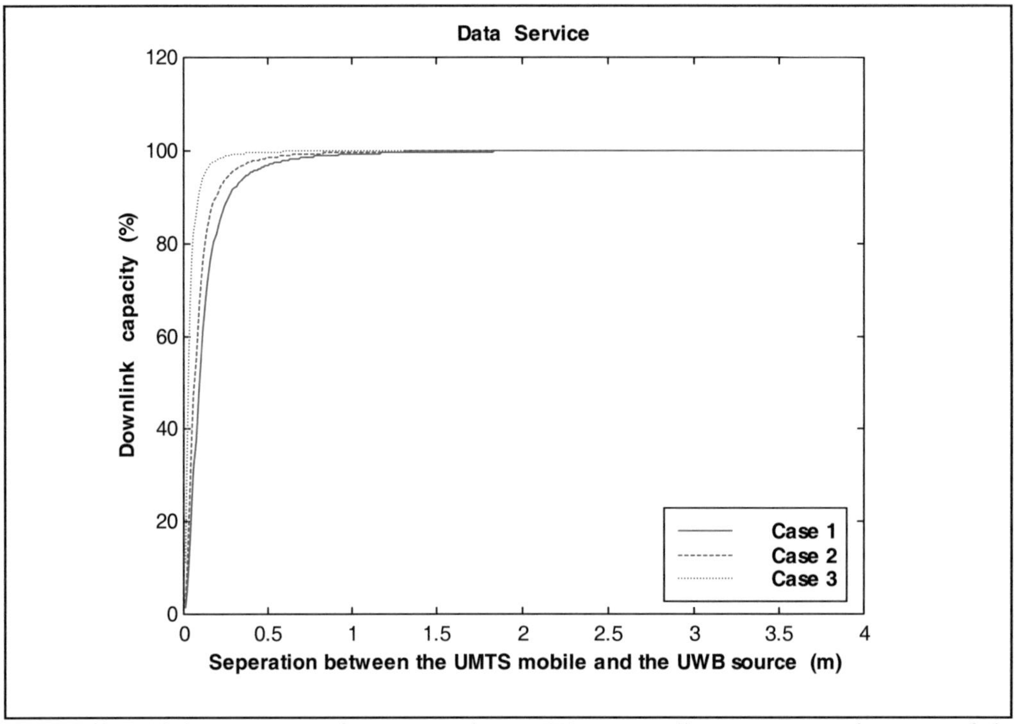

Fig. 7. Effect of the UWB interference on the UMTS microcell capacity as a function of the separation between the UWB transmitter and the UMTS mobile (P_{UWB} = -60 dBm/MHz).

Table 3 shows the distance d_C at which the microcell capacity is 95% of its value without the UWB interference. It also shows the distance d_R at which the microcell range is 95% of its value without the UWB interference.

Table 4 shows the distance d_C, between the UMTS mobile and the UWB transmitter, at which the microcell capacity is 99% of its value without the UWB interference. It also shows the distance d_R at which the microcell range is 99% of its value without the UWB interference. Form Table 4, it can be noticed that the UMTS system can easily tolerate a -80 dBm/MHz UWB interference with quasi null effect (less than 1% reduction in range or capacity) when the distance between the UWB transmitter and the UMTS receiver is higher than 1m.

UWB Power density (dBm/MHz)	$d_{R\,95\%}$ (m)	$d_{C\,95\%}$ (m)
-50	6.5	12.3
-55	3.7	6.9
-60	2.1	3.9
-65	1.2	2.2
-70	0.7	1.3
-75	0.4	0.7

Table 3. Distance d_C at which the microcell capacity is 95% of its value without the UWB interference and the distance d_R at which the microcell range is 95% of its value without the UWB interference.

UWB Power density (dBm/MHz)	$d_{R\,99\%}$ (m)	$d_{c\,99\%}$ (m)
-60	4.4	8.8
-65	2.5	5.0
-70	1.4	2.8
-75	0.8	1.6
-80	0.45	0.9
-85	0.25	0.5

Table 4. Distance d_C at which the microcell capacity is 99% of its value without the UWB interference and the distance d_R at which the microcell range is 99% of its value without the UWB interference.

Now we study the case when N_{UWB} transmitters are distributed uniformly within a circle around the UMTS mobile receiver (Multi transmitter case) assuming P_{UWB} of-55 dBm/MHz and six UWB transmitters. Fig. 8 shows the downlink microcell range as a function of the circle radius. It can be seen that the UWB signal creates a high interference (which reflects a microcell range reduction) when the circle radius is less than 5 m. At a radius of 20 m, the effect of the UWB transmitters is very small.

Fig. 9 shows the downlink microcell normalized capacity as a function of the circle radius. It can be noticed a high microcell capacity reduction when the circle radius is lower than 10 m. At a radius of 30 m, the capacity reduction is negligible.

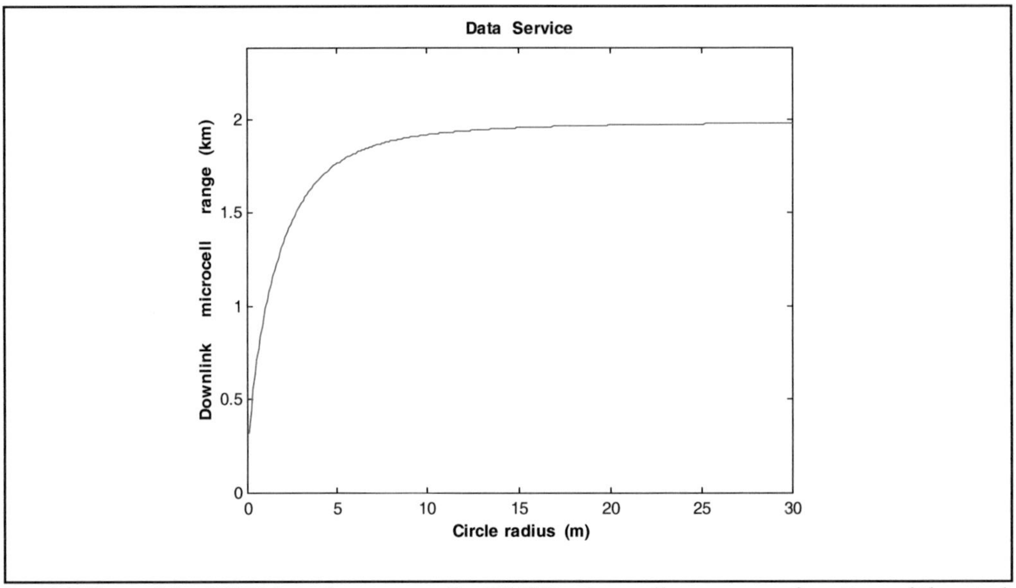

Fig. 8. Effect of the UWB interference on the UMTS microcell range as a function of the circle radius (N = 6, P_{UWB} = -55dBm/MHz).

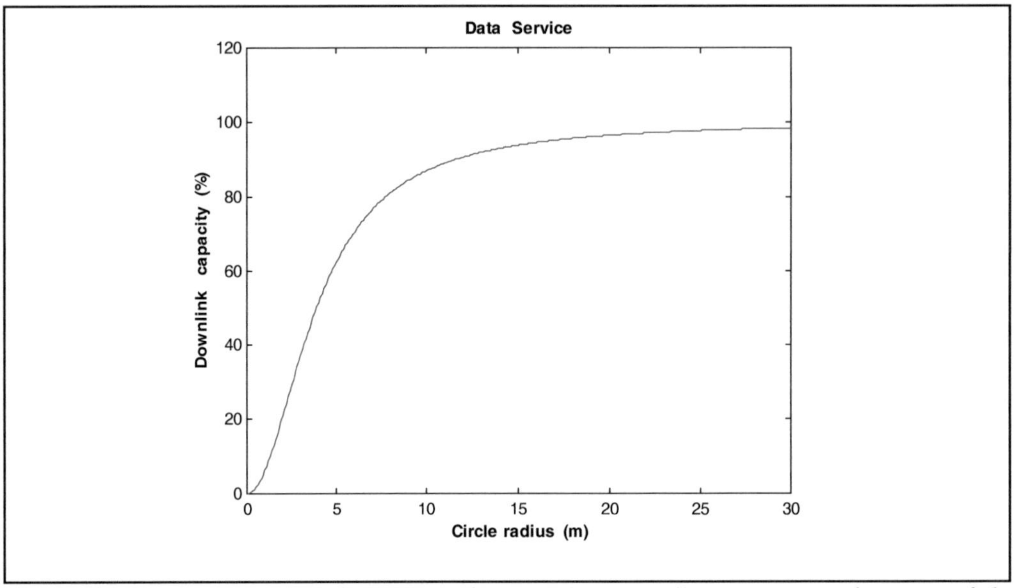

Fig. 9. Effect of the UWB interference on the UMTS microcell capacity as a function of the circle radius (N = 6, P_{UWB} = -55 dBm/MHz).

Now we study the case of UWB multi transmitters when the UWB power density is -87 dBm/MHz and N = 6. Fig. 10 shows the downlink microcell range as a function of the circle radius. It can be noticed that the UWB signal creates a very low interference (which reflects in a microcell range reduction of less than 1%) when the circle radius is 0.5 m or more.

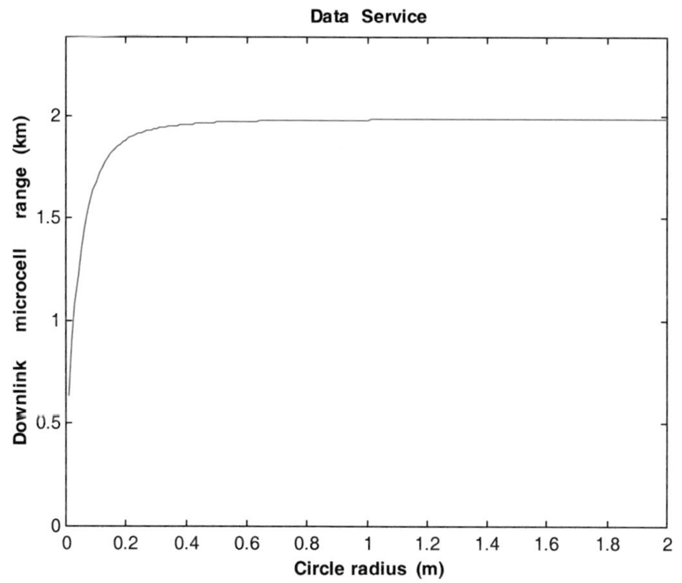

Fig. 10. Effect of the UWB interference on the UMTS microcell range as a function of the circle radius (N = 6, P_{UWB} = -87 dBm/MHz).

Fig 11 shows the downlink microcell normalized capacity as a function of the circle radius. It can be noticed that the microcell capacity reduction is low (1%) when the circle radius is 1 m.

Table 5 shows the distance d_C at which the microcell capacity is 99% of its original value and the distance d_R at which the microcell range is 99% of its original value for the case of multi UWB transmitters (N = 6).

Next we study the case of the GSM1800 system. Fig. 12 shows the GSM1800 downlink microcell range as a function of the separation between the GSM1800 mobile and the UWB transmitter when the UWB power density is – 80 dBm/MHz. It can be noticed that the UWB signal creates a high interference (which reflects a microcell range reduction) when the separation is less than 0.2 m. For larger separation, the interference is lower. At a distance higher than 1 m, the effect of the interference is quasi null (less than 1% range reduction). The GSM1800 microcell downlink original range is 3.43 km.

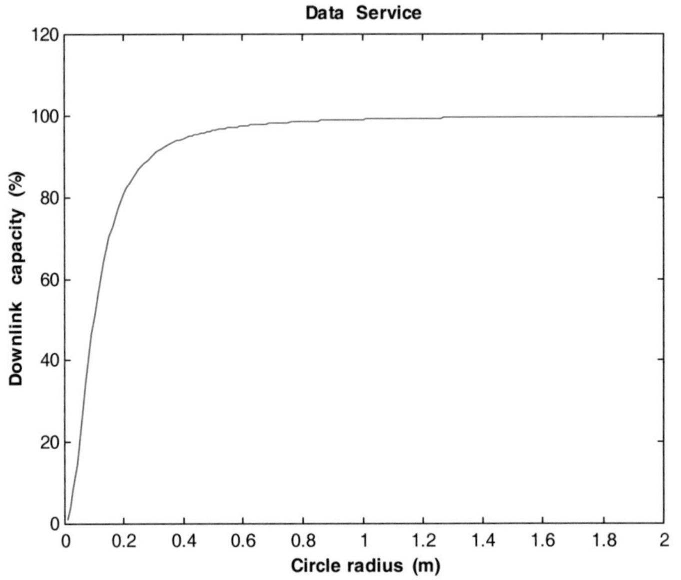

Fig. 11. Effect of the UWB interference on the UMTS microcell capacity as a function of the circle radius (N = 6, PUWB = -87 dBm/MHz).

UWB Power density (dBm/MHz)	$d_{R\ 99\%}$ (m)	$d_{c\ 99\%}$ (m)
-65	5.9	12.2
-70	3.3	6.9
-75	1.9	3.9
-80	1.1	2.2
-85	0.6	1.3
-90	0.34	0.7

Table 5. Distance d_C at which the microcell capacity is 99% of its value without the UWB interference and the distance d_R at which the microcell range is 99% of its value without the UWB interference for the UWB multi transmitter case.

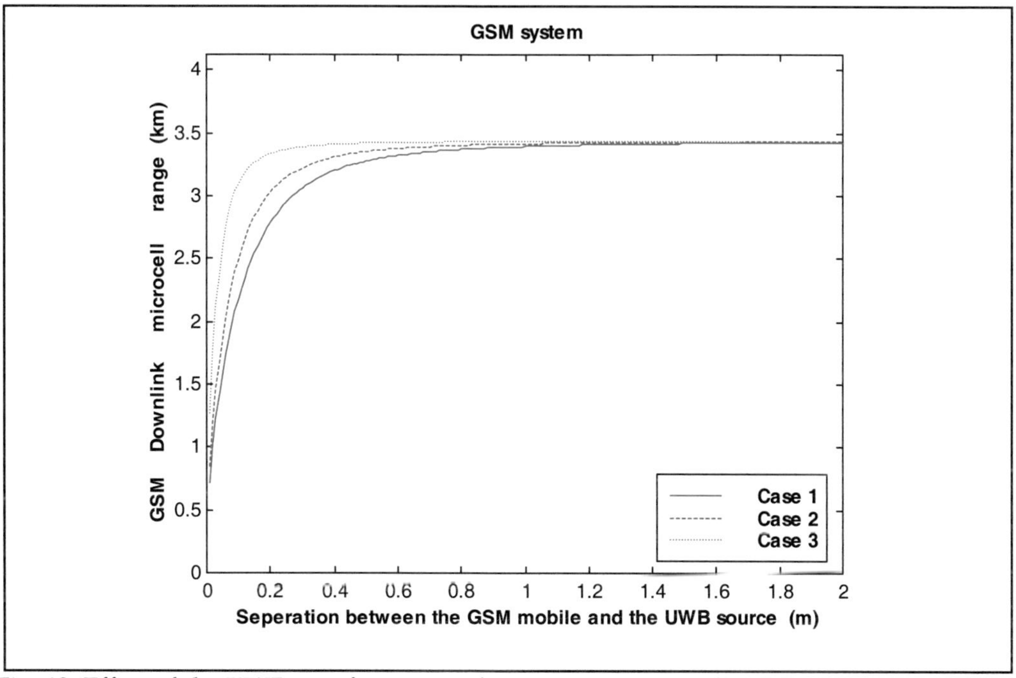

Fig. 12. Effect of the UWB interference on the GSM1800 microcell range as a function of the separation between the UWB transmitter and the GSM1800 mobile (P_{UWB} = -80 dBm/MHz).

Fig. 13 shows the GSM1800 downlink microcell range as a function of the separation between the GSM1800 mobile and the UWB transmitter when the UWB power density is - 86 dBm/MHz. It can be noticed that the UWB signal creates a high interference (which reflects a microcell range reduction) when the separation is less than 0.1 m. For larger separation, the interference is lower. At a distance equal to or higher than 0.5 m, the effect of the interference is quasi null (less than 1% range reduction).

Finally we study the case of the GSM900 system. Fig. 14 shows the GSM900 downlink microcell range as a function of the separation between the GSM900 mobile and the UWB transmitter when the UWB power density is - 87 dBm/MHz. It can be noticed that the UWB signal creates a high interference (which reflects a microcell range reduction) when the separation is less than 0.2 m. For larger separation, the interference is lower. At a distance equal to or higher than 1 m, the effect of the interference is quasi null (less than 1% range reduction). The GSM900 microcell downlink original range is 6.696 km.

Fig. 15 shows the GSM900 downlink microcell range as a function of the separation between the GSM900 mobile and the UWB transmitter when the UWB power density is -93 dBm/MHz. It can be noticed that the UWB signal creates a high interference (which reflects a microcell range reduction) when the separation is less than 0.1 m. For larger separation, the interference is lower. At a distance equal to or higher than 0.5 m, the effect of the interference is quasi null (less than 1% range reduction).

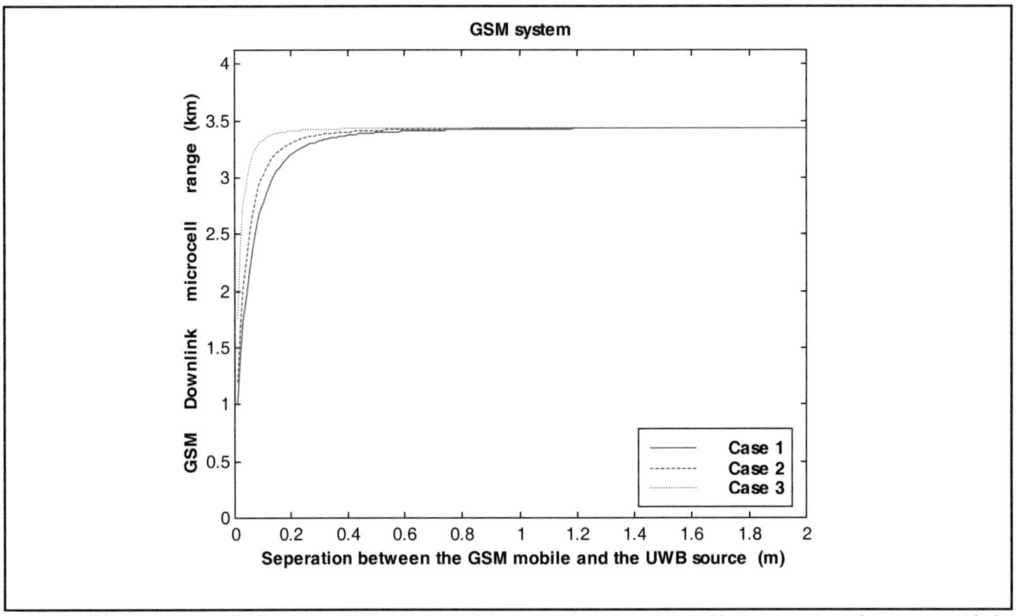

Fig. 13. Effect of the UWB interference on the GSM1800 microcell range as a function of the separation between the UWB transmitter and the GSM1800 mobile (P_{UWB} = -86 dBm/MHz).

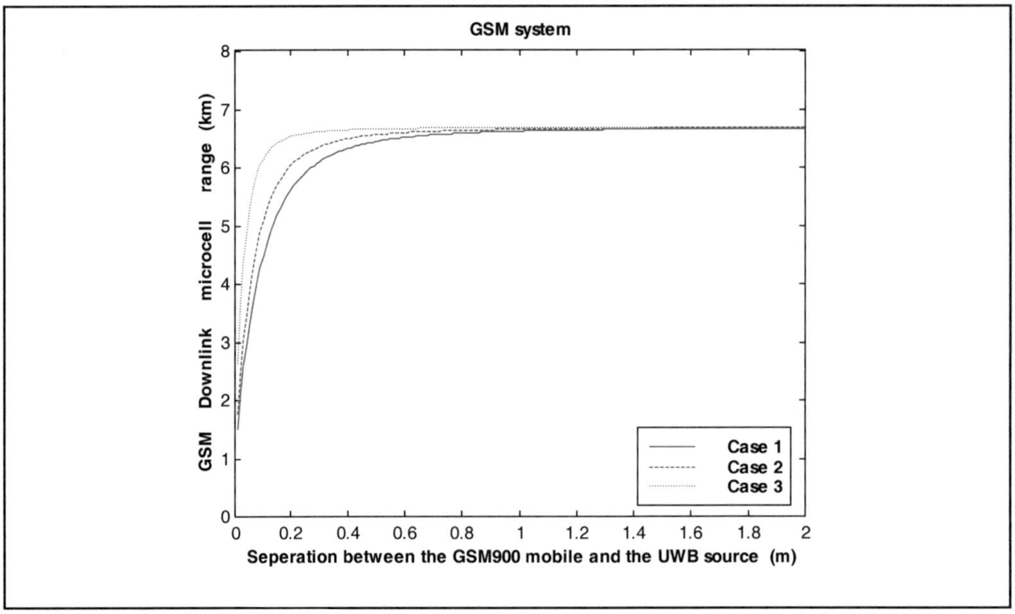

Fig. 14. Effect of the UWB interference on the GSM900 microcell range as a function of the separation between the UWB transmitter and the GSM900 mobile (P_{UWB} = -87 dBm/MHz).

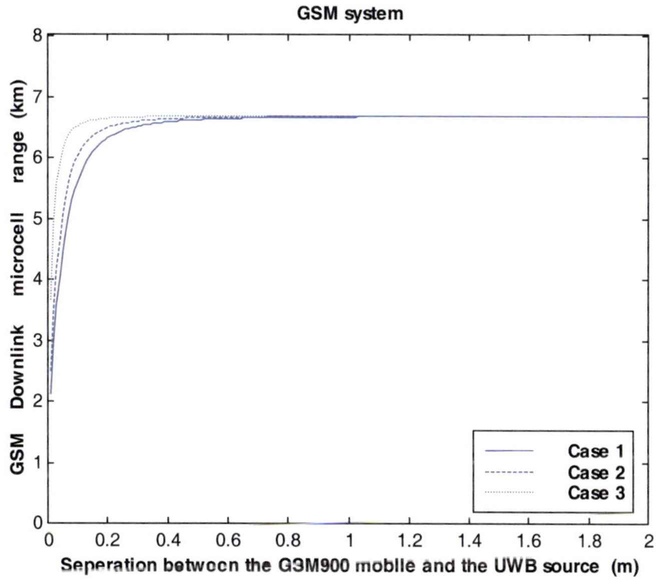

Fig. 15. Effect of the UWB interference on the GSM900 microcell range as a function of the separation between the UWB transmitter and the GSM900 mobile (P_{UWB} = -93 dBm/MHz).

5. Conclusions

The effect of the UWB transmitters on the UMTS microcell downlink has been presented for different configuration and environments. For the case of single UWB transmitters, the effect of the UWB signals is quasi null when the distance between the UWB transmitter and the UMTS receiver is 1 m or more and the UWB power density is -80 dBm/MHz or less. For the case of multi UWB transmitters, the effect of the UWB signals is quasi null when the distance between the UWB transmitter and the UMTS receiver is 1 m or more and the UWB power density is -87 dBm/MHz or less.

For the case of single UWB transmitters, the effect of the UWB signals is quasi null when the distance between the UWB transmitter and the GSM1800 receiver is 1 m or more and the UWB power density is -80 dBm/MHz or less. For the case of multi UWB transmitters , the effect of the UWB signals is quasi null when the distance between the UWB transmitter and the GSM1800 receiver is 1 m or more and the UWB power density is -86 dBm/MHz or less.

For the case of single UWB transmitters, the effect of the UWB signals is quasi null when the distance between the UWB transmitter and the GSM900 receiver is 1 m or more and the UWB power density is -87 dBm/MHz or less. For the case of multi UWB transmitters, the effect of the UWB signals is quasi null when the distance between the UWB transmitter and the GSM900 receiver is 1 m or more and the UWB power density is -93 dBm/MHz or less.

6. References

Ahmed, B. T., Calvo Ramón, M., Haro Ariet, L. H. (2007), On the Impact of Ultra Wide Band (UWB) on Macrocell Downlink of CDMA-PCS System, *Wireless Personal Communications Journal*, Vol. 43, No. 2, pp.355-367.

Ahmed, B. T, Calvo Ramón, M. (2008), On the Impact of Ultra-Wideband (UWB) on Macrocell Downlink of UMTS and CDMA-450 Systems, *IEEE Electromagnetic Compatibility*, Vol. 5, No. 2, pp. 406-412.

Giuliano, R., Mazzenga, F., Vatalaro, F. (2003), On the interference between UMTS and UWB system, , *IEEE Conference on Ultra Wideband Systems and Technologies*, 2003 pp:339 - 343.

Hamalainen, M. , Hovinrn, V., Tesi, R., J. Iinatti, and M. Latava-aho (2002), " On the UWB System Coexistence with GSM900, UMTS/WCDMA, and GPS", *IEEE Journal on Selected Areas in Communications*, Vol. 20, No. 9, pp. 1712-1721.

Hamalinen, M., R. Tesi., J. Iinatti (2004), UWB co-existence with IEEE802.11a and UMTS in modified saleh-valenzuela channe, *Ultra Wideband Systems, 2004*, p.p:45 - 49.

Holma, H., Toskala, A. (2002), *WCDMA for UMTS*, John Wiley & Sons.

Tsai, Y. R., Chang, J. F. (1996), Feasibility of Adding a Personal Communications Network to an Existing Fixed-service Microwave System , *IEEE Transactions on Communications*, Vol. 44, N°. 1, pp 76-83.

3

Parallel channels using frequency multiplexing techniques

Magnus Karlsson, Allan Huynh and Shaofang Gong
Linköping University
Sweden

1. Introduction

The principle of frequency (de-) multiplexing provides the opportunity to either split a wide frequency-band into several parallel sub-bands or to combine parallel sub-bands into one wide frequency band. A typical de-multiplexing operation is that a wideband signal from a single broadband antenna is divided into sub-bands for parallel data processing. Similarly, several services from a single antenna can be separated utilizing a de-multiplexing technique during reception, and combined with multiplexing during transmission. Moreover, the relation can be the opposite, i.e., a system containing several narrowband antenna can be connected to a single transceiver using the (de-) multiplexing technique. This chapter presents stand-alone components as well as UWB radio front-end configurations, utilizing multiplexing techniques. Implementations are demonstrated both with conventional multi-layer and flex-rigid printed circuit board technologies. Fig. 1 shows the principle of (de-) multiplexing, where FMN is the abbreviation of frequency multiplexing network.

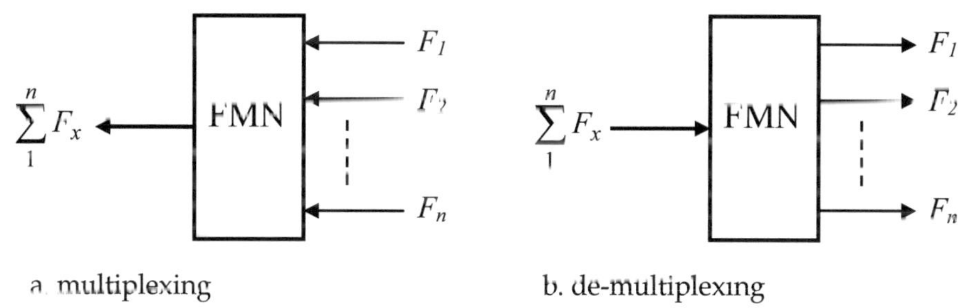

Fig. 1. The principle of frequency (de-) multiplexing.

In multi-band systems, frequency multiplexers are used to replace switches, and for channel parallelism. The concept of multiple frequency channels has been around for roughly half a century. For instance, (Coale, 1958) suggested to use directional filters as basic building blocks for frequency multiplexing, and a waveguide solution for operation in the X-band is shown as a demonstrator. A few years later (Rhodes & Levy, 1979) presents a generalized manifold theory. In brief terms the manifold (Bandler et al., 1987) presents an optimization algorithm for waveguide multiplexers. The algorithm is demonstrated with a 12-channel narrow-band waveguide multiplexer around 12 GHz. Three sub-bands multiplexed to one common frequency-band is also known as a triplexer, e.g., (Mansour, 1994) demonstrates a triplexer using dual-mode high-temperature superconductor thin-film filters and cryogenic circulators. In general manifolds suffer from the drawback of a large number of network variables that must be solved simultaneously. Various optimization techniques and algorithms to ease design and implementation have been proposed. Utilizing prototype circuits based on infinite-array logarithmic-periodic principles (Rauscher, 1994) showed two multiplexer solutions using transmission lines, resonators and coupling capacitors. (Kirilenko et al., 1994) demonstrates procedures for minimizing the need of experimental correction when using computer-aided design. Waveguide technology is quite common in manifold multiplexers since sharp sub-band filter cut-offs increases neighbouring sub-band to sub-band isolation, i.e., matching the circuitry is easier. A waveguide duplexer and a four-channel multiplexer are designed using electromagnetic simulation. (Matthaei et al., 1996) presents a lumped element and manifold microwave multiplexer using the high-temperature superconductor technology. Classically frequency-multiplexed selection relies on band-pass filtering. Reversing the principle by blocking out of sub-band frequencies using band-stop filters has also been shown. (Bariant et al., 2002) presents a microstrip duplexer using band-stop filters. The band-stop filtering is achieved using open circuit stubs. (Ohno et al., 2005) presents both a duplexer and a triplexer for printed circuit board integration. However, the design still involves some lumped components and the sub-bands are fairly small, having large guard-bands. In reference (Chen et al., 2006) a duplexer using microstrips is presented, but requires structural redesign to extend the number of ports. Paper (Lai & Jeng, 2005) proposes a stepped-impedance multiplexer for UWB and WLAN coexistence. In reference (Mallegol et al., 2007) a narrow-band four-channel multiplexer using open loop resonators for multi-band on-off keying UWB is demonstrated. Papers (Stadius et al., 2007; Tarng et al., 2007) show two channel-select multiplexers intended for UWB local oscillator signal selection, i.e., only one sub-band is active at the time.

2. Printed Circuit Board Build-up

Multi-layer printed circuit boards are commonly used to build space efficient electronics. Standard printed circuit board processes can today provide many choices when it comes to material selection and stack build-up techniques. Fig. 2 shows two different alternatives. Fig. 2(a) and (b) show a regular four metal-layer and flex-rigid (four metal-layer in the rigid part, and two metal-layers in the flexible part) printed circuit boards, respectively. In detail Fig. 2(a) is built-up as follows: Two dual-layer Rogers 4350B (RO4350B) boards processed together with a Rogers 4450B (RO4450B) prepreg. RO4450B prepreg is a sheet material (e.g., glass fabric) impregnated with a resin cured to an intermediate stage, ready for one stage printed circuit board bonding. The flex-rigid printed circuit board in Fig. 2(b) is built-up similarly but the choices of material must be such that the rigid contour can be cut out with depth controlled laser milling. Using LF8520, LF0100, LF0110 and AP8525 from DuPont™ Pyralux® laminate series. AP series is polyimide only materials, used for the flexible substrate layer. LF8520 is a combination of polyimide and fully cured adhesives, more physically stiff than an AP series material. LF0100 is an adhesive used for printed circuit board bonding, while the LF0110 is commonly used as protective coating on flexible substrate layers. The rigid and the flexible substrates are processed together in a printed circuit board bonding process, i.e., the adhesive layers are used to bond the polyimide layers. The flex-rigid technology provides additional possibilities compared to regular boards when it comes to printed circuit board component integration. For instance, the antenna is placed in the flexible part for best connectivity, while the rest of the transceiver is space efficiently built in the rigid part. Moreover, distributed components like a balun or a triplexer can be integrated in the printed circuit board as if the rigid part was a regular four metal-layer printed circuit board.

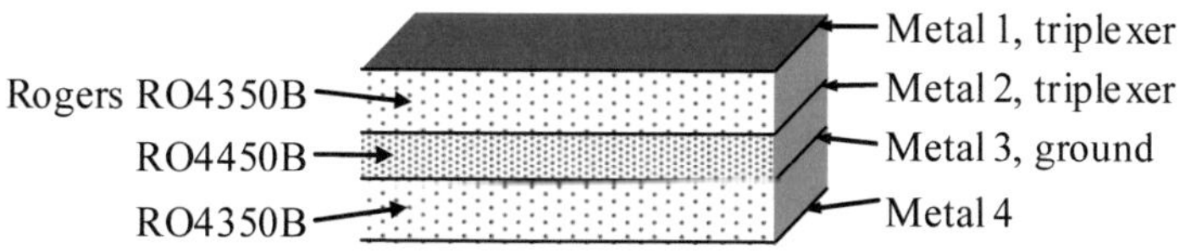

a. conventional printed circuit board

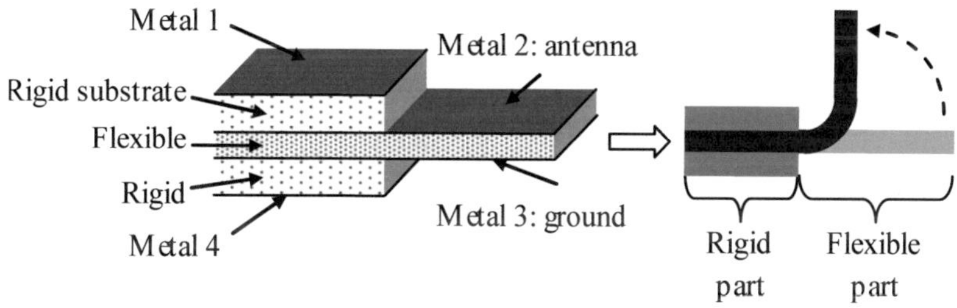

b. flex-rigid printed circuit board

Fig. 2. Printed circuit board structures.

3. Circular Dipole Antenna

Fig. 3 shows circular dipole antenna for UWB realized using the flex-rigid substrate. The antenna is positioned in the x-y plane, and $\phi=0$ (Horizontal plane) is along the x axis. It is seen that the radiating antenna element is placed entirely on the flexible part of the substrate. Furthermore, the balun is integrated in the rigid part of the substrate (Karlsson & Gong, 2008). A balun is needed to convert the differential port of the dipole antenna to a single-ended port, i.e., to connect to a single-ended front-end. The backside of the rigid part (Metal 4) is completely covered with metal to make through-board ground vias possible, and to provide additional solderable ground-junctions for the SMA connector (Karlsson & Gong, 2009). Drilled vias with a diameter of 0.3 mm are used for grounding. For a detailed study of the performance of the Mode 1 antenna, see (Karlsson & Gong, Oct. 2009). Antenna solutions for both the Mode 1 and the 6-9 GHz frequency bands was originally presented in (Karlsson et al., Sept. 2009).

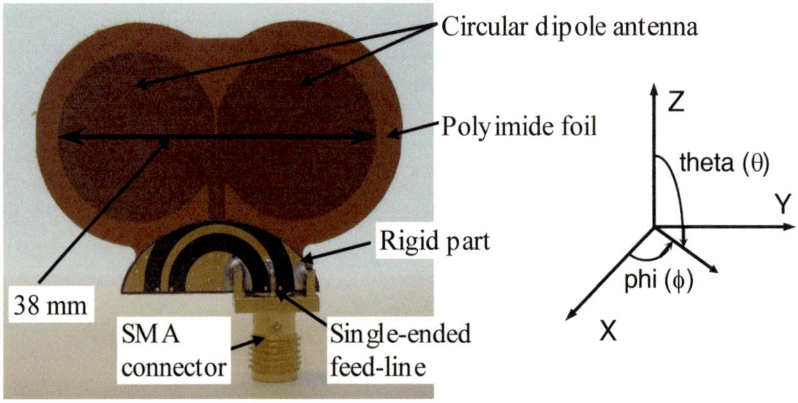

a. Mode 1 UWB antenna

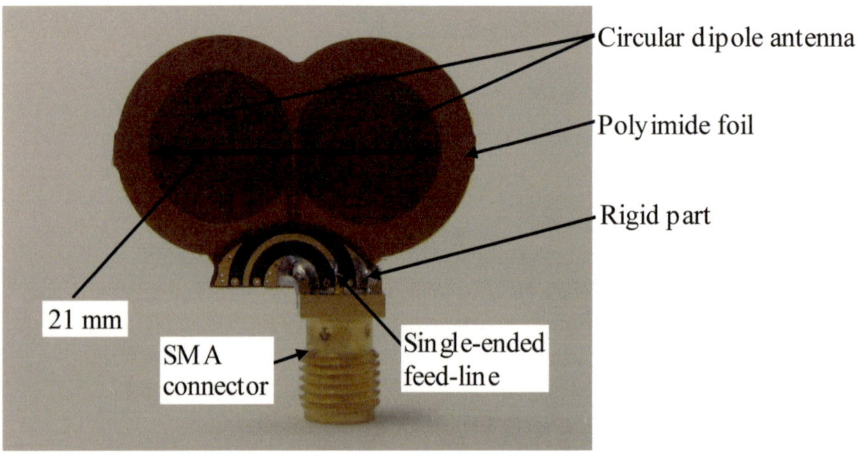

b. 6-9 GHz antenna

Fig. 3. Circular dipole UWB antenna: (a) Mode 1 antenna (3.1-4.8 GHz), and (b) 6-9 GHz antenna.

Fig. 4(a) and (b) show voltage standing wave ratio (VSWR) simulations and measurements of the circular dipole antenna on the flex-rigid substrate. The VSWR simulation and measurement results with the balun are shown. It is seen in the simulated and measured results that the circular dipole antenna for the upper UWB band (6-10.6 GHz) has a wide impedance bandwidth (a VSWR<2.5 bandwidth from 5.5 to 11.0 GHz). A small shift in frequency is also seen in both graphs, which is likely due to the fact that the simulated phase velocity is lower than the actual one (Karlsson & Gong, 2009). Fig. 4(c) shows simulated and measured gain in dBi at the boresight direction of the Mode 1 antenna. A match between simulation and measurement is seen within the Mode 1 UWB frequency-band (3.1-4.8 GHz), and a gain around 2 dBi is observed. However, some difference between simulation and measurement is seen, especially outside the Mode 1 UWB frequency-band. This is also due to the fact that the effect of the balun is not included in the radiation simulation (Karlsson & Gong, 2009).

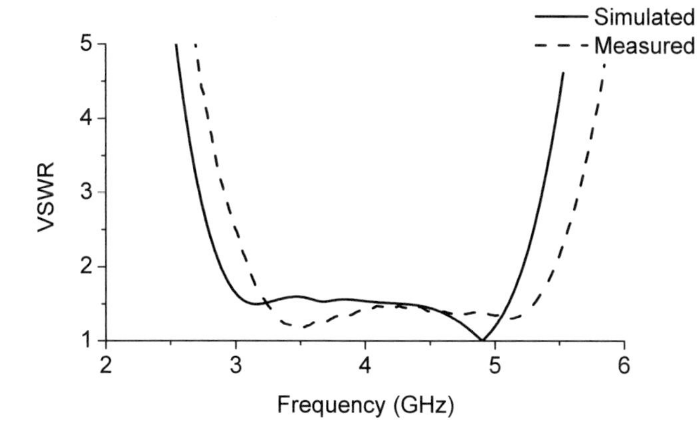

a. VSWR simulation and measurement of the Mode 1 UWB antenna

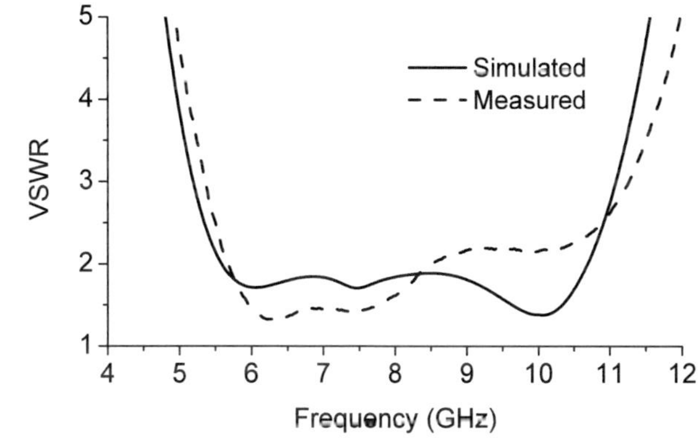

b. VSWR simulation and measurement of the 6-9 GHz UWB antenna

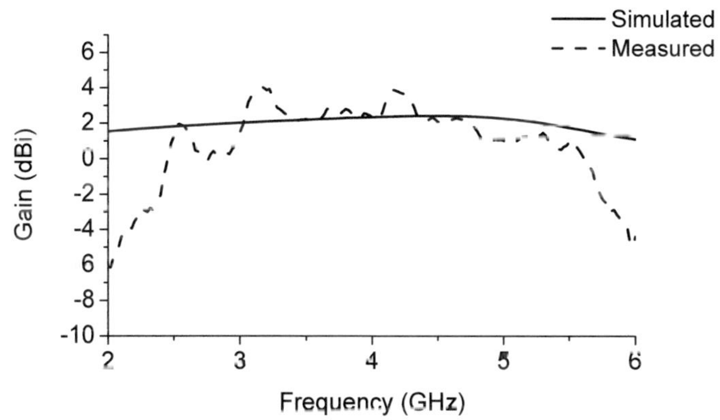

c. gain simulation and measurement of the Mode 1 UWB antenna

Fig. 4. Circular dipole antenna simulations and measurements.

4. Triplexer

Fig. 5 shows a schematic of a multiplexer with three sub-bands, i.e., a triplexer. The triplexer consists of three series quarter-wavelength transmission lines, three bandpass filters, and three transmission lines for tuning of the filter impedance. The principle of operation is that each sub-band has a matched input impedance (50 Ω in this design) at the junction, but a high input impedance at the input of other sub-bands. The series transmission lines of three different quarter wavelengths provide a high impedance at the respective frequency band, i.e., preventing sub-band #1 signals to reach sub-band #2 and #3. The filter tuning lines at the junctions optimize the stop band impedance of each filter, to provide a high stop band impedance in the neighbouring bands. Neighbouring sub-bands are most critical to a sub-band since the band-pass filter has limited rejection close to its pass-band. The entire network is optimized together with the filters to achieve flat passbands and a symmetric performance between the sub-bands (Karlsson et al., 2006; Karlsson & Gong, 2007; Karlsson et al. Nov. 2008).

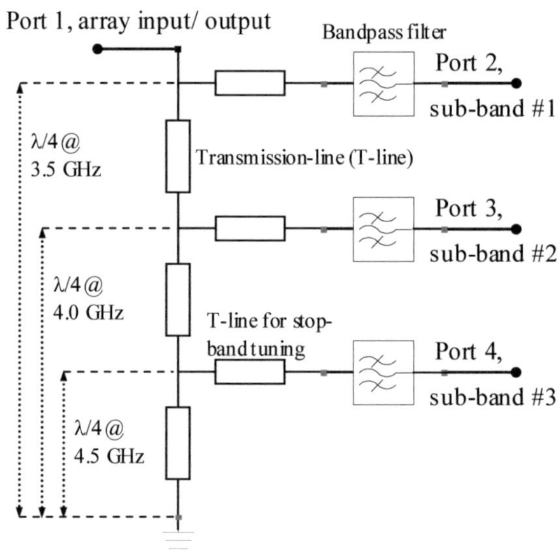

Fig. 5. Triplexer utilizing the manifold principle.

4.1 Combined Broadside- and Edge-coupled Filter Technology

Fig. 6(a) and (b) show the broadside-coupling and edge-coupling, respectively. All implementations are made using microstrips. Fig. 6(c) shows the combined broadside- and edge-coupled filter. The start and the stop segments are placed on Metal layer 1 (see Fig. 6(c)), and the rest of the filter is placed on Metal layer 2. A fifth order band-pass filter, two orders from broadside-coupling and three orders from edge-coupling are utilized.

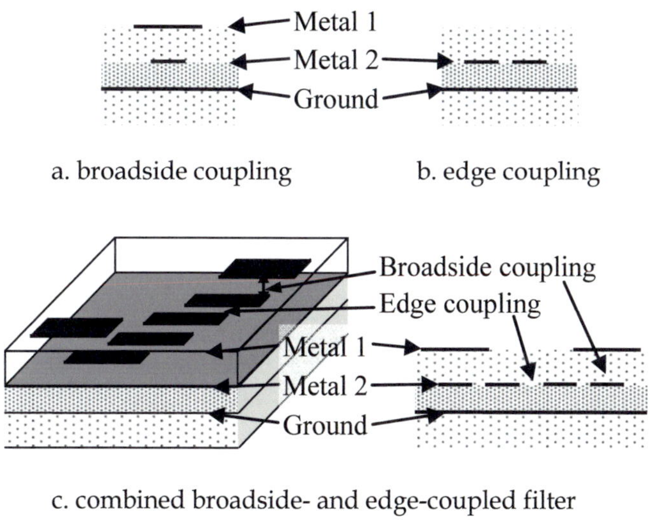

Fig. 6. Filter structures.

4.2 Implementation with Conventional Multi-layer Printed Circuit Board

Fig. 7 shows a photo of the implementation with the substrate shown in Fig. 2(a). The size of the triplexer prototype is 53 x 60 mm. Three of the four soldered Sub-Miniature A (SMA) connectors are seen. SMA connectors mounted from the side connect the three input sub-bands. Port 2 is for sub-band #1 (3.432 GHz), Port 3 is for sub-band #2 (3.960 GHz), and Port 4 is for sub-band #3 (4.488 GHz). The fourth output connector (Port 1) is mounted on the backside of the printed circuit board, i.e., only the soldered signal pin is seen. Moreover, it is

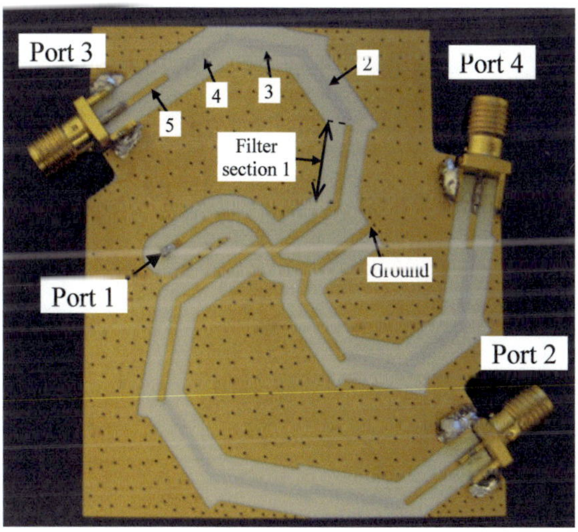

Fig. 7. Photo of the implementation.

seen that the prototype has a bend shape, which was done to achieve a more compact design. The design relies on impedance-controlled microstrip-lines, so the bending has no noticeable effect on the filter characteristic. Design and simulation were done with Advanced Design System (ADS) from Agilent technologies Inc. Measurements were done with a Rhode&Schwartz ZVM vector network analyzer.

Fig. 8(a) and (b) show the simulation and measurement results of forward transmission of the triplexer, respectively. A fairly flat passband response is seen. The transmission line network is optimized together with the filters to achieve high blocking of neighbouring bands. A good match between simulation and measurement results is seen. The complete multi-layer structure was simulated with radiation characteristics enabled in ADS for the best accuracy. However, some limitations still exist in the simulations. The SMA connectors are not included, and moreover ADS Momentum (ADS electromagnetic simulator) does not take surface roughness into count. The simulated insertion loss is 1.3-1.6 dB, and measured insertion loss is 3.1-3.5 dB for the three sub-bands. All sub-bands have at least 500 MHz bandwidth at -3 dB from the top. Fig. 8(c) and (d) show the simulation and measurement results of return loss of the triplexer, respectively. Due to the narrow guard-band blocking of neighbouring bands a smooth forward transmission was prioritized over low return loss, as seen in Fig. 8(a)-(d). The design freedom to achieve a low return-loss and smooth forward transmission is therefore limited. However, to use higher order than the fifth order band-pass filters would increase the design freedom but losses will increase. Fig. 8(e) and (f) show simulated and measured group delay, respectively. It is seen that for all the 500 MHz sub-bands the group delay is around 3.0 ns and the variation is approximately 1.0 ns within each sub-band. Fig. 8(g) shows isolation between Ports 2-4. It is seen that the minimum isolation is 23 dB. The minimum isolation occurs at the boundary of the neighbouring sub-bands, so in the three passbands the isolation is better than 23 dB. The isolation between the non-neighbouring alternate sub-bands is 51 dB. This work was originally presented in (Karlsson et al. Nov. 2008).

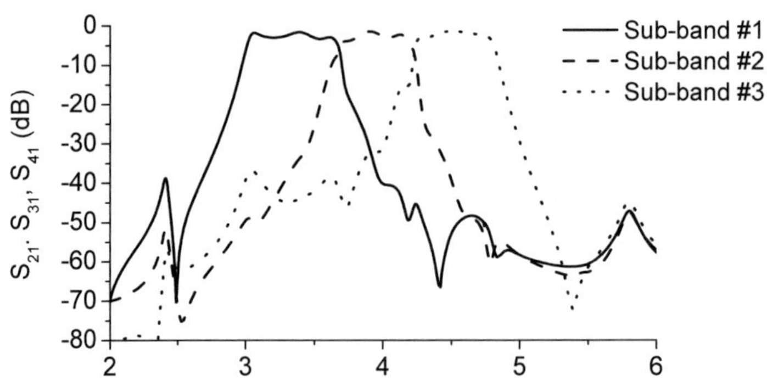

a. simulation of forward transmission

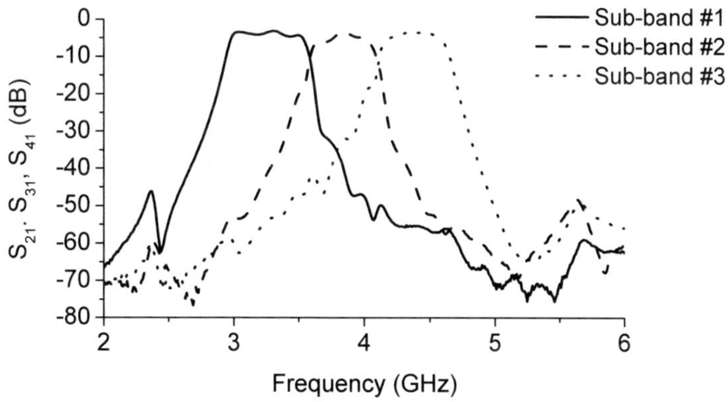

b. measurement of forward transmission

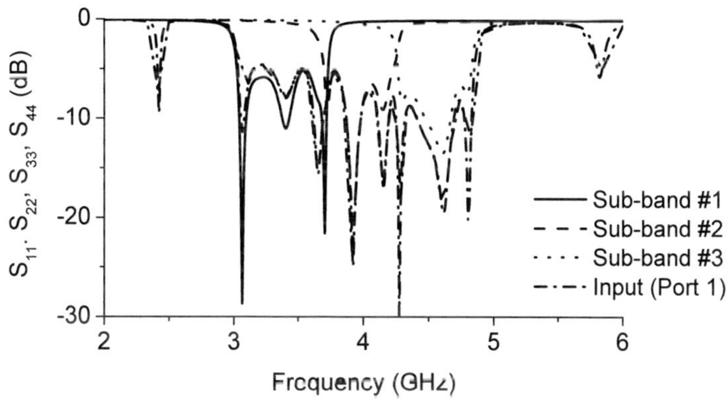

c. simulation of return loss

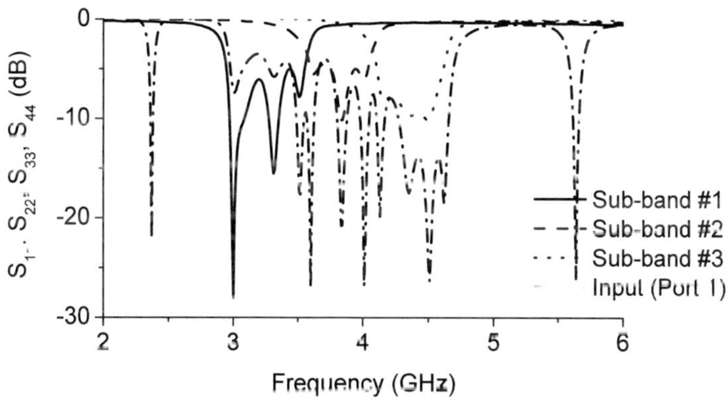

d. measurement of return loss

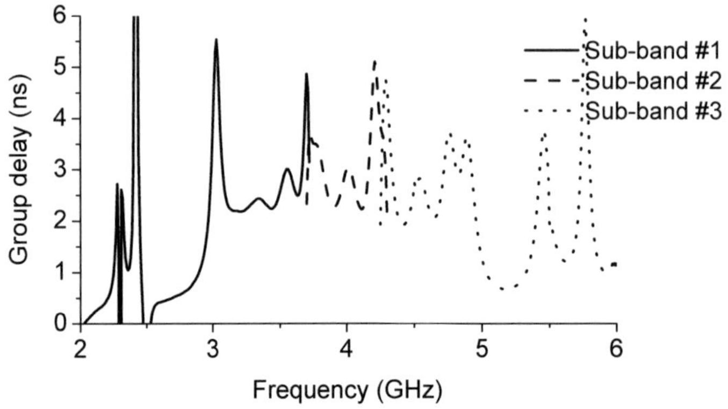

e. simulation of group delay

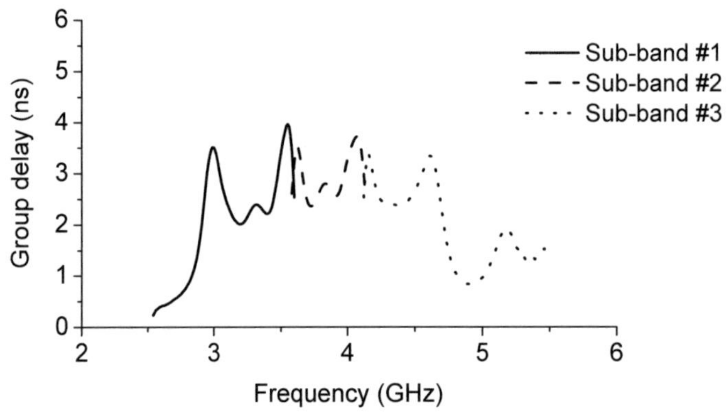

f. measurement of group delay

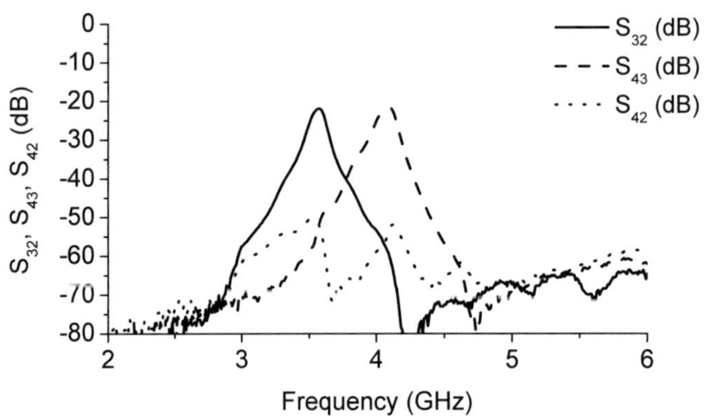

g. measurement of isolation between neighboring and alternate sub-bands

Fig. 8. Triplexer simulations and measurements.

4.3 Implementation with the Flex-rigid Substrate

Fig. 9 shows a photo of the implementation with the substrate shown in Fig. 2(b). The network is realized with a microstrip technology in the rigid part. The size of the triplexer prototype is 25 x 48 mm. Three of the four soldered Sub-Miniature A (SMA) connectors are seen. SMA connectors mounted from the side connect the three input sub-bands. Port 1 is the array input/ output (6-9 GHz), Port 2 is for sub-band #1 (6-7 GHz), Port 3 is for sub-band #2 (7-8 GHz), and Port 4 is for sub-band #3 (8-9 GHz).

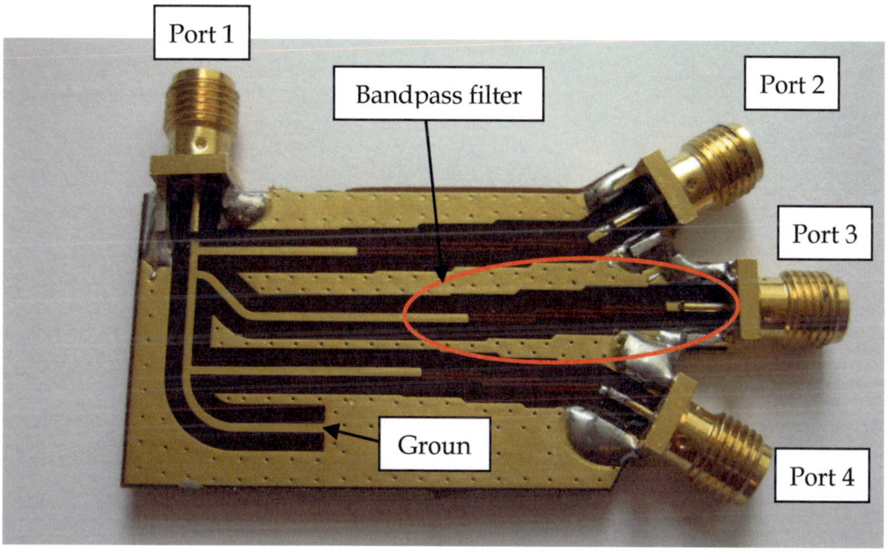

Fig. 9. Triplexer prototype photo.

Fig. 10(a) shows the simulation and measurement results of forward transmission of the triplexer. A fairly flat passband response is seen. The transmission line network is optimized together with the filters to achieve high blocking of neighbouring bands. A good match between simulation and measurement results is seen. The complete multi-layer structure was simulated with radiation characteristics enabled in ADS for the best accuracy. However, some limitations still exist in the simulations. The SMA connectors are not included, and as previously mentioned ADS Momentum does not take surface roughness into count. The simulated insertion loss is 3.35-3.85 dB, and measured insertion loss is 3.41-4.10 dB for the three sub-bands. All sub-bands have at least 1 GHz bandwidth at -3 dB from the top. Fig. 10(b) and (c) show the simulation and measurement results of return loss of the triplexer, respectively. Due to the narrow guard-band blocking of neighbouring bands a smooth forward transmission was prioritized over low return loss, as seen in Fig. 10(a)-(c). However, to use higher order than the fifth order band-pass filters would increase the design freedom but losses will increase. The only noticeable difference is a small frequency shift, due to the fact that the simulated phase velocity likely differs from the actual (Karlsson et al., 2008). Because of that known issue a scaled version of the triplexer was also designed, fabricated and measured, see the doted line labelled -5 % in Fig. 10(a). The -5 % notation is with respect to frequency, i.e., all electrical lengths were scaled up with 5 %. Fig. 10(d) shows measured isolation between Ports 2-4. It is seen that the minimum isolation is 15 dB. The minimum isolation occurs at the boundary of the neighbouring sub-bands, so in the three passbands the isolation is better than 15 dB. The isolation between the non-neighbouring alternate sub-bands is 45 dB. Fig. 10(e) shows measured phase response. It is seen that all three sub-bands have a high degree of linearity within their respective passbands. Fig. 10(f) shows measured group delay. It is seen that for all the 1 GHz sub-bands the group delay is around 1.0 ns and the variation is approximately 0.4 ns within each sub-band. It is the filter type and filter order that dominate the delay (Karlsson et al., 2008).

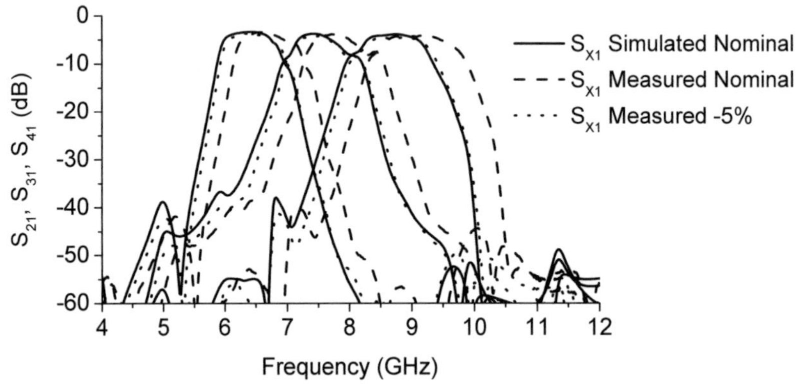

a. simulation and measurement of forward transmission

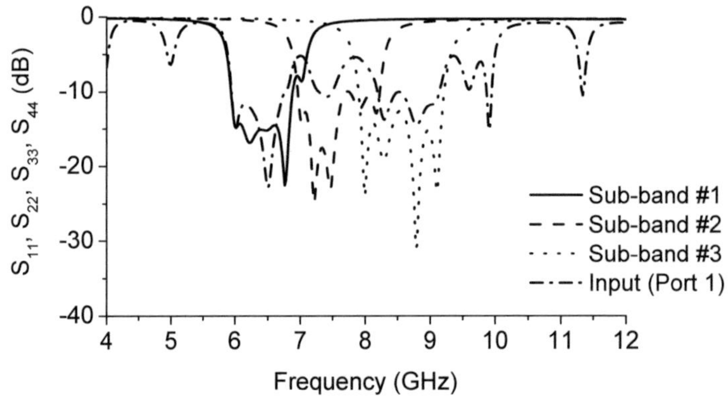

b. simulation of return loss

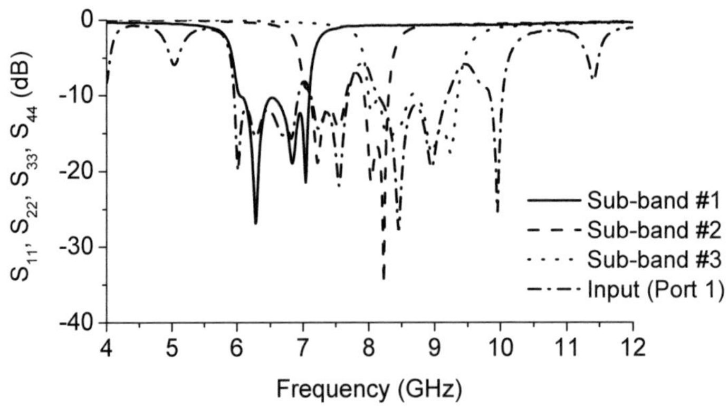

c. measurement of return loss

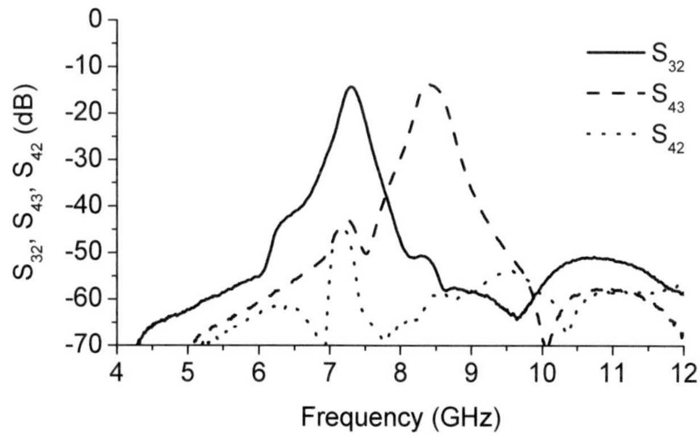

d. measurement of isolation between neighboring and alternate sub-bands

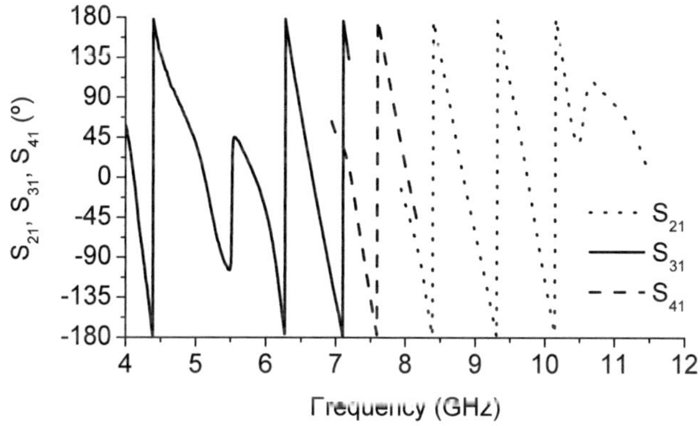

e. measurement of sub-band phase response

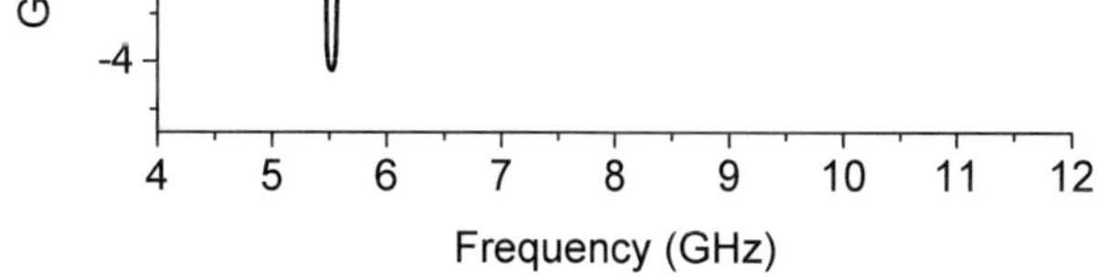

f. measurement of group delay

Fig. 10. Triplexer simulations and measurements.

5. Radio Front-end

A single wideband antenna is used to transmit three parallel channels (Fig. 5). A suitable wideband antenna can be those presented in Section 3.

5.1 Antenna

Fig. 11(a) shows the measured S_{21} phase response from a transmission between two identical circular dipole antenna (Fig. 3a), including the contribution from one transmitter antenna and one receiver antenna. It is seen that the established radio link has good phase linearity.

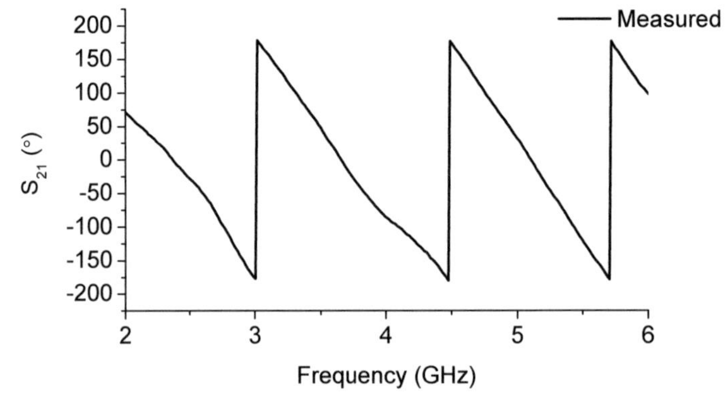

a. measurement of phase response, two Mode 1 UWB antenna

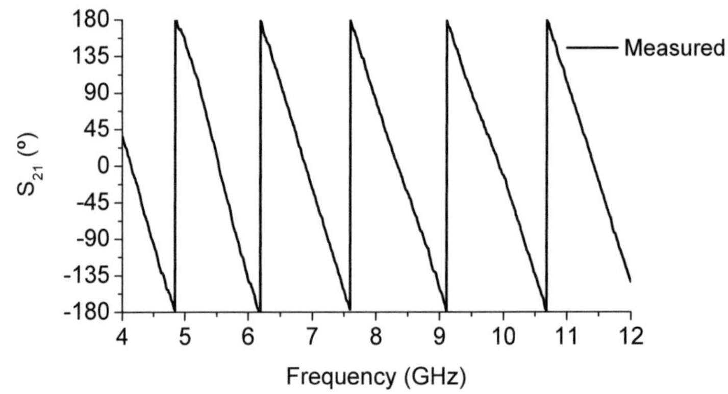

b. measurement of phase response, two 6-9 GHz antenna

Fig. 11. Measured S21 phase response (transmission between two circular dipole antenna).

5.2 System

Transmission using two antenna plus a triplexer, i.e., to receive three parallel sub-bands is shown in Fig. 12. The triplexer provides equal performance between the three different sub-bands. A wide band signal is received and divided into three parallel sub-bands using the triplexer. Moreover, both the triplexer and the antenna are bi-directional, e.g., suitable for both transmit and receive operations. For instance, the triplexer can be used to connect one antenna to three parallel transceiver channels or three antenna to one common transceiver.

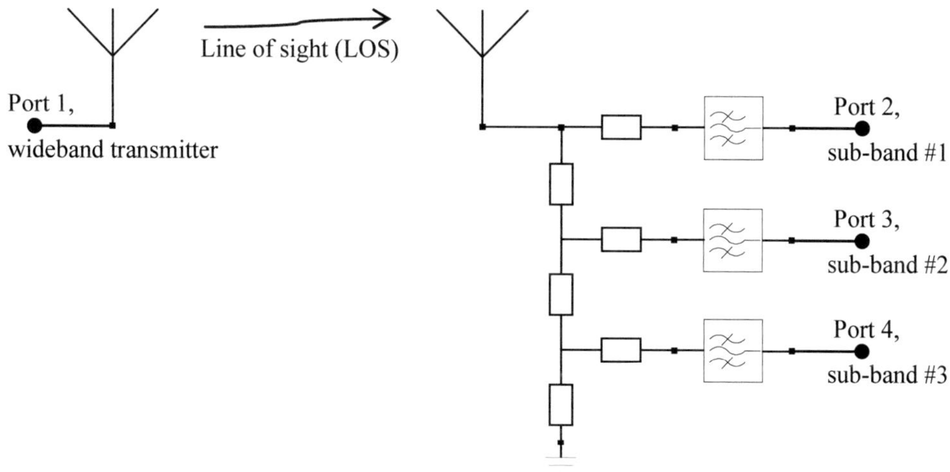

Fig. 12. Measured parallel channel transmission.

In this section a demonstration of a system providing three 500 MHz channels is shown. In theory an arbitrary number of sub-bands, of equal or unequal bandwidth can be combined with manifold multiplexing The limitations are in general on the actual physical implementation. For instance, the chosen filter topology should be suitable for the actual relative bandwidth. In the design with three equal size sub-bands having almost the same relative bandwidth it is natural to have the same kind of band-pass filter in all sub-bands. Otherwise, it ought to be beneficial to utilize different filter technologies for wide or narrow sub-bands

During radiation measurements it is important to separate near-field and far-field, i.e., to separate point-dependant electromagnetic coupling from plane wave propagation. The near-far field crossover distance is commonly noted R_{ff}, see equation 1 (Pozar, 2001). The distance depends on the quote between the largest dimension of the source (upper case D) in square and the wavelength (λ); c and f are the speed of light in vacuum in metres per second and the frequency in hertz, respectively. If the distance between the transmitting and receiving antenna is larger than R_{ff}, then it is a far field measurement (Fraunhofer diffraction) and if the measuring distance is less than R_{ff}, it is a near field measurement (Fresnel zone).

$$R_{ff} = \frac{2D^2}{\lambda} = \frac{2D^2 f}{c} \tag{1}$$

Free-space path loss (FSPL) is the loss in signal strength of a propagating wave from a line-of-sight path through free space (Pozar, 2001; Fusco, 2005), assuming that no obstacles nearby causes reflection or diffraction. Moreover, it does not take such factors into count as the gain of the antenna at the transmitter and receiver sides or any loss in the transceiver hardware. Lower case d is the distance between the transmitter and receiver antenna in meters, λ, c and f are defined as above.

$$\mathrm{FSPL} = \left(\frac{4\pi d}{\lambda}\right)^2 = \left(\frac{4\pi df}{c}\right)^2 \tag{2}$$

and in decibels (dB):

$$\mathrm{FSPL}_{dB} = 10\log_{10}\left(\frac{4\pi df}{c}\right)^2 \tag{3}$$

Using equation (1) the maximum R_{ff} distance for the "Mode 1 UWB antenna" within the Mode 1 frequency-band is calculated to 4.6 centimetres (cm) at 4.8 GHz. Furthermore, a measurement distance of 20 cm was chosen, which is four times of the maximum R_{ff} distance. Using equation (3), the estimated FSPL_{dB} ranges from -28 to -32 dB (from 3.1 to 4.8 GHz). Fig. 13(a) shows the measured results of forward transmission of the front-end. A relatively flat passband response is seen, as expected from the triplexer filter characteristics. Fig. 13(b) shows only the passband, it is seen that all channels have more than 500 MHz bandwidth at -3 dB from the top value within each sub-band. Moreover, it is seen that the three sub-bands have a similar performance. Comparing the sub-bands it should also be considered that the loss contribution due to free space path loss is frequency dependant, i.e., it increases with the square of the frequency. As shown in detail in section 4.2 the measured insertion loss (IL) of the three triplexer sub-bands was measured to be 3.1-3.5 dB, see Fig. 8(b). As shown in section 3 the circular dipole Mode 1 UWB antenna has a simulated and measured gain around 2 dBi, see Fig. 4(c). A coaxial cable with 1 dB loss that was not included in the instrument calibration was used to connect the antenna to the triplexer. Expected S_{x1} (dB) will then be FSPL_{dB} + transmitter antenna gain (2 dBi) + receiver antenna gain (also 2 dBi) – cable loss (1 dB) – triplexer IL (3.1-3.5 dB). Considering antenna gain, losses and the calculated FSPL it is seen that the results in Fig. 13(a) correlates very well with the theoretical expectations. The phase response in Fig. 13(c) shows that all sub-bands have good linearity within their respective frequency ranges, which is also recognized in the low group delay variation seen in the plot, in Fig. 13(d).

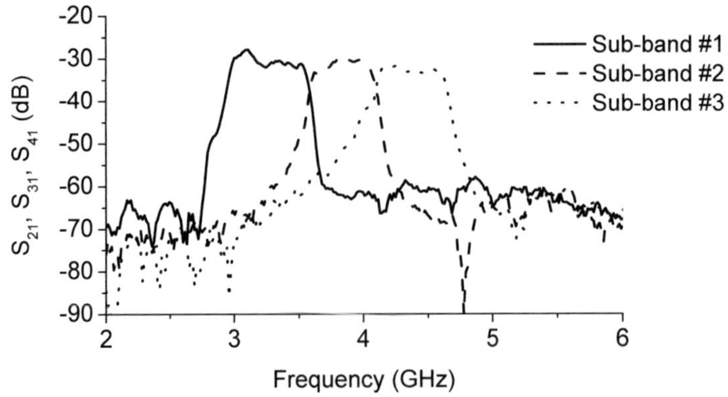

a. measurement of forward transmission of the radio link

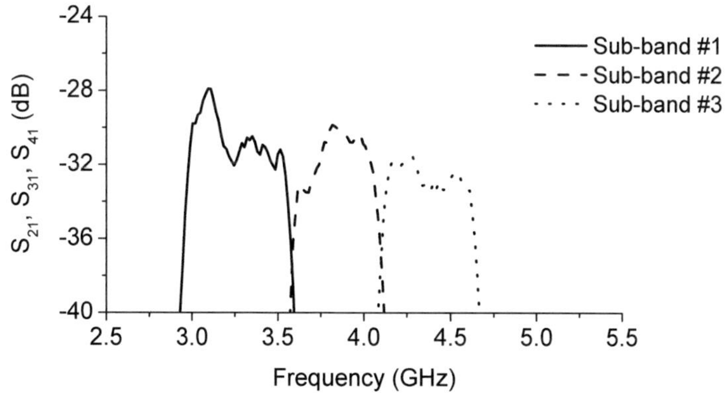

b. measurement of forward transmission (pass-band only)

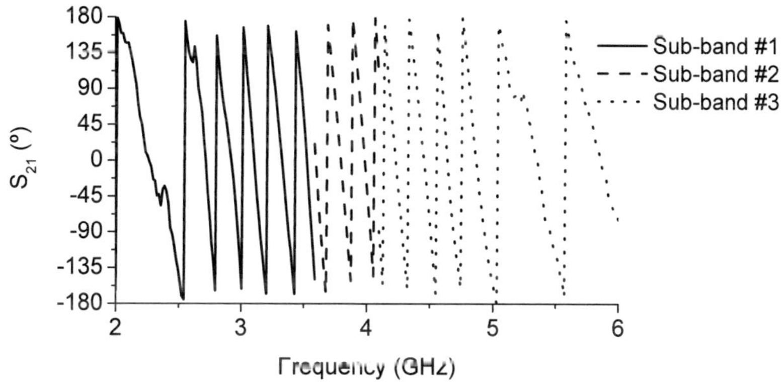

c. measurement of phase response

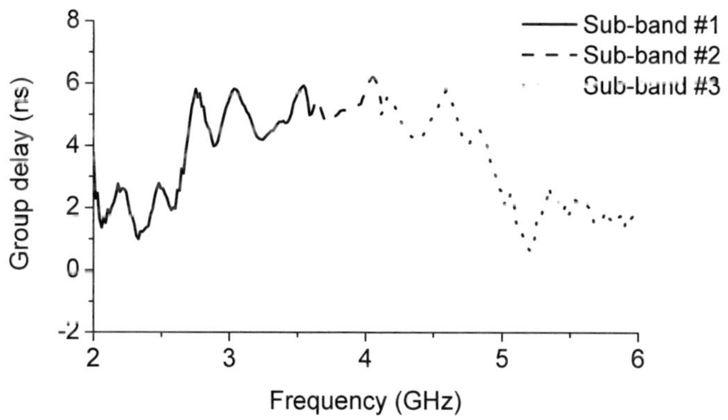

d. measurement of group delay

Fig. 13. Measured parallel channel transmission.

6. Conclusion

A fully integrated planar triplexer using microstrips for multi-band UWB has been presented. Three flat sub-bands in the frequency band 3.1-4.8 GHz and 6-9 GHz for multi-band UWB have been achieved. The triplexer can be integrated into a printed circuit board using a commercial process at low cost, even though the guard-band has only a relative bandwidth of 0.7 % between the three sub-bands. The triplexer uses three filters with a combined broadside- and edge-coupled structure. It is verified that this kind of combined broadside- and edge-coupled filters has higher performance than that of conventional edge-coupled filters.

Two circular dipole antenna with integrated baluns using the flex-rigid substrate can cover the lower UWB frequency band (3.1-4.8 GHz) and the upper UWB band (6-9 GHz) at a measured VSWR around 2. Furthermore, a wide and stable radiation pattern is achieved. Moreover, good phase linearity is observed when the antenna is used in a wireless transmission, i.e., good linearity in both transmitting and receiving operations. With these excellent properties the antenna can be either used as stand-alone components or integrated in a UWB system.

It is shown that using a triplexer and a circular dipole antenna 500 MHz sub-bands can be processed in parallel with equal performance. Moreover, the whole system, i.e., antenna, balun, and triplexer including filters is implemented using only distributed components. The passband shape of the transmitted sub-channels is very close to the shape of the sub-bands in the stand-alone triplexer, indicating that the passband of the filters dominates the shape of the passbands of the transmitted channels. Moreover, a linear phase response and a group delay variation of 1 ns for each transmitted sub-band are obtained.

7. References

Coale, F. S. (1958). Applications of Directional Filters for Multiplexing Systems. *Trans. Microwave Theory and Tech.*, Vol. 6, No. 4, pp. 450-453

Rhodes, J. D. & Levy, R. (1979). A generalized multiplexer theory. *Trans. Microwave Theory and Tech.*, Vol. 27, No. 2, pp. 99-111, Feb. 1979

Rhodes, J. D. & Levy, R. (1979). Design of General Manifold Multiplexers. *Trans. Microwave Theory and Tech.*, Vol. 27, No. 2, pp. 111-123, Feb. 1979

Bandler, J. W.; Kellermann, W. & Madsen, K. (1987). A nonlinear l_1 optimization algorithm for design, modeling, and diagnosis of networks. *IEEE Trans. Circuits and Systems*, Vol. 34, No. 2, pp. 174-181, Feb. 1987

Mansour, R. R. (1994). Design of Superconductive Multiplexers Using Single-Mode and Dual-Mode Filters. *Trans. Microwave Theory and Tech.*, Vol. 41, No. 7, pp. 1411-1418, Jul. 1994

Rauscher, C. (1994). Efficient design methodology for microwave frequency multiplexers using infinite-array prototype circuits. *Trans. Microwave Theory and Tech.*, Vol. 42, No. 7, pp. 1337-1346, Jul. 1994

Kirilenko, A. A.; Senkevich, S. L.; Tkachenko, V. I. & Tysik, B. G. (1994). Waveguide duplexer and multiplexer design. *Trans. Microwave Theory and Tech.*, Vol. 42, No. 7, pp. 1393-1396, Jul. 1994

Matthaei, G. L.; Rohlfing, S. M. & Forse, R. J. (1996). Design of HTS, lumped-element, manifold-type microwave multiplexers. *Trans. Microwave Theory and Tech.*, vol. 44, no. 7, pp. 1313-1321, Jul. 1996

Bariant, D.; Bila, S.; Baillargeat, D.; Verdeyme, S.; Guillon, P.; Pacaud, D. & Herren, J. J. (2002). Method of spurious mode compensation applied to manifold multiplexer design, in *IEEE MTT-S Int. Microwave Symp. Dig.*, 2002, Vol. 3, pp. 1461-1464

Ohno, T.; Wada, K. & Hashimoto, O. (2005). Design methodologies of planar duplexers and triplexers by manipulating attenuation poles. *IEEE Trans. Microwave Theory and Tech.*, Vol. 53, No. 6, pp. 2088-2095, Jun. 2005

Chen, C.-F.; Huang, T.-Y.; Chou, C.-P. & Wu, R.-B. (2006). Microstrip duplexers design with common resonator sections for compact size, but high isolation. *Trans. Microwave Theory and Tech.*, Vol. 54, No. 5, pp. 1945-1952, May 2006

Cameron, R. I. & Yu, M. (2007). Design of manifold-coupled multiplexers," *Microwave Magazine, IEEE*, vol. 8, no. 5, pp. 46-59, Oct. 2007

Lai, M.-I. & Jeng, S.-K. (2005) A microstrip three-port and four-channel multiplexer for WLAN and UWB coexistence. *Trans. Microwave Theory and Tech.*, Vol. 53, No. 10, pp. 3244-3250, Oct. 2005

Mallegol, S.; Coupez, J.-P.; Person, C.; Lespagnol, T.; Paquelet, S. & Bisiaux, A. (2006) Microwave (De)Multiplexer for Ultra-Wideband (UWB) Non-Coherent High Data Rates Transceiver, in *Proc. 3rd European Radar Conference, EuRAD 2006*, pp. 346-349

Stadius, K.; Rapinoja, T.; Kaukovuori, J.; Ryynanen, J. & Halonen, K. A. I. (2007). Multitone Fast Frequency-Hopping Synthesizer for UWB Radio. *Trans. Microwave Theory and Tech.*, Vol. 55, No. 8, pp.1633-1641, Aug. 2007

Tarng, S.-H.; Tsai, Y.-C.; Shen, Y.-S. & Jou, C. F. (2007) A Signal Generator for MB-OFDM UWB System in 0.18 μm CMOS Process, in *IEEE MTT-S Int. Microwave Symp.*, 2007, pp. 2157-2160

Galbraith, C.; Rebeiz, G. M. & Drangmeister, R. (2007) A Cochlea-based Preselector for UWB Applications, in *IEEE Radio Frequency Integrated Circuits (RFIC) Symp.*, 2007, pp. 219-222

Karlsson, M. & Gong, S. (2008) Monopole and Dipole Antenna for UWB Radio Utilizing a Flex-rigid Structure, *ISAST Transactions on Electronics and Signal Processing*, Vol. 2, No. 1, pp. 59-63, 2008

Karlsson, M.; Osth, J.; Owais; Serban, A. & Gong, S. (2009) Circular dipole antenna for lower and upper UWB bands with integrated balun, *IEEE International Conference on Ultra-Wideband, ICUWB 2009*, pp.658-663, 9-11 Sept. 2009

Karlsson, M. & Gong, S. (2009) Circular Dipole Antenna for Mode 1 UWB Radio with Integrated Balun Utilizing a Flex-rigid Structure, *IEEE Trans. Antenna and Propag.*, Vol. 57, No. 10, pp. 2967-2971, Oct. 2009

Karlsson, M.; Håkansson, P.; Huynh, A. & Gong, S. (2006) Frequency-multiplexed Inverted-F Antenna for Multi-band UWB, *IEEE Wireless and Microwave Conf. 2006*, pp. 2.1-2.3, 2006

Karlsson, M. & Gong, S. (2007) A Frequency-Triplexed Inverted-F Antenna System for Ultra-wide Multi-band Systems 3.1-4.8 GHz, ISAST Transactions on Electronics and Signal Processing, Vol. 1, No. 1, pp. 95-100, 2007

Karlsson, M.; Håkansson, P. & Gong, S. (2008) A Frequency Triplexer for Ultra-Wideband Systems Utilizing Combined Broadside- and Edge-Coupled Filters, *IEEE Trans. on Advanced Packaging*, Vol. 31, No. 4, pp. 794-801, Nov. 2008

Pozar, D. M. (2001) Microwave and RF Design of Wireless Systems, John Wiley & Sons Inc., ISBN 0-471-32282-2, USA, 2001

Fusco, V. F. (2005) Foundations of Antenna Theory and Techniques, Pearson Education Limited, Edinburgh Gate, Harlow, Essex, England, ISBN 0-130-26267-6, 2005

4

Performance of a TH-PPM UWB system in different scenario environments

Moez HIZEM and Ridha BOUALLEGUE
Research Unit 6'Tel, Sup'Com
Tunisia

1. Introduction

Ultra Wideband (UWB) communication technology has attracted considerable attention by researchers in recent years because of its appealing features and its several applications it offers in many areas (Win & Scholtz, 1998; Fontana, 2007; Ghavami et al, 2007). An UWB system is characterised by very short-duration pulses (usually on the order of a nanosecond) with a low duty cycle. It offers low power transmission, a fine path resolution and it easily supports multi-user communication (Di Benedetto, 2004). These properties make UWB technology an attractive candidate for short-range, high-speed wireless multiple access communication and ad hoc networking, with simple baseband and the capability to overlay legacy wireless systems. All this gives us many features such as wireless radar, communications, networking, imaging and positioning systems (Yang & Giannakis, 2004).
Historically, UWB systems are based on impulse radio (IR) concepts. In an IR UWB system, a number of pulses are transmitted per information symbol and information is usually conveyed by the positions or the polarities of the pulses. In order that impulse radios, operating in the highly frequency range below a few GHz, do not interfere with narrowband radio systems operating in the same frequency band, the use of spread-spectrum techniques is necessary. A simple mean to spread the spectrum of these UWB pulse trains is Time Hopping (TH), with data modulation achieved in the rate of many pulses per data symbol (Win & Scholtz, 1998, a). In UWB systems, there are several basic methods of modulation but the most common impulse radio based UWB concepts are based on Pulse Position Modulation combined with Time Hopping (TH-PPM) where each pulse is delayed in advance of a regular time scale. Thereafter, we will describe this concept with further details. The study of digital communications system performance over the AWGN (Additive White Gaussian Noise) channels starts generally with statistically independent zero-mean Gaussian noise samples. Due to the Gaussian statistics of the noise samples, the probability of error can therefore be written in terms of a Q-function.
There exists a set of efficient techniques for performance analysis when the system is distorted by AWGN and Rayleigh fading. We shall focus on the analytical methods that are useful in addressing the characteristics unique to UWB systems, such as the different modulation schemes and the large number of resolvable paths available to the receiver. In a UWB system rather realistic, the received pulses may overlap others causing inter-pulse

interference (IPI). Performance analysis taking into account IPI is commonly very complex and will not be developed in this chapter. This topic is studied and evaluated in (Zhao & Liu, 2005). A method to estimate the Bit Error Rate (BER) of UWB TH-PPM in the presence of multi-user interference (MUI) and AWGN channel is proposed by using Gaussian quadrature rules (GQR). Applied to UWB system performance analysis, its major improvement is to surmount the problem of exactly evaluating the MUI (Durisi & Benedetto, 2003). Studies of multiple-access system for the TH-PPM modulation were conducted in (Scholtz, 1993; Zhao & Haimovich, 2002), using a Gaussian approximation (GA) to statically model the multiple access interference (MAI). However, it was shown in (Durisi & Romano, 2002) that the GA significantly underestimates the BER of practical TH-PPM systems. A method is proposed for precisely calculating the BER of a TH-BPPM UWB system with MAI. The analytical expression is validated by simulation and used to assess the inaccuracy of the GA (Hu & Beaulieu, 2003). An analytical method based on exact statistical modeling of MAI is proposed for exact BER computation of TH-PPM UWB systems. The proposed modeling considers full asynchronism (Niranjayan et al, 2004). The system robustness and real indoor channel measurements in dense multipath environments have been studied. The results show that the UWB signal does not suffer from multipath fading. Therefore, little fading margin is necessary to undertaking reliable communications (Win & Scholtz, 1998, b).

In this chapter, however, we focus on an ideal multiple-access channel, i.e., an additive white Gaussian noise (AWGN) channel. An exact BER calculation for UWB systems is usually unwieldy. Our purpose is to provide an accurate approach for the evaluation of the ultra wideband system performance in a TH-BPPM scheme in the presence of an AWGN channel. This performance was illustrated using an analytical method based on the evaluation of the exact bit error rate (BER) probability versus signal to noise ratio (SNR). This is based on the decision that enables to decode the information transmitted over our UWB system model. This decision is then developed by equations in order to precisely compute the performance in terms of errors rate by bit. In order to emphasize the fundamental analysis techniques, we will firstly focus on a single-user and single-path system (no co-channel interference) that utilizes binary signaling, and suppose that there is no narrowband interference or inter-symbol interference (ISI). We will extend the used method in different scenario environments and a comparison is made between them.

The rest of this chapter is organized as follows. We present a detailed description of the TH-PPM UWB system in Section.2, and then we develop an error performance analysis for only one user and one path environment in Section.3. In Section.4, this analytical analysis is extended for multi-user TH-PPM UWB systems. The performance of multipath TH-PPM UWB systems is developed in Section.5 from the same method used previously. Section.6 presents the performance of simultaneously multipath and multi-user TH-PPM UWB systems always with this same analysis and a comparison between different scenario environments performance. This comparison is illustrated by simulation results. And finally, we conclude this chapter in Section.7.

2. TH-PPM UWB System Model

Common multiple access techniques implemented for pulse based UWB systems are Time Hopping (TH) and Direct Sequence (DS). Appropriate modulation techniques include OOK

(Foerster et al, 2001) and particularly PPM and PAM (Hämäläinen et al, 2002). A given UWB communication system will be a mixture of these techniques, leading to signals based on, for example, TH-PPM, TH-BPAM or DS-BPAM. TH-PPM is almost certainly the most frequently adopted scheme and will be applied in the following as an example for determining the resources existing in a UWB system.

2.1 Pulse Position Modulation (PPM)

With pulse position modulation (PPM), the selected bit to be transmitted influences the position of the UWB pulse. That denotes that while bit '0' is represented by a pulse originating at the time instant 0, bit '1' is shifted in time by the amount of δ from 0.
Analytically, the signal PPM x(t) can be represented as

$$x(t) = w_{tr}(t - \delta d_j) \tag{1}$$

Where $w_{tr}(t)$ is the transmitted pulse waveform and d_j assumes the following values, depending on the bit chosen to be transmitted,

$$d_j = \begin{cases} 0, & j = 0 \\ 1, & j = 1 \end{cases}$$

The advantages of PPM mainly arise from its simplicity and the ease with which the delay may be controlled. On the other hand, for the UWB system extremely fine time control is necessary to modulate pulses to sub-nanosecond accuracy.

2.2 Data Modulation with Time Hopping

In TH-mode, the pulse transmission instant is defined by the pseudo-random code. One data bit is spread over the multiple pulses to achieve a processing gain due to the pulse repetition. The processing gain is also increased by the low transmission duty cycle.
The time hopping randomizes the signal in both time and frequency domains (Withington et al., 1999). Pseudo random time hopping also reduces collisions between users in multiple access systems, where each user has a distinct pulse shift pattern (Win & Scholtz, 1997a).

2.3 Description of TH-PPM UWB System Model

TH-UWB impulse radio is built upon position shift of pulses with a certain shape in the time domain. The studied system's model is based on Time Hopping (TH) combined with pulse position modulation (PPM) scheme applied in the context of UWB. The TH-PPM block diagram used in our case is shown in Fig. 1.

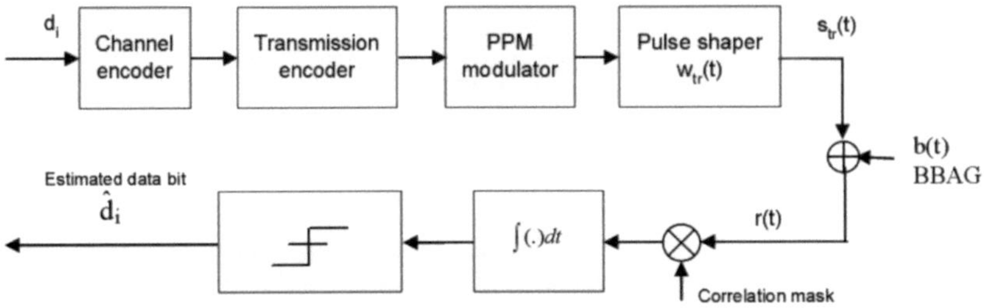

Fig. 1. Description of the used UWB TH-PPM scheme block diagram

The transmitted signal $S_{tr}(t)$ in the UWB TH-PPM systems is described by the following model (Durisi & Benedetto, 2003):

$$S_{tr}(t) = \sum_{k=1}^{+\infty} a_k \sum_{i=-\infty}^{+\infty} \sum_{j=0}^{N_h-1} w_{tr}\left(t - iT_s - jT_f - c_j^{(k)}T_s - d_i^{(k)}\delta\right) \tag{2}$$

Where $w_{tr}(t)$ is the transmitted pulse waveform, which is usually referred to monocycle. T_s is the symbol (or bit) duration, K is the number of users and a_k is the amplitude of different users. In order to allow the channel to be shared by many users and eliminate catastrophic collision, each user is assigned a distinctive time-shift pattern $c_j^{(k)}$ called as TH sequence, which takes values in $\{0,1,\ldots,N_h\text{-}1\}$. The frame time T_f and the chip time T_c are chosen to satisfy $N_hT_c \le T_f$. The binary information stream $\{d_i^{(k)}\}$ is transmitted employing a PPM modulation format and introducing an additional shift δ to distinguish between pulses carrying the bit 0 and the bit 1.

In binary PPM modulation scheme, the information is transmitted with time lags between the nominal and real moments of transmission of impulse. If the impulsion is sent during the real time of transmission which is defined by the pseudo-random code specific to the user, the bit is '0'. If the moment of transmission is delayed of a certain time which is connected to the index of modulation of the system, the bit transmitted is '1'. This is described by the Fig. 2 which represents two cases of transmission ('0' and '1') for $N_f = 4$ (bit represented on 4 impulses), $N_h = 3$ (3 chips).The TH code is given by [1 *0 0* 2], which means that the pulse in the first frame is shifted by $1T_c$ seconds, the ones in the second and the third frame are not shifted and the one in the fourth frame is shifted by $2T_c$ seconds.

We suppose that the model of the TH-PPM system is synchronized. This enables us to avoid dealing with the problems involved in synchronization.

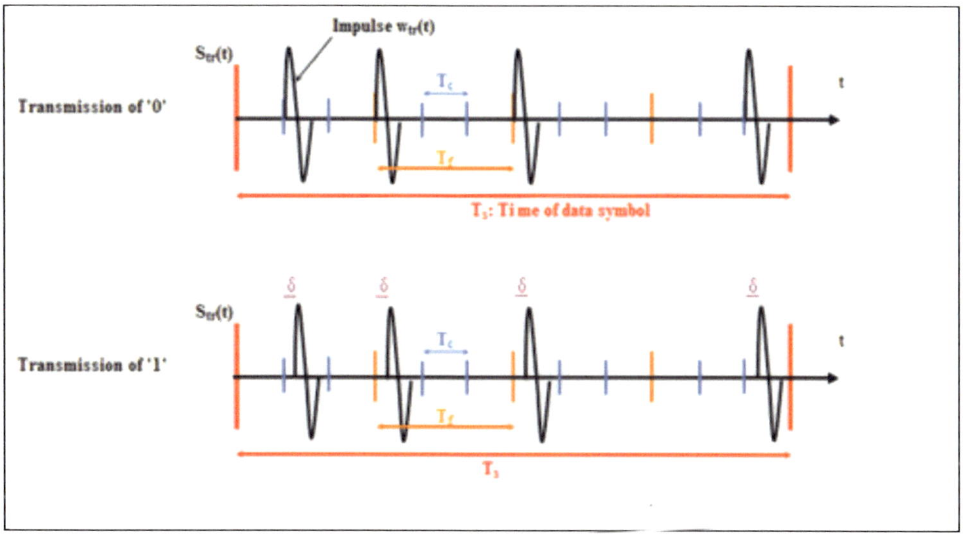

Fig. 2. Transmission of a TH-PPM signal

3. Analytical Analysis of BER in the UWB TH-PPM System Model

In order to determine the probability of error, we will first of all start by studying the reception of the UWB TH-PPM system model for only one user and one path (Hizem & Bouallegue, 2008).

This translates into the following equation which is basically the decision at the reception (Multiplication of the emitted symbol expression by the difference between the received symbols expression '0' and '1'),

$$D_i = \int_{[T_s]} \left[\sum_{j=0}^{N_h-1} w_{tr}\left(t - jT_f - c_jT_c - d_i\delta\right) + b(t) \right] \times \left[\sum_{j=0}^{N_h-1} \left(w_{tr}\left(t - jT_f - c_jT_c\right) - w_{tr}\left(t - jT_f - c_jT_c - \delta\right) \right) \right] dt \quad (3)$$

We will suppose that the temporal support in this case is disjoins. After calculation, we obtain the equation (4) derived from (3):

$$D_i = N_h R_w(d_i\delta) - N_h\left((1 - d_i)\delta\right) + \tilde{b} \quad (4)$$

With $R_w(d_i\delta) = \int_{[T_s]} w_{tr}(t) w_{tr}(t - d_i\delta)dt$, $\tilde{b}$ determines the noise power and R_w represents the autocorrelation function of the transmitted signal. In the noise less case ($b(t) = 0$), we obtain:

$$d_i = 0; \qquad D_i = N_h[R_w(0) - R_w(\delta)] > 0$$
$$d_i = 1; \qquad D_i = N_h[R_w(\delta) - R_w(0)] < 0$$

By definition, the probability of error represents the percentage of error of the received sequences $\widehat{d_i}$ compared to the emitted sequences d_i. This is given by:

$$P_e = \text{Prob}\left(\widehat{d_i} \neq d_i\right) \tag{5}$$

Since the d_i are equiprobable, the equation (5) becomes:

$$P_e = \text{Prob}\left(\widehat{d_i} \neq d_i \,/\, d_i = 0\right) = \text{Prob}(D_i < 0 \,/\, d_i = 0) \tag{6}$$

After calculation, we find the expression of the probability of error:

$$P_e = \text{Prob}\left(\frac{\tilde{b}}{\sigma_b^2} > \frac{N_h[R_w(0) - R_w(\delta)]}{\sigma_b^2}\right) \tag{7}$$

To be able to calculate the autocorrelation functions $R_w(0)$ and $R_w(\delta)$, we consider the expression of Gaussian monocycle which can be defined as the first derivative of the Gaussian function. The Gaussian monocycle in time domain $w_{tr}(t)$ can be mathematically defined using the formula (Win & Scholtz, 2000):

$$w_{tr}(t) = \left(\frac{t}{\tau}\right)\exp\left(-\left(\frac{t}{\tau}\right)^2\right) \tag{8}$$

Thus, we obtain the expressions of $R_w(0)$ and $R_w(\delta)$,

$$R_w(0) = \frac{\sqrt{2\pi}}{8}\tau$$

$$R_w(\delta) = \frac{\sqrt{2\pi}}{8}(\tau^2 - \delta^2)\exp\left(-\frac{\delta^2}{2\tau^2}\right)$$

After having made calculation of $R_w(0)$ and $R_w(\delta)$, the equation (7) will become:

$$P_e = \text{Prob}\left(\frac{\tilde{b}}{\sigma_b^2} > \frac{\sqrt{2\pi}N_h\left[\tau - (\tau^2 - \delta^2)\exp\left(-\frac{\delta^2}{2\tau^2}\right)\right]}{8\sigma_b^2}\right) \tag{9}$$

Since the signal power is given by:

$$P_s = N_h \int w_{tr}^2(t)dt = N_h\tau\frac{\sqrt{2\pi}}{8} \tag{10}$$

We can rewrite the equation (9) in another way:

$$P_e = \text{Prob}\left(\frac{\tilde{b}}{\sigma_b^2} > \frac{P_s}{\sigma_b^2} - \frac{\sqrt{2\pi}}{8}N_h\left(\frac{\tau^2 - \delta^2}{\sigma_b^2}\right)\exp\left(-\frac{\delta^2}{2\tau^2}\right)\right)$$

$$= \mathrm{Prob}\left(\frac{\tilde{b}}{\sigma_{\tilde{b}}^2} > SNR - \frac{\sqrt{2\pi}}{8}\mathrm{N_h}\left(\frac{\tau^2-\delta^2}{\sigma_{\tilde{b}}^2}\right)\exp\left(-\frac{\delta^2}{2\tau^2}\right)\right)$$

After having developed the expression of P_e, we obtain the equation (11):

$$P_e = \int_{\beta}^{+\infty} \frac{1}{\sqrt{2\pi}} \exp\left(-\frac{x^2}{2}\right) dx \tag{11}$$

With $\beta = \mathrm{SNR} - \frac{\sqrt{2\pi}}{8}\mathrm{N_h}\left(\frac{\tau^2-\delta^2}{\sigma_{\tilde{b}}^2}\right)\exp\left(-\frac{\delta^2}{2\tau^2}\right)$

Knowing that $\sigma_{\tilde{b}}^2$ is the noise power and the signal power is equal to $R_w(0)$, we find the equation (12) derived from (11):

$$P_e = Q\left(\mathrm{SNR}\left(1-\tau\left(1-\frac{\delta^2}{\tau^2}\right)\exp\left(-\frac{\delta^2}{2\tau^2}\right)\right)\right) \tag{12}$$

The above equation represents the performance of an UWB TH-PPM system for the case of one user and one path, where Q characterizes the Marcum function and, by definition, is the complementary error function.

The Fig. 3 gives us an outline of the comparison, point of view probability of error, between the analytical approach and simulation by the Matlab tool. According to the figure, we can see that the probability of error in the analytical case and the simulation case are almost the same.

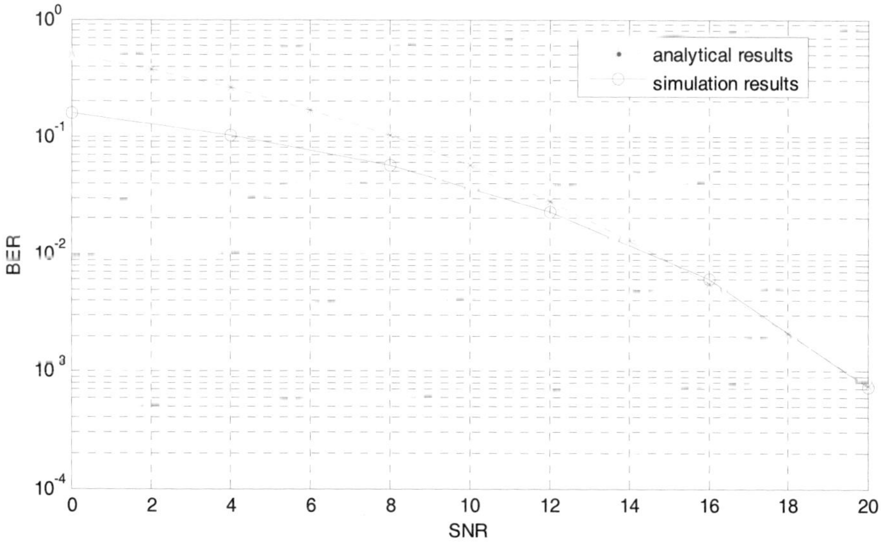

Fig. 3. Comparison between analytical and simulation results

4. Analytical Analysis of BER in the UWB TH-PPM System Model in Multi-user environments

In this section, we are interested in performance of UWB TH-PPM system model in multi-user environments. We assume that the amplitudes a_k of different users are known (assuming that we use later in our analytical analysis). The Fig. 4 shows a particular case of emission of three users. These emitters have some TH different codes and each sends a symbol (either '0' or '1') according to its own TH code.

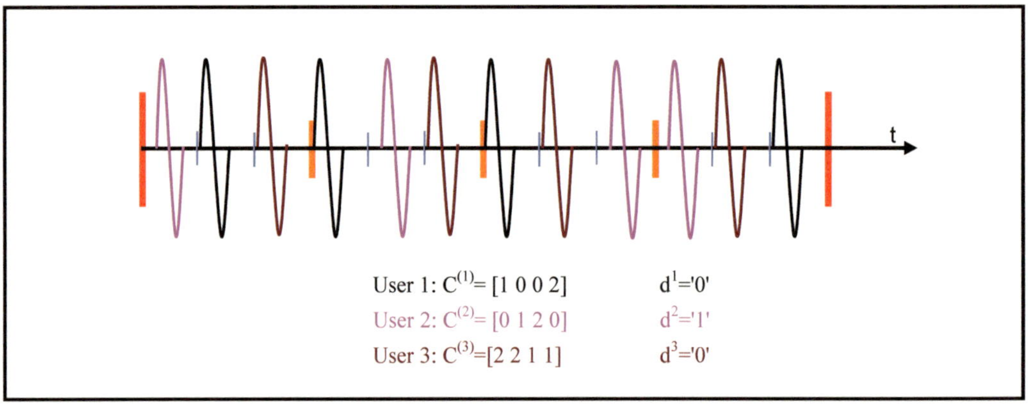

Fig. 4. Transmission of an UWB TH-PPM signal in multi-user environments

As before, we begin by studying the reception of this system translated by the following equation which is the decision making at the reception (Hizem & Bouallegue, 2009a; Hizem & Bouallegue, 2009b),

$$D_i = \int_{[T_s]} \left[\sum_{k=1}^{K} a_k \sum_{j=0}^{N_h-1} w_{tr}\left(t - jT_f - c_j^{(k)}T_c - d_i^{(k)}\delta\right) + b(t) \right] \times \left[\sum_{j=0}^{N_h-1} \left(w_{tr}(t - jT_f - c_jT_c) - w_{tr}(t - jT_f - c_jT_c - \delta) \right) \right] dt \tag{13}$$

Considering the same assumptions as for the previous section and developing the above equation,

$$D_i = \int_{[T_s]} \left[\sum_{k=1}^{K} a_k \left(\sum_{j=0}^{N_h-1} w_{tr}\left(t - jT_f - c_j^{(k)}T_c - d_i^{(k)}\delta\right) w_{tr}(t - jT_f - c_jT_c) - w_{tr}\left(t - jT_f - c_j^{(k)}T_c - d_i^{(k)}\delta\right) w_{tr}(t - jT_f - c_jT_c - \delta) \right) \right] dt + \tilde{b} \tag{14}$$

To simplify our calculation, we take first the case of 2 users and then try to generalize the found results for K users. After developing the equation (14) and made an appropriate change of variable, we obtain the following equation:

$$D_i = \int_{[T_s]} \left[\left(a_1 \sum_{j=0}^{N_h-1} w_{tr}\left(t - d_i^{(1)}\delta\right) w_{tr}(t) + a_2 \sum_{j=0}^{N_h-1} w_{tr}\left(t - d_i^{(2)}\delta\right) w_{tr}(t) \right) - \left(a_1 \sum_{j=0}^{N_h-1} w_{tr}\left(t - d_i^{(1)}\delta\right) w_{tr}(t-\delta) + a_2 \sum_{j=0}^{N_h-1} w_{tr}\left(t - d_i^{(2)}\delta\right) w_{tr}(t-\delta) \right) \right] dt + \tilde{b} \tag{15}$$

By replacing the integral in the above equation with N_h, we obtain:

$$D_i = \int_{[T_s]} \left[N_h a_1 \left(w_{tr}\left(t - d_i^{(1)}\delta\right) w_{tr}(t) - w_{tr}\left(t - d_i^{(1)}\delta\right) w_{tr}(t-\delta) \right) + N_h a_2 \left(w_{tr}\left(t - d_i^{(2)}\delta\right) w_{tr}(t) - w_{tr}\left(t - d_i^{(2)}\delta\right) w_{tr}(t-\delta) \right) \right] dt + \tag{16}$$

To simplify our calculation, we can rewrite the equation (16) in another way,

$$D_i = N_h a_1 \left[R_w\left(d_i^{(1)}\delta\right) - R_w\left((1 - d_i^{(1)})\delta\right) \right] + N_h a_2 \left[R_w\left(d_i^{(2)}\delta\right) - R_w\left((1 - d_i^{(2)})\delta\right) \right] + \tag{17}$$

With

$$R_w\left(d_i^{(1)}\delta\right) = \int_{[T_s]} w_{tr}(t)\, w_{tr}\left(t - d_i^{(1)}\delta\right) dt$$
$$R_w\left(d_i^{(2)}\delta\right) = \int_{[T_s]} w_{tr}(t)\, w_{tr}\left(t - d_i^{(2)}\delta\right) dt$$

The performance will be determined in relation to the user 1. Obviously, it will be the same as for the user 2. In the noise less case ($b(t) = 0$), we obtain:

$$d_i^{(1)} = 0; \quad D_i = N_h a_1 [R_w(0) - R_w(\delta)] + N_h a_2 \left[R_w\left(d_i^{(2)}\delta\right) - R_w\left((1 - d_i^{(2)})\delta\right) \right] > 0$$
$$d_i^{(1)} = 1; \quad D_i = N_h a_1 [R_w(0) - R_w(\delta)] + N_h a_2 \left[R_w\left((1 - d_i^{(2)})\delta\right) - R_w\left(d_i^{(2)}\delta\right) \right] < 0$$

Then, from this expression, we can determine the probability of error for the user 1,

$$P_e^{U_1} = \mathrm{Prob}\left(\frac{\tilde{b}}{\sigma_{\tilde{b}}^2} > \frac{N_h a_1 [R_w(0) - R_w(\delta)] + N_h a_2 \left[R_w\left(d_i^{(2)}\delta\right) - R_w\left((1 - d_i^{(2)})\delta\right) \right]}{\sigma_{\tilde{b}}^2} \right) \tag{18}$$

As in the previous section, we consider the expression of a Gaussian pulse. $R_w(0)$ and $R_w(\delta)$ already being calculated, remains to be determined the expressions of $R_w\left(d_i^{(2)}\delta\right)$ and $R_w\left((1-d_i^{(2)})\delta\right)$. Thus, we obtain:

$$R_w\left(d_i^{(2)}\delta\right) = \frac{\sqrt{2\pi}}{8}\left[\tau^2 - \left(d_i^{(2)}\delta\right)^2\right]\exp\left(-\frac{\left(d_i^{(2)}\delta\right)^2}{2\tau^2}\right)$$

$$R_w\left((1-d_i^{(2)})\delta\right) = K\frac{\sqrt{2\pi}}{8}\left[\tau^2 + \delta^2\left(1-d_i^{(2)}\right)\left(1-3d_i^{(2)}\right)\right]$$

With $$K = \exp\left(-\frac{3}{4}\delta^2\right)\exp\left(-\frac{\delta^2}{2}d_i^{(2)}\right)\exp\left(\frac{3}{4}\delta^2\left(d_i^{(2)}\right)^2\right)$$

Based on the foregoing, it is clear that the probability of error for the user 1 depends on $d_i^{(2)}$. Therefore, there are two cases following that $d_i^{(2)}$ = '0' or $d_i^{(2)} = 1$.

4.1 First Case: $d_i^{(2)}$ = '0'

Therefore, $K = exp\left(-\frac{3}{4}\delta^2\right)$ and the probability of error for the user 1 will have as expression (knowing that $P_s = N_h\tau\frac{\sqrt{2\pi}}{8}$),

$$P_e^{U_1} = Q\left(a_1 SNR\left(1-\tau\left(1-\frac{\delta^2}{\tau^2}\right)\exp\left(-\frac{\delta^2}{2\tau^2}\right)\right) + a_2 SNR\left(\tau\left(1-\exp\left(-\frac{3}{4}\delta^2\right)\right)-\frac{\delta^2}{\tau^2}\exp\left(-\frac{3}{4}\delta^2\right)\right)\right) \quad (19)$$

4.2 Second Case: $d_i^{(2)}$ = '1'

Therefore, $K = exp\left(-\frac{\delta^2}{2}\right)$ and the probability of error for the user 1 will have as expression,

$$P_e^{U_1} = Q\left(a_1 SNR\left(1-\tau\left(1-\frac{\delta^2}{\tau^2}\right)\exp\left(-\frac{\delta^2}{2\tau^2}\right)\right) + a_2 SNR\left(\left(\tau-\frac{\delta^2}{\tau}\right)\exp\left(-\frac{\delta^2}{2\tau^2}\right)-\tau\exp\left(-\frac{\delta^2}{2}\right)\right)\right) \quad (20)$$

The Fig. 5 compares the probability of error for the two cases $d_i^{(2)}$ = '0' and $d_i^{(2)} = 1$. We notice according to this figure that there is very little difference between the two performances. Therefore, we can conclude that the choice of the impulsion ('0'or '1') doesn't influence the performance of this arrangement of modulation.

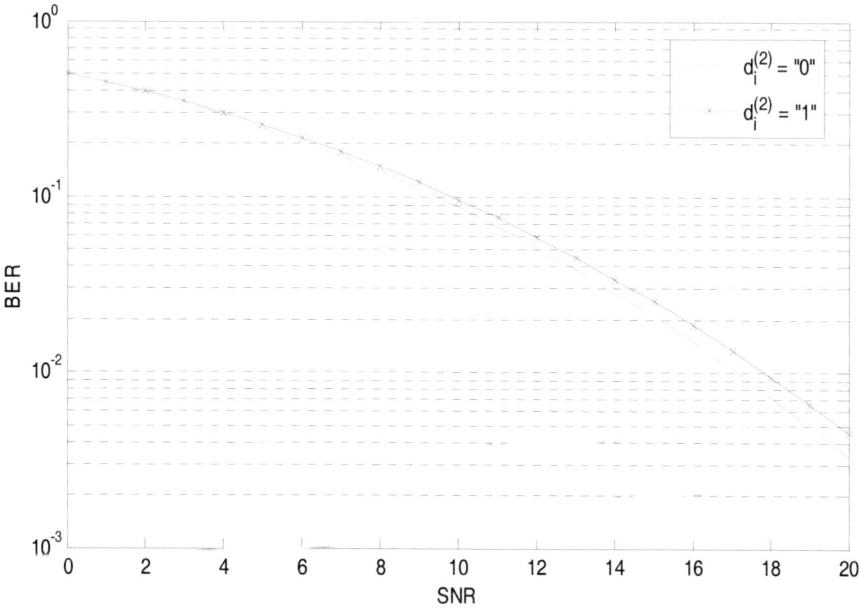

Fig. 5. Comparison of the error probability for $d_i^{(2)} = '0'$ and $d_i^{(2)} = '1'$

From this result for 2 users, we can deduce the expression of the error probability in an arrangement of UWB TH-PPM modulation in multi-user environments,

$$P_e^{U_1} = Q\left(\frac{N_h}{\sigma_b^2}\left[d_1[R_w(0) - R_w(\delta)] + \sum_{k=2}^{K} a_k\left[R_w\left(d_i^{(k)}\delta\right) - R_w\left(\left(1-d_i^{(k)}\right)\delta\right)\right]\right]\right) \quad (21)$$

With
$$R_w\left(d_i^{(k)}\delta\right) = \frac{\sqrt{2\pi}}{8}\left[\tau^2 - \left(d_i^{(k)}\delta\right)^2\right]\exp\left(-\frac{\left(d_i^{(k)}\delta\right)^2}{2\tau^2}\right)$$
$$R_w\left(\left(1-d_i^{(k)}\right)\delta\right) = K^{(k)}\frac{\sqrt{2\pi}}{8}\left[\tau^2 + +\delta^2\left(1-d_i^{(k)}\right)\left(1-3d_i^{(k)}\right)\right]$$

Knowing that
$$K^{(k)} = exp\left(-\frac{3}{4}\delta^2\right) exp\left(-\frac{\delta^2}{2}d_i^{(k)}\right) exp\left(\frac{3}{4}\delta^2\left(d_i^{(k)}\right)^2\right)$$

The Fig. 6 represents the performance of a modulation arrangement UWB TH-PPM for 1, 2 and 3 users. According to this figure, it is clear that more the number of users increases more the performance deteriorates. This result confirms our forecasts and previous work.

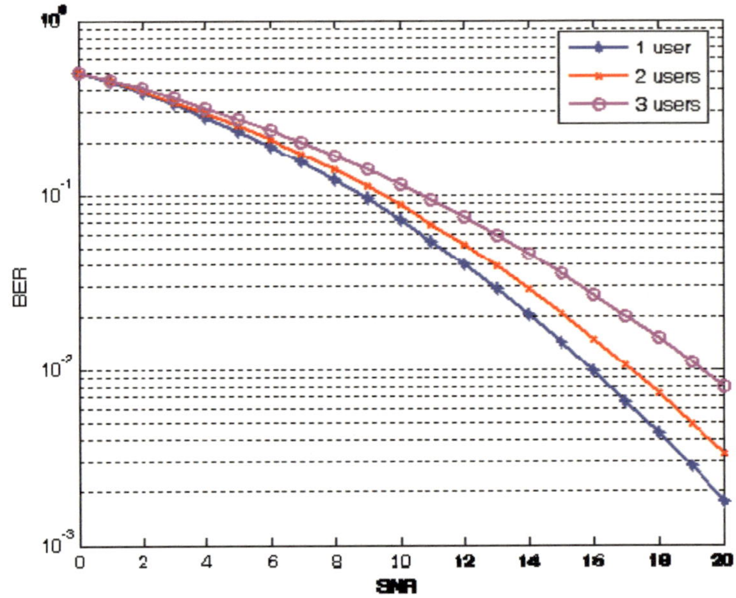

Fig. 6. Performance of TH-PPM UWB system in multi-user environments

5. Analytical Analysis of BER in the UWB TH-PPM System Model in Multipath Environments

In this section, we are interested in performance of UWB TH-PPM system model in multipath environments. In our case, we take as channel model a Rayleigh channel and we assume that their parameters are known (assuming that we use later in our analytical analysis).
The impulse response Rayleigh channel is given by:

$$h(t) = \sum_{l=1}^{L} \alpha_1 \delta(t - \tau_1) \tag{22}$$

Where is the (real) amplitude of the lth path, their delay and L is the paths number. A block diagram of a multipath channel is shown in Fig. 7.

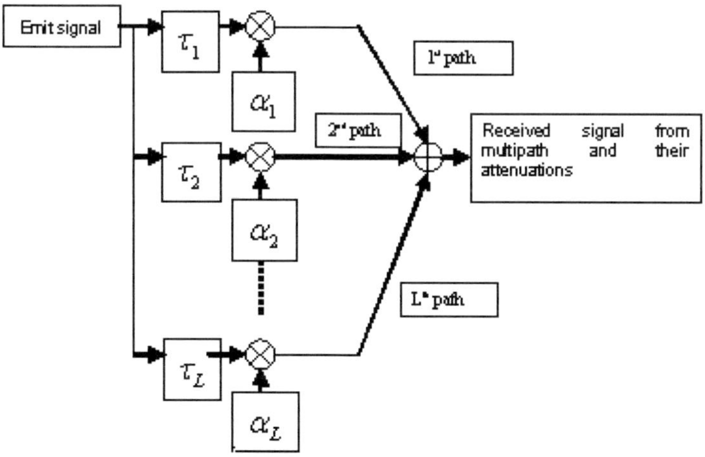

Fig. 7. Block diagram of a multipath channel

As before, we begin by studying the reception of this system translated by the following equation which is the decision making at the reception (Hizem & Bouallegue, 2009c),

$$D_i = \int_{[T_s]} \left[\sum_{j=0}^{N_h-1} \sum_{l=1}^{L} \alpha_l w_{tr}\left(t - jT_f - c_j T_c - \tau_l - d_i\delta\right) + b(t) \right] \times \left[\sum_{j=0}^{N_h-1} \sum_{l=1}^{L} \alpha_l \left(w_{tr}\left(t - jT_f - c_j T_c - \tau_l\right) - w_{tr}\left(t - jT_f - c_j T_c - \tau_l - \delta\right) \right) \right] dt \quad (23)$$

To simplify our calculation, we take first the case of 2 paths and then try to generalize the found results for L paths. After developing the equation (23), used the same hypothesis as for the preceding sections (disjoins temporal support, perfect synchronization) and made an appropriate change of variable, we obtain the following equation:

$$D_i = \int_{[T_s]} \left[\left((\alpha_1)^2 \sum_{j=0}^{N_h-1} w_{tr}(t - \tau_1 - d_i\delta)\, w_{tr}(t - \tau_1) + (\alpha_2)^2 \sum_{j=0}^{N_h-1} w_{tr}(t - \tau_2 - d_i\delta)\, w_{tr}(t - \tau_2) \right) - \left((\alpha_1)^2 \sum_{j=0}^{N_h-1} w_{tr}(t - \tau_1 - d_i\delta)\, w_{tr}(t - \tau_1 - \delta) + (\alpha_2)^2 \sum_{j=0}^{N_h-1} w_{tr}(t - \tau_2 - d_i\delta)\, w_{tr}(t - \tau_2 - \delta) \right) \right] dt + \tilde{b} \quad (24)$$

By replacing the integral in the equation (24) with N_h (consequence of assumptions made before), we obtain:

$$D_i = [N_h(\alpha_1)^2 + N_h(\alpha_2)^2][R_w(-d_i\delta) - R_w((1-d_i)\delta)] + \tilde{b} \tag{25}$$

With $$R_w(-d_i\delta) = \int_{[T_s]} w_{tr}(t-\tau_1)\, w_{tr}(t-\tau_1-d_i\delta)dt = \int_{[T_s]} w_{tr}(t-\tau_2)\, w_{tr}(t-\tau_2-d_i\delta)dt$$

Where the noise is null (less noise case: b (t) = 0), we get:

$$d_i = 0;\quad D_i = N_h(\alpha_1)^2[R_w(0) - R_w(-\delta)] + N_h(\alpha_2)^2[R_w(0) - R_w(-\delta)] > 0$$
$$d_i = 1;\quad D_i = N_h(\alpha_1)^2[R_w(-\delta) - R_w(0)] + N_h(\alpha_2)^2[R_w(-\delta) - R_w(0)] < 0$$

From this expression, we can determine the probability of error,

$$P_e = \text{Prob}\left(\frac{\tilde{b}}{\sigma_b^2} > \frac{N_h[(\alpha_1)^2 + (\alpha_2)^2][R_w(0) - R_w(-\delta)]}{\sigma_b^2}\right) \tag{26}$$

As in the previous sections, we consider the expression of a Gaussian pulse. $R_w(0)$ already being calculated and $R_w(-\delta) = R_w(\delta)$. Thus, we obtain:

$$P_e = Q\left(\text{SNR}[(\alpha_1)^2 + (\alpha_2)^2]\left[1 - \tau\left(1 - \frac{\delta^2}{\tau^2}\right)\exp\left(-\frac{\delta^2}{2\tau^2}\right)\right]\right) \tag{27}$$

From this result for 2 paths, we can deduce the expression of the probability of error in an arrangement of TH-PPM modulation in multipath environments,

$$P_e = Q\left(\text{SNR}\left[\sum_{l=1}^{L}(\alpha_l)^2\right]\left[1 - \tau\left(1 - \frac{\delta^2}{\tau^2}\right)\exp\left(-\frac{\delta^2}{2\tau^2}\right)\right]\right) \tag{28}$$

The Fig. 8 represents the performance of an arrangement of modulation TH-PPM for 1, 2 and 3 paths. According to this figure, it is clear that more the number of paths increases more the performance deteriorates. Note that the system performance even in the presence of several paths remains correct. This is one of the characteristics of the ultra wideband technology. This result confirms our forecasts and previous work.

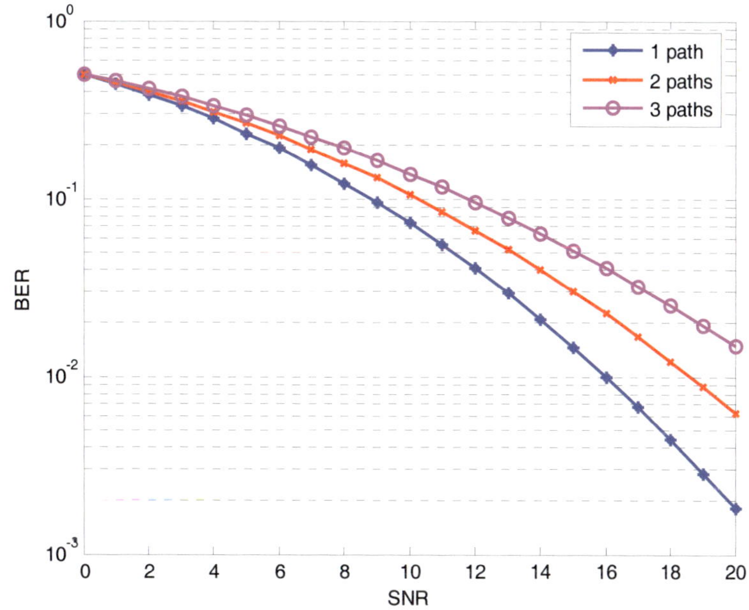

Fig. 8. Performance of TH-PPM UWB system in multipath environments

6. Analytical Analysis of BER in the UWB TH-PPM System Model in Simultaneously Multipath and Multi-user Environments

This final part is a combination of previous analytical approaches. In this section, we are interested in performance of UWB TH-PPM system model in simultaneously multipath and multi-user environments. In our case, we take a Rayleigh channel and we assume that their parameters are known. In the same way, we suppose that the amplitudes a_k of different users are known. These hypotheses are used later in our analytical analysis.

As before, we begin by studying the reception of this system translated by the following equation which is the decision making at the reception (Hizem & Bouallegue, 2009d),

$$D_i = \int_{[T_s]} \left[\sum_{k=1}^{K} \sum_{j=0}^{N_h-1} \sum_{l=1}^{L} a_k \alpha_l w_{tr}\left(t - jT_f - c_j^{(k)} T_c - \tau_l - d_i^{(k)} \delta\right) + b(t) \right] \times \left[\sum_{j=0}^{N_h-1} \sum_{l=1}^{L} \alpha_l \left(w_{tr}\left(t - jT_f - c_j^{(k)} T_c - \tau_l\right) - w_{tr}\left(t - jT_f - c_j^{(k)} T_c - \tau_l - \delta\right) \right) \right] dt \qquad (29)$$

We will not repeat the same steps of calculation since it is the same as the previous sections. As in the previous section, we consider the expression of a Gaussian pulse. To simplify our calculation, we take first the case of 2 paths and 2 users and then try to generalize the found results for L paths and K users. And after computation, we obtain the error probability expression with a UWB TH-PPM modulation arrangement in simultaneously multipath and multi-user environments,

$$P_e = Q\left(SNR\left[1-\tau\left(1-\frac{\delta^2}{\tau^2}\right)\exp\left(-\frac{\delta^2}{2\tau^2}\right)\right]\left[\left(\sum_{k=1}^{K} a_k\right)^2\left(\sum_{l=1}^{L}(\alpha_l)^2\right)\right] + \tau SNR\left[\sum_{i\neq j}\alpha_i\alpha_j\left(\sum_{k=1}^{K} a_k\right)^2\right]\left[\left(1-\sum_{i\neq j}(\tau_i-\tau_j)^2\right)\exp\left(-\frac{1}{2}\sum_{i\neq j}(\tau_i-\tau_j\right. - \left(1-\sum_{i\neq j}(\tau_i-\tau_j+\delta)^2\right)\exp\left(-\frac{1}{2}\sum_{i\neq j}(\tau_i-\tau_j+\delta)\right)\right]\right) \quad (30)$$

The Fig. 9 represents the performance of a UWB TH-PPM modulation arrangement for simultaneously 2 users and 2 paths, 3 users and 3 paths. According to this figure, it is clear that more the number of paths and users increases more the performance deteriorates. This result confirms our forecasts and previous work. The Fig. 10 gives a comparison between different scenario environments performance and computer simulation results show the conformity of this method since we see that performance in the case of 2 users and 2 paths simultaneously is worse than other cases.

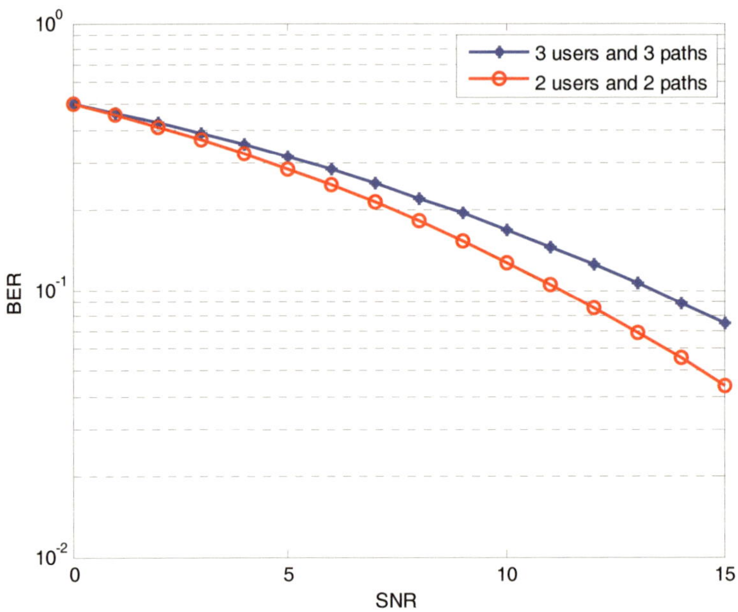

Fig. 9. Performance of TH-PPM UWB system in simultaneously multipath and multi-user environments

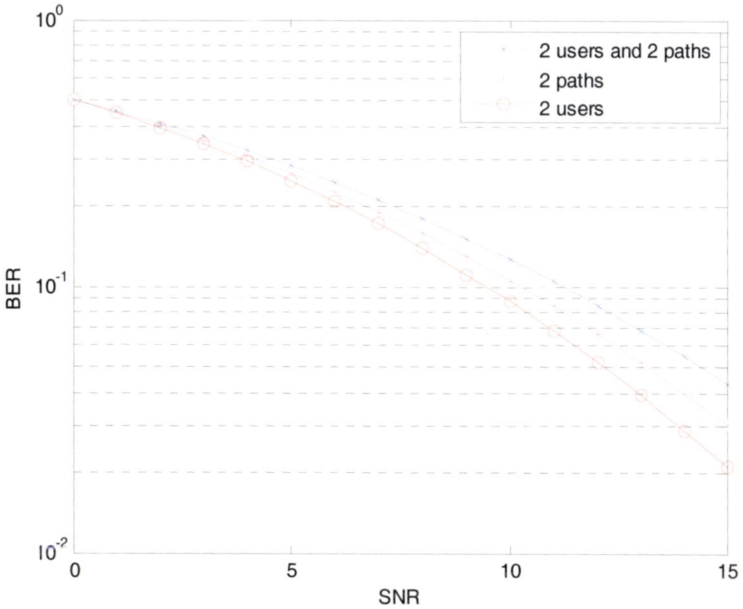

Fig. 10. Comparison between different scenario environments performance

7. Conclusion and Future Research

In this chapter, we have discussed the problem of TH-PPM UWB system performance in different environments. While there is a rich body of literature addressing this problem most of which has emerged recently, this topic is far from being mature. In this context, developing novel analytical methods with relatively low complexity still represents crucial task in meeting the challenges of UWB communications.

We first gave an outline of pulse position modulation and time hoping spectrum spreading and then describe the TH-PPM UWB system model. In the rest of this chapter, we have derived an accurate, analytical expression for the bit error rate of TH-PPM UWB systems. Compared with other methods employed in the performance analysis of UWB systems, our analysis provides a powerful tool for calculating BER's to any desired precision with very low complexity. It was verified by comparisons with simulation results the conformity of this method compared to previous work in this domain and therefore is usable in a UWB communication system.

Finally, we extend this method to multi-user, multipath and simultaneously multipath and multi-user environments. The results have confirmed our forecasts and demonstrated the ability to give simple expressions that allows us further to use them in more complexes cases and therefore benefit in computing time.

The presented analytical method has been only for scenarios with perfect synchronization. A natural extension will be to use dynamic and more realistic scenarios in order to fully describe the UWB radio channels. In future work, we shall try to study the other channel's models more close to the reality and other modulation's schemes to see which one gives us of better performances.

8. References

Di Benedetto, M. G. (2004). *Understanding Ultra Wide Band Radio Fundamentals,* Prentice Hall, ISBN: 9780132441308, Upper Saddle River, NJ

Durisi, G. & Romano, G. (2002). On the Validity of Gaussian Approximation to Characterize the Multiuser Capacity of UWB TH-PPM, *Proceedings of IEEE Conference on Ultra Wideband Systems and Technologies,* May. 2002, Baltimore, MD

Durisi, G. & Benedetto, S. (2003). Performance Evaluation of TH-PPM UWB Systems in the Presence of Multiuser Interference, *IEEE Commun. Lett.,* Vol. 7, No. 5, (May. 2003), pp. 224-226, ISSN 1089-7798

Foerster, J.; Green, E.; Somayazulu, S. & Leeper, D. (2001) Ultra-Wideband Technology for short or medium range wireless communications, *Intel Technology Journal,* Q2, 11p

Fontana, R. J. (2007) Ultra-Wideband, Short-Pulse Electromagnetics 5, Springer US, ISBN: 978-0-306-47948-9, pp. 225-234

Ghavami, M.; Michael, L. & Kohno, R. (2007) Ultra Wideband Signals and Systems in Communication Engineering, John Wiley & Sons Ltd, ISBN: 0470027630

Hämäläinen, M.; Hovinen, V. & Latva-aho, M. (2002) On the UWB System Coexistence with GSM900, UMTS/WCDMA and GPS, *IEEE Journal on Selected Areas in Communications,* Vol. 20, No. 9, (Dec. 2002), pp. 1712-1721, ISSN 0733-8716

Hizem, M. & Bouallegue, R. (2008) Analytical probability of error in TH-PPM and TH-PAM Ultra Wideband Systems, *Proceedings of IEEE International Conference on Electronics, Circuits and Systems (ICECS 2008),* pp. 930-930, Sep. 2008, St Julians, Malta

Hizem, M. & Bouallegue, R. (2009a) Performance of TH-PPM Ultra Wideband Systems in Multi-User Environments, *Proceedings of International Multi-Conference on Systems, Signals and Devices (SSD 2009),* Mars. 2009, Djerba, Tunisia

Hizem, M. & Bouallegue, R. (2009b) Performance of a TH-PPM Ultra Wideband System in Different Scenarios Environments, *IJCSNS International Journal of Computer Science and Network Security,* Vol. 9, No. 11, (Nov. 2009), pp. 319-321

Hizem, M. & Bouallegue, R. (2009c) Performance of TH-PPM Ultra Wideband Systems in Multipath Environments, *Proceedings of IEEE International Conference on Telecommunications (ICT 2009),* pp. 109-112, ISBN 978-1-4244-2936-3, May. 2009, Marrakech, Morocco

Hizem, M. & Bouallegue, R. (2009d) Study of Different Pulse Waveforms and Performance of TH-PPM Ultra Wideband Systems in Multipath and Multi-User Environments Simultaneously, *Proceedings of IEEE International Conference on Electronics, Circuits and Systems (ICECS 2009),* Dec. 2009, Hammamet, Tunisia

Hu, B. & Beaulieu, N. C. (2003). Exact Bit Error Rate Analysis of TH-PPM UWB Systems in the Presence of Multiple-Access Interference, *IEEE Commun. Lett.,* Vol. 7, No. 12, (Dec. 2003), pp. 572-574, ISSN 1089-7798

Niranjayan, S.; Nallanathan A. & Kannan, B. (2004). A New Analytical Method for Exact Bit Error Rate Computation of TH-PPM UWB Multiple Access System, *Proceedings of IEEE International Symposium on Personal, Indoor, and Mobile Radio Communications (PIMRC 2004),* pp. 2968-2972, ISBN 0-7803-8523-3, Sep. 2004, Barcelona, Spain

Scholtz, R. A. (1993). Multiple Access with Time-Hopping Impulse Modulation, *Proceedings of IEEE Military Communications Conference (MILCOM'93),* pp. 447-450, Oct. 1993, Boston, Mass, USA

Win, M. Z. & Scholtz, R. A. (2000). Ultra-wide Bandwidth time-hopping spread-spectrum impulse radio for wireless multiple-access communications, *IEEE Trans. Commun.*, Vol. 48, No. 4, (Apr. 2000), pp. 679-689, ISSN 0090-6778

Win, M. Z. & Scholtz, R. A. (1998a). Impulse Radio: How it Works, *IEEE Commun. Lett.*, Vol. 2, No. 2, (Feb. 1998), pp. 36-38, ISSN 1089-7798

Win, M. Z. & Scholtz, R. A. (1998b). On the Robustness of Ultra-Wide Bandwidth Signals in Multipath Environments, *IEEE Commun. Lett.*, Vol. 2, No. 2, (Feb. 1998), pp. 51-53, ISSN 1089-7798

Win, M. Z. & Scholtz, R. A. (1997). Comparisons of analogue and digital impulse radio for wireless multiple access communications, *Proceedings of the 1997 IEEE International Conference on Communications (ICC'97)*, Montreal, Canada, pp. 91-95

Withington, P.; Reinhardt, R. & Stanley, R. (1999). Preliminary Results from Ultra-Wideband (Impulse) Scanning Receivers, *Proceedings of the IEEE Military Communications Conference (MILCOM'99)*, Vol. 2, (Nov. 1999), Atlantic City, NJ, USA, pp. 1186-1190, ISBN 0-7803-5538-5

Yang, L. & Giannakis, G. B. (2004). Ultra-Wideband Communications: An Idea Whose Time Has Come, *IEEE Signal Process. Magn.*, Vol. 21, No. 6, (Nov. 2004), pp. 26-54, ISSN 1053-5888

Zhao, L. & Haimovich, A. M. (2002). Multi-user capacity of M-ary PPM ultra-wideband communications, *Proceedings of IEEE Conference on Ultra Wideband Systems and Technologies*, May. 2002, Baltimore, MD

Zhao, S. & Liu, H. (2005). On The Optimum Linear Receiver for Impulse Radio System in the Presence of Pulse Overlapping, *IEEE Commun. Lett*, Vol. 9, No. 4, (Apr. 2005), pp. 340-342, ISSN 1089-7798

5

High performance analog optical links based on quantum dot devices for UWB signal transmission

M. Ran, Y. Ben Ezra and B.I. Lembrikov
Holon Institute of Technology (HIT),
P.O.Box 305, 58102, 52 Golomb Str., Holon
Israel

1. Introduction

In this chapter, we discuss the possibility of quantum dot (QD) laser and QD semiconductor optical amplifier (SOA) applications in ultra-wideband (UWB) communication systems. We mainly concentrate on novel methods of UWB pulse photonic generation, UWB over optical fiber (UROOF) technology, and in particular, performance of analogous optical links in UROOF systems. We demonstrate that QD devices are promising candidates for different applications in the communication systems due to their low bias current, high temperature stability, extremely high operation rate, and the possibility of the light generation in a wide range of optical frequencies. We briefly discuss the state-of-the-art in UWB technology and present original results concerning UWB pulse photonic generation based on passive elements, and application of a QD laser in an analogous optical link.
The chapter is constructed as follows. In Section 2, we discuss the UWB communication state-of-the-art. In Section 3, we discuss the photonic generation of the UWB pulses and present original experimental results concerning the generation of UWB Gaussian pulses with passive elements. In Section 4, we describe the novel approach to UWB communication systems known as UROOF technology which permits to increase dramatically the distance of the UWB signal transmission and to improve the UWB system performance. In Section 5, we analyze the structure and performance of an analog optical link as a key element of the UROOF communication system. The improvement of the analog optical link performance, especially with respect to operation rate and bandwidth, can be achieved by implementation of integrated photonic and electronic circuits. The possibilities of Si photonics applications in UROOF technology are discussed in Section 6. The key element of UROOF communication system is a laser diode as a source of a directly modulated optical carrier. The structure, operation principle and dynamics of QD lasers are discussed in Section 7. We have carried out numerical simulations for the analogous optical link with the QD laser instead of a conventional vertical cavity surface emitting laser (VCSEL) using the coupled rate equations. The theoretical results predict a high performance of such a link. Conclusions are presented in Section 8.

2. UWB Communications

UWB radar systems were developed primarily for radar and military applications Ghawami (2005), Chong (2006). Recently, UWB technology has been focused on consumer electronics and communications Ghawami (2005). Possible UWB communication system applications include radars, wireless personal area networks (WPAN), sensor networks, imaging systems, UWB positioning systems, etc. Yang (2004), Kshetrimayum (2009). UWB transmission is characterized by high data rate, availability of low-cost transceivers, low transmit power, and low interference Ghawami (2005), Qui (2006). UWB systems have low power spectral density (PSD), and consequently can coexist with cellular systems, wireless local area networks (WLAN), global positioning systems (GPS) etc. Chong (2006). UWB operate at the noise level or even below it, and for this reason they are inherently covert and difficult for unintended users to detect Chong (2006).
The three main types of UWB technologies are following Ran (2009).

1. Impulse radio (IR-UWB).
2. Direct sequence (DS-UWB).
3. Multi-band orthogonal frequency division multiplexing (MB-OFDM).

In IR-UWB, information is carried by a set of narrow electromagnetic pulses with bandwidth inversely proportional to the pulse width. The center frequency in IR-UWB is determined by the zero crossing rate of the pulse waveform. Various data modulation format (DMFs) may be used in the case of IR-UWB such as pulse amplitude modulation (PAM), pulse position modulation (PPM) and pulse shape modulation (PSM). DS-UWB is based on concepts of conventional DS spread spectrum (DS-SS). MB-OFDM is based on subdividing the UWB spectrum into 5 band groups and 14 sub-bands of $528MHz$ width composed of 128 sub-carriers OFDM modulated signals. The MB UWB OFDM technology combines the advantages of spectral efficiency (SE) DMFs and OFDM. OFDM has emerged as the leading physical-layer interface in broadband wireless communication systems because it is characterized by a comparatively low intersymbol interference (ISI), and it transfers the complexity of transmitters and receivers from the analog to the digital domain Shieh (2008), Armstrong (2009). In OFDM the spectra of individual subcarriers overlap, but for linear channels the subcarriers can be demodulated without interference and without an analog filtering to separate the received subcarriers Armstrong (2009). Optical OFDM has been proposed which is based on electronic signal processing before the optical modulator and after the photo detector (PD) Shieh (2008).
UWB signals are based on short pulses rather than the harmonic sine waves Qui (2006). UWB can be described as baseband, carrier-free and impulse technology Ghawami (2005). The extremely short UWB pulses can be distinguished from unwanted multipath reflections which leads to the multipath immunity; UWB pulses' low frequency components enable the signals propagate through materials; extremely high data rates can be achieved due to the large bandwidth; UWB transmitters and receivers are compact, low-cost, have low power consumption as compared to conventional narrow-band communication systems; they do not require expensive and large modulators and demodulators Ghawami (2005). According to the Federal Communications Commission (FCC) decision, the unlicensed frequency band between 3.1 and $10.6GHz$ is reserved for indoor UWB wireless communication systems Qui (2006). It is seen from the well known Shannon's capacity equation

$$C = B \log\left(1 + \frac{S}{N}\right) \tag{1}$$

that UWB systems have a great potential for high-capacity wireless communications Ghawami (2005). Here C is the maximum channel capacity in $bits/s$, B is the channel bandwidth, in Hz, S is the signal power, in *watts*, and N is the noise power, in *watts*. PSD of UWB is defined as $PSD = P/B$ where P is the transmitted power in watts Ghawami (2005). It is very low compared to conventional systems due to a very large bandwidth B. For instance, for UWB power $P = 1mW$, we obtain $PSD = 0.013W/MHz$ Ghawami (2005).
After transmission, an electromagnetic signal travels by various paths to the receiver which is called a multipath phenomenon Ghawami (2005). It is caused by the physical effects such as reflection, absorption, diffraction, and scattering, and leads, in particular, to ISI and a time delay Ghawami (2005). The multipath interference can be diminished by decreasing the pulse width, or by increasing the time delay between pulses, i.e. by decreasing the duty cycle of the system Ghawami (2005). UWB systems are immune to multipath fading and capable of resolving multipath components (MPCs) in dense multipath environments Chong (2006). Gaussian monocycle and doublet pulses provide better multipath performance among other impulse signals Yao (2009). However, it is difficult and expensive to generate such pulses with a fractional bandwidth greater than 100% at the central frequency of about $7GHz$ Yao (2007). The penetration capabilities of UWB are determined by the lower frequency components of about $1GHz$, and they have substantially decreased due to the increase of the UWB lower frequency limit up to $3.1GHz$ Ghawami (2005). They can operate under both line-of-sight (LOS) and non-LOS conditions Chong (2006). UWB applications are targeting the data rate up to $500Mbps$ that is much larger than the bit rate of Bluetooth, or the wireless local area network (WLAN) standards Ghawami (2005), Qui (2006). Low complexity and consequently low cost of UWB technology are determined by nearly "all-digital" structure of UWB systems Ghawami (2005), Qui (2006). They can be implemented on a single chip architecture Chong (2006). However, the UWB communication distances are limited by less than $10m$ due the FCC constraints on allowed emission levels Ran (2009). In order to increase the area of coverage a novel approach based on the UROOF technology has been recently proposed Ran (2009), Yao (2009). The state-of-the-art optical fibers possess low loss and broad bandwidth, and for this reason the UROOF technology is a promising solution Ran (2009), Yao (2009). In order to distribute UWB signals over the optical fiber, it is desirable to generate these signals directly in the optical domain without extra electrical-to-optical (E/O) conversion Yao (2007), Yao (2009).

3. Photonic Generation of UWB Pulses

UWB pulses are of nanosecond or picosecond order, with a typical pulse shape approximating a Gaussian function y_{g1}, a Gaussian monocycle y_{g2} and a Gaussian doublet y_{g3} given by the first and the second derivative of a Gaussian pulse, respectively Ghawami (2005)

$$y_{g1} = K_1 \exp\left(-\frac{t^2}{\tau^2}\right) \quad (2)$$

$$y_{g2} = K_2 \left(-\frac{2t}{\tau^2}\right) \exp\left(\frac{t^2}{\tau^2}\right); \; y_{g3} = K_3 \left(-\frac{2}{\tau^2}\right)\left(1 - \frac{2t^2}{\tau^2}\right) \exp\left(-\frac{t^2}{\tau^2}\right) \quad (3)$$

where $\infty < t < \infty$, τ is the time-scaling factor, and $K_{1,2,3}$ are normalization constants. Gaussian pulses are the most widely used waveforms due to their simplicity and feasibility Yao (2007). The important property of the Gaussian pulses (2), (3) is that they are almost uniformly distributed over their frequency spectrum Ghawami (2005).

A number of optically based methods of the Gaussian IR UWB monocycles and doublets generation for low-cost high-data rate UWB wireless systems have been proposed Lin (2005), Le Guennec (2007), Yao (2007), Zeng (April 2006), Zeng (October 2006), Zeng (2007), Ben Ezra (2008). The advantages of these methods are following: the decreasing of interference between electrical devices, low loss and light weight of optical fibers Lin (2005), Yao (2007), Wang (2006). The all-optical methods of IR UWB generation have been reviewed in detail Yao (2007), Ben Ezra (2009). In particular, we concentrated on the all-optical methods of UWB pulse generation based on cross phase modulation (XPM) and cross gain modulation (XGM) in SOAs. We proposed a theoretical analysis of a novel all-optical method of the IR UWB pulse generation in an integrated Mach-Zehnder interferometer (MZI) with QD SOA as an active element inserted into one arm of the integrated MZI which results in an intensity dependent optical signal interference at the output of MZI Ben Ezra (2008).
Recently, a novel method of photonic passive generation of UWB pulse in the form of the Mexican hat mother wavelet (MHMW) proportional to the Gaussian doublet Rao (1998) has been proposed based on the system of two unbalanced Mach-Zehnder Interferometers (UMZIs) connected in parallel that does not contain any active elements Ben Ezra (June 2009). The proposed method provides the pulse shaping directly in the time domain and does not require additional optical filters and FBG. The block diagram of the UMZIs connected in parallel is shown in Fig. 1. The UMZIs are chosen in such a way that the phase difference of the interfering signals at the output is equal to π. As a result, at the output of the UMZIs the interfering optical signals modulated by a Gaussian UWB pulse form the first-order difference approximating the Gaussian monocycle and the second-order difference approximating the Gaussian doublet. At the output of the system, the UWB monocycles and doublets can be converted to a UWB signal by means of a homodyne detection where the local oscillator frequency ω_{LO} coincides with the optical carrier frequency ω Agrawal (2002). In such a case the homodyne detected signal is proportional to the UWB modulated optical signal amplitude Agrawal (2002), i.e. to the Gaussian monocycle or doublet in our case.

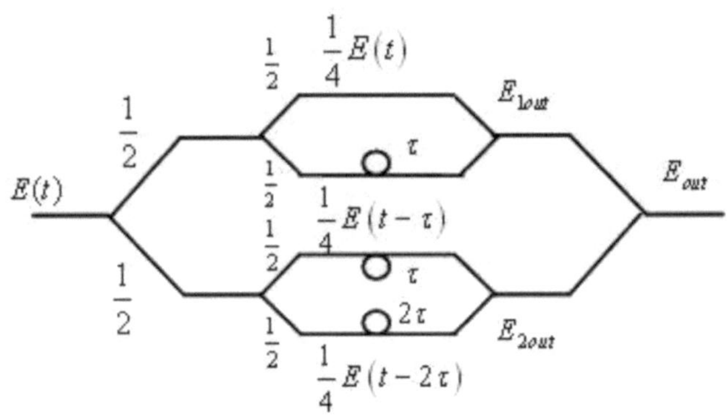

Fig. 1. The UMZIs connected in parallel

The UWB modulated optical carrier field $E(t) = A(t)\exp[-i(\omega t + \phi)]$ is split in the two equal parts at the input of the system, and then the each signal is split equally once more at the input of the both UMZIs. Here $A(t), \phi$ are the amplitude and phase of the input signal, respectively. Assuming the delay time τ of the lower arm of the upper UMZI1 and of the upper arm of the lower UMZI2 and the delay time 2τ of the lower arm of the lower UMZI2 we can describe the interfering optical fields as follows.

$$E_{1,2in} = \frac{1}{2}E(t); E_{1up} = \frac{1}{4}E(t); E_{1low} = \frac{1}{4}E(t-\tau) \quad (4)$$

$$E_{2up} = \frac{1}{4}E(t-\tau); E_{2low} = \frac{1}{4}E(t-2\tau) \quad (5)$$

$$E_{1out} = E_{1up} - E_{1low} = \frac{1}{4}[E(t) - E(t-\tau)] \quad (6)$$

$$E_{2out} = E_{2up} - E_{2low} = \frac{1}{4}[E(t-\tau) - E(t-2\tau)] \quad (7)$$

$$E_{out} = E_{1out} - E_{2out} = \frac{1}{4}[E(t) - 2E(t-\tau) + E(t-2\tau)] \quad (8)$$

It is easy to see from eqs. (6)-(8) that the output fields E_{1out}, E_{2out} of the UMZI1 and UMZI2, respectively, correspond to the first-order difference of the input signal $E(t)$, and the system output signal $E_{out}(t)$ corresponds to the second-order difference of $E(t)$ which represent the approximations of the first and second derivative of $E(t)$, respectively Yao (2007). Similarly, in the case of the UMZIs connected in cascade shown in Fig. 2 we have for the interfering fields at the outputs of the UMZI1 and UMZI2.

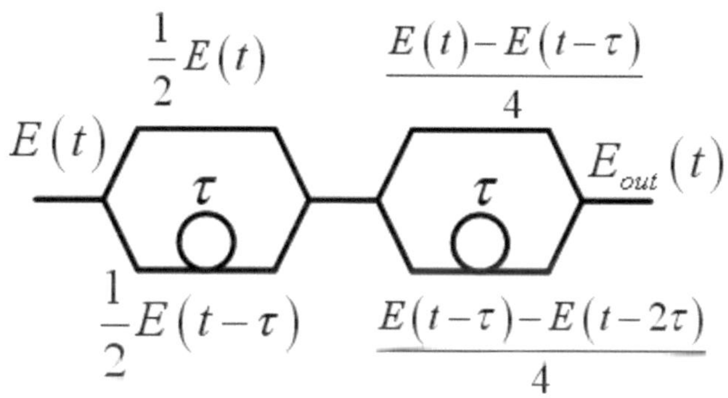

Fig. 2. The UMZIs connected in a cascade

$$E_{1,2in} = \frac{1}{2}E(t); E_{1up} = \frac{1}{2}E(t); E_{1low} = \frac{1}{2}E(t-\tau) \quad (9)$$

$$E_{1out} = E_{1up} - E_{1low} = \frac{1}{2}[E(t) - E(t-\tau)] \quad (10)$$

$$E_{2up} = \frac{E(t) - E(t-\tau)}{4}; E_{2low} = \frac{E(t-\tau) - E(t-2\tau)}{4} \quad (11)$$

and expression (8), respectively. Evidently, in the both cases the output fields correspond to the Gaussian monocycles and doublets. The system can be made tunable by including into UMZIs a tunable delay line.

In order to down-convert the output monocycle and doublet modulated optical signals, the coherent-detection technique is used where the local oscillator frequency $\omega_{LO} = \omega$ Agrawal (2002). In order to improve the accuracy of the homodyne detection we use the same laser as a source of the externally UWB modulated optical signal and the continuous wave (CW) optical signal. The detector photocurrent $I(t)$ is given by Agrawal (2002)

$$I(t) = R(P_{out} + P_{LO}) + 2R\sqrt{P_{out}P_{LO}}\cos(\phi_{out} - \phi_{LO}) \quad (12)$$

where R is the detector responsivity, $P_{out} = KA_{out}^2$, $P_{LO} = KA_{LO}^2$, A_{out}, A_{LO}, ϕ_{out}, ϕ_{LO} are the output signal and local oscillator optical powers, amplitudes and phases, respectively, K is a constant of proportionality. The phase difference $\phi_{out} - \phi_{LO}$ can be eliminated by using a phase shifter. Then, the homodyne signal is given by Agrawal (2002)

$$I_h(t) = 2R\sqrt{P_{out}P_{LO}} = 2R\sqrt{KP_{LO}}A_{out}(t) \sim |E_{out}| \tag{13}$$

Eq. (13) shows that the homodyne signal is proportional to the Gaussian doublet. Obviously, down-conversion of the output signals of MZI1 or MZI2 yields the homodyne signal proportional to the Gaussian monocycle. Typically, the local oscillator power is much larger than the output signal, and optical losses in the MZI system can be neglected: $P_{LO} \gg P_{out} \sim |A(t)|^2$. For the typical values of $R = (0.4 - 0.9)\,A/W$ Agrawal (2002), $P_{LO} = 10mW$, $P_{out} = 0.1mW$ we obtain $I_h(t)_{\max} \approx (0.8 - 1.8)\,mA$.

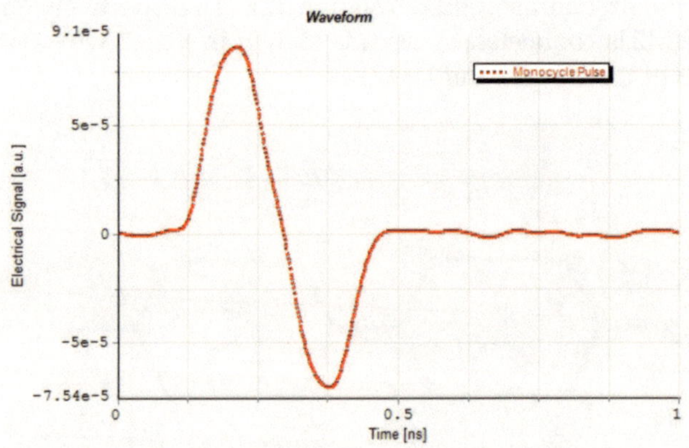

Fig. 3. Simulation results for the Gaussian monocycle at the output of the passive UMZI system

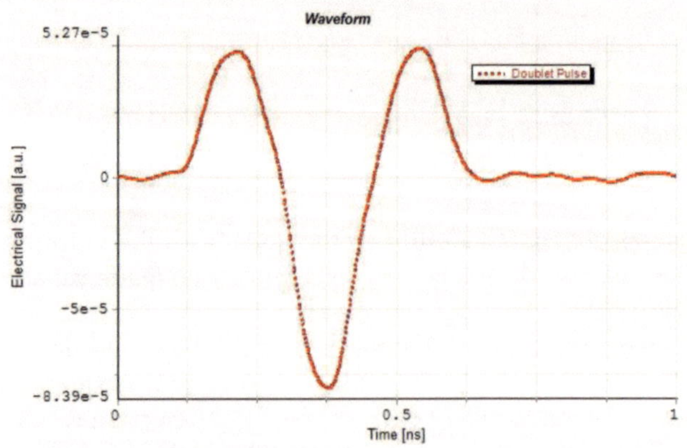

Fig. 4. Simulation results for the Gaussian doublet at the output of the passive UMZI system

The Gaussian monocycle and doublet obtained by using numerical simulations based on eqs. (4)-(8) and eqs. (9)-(11) are shown in Figs. 3, 4. The Gaussian doublet shown in Fig. 4 is generated at the output of the UMZI system as a result of the monocycle interference and further coherent homodyne detection. We have used the following data: the time window is $6.4 \times 10^{-9}s$, the sample mode bandwidth is $1.28THz$, the carrier sample mode frequency is $193.1THz$, the sampling rate is $160 \times 10^{9}Hz$, the impulse bit rate $10Gb/s$, the delay time of the optical delay line is $166ps$.
We have carried out experimentally the generation of the UWB monocycles and doublets for the case of the UMZIs connected in cascade. Block diagram of the experimental setup is shown in Fig. 5.

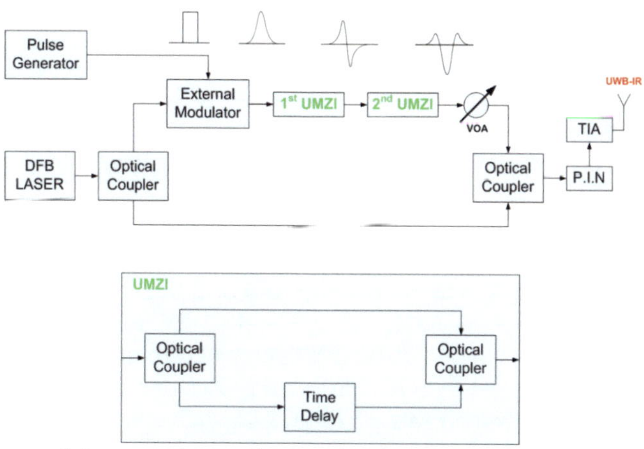

Fig. 5. Block diagram of the experimental setup for the photonic generation of UWB Gaussian monocycles and doublets

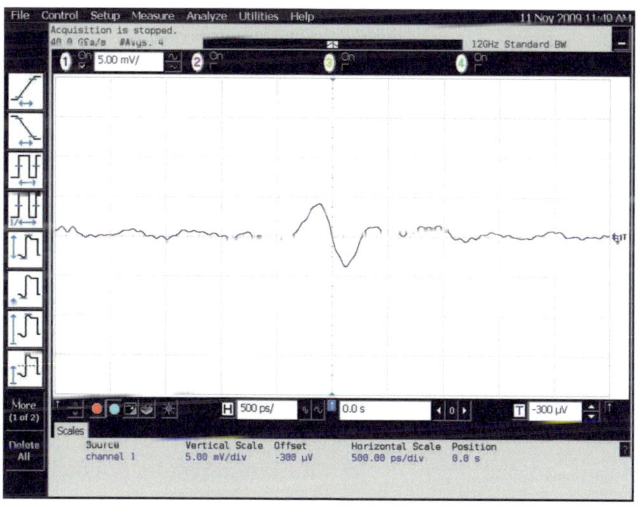

Fig. 6. The measured Gaussian monocycle at the output of UMZI1

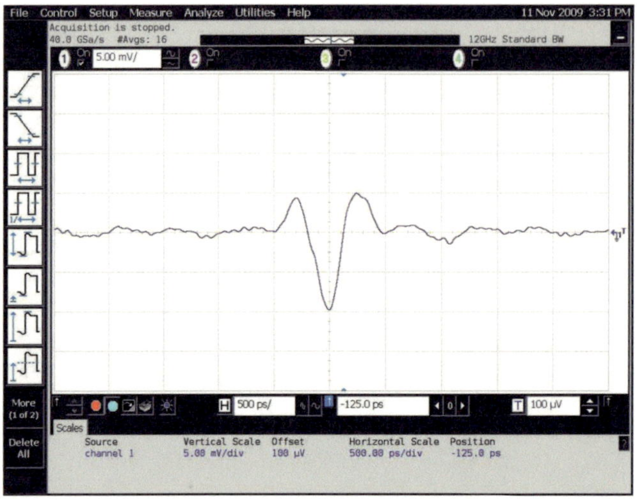

Fig. 7. The measured Gaussian doublet at the output of the passive UMZI system

It consists of the following components: $1550nm$ distributed feedback (DFB) coaxial laser, $10Gb/s$ amplitude modulator, single mode wideband optical couplers (OCs), analog PIN detector, a monolithic broadband amplifier GALI 39+, 50Ω, DC to $7GHz$, a variable optical attenuator, and connecting single mode fibers (SMFs). The UWB modulated optical signal from the laser is fed into a MZM after the OC. Electrical pulses of a fixed pattern, corresponding to one "1" every 128 bits with a bit rate of $10GHz$, in such a way that the repetition rate is $78.125MHz$ come from a pulse pattern generator Anritsu MP1763B driving the MZM. Full-width at half-maximum (FWHM) of the optical pulse is $\tau = 100ps$.

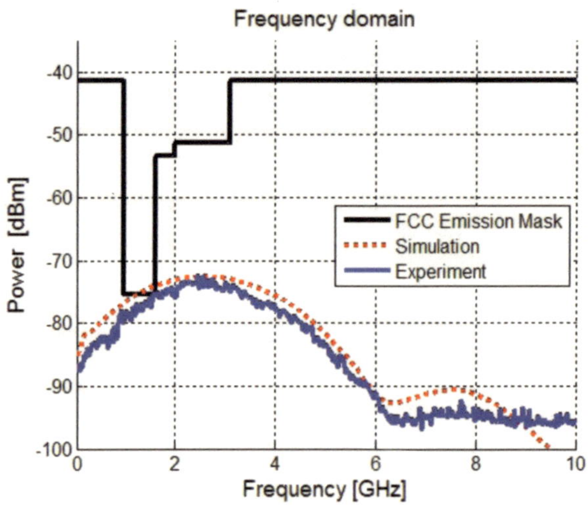

Fig. 8. Spectrum of the Gaussian monocycle: simulation results (dashed line) and experimental results (solid line)

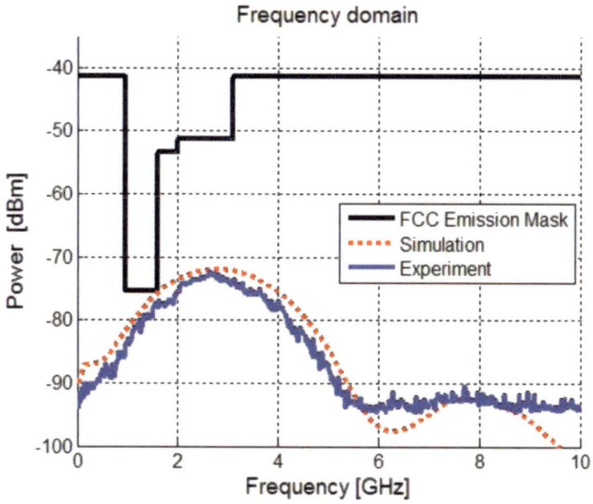

Fig. 9. The spectrum of the Gaussian doublet: the simulation results (dashed line) and the experimental results (solid line)

The measured Gaussian monocycle and doublet are shown in Figs. 6, 7. The simulation results together with the experimental results for the monocycle and doublet spectrum evaluated by using of the fast Fourier transform (FFT) are shown in Figs. 8, 9. The spectrum is limited by the FCC spectral mask. The simulation and experimental results are in a good accord as it is seen from Figs. 3, 4, 6-9.

Recently, self-organized In(Ga)As/Ga(Al)As QD lasers grown directly on Si have been demonstrated Mi (2009). In the framework of an integrated all-optical signal processing system, such an externally or directly modulated QD laser can be used as a source of UWB modulated optical carriers. Integrated UMZIs based on Si waveguides can then generate UWB Gaussian monocycles and doublets.

4. UWB over Optical Fiber (UROOF) Technology

Fiber-optic communication systems use carrier frequencies in the visible or near-infrared region of the electromagnetic radiation spectrum, i.e. about 10^{14} Hz, and can be applied for the information transfer from one place to another. Fiber-optic communications have the following advantages Agrawal (2002):

1. Extremely low fiber losses exhibiting a minimum loss of about $0.2dB/km$ near the wavelength $\lambda = 1.55\mu m$
2. Compatibility with semiconductor lasers and SOAs.
3. The possibility of operation as Erbium doped fiber amplifier (EDFA), or Raman fiber amplifier.
4. High bit rate of information transmission.
5. Large transmission distances.
6. The possibility of a system capacity increase by virtue of OFDM technology.
7. Soliton communications.

Fiber-optic communication system can be divided into three groups: (i) point-to-point links; (ii) distribution networks; (iii) local area networks (LAN) Agrawal (2002). In particular, the UROOF concept enables the transmission of UWB radio frequency (RF) signals over optical fibers by superimposing the UWB RF signals of several GHz on the optical CW carrier Ran (2009), Yao (2009). UROOF applications are related to the short-haul case Ran (2009). UROOF technology can be successfully applied in WPAN, security systems with a large number of sensors and cameras equipped with UWB, and broadband multimedia Ran (2009). In a typical application of a broadband indoor system, UWB signals are generated and encoded in a central office and distributed over optical fiber to the access points where the UWB signals are down-converted from the optical domain to the electrical domain and the detected UWB signals radiate to free space Ran (2009), Yao (2009). UROOF technology has the following advantages Ran (2009), Yao (2009):

1. The conversion process becomes transparent to the UWB modulation method.
2. The high costs of additional electronic components required for synchronization and other processes can be avoided.
3. The integration of all the RF and optical transmitter/receiver components on a single chip is possible.

For the sake of definiteness, we consider the analog optical communication systems which permit the transmission of multilevel modulated radio signals as an envelope of the optical carrier over the optical fiber Ran (2009).

5. UWB Analog Optical Link

In this section we briefly discuss the problems related to the high-performance optical links in UROOF communication systems. UWB high-speed optical link includes E/O converter, an optical fiber, and optical/electrical (O/E) converter Ran (2009). We need to carry out the modulation of an optical signal, or up-conversion, at the input of the UROOF system, and separation of the electrical signal envelope from the optical carrier, or down-conversion (detection), at the output of the UROOF system Ran (2009). After the O/E conversion, a conventional radio receiver can be used for the further detection of a multilevel modulated signal Ran (2009). The optical link block diagram is shown in Fig. 10.

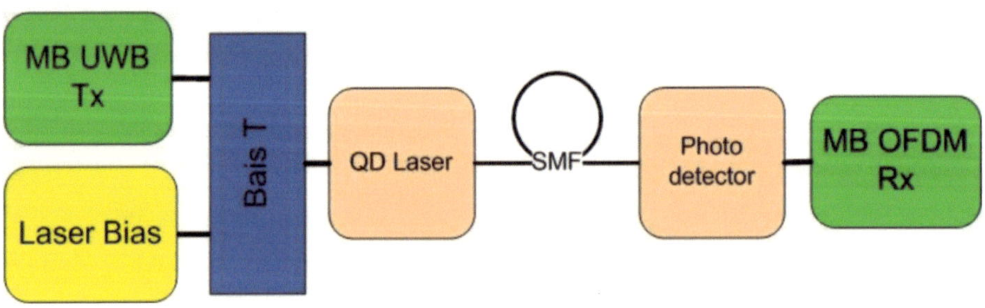

Fig. 10. Block diagram of the optical link. MB UWB Tx - transmitter, MB UWB Rx -receiver, SMF - single mode fiber

During E/O conversion process, UWB analog signals are imparted onto the optical carrier via an optical modulation device where any parameter of the optical carrier can be modulated

such as intensity, phase, frequency, or polarization. The intensity modulation is commonly used in analog optical links. There are two main methods of optical carrier intensity modulation: direct modulation and external modulation. In the first case, the analog UWB signal modulates the intensity of the diode laser which possesses a sufficient bandwidth; in the second case, the laser operates in a CW regime and the intensity modulation is imposed via an external device Cox (2003). A directly modulated link combines a diode laser with a photodiode detector Cox (2003). External modulation is usually realized by MZI fabricated in electro-optic crystal $LiNbO_3$, and an externally modulated link combines a CW laser, MZI modulator and a photodiode Cox (2003).
The performance of the analog optical link is characterized by three most common and basic parameters: the intrinsic link gain, noise figure (NF), and intermodulation-free dynamic range (IMFDR) Cox (2003). These parameters are defined as follows Cox (2003). The intrinsic link gain g_i (without any amplifiers) is defined as the available power gain between the input to the modulation device and the output of the photodetection device. NF specific for the modulation links has the form.

$$NF\,(dB) = 10\log\left[\frac{(S/N)_{in}}{(S/N)_{out}}\right] = 10\log\left(\frac{N_{out}}{kTg_i}\right) \tag{14}$$

where $(S/N)_{in}$, $(S/N)_{out}$ are signal-to-noise ratio (SNR) at the input and output, respectively, T is the temperature in K, the input noise N_{in} is taken as thermal noise at $T = 290K$,

$$N_{out} = g_i N_{in} + N_{link} \tag{15}$$

and the link noise N_{link} consists of the sum of laser relative intensity noise (RIN) and thermal noise of the modulation and photodetection devices. The IMFDR is defined as the SNR for which the non-linear distortion terms are equal to the noise floor. The two most common IMFDRs are the second- and third-order non-linear distortions Cox (2003). The advantages of the direct modulation are the simplicity and low cost. The most promising laser diodes for the direct modulation in UROOF optical links are low cost, compact, easily packaged VCSELs Ran (2009). The low level of RIN and coupling losses can be achieved in the case of a single-mode VCSEL. However, the VCSEL performance in analog communication systems is significantly lower than in digital ones Ran (2009). For instance, the strong nonlinearity in VCSELs gives rise to IMFDR related mainly to the third order intermodulation which results in the dynamic range limitation. For this reason, lasers with better performance are needed. In the following sections we consider QD lasers as promising candidates for the improvement of the optical link performance.

6. Possible Si Photonics Applications in UROOF Technology

The existing UROOF systems are relatively large and expensive since they are based on discrete photonic and microwave components made from III-V based compounds such as GaAs, InP, or the electro-optic crystal $LiNbO_3$ Reed (2004), Yao (2009). In order to reduce size and lower the cost of the components, it is necessary to develop novel O/E and E/O components and subsystems for the UROOF based on Si photonic integrated circuits (PICs) Yao (2009). Generally, the Si photonics development is crucial for UROOF system performance improvement. The advantages of the Si photonics are the compatibility with the silicon manufacturing, low cost, the highest crystal quality, the strong optical confinement, the possibility of strongly pronounced nonlinear optical effects, high-quality silicon-on-insulator (SOI) wafers serving

as an ideal platform for planar waveguide circuits Jalali (2006). Silicon photonics may provide such devices as integrated transceivers for synchronous optical networks, optical attenuators, optical interconnects for CMOS electronics, photonic crystals, waveguide-to-waveguide couplers, Mach-Zehnder interferometers, arrayed waveguide gratings (AWG), etc. Reed (2004), Jalali (2006). The principal goal of electronic and photonic integrated circuits (EPIC) development is the monolithic integration of silicon very large scale integration (VLSI) electronics with Si nanophotonics on a single silicon chip in a commercial state-of-the-art CMOS SOI production plant Soref (2006). The serious challenge of the Si based photonic integrated circuit is the fabrication of Si-based, electrically pumped light-emitting devices (LEDs) since Si possesses an indirect band gap with a low probability for radiative electron-hole recombination Reed (2004). In order to prevent carrier diffusion to nonradiative centres the low-dimensional structures such as porous silicon, nano-crystals, Er-doped nano-crystals have been proposed Reed (2004). The performance of light-emitting devices based on the crystalline, amorphous and Er-doped Si nanostructures has been investigated, and a stable electroluminescence (EL) at $850nm$ and $1.54\mu m$ has been demonstrated Iacona (2006). Si QDs embedded in the silicon nitride thin films may provide an alternative possibility for a Si-based full-color emission Sung (2006). Still, the electrical carrier injection and the efficient extraction of the emitted are the main obstacles for the fabrication of the highly efficient Si based LED Sung (2006).
Recently, InGaAs QD lasers on Si have been developed and monolithically integrated with crystalline and amorphous Si waveguides and InGaAs quantum well (QW) electroabsorption modulators (EAM) Mi (2009). The measured threshold current for such QD lasers is still much larger than that of QD lasers grown on GaAs. However, under certain technological conditions, the performance of QD lasers on Si may be essentially improved, and the characteristics comparable to the QD lasers grown on GaAs substrates can be achieved Mi (2009). Then, the high performance 1.3 and $1.55\mu m$ QD lasers on Si can be realized Mi (2009). In the framework of an integrated all-optical signal processing system, such an externally or directly modulated QD laser can be used as a source of UWB modulated optical carriers. Integrated UMZIs based on Si waveguides can then generate UWB Gaussian monocycles and doublets.
Taking into account the unique possibilities of the Si photonic integrated circuits combined with InGaAs QD lasers we may predict the essential improvement of the UWB optical links based on such devices. We used the QD laser rate equations and investigated theoretically the direct modulation of QD laser radiation and its influence on the optical link performance.

7. QD Lasers

In this section we briefly describe the structure and optical properties of QDs. Then, we discuss the QD laser dynamic model based on the coupled rate equations for carrier population. We present the original results based on the numerical simulations for the analog optical link containing a QD laser.

7.1 QD Structure

Quantization of electron states in all three dimensions results in a creation of a novel physical object - a macroatom, or QD containing a zero dimensional electron gas. Size quantization is effective when the QD three dimensions are of the same order of magnitude as the electron de Broglie wavelength which is about several nanometers Ustinov (2003). QD is a nanomaterial confined in all the three dimensions, and for this reason it has unique electronic and optical properties that do not exist in bulk semiconductor material Ohtsu (2008). An electron-hole pair created by light in a QD has discrete energy eigenvalues caused by the electron-hole confinement in the material. This phenomenon is called a quantum confinement effect Ohtsu (2008).

The different types of QDs based on different technologies and operating in different parts of spectrum are known such as In(Ga)As QDs grown on GaAs substrates, InAs QDs grown on InP substrates, and colloidal free-standing InAs QDs. QD structures are commonly realized by a self-organized epitaxial growth where QDs are statistically distributed in size and area. A widely used QDs fabrication method is a direct synthesis of semiconductor nanostructures based on the island formation during strained-layer heteroepitaxy called the Stranski-Krastanow (SK) growth mode Ustinov (2003). The spontaneously growing QDs are said to be self-assembling. SK growth has been investigated intensively for InAs on GaAs, InP on GaInP, and Ge on Si structures Ustinov (2003). The energy shift of the emitted light is determined by size of QDs that can be adjusted within a certain range by changing the amount of deposited QD material. Evidently, smaller QDs emit photons of shorter wavelengths Ustinov (2003).

The simplest QD models are described by the spherical boundary conditions for an electron or a hole confinement in a spherical QD with a radius R, or by the cubic boundary conditions for a parallelepiped QD with a side length $L_{x,y,z}$ Ohtsu (2008). In the first case, the electron and hole energy spectra $E_{e,nlm}$ and $E_{h,nlm}$ are given by, respectively Ohtsu (2008)

$$E_{e,nlm} = E_g + \frac{\hbar^2}{2m_e}\left(\frac{\alpha_{nl}}{R}\right)^2 ; E_{h,nlm} = \frac{\hbar^2}{2m_h}\left(\frac{\alpha_{nl}}{R}\right)^2 \tag{16}$$

where

$$n = 1,2,3,...; l = 0,1,2,...n-1; m = 0, \pm 1, \pm 2, .. \pm l \tag{17}$$

E_g is the QD semiconductor material band gap, $m_{e,h}$ are the electron and hole effective mass, respectively, $\hbar = h/2\pi$, h is the Planck constant, and α_{nl} is the n-th root of the spherical Bessel function. In the second case, the energy eigenvalues $E_{e,nlm}$ and $E_{h,nlm}$ are given by, respectively Ohtsu (2008)

$$E_{e,nlm} = E_g + \frac{\hbar^2\pi^2}{2m_e}\left[\left(\frac{n}{L_x}\right)^2 + \left(\frac{l}{L_y}\right)^2 + \left(\frac{m}{L_z}\right)^2\right] \tag{18}$$

$$E_{h,nlm} = \frac{\hbar^2\pi^2}{2m_h}\left[\left(\frac{n}{L_x}\right)^2 + \left(\frac{l}{L_y}\right)^2 + \left(\frac{m}{L_z}\right)^2\right]$$

The density of states (DOS) $\rho_{QD}(E)$ for an array of QDs has the form Ustinov (2003)

$$\rho_{QD}(E) = \sum_n \sum_m \sum_l 2n_{QD}\delta\left(E - E_{e,nlm}\right) \tag{19}$$

where $\delta\left(E - E_{e,nlm}\right)$ is the δ-function, and n_{QD} is the surface density of QDs.

Detailed theoretical and experimental investigations of InAs/GaAs and InAs QDs electronic structure taking into account their more realistic lens, or pyramidal shape, size, composition profile, and production technique (SK, colloidal) have been carried out Bimberg (1999), Bányai (2005), Ustinov (2003). A system of QDs can be approximated with a three energy level model in the conduction band containing a spin degenerate ground state GS, fourfold degenerate excited state (ES) with comparatively large energy separations of about $50-70meV$, and a narrow continuum wetting layer (WL). The electron WL is situated $150meV$ above the lowest electron energy level in the conduction band, i.e. GS and has a width of approximately

$120meV$. In real cases, the QDs vary in size, shape, and local strain which leads to the fluctuations in the quantized energy levels and the inhomogeneous broadening in the optical transition energy. The QDs and WL are surrounded by a barrier material which prevents direct coupling between QD layers. The absolute number of states in the WL is much larger than in the QDs. GS and ES in QDs are characterized by homogeneous and inhomogeneous broadening Bányai (2005). The homogeneous broadening caused by the scattering of the optically generated electrons and holes with imperfections, impurities, phonons, or through the radiative electron-hole pair recombination Bányai (2005) is about $15meV$ at room temperature. The eigenspectrum of a single QD fully quantized in three dimensions consists of a discrete set of eigenvalues depending only on the number of atoms in it. Variations of eigenenergies from QD to QD are caused by variations of QD's strain and shape. The finite carrier lifetime results in Lorentzian broadening of a finite width Ustinov (2003). The optical spectrum of QDs consists of a series of transitions between the zero-dimensional electron gas energy states where the selections rules are determined by the form and symmetry of QDs Ustinov (2003). In(Ga)As/GaAs QDs are characterized by emission at wavelengths no longer than $\lambda = 1.35\mu m$, while the InAs/InP QDs have been proposed for emission at the usual telecommunication wavelength $\lambda = 1.55\mu m$ Ustinov (2003).

7.2 Dynamics of QD Lasers

Fabrication techniques, structure, electrical and optical properties as well as possible applications of QD lasers have been thoroughly investigated Ustinov (2003), Ledentsov (2008), Mi (2009). QD lasers based on self-organized InGaN, InAs, InGaAlP nanostructures have been proposed for different applications from the ultraviolet (UV) to the far infrared (IR) spectral range Ledentsov (2008). They demonstrate extremely low threshold current densities, high temperature stability, potential low wavelength chirp, fast carrier dynamics, and modified DOS function which should lead to the improved performance Ustinov (2003), Thompson (2009). In particular, the InAs/GaAs QD lasers based on 3-D nanometer scale islands with dimensions of about $10nm$ are promising in fiber optic applications in the $1.3\mu m$ wavelength range. QD edge-emitting lasers and VCSELs can be realized Ustinov (2003), Ledentsov (2008). In UWB optical link applications the QD laser direct modulation is essential. The detailed study of QD laser dynamics is necessary for the evaluation of signal dispersion, modulation-induced chirping, linewidth, etc. Tan (2009). Modulation characteristics of QD lasers are limited by small area density of QDs grown by SK technique and the inhomogeneous gain broadening caused by the QD size fluctuations Sakamoto (2000), Sugawara (2002), Sugawara (2004), Ledentsov (2008). A Gaussian distribution may be used for the description of the QD sizes, and it shows that the discrete resonances merge into a continuous structure with widths around 10% Bányai (2005). The ensemble of QDs should be divided into groups by their resonant frequency of the GS transition between the conduction and valence bands Sugawara (2002), Sugawara (2004). However, in some cases the gain broadening is desirable providing a stable VCSEL operation in a wide temperature range Ledentsov (2008). It may be also helpful in the case of single-source multichannel data transmission systems Ledentsov (2008). It has been shown theoretically that the inhomogeneous broadening in QD SOA limits the pulse duration to nanoseconds or even several dozen picoseconds for a large enough bias current Ben Ezra (2007). Unlike bulk and QW lasers, the modulation bandwidth in QD lasers is essentially determined by the carrier relaxation and radiative recombination due to the complete quantization of the energy levels Chow (2005).

The analysis of QD laser dynamic behavior can be derived from the phenomenological rate equations, or from quantum mechanical theories. A semiclassical approach is based on the laser field and active medium description by the Maxwell-Bloch equations which account for nonequilibrium effects on time scales from subpicosecond to nanoseconds Chow (2005). This microscopic approach is extremely complicated due to a large number of effects to be included in general case.

The alternative phenomenological approach based on the coupled rate equation system for the carriers is widely used both for QD lasers and for QD SOAs Berg (2001), Berg (2004), Berg (November 2004), Ben Ezra (September 2005), Ben Ezra (October 2005), Ben Ezra (2007), Ben Ezra (2008), Qasaimeh (2003), Qasaimeh (2004), Sakamoto (2000), Uskov (2004), Yavari (2009), Tan (2009), Kim (2009). Typically, the electron-hole pair is considered as a one bound state, or an exciton, and only the carrier dynamics in conduction band is investigated. Recently, a more complicated model has been proposed for QD SOA where the dynamics of electrons and holes has been considered separately Kim (2009).

We use the standard approach where the hole dynamics is neglected. The QD laser model includes WL, upper continuum state (CS), GS and ES where the carriers are injected into WL, then they relax to CS serving as a carrier reservoir, and finally to GS and ES in each QD ensemble Yavari (2009), Tan (2009). The energy band structure of the QD laser is shown in Fig. 11.

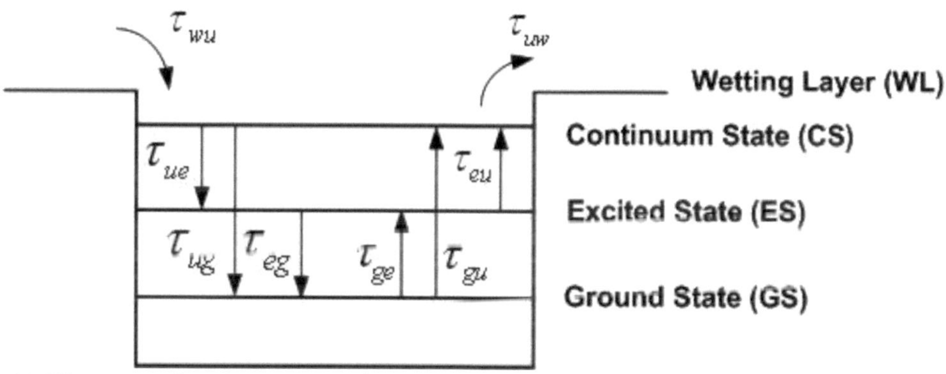

Fig. 11. The energy band structure of a QD laser

Carrier thermal emission occurs among CS, ES, and GS, and separately, between CS and WL Tan (2009). The stimulated emission of photons occurs above the threshold bias current due to the carrier transitions from GS Yavari (2009), Tan (2009). The system of the coupled rate equations has the form Tan (2009).

$$\frac{dN_w}{dt} = \frac{\eta_i I}{q} - \frac{N_w}{\tau_{wr}} - \frac{N_w}{\tau_{wu}} + \frac{1}{\tau_{uw}} \sum_j N_{u,j} \tag{20}$$

$$\frac{dN_{u,j}}{dt} = \frac{N_w G_n}{\tau_{wu,j}} + \frac{N_{g,j}}{\tau_{gu,j}} + \frac{N_{e,j}}{\tau_{eu,j}} - \frac{N_{u,j}}{\tau_{ug,j}} - \frac{N_{u,j}}{\tau_{ue,j}}$$
$$- \frac{N_{u,j}}{\tau_{uw}} - \frac{N_{u,j}}{\tau_r} - \frac{c\Gamma}{n_r} \sum_m g_{mn} S_m \tag{21}$$

$$\frac{dN_{e,j}}{dt} = \frac{N_{u,j}}{\tau_{ue,j}} + \frac{N_{g,j}}{\tau_{ge,j}} - \frac{N_{e,j}}{\tau_{eu,j}} - \frac{N_{e,j}}{\tau_{eg,j}} - \frac{N_{e,j}}{\tau_r} - \frac{c\Gamma}{n_r}\sum_m g_{mn} S_m \tag{22}$$

$$\frac{dN_{g,j}}{dt} = \frac{N_{u,j}}{\tau_{ug,j}} + \frac{N_{e,j}}{\tau_{eg,j}} - \frac{N_{g,j}}{\tau_{gu,j}} - \frac{N_{g,j}}{\tau_{ge,j}} - \frac{N_{g,j}}{\tau_r} - \frac{c\Gamma}{n_r}\sum_m g_{mn} S_m \tag{23}$$

Here I is the current injection, η_i is the internal quantum efficiency, q is the electron charge, the subscript j refers to the jth group of QDs, the subscripts w, u, e and g refer to WL, CS, ES and GS, respectively; N_w, $N_{u,j}$, $N_{e,j}$, $N_{g,j}$ are the carrier populations in the WL, CS, ES, and GS of the jth QD group, respectively; S_m is the number of photons in the mth mode, c is the free space light velocity, Γ is the optical confinement factor, g_{mn} is the linear optical gain of the nth QD group contributing to the mth mode photons, τ_{wr} is the recombination lifetime constant in the WL, $\overline{\tau}_{wu}$ is the average carrier relaxation time from WL to CS, τ_r is the common recombination lifetime in each group of QDs, τ_{uw} is the excitation lifetime from CS to WL. The total active region volume V_A is given by Tan (2009).

$$V_A = HdLn_w \tag{24}$$

where H is the QD height, L is the laser cavity length, d is the width of the device, n_w is the number of dot layers in the active region.

7.3 Direct Modulation of QD Lasers by UWB Signals in an Analog Optical Link

In order to investigate the performance of the analog optical link containing a QD laser, we have carried out the numerical simulations of the QD laser direct modulation in the MB OFDM case using rate equations (20)-(23). The typical values of the essential device parameters used in our simulations are similar to the ones used in Refs. Yavari (2009), Tan (2009). For instance, a WL thickness is $1nm$, $L = 800\mu m$, the volume density of QDs is $N_D = 1.67 \times 10^{23} m^{-3}$, the volume of active region is $9.6 \times 10^{-16} m^3$, $\overline{\tau}_{wu} = 1ps$, $\tau_{uw} = 10ps$, $\tau_{wr} = 0.4ns$, $\tau_r = 1ns$, spontaneous emission lifetime $2.8ns$. The QD laser is biased with the dc current $I = 10mA$ and MB OFDM UWB signal at the power level of $-14dBm$. The resulting modulated optical signal in shown in Fig. 12. The corresponding spectra of the modulated bandpass and baseband

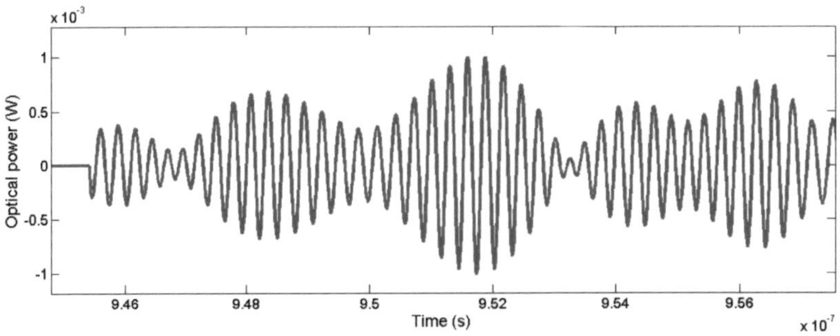

Fig. 12. Directly modulated optical power of the QD laser in the analogous optical link

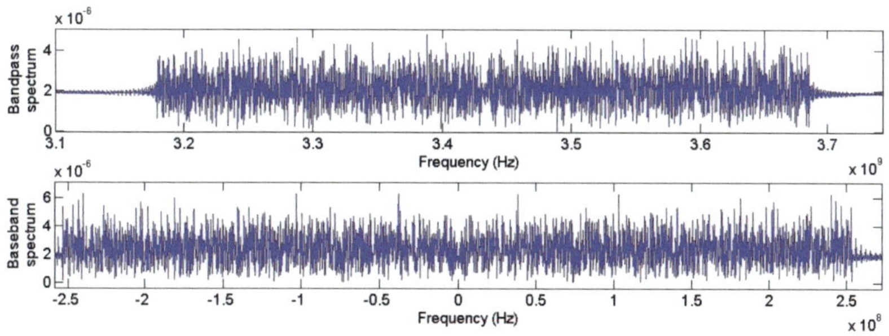

Fig. 13. Spectrum of the directly modulated QD laser radiation (upper box); spectrum of the baseband signal (lower box)

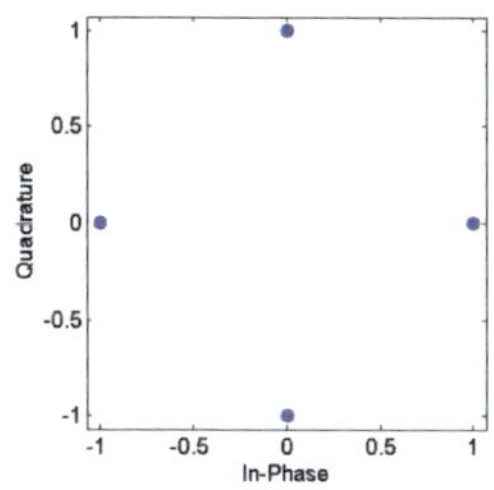

Fig. 14. Constellation diagram of the signal transferred through the analogous optical link

signals are shown in Fig. 13. The modulated signal was transmitted over SMF of a $1km$ length and detected with a photodiode (PD). The responsivity of PD was $R = 0.95A/W$ and the radio frequency bandwidth was $10GHz$. The constellation diagram of the received baseband UWB signal is shown in Fig. 14. The constellation diagram clearly shows the high quality of the transmission over the optical link containing QD laser which corresponds to the non-distorted form of the optical signal and its spectrum.

8. Conclusions

We have discussed state-of-the-art of the UWB communications, the novel trends such as UROOF technology, theoretical and experimental results for the photonic generation of UWB pulses, the importance of the high level integration of novel photonic and electronic components for UWB communications, and applications of QD lasers and QD SOAs. The integration of QD lasers with the Si photonics on a Si platform can significantly improve the performance of UWB communication systems and reduce the cost. We have carried out the numerical simulations for the analog optical link containing the QD laser. The performance of the optical link is significantly improved due to high linearity, large bandwidth and low noise of the QD laser. Further detailed theoretical and experimental investigations in the field of QD devices are required in order to develop new generations of UWB communication systems mainly based on the all-optical signal processing.

9. References

Agrawal, G.P. (2002). *Fiber-Optic Communication Systems*. Wiley, ISBN 0-471-21571-6, New York

Armstrong, J. (2009). OFDM for Optical Communications, *IEEE Journal of Lightwave Technology*, Vol. 27, No. 3 (February 2009) 189-204, ISSN 0733-8724

Bányai, L. & Koch, S. W. (2005). *Semiconductor Quantum Dots* (Second Edition). World Scientific, ISBN 9810213905, London

Ben-Ezra, Y.; Haridim, M. & Lembrikov, B. I. (2005). Theoretical analysis of gain-recovery time and chirp in QD-SOA. *IEEE Photonics Technology Letters*, Vol. 17, No. 9, (September 2005) 1803-1805, ISSN 1041-1135

Ben-Ezra, Y.; Lembrikov, B. I. & Haridim, M. (2005). Acceleration of gain recovery and dynamics of electrons in QD-SOA. *IEEE Journal of Quantum Electronics*, Vol. 41, No. 10, (October 2005) 1268-1273, ISSN 0018-9197

Ben-Ezra, Y.; Lembrikov, B. I. & Haridim, M. (2007). Specific features of XGM in QD-SOA. *IEEE Journal of Quantum Electronics*, Vol.43, No. 8, (August 2007) 730-737, ISSN 0018-9197

Ben Ezra, Y.; Haridim, M.; Lembrikov, B.I. & Ran, M. (2008). Proposal for All-optical Generation of Ultra Wideband Impulse Radio Signals in Mach-Zehnder Interferometer with Quantum Dot Optical Amplifier. *IEEE Photonics Technology Letters*, Vol. 20, No. 7 (April 2008) 484-486, ISSN 1041-1135

Ben Ezra, Y.; Lembrikov, B.I.; Ran, M. & Haridim, M. (2009). All Optical Generation and Processing of IR UWB Signals", In: *Optical Fibre, New Developments*. Christophe Lethien (Ed.), In-Tech, 2009, Vukovar, Croatia, pp. 425-444, ISBN 978-953-7619-50-3

Ben Ezra, Y. & Lembrikov, B.I. (June 2009). Optical wavelet signal processing. *11th Int'l. Conf. on Transparent Optical Networks (ICTON 2009)*. Azores, Portugal, 28 June-2 July 2009, We. A.2.2, pp. 1-4, ISBN 978-1-4244-4826-5

Berg, T.W.; Bischoff, S.; Magnusdottir, I. & Mørk, J. (2001). Ultrafast gain recovery and modulation limitations in self-assembled quantum-dot devices. *IEEE Photonics Technology Letters*, Vol. 13, No. 6 (June 2001) 541-543, ISSN 1041-1135

Berg, T.W.; Mørk, J. & Hvam, J.M. (2004). Gain dynamics and saturation in semiconductor quantum dot amplifiers. *New Journal of Physics*, Vol. 6, No. 178, (2004) 1-23, ISSN 1367-2630

Berg, T.W. & Mørk, J. (2004). Saturation and Noise Properties of Quantum-Dot Optical Amplifiers. *IEEE J. of Quantum Electronics*, Vol. 40, No. 11, (November 2004) 1527-1539, ISSN 0018-9197

Bimberg, D.; Grundmann, M. & Ledentsov, N. N. (1999). *Quantum Dot Heterostructures*. John Wiley, ISBN 047 1973882, New York

Chong, C.-C.; Watanabe, F. & Inamura, H. (2006). Potential of UWB technology for the next generation wireless communications. *Proceedings of 2006 IEEE Ninth International symposium on Spread Spectrum Techniques and Applications, Manaus, Amazon, Brazil* (28-31 August 2006) 422-429, ISBN 0-7803-9779-7

Chow, W.W. & Koch, S. W. (2005). Theory of semiconductor quantum-dot laser dynamics. *IEEE J. of Quantum Electronics*, Vol. 41, No. 4, (April 2005) 495-505, ISSN 0018-9197

Cox, III, C.H. (2003). Analog optical links: models, measures and limits of performance. In: *Microwave Photonics* Vilcot, A., Cabon, B. & Chazelas, J. (Eds.), 210-219, Kluver, ISBN 1-4020-7362-3, Boston

Ghavami, M.; Michael, L.B. & Kohno, R. (2005). *Ultra Wideband Signals and Systems in Communication Engineering*, Wiley, ISBN-10 0-470-86571-5(H/B), Chichester, England

Iacona, F.; Irrera, A.; Franzò, G.; Pacifici, D.; Crupi, I.; Miritello, M.; Presti, C.D. & Priolo, F. (2006). Silicon-based light-emitting devices: properties and applications of crystalline, amorphous and Er-doped nanoclusters. *IEEE Journal of Selected Topics in Quantum Electronics*, Vol. 12, No. 6 (November/December 2006) 1596–1606, ISSN 1077-260X

Jalali, B. & S. Fathpour, S. (2006). Silicon Photonics, *Journal of Lightwave Technology*, Vol.24, No. 12, (December 2006) 4600-4615, ISSN 0733-8724

Kim, J.; Laemmlin, M.; Meuer, C.; Bimberg, D. & Eisenstein, G. (2009). Theoretical and experimental study of high-speed small-signal cross-gain modulation of quantum-dot semiconductor optical amplifiers. *IEEE J. of Quantum Electronics*, Vol. 45, No. 3, (March 2009) 240-248, ISSN 0018-9197

Kshetrimayum, R. S. (2009). An Introduction to UWB Communication Systems. *Potentials, IEEE*, Vol. 28, Issue 2, (March-April 2009) 9-13, ISSN 0278-6648

Ledentsov, N.N.; Bimberg, D. & Alferov, Zh.I. (2008). Progress in epitaxial growth and performance of quantum dot and quantum wire lasers, *Journal of Lightwave Technology*, Vol.26, No. 11, (June 2006) 1540-1555, ISSN 0733-8724

Le Guennec, Y. & Gary, R. (2007). Optical frequency conversion for millimeter-wave ultra-wideband-over-fiber systems. *IEEE Photonics Technology Letters*, Vol. 19, No. 13, (July 2007) 996-998, ISSN 1041-1135

Lin, W.-P. & Chen, J.-Y. (2005). Implementation of a new ultrawide-band impulse system, *IEEE Photonics Technology Letters*, Vol. 17, No. 11, (November 2005) 2418-2420, ISSN 1041-1135

Mi, Z.; Yang, J.; Bhattacharya, P.; Qin, G. & Ma, Z. (2009). High-Performance quantum dot lasers and integrated optoelectronics on Si. *Proceedings of the IEEE*, Vol. 97, No. 7, (July 2009) 1239-1249, ISSN 0018-9219

Ohtsu, N.; Kobayashi, K.; Kawazoe, T.; Yatsui, T. & Naruse, N. (2008). *Principles of Nanophotonics*, CRC Press, ISBN-13 978-1-58488-972-4, London

Qasaimeh, O. (2003). Optical gain and saturation characteristics quantum-dot semiconductor optical amplifiers. *IEEE J. of Quantum Electronics*, Vol. 39, No. 6, (June 2003) 793-798, ISSN 0018-9197

Qasaimeh, O. (2004). Characteristics of cross-gain (XG) wavelength conversion in quantum dot semiconductor optical amplifiers. *IEEE Photonics Technology Letters*, Vol. 16, No. 2, (February 2004) 542-544, ISSN 1041-1135

Qui, R. C.; Shen, X.; Guizani, M. & Le-Ngoc, T. (2006). Introduction, In: *Ultra-wideband wireless communications and networks*, Shem, X., Guizani, M., Qui, R. C., Le-Ngoc, T. (Ed.), 1-14, Wiley, ISBN 0-470-01144-0, Chichester, England

Ran, M; Ben Ezra, Y. & Lembrikov B.I. (2009). Ultra-wideband Radio-over-optical-fibre Technologies, In: *Short-Range Wireless Communications*, Kraemer, R. & Katz, M. D. (Eds.), 271-327, Wiley, ISBN 978-0-470-69995-9 (H/B), Chichester, England

R.M. Rao and A.S. Bopardikar (1998). *Wavelet Transforms. Introduction to Theory and Applications*. Addison-Wesley, Addison-Wesley, ISBN-10: 020 16 34 635, Reading, Massachusetts

Reed, G.T. & Knights, A.P. (2004). *Silicon Photonics*, Wiley, ISBN 0-470-87034-6, Chichester, England

Sakamoto, A. & Sugawara, M. (2000). Theoretical calculation of lasing spectra of quantum-dot lasers: effect of homogeneous broadening of optical gain, *IEEE Photonics Technology Letters*, Vol. 12, No. 2, (February 2000) 107-109, ISSN 1041-1135

Shieh, W.; Bao, H. & Tang, Y. (2008). Coherent optical OFDM: theory and design. *Optics Express*, Vol.16, No. 2, (January 2008) 841-859, ISSN 1094-4087

R. Soref, R. (2006). The Past, present, and future of Si photonics, *IEEE Journal of Selected Topics in Quantum Electronics,* Vol.13, No. 6, (November/December 2006) 1678-1687, ISSN 1077-260X

Sugawara, M.; T. Akiyama, T.; N. Hatori, N. ; Y. Nakata, Y.; Ebe, H. & H. Ishikava, H. (2002). Quantum-dot semiconductor optical amplifiers for high-bit-rate signal processing up to 160 Gbs^{-1} and a new scheme of 3R regenerators, *Meas. Sci. Technol.*, Vol. 13, (2002), 1683-1691, ISSN 0957-0233

Sugawara, M.; Ebe, H.; Hatori, N.; Ishida, M.; Arakawa, Y.; Akiyama, T.; Otsubo, K. & Nakata, Y. (2004) Theory of optical signal amplification and processing by quantum-dot semiconductor optical amplifiers. *Phys. Rev.B,* Vol. 69, No. 23 (June 2004) 235332-1-39, ISSN 1098-0121

Sung, G.Y. & al (2006). Physics and device structures of highly efficient silicon quantum dots based silicon nitride light-emitting diodes. *IEEE Journal of Selected Topics in Quantum Electronics,* Vol. 12, No. 6 (November/December 2006) 1545–1555, ISSN 1077-260X

Tan, C. L.; Wang, Y.; Djie, H. S. & Ooi, B. S. (2009). The dynamic characteristics and linewidth enhancement factor of quasi-supercontinuum self-assembled quantum dot laser, *IEEE Journal of Quantum Electronics,* Vol. 45, No. 9, (September 2009) 1177-1182, ISSN 0018-9197

Thompson, M.G.; Rae, A.R.; Xia, M.; Penty, R.V. & White, I.H. (2009). InGaAs quantum-dot mode-locked laser diodes. *IEEE Journal of Selected Topics in Quantum Electronics,* Vol. 15, No. 3 (May/June 2009) 661–672, ISSN 1077-260X

Uskov, A.V. ; Berg, T.W. & Mørk, J. (2004). Theory of pulse-train amplification without patterning effects in quantum-dot semiconductor optical amplifiers. *IEEE J. of Quantum Electronics,* Vol. 40, No. 3, (March 2004) 306-320, ISSN 0018-9197

Ustinov, V.M.; Zhukov, A.E.; Egorov, A. Yu. & Maleev, N. A. (2003). *Quantum Dot Lasers,* Oxford University Press, ISBN 0 19 852679 2, Oxford

Wada, O. (2007). Femtosecond all-optical devices for ultrafast communication and signal processing, In: *Microwave Photonics,* Lee, C. H. (Ed), 31-75, CRC Press, ISBN-10: 0-8493-3924-3

Wang, Q. & Yao, J. (2006). UWB doublet generation using nonlinearly-biased electro-optic intensity modulator, *Electronic Letters,* Vol. 42, No. 22, (October 2006)1304-1305, ISSN 0013-5194

Yang, L. & Giannakis, G.B. (2004). Ultra-Wideband Communications. *IEEE Signal Processing Magazine,* Vol. 21, No. 6; (November 2004) 26-54, ISSN 1053-5888

Yao, J.; Zeng, F. & Wang, Q. (2007). Photonic generation of ultrawideband signals. *Journal of Lightwave Technology,* Vol. 25, No. 11, (November 2007) 3219-3235, ISSN 0733-8724

Yao, J. (2009). Photonics for ultrawideband communications, *IEEE Microwave Magazine,* Vol. 10, No. 4, (June 2009) 82-95, ISSN 1527-3342

Yavari, M.H. & Ahmadi, V. (2009). Circuit-level implementation of semiconductor self-assembled quantum dot laser. *IEEE Journal of Selected Topics in Quantum Electronics,* Vol. 15, No. 3 (May/June 2009) 774–779, ISSN 1077-260X

Zeng, F. & Yao, J. (2006). An approach to ultrawideband pulse generation and distribution over optical fiber. *IEEE Photonics Technology Letters,* Vol. 18, No. 7, (April 2006) 823-825, ISSN 1041-1135

Zeng, F. & Yao, J. (2006). Ultrawideband impulse radio signal generation using a high-speed electrooptic phase modulator and a fiber-Bragg-grating-based frequency discriminator. *IEEE Photonics Technology Letters,* Vol. 18, No. 19, (October 2006) 2062-2064, ISSN 1041-1135

Zeng, F.; Wang, O. & Yao, J.P. (2007). All-optical UWB impulse generation based on cross-phase modulation and frequency discrimination. *Electronic Letters,* Vol. 43, No. 2, (January 2007) 119-121, ISSN 0013-5194

6

Portable ultra-wideband localization and asset tracking for mobile robot applications

Jong-Hoon Youn* and Yong K. Cho**
*University of Nebraska-Omaha**
*University of Nebraska-Lincoln***
USA

1. Introduction

This chapter introduces our on-going research at the Peter Kiewit Institute, Omaha, Nebraska, to investigate the performance of Ultra-Wideband (UWB) localization technologies that can be applied to sensor-aided intelligent mobile robots for high-level navigation functions for construction site security and material delivery.

Security at construction sites, especially in the commercial construction industry, is a widespread problem. Construction site can be jeopardized by thieves and vandals, which can cause job delays, downtime for operators, higher insurance premiums, possible cancellation of insurance policies, and diminished profitability of projects under construction (Berg & Hinze, 2005). The U.S. construction industry lost nearly $1 billion in 2001 due to theft of equipment and tools, according to the National Insurance Crime Bureau (McDowall, 2002), and the annual insurance claims in Canada represent theft losses of more than $46 million (Mechanical, 1999). McDowall (McDowall, 2002) reported that 90% of the equipment and tool thefts occur on job sites with little security and where assets remain unattended over the weekends or holidays. A typical construction site turns into a "ghost town" after 4 or 5 p.m., which often makes it vulnerable to theft and vandalism. Interestingly, research has shown that the majority of theft and vandalism incidents are not caused by strangers, but rather by individuals familiar with the jobsite (Gardner, 2006).

Unlike fixed facilities, tracking the location of mobile assets in a dynamic indoor environment is not an easy task. Emerging technologies such as mobile devices and wireless technologies have already demonstrated the capability of identifying the location of mobile assets. However, the penetration of these technologies into indoor building environments has been limited, especially in highly congested areas with room partitions, metal structures, furniture, and people. In this chapter, we present the results of our experimental investigations on the accuracy of an Ultra Wideband (UWB) system for tracking mobile assets in various indoor environments and scenarios. We also demonstrate the integration of a UWB tracking technology into a path planning system of mobile robots for improved navigation.

2. Mobile Robot Platform and Graphical User Interface

In order to operate independently and effectively, a robot must be able to autonomously explore its own space. Autonomous navigation is the ability of a wheeled mobile robot system to purposefully steer its course through a physical medium with the knowledge of where it is, other places it might want to go, and paths it would take to get there safely. Therefore, the precise position information of the robot is a key to the development of an autonomous navigation system.

2.1 Issues in indoor localization of mobile robots

Autonomous navigation is one of the most basic behaviors needed in many applications and especially in mobile robotics. However, it is quite challenging since mobile robots are plagued with communication problems. Wireless communications between a robot and an operator suffer from multi-path interference, signal loss, and non-Line of Sight (NLOS) as a robot penetrates deeper into an unknown environment (Farrington, 2004).

Localization is a major area of mobile robotics and sensor-based exploration enables a robot to localize its position, explore an environment and build a map of that environment using sonar sensors, a laser rangefinder, and a 3D laser sweeper. However, these technologies require a line of sight to register the robot's location in a map, which limits its applicability to open space only.

In this study, five mobile robot platforms were obtained from Dr. Robot Inc. (Dr. Robot, 2010). The robots were not rugged enough for real-world applications, but they were sufficient enough to represent wireless robots for the purpose of control algorithms and graphical user interface development in our testbed. As shown in Fig. 1, each robot was equipped with six ultrasonic range sensor modules, nine infrared distance measuring sensors, two wheel encoders, and two human detect/motion sensors detecting infrared energy radiation from human bodies within a 5-meter range. A camera, microphone and speaker were installed on each robot. The camera system has a color image module with a mini-color camera head which is a CMOS image sensor module that can be connected directly to its multimedia controller board. The image size and frame rate can be up to 353x288 pixels and 15fps respectively.

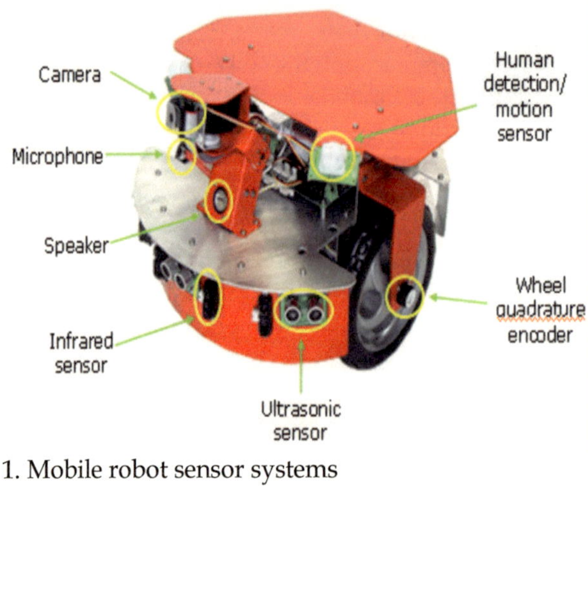

Fig. 1. Mobile robot sensor systems

Each robot was assigned with its own IP address. With its integrated WiFi 802.11 wireless module, the system can transmit all sensor data to a PC or server. Commands and data can be also sent to the robots via the same wireless link for real-time control and access. In this study, the robot control program was programmed to manually or autonomously maneuver around the building while avoiding static or mobile obstacles using the aforementioned sensors. Fig. 2 shows the robot control and communication architecture.

AutoCAD™ and Microsoft Visual Studio were used to develop a graphical user interface (GUI) for multi-robot control. Theoretically, one can determine the (x, y) coordinates of the robot using dead-reckoning, a process that determines the robot's location by integrating data from wheel encoders that count the number of wheel rotations. However, in general, dead reckoning fails to accurately position the robot for many reasons, including wheel slippage. If the robot slips, the wheel rotation does not correspond to the robot's motion and thus encoder data, which reflects the state of the wheel rotation, do not reflect the robot's net motion, thereby causing positioning errors (Choset & Nagatani, 2001). In addition, each robot's wheel encoders need to be calibrated to their respective control programs. According to the results of our experiments at PKI using the mobile robot platform shown in Fig. 1, deadreckoning showed about 35cm positional error when the robot traveled about 7 meters, mainly due to a built-in inconsistent rpm for each wheel motor which tended to cause curving paths even for a straight movement command (Cho et al., 2007).

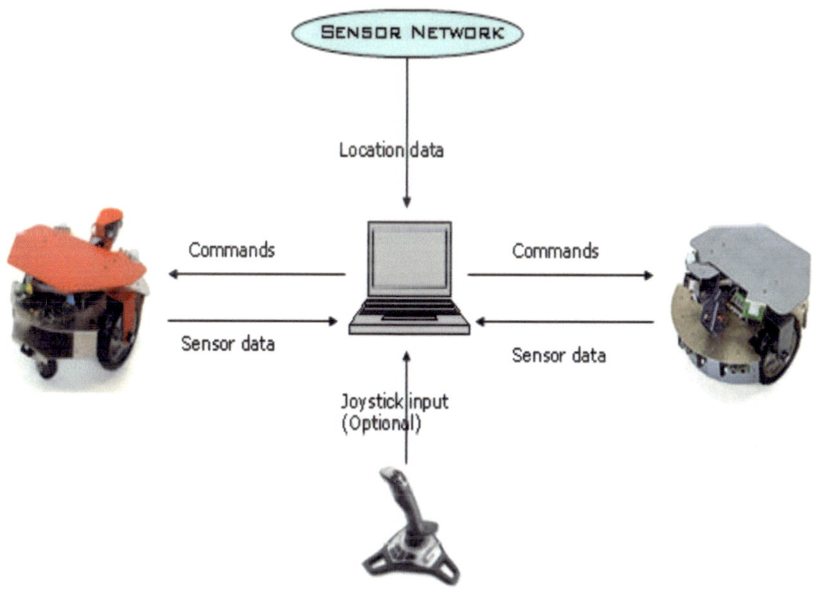

Fig. 2. Wireless robot control system architecture within a UWB sensor system

2.2 Real-time graphical user interface (GUI) for mobile robots

In this study, software modules for a robot control and a UWB position tracking were developed, which can be easily imbedded into standard CAD programs such as Microstation (Microstation, 2010) and AutoCAD (AutoCAD, 2010). Since most of the building construction projects already have either 2D or 3D CAD floor drawings available,

the developed modules can save enormous amounts of time in generating a new graphical user interface when applied to different building applications.
Integrated with the GUI, the robot's actual location and orientation is displayed on the CAD building map. Once sensor data is received from wheel encoders, the robot's location is displayed to the GUI in real time. Simultaneously, another position symbol is displayed based on position data received from the UWB location system. Fig. 3 (a) shows a dead reckoning position as a capital letter *A* and a UWB sensor network position as a capital letter *B*. The UWB position is referred as a phantom of robot since the sensed position may rapidly change and move around the dead reckoning position within its position accuracy range even when the robot does not move. Fig. 3 (b) shows a visual representation of the robot's control interface.

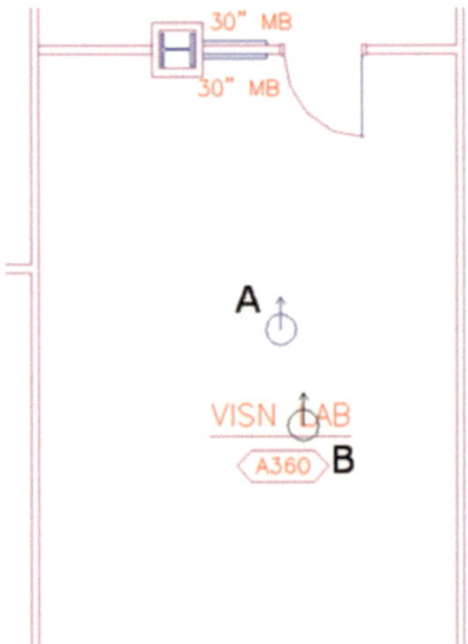

(a) Robot's dead reckoning position (A) and UWB position (B)

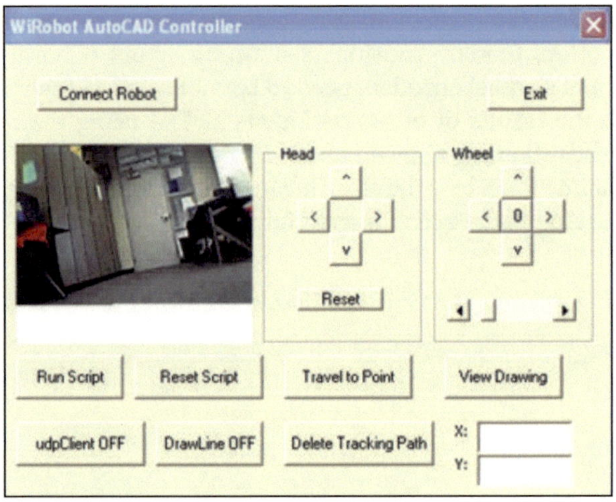

(b) Real-time robot control GUI

Fig. 3. GUI showing the robot's position along with a robot control program.

3. Accuracy of Ultra-wideband (UWB) Positioning Systems

In this study, a commercial UWB system developed by Ubisense (Ubisense, 2010) was used for implementation and performance analysis in several building spaces. The hardware of the ultra-wideband sensor network consists of tags and sensors. A tag is attached to an object that requires location tracking. As each tag emits an UWB signal, location is calculated using both the time difference of arrival between different sensors (a.k.a., receivers) and the angle of arrival at each sensor. Each sensor employs a minimum of four UWB receivers which allow the angle of arrival to be determined (Ubisense, 2010).
The standard UWB configuration consists of a single master sensor and three slave sensors, and requires wired communication cables and timing cables. In order to properly calculate the time of arrival, each slave sensor must synchronize with the master sensor. In the standard configuration, this is done through timing cables between each slave sensor and the master sensor. The Ubisense system spans 5.8-7.2 GHz bandwidth. The system measures time of flight and angle of arrival using directional antennas.

In the next sub-sections, we present our experimental results of the UWB positioning system. To evaluate the sensitivity of multi-path signal problems, the accuracy of UWB sensors was tested in an open space as well as a closed space.

3.1 Open space test

The open space test was conducted in a local building's basement. Four sensors were mounted on tripods and multiple known positions were marked on a floor. Then, a total station was used to get the (x, y, z) position of the sensors and the points on the floor. Fig. 4 shows the surveyed positions of the sensors (402-405) and points on the floor (400, 1000-10013). A UWB tag was then placed on each marked point on the floor to measure the accuracy in difference in distance between a surveyed known position and a wirelessly estimated tag position. The four sensors can cover about 400 square meters.

The obtained average accuracy of the open space test was 19.1cm when the UWB tags were placed on the floor. When the tag was raised by 35cm from the floor level, there was a slight accuracy improvement (1.7 cm) for most of the central points (1001, 1004, 400, 1009 and 1012), as shown in Fig. 4. However, there was a significant accuracy improvement by 13.5 cm for the outermost points (1000-1002 and 1011-1013) when the tag was raised by 35 cm. The results of our open space test verify that, in order to accurately determine a tag position, a multiple number of receivers (typically three) must have a direct line-of-sight or at least a strong attenuated line-of-sight transmission path (Fontana 2003). In particular, the receiver did not catch a signal from the tag when the tag was located just below the receiver. Therefore, it is recommended to install the receiver as high as possible from the floor and face down to cover a large area of the space.

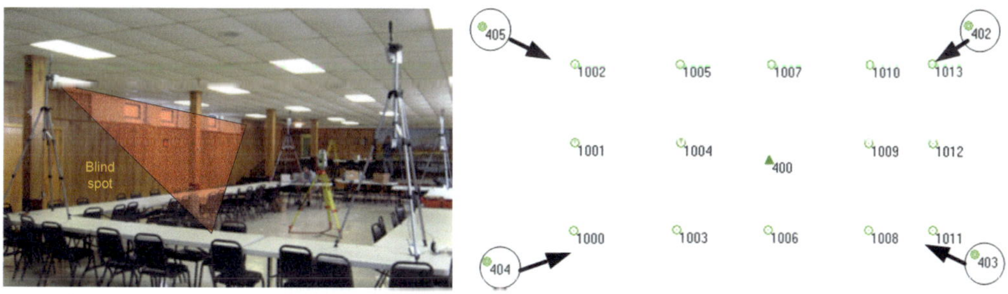

Fig. 4. Open space test in a basement (up) and test area layout (down)

3.2 Closed space test

To conduct a closed space test, an office area of the Peter Kiewit Institute (PKI) at the University of Nebraska-Omaha was selected. The PKI building was the most challenging environment in which to test the UWB system because the building (1) was built with steel frames and metal studs, (2) was furnished with all metal furniture and electronics such as printer and copy machines, and (3) had computer electronics and wireless telecommunication labs nearby the test area which may cause interference with the UWB communication system. In addition, heavy people traffic in this area also negatively impact on the accuracy of the positioning system, since human bodies can absorb wireless signals. Especially, 5.8 GHz cordless phones should be turned off before testing the UWB system because 5.8 GHz phones may significantly interfere with signals from the UWB positioning system which uses 5.8-7.2 GHz frequency bands.

Fig. 5 shows the test area layout with four receiver positions (left) and measured tag positions (marked "+" in the right figure of Fig. 5). The first set of tests was conducted by placing a tag at the floor level. Then the tag was raised by 104 cm for the second test set. Each set of tests was conducted twice. The average of floor level (0 height) tests showed 41 cm accuracy. When the tag was raised by 104 cm, the test showed 48cm accuracy. Unlike the previous open space test which used a stand to raise the tag position, the tag was carried by a human subject in the closed space testbed. Although it was identified that a higher position of the tag showed better accuracy to improve the line-of-sight transmission path, it was noted in the closed space test that the human carrier significantly affected the accuracy based on its orientation.

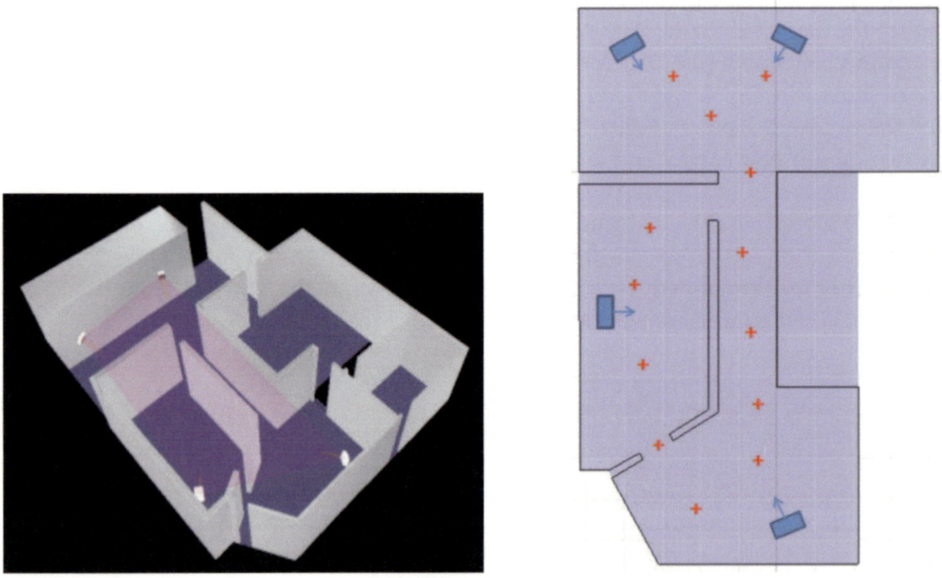

Fig. 5. Closed space test area layout (left) and data points (right).

4. Integration with Ultra-wideband (UWB) Positioning Systems

As mentioned earlier, many outside factors such as wheel slippage can have an adverse effect upon dead reckoning values, which make the technique unreliable. For example, often a robot's infrared and ultrasonic sensors do not recognize thin-leg chairs, and a robot may get stuck in one place while the wheels are still running. This means that the dead reckoning position keeps changing in the GUI while reality does not. Therefore, a more effective method of position tracking and movement control is required.

To remedy this situation, the position information was integrated into the navigation algorithm in this study. If the dead reckoning position is beyond the precision range of the UWB positioning system, the path planning algorithm adjusts the robot's position based on the recent samples of UWB location data.

4.1 Portable Ultra Wideband Positioning System

The basic UWB positioning system consists of a single master sensor and three slave sensors, and requires wired communication cables and timing cables. In order to properly calculate the time of arrival, each slave sensor must be synchronized with the master sensor. In a standard configuration, this is done through timing cables between each slave sensor and the master sensor. However, a dynamically changing environment may not have a wireless infrastructure installed yet. For example, in a construction site, determining a fixed location (e.g., ceiling, wall, and column) for UWB sensors is not an easy task in the middle of construction unless the construction is near completion, because the surface should be finished before a sensor node is attached to it.

To apply this technology at dynamic sites, we decided to design a stand-alone wireless UWB configuration for each sensor which can be easily relocated as needed. In order to remove the Ethernet cables, each slave sensor is connected to a wireless bridge, and the master sensor is connected to a wireless router. The wireless router provides a gateway through which a laptop is able to access sensor readings. Furthermore, the software configuration of the UWB sensors is changed to synchronize them via wireless channels. The untethered configuration of the Ubisense positioning system is shown in Fig. 6.

In the proposed system, the communication between the UWB sensors and a laptop is also performed wirelessly through the 802.11 network, and each UWB sensor drains power from a portable battery in order to operate. The sensors are mounted on tripods which allows for easy transport and deployment. In addition, each sensor is connected to a wireless bridge which is then connected to the laptop. The laptop transmits the boot files to the sensors, allows the user to configure the system's behavior and collects position information.

After surveying the relative coordinates of four UWB sensors using a total station, we are able to track a tag by collecting and analyzing the received wireless signals from the tag. This position data is produced by the estimation of UWB signals between sensors on tripods and a tag placed on a mobile robot.

The relative local values from the UWB sensors are reconciled with the global drawing coordinate system by allowing the user to specify the origin (0, 0, 0) of the sensor network on the drawing during operation.

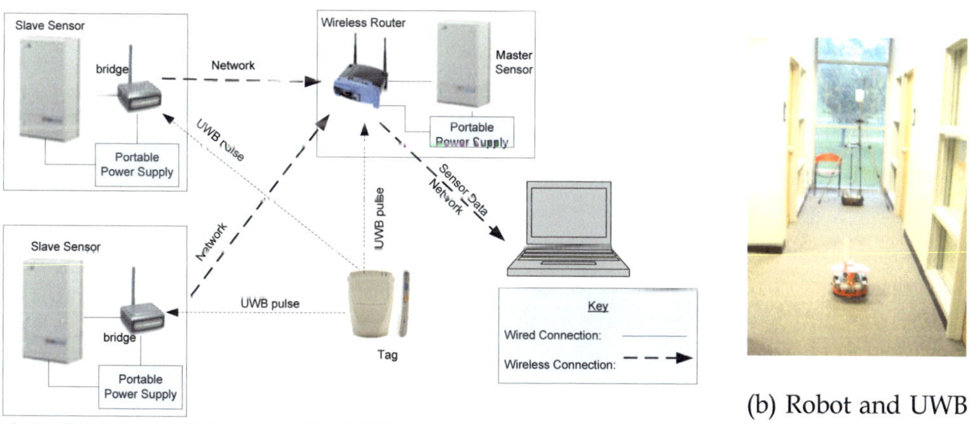

(a) Architecture of the portable UWB system

(b) Robot and UWB sensor on a tripod

Fig. 6. A proposed portable UWB tracking system architecture

Location values are collected as a relative (x, y, z) coordinate on a per request basis. Each robot is assigned a tag. The location of the robot is updated when the controller sends a request for the location of a particular tag. Multiple robots using multiple tags are able to operate simultaneously.

Unfortunately, the UWB sensors come with some difficulties in setup and configuration. Configuring the system from a tethered to untethered system requires a great deal of experience and knowledge of the wireless connections between sensors and a controller. One of the main limitations of the UWB system used in this study is that the system suffers from interference from IEEE 802.11a wireless local networks and 5.8 GHz cordless phones.

4.2 Path finding and planning algorithm

Accurate sensor data is vital for the object avoidance algorithm and position reporting. Any incorrect sensor values will create inconsistent robot behavior and/or location reporting. As mentioned earlier, we are currently investigating a fuzzy logic model for cleaning up the noisy readings because each sensor reading is, by itself, unreliable. Fig. 7 shows a fuzzy logic model which will be developed in the course of this study.

Rather than defining specific slow and stop distances for ultrasonic and infrared sensor values, we create membership functions for far, medium, and near which map to a truth value between 0 and 1. Using these truth values, our navigation model can appropriately change speed or halt the robot.

Our filtering model also performs simple checks such as comparing incoming sensor values against their pre-defined minimum and maximum thresholds to ensure they are within bounds. For example, location data from the UWB sensors are checked using the robot's maximum speed of 1 meter/second as the greatest possible change in position. If an incoming positioning value indicates that the robot is traveling more than several meters per second, the value will be ignored. The flow chart of the algorithm can be seen in Fig. 7 (b).

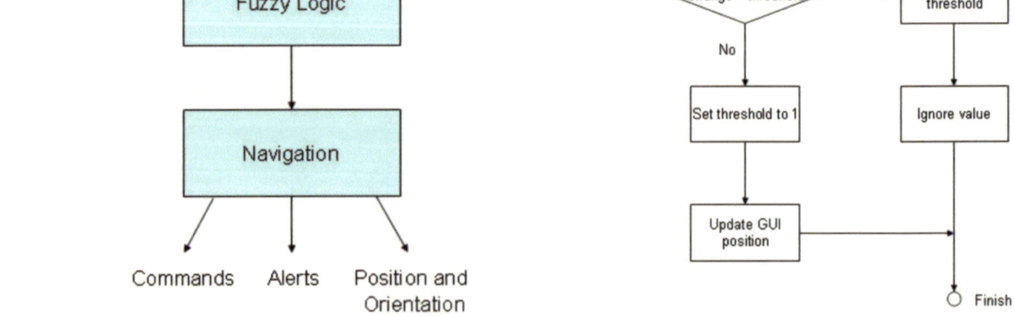

(a) Fuzzy logic and navigation (b) Fuzzy logic flow chart

Fig. 7. Path planning and fuzzy logic

The path planning algorithm is divided into two levels. The first is reaction control which handles avoiding obstacles not present in our drawing. This level also uses human detection readings to avoid and/or report human presence. If human presence is detected, the robot controller would send an alert to the user and stop any current movement so the user could intervene and act appropriately.
The second part is the rail-based movement control scheme. Fig. 8 shows the rail paths deployed in the AutoCAD™ graphical user interface (GUI). To construct this network of rails, a graph of points and lines is added to the CAD drawing. A line follows the center of each hallway with points on this line perpendicular to doorways. Lines then connect this hallway point with a point within the room at each door. Here, a well-known all-to-all shortest path algorithm, Floyd-Warshall's algorithm (Cormen et al., 1990), is used to pre-compute the shortest path from room to room or to the hallway along the rails graph. When the user selects a start and end point, the robot is guided to the starting point and follows the rail paths of the graph along the shortest route to the end point.

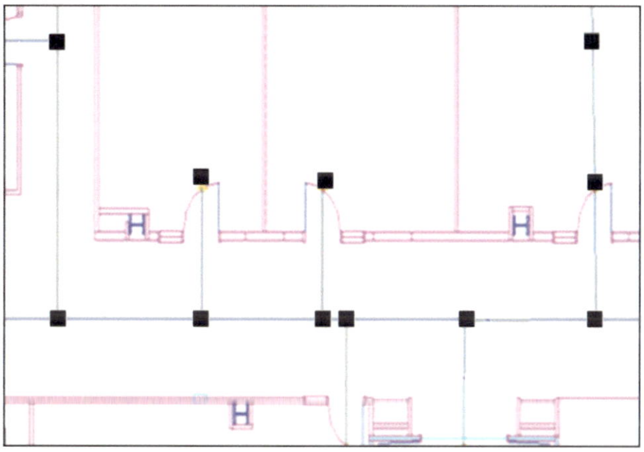

Fig. 8. Rail paths

4.3 Positional error analysis

A preliminary positional error test has been conducted to verify the accuracy of a fully-untethered UWB configuration. Fig. 9 displays the test results. Using the Pythagorean Theorem, positional errors are computed by comparing known points (x, y, z) with points reported from the UWB system. Category 1 describes the error for the fully wired configuration of the UWB setup, Category 2 describes the results of wireless communications using wireless bridges (with synchronization via wired timing cables), and Category 3 describes the results of the fully-untethered configuration with wireless bridges.
Table 1 summarizes the analyzed average positional errors shown in Fig. 9. The fully untethered configuration yielded higher errors than the other two configurations, although 35.6cm is a still acceptable level of accuracy for this study's application. UWB sensors provide positional data that are sufficiently accurate for the robot navigation, but require additional time and effort to set up properly. Since the range of sensors restricts the range of the robot, additional sensors may be added to the network cell to increase range and accuracy. Once the robot moves outside of the sensor network cell, the robot controller

application must recognize this and attempt to return the robot to the sensor cell, if necessary for that scenario.

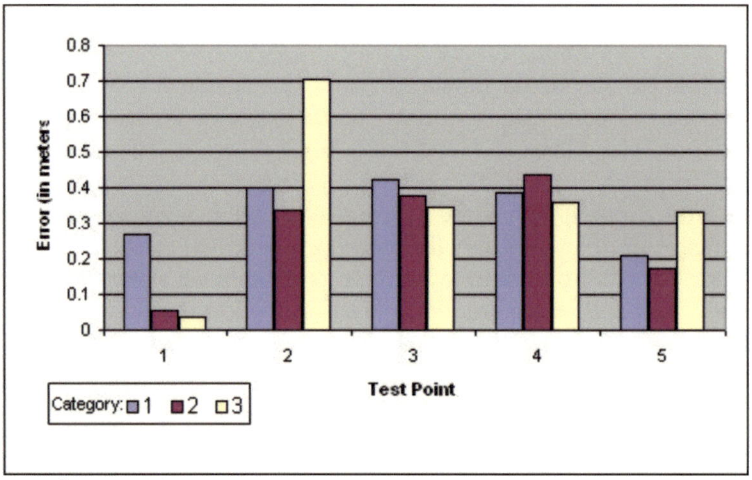

Fig. 9. Error over five positions

Configuration	Error (cm)
Standard (Category 1)	26.3
Wireless bridges (Category 2)	27.5
Untethered with wireless bridges (Category 3)	35.6

Table 1. UWB average error

The proposed rail-based movement algorithm may provide a simple way to implement the method of end-to-end path traversal, but it has some problems that must be addressed. For example, the controller must be able to identify if an obstacle is blocking one of the points on the graph in its path and react appropriately.

5. Conclusion and Future Work

According to the results of our experimental study, the accuracy of the UWB position system depends upon several factors, including precise knowledge of all receiver and reference tag locations. Absolute tag position accuracy of better than 19 cm has been demonstrated in an open space and 48 cm for a closed space. It is recommended that the receiver be located as high as possible to cover a larger area. Also, it is important to strategically select the direction of the receiver and have a minimum of one set of line of sight between a receiver and a tag in any location, which can significantly affect a tag's position accuracy.

This chapter also presented a methodology for autonomous end-to-end navigation of mobile wireless robots for automated construction applications when the working environment is known a priori. As an on-going research effort, this study investigates methods to determine

position and direction along with a process to detect and avoid incorrect sensor values. The key advantages of the proposed approach are: (1) this approach is a fully untethered self-powered ad-hoc wireless networking system which is mainly designed for construction sites or locations where communication infrastructure may not be installed, and (2) the developed position tracking and robot control software modules can be easily imbedded into a standard CAD package (e.g., AutoCAD, Microstation), thus reducing computational burden on developing a new graphical user interface (GUI) for different building applications.
Future challenges include minimizing UWB errors caused by reflection from metal obstacles, maximizing the battery lifespan of the tags, rectifying orientation errors produced by a digital compass when interfering with surrounded magnetic objects, and developing effective dynamic pathing algorithms which best coordinate location data, robot sensor data, and floor plan information.

6. References

AutoCAD (2010), http://usa.autodesk.com/, May 12, 2010

Berg, R. and Hinze, J. (2005), Theft and Vandalism on Construction Sites, In: *Journal of Construction Engineering and Management*, ASCE, 131 (7), pp.826-833

Cormen, Thomas H.; Leiserson, Charles E., Rivest, Ronald L. (1990). *Introduction to Algorithms*, MIT Press and McGraw-Hill, 1990

Cho Y.; Youn, J. (2006), Wireless Sensor-driven Intelligent Navigation Robots for Indoor Construction Site Security and Safety, *Proceedings of 23rd International Symposium on Automation and Robotics in Construction (ISARC)*, Tokyo, Japan, October 3-5, pp. 493 - 499, 2006

Cho, Y.; Youn, J.; Martinez, D. (2010), Error modeling for an untethered ultra-wideband system for construction indoor asset tracking, *Automation in Construction*, Elsevier, Volume 19, Issue 1, page 43-54, January 2010

Choset, H.; Nagatani, K. (2001), Topological simulation localization and mapping (SLAM): toward exact localization without explicit localization, In: *IEEE Transactions on Robotics and Automation*, 17 (2), pp.1254-137, April, 2001

Dr. Robot. Inc. (2010), http://www.drrobot.com/products.asp, May 12, 2010

Farrington, N.; Nguyen, H.; Pezeshkian, N.(2004), Intelligent behaviors for a convoy of indoor mobile robots operating in unknown environments, *Proceedings of SPIE Proc. 5609: Mobile Robots XVII*, Philadelphia, PA, October 27-28, 2004

Fontana, R.; Richley, E.; Barney, J. (2003), Commercialization of an Ultra Wideband Precision Asset Location System, *IEEE conference on Ultra Wideband Systems and Technologies*, Reston, VA, November 2003.

Gardner, T. (2006), *Security in Construction and Beyond; Protecting Your Site, Even During Build-up*, Virgo Publishing, Inc. May 25, 2006

Grabowski, R.; Khosla, P.; Choset, H. (2003), Autonomous Exploration via Regions of Interest, *Proceedings of IEEEE/RSJ intl. conference on intelligent Robots and Systems*, Las Vegas, Nevada, October, pp.-1691-1696, 2003

McDowall, J. (2002). Backhoes, Air Compressors, Skid-steers, Generators head the Hit List, *Rental Management*, Nov. 2002

Mechanical Contractors Association of Toronto (1999), Combating Construction Theft: TCA Partners With Crime Stoppers. *Pipeline*, Vol. 1, Fall 1999

Microsoft Visual Studio (2010), http://msdn.microsoft.com/en-us/vbasic/, May 12, 2010

Microstation (2010), http://www.bentley.com/en-US/Products/, May 12, 2010

(2002). Japanese Theft Gang Tied to U.S., *Rental Equipment Registrar Magazine*. March 11, 2002

Ubisense (2010), http://www.ubisense.net/, May 12, 2010

Williams, C.; Cho, Y.; Youn, J. (2007), Wireless Sensor-driven Intelligent Navigation Method for Mobile Robot Applications in Construction, *Proceedings of* ACSE International Workshop on computing in Civil Engineering, Pittsburg, Pennsylvania, pp. 640 - 647, July 24-27, 2007

7

Transient Modelling of Ultra Wideband (UWB) Pulse Propagation

Qingsheng Zeng and Arto Chubukjian
Communications Research Centre Canada
Ottawa, Ontario K2H 8S2, Canada

1. Introduction

Transient modeling of electromagnetic pulse propagation can be traced back to the beginning of the last century, has become a powerful tool for ultra wideband (UWB) technology, and has been of great interest with a variety of applications, such as short range communication, material characterization, geophysical probing and medical imaging. When an appropriate model has been adopted for the medium, one can manage to work out the frequency-domain solution for wave propagation in this medium. The main difficulties are encountered when trying to transform from the frequency-domain to the time-domain. An inverse fast Fourier transform (IFFT) can be employed to yield the desired transient result. However, several investigations have shown that a large number of sample points are required if one desires to reduce aliasing so that an accurate characterization can be obtained. Besides, when a frequency-domain solution has singular behaviors at some frequencies, direct use of IFFT is inappropriate and some preprocessing must be done for removing these singularities. Furthermore, it is preferable to solve the problems directly in the time-domain under certain circumstances, in which time-varying media or nonlinear systems are involved, or a time-domain response persists very long time.

Other techniques have their own inherent problems. Numerical integration algorithms are free from the problem of aliasing, but the highly oscillatory integrands that are encountered mandate a large number of sample points for the integration and correspondingly a relatively large amount of computation time. Asymptotic techniques are computationally efficient and provide valuable insight into the physical mechanism. However, an asymptotic analysis can be quite cumbersome and the resulting asymptotic expressions can be applied only to parameter values that fall within the range of applicability for the asymptotic expansion. The finite-difference time-domain (FDTD) technique has the advantage that it can be applied to relatively complex, inhomogeneous media, but it also has the following disadvantages. Firstly, the FDTD method does not accurately fulfill the boundary conditions at material interfaces posed by Maxwell's equations, and can cause high calculation costs even in combination with surface impedance boundary conditions for achieving high accuracy under some circumstances. Secondly, when the widths of signal pulses are very narrow and the calculation time domain is large, FDTD solutions may become computationally intractable. Thirdly, the standard FDTD approach cannot handle simulations of long propagation distances because of finite computer memory resources and accumulation of phase errors associated with numerical dispersion. Another common drawback of the FDTD technique, fast Fourier transform (FFT) and numerical integration is that all the three techniques are purely numerical, and therefore it is difficult to extract the physical phenomenology from the numerical data.

The advancement of UWB technology has been driving the need to develop efficient techniques for transient analyses of electromagnetic pulses. The objective of this chapter is to introduce some new technique that is based on numerical inversion of Laplace transform into transient modeling of UWB pulse propagation. In this chapter, first of all, the previous related investigations, majority of which are not based either on FFT, or on FDTD, or on other purely numerical methods, are overviewed, and some limitations of these methods are discussed. Then numerical inversion of Laplace transform and Prony's method are addressed. Next, the approach combining a numerical inversion of the Laplace transform with Prony's method is applied to the analyses of pulses reflected from a conductive interface. Meanwhile, a mathematical proof is presented, showing that the numerical inversion of the Laplace transform is applicable to the characterization of the reflected pulse due to an incident pulse that is a linear combination of exponential signals and is impinging upon a conductive interface at any incident angle for both horizontal and vertical polarizations. Numerical results are illustrated and compared with those published in the literature. A good agreement between the two validates the correctness and effectiveness of this approach. Furthermore, a time domain multipath model is utilized to characterize hallway UWB signal propagation. With the evaluation of direct and reflected waves in time domain, the performance analysis is conducted for binary UWB communications, and the impacts of multipath components on pulse distortion and UWB system performance are discussed. After that, based on the studies of pulses reflected from a conducting half space, characterization of pulses propagating through a lossy dielectric slab is pursued. Our results are shown to be comparable to the previously published results and agree well with those obtained using the FDTD technique. Moreover, the transmission loss is discussed for different parameters and the results are shown to be consistent with those published in the literature. The corresponding results for an incident angle close to 90^0 are also provided, which can not be generated with the previous approaches. In addition, the concern on whether the treatment of permittivity and conductivity in this chapter accords with the Kramers-Kronig relations is properly adressed. Finally, this approach is summarized and the significance of this work is discussed.

2. Overview of Previous Investigations

Theoretical investigations of pulse propagation through different media and interaction with objects have been performed since the days of Sommerfeld during the early last century (Sommerfeld, 1914). These investigations involved calculations of the reflected and/or transmitted fields at the interface between two different media. The problem involving a time-harmonic plane wave obliquely incident on a finite conductive half-space is a classic boundary value problem in electromagnetic theory that is thoroughly treated in standard textbooks, for instance, those by Stratton (Stratton, 1941) and by Balanis (Balanis,

1989). However, due to the mathematical complexity, it is not easy to analytically integrate the required inverse Laplace transform. Dudley et al. (Dudley et al., 1974) undertook a thorough investigation of TE and TM reflected waves associated with a double exponential, obliquely incident plane wave. They utilized contour integration techniques to rewrite the inverse Fourier transform representation for the reflected fields in terms of a residue term and an integral around the branch cut. The contribution of this branch cut was calculated using numerical integration. Papazoglou (Papazoglou, 1975) extended the analysis to the treatment of TE and TM transmitted waves. He also studied a Debye model which accounted for the frequency dependence in the electrical properties of the conductive media. Klaasen (Klaasen, 1990) showed that the TE transmitted and reflected fields associated with a unit-step, obliquely incident plane wave can be represented in terms of convolution integrals involving exponential functions and modified Bessel functions. Klassen employed a time marching procedure to evaluate the required convolution integrals. The FDTD technique was applied to this problem (Maloney et al., 1990), but computation costs are high even in combination with surface impedance boundary conditions (Maloney & Smith, 1992). The approximate form of a frequency-domain reflection coefficient permits one analytical expression for the impulse response of a lossy half space (Barnes & Tesche, 1991), but makes the solutions inaccurate or even invalid in some cases, e.g., for large incident angles relative to the normal to the interface and/or for relative dielectric constants below the order of 10. Pao et al (Pao et al, 1996, a) (Pao et al, 1996, b) developed a method for the analytical evaluation of the inverse Laplace transform representations for transient TE and TM plane waves, obliquely incident on a conductive half space. They assumed that the permittivity and conductivity of the dispersive half space are independent of frequency. The time-domain expressions for the reflected and transmitted waves are first represented as inverse Laplace transform. The transient fields are then shown to consist of two canonical integrals that in turn are solved analytically, thus leading to solutions involving incomplete Lipschitz-Hankel integrals (ILHI's). Rothwell and Suk introduced a rapidly converging series of the time-domain reflection coefficient into the analysis of transient reflection from a lossy half space, which is valid for all incident angles for the horizontal polarization (Rothwell & Suk, 2003), and for incident angles less than the Brewster angle for the vertical polarization (Rothwell, 2005). Few terms provide good accuracy for late time, while many more terms may be required to approach acceptable accuracy for early time. Pantoja et al (Pantoja et al., 2009) compared the method in (Rothwell & Suk, 2003) (Rothwell, 2005) with that in (Barnes & Tesche, 1991) by changing angles of incidence and constitutive parameters of half-spaces, and presented the accuracy and errors for the direct computation of the time-domain plane wave reflection coefficients for TE and TM plane waves incident on a lossy half-space.

3. Numerical Inversion of Laplace Transform and Prony's Method

3.1 Numerical Inversion of Laplace Transform

The Laplace transform (image function in the complex frequency domain) $F(s)$ and the inverse Laplace transform (original function in the time domain) $f(t)$ are related by the forward transformation

$$Lf(t) = F(s) = \int_0^\infty f(t) e^{-st} dt \tag{1}$$

and the inverse transformation

$$L^{-1}F(s)=f(t)=\frac{1}{2\pi j}\int_{\gamma-j\infty}^{\gamma+j\infty}F(s)e^{st}ds\,. \tag{2}$$

In general, it is straightforward to take the Laplace transform of a function. However, the inverse transformation is often difficult. In many cases, the method using simple rules and a table of transforms, and the method using the Bromwich integral and Cauchy integral theorem do not work well, and some numerical technique must be utilized. In this work, the method proposed by Hosono (Hosono, 1981) is applied. To implement the numerical inversion method, the following conditions should be satisfied: 1) $F(s)$ is defined for $\mathrm{Re}(s)>0$; 2) $F(s)$ is nonsingular; 3) $\lim_{s\to\infty}F(s)=0$ for $\mathrm{Re}(s)>0$; 4) $F^*(s)=F(s^*)$, where the asterisk denotes complex conjugate.

The most distinctive feature of this method lies in the approximation for e^{st}. Its main points are:

i)
$$e^{st}=\lim_{\rho\to\infty}\frac{e^{\rho}}{2\cosh(\rho-st)}=e^{st}-e^{-2\rho}e^{3st}+e^{-4\rho}e^{5st}-\cdots \tag{3}$$

ii)
$$e^{st}\approx E_{ec}(st,\rho)=\frac{e^{\rho}}{2\cosh(\rho-st)}=\frac{e^{\rho}}{2}\sum_{n=-\infty}^{\infty}\frac{(-1)^n j}{st-\left[\rho+j(n-0.5)\pi\right]} \tag{4}$$

iii) The Bromwich integral is transformed to the integral around the poles of $E_{ec}(st,\rho)$.

Then $f(t)$ is approximated by $f_{ec}(t,\rho)$, which is expressed by

$$f_{ec}(t,\rho)=\frac{1}{2\pi j}\int_{\gamma-j\infty}^{\gamma+j\infty}F(s)E_{ec}(st,\rho)\,ds=f(t)-e^{-2\rho}f(3t)+e^{-4\rho}f(5t)-\cdots=\left(e^{\rho}/t\right)\sum_{n=1}^{\infty}F_n \tag{5}$$

where $t>0$, and

$$F_n=(-1)^n\,\mathrm{Im}\,F\left\{\left[\rho+j(n-0.5)\pi\right]/t\right\} \tag{6}$$

Equation (5) shows that the function $f_{ec}(t,\rho)$ gives a good approximation to $f(t)$ when $\rho>>1$, and can be used for error estimation. Equations (5) and (6) are derived by substituting $E_{ec}(st,\rho)$ from (4), and can be applied to the numerical inversion of the Laplace transform. In practice, the infinite series in (5) has to be truncated after a proper number of terms. Since the infinite series is a slowly convergent alternating series, truncating to a small number of terms leads to a significant error. An effective approach using the Euler transformation has been developed, which works under the following conditions (Hosono, 1981): a) There exists an integer $k\geq 1$ such that the signs of F_n alternate for $n\geq k$; b) For $n\geq k$, $\frac{1}{2}<\left|F_{n+1}/F_n\right|\leq 1$. With conditions a) and b), (5) can be truncated with $f_{ec}^{lm}(t,a)$, which has $N=l+m$ terms and is given by

$$f_{ec}^{l\,m}(t,\rho)=\left(e^{\rho}/t\right)\left(\sum_{n=1}^{l-1}F_n+2^{-m-1}\sum_{n=0}^{m}A_{mn}F_{l+n}\right) \tag{7}$$

where A_{mn} are defined recursively by

$$A_{mm}=1\,, \qquad A_{mn-1}=A_{mn}+\binom{m+1}{n}. \tag{8}$$

In this method, the upper bound for the truncation errors is given by

$$R^{l\,m}=\left|f_{ec}^{l+1,m}(t,\rho)-f_{ec}^{l,m}(t,\rho)\right| \tag{9}$$

while the upper bound for the approximation errors is given by

$$\left|f_{ec}(t,\rho)-f(t)\right|\approx Me^{-2\rho}\,, \tag{10}$$

If

$$\left|f(t)\right|\le M \qquad \text{for all} \qquad t>0\,.$$

As indicated in (10), the relative approximation errors are less than $e^{-2\rho}$, while the truncation errors increase with t and decrease with N. For a typical value of t, the calculation is repeated by increasing N to determine a proper number of terms in (5), which makes the truncation errors small enough.

3.2 Prony's Method and Its Application to Decomposition of UWB Signals

An incident signal can be represented as a superposition of exponential functions, i.e.,

$$E(t)=\sum_{p=1}^{q}C_p e^{-\alpha_p t} \tag{11}$$

where q is the number of exponential functions, and can be infinite or a finite number. In this article, only the case where q is finite or can be truncated to a finite is considered. C_p and α_p can be determined directly from one set of sample values of $E(t)$. This technique is known as Prony's method. When α_p is nonnegative, C_p is a real; when α_p is a complex number with a nonnegative real part, C_p is a complex number, and the corresponding conjugate term, $C_p^* e^{-\alpha^* t}$, must be included in (11) in this case.

Following the discussion of Prony's method in (Zeng, 2010), q is selected through a series of numerical trials to meet some requirement of accuracy. In this work, a Gaussian doublet is used as the incident pulse. For approximating a Gaussian doublet by a series of exponentials within some time interval, the numerical trials in (Zeng, 2010) show that the accumulative error first decreases rapidly with the number of exponentials, and then does not significantly decrease if the number of exponentials is above 20. Hence, more than 20 exponential functions should be used for approximating a Gaussian doublet pulse with good accuracy.

4. Reflection of UWB Pulses from a Conducting Half Space

In this section, how to apply the above approach to modeling pulses reflected from a conductive interface is demonstrated, and the comparisons between our results and the published ones are made, showing a good agreement between them. A pulse which is a linear combination of a finite number of exponential functions is expressed by (11), and is incident from free space onto an interface between free space and a lossy material with conductivity σ and relative dielectric constant ε_r. The reflection coefficients in complex frequency domain for vertical and horizontal polarizations are

$$R_v(s)=\frac{\left(\varepsilon_r+\dfrac{\sigma}{s\varepsilon_0}\right)cos\,\theta-\sqrt{\varepsilon_r+\dfrac{\sigma}{s\varepsilon_0}-sin^2\theta}}{\left(\varepsilon_r+\dfrac{\sigma}{s\varepsilon_0}\right)cos\,\theta+\sqrt{\varepsilon_r+\dfrac{\sigma}{s\varepsilon_0}-sin^2\theta}} \tag{12}$$

and

$$R_h(s)=\frac{cos\,\theta-\sqrt{\varepsilon_r+\dfrac{\sigma}{s\varepsilon_0}-sin^2\theta}}{cos\,\theta+\sqrt{\varepsilon_r+\dfrac{\sigma}{s\varepsilon_0}-sin^2\theta}}, \tag{13}$$

respectively, where ε_0 is the permittivity of free space, θ is the incidence angle relative to the normal to the interface, and s is the complex frequency. The image function of $E(t)$ in (11) is

$$E(s)=\sum_{p=1}^{q}\frac{C_p}{s+\alpha_p} \tag{14}$$

The final image functions, $F_v(s)=R_v(s)E(s)$ and $F_h(s)=R_h(s)E(s)$, obviously satisfy conditions 1) - 4) listed in Section 3. A proof is given below that, for $s=\left[\rho+j(n-0.5)\pi\right]/t$, $F_v(s)$ and $F_h(s)$ also obey the above two conditions a) and b) described in Section 3, under which $f_{ec}^{lm}(t,\rho)$ can be used to approximate $f_{ec}(t,\rho)$.

Here only the proof for $F_v(s)$ with α_p and C_p being real numbers is given, since the proofs for $F_v(s)$ with α_p and C_p being complex numbers and for $F_h(s)$ are similar. If we let

$$\left(\varepsilon_r+\frac{\sigma}{s\varepsilon_0}\right)cos\,\theta=a+jb\,, \tag{15}$$

$$\varepsilon_r + \frac{\sigma}{s\varepsilon_0} - sin^2\theta = c_1 + jd_1 , \tag{16}$$

$$\sqrt{\varepsilon_r + \frac{\sigma}{s\varepsilon_0} - sin^2\theta} = c + jd , \tag{17}$$

$$a = \left(\varepsilon_r + \frac{\rho\sigma t}{B}\right)cos\theta , \quad b = -\frac{(n-0.5)\pi\sigma t}{B}cos\theta , \quad B = \left[\rho^2 + (n-0.5)^2\pi^2\right]\varepsilon_0 , \tag{18}$$

$$c_1 = \varepsilon_r - sin^2\theta + \frac{\rho\sigma t}{B} , \qquad d_1 = -\frac{(n-0.5)\pi\sigma t}{B} , \tag{19}$$

$$c = \pm\sqrt{\frac{c_1 + \sqrt{c_1^2 + d_1^2}}{2}} , \qquad d = \pm\frac{d_1}{|d_1|}\sqrt{\frac{\sqrt{c_1^2 + d_1^2} - c_1}{2}} . \tag{20}$$

If we denote

$$\sum_{p=1}^{q}\frac{C_p}{s+\alpha_p} = \sum_{p=1}^{q}\left(u_p + jv_p\right) , \tag{21}$$

then

$$u_p = \frac{(\rho + \alpha_p t)C_p t}{A} , \qquad v_p = -\frac{(n-0.5)\pi C_p t}{A} , \qquad A = (\rho + \alpha_p t)^2 + (n-0.5)^2\pi^2 . \tag{22}$$

From $F_v(s) = R_v(s)E(s)$,

$$F_v(s) = \sum_{p=1}^{q}\frac{(a+jb)-(c+jd)}{(a+jb)+(c+jd)}\left(u_p + jv_p\right) , \tag{23}$$

then

$$F_n = (-1)^n Im\left(F_v(s)\right) = (-1)^n\frac{F_v(s) - F_v^*(s)}{2j} = \sum_{p=1}^{q}\frac{(-1)^n\left(v_p g + u_p h\right)}{(a+c)^2 + (b+d)^2} , \tag{24}$$

where

$$g = \left(a^2 + b^2\right) - \left(c^2 + d^2\right) , \qquad h = 2\left(bc - ad\right) . \tag{25}$$

When n becomes large,

$$F_n \to \sum_{p=1}^{q}(-1)^n\left(-\frac{C_p t}{n\pi}\right)\frac{\varepsilon_r cos\theta - \sqrt{\varepsilon_r - sin^2\theta}}{\varepsilon_r cos\theta + \sqrt{\varepsilon_r - sin^2\theta}} .$$

Thus, the signs of F_n alternate, and furthermore, $|F_{n+1}| < |F_n|$ but $|F_{n+1}| \to |F_n|$, viz., $F_v(s)$ satisfies the two conditions a) and b) described in Section 3.

For comparing our result with that in (Qiu, 2004), the same Gaussian doublet pulse as that in (Qiu, 2004) is used as the incident pulse, which is the second derivative of a Gaussian pulse and is given by

$$E(t)=\left[1-4\pi\left(\frac{t-t_s}{\tau_p}\right)^2\right]\exp\left(-2\pi\left(\frac{t-t_s}{\tau_p}\right)^2\right) \tag{26}$$

where the amplitude has been normalized to unity, the waveform parameter τ_p = 1.7262 ns and the time shift t_s = 0.75 ns in the calculation. Fig. 1 plots the incident pulse and the approximating pulse with 40 exponential functions, showing a good approximation.

Equations (12) and (13) are used for the final image functions. The reflected field is calculated when $\theta = 45^0$, ε_r = 10, 25, 40 and $\sigma = 0.1$ mho/m, and is plotted in Fig. 2 and in Fig. 3 for the horizontal and vertical polarizations, respectively. These two figures illustrate that the reflected pulse has less distortion for both polarizations in this case, and the peak amplitude of the reflected pulse increases with the increase of ε_r. Comparison between the two figures indicates that the reflected pulse has smaller peak amplitudes for the vertical polarization than for the horizontal polarization. Fig. 3 compares our results with those in (Qiu, 2004) and shows a good agreement between them. It is worthwhile to point out that the result in (Qiu, 2004) is accurate in this case where the incident angle is not large and the relative electric constant is on the order of 10.

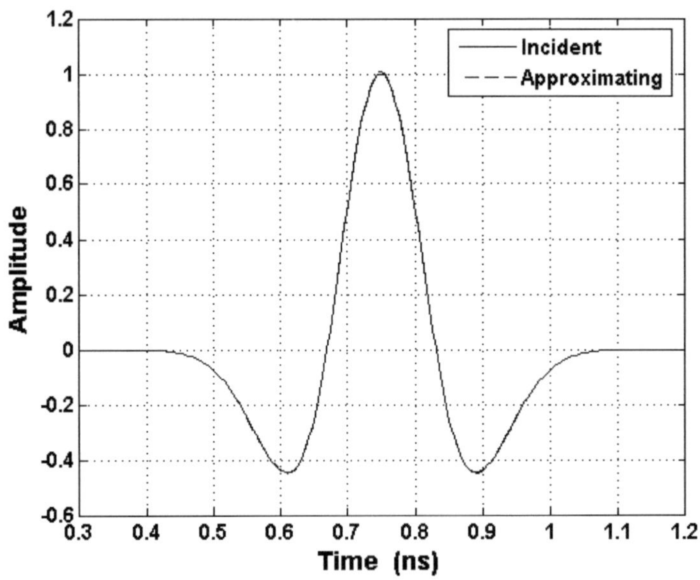

Fig. 1. Incident pulse and approximating pulse with 40 exponentials.

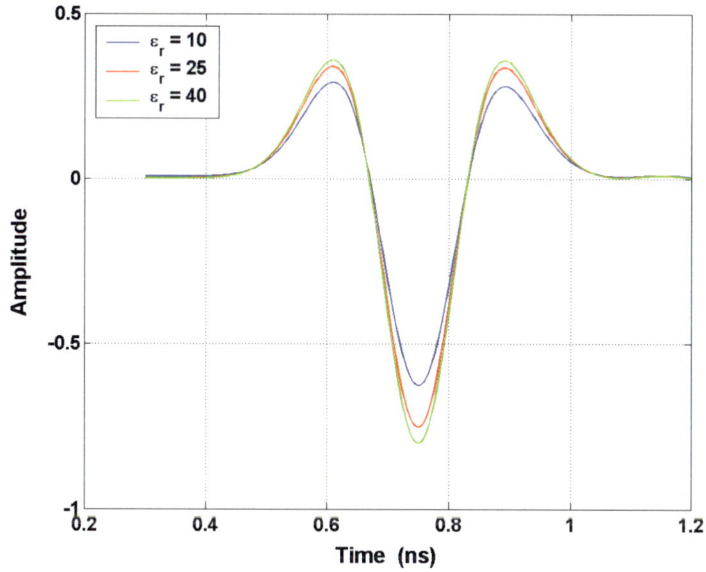

Fig. 2. Reflected field for the horizontal polarization ($\theta = 45^0$, $\varepsilon_r = 10, 25, 40$ and $\sigma = 0.1$ mho/m).

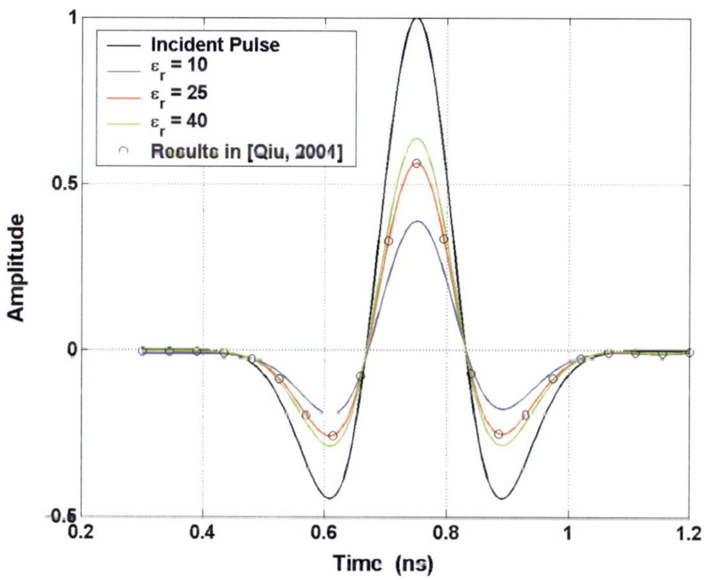

Fig. 3. Reflected field for the vertical polarization ($\theta = 45^0$, $\varepsilon_r = 10, 25, 40$ and $\sigma = 0.1$ mho/m).

5. Performance Analysis of UWB Communication in a Hallway Environment

Recently pulse distortion in time domain (or frequency dependence in frequency domain) has received considerable attention (Qiu, 2006). Studies on pulse distortion are important in various areas including channel modeling (Qiu, 2004) and UWB system analysis and design. So far, in the most investigations, the received UWB signal waveforms are assumed on the basis of measurement data for some kind of transmitted signals and specific scenarios (Ramírez-Mireles, 2002). This approach for determining received waveforms could not have generality. It would be difficult to use this approach to clarify the mechanisms causing pulse shape distortion and to connect system performance parameters such as bit error rate (BER) with propagation environment parameters such as transmitter and receiver heights, transmitter-receiver separations, wave polarizations, material parameters of reflecting surfaces, etc.

A new theoretical framework is being set up currently (Qiu, 2004) (Qiu, 2006), making it possible to predict UWB system performances directly from propagation environment parameters. In a multipath channel, normally reflected waves have most significant impacts on pulse distortion. In the new framework, the impulse response of a lossy interface developed in (Barnes & Tesche, 1991) is utilized, and then reflected waves are evaluated in time domain by convolving the incident field waveform with the impulse response. This impulse response contains an infinite sum of modified Bessel functions that evaluates the response term persisting in time. In order to apply this expression to practical problems, truncation of the infinite sum of modified Bessel functions is needed. Few terms permits a simple evaluation but makes the accuracy degrade, while many more terms are required to approach an acceptable accuracy but makes calculation complicated and time-consuming. Furthermore, this impulse response was derived from the approximate Fresnel reflection coefficient, which holds under the conditions that the relative dielectric constant ε_r is on the order of 10 or more and that the incident angle θ with the interface is small. Hence, the accuracy of the evaluation of reflected waves is questionable for incident angles larger than 80^0 and/or ε_r less than 10, particularly for vertical polarization.

In this section, a time domain multipath model is utilized to characterize UWB signal propagation in a hallway. Transient waves reflected from conducting interfaces for both vertical and horizontal incidence are calculated through numerical inversion of Laplace transform, which is simple and accurate. With the evaluation of direct and reflected waves in time domain, the performance analysis is conducted for binary UWB communications, and the impacts of multipath signals on pulse distortion and UWB system performance are discussed. This approach does not need the conditions on the relative dielectric constant ε_r and the incident angle θ, and can achieve satisfactory accuracy in both late and early time.

This work is classified as "deterministic channel modeling", and has a conceptual foundation based on per-path pulse shapes. The signal model is such that the received deterministic signals governed by electromagnetic wave equations are distorted by the background noise. The system model is such that the receiver is optimal in some sense, which is determined by the statistical communication theory. The wave-based solutions provide the response of the channel where each wave arrives separately. The availability of the channel response allows the receiver to match with the entire received signal composed of a linear superposition of many mutipath pulses. Hence, the system performance is jointly determined by electromagnetic and statistical communication theories.

Hallway is a special indoor environment in the sense of its long and narrow geometrical configuration, where the light of sight (LOS) ray together with multiple reflection rays dominate the received signal. In a hallway whose size is quite large relative to wavelength of UWB signal, ray tracing should be applicable. Furthermore, because of the transient characteristics of UWB pulses, it should be more convenient to analyze the performance of UWB communication in time domain. Specular reflection is assumed for all the reflections undergoing in a hallway environment, which is resonable considering the roughness of the walls is far less than the wavelength of the propagation signal. It is also assumed that all the reflection interfaces are made of the same material (Zhou & Qiu, 2006).

Fig. 4 illustrates the direct (light of sight) path AB, single reflection paths AC_1B and AC_2B, double reflection paths AD_1E_2B and AD_2E_1B, triple reflection paths $AF_1G_2H_1B$ and $AF_2G_1H_2B$, fourfold reflection paths $AI_1J_2K_1L_2B$ and $AI_2J_1K_2L_1B$. In the following analysis, it is assumed that the multipath signals through the fivefold and multifold reflection paths have smaller magnitudes than the signals via the less than fivefold reflection paths. Then the signals through the direct, single, double, triple and fourfold reflection paths are only taken into account in the performance analysis of a binary UWB communication system. Furthermore, the reflected rays are divided into two groups: one is for those with the first reflection occuring on the floor (AC_1B, AD_1E_2B, $AF_1G_2H_1B$ and $AI_1J_2K_1L_2B$); another one is for those with the first reflection happening on the ceiling (AC_2B, AD_2E_1B, $AF_2G_1H_2B$ and $AI_2J_1K_2L_1B$).

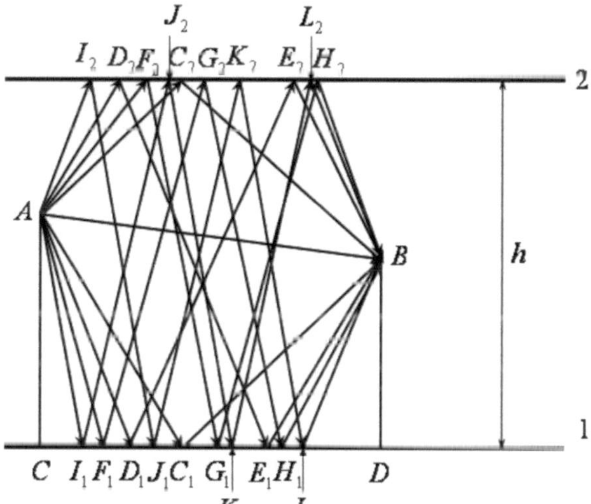

Fig. 4. UWB signal propagation in a hallway environment. AC=1.8 m, BD=1.5 m, $h = 3$ m, CD=2.0 m, $\varepsilon_r = 25$, $\sigma = 0.1$ S/m.

The electric field of a ray from the transmitter to the receiver can be calculated by the following equations.

For the direct ray,

$$E_{LOS}(s) = E(s)\frac{exp(-jkr_0)}{r_0} \tag{27}$$

where $E(s)$ is the electric field emitted by the transmitter in complex frequency (s) domain and can be accurately and approximately given by (14) for any exponential and non exponential signals, respectively, k is the wave number, r_0 is the distance that the ray travels from the transmitter to the receiver and is given by

$$r_0 = \sqrt{(h_t - h_r)^2 + d^2} \tag{28}$$

with d representing the distance of the transmitter-receiver separation (CD) and h_t and h_r representing the heights of transmitting and receiving antennas (AC and BD), respectively.

For reflected rays,

$$E_{reflected}(s) = [R(s)]^i E(s)\frac{exp(-jkr_i)}{r_i} \tag{29}$$

where $R(s)$ is reflection coefficient in s domain and is given by (12) and (13) for vertical and horizontal polarizations, respectively, and r_i is the length of the reflection path, along which the ith ray travels and undergoes i-fold reflections, and is given by

$$r_i = \sqrt{l_i^2 + d^2} \tag{30}$$

with

$$l_i = \begin{cases} (h_t + h_r) + (i-1)h & i\ is\ odd \\ (h_t - h_r) + i\,h & i\ is\ even \end{cases}, \tag{31}$$

where h is the height of the hallway. For different rays, reflection angles in $R(s)$ are different. The reflection angle for the ith ray, θ_i, can be determined by

$$\theta_i = arctan\left(\frac{d}{r_i}\right). \tag{32}$$

The contribution from the first group of reflected rays can be expressed as

$$E_{group1}(s) = \sum_{i=1}^{I}[R(s)]^i E(s)\frac{exp(-jkr_i)}{r_i} \tag{33}$$

with $I = 4$ corresponding to the case in Fig. 4 where the rays with a maximum of 4 reflections have been traced.

Since the second group of reflected rays follow the same laws as the first group of reflected rays, we can still use (33) and simply replace h_t and h_r with $h - h_t$ and $h - h_r$, respectively, to obtain the contribution from the second group of reflected rays, $E_{group2}(s)$.

The total received electric field at the receiver is given by

$$E_{total}(s) = E_{LOS}(s) + E_{group1}(s) + E_{group2}(s)\,. \tag{34}$$

The corresponding waveform $E_{total}(t)$ can be achieved using numerical inversion of Laplace transform based on the discussion in Section 4. With a signal waveform $f(t)$, one of the most important system performance parameters, bit error rate (BER), can be determined by the equations below (Ramírez-Mireles, 2002).

The normalized signal correlation function of $f(t)$ is defined as the inner product of $f(t)$ with a shifted version $f(t-\tau)$

$$\gamma(\tau) = \frac{1}{E_f}\int_{-\infty}^{\infty} f(t) f(t-\tau)\,dt \tag{35}$$

where

$$E_f = \int_{-\infty}^{\infty} \left|f(t)\right|^2 dt \tag{36}$$

is the energy of the signal. Hence, if the received signal is $f(t)$, the squared distance between received signals is

$$d^2(\tau) = \frac{1}{2E_f}\int_{-\infty}^{\infty} \left|f(t) - f(t-\tau)\right|^2 dt = \left(1-\gamma(\tau)\right). \tag{37}$$

The binary bit error rate (BER) is

$$P_e(\tau) = Q\left(\sqrt{\frac{\Lambda \cdot d^2(\tau)}{2}}\right) \tag{38}$$

where Λ is the signal-to-noise (SNR) value and $Q(\bullet)$ denotes the Gaussian tail integral.

We still use the normalized Gaussian doublet pulse, given by equation (26) but with the waveform parameter τ_p = 6 ns and the time shift t_s = 15 ns. Fig. 5 plots the direct field, reflected fields and total received field at the receiver for vertical and horizontal polarizations. Fig. 6 shows the bit error rates (BERs) of non-multipath (Gaussian) and multipath channels for vertical and horizontal polarizations, which are calculated on the basis of the waveforms in Fig. 5.

Fig. 5 and Fig. 6 demonstrate that the multipath components with one, two and three reflections have significant impacts on the waveforms of received signals and on the system performance. Fig. 6 shows no significant difference between the impacts of the components through triple and fourfold reflection paths, indicating that multipath components with five and more reflections can be ignored. Moreover, it can be seen from Fig. 6 that multipath signals have a larger influence on the bit error rate for vertical polarization than for horizontal polarization.

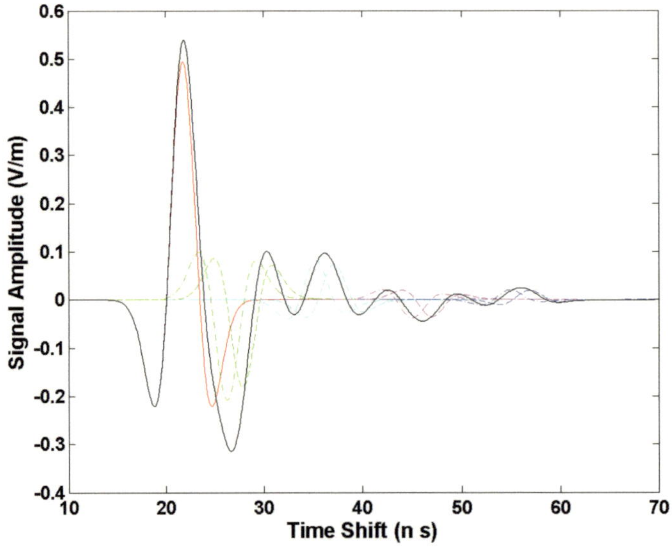

(a)

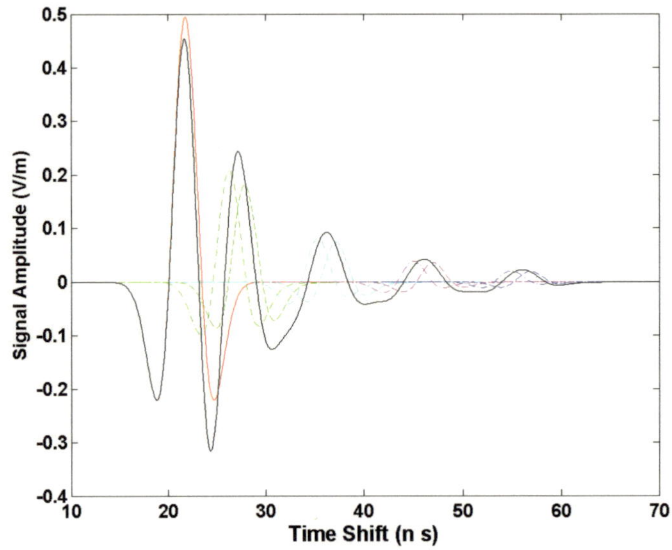

(b)

Fig. 5. Waveforms of direct field, reflected fields and their summations at receiver.
(a) horizontal polarization; (b) vertical polarization.
Red solid line: direct (LOS) path AB;
Green dashed and dash-dot lines: single reflection path AC_1B and AC_2B;
Cyan dashed and dash-dot lines: double reflection paths AD_1E_2B and AD_2E_1B;
Magenta dashed and dash-dot lines: triple reflection paths $AF_1G_2H_1B$ and $AF_2G_1H_2B$;
Blue dashed and dash-dot lines: fourfold reflection paths $AI_1J_2K_1L_2B$ and $AI_2J_1K_2L_1B$;
Black solid line: total received field.

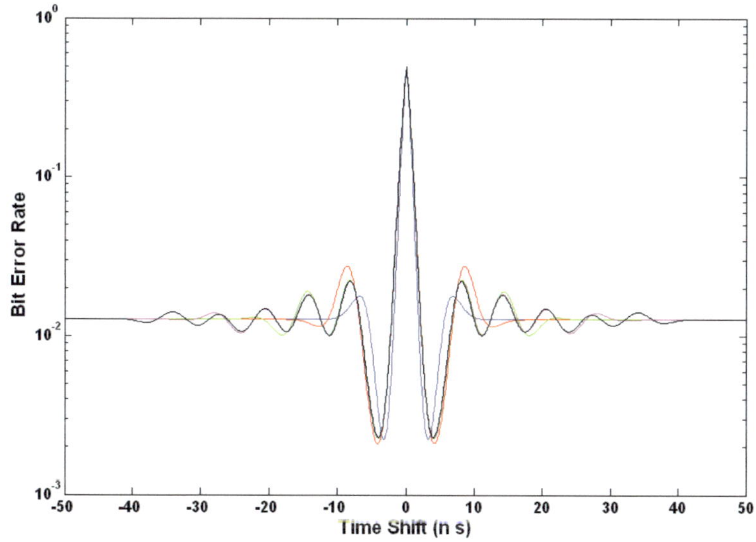

(a)

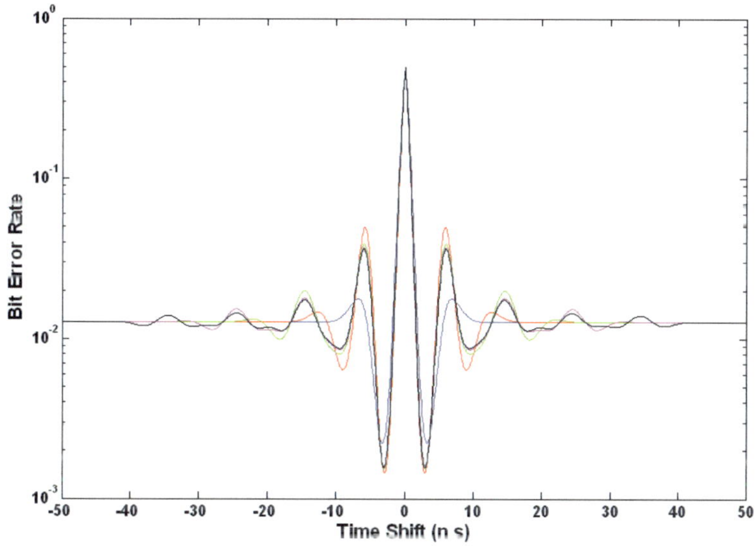

(b)

Fig. 6. Time-domain bit error rates of non-multipath channel AB (blue line), multipath channels $AB + AC_1B + AC_2B$ (red line), $AB + AC_1B + AC_2B + AD_1E_2B + AD_1E_2B$ (green line), $AB + AC_1B + AC_2B + AD_1E_2B + AD_1E_2B + AF_1G_2H_1B + AF_2G_1H_2B$ (magenta line), and $AB + AC_1B + AC_2B + AD_1E_2B + AD_1E_2B + AF_1G_2H_1B + AF_2G_1H_2B + AI_1J_2K_1L_2B + AI_2J_1K_2L_1B$ (black line) for (a) horizontal polarization and (b) vertical polarization.

6. Propagation of UWB Pulses through a Lossy Dielectric Slab

The transient analysis of pulses propagating through a lossy dielectric slab is of great significance in a number of engineering fields, such as material characterization and diagnosis, wall penetration radar, and pulse radio. In fact, this kind of analysis can provide valuable insights into the appreciation of the capabilities and limitations of UWB communication for indoor and indoor-outdoor scenarios. As discussed in Section 2, the approximation to a frequency-domain reflection coefficient permits one analytical expression of the impulse response of a lossy half space (Barnes & Tesche, 1991), but makes the solutions inaccurate or even invalid in some cases, e.g., for large incident angles. Based on the approximate form in (Barnes & Tesche, 1991), the time domain solutions for pulse transmission through a lossy dielectric slab were achieved and some related UWB issues were addressed (Qiu, 2004) (Chen et al., 2004). These solutions contain infinite sums of modified Bessel functions and time domain convolutions, and are implemented in three directions, parallel polarization, normal and tangential perpendicular polarizations (Chen et al., 2004), leading to considerable calculations.

In this section, based on the discussion in Section 3 and Section 4, the technique combining numerical inversion of Laplace transform with Prony's method is extended to the transient analysis of pulses propagating through a lossy dielectric slab. Comparison between our results obtained and those obtained using the FDTD technique indicates a good agreement. The waveforms and strengths of the transmitted signals are governed by four main parameters, thickness, relative permittivity and conductivity of the slab and incident angles. The analysis of transmitted signal waveforms is conducted for four different parameters and the results are shown to be comparable to those given by (Chen et al., 2004). Based on this waveform analysis, the transmission loss is discussed for different parameters and the results are shown to be consistent with the previously published results (Chen et al., 2004). Our approach also yields the results for a large incident angle, these being unavailable using alternative approaches (Chen et al., 2004).

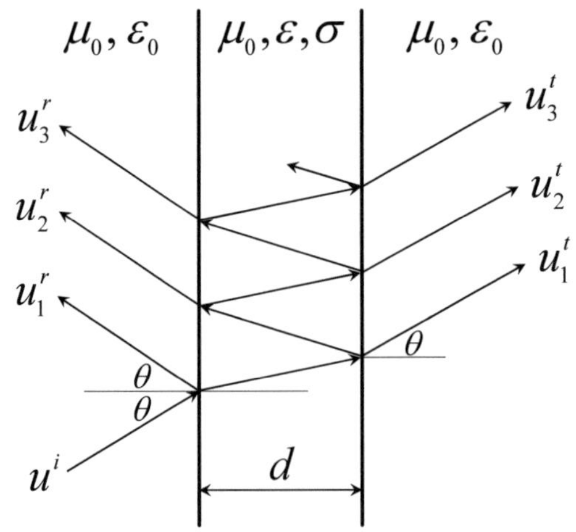

Fig. 7. Pulse is impinging on lossy dielectric slab.

In this investigation, the Gaussian doublet pulse with the same waveform parameter and time shift as in Section 4 is used as the incident pulse. Fig. 7 shows that the pulse is impinging on a homogeneous lossy slab at an incident angle of θ. The slab has an thickness of d, permeability of μ_0, conductivity σ and permittivity of $\varepsilon = \varepsilon_0 \varepsilon_r$ where ε_0 is the permittivity of vacuum and ε_r is the relative permittivity of the slab. The transmission through a dielectric layer is governed by the equation (Yeh, 1988)

$$T = \frac{t_{0n}\, t_{n0}\, e^{-j\varphi}}{1 - r_{0n}\, r_{n0}\, e^{-j2\varphi}} \tag{39}$$

where r and t denote the reflection and transmission coefficients of the interface, respectively. The subscripts $0n$ and $n0$ mean that the pulse is incident from air onto the layer and from the layer onto air. The quantity φ is the complex frequency dependent electrical length of the layer as seen by the wave and is given by

$$\varphi(s) = \frac{s\, d}{j\, c}\sqrt{\varepsilon_r - \sin^2\theta + \frac{\sigma}{s\,\varepsilon_0}} \tag{40}$$

s is the complex frequency and c is the phase velocity of the wave in vacuum. With $t_{0n}t_{n0} - r_{0n}r_{n0} = 1$ and $r_{0n} = -r_{n0}$ (Yeh, 1988), (39) is written as

$$T(s) = \frac{\left(1 - r_{0n}^{\;2}(s)\right)e^{-j\varphi(s)}}{1 - r_{0n}^{\;2}(s)\, e^{-j2\varphi(s)}} \tag{41}$$

where $r_{0n}(s)$ is the reflection coefficient in complex frequency domain and is given by (12) for vertical polarization, or by (13) for horizontal polarization.

The image function of the approximating pulse is

$$E^{inc}(s) = \sum_{p=1}^{q} \frac{C_p}{s + \alpha_p}. \tag{42}$$

The final image functions is

$$F(s) = T(s)\, E^{inc}(s). \tag{43}$$

It satisfies the four conditions specified in Section 3 under which $f(t)$ can be approximated by $f_{ec}(t,\rho)$. For $s = [\rho + j(n-0.5)\pi]/t$, $F(s)$ does not obey the two additional conditions in Section 3 under which $f_{ec}^{lm}(t,\rho)$ can be used to approximate $f_{ec}(t,\rho)$.

The total transmitted field can be decomposed into a series of successive transmitted components,

$$T = u_1^t + u_2^t + u_3^t + \cdots = t_{0n}\, t_{n0}\, e^{-j\varphi}\left[1 + r_{n0}^{\ 2}\, e^{-j2\varphi} + \left(r_{n0}^{\ 2}\, e^{-j2\varphi}\right)^2 + \cdots\right]. \tag{44}$$

Consider the first term modeling two transmissions through two surfaces of the layer,

$$u_1^t = t_{0n}\, t_{n0}\, e^{-j\varphi} = \left(1 - r_{0n}^{\ 2}\right) e^{-j\varphi}. \tag{45}$$

$F_1(s) = u_1^t(s)\, E^{inc}(s)$ still does not satisfy the two additional conditions for Euler summation due to the phase factor $e^{-j\varphi}$ when $s = [\rho + j(n - 0.5)\pi]/t$.

From (40), it is observed that, when $s \to \infty$,

$$\varphi(s) \to \varphi_m(s) = \frac{s}{j}\frac{d}{c}\sqrt{\varepsilon_r - \sin^2\theta}. \tag{46}$$

The replacement image function for $F_1(s)$ is defined as

$$F_{r1}(s) = u_1^t(s)\, E^{inc}(s)\, e^{j\phi_m(s)} = F_1(s)\, e^{s\tau} \tag{47}$$

and satisfies the four conditions and the two additional conditions listed in Section 3, where $e^{j\varphi_m(s)}$ is the modifying phase factor and the time shift is

$$\tau = \frac{d}{c}\sqrt{\varepsilon_r - \sin^2\theta}. \tag{48}$$

Hence, (7) is applicable to calculate $f_{r1,ec}^{lm}(t,\rho)$ which approximates $f_{r1,ec}(t,\rho)$, the original function of $F_{r1}(s)$. From (47), the relationship between $f_{r1,ec}^{lm}(t,\rho)$ and $f_{1,ec}^{lm}(t,\rho)$ which approximates $f_{1,ec}(t,\rho)$, the original function of $F_1(s)$, is given by

$$f_{1,ec}^{lm}(t,\rho) = f_{r1,ec}^{lm}(t - \tau, \rho). \tag{49}$$

Similarly, consider the second term in (44), which characterizes two transmissions through two surfaces and two reflections between two surfaces,

$$u_2^t = t_{0n}\, t_{n0}\, r_{n0}^2\, e^{-j3\varphi} = \left(1 - r_{0n}^{\ 2}\right) r_{n0}^2\, e^{-j3\varphi}. \tag{50}$$

$F_2(s) = u_2^t(s)\, E^{inc}(s)$ does not satisfy the two additional conditions specified in Section 3 due to the phase factor $e^{-j3\varphi}$ when $s = [\rho + j(n - 0.5)\pi]/t$. The replacement image function for $F_2(s)$ is

$$F_{r2}(s) = u_2^t(s)\, E^{inc}(s)\, e^{j3\phi_m(s)} = F_2(s)\, e^{3s\tau} \tag{51}$$

and meets the four conditions in Section 3 and the two additional conditions for Euler summation. $f_{r2,ec}^{lm}(t,\rho)$ can be calculated by using (7), and is a good approximation to $f_{r2,ec}(t,\rho)$, the original function of $F_{r2}(s)$. From (51), the relationship between $f_{r2,ec}^{lm}(t,\rho)$ and $f_{2,ec}^{lm}(t,\rho)$ which approximates $f_{2,ec}(t,\rho)$, the original function of $F_2(s)$, is given by

$$f_{2,ec}^{lm}(t,\rho) = f_{r2,ec}^{lm}(t - 3\tau, \rho). \tag{52}$$

Following the above procedure, $f_{i,ec}^{lm}(t,\rho)$ can be achieved and is a good approximation to $f_{i,ec}(t,\rho)$, the original functions of $F_i(s) = u_i^t(s) E^{inc}(s)$, $i = 1, 2, 3, \cdots$. From

$$F = F_1 + F_2 + F_3 + \cdots, \tag{53}$$

the final original function can be given approximately by

$$\begin{aligned} f(t) &\approx f_{ec}(t,\rho) = f_{1,ec}(t,\rho) + f_{2,ec}(t,\rho) + f_{3,ec}(t,\rho) + \cdots \\ &\approx f_{1,ec}^{lm}(t,\rho) + f_{2,ec}^{lm}(t,\rho) + f_{3,ec}^{lm}(t,\rho) + \cdots \end{aligned} \tag{54}$$

In general, the terms beyond the first term have much weaker impacts than the first one in (54), and then only taking the first term $f_{r1,ec}^{lm}(t,\rho)$ leads to a high accuracy. If a very high accuracy is required for some specific purposes, the first several terms in (54) will be added together. In the following discussion, only the first term in (54) is taken into account. Fig. 8 plots the waveform of the transmitted pulse at the layer's back surface, and shows that our results agree quite well with FDTD results. The comparison between our results and FDTD results for vertical polarization also leads to a quite good agreement but is omitted here to save the space.

Figures 9-12 illustrate the waveforms of the transmitted signal through a slab with different thickness, relative permittivity, conductivity and incident angles. With reference to the incident pulse shown in Fig. 1, the attenuation, delay and distortion of the transmitted pulse can be seen and compared with each other in the different cases. Fig. 9 shows that the amplitude of the transmitted signal decreases, the delay increases and the distortion becomes larger with the increase of the thickness. In Fig. 10, the amplitude becomes a little smaller, the distortion becomes a little larger and it takes longer for the pulse to go through the layer as the relative permittivity increases. Fig. 11 illustrates that the amplitude decreases, the distortion increases but the delay almost remain the same when the conductivity increases.

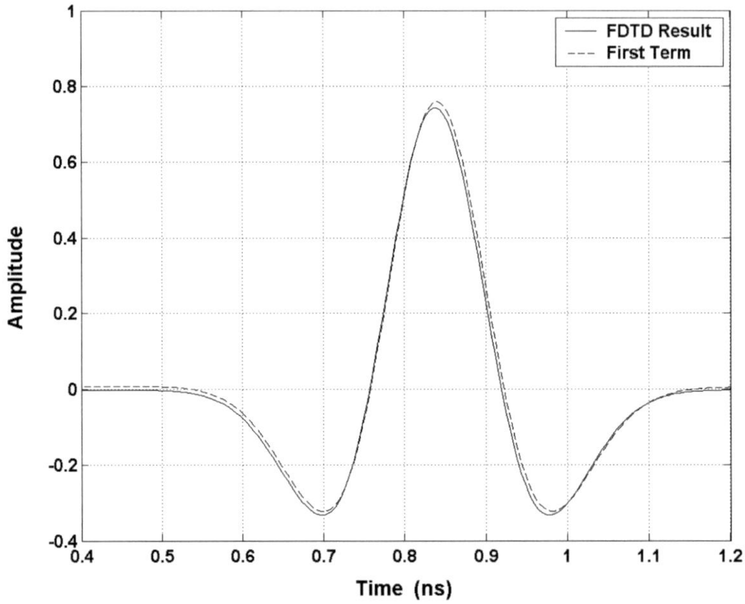

Fig. 8. Waveforms of transmitted signal obtained using this method and using FDTD for horizontal polarization. $d = 0.02$ m, $\varepsilon_r = 2$, $\sigma = 0.1\ \mathrm{S/m}$ and $\theta = 30^0$.

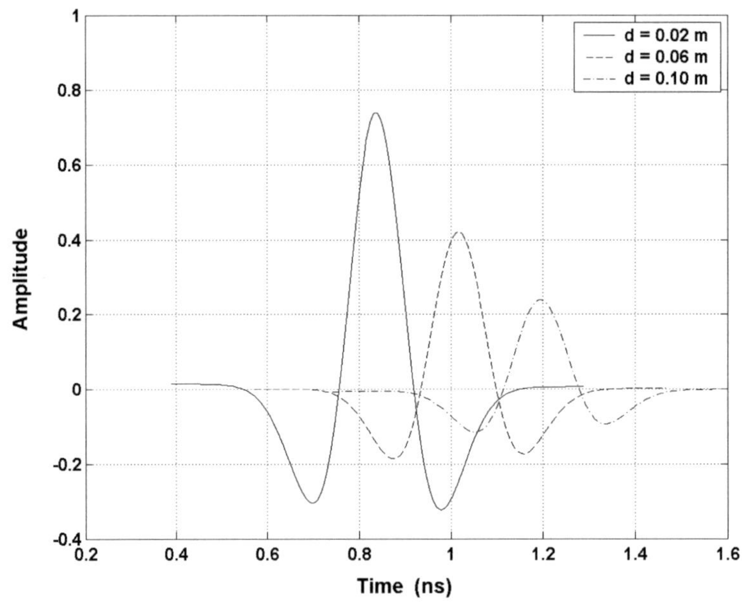

Fig. 9. Waveforms of transmitted signal for horizontal polarization. Varying d, $\varepsilon_r = 2$, $\sigma = 0.1\ \mathrm{S/m}$ and $\theta = 30^0$.

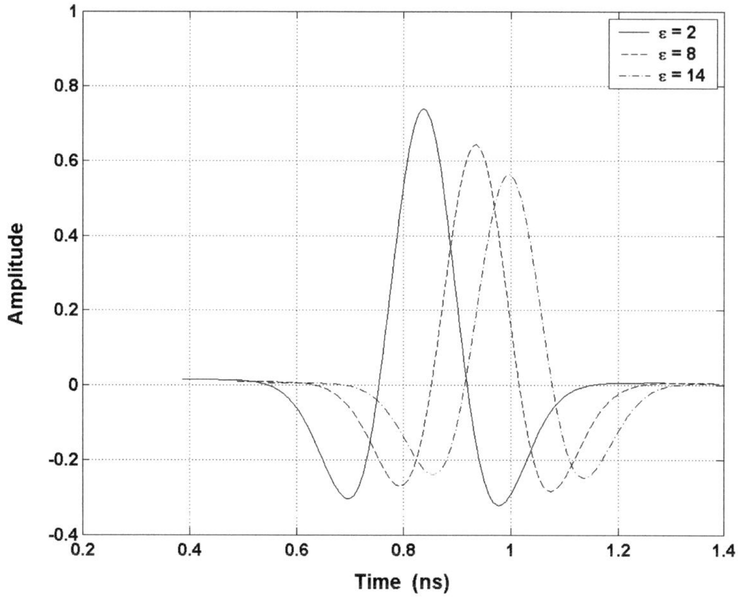

Fig. 10. Waveforms of transmitted signal for horizontal polarization. Varying ε_r, $d = 0.02$ m, $\sigma = 0.1$ S/m and $\theta = 30^0$.

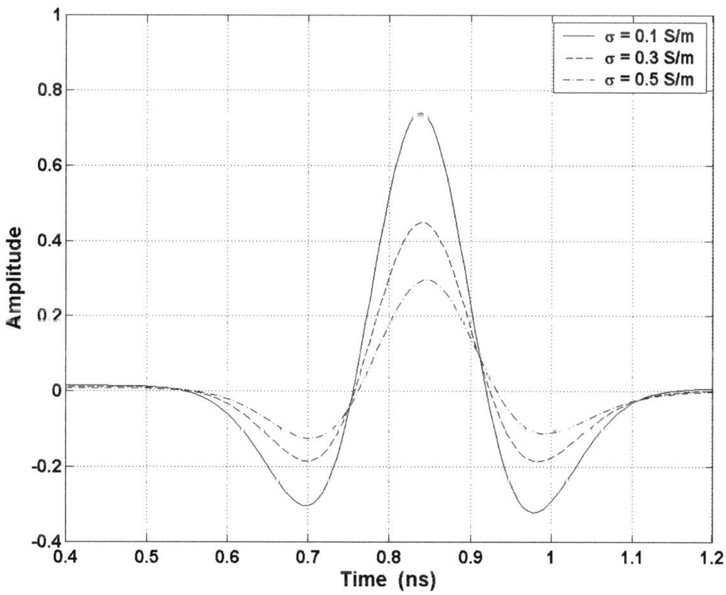

Fig. 11. Waveforms of transmitted signal for horizontal polarization. Varying σ, $d = 0.02$ m, $\varepsilon_r = 2$ and $\theta = 30^0$.

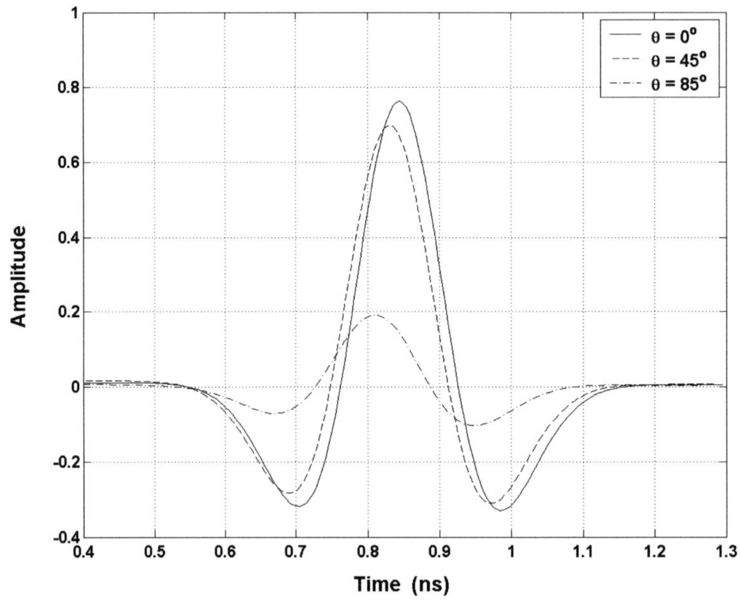

(a)

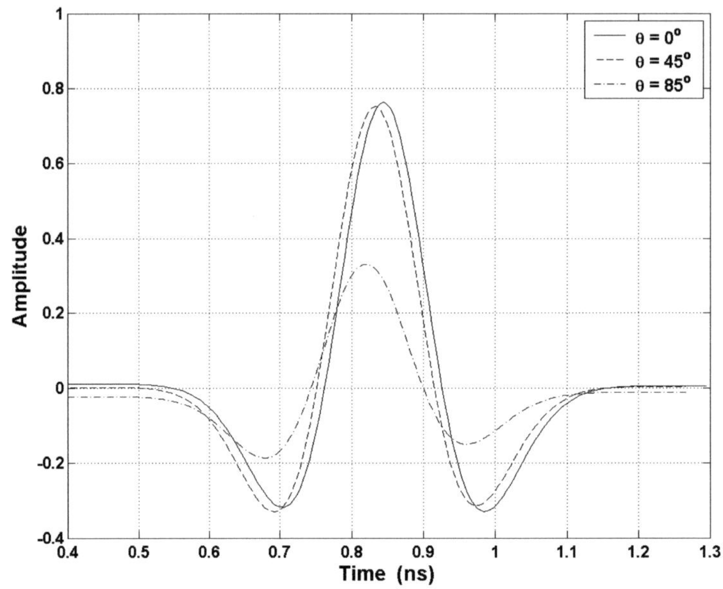

(b)

Fig. 12. Waveforms of transmitted signal. (a) horizontal polarization; (b) vertical polarization. Varying θ, $d = 0.02$ m, $\varepsilon_r = 2$ and $\sigma = 0.1$ S/m.

Although Figures 9-11 plot the results only for horizontal polarization due to a limited space, it is worthwhile to indicate that, when the incident angle is fixed and the other three parameters are varying, the transmitted pulse experiences roughly the same variation for both polarizations in the above three cases. On the other hand, when the incident angle is varying, the transmitted pulse undergoes different variations for two different polarizations. As shown in Fig. 12, when the incident angle increases, the amplitude decreases, the delay decreases slightly and the distortion becomes larger. Meanwhile, the transmitted pulse undergoes larger variation for horizontal polarization than for vertical polarization. The above results accord with those in (Chen et al., 2004). Nevertheless, Fig. 12 demonstrates that the amplitude and distortion largely change when the incident angle is close to 90^0. This case was not discussed in (Chen et al., 2004).

On the basis of the above results, the transmission loss through a layer is discussed for different parameters. Fig. 13 (a) illustrates that the transmission loss is basically proportional to the thickness and increases with the increase of the conductivity. As the conductivity becomes larger, the change rate of the transmission loss with the thickness becomes larger. Fig. 13 (b) shows that the transmission loss has the minimal value for a normal incidence, and slightly increases as the relative permittivity increases. The comparison between Fig. 13 (a) and Fig. 13 (b) indicates that the thickness and conductivity have much larger impacts on the transmission loss than the other two parameters, the relative permittivity and incident angle. These conclusions are consistent with those drawn in (Chen et al., 2004). In Fig. 13 (b), it is seen that the transmission loss for the incident angle close to 90^0 is much larger, and increases much faster with the increase of the relative permittivity than that for a small incident angle, which is not addressed in (Chen et al., 2004) and then is added here.

7. Additional Comments

As is well known, the principle of causality stating that the response cannot come before the stimulus leads to the Kramers-Kronig relations describing the interdependence of the real and imaginary parts of the susceptibility $\chi(\omega)$ (Rothwell & Cloud, 2001). The Kramers-Kronig relations compose one of the most elegant and general theorems in physics, since they depend for their validity only on the principle of causality. As applied to wave propagation, the real part of susceptibility describes essentially the index of refraction and imaginary part the absorbstion coefficient of a medium. Thus, the Kramers-Kronig relations explain in the most fundamental and general terms, completely independent of the underlying physical mechanisms, the intimate connection between refraction and absorption. Actually, given one, the other follows immediately. The Kramers-Kronig relations are given by

$$\mathrm{Re}\left[\chi(\omega)\right]=\frac{1}{\pi}P\int_{-\infty}^{\infty}\frac{\mathrm{Im}\left[\chi(\Omega)\right]}{\omega-\Omega}d\Omega \tag{55}$$

$$\mathrm{Im}\left[\chi(\omega)\right]=-\frac{1}{\pi}P\int_{-\infty}^{\infty}\frac{\mathrm{Re}\left[\chi(\Omega)\right]}{\omega-\Omega}d\Omega \tag{56}$$

where P stands for principal part. The expressions show that causality requires the real and imaginary parts of the dielectric susceptibility (permittivity) or magnetic susceptibility (permeability) to depend on each other through the Hilbert transform pair.

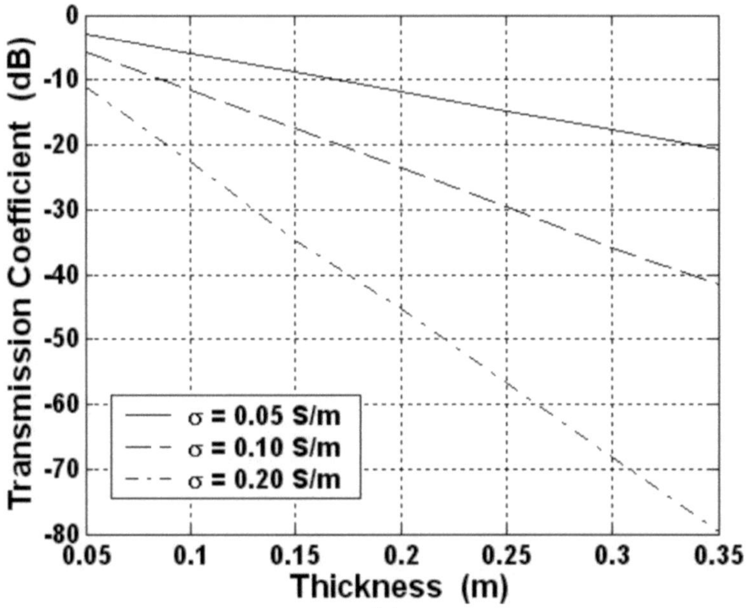

(a)

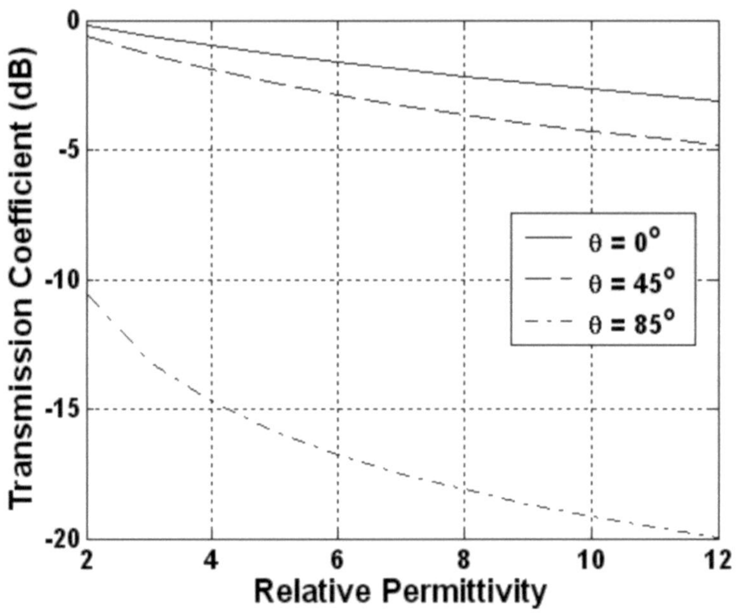

(b)

Fig. 13. Transmission coefficient of slabs with different parameters. (a) thickness and conductivity; (b) relative permittivity and incident angle.

In Section 4 and Section 6, $\varepsilon(\omega)$ varies when $\sigma(\omega)$ is fixed, and $\sigma(\omega)$ varies when $\varepsilon(\omega)$ is fixed. This seems not to obey the Kramers-Kronig relations but can be considered as the approximations of permittivity and conductivity of a conductive dielectric at low frequencies. The complex permittivity of a dielectric is best described by the resonance model (Rothwell & Cloud, 2001)

$$\varepsilon_c(\omega) = \varepsilon(\omega) + j\,\varepsilon''(\omega) = \varepsilon(\omega) - j\,\frac{\sigma(\omega)}{\omega} = \varepsilon_0 + \sum_i \frac{\varepsilon_0\,\omega_{pi}^2}{\omega_i^2 - \omega^2 + j\,\omega\,2\,\Gamma_i^2}, \tag{57}$$

where $\omega_{pi}^2 = N_i e^2 / m_i \varepsilon_0$ is the plasma frequency of the ith resonance component, and ω_i and Γ_i are the oscillation frequency and damping coefficient, respectively, of this component. Splitting the permittvity into real and imaginary parts we have

$$\varepsilon(\omega) = \varepsilon_0\left(1 + \sum_i \frac{\omega_{pi}^2\left(\omega_i^2 - \omega^2\right)}{\left(\omega_i^2 - \omega^2\right)^2 + 4\,\omega^2\,\Gamma_i^2}\right), \tag{58}$$

$$\varepsilon''(\omega) = -\varepsilon_0 \sum_i \frac{2\,\omega\,\Gamma_i\,\omega_{pi}^2}{\left(\omega_i^2 - \omega^2\right)^2 + 4\,\omega^2\,\Gamma_i^2}, \tag{59}$$

and then

$$\sigma(\omega) = -\omega\,\varepsilon''(\omega) = \varepsilon_0 \sum_i \frac{2\,\omega^2\,\Gamma_i\,\omega_{pi}^2}{\left(\omega_i^2 - \omega^2\right)^2 + 4\,\omega^2\,\Gamma_i^2}. \tag{60}$$

For low frequencies,

$$\varepsilon(\omega) \approx \varepsilon_0\left(1 + \sum_i \frac{\omega_{pi}^2}{\omega_i^2}\right), \tag{61}$$

which is the static permittivity of material. A conductive dielectric has such small values of ω_i that the electrons become unbound. At low frequencies,

$$\sigma(\omega) \approx \varepsilon_0 \sum_i \frac{\omega_{pi}^2}{2\,\Gamma_i}, \tag{62}$$

which is the dc conductivity. Hence, it is not unreasonable for a conductive dielectric at low frequencies that $\varepsilon(\omega)$ and $\sigma(\omega)$ are approximately frequency independent and one of them varies when another is fixed. Even for modeling propagation of UWB signals in a typical band from 3 GHz to 10 GHz, the permittivity and conductivity of a construction material are still considered as constants independent in (Ghavami et al, 2004). In (Ho & Lai, 2007), the permittivity (or conductivity) of a lossy dielectric varies when the conductivity (or permittivity) is fixed. In (Suk, 2000), one of the permittivity, permeability and conductivity of a conductive medium varies when fixing the rest.

8. Conclusion

Numerical inversion of Laplace transform and Prony's method are discussed. The conditions under which numerical inversion of Laplace transform can be applied in practice are clarified. The approach combining numerical inversion of Laplace transform with Prony's method is applied to the analysis of transient reflection of UWB pulses from a conductive interface. Numerical results are illustrated and compared with those published in the literature. A good agreement between them validates the correctness and effectiveness of this approach.

With the evaluation of transient direct and reflected waves, the impacts of multipath components on pulse distortion and UWB system performance in a hallway environment are discussed. The significance of this work is twofold: First, the methodology combines the time domain electromagnetics and the UWB system theory, and lends us the powerful methods and rich solutions already available to gain insight into UWB problems. Second, the efficiency of the methodology is improved, leading to simple implementation, low computation cost, easy estimation and control of errors.

Based on the studies of pulses reflected from a conducting interface, characterization of pulses propagating through a lossy dielectric slab is pursued. Our results are shown to be comparable to the previously published results and agree well with those obtained using the FDTD technique. Furthermore, the corresponding results for an incident angle close to 90^0 can be provided with this technique, which can not be generated with the previous approaches. This efficient time domain technique can be extended in a straightforward manner to the transient analysis of multiple reflections and transmissions in lossy media, and thus provide a powerful tool for electromagnetic analysis and design.

9. References

Balanis, C. (1989). *Advanced Engineering Electromagnetics,* John Wiley & Sons, New York, NY, USA.

Barnes, P. & Tesche, F. (1991). On the direct calculation of a transient plane wave reflected from a finitely conducting half space. *IEEE Trans. Electromagn. Compat.,* Vol. 33, May 1991, pp. 90-96.

Chen, Z.; Yao, R. & Guo, Z. (2004) The characteristics of UWB signal transmitting through lossy dielectric slab. *Proceedings of IEEE Radio and Wireles Conference 2004,* pp. 134-138, Atlanta, GA, USA, Sept. 19–22, 2004.

Dudley, D.; Papazoglou, T. & White, R. (1974). On the interaction of a transient electromagnetic plane wave and a lossy half-space. *J. Appl. Phys.,* Vol. 45, Mar. 1974, pp. 1171-1175.

Ghavami, M.; Michael, L. & Kohno, R. (2004). *Ultra Wideband Signal and Systems in Communcation Engineering,* Section 4.3, pp. 110-121, John Wiley & Sons, Chichester, England; Hoboken, NJ, USA.

Ho, M. & Lai, F.-S. (2007). Effects of medium conductivity on electromagnetic pulse propagation onto dielectric half space: One-dimensional simulation using characteristic-based method. *J. Electromagn. Wave Appl.*, Vol. 21, No. 13, 2007, pp. 1773-1785.

Hosono, T. (1981). Numerical inversion of Laplace transform and some applications to wave optics. *Radio Sci.*, Vol. 16, No. 6, Nov.-Dec. 1981, pp. 1015-1019.

Klaasen, J. (1990). Time-domain analysis of one-dimensional electromagnetic scattering by lossy media. *Rep. FEL-90-A211*, TNO Phys. Electron. Lab., The Hague, Oct. 1990.

Maloney, J.; Smith, G. & Scott, Jr., W. (1990). Accurate computation of the radiation from simple antennas using the finite-difference time-domain method. *IEEE Trans. Antennas Propagat.*, Vol. 38, July 1990, pp. 1059-1068.

Maloney, J. & Smith, G. (1992). The use of surface impedance concepts in the finite-difference time-domain method. *IEEE Trans. Antennas Propagat.*, Vol. 40, Jan. 1992, pp. 38-48.

Pantoja, M.; Yarovoy, A. & Bretones, A. (2009). On the direct computation of the time-domain plane-wave refelction coefficients. *ACES (Applied Computational Electromgnetics Society) Journal*, Vol. 24, No. 3, June 2009, pp. 294-299.

Pao, H.-Y.; Dvorak, S. & Dudley, D. (1996, a). An accuate and efficient analysis for transient plane waves obliquely incident on a conductive half space (TE case). *IEEE Trans. Antennas Propagat.*, Vol. 44, No. 7, July 1996, pp. 918-924.

Pao, H.-Y.; Dvorak, S. & Dudley, D. (1996, b). An accuate and efficient analysis for transient plane waves obliquely incident on a conductive half space (TM case). *IEEE Trans. Antennas Propagat.*, Vol. 44, No. 7, July 1996, pp. 925-932.

Papazoglou, T. (1975). Transmission of a transient electromagnetic plane wave into a lossy half-space. *J. Appl. Phys.*, Vol. 46, Aug. 1975, pp. 3333-3341.

Qiu, R. (2004). A generalized time domain multipath channel and its application in ultra-wideband (UWB) wireless optimum receiver design–Part II: Physics-based system analysis. *IEEE Trans. Wireless Comm.*, Vol. 3, No. 6, Nov. 2004, pp. 2312-2324.

Qiu, R. (2006). A generalized time domain multipath channel and its application in ultra-wideband (UWB) wireless optimum receiver–Part III: System performance analysis. *IEEE Trans. Wireless Comm.*, Vol. 5, No. 10, Oct. 2006, pp. 2685-2695.

Ramírez-Mireles, F. (2002). Signal design for ultra-wide-band communications in dense multipath. *IEEE Trans. Veh. Tech.*, Vol. 51, No. 6, Nov. 2002, pp. 1517-1521.

Rothwell, E. & Cloud, M. (2001). *Electromagnetics*, Chapter 4, pp. 189-348, CRC Press, Boca Raton, FL, USA.

Rothwell, E. & Suk, J. (2003). Efficient computation of the time-domain TE plane-wave reflection coefficient. *IEEE Trans. Antennas Propagat.*, Vol. 51, No. 12, Dec. 2003, pp. 3283-3285.

Rothwell, E. (2005). Efficient computation of the time-domain TM plane-wave reflection coefficient. *IEEE Trans. Antennas Propagat.*, Vol. 53, No. 10, Oct. 2005, pp. 3417-3419.

Sommerfeld, A. (1914). Über die Fortpflanzung des Lichtes in dispergierenden Medien. *Ann. Phys.*, Vol. 44, 1914, pp. 177-202.

Stratton, J. (1941). *Electromagnetic Theory*, McGraw-Hill, New York, NY, USA.

Suk, J. (2000). *Transient analysis of plane-wave scattering in a layered medium*, Ph.D. dissertation, Michigna State University, East Lansing, MI, USA, December 2000.

Yeh, P. (1988). *Optical Waves in Layered Media,* pp. 66 and pp. 86–88, John Wiley & Sons, New York, NY, USA.

Zeng, Q. (2010). *Transient Analysis of Electromagnetic Waves Based on Numerical Inversion of Laplace Transform,* Ph.D. dissertation, University of Ottawa, Ottawa, Ontario, Canada, May 2010.

Zhou, C. & Qiu, R. (2006). Spatial focusing of time-reversed UWB electromagnetic waves in a hallway environment. *Proceedings of IEEE 38th Southeastern Symposium on System Theory,* Cookeville, TN, USA, 2006.

8

Pulse generator design

S. Bourdel, R. Vauché and J. Gaubert
Aix-Marseille University, IM2NP, and CNRS, IM2NP (UMR 6242), France

1. Analysis of the current state of the art

The techniques normally used for generating pulses in low-cost monolithic technology (CMOS or BiCMOS) are different from those usually used in hybrid technologies. The latter mainly use edge combination methods generated from SRD diodes via quarter-wave lines or stubs (Jeongwoo Han et al., 2004). In a low-cost context, these techniques are not possible, as they cannot be integrated into the desired technologies. We shall present here only the following techniques:

- Baseband pulse transposition
- Baseband pulse filtering
- Synthesis by pulse combination.

This analysis is performed using circuits that have been built and measured and that can be found in the literature. Before commencing this analysis, it is necessary to point out that the figure of merit often used in pulse generation is the energy consumed by the pulse. This criteria is subject to a caveat, as it often fails to take into account the power consumed between two pulses, which means it is only relevant if the system is combined with power management (sometimes difficult to achieve, depending on the topology of the circuit). This is why we shall be presenting, wherever possible, an estimate of the total energy consumed by the pulse ($Ec_t=P_{DC}/D_S$) that take into account the average consumption between two pulses. The energy consumed per pulse will then be used to quantify the energy consumed during the pulse alone (τ), and if this is not given, it will be approximated as follows: $E_c=P_{DC}*\tau$. Moreover, in order to be completely suitable, the energy consumed by the total pulse must be compared to the energy of the pulse produced (E_p) by way of the energy efficiency per pulse ($n=E_p/Ec_t$). As this energy is rarely given, it will be estimated by assuming that the pulse is a sinusoid modulated by a gate of width τ and amplitude V_p ($E_p=\tau.V_p^2/2R_0$).

1.1. Baseband pulse transposition

This technique, described in Fig. 1, makes it possible to transpose a baseband pulse in a frequency band. This technique has the great advantage of being able to change the frequency band by varying the local oscillator (LO) frequency, as well as varying the bandwidth by the width of the baseband pulse. Furthermore, the doubling of the spectrum due to the frequency transposition allows the use of baseband pulses with a width of τ=2/BW. In addition, these techniques are not very sensitive to LO phase noise which only degrades the spectral purity of the lines of the discrete spectrum and does not affect the Power Spectral Density (PSD) envelope.

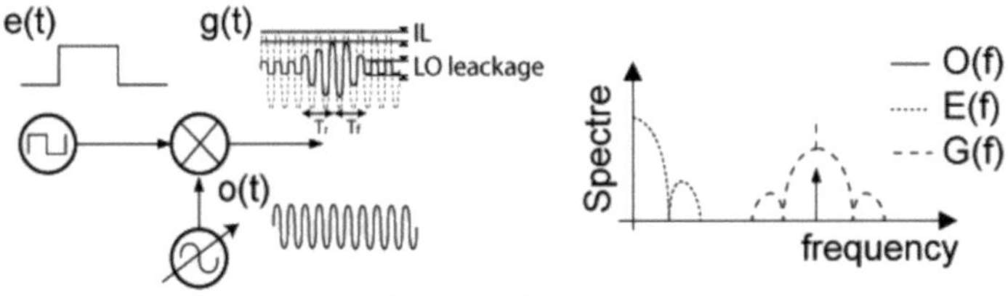

Fig. 1. Principle of frequency transposition architectures

A first transposition technique is based on the use of a switching circuit (Rui Xu et al., 2006), usually a CMOS switch or a mixer. The performance of these architectures is mainly determined by the switching circuit, since the control signal gives the envelope of the baseband pulse transmitted. The performance of these architectures mainly depends on the off-on switching time (Tr), the on-off switching time (Tf), the insertion losses (IL), and the isolation between the LO and the output, as all these parameters influence the spectrum of g(t) (G(f) in Fig. 1). The simplest architecture found in literature is based on the use of a single transistor. This topology is very limited, as its sizing makes it impossible to optimize all the performance criteria at the same time. Indeed, reducing the insertion losses involves increasing the size of the transistor, leading to increased stray capacitances, which degrades the insertion losses at high frequencies and reduces isolation from the output (Rui Xu et al., 2006).

The switching circuit can also be achieved using a double balanced mixer similar to a Gilbert cell (Wentzloff & Chandrakasan, 2006) (Datta et al., 2007). In (Wentzloff & Chandrakasan, 2006), the currents in the differential pairs are summed in order to cancel out LO leakage and improve isolation. Moreover, this topology makes it possible to generate BPSK signals by switching the baseband signal between the + or − inputs. In addition, the use of a mixer allows a better control of the signal spectrum by changing the baseband pulse shape. In (Datta et al., 2007), a passive Gaussian filter is used to shape the baseband pulse and a Gilbert cell is used to generate the bipolar signals. However, because of the LO leakages, these structures require small signals to be used for the switching (LO input). As shown in Table 1, this results in low output amplitudes and implies the use of power amplifiers (PA). In addition, the switching times of these architectures are greater than those of a single transistor. This difficulty in producing wideband mixers prevents the generation of very short (<1 ns) pulses using this topology.

Even though none of the circuits here includes the LO, the consumption is poor because of the consumption of the mixers. This implies the use of power management to turn off the LO between two pulses.

These considerations concerning LO power management have given rise to a technique that consists of switching the LO directly (On/Off LO or Switched LO) rather than its output, solving not just the problem of consumption between two pulses, but also the leakage problem. This method allows performance to be achieved (see Table 1) that represents the state of the art in 2009 in terms of consumption and amplitude, for generating 500 MHz bandwidth signals in the 3-5 GHz band. In the case of an LC LO, (Phan et al., 2008) shows that the rise and fall times (t_r and t_f) can be equal and give rise to 3.5 ns wide pulses with component values that can be integrated into the technology used (0.18 μm CMOS). Furthermore, the use of switched capacitors makes it possible to change the oscillation frequency and to address different channels, making this technique applicable for systems to the 802.15.4 standard. The major drawback of this technique lies in the low pulse amplitude.

To improve start-up time, (Barras et al., 2006) proposes a structure that gives the LO initial conditions that are greater than those generally produced by noise. This technique also allows the modification of the start phase, thereby offering the possibility of performing BPSK modulation. As reported in Table 1, this technique makes it possible to achieve very good performance in terms of amplitude.

In order to mitigate the excessively long start-up times for LC LOs, (Sanghoon Sim et al., 2009) proposes using ring oscillators. This structure allows the pulse widths to be around 0.5 ns. Furthermore, the digital structure of these LOs makes it possible to use inverters as output buffers with better performance than voltage followers, allowing amplitudes greater than 600 mV_{pp} for a consumption of 27 pJ/Pulse in the 6-10 GHz band.

Ref.	Arch.	LO leakage PWM6	τ (ns)	V_{pp}	Ec (pJ/P)	Ec_t (pJ/P)	Ep (pJ/P)	n	Pcons	Size (mm^2)	Techn.	Mod.	Integ.
0	Gated-LO (SW)	10	0.4	1.2	0.7*	120	1.44	0.012	1.8 mW @ 15 MHz	0.6	0.18 CMOS	OOK	Ext. LO
0	Gated-LO (Mix)	~10	1.7 – 3.3	0.25	100*	313	0.52	0.0016	31.3 mW @ 100 MHz	nc	0.18 SiGe	BPSK	Ext. LO
0	Gated-LO (Mix)	5	1	0.014	15*	120	0.0005	4.10^{-6}	15 mW @ 125 MHz	nc	0.25 SiGe	BPSK	Full
0	On/Off-LO (LC)	0	3.5	0.18	18	18	0.284	0.016	6.52 mW @ 125 MHz	0.39	0.18 CMOS	OOK	Full
0	On/Off-LO (LC)	0	2.5	0.9	180	180	5.06	0.028	1.8 mW @ 10 Mp/s	0.57	0.18 CMOS	BPSK	Full
0	On/Off-LO (rings)	0	0.5	0.673	27	nc	0.56	0.021**	nc	0.11	0.18 CMOS	OOK	Full

* Estimate (Ec=Pdc*τ), ** (Ec/Ep)

Table 1. Main characteristics of LO switching generators.

Table 1 lists the key characteristics of the works presented. With this technique, efficiencies of the order of 1 % and levels below 1 V are reached. Let us note here that only the works presented in 0 and 0 consume no power between two pulses ($Ec - Ec_t$).

1.2. Baseband pulse filtering

The principle of this technique, represented in Fig. 2, is based on the excitation of a filter by one or more baseband pulses produced by the combination of logic edges.

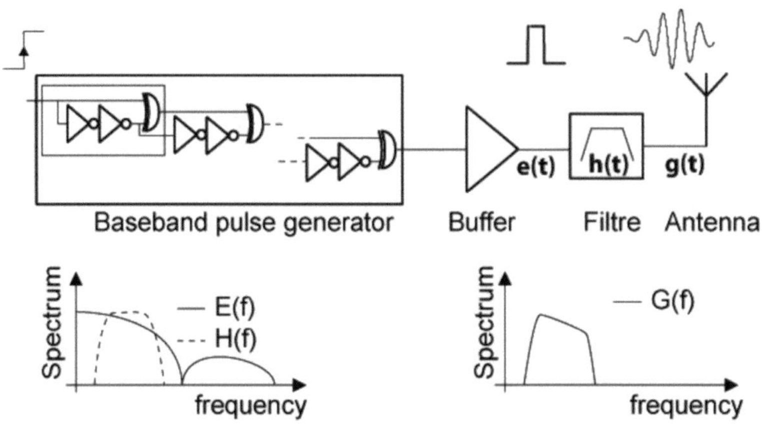

Fig. 2. Principle of baseband pulse filtering.

The expression of the generated pulse (g(t)) and its Fourier transform (G(f)) are dependent on the baseband pulses (e(t)) and the filter's transfer function in the manner described by 0 and 0. In particular, the filter makes it possible to adapt the signal's spectrum to a particular frequency band.

$$g(t) = e(t) * h(t) \quad (1)$$

$$G(f) = E(f).H(f) \quad (2)$$

This technique is particularly interesting for a low cost on package integration (System on Package - SoP) of the generator (Lee et al., 2008), as the generation of baseband pulse can be easily achieved in CMOS (here, 0.35 µm CMOS) and the filter can easily be produced "Off Chip" with coplanar or micro-strip technology at the same time as the interconnection with the antenna. In this work, excitation is achieved by a 2 ns wide pulse with an amplitude of 2.8 V, produced by a logic edge combiner which is described in Fig. 2. The signal is then filtered by a stub filter integrated onto a low-cost substrate (FR4). This technique makes it possible to generate pulses of substantial amplitude (0.65 V_{pp}) thanks to the filter's modest insertion loss (2.3 dB) and the strong excitation. Moreover, the total SoP size does not exceed 40 mm * 40 mm.

In order to be independent of the production of the chip carrier inherent to SoP technologies, it is possible to implement this technique in a System on Chip (SoC) with 0.13 µm CMOS technology (Bourdel et al., 2009). Indeed, in the case of UWB signals occupying the whole FCC band, the constraints on the filter are fairly minimal, and a 3rd-order is enough to meet the FCC mask, which leads to reasonable losses despite the poor quality of passive circuits of these technologies. Here, the filter is current driven by a C class biased transistor, which reduces the consumption (Ec) to 2.2 pJ/Pulse for a 1 V_{pp} pulse. Moreover, the authors show that the use of SoP technology would improve generator performance and that the use of conventional (non-ECL) logic would reduce the static consumption to 0 W. This performance represents the state of the art in terms of pulses generation covering the whole FCC band, and will be presented in detail in this chapter.

However, these techniques are limited when the filter order increases in order to generate pulses with lower spectral occupation (Bourdel et al., 2007). Filtering a 75 ps elementary pulse requires a 5th order to meet the ECC mask. It is then necessary to use an active filter in order to compensate the integrated filter's losses, which heavily penalizes the consumption, as shown by the circuit characteristics presented in Table 2. Furthermore, such a filter requires a significant number of inductors, which greatly increases the circuit's size.

In order to relax the constraints on the filtering, it is possible to use a sequence of elementary pulses instead of a single pulse (Smaini et al., 2006). In this way, it is possible to concentrate the pulse energy around the pseudo frequency of the sequence, thereby making filtering around this frequency easier. This technique can be used to generate pulses with a bandwidth of 500 MHz for applications in the 802.15.4 standard (Wentzloff & Chandrakasan, 2007). Eleven 120 ps elementary pulses at 120 ps spacing make it possible to generate a pulse in Channel 2 (4.05 GHz) after a simple filtering of the DC component. Varying the width, spacing, and number of pulses makes it possible to address different bands. Here, the consumption increases compared with the previous works presented, but it remains acceptable when compared with the energy of the pulse produced. However, it is not possible to achieve the consumption performance of the LO swintching designed for this same type of application using this technique, whereas small size (0.08 mm²) can be achieved due to the absence of inductors.

Table 2 summarizes the main characteristics of generators using pulse filtering. Here too, efficiencies are of the order of 1 % and levels do not exceed 1 V. However, this technique makes it possible to achieve higher bandwidths than those obtained with LO switching.

Ref.	t (ns)	BW (GHz)	Vpp (V)	Ep (pJ/P)	Ep (pJ/P)	Ep (pJ)	n	Pdc	Size (mm^2)	Techn.	Mod.	Integ.
0	2	nc	0.65	nc	nc	2.11	nc	nc	0.5	0.35 CMOS	OOK	SoP
0	0.6	4.3	1	2.25	13.5	2.16	0.16	2.7mW@200MHz	0.54	0.13 CMOS	OOK	SoC
0	1.8	2.5	0.35	23.6*	52.4	0.55	0.01	13.1mW@250MHz	1.02	0.13 CMOS	BPSK	SoC
0	0.6-0.8	2-4	0.35–0.45	8*	62.5	0.41	0.006	10mW@160MHz	1.56	0.13 CMOS	BPSK	SoP
0	3	0.5	0.65	47	nc	3.17	0.07**	nc	0.08	0.09 CMOS	BPSK	SoC

* Estimate (Ec=Pdc*τ), ** Ep/Ec

Table 2. Performance of baseband pulse filtering generators.

1.3. Synthesis by pulse combination

This technique is based on the principle (described in Fig. 3) that multi-cycle pulses s(t) are a combination of elementary single-cycle pulses $e_n(t)$.

$$s(t) = \sum_{n=0}^{N-1} g_n . e_n \left(t - \sum_{n=0}^{N-1} \tau_{n-1} \right) \quad (3)$$

$$with \ \tau_{-1} = 0$$

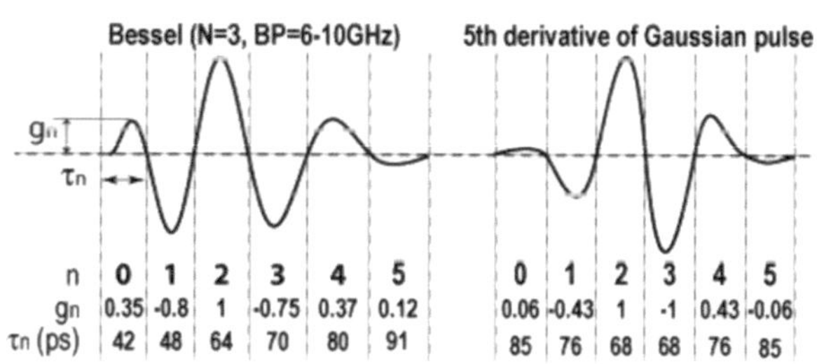

Fig. 3. Principle of synthesis by pulse combination.

It appears that varying the shape of the elementary pulse has little influence on the final spectrum, and that only its amplitude and width have any real influence (Vauché et al., 2009). Hence it is possible to synthesize a complex pulse using a same pulse e(t) delayed and amplified. The major advantage of this technique lies in the fact that it is no longer necessary to use filters or oscillators and that it can be achieved without inductors. This gives to this technique a great deal of potential, particularly with the developments of submicronic technologies. The other major interest of this technique lies in its programmability. Indeed, it then becomes possible to adapt the pulse to a channel, to change its frequency band, to produce predistortion, or to compensate for process variation associated with manufacturing. However, this technique is not mature and few circuits have so far been produced.
The main studies carried out to date use the same technique for generating elementary pulses, namely an edge combiner based on a voltage controlled delay line (VCDL). However, these studies are characterized by the use of different combination methods. The elementary pulses can be current-combined by transistors of different sizes (Kim et al., 2004). The nature of the transistor (P or N) makes it possible to achieve the positive or negative alternation of the pulses. The consumption is very good (15 mW @ 500 MHz) as the output stage is unbiased and operates in switching mode. It is also possible with this technique to address different frequency bands by varying the combiner delays (Kim et al., 2006) (Kim et al., 2005). However, this topology remains limited in terms of programmability, as it is not possible to change the number of amplitude of the elementary pulses.

It is also possible to use current combination with differential pairs, which makes it possible to control the amplitude of the pulses by varying the biasing of the pairs (Bourdel et al., 2007). The positive and negative alternation of the pulses is achieved by cross-connecting the path of the differential pairs. Here, the number and amplitude of the pulses are not limited, which gives a great deal of latitude in programming. However, an output stage configured as a voltage follower is necessary to drive the power into a 50 Ω load. This output stage limits the performance in terms of amplitude ($0.6V_{pp}$ simulated using a 0.13 μm CMOS Design Kit) and static consumption. The energy consumed per pulse remains acceptable (26.4 pJ/P) if high-performance power management is used, otherwise the circuit consumes 202 pJ/P @ 100 Mbs^{-1}.
The principle of current summing using differential pairs can be used to produce bipolar pulses, or to relieve the constraints on the filtering in order to be able to achieve complete integration (SoC), using only an integrated output transformer (Demirkan et al., 2008). The circuit's consumption is substantial (71 pJ/P) because of the high data rate. However, the principle of this approach is validated with a measured pulse amplitude of 220 mV_{pp}.
Triangular pulses and a charge pump can also be used to vary the amplitudes of the elementary pulses (Norimatsu et al., 2007). The value of the current in the charge pump sets the amplitude of the triangle. This circuit produces a pulse using just digital cells, and the size of the circuit reaches 0.4 mm^2 in 0.18 μm CMOS technology. Moreover, the circuit achieves good performance in terms of amplitude and pulse width ($1.24V_{pp}$ measured for a width of 1.75 ns). The main limitations lie in the consumption (29.7 mW @ 36 MHz) and the use of a discrete transformer for the positive and negative alternations of the elementary pulses.

Ref.	t (ns)	BW (GHz)	Vpp	Ec (pJ/P)	Ect (pJ/P)	Ep (pJ)	n	Pdc	Size (mm^2)	Techn.	Mod.	Integ.
0	0.38	7.2	0.7	5.7*	30	0.47	0.015	15 mW @ 500 MHz	nc	0.18 CMOS	OOK	No
0	0.38	7.2	0.92	0.74*	23.41	0.84	0.034	1.88 mW @ 77 MHz	0.78	0.18 CMOS	BPSK	No
0	0.36	6	0.6	26.4	202	0.32	0.002	20.24 mW @ 100 MHz	nc	0.13 CMOS	BPSK	No
0	0.53	4	0.22	68.4*	71.7	0.06	0.008	129 mW @ 1.8 GHz	2.83	0.09 CMOS	BPSK	SoC
0	1.75	1.4	1.24	52*	825	6.73	0.008	29.7mW @ 36 MHz	0.4	0.18 CMOS	BPSK	SoP

* Estimate (Ec=Pdc.τ)

Table 3. Main characteristics of pulse synthesis generators.

1.4. Conclusions on the state of the art

This analysis of the state of the art highlights the major efforts that have been made to reduce pulse generator consumption, since the energy efficiency per pulse produced has gone from around 0.10 % to nearer 10 % in just a few years. In this context, baseband pulse filtering seems to have the greatest potential in terms of efficiency. It proves capable of generating pulses of large amplitude and of widths making it possible to address different bands, and particularly the broadest bands. However, "narrowband" (500 MHz) generation, particularly at higher frequencies, requires the use of a significant number of delays and logic functions in the combiner. This worsens consumption, as well as integration because of the balance needed for each path when designing the masks. For applications in the 500 MHz bands, the LC LO switching techniques yield the best results. However, the times response and the output buffers limit the pulse amplitude as well as efficiency, preventing these architectures from being able to address the highest bands. The use of a ring VCO (Sim et al., 2009) is an interesting example of convergence between these two techniques (pulse filtering and LO switching). Indeed, on the one hand the long delay lines needed for generating in the 500 MHz bands of the high band (> 6.5 GHz) seem destined to be replaced by switched ring VCOs, while on the other, using this type of function requires a shaping filter because of the high energy levels it generates in the lower bands. As far as pulse synthesis is concerned, this is currently slightly behind in terms of efficiency. The future of these techniques depends on the development of the technologies or on the needs of applications which may justify this increase in consumption that is inherent in pulse programming.

2. Analysis of the FCC and ECC standards

This section gives an analysis of the FCC and ECC standards using theoretical models, in order to evaluate the potential of UWB-IR systems in terms of range and data rate. In the case of switched signals, it appears that PSD increases as a function of the level of the pulse and as a function of the data rate. It is then possible to reduce the data rate in order to increase pulse amplitude (and hence detection) while maintaining a PSD that meets the standard. However, there is also a restriction on the peak value of the transmitted signal with the peak PSD limit, in order to restrain this practice. By analysing the average PSD (PSD_{av}) and peak PSD (PSD_{pk}) together we can evaluate the maximum amplitude value (g_{0max}) allowed for a given modulation and the associated data rate. This analysis is performed in the case of linear modulations (OOK, BPSK, PAM) for which the transmit signal (s(t)) and its PSD ($S_{ss}(f)$) are expressed as:

$$s(t) = \sum_{k=0}^{K-1} q_k g\left(t - kT_k\right) \tag{4}$$

$$S_{SS}(f) = \frac{\sigma_q^2}{T_s}\left|G(f)\right|^2 + \frac{\mu_q^2}{T_s^2}\left|G(f)\right|^2 .W_{Fs}(f) \tag{5}$$

where q_k is a random sequence with mean value μ_q and variance σ_q, $g(t)$ is the pulse waveform, and $G(f)$ its Fourier transform. This analysis especially gives the potential of OOK and BPSK modulations in terms of detection and data rate in order to see which types of applications they are compatible with. Lastly, we assume here an ideal pulse with a spectrum defined by the FCC or ECC masks, in order to evaluate the maximum theoretical amplitude value and the associated data rate value.

2.1. Mean PSD

The mean PSD of a UWB signal is limited by the masks shown in Fig. 4

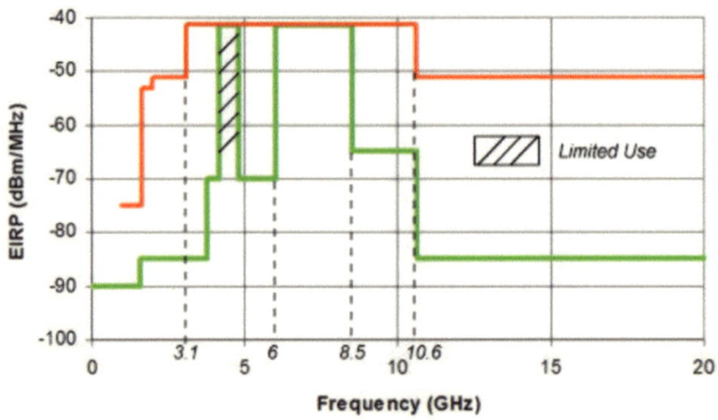

Fig. 4. FCC and ECC masks

If we ignore the power in the unallocated bands, the spectrum of the signal with the best spectral occupation is given by equation (3). It is a square function with a width (BW_{TOT}) defined by the allocated band, and which is centred on the middle of this band (f_0). Its inverse Fourier transform gives the ideal base pulse (equation 0).

$$G(f) = G_0\left[\Pi_{BW_{TOT}}\left(f - f_0\right) + \Pi_{BW_{TOT}}\left(f + f_0\right)\right] \tag{6}$$

$$g(t) = 2.G_0.BW_{TOT}.\text{sinc}\left(\pi BW_{TOT} t\right).\cos(2\pi f_0 t) \tag{7}$$

with (for the FCC standard): $BW_{TOT} = 7.5$ GHz and $f_0 = 6.85$ GHz and (for the ECC standard): $BW_{TOT} = 2.5$ GHz and $f_0 = 7.25$ GHz. The peak amplitude of the ideal pulse is then given by:

$$g_0 = 2G_0 BW_{TOT} \tag{8}$$

The ECC and FCC standards require the use of a spectrum analyser whose resolution filter bandwidth (RBW_{av}) is set to 1 MHz. The measured PSD (single-sided) can then be expressed as follows, from 0:

$$DSP_{av}^{+}(f) = 2\frac{|G(f)|^2}{Z_0} D_s \left\{ RBW_{av}.\sigma_q^2 + D_s \mu_q^2 W_{FS} \right\} \tag{9}$$

For both standard, the maximum value of the average PSD is set to −41.3 dBm/MHz and can be expressed as follows:

$$DSP_{\max} = \max\left\{ \frac{2\sigma_q^2}{Z_0} D_s RBW_{av} G_0^2 ; \frac{2\mu_q^2}{Z_0} D_S^2 G_0^2 \right\} = 10^{-7.13} \tag{10}$$

Using 0 and 0, it is then possible to establish a relationship between the maximum amplitude allowed by the standard and the symbol rate as follow:

$$g_{0\max} = \min\left\{ \left(\frac{2BW_{TOT}^2 Z_0 .DSP_{\max}}{D_s RBW_{av} \sigma_q^2} \right)^{1/2}, \left(\frac{2BW_{TOT}^2 Z_0 .DSP_{\max}}{D_s^2 \mu_q^2} \right)^{1/2} \right\} \tag{11}$$

In Fig. 6, $g_{0\max}$ is represented as a function of D_s for OOK and BPSK modulation. However, it appears that if we consider only the limit imposed by the mean PSD, the maximum magnitude allowed value for data rates of the order of 10 kbs^{-1} exceeds 100 V. It is then necessary to evaluate the peak PSD.

2.2. Peak PSD

The ECC and FCC standards limit the peak power as follows. The peak PSD of the transmitted signal must be measured using a spectrum analyser in "peak detection" mode and in a 50 MHz resolution bandwidth (*RWB_{pk}*). At the frequency where the mean PSD is maximum, the peak PSD must not exceed 0 dBm. This measurement can be interpreted in the following way: the peak power of an elementary pulse filtered by an ideal 50 MHz bandpass filter centred on f_0 must not exceed 0 dBm. This interpretation is only valid where the symbol data rate is less than the spectrum analyser's RBW. Above this limit, the filter does not have the time to respond and the peak detector measures the power of the filter response to several pulses. However, it is at lower data rates (< 50 MHz) that this measurement is most meaningful, and this area of validity is sufficient for estimating the maximum allowed pulse magnitude.

Since the spectrum of the ideal pulse defined above is flat, the spectrum of the pulse filtered by the resolution filter (assumed to be ideal) together with its inverse Fourier transform can be expressed as follows:

$$G_{pk}(f) = G_0\left[\Pi_{RBW_{pk}}(f - f_0) + \Pi_{RBW_{pk}}(f + f_0)\right] \tag{12}$$

$$g_{pk}(t) = 2G_0.RBW_{pk}.\text{sinc}\left(\pi RBW_{pk}t\right).\cos(2\pi f_0 t) \tag{13}$$

From 0, the peak power of the resolution filter output signal (which is the image of the peak PSD defined by the standard) can be expressed with G_0 as follow:

$$P_{pk} = \frac{4.G_0^2.RBW_{pk}^2}{Z_0} = DSP_{pk} \text{ for Ds < 50 MHz} \tag{14}$$

This interpretation of the evaluation of the peak PSD is validated by the measurements given in Fig. 5. Here, the peak PSD obtained from (11) is compared to the measurement, performed under the conditions imposed by the FCC standard, of an OOK sequence using RZ (Return to Zero) pulses of width $\tau = 1$ ns and amplitude $A = 1$ V. Let us note that the standard allows this measurement to be performed using an RBW lower than 50 MHz (but necessarily greater than 1 MHz). In this case, the measurement must be corrected by a factor equal to 20 log (RBW/50 MHz).

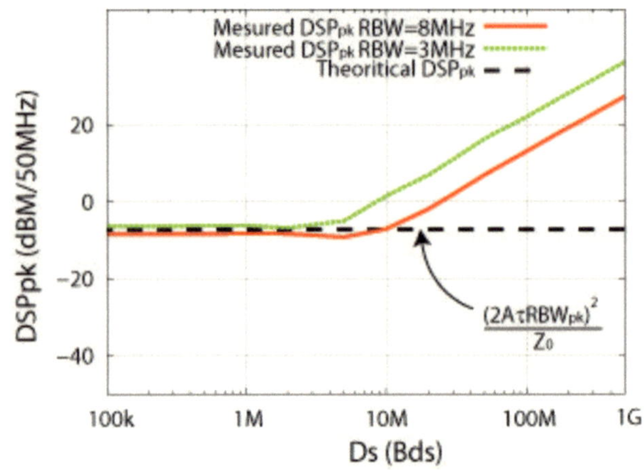

Fig. 5. Comparison of the model of the peak PSD and its measurement for OOK modulation using RZ pulses with an amplitude of A=1 V and a width of τ=1 ns.

From 0 and (11), the peak PSD can be expressed as a function of D_s in the case where the pulse amplitudhe is adjusted to achieve the maximum allowed PSD ($g_0 = g_{0max}$).

$$P_{pk} = \min\left\{\frac{2.DSP_{\max}.RBW_{pk}^2}{D_s\sigma_q^2.RBW_{av}};\frac{2.DSP_{\max}.RBW_{pk}^2}{D_s^2\mu_q^2}\right\} \tag{15}$$

2.3. Interpretation

Fig. 6 and Fig. 7 (for the FCC and ECC standards respectively) show the maximum value of the ideal emitted pulse (g_{0max}) given by 0 and the peak PSD (P_{pk}) given by 0 in the case where the value of the mean PSD is the maximum allowed by the standards ($DSP_{max} = 10^{-7.13}$). OOK and BPSK modulations are being considered here to compare their potential for low-cost applications.

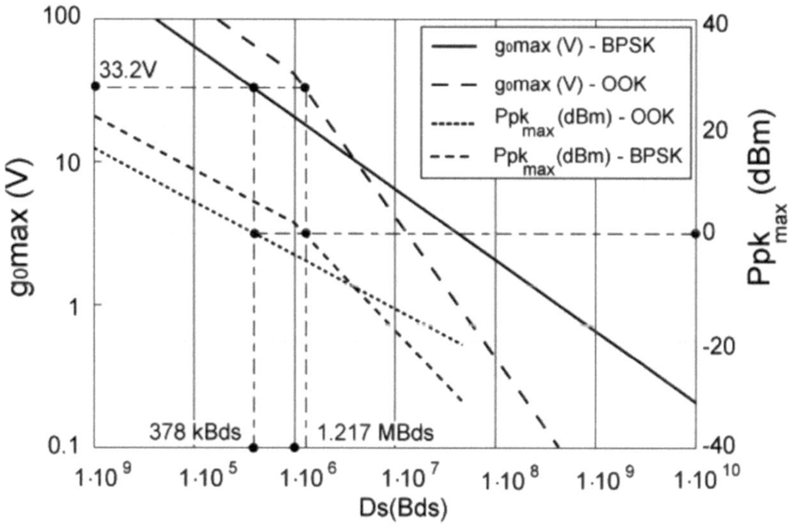

Fig. 6. Maximum value of the transmitted pulse (g_{0max}) and peak PSD (P_{pk}) as a function of the data rate (Ds) for $PSDav_{max} = 10^{-7.13}$ in the case of the FCC standard.

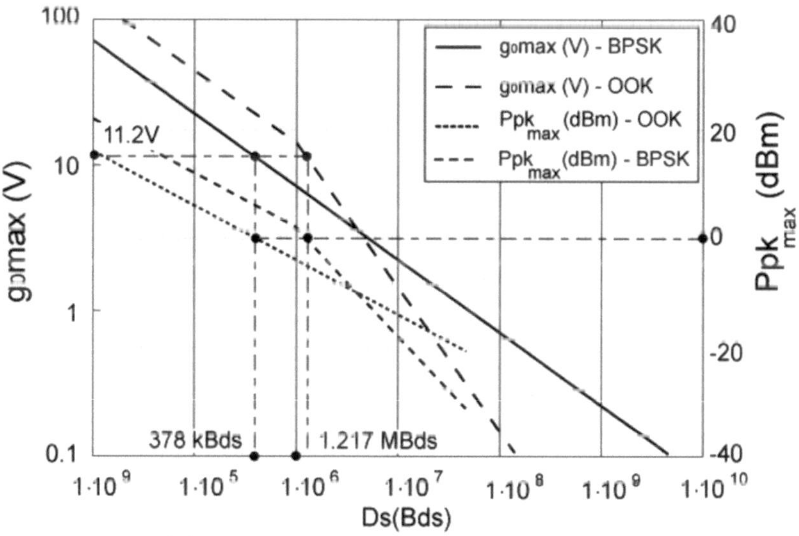

Fig. 7. Maximum value of the transmitted pulse (g_{0max}) and peak PSD (P_{pk}) as a function of the data rate (Ds) for $PSDav_{max} = 10^{-7.13}$ in the case of the ECC standard.

Looking at $g_{0max}(D_s)$, the discontinuous spectrum limit in the case of OOK modulation appears clearly for data rates greater than RBW_{av}. In fact, for data rates above 4 Mbs^{-1}, BPSK modulation has greater potential. However, it is possible to generate pulses greater than 1 V in OOK u to 40 Mbs^{-1} for the FCC standard and 14 Mbs^{-1} for ECC For data rates below 4 Mbs^{-1}, OOK modulation has greater potential than BPSK, because of the different variance. Let us note, moreover, that the values permitted by the FCC standard are higher than those of the ECC standard, since as the band is wider, the pulse energy is lower.

Observing the peak PSD shows that it is possible to reduce the data rate in order to increase the amplitude of the pulse up to 1.217 Mbs^{-1} in OOK and 378 kbs^{-1} in BPSK. Beyond these values, it is no longer possible to increase the amplitude by reducing Ds due to the peak power limitation. For these limit values, the pulse amplitude is 33.2 V in FCC and 11.2 V in ECC. In the case of 500MHz bandwidth signals, this value drop to 2V. Here again, OOK modulation has the greater potential.

In conclusion, it is preferable to choose OOK modulation when the intended data rates are lower than 4Mbs^{-1} and BPSK when data rates are above 40 Mbs^{-1} in FCC and 14 Mbs^{-1} in ECC. The choice between the two may be influenced by the application needs and technical constraints. In an integrated circuit context where it is difficult to generate pulse amplitudes exceeding 1 V, OOK modulation is sufficient to achieve such a level up to 40 Mbs^{-1} (or 14 Mbs^{-1} in ECC). If application requirements in terms of detection (range) or data rate is more stringent so demand, BPSK modulation may be considered, at the expense of increased complexity.

3. Designing an FCC generator using elementary pulse filtering

The technique described here has been used in various works (Bourdel et al., 2009) (Bourdel et al. 2010) (Bachelet et al., 2006) and performs the best results in terms of amplitude and energy per pulse for frequency bandwidth above a few GHz. The principle of this technique is that given in Fig. 2. It is applied for the whole FCC band for an application requiring a data rate of 36 Mbs^{-1} and an amplitude $g_0 > 1$ V.

3.1. Sizing

The first step in the design of the device shown in Fig. 2 consists in sizing the transmit filter. Several combinations of filters (h(t)) and baseband pulses (e(t)) can meet the FCC mask. In the case where e(t) is modelled by a square function ($\pi_\tau(t)$) of width τ and amplitude A, g(t) and its Fourier transform are:

$$g(t) = \frac{A}{\sqrt{l}}.\pi_\tau(t) * h_e(t) \tag{16}$$

$$G(f) = \frac{A\tau \text{sinc}(\pi\tau f).H_e(f)}{\sqrt{l}} \tag{17}$$

where h(t) is the ideal pulse response of the filter, and *l* the power losses.

Fig. 8 shows the spectrum, evaluated from 0, of four pulses defined for different *h(t)* and different τ. Because of its very broad nature, the FCC mask can be satisfied using low-order filters, which is a major advantage for monolithic design in CMOS technology, where inductances have substantial losses.

Of all these different pulses, *pulse 2* (Fig. 8b) exhibits the best compromise. First of all, it has good voltage efficiency (α), which represents the ratio between the amplitude (A) of the drive pulse (e(t)) and the amplitude (g_0) of the filter output pulse (g(t)). Furthermore, the value of τ is higher, which relaxes the constraints on the baseband generator. Lastly, the component values needed to produce it (Table 4) are compatible with the intended technology.

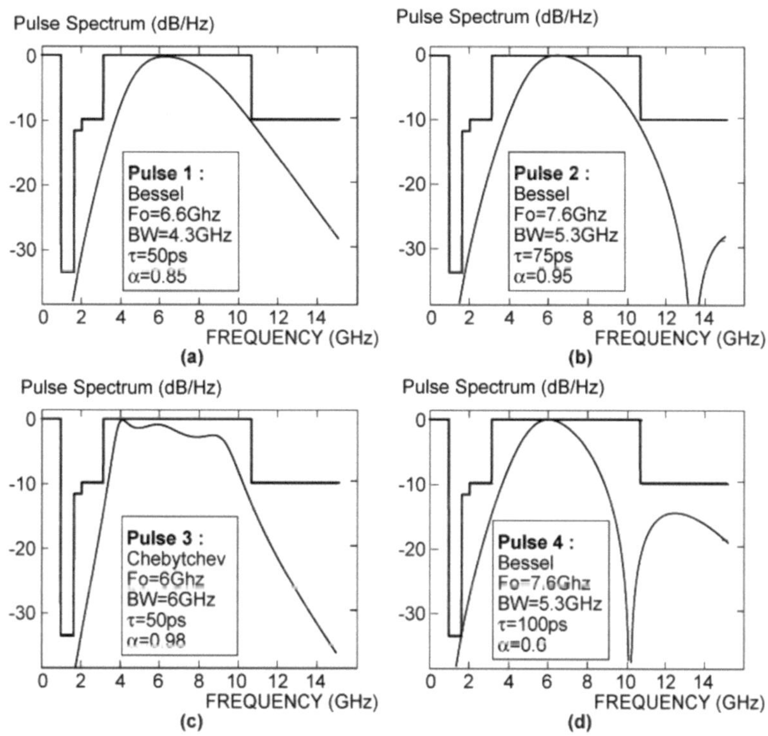

Fig. 8. Normalized spectral density ($|G(f)|^2/G_0$) for different 3rd-order filters and different pulse widths.

The Fig. 6 shows that it is theoretically allowed to generate pulses exceeding 1 V magnitude with a data rate of $36Mbs^{-1}$ when using OOK modulation. For the case study presented here, the same analysis as presented in section 2 can be performed with a pulse g(t) given by 0 instead of 0 (Bourdel et al., 2010). From this analysis, a more accurate specification for the generator characteristics can then be deduced. In the case of *pulse 2*, we then have $g_0 = 1.73$ V. 0 enables us then to evaluate the amplitude of e(t): A = 2.56 V.

3.2. Design

The architecture of the circuit presented is given in Fig. 9. The generator consists of a digital edge combiner (also referred to as a triangular pulse generator) producing the baseband pulse, a driver, and an integrated filter. The filter is driven in current mode in order to provide an amplitude (A) at its input greater than the supply voltage (V_{DD} = 1.2V).

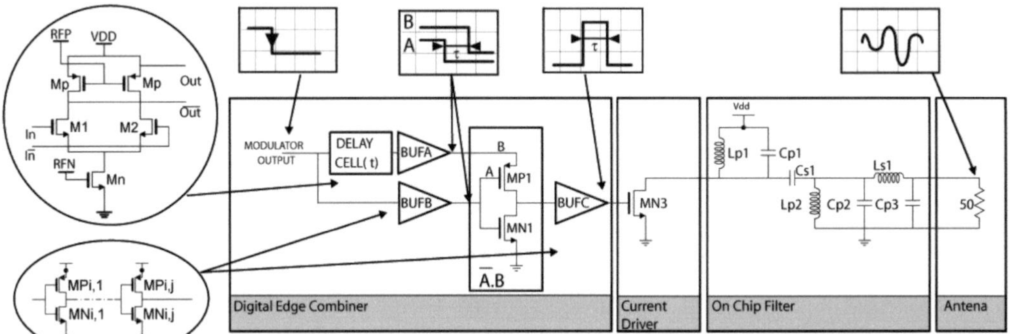

Fig. 9. Architecture of the FCC generator.

The design of the integrated filter is highly determined by the performances of the passive circuits available in the technology, especially the inductors. A preliminary study must be achieved to evaluate these performances. Inductor losses and self-resonance frequencies (srf) are actually heavily dependent on the inductor value (*L*). In the technology used in this design (0.13 µm CMOS), best performance is achieved by inductors with 0.4nH<*L*<1.5 nH. For these values, the Q remains greater than 10 over the whole FCC band and the srf remains above 15 GHz. The capacitors exhibit better RF performance, as the range of values that ensure proper operation (Q > 50 and srf > 24 GHz) is from 100 fF to 2 pF. However, for higher values, a significant discrepancy between the nominal value and the value at 7 GHz is noted (10 % for 2 pF) and will need to be taken into account during the design.
The narrow range of possible inductor values imposes the major restriction on the choice of filter. Very fortunately, the relative bandwidth of the FCC band is close to unity, which limits the spread of component values. For any one filter, several topologies are possible, and the choice is determined by the value of the components they require. The topology chosen here (which is not a classic ladder filter topology) gives the component values given in Table 4.

Lp1 (nH)	Cp1 (pF) (ideal)	Cp1 (pF) (Real)	Cs1 (fF)	Ls1 (nH)	Lp2 (nH)	Cp2 (fF)	C3 (fF)
460	1.43	0.5	677	1.15	1.08	420	260

Table 4. Component values for the integrated filter.

From the filter values it is then possible to size the current driver (MN3). The size of the transistor depends on A and the filter's input impedance R_{in}, for which this filter topology is the same as R_{out} = 50 Ω (antenna impedance). As the baseband pulse (0–V_{DD}) is applied to the gate of MN3, the current supplied to the filter by the transistor during the conduction time (τ) can be approximated according to the small signal theory. The size of the transistor can then be expressed as follows:

$$W = \frac{L.A_{max}}{R_{IN}.\mu_0.C_{ox}\left(V_{DD}-V_t\right)^2} \quad (18)$$

The current needed to drive 2.56 V into 50 Ω is I_0 = 51 mA, leading to a very large transistor. For such a transistor, the output impedance (R_{ds} and C_{ds} shown in Fig. 10) must be matched to the filter.

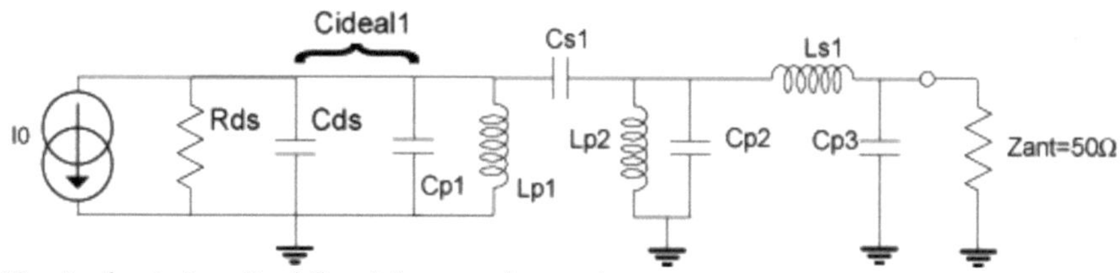

Fig. 10. Equivalent circuit of the driver and transistor.

Due to the high capacitance value in the first resonator, the effect of C_{ds} can easily be compensated for with C_{p1}. However, using such a simple topology, power matching (R_{ds}=R_{in}) cannot be achieved independently of the value of I_0. The size of the transistor then becomes a compromise between the value of I_0, the matching (R_{ds}), and the driver consumption (size of MN3), which is the highest in the circuit. The size finally adopted (W = 100 µm) provides a current of 58 mA (close to A_{max}/R_{out}) leading to an output of g_0 = 1.73 V. The value of R_{ds} is 122 Ω. Better matching would have been obtained with a larger transistor, at the expense of an increased consumption.

The edge combiner's delay cells are made using mode current differential logic (MCDL) as shown in Fig. 9. The main interest of this logic is its speed, together with its low dynamic consumption. The delays can be varied by applying a control voltage to the gates of the P transistor, thereby modifying their dynamic resistance. Each cell produces a delay that can vary from 17 ps to 300 ps, thereby making it possible to compensate for variations in the manufacturing process and achieve the desired value of τ. The edge combination is performed in a logic cell ($A.\overline{B}$) using only two transistor, in this way making it possible to generate pulses of up to 50 ps. Lastly, buffers are needed to match the sizes of the transistors between the logic circuits, which use smaller transistors, and the driver. In order not to place all the constraint on buffer C, an initial series of buffers (buffers A and B) are placed between the delays and the logic function.

3.3. Results

The main measurement results are given in Fig. 11. The circuit (shown in Fig. 11a) occupies 0.54 mm². Pulse amplitude is 1.4 V_{pp} with a 1.2 V supply as presented in Fig. 11b and the spectrum of the generated pulses is FCC compliant as shown in Fig. 11c. Moreover, the FCC mask is satisfied for a 36 Mbs^{-1} data rate (Fig. 11d). The mean consumption is 3.8 mA @ 100 MHz. The energy consumed per pulse is estimated at 9 pJ, especially due to the driver (MN3), which operates in C class. However, this performance can only be achieved if power management is used, as this estimation does not take DC consumption between two pulses into account. Indeed, like most of previous published works present in the literature, this generator dissipates DC power, making the total energy consumed per pulse (Ec_t) dependent on the data rate.

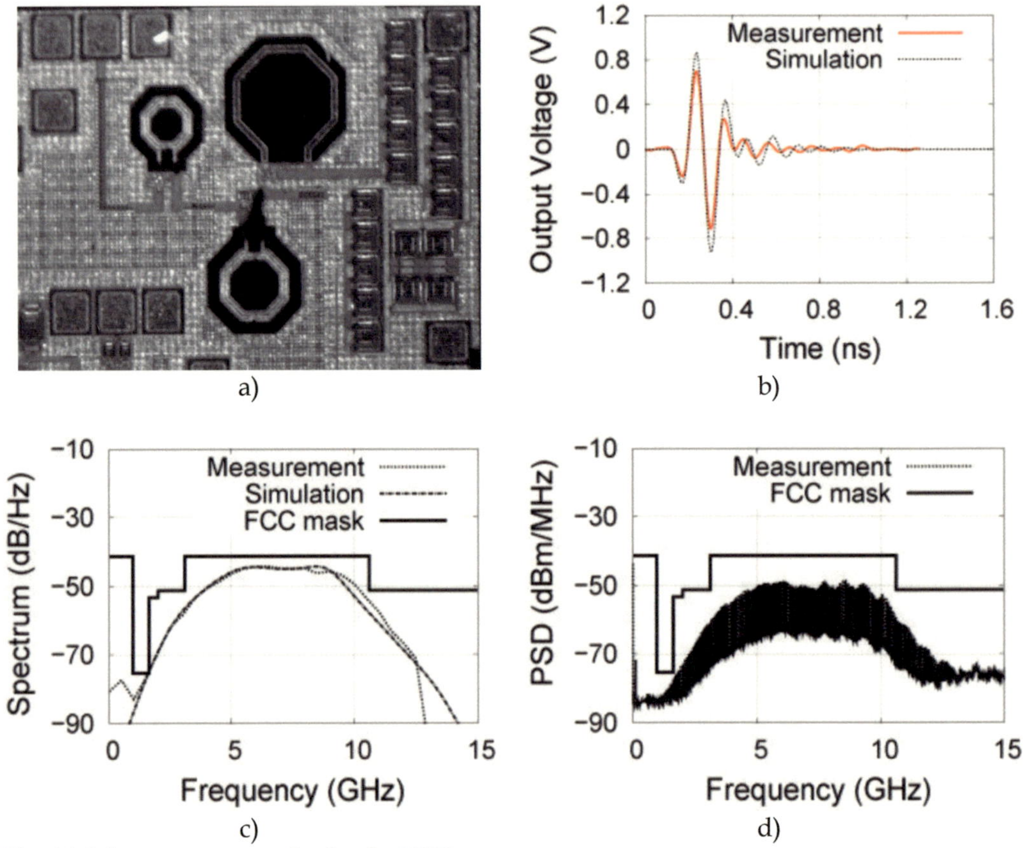

Fig. 11. Measurement results for the FCC generator.

4. Designing a pulse synthesizer for the FCC band

4.1. Principle

The principle of the pulse synthesizer is shown in Fig. 12. It uses the elementary pulse combination method presented in section 1.3. With this technique different pulse shapes can be synthesized using a single generator, in particular to compensate for PVT variations. The study presented here demonstrates the effectiveness of this technique in terms of programming and integration. The synthesizer is dimensioned to enable generation of the 5th derivative of a Gaussian pulse, together with the impulse responses of a Bessel filter presented in Fig. 3. In order to achieve this, the generator must include six stages in order to generate the six elementary pulses shown in Fig. 3**Error! Reference source not found.**.

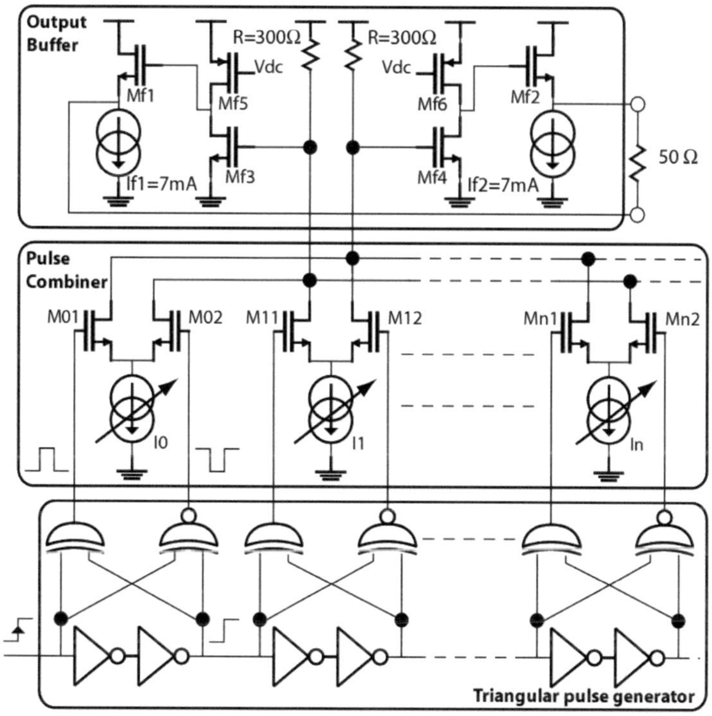

Fig. 12. Principle of combination using cross-connected differential pairs.

One of the main difficulties in pulse combination lies in the need to alternate the polarity of successive elementary pulses. The use of cross-connected differential pairs resolves this issue. Current summing is achieved into a load and each output is alternately cross-connected with the next in order to achieve the polarity alternation. The bias current (I_n) in each pair then sets the absolute value of g_n.

4.2. Design

The use of differential pairs implies the use of a differential elementary pulse. In principle, this necessity does not prevent the use of a logic combiner. However, this introduces an asymmetry into the combiner, which has to use complementary logic functions to produce the positive pulse and its complement. Given that the width needed for a Gaussian pulse ($\tau_n = 75$ ps) is close to the minimum achievable in the considered technology (0.13 µm CMOS), this asymmetry (represented in Fig. 14c) will lead to an imperfection in the driving of the differential pairs and the generation of a common mode. The delay cells used in the combiner are the ones given in Fig. 9 of the section 3. The complementary logic functions (shown in Fig. 13a) are ($A.\overline{B}$) and ($\overline{A}+B$) because these can be achieved using only two transistors, involving high speed performances.

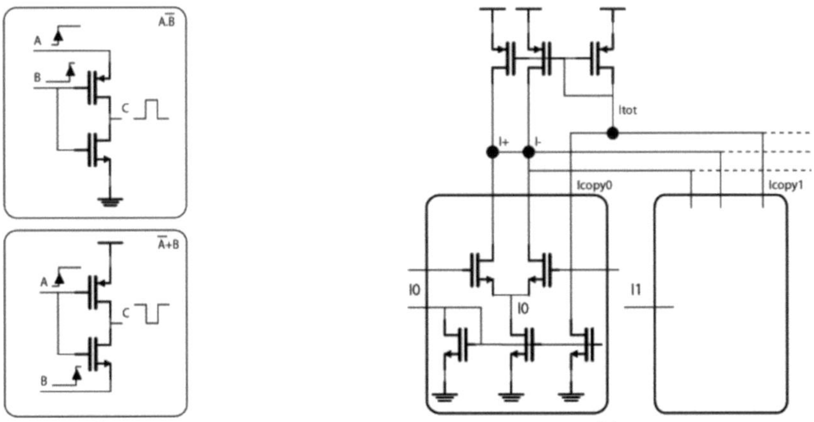

a) b)

Fig. 13. Generating the elementary pulse and its complement (a), current mirroring (b).

Moreover, driving a high-amplitude signal into the 50 Ω load imposed by the antenna constitutes one of the main constraints of this design. Indeed, insofar the use of inductors must be avoided to optimize integration, the gain-bandwidth product of the active cells that can be achieved in 0.13 µm CMOS technology considerably limits the amplitude of the transmitted pulse. In fact, the size of the transistors needed to drive such a load imposes cut-off frequencies well below 10 GHz. Several solutions have been implemented to mitigate this problem. First of all, the differential structure imposed by the combination structure is maintained right up to the antenna, thereby making it possible to double the output voltage. Common-mode rejection can be problem in a differential structure, however here, the distortion introduced by this common mode can be compensated for by the value of the g_n co-efficients. In our case, the time constant for establishing this common mode, represented Fig.14a, is much slower than the elementary pulse, which leads to stretching of the final pulse s(t). This stretching can be cancelled out by adding an extra stage with a gain inverse to the common-mode value observed at the end of the pulse. The comparison of the current values I_n with the normalized value of g_n (given in Table 5) highlights this common-mode compensation. This specific feature demonstrates this structure's ability to compensate for distortions.

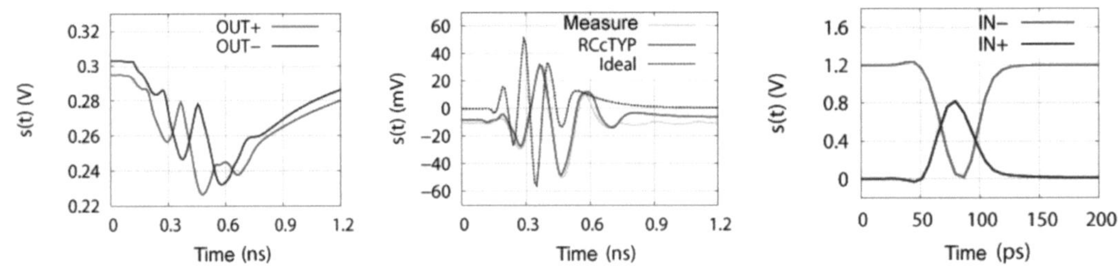

a) b) c)

Fig. 14. ("post-layout") simulation of the single (a) and differential (b) output pulses and the drive (c).

N	0	1	2	3	4	5	6
g_n	0.06	−0.43	1	−1	0.43	−0.06	0
I_n (mA)	0.005	0.82	2.2	3.4	2.28	0.63	0.1

Table 5. Comparison of g_n and I_n values for the 5th derivative of a Gaussian pulse.

The differential pairs are combined into an active load biased by the mirroring of the I_n currents (shown in Fig.13b) making it possible to ensure a constant output stage gate voltage (Mf3 and Mf4), regardless of the values of g_n required to produce the pulse. The differential pair transistors are dimensioned to ensure the maximum gain into a high-impedance load, leading to a small size (3 μm).
The output stage allows matching to the antenna. Several circuit arrangements have been envisaged. The voltage follower (SF) used in (Bourdel et al., 2007) was ultimately replaced by a common source (CS) circuit with a resistive load. Indeed, even though the SF circuit offers an output impedance of $r_0 = 1/g_m$ over a very wide bandwidth (allowing it to perform "active" matching, coupling it to the CS buffering circuit (Mf3/Mf5 and Mf4/Mf6) leads to a total gain (CS plus SF) of significantly less than unity (Razavi, 2001). Furthermore, the DC current required by the output stage (7 mA) to achieve $1/g_m$ close to 50 Ω degrades the consumption performance.

Lastly, the measurements of this structure, given in Fig. 15, show an amplitude of 160 mV_{pp} (200 mV_{pp} allowing for the 2 dB loss in the measuring cable) for pulses meeting the FCC mask. These voltage levels are obtained using a modest technology (0.13 μm CMOS), without the use of inductors, and for signals with a 10 dB bandwidth of 3.5 GHz, which constitutes a good performance. However, these levels are still low and do not make it possible to achieve the ranges necessary for the intended applications. Hence other structures need to be studied in order to get over this limit.

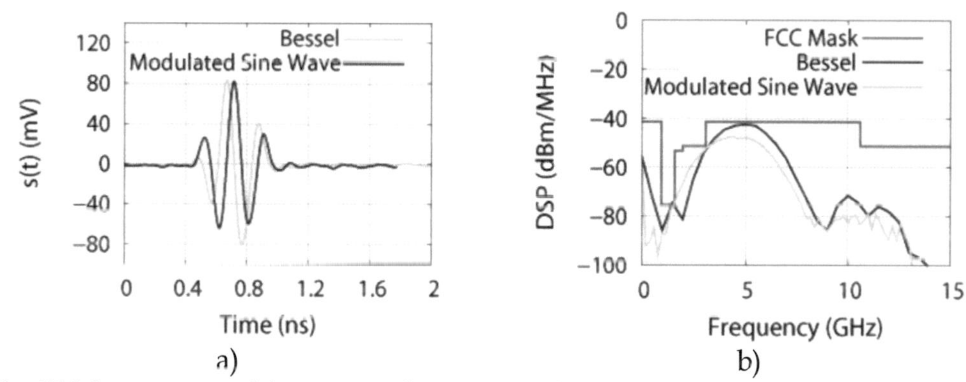

Fig. 15. Measurement of the various elementary pulses a) and their spectrum b).

The circuit's total consumption is 38.4 mW @ 100 MHz, while the consumption per pulse during the pulse time (achievable assuming the use of power management) is 72 pJ. This performance is lower than that of the non-programmable structure. However the area occupied is very small (0.06 mm²) as no inductors are used and the programming ability offers the possibility of compensating for PVT variations or transmission distortion. This shows the great potential of this approach if the consumption bottleneck is overcame.

5. Conclusion

In this chapter, several aspects relating to the generation of UWB pulse signals have been addressed. The bibliographic study presented at the beginning of this chapter shows the advantages and limitations of the various techniques that are mainly being used. It also shows the significant effort put in to reducing the consumption of the generators and their great potential in terms of power saving, but also the limitations imposed by the technologies on the pulse amplitude and programming.

The standards appear to have a considerable effect on transmitter design. They have a high incidence not only on the spectrum of the transmitted pulse, but also on the modulation, the data rate, and the amplitude of the transmitted signal. Especially, understanding the relationship between the data rate and pulse amplitude enables the designer to best select the modulation required for an application, as well as to best size the generator.

Substantial research effort has recently been devoted to optimizing consumption and pulse amplitude in order to meet the requirements of low-cost and low-power applications. In this context, the generation technique based on exciting an integrated filter shows a great deal of potential. This technique makes it possible to produce pulse generators with the lowest dynamic consumption quoted in the literature to date for output amplitudes over 1 V, also giving them the best dynamic efficiency (Bourdel et al., 2009) (Bourdel et al., 2010).

In the field of programmable generators, research efforts have recently been begun with the aim of producing generators able to generate different pulse shapes, at high amplitudes, and occupying a limited area of silicon. Pulse programming needs to make it possible to address several frequency bands, as well as to compensate for PVT variations. An initial study based on pulse synthesis shows the feasibility making fully-programmable generator that consumes very small silicon area.

6. References

Rui Xu; Jin, Y.; Nguyen, C.; (2006). Power-efficient switching-based CMOS UWB transmitters for UWB communications and Radar systems. *Microwave Theory and Techniques, IEEE Transactions on*, Volume 54, Issue 8, Aug. 2006 Page(s): 3271–3277.

Wentzloff, D.D.; Chandrakasan, A.P. (2006). *Gaussian pulse Generators for subbanded ultra-wideband transmitters;* Microwave Theory and Techniques, IEEE Transactions on; Volume 54, Issue 4, Part 2, June 2006 Page(s): 1647–1655.

Datta, P.K.; Xi Fan; Fischer, G. (2007). *A Transceiver Front-End for Ultra-Wide-Band Application;* Circuits and Systems II: Express Briefs, IEEE Transactions on; Volume 54, Issue 4, April 2007 Page(s): 362–366.

Phan, A. T.; Lee, J.; Krizhanovskii, V.; Le, Q.; Han, S.-K.; Lee, S.-G. (2008). *Energy-Efficient Low-Complexity CMOS Pulse Generator for Multiband UWB Impulse Radio;* Circuits and Systems I: Regular Papers, IEEE Transactions on; Volume 55, Issue 11, Dec. 2008 Page(s): 3552–3563.

Barras, D.; Ellinger, F.; Jackel, H.; Hirt, W.(2006). *Low-power ultra-wideband wavelets generator with fast start-up circuit;* Microwave Theory and Techniques, IEEE Transactions on; Volume 54, Issue 5, May 2006 Page(s): 2138–2145.

Sanghoon Sim; Dong-Wook Kim; Songcheol Hong. (2009). *A CMOS UWB Pulse Generator for 6–10 GHz Applications,* Microwave and Wireless Components Letters, IEEE; Volume 19, Issue 2, Feb. 2009 Page(s): 83–85.

Lee, J.; Park, Y. J.; Kim, M.; Yoon, C.; Kim, J.; Kim, K. H. (2008). *System On Package Ultra-Wideband transmitter using CMOS impulse generator;* Microwave Theory and Techniques, IEEE Transactions on; Volume 54, Issue 4, Apr. 2008 Page(s): 1667-1673.

S. Bourdel, J. Gaubert, O. Fourquin, R. Vauche, and N. Dehaese, (2009). *CMOS UWB Pulse Generator Co-Designed with Package Transition,* IEEE Radio Frequency Integrated Circuits (RFIC) Symposium 2009, Publication Year: 2009 , Page(s): 539 - 542.

Bourdel, S.; Gaubert, J.; Battista, M.; Bachelet, Y.; Bas, G. (2007). *CMOS UWB transceiver for Impulse Radio;* Ultra-Wideband, 2007. ICUWB 2007. IEEE International Conference on 24–26 Sept. 2007 Page(s): 188–193.

Smaini, L.; Tinella, C.; Helal, D.; Stoecklin, C.; Chabert, L.; Devaucelle, C.; Cattenoz, R.; Rinaldi, N.; Belot, D. (2006). *Single-chip CMOS pulse generator for UWB systems;* Solid-State Circuits, IEEE Journal of; Volume 41, Issue 7, July 2006 Page(s): 1551-1561.

Wentzloff, D.D.; Chandrakasan, A.P. (2007). *A 47 pJ/pulse 3.1-to-5 GHz All-Digital UWB Transmitter in 90 nm CMOS;* Solid-State Circuits Conference, 2007. ISSCC 2007. Digest of Technical Papers. IEEE International; 11–15 Feb. 2007 Page(s): 118–591.

H. Kim, D. Park, and Y. Joo, (2004). *All-Digital Low-Power CMOS Pulse Generator for UWB system,* Electronic Letters, vol. 40, November 2004. pp no. 24, 25

Kim, H.; Joo, Y.; Jung, S. (2006). *A Tunable CMOS UWB Pulse Generator;* Ultra-Wideband, The 2006 IEEE 2006 International Conference on, 24–27 Sept. 2006 Page(s): 109–112.

Hyunseok Kim; Youngjoong Joo; Sungyong Jung. (2005). *Digitally controllable bi-phase CMOS UWB pulse generator;* Ultra-Wideband, 2005. ICUWB 2005. 2005 IEEE International Conference on; 5-8 Sept. 2005 Page(s): 442 445

S. Bourdel, Y. Bachelet, J. Gaubert, M. Battista, M. Egels, N. Dehaese, (2007). *Low-Cost CMOS Pulse Generator for UWB Systems,* Electronic Letters, vol. 43, issue 25, pp. 1425–1427, 6 December 2007.

Demirkan, M.; Spencer, R.R. (2008). *A 1.8 Gpulses/s UWB Transmitter in 90 nm CMOS;* Solid-State Circuits Conference, 2008. ISSCC 2008. Digest of Technical Papers. IEEE International; 3–7 Feb. 2008 Page(s): 116–600

Norimatsu, T.; Fujiwara, R.; Kokubo, M.; Miyazaki, M., Maeki, A.; Ogata, Y.; Kobayashi, S.; Koshizuka, N.; Sakamura, K. (2007). *A UWB-IR Transmitter With Digitally Controlled Pulse Generator;* Solid-State Circuits, IEEE Journal of; Volume 42, Issue 6, June 2007 Page(s): 1300–1309

R. Vauché, S. Bourdel, N. Dehaese, O. Fourquin, J. Gaubert; (2009). *Fully Tunable UWB Pulse Generator with Zero DC Power Consumption;* ICUWB 2009. IEEE International Conference on; Publication Year: 2009 , Page(s): 418 - 422

Cubillo, J. R.; Gaubert, J.; Bourdel, S.; Barthelemy, H. (2008). *RF Low-Pass Design Guiding Rules to Improve PCB to Die Transition Applied to Different Types of Low-Cost Packages;* Advanced Packaging, IEEE Transactions on; Volume 31, Issue 3, Aug. 2008 Page(s): 527–535

Bachelet, Y.; Bourdel, S.; Gaubert, J.; Bas, G.; Chalopin, H. (2006). *Fully integrated CMOS UWB pulse generator,* Electronics Letters, Volume 42, Issue 22, Oct. 26 2006, Page(s): 1277–1278

Jia-Sheng Hong, M.J. Lancaster; (2001). *Microstrip Filters for RF/Microwave Application,* Wiley-Interscience Publication.

Behzad Razavi (2001) "Design of CMOS Integated Circuit" McGrawHill pub.

S. Bourdel, Y. Bachelet, J. Gaubert, R. Vauché, O. Fourquin, N. Dehaese, and H. Barthelemy; (2010). *A 9 pJ/Pulse 1.42 Vpp OOK CMOS UWB Pulse Generator for the 3.1–10.6 GHz FCC Band* Microwave Theory and Techniques, IEEE Transaction on; Volume: 58 , Issue: 1, Publication Year: 2010 , Page(s): 65 - 73.

Jeongwoo Han; Cam Nguyen. (2004). *Ultra-wideband electronically tunable pulse generators;* Microwave and Wireless Components Letters, IEEE; Volume 14, Issue 3, March 2004 Page(s): 112–114.

9

Ultra wideband oscillators

Dr. Abdolreza Nabavi
Associate Professor
Faculty of Electrical and Computer Engineering
Tarbiat Modares University
Tehran, Iran, 14115-143

1. Ultra Wideband Oscillators

1.1 Introduction

Ultra wideband (UWB) wireless technology has promoted designing devices covering wide bandwidth over several gigahertz. Among them are UWB oscillators that should achieve very wide tuning range along with low phase noise performance.

An effective solution to this has been to use multiple narrowband VCOs, each covering a portion of the required range. This solution requires high cost and increased design complexity. Alternatively, varactors, switched capacitors, variable inductors, and tunable active inductors are proposed to extend the tuning range of VCOs. However, there are several challenges in realizing integrated VCOs with these techniques.

This chapter deals with the analysis and design of integrated oscillator circuits, with emphasis on Ultra Wideband (UWB) application. First, VCO fundamentals are introduced and the impacts of wideband operation on VCO performance are discussed. After that, the general guidelines in doing layout for active and passive devices will be presented. Focus will be placed on the optimum RF performance of components. Then, the design considerations along with various tuning methods for wideband oscillation will be introduced. In each case, the achieved tuning range realized through these methods is mentioned. Finally, the design and implementation of two Ultra wideband (UWB) VCOs are described, with the experimental results in a 0.18-µm CMOS technology.

1.2 Specification of Oscillator Properties

The most critical performance specification for an oscillator is its spectral purity, usually characterized by phase noise. In a receiver, the phase noise of the local oscillator (LO) degrades the received signal-to-noise ratio (SNR) of the desired signal at IF by a process often referred to as reciprocal mixing. This limits the ability to detect a weak signal in the presence of a strong signal in an adjacent channel. Phase noise also corrupts the information present in phase-modulated signals by effectively rotating the symbol constellation, degrading the bit error rate (BER) of communication systems. In a transmitter, LO phase noise is modulated onto the desired signal and results in energy being transmitted outside of the desired band.

Since many wireless transceivers are battery-powered, it is required to minimize the power consumption in oscillator. There is a trade-off between phase noise and power consumption until the voltage swing is maximized. Beyond this swing level, raising the current will increase the phase noise, and will waste power.

1.3 Single Transistor Oscillator

Colpitts and Hartley oscillators are two most popular single transistor topologies, as illustrated in Figure 1. The Colpitts oscillator has a capacitively tapped resonator, with a positive feedback provided by an active device.
In Hartley oscillator, the LC network has two inductors and one capacitance. The NMOS amplifier is connected in a common gate configuration. The capacitance C3 has one port connected to L1 and the other port connected to L2. There is no way to replace this capacitance with the load capacitance.

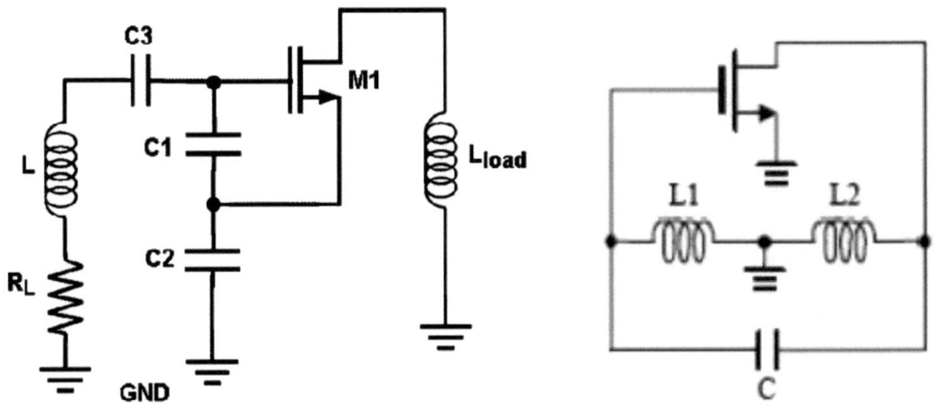

(a) *(b)*
Fig. 1. AC equivalent circuit a) Colpitts VCO with a load inductor **b)** Hartley Oscillator

1.4 Differential Oscillators

The single-switch VCO (SS-VCO) and the double-switch VCO (DS-VCO) are two popular topologies used in the design of integrated oscillators. Figure 2 shows the simplified circuit schematic of both topologies. The transconductance in both circuits, which is set by the bias condition and the dimensions of the cross-coupled pair transistors, provides a negative resistance to compensate the losses in the resonator.
To control the negative resistance and hence set the oscillation amplitude, a tail current source is employed (transistor M3 in Fig. 2(a) and (b)). The presence of the tail current source, which reduces the oscillation headroom, affects the up-conversion of 1/f and thermal noise to phase noise as well [1].
In the SS-VCO two integrated inductors or a single center-tapped differential inductor may be employed, while a single center-tapped can be used in the DS-VCO. The parasitic capacitances associated with the transconductor cell are larger in the DS-VCO than in the SS-VCO. The parasitic capacitances reduce both the tuning range and the maximum oscillation frequency. The oscillation amplitude of the DS-VCO, for identical resonators and equal power consumption, is anticipated to be twice as large as in the SS-VCO [2]. Thus, DS-

VCO exhibits better phase noise performance compared to the SS-VCO. However, the former requires a larger supply voltage than the latter, due to the additional stacking of the PMOS pair.

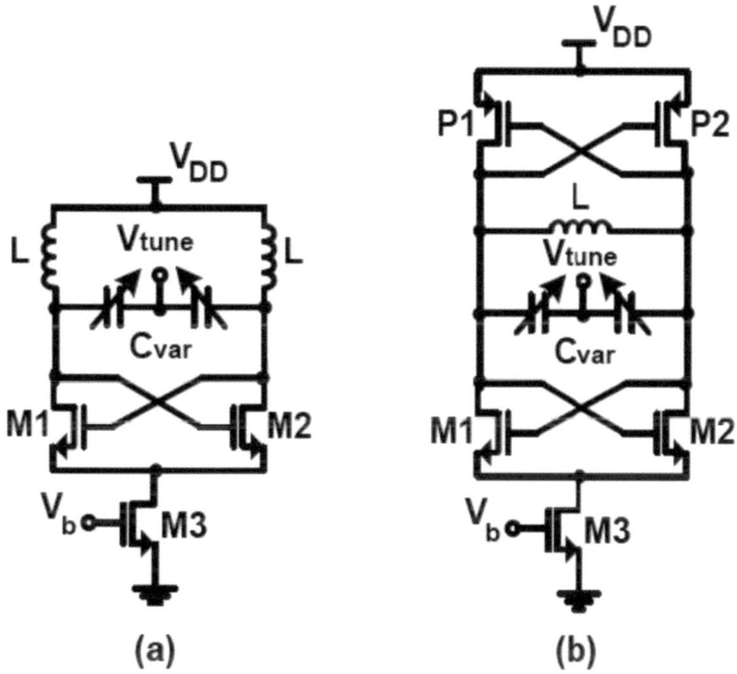

Fig. 2. Simplified circuits schematic of (a) the SS-VCO and (b) the DS-VCO.

1.5 Phase Noise

The most critical performance specification for an oscillator is its spectral purity. In any practical oscillator, the spectrum has power distributed around the desired oscillation frequency ω_0, known as *phase noise,* in addition to power located at harmonic frequencies, as shown in Figure 3.

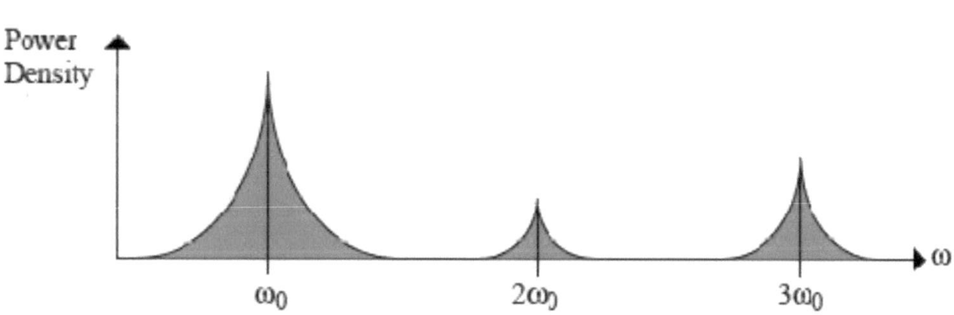

Fig. 3. Practical oscillator spectrum.

An oscillator can usually either be viewed as a single two-port feedback circuit, or as two one-port circuits connected together. Consider the linear feedback model depicted in Figure 4.

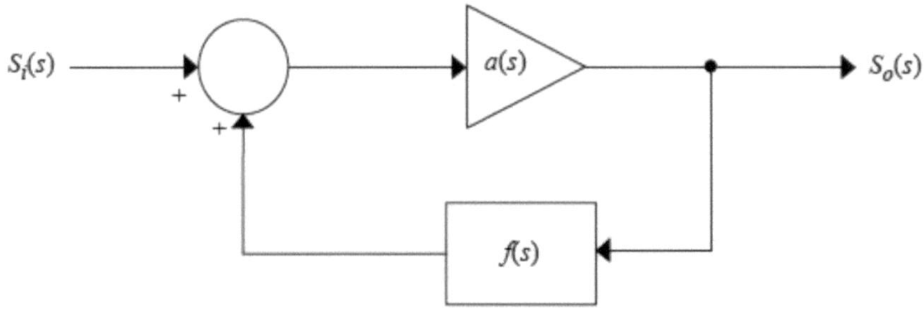

Fig. 4. Basic Oscillator feedback model

The overall transfer function from input to output is given by

$$\frac{S_o(s)}{S_i(s)} = \frac{a(s)}{1 - a(s)f(s)} \tag{1}$$

This system can have a non-zero output without any input as long as the quantity *a(s)f(s)*, i.e. the *loop gain*, is one and the phase shift around the loop is zero.
However, an initial loop gain magnitude greater than one is typically designed and then nonlinearities in the amplifier will reduce the magnitude to exactly one in steady-state operation.
Assuming *a(s)* has zero phase shift, we can implement *f(s)* as a resonator, realized with a parallel *LC* tank, having zero phase shift at the desired oscillation frequency.

Another way to view an oscillator is to break it up into two one-port networks, an active circuit and a resonator, as depicted in Figure 5. When the equivalent parallel resistance R_T of the resonator is exactly balanced by a negative resistance $-R_a$ of the active circuit, the negative resistance compensates the losses in the resonator and steady-state oscillation is achieved.

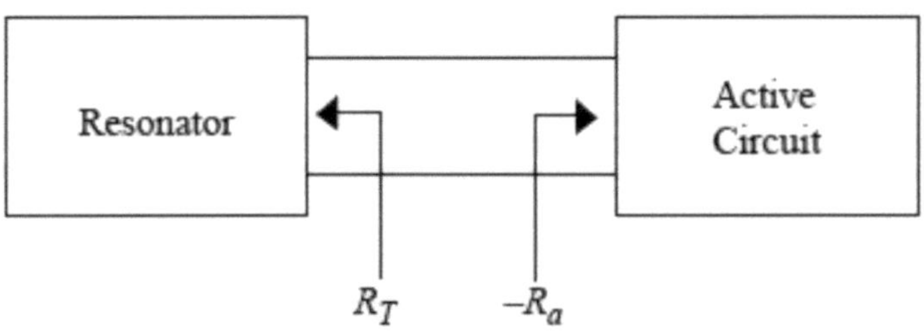

Fig. 5. Two One-port networks view of an oscillator.

1.5.1 One-Port View of Phase Noise

Figure 6 shows an equivalent one-port model of an *LC* oscillator, in which $i_n(\omega)$ denotes all noise sources in the circuit. Suppose the mean square noise current density is $\overline{i_n^2}/\Delta\omega$.

Assuming linear time-invariant behavior, total noise power density $P_n(\omega)/\Delta\omega$ can be calculated as [1]:

$$\frac{P_n(\omega)}{\Delta(\omega)} = \frac{\bar{i}_n^2}{\Delta(\omega)} \cdot |Z(\omega)| \tag{2}$$

where, $|Z(\omega)|$ is the tank's magnitude response.

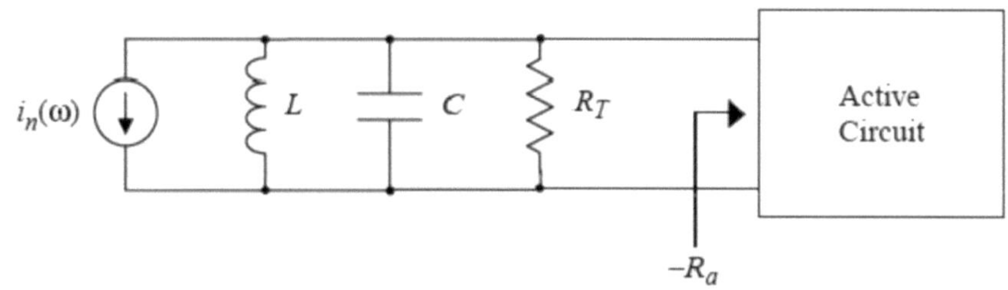

Fig. 6. One-port model of an LC oscillator.

Two ways to decrease phase noise are suggested by (2). First, we should use as few active devices as possible to minimize the number of noise sources in the oscillator. Second, the tank's magnitude response $|Z(\omega)|$ should be made as narrow as possible, i.e. a high quality factor (Q) should be employed for the LC-tank.

1.5.2 Two-Port View of Phase Noise

Returning to the two-port model shown in Figure 4, we now consider *f(s)* to be a parallel RLC tank as shown in Figure 7(a). The magnitude and phase responses of such a network are given in Figure 7 (b). As discussed before, we need zero degrees net phase shift around the feedback loop (any integer multiple of 360 degrees). Since noise sources in the oscillator circuit will cause temporary phase shifts in the feedback loop, the instantaneous oscillation frequency will be changing such that the tank produces a compensating phase shift, keeping the total phase shift around the loop equal to zero. Thus, phase noise can also be viewed as short-term instability in the frequency of oscillation [3].

The phase noise denoted by L{Δω}is defined as

$$L\{\Delta\omega\} = 10.\log\left[\frac{P_{1HZ}(\omega_0 + \Delta\omega)}{P_s}\right] \tag{3}$$

where, $P_{1Hz}(\omega_0 + \Delta\omega)$ represents the single sideband power measured in a 1-Hz bandwidth and located at a frequency offset Δω from the oscillation frequency ω_0. P_s represents the total signal power. A typical plot of L{Δω}is shown in Figure 8. Note the existence of regions of various slopes, as discussed in [1].

As mentioned above, to reduce the phase noise the magnitude response of the tank should be as sharp as possible, i.e. it should have a very narrow bandwidth or simply a high quality factor Q.

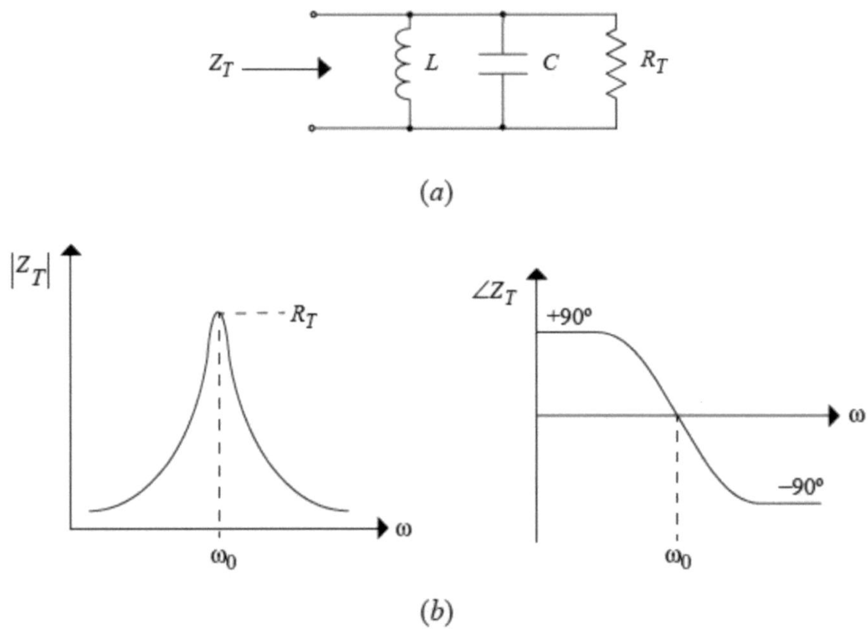

Fig. 7. (*a*) Parallel RLC tank. (*b*) Magnitude and phase response.

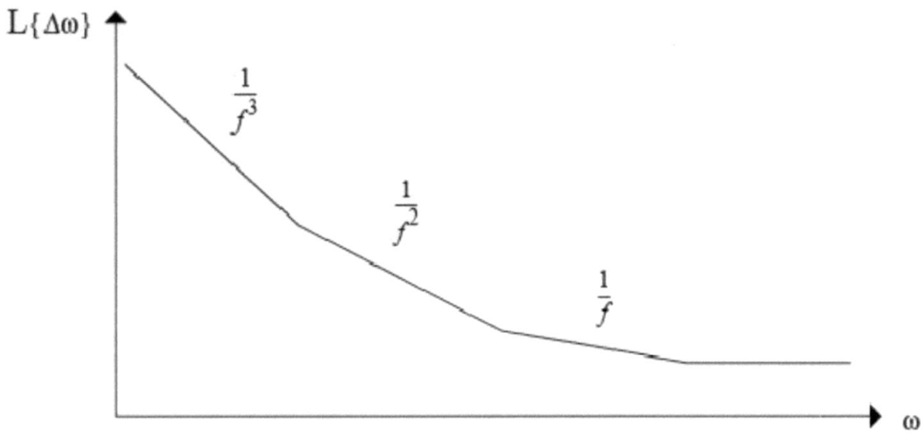

Fig. 8. General appearance of single-sideband phase noise.

I.5 Quality Factor

LC tanks, often referred as *LC* resonators, are represented as series or parallel *RLC* networks, since practical *LC* tanks contain additional resistive components. At resonance frequency, $\omega_0 = 1/\sqrt{LC}$, the tank impedance is purely resistive, and the phase of the impedance response is exactly zero. At frequencies below (above) resonance, the tank impedance of the parallel RLC network is mainly inductive (capacitive). For series RLC networks, this scenario is exactly opposite.

The resonator's quality factor, Q, is generally defined as:

$$Q = \omega.\frac{Energy\ stored}{Average\ power\ dissipated} \tag{4}$$

The quality factor, which indicates the ability of the tank to retain energy, often determines the phase noise performance of LC VCOs. Also, Q indicates the steepness of the impedance near ω_0 or the sharpness of the peak impedance at ω_0. Therefore, Q can also be described by:

$$Q = \frac{\omega_0}{\Delta\omega_{-3dB}} \tag{5}$$

where, $\Delta\omega_{-3dB}$ is the −3dB bandwidth of the impedance response. Clearly, a larger Q results in a higher rejection of spectral energy away from the resonant frequency, leading to more purity of the oscillator output spectrum.

At resonance, the Q of the RLC networks is given by:

$$Q = \frac{R}{\omega_0 L} = \omega_0 RC \qquad (parallel\ RLC) \tag{6}$$

$$Q = \frac{\omega_0 L}{R} = \frac{1}{\omega_0 RC} \qquad (series\ RLC) \tag{7}$$

where, the dual nature of series and parallel RLC networks is apparent.

In wide-band VCOs, the equivalent tank impedance changes considerably along the tuning range. Figure 9 shows the simulated Q of a standard available on-chip inductor in a 0.18µm CMOS technology [2]. It is observed that the Q is linearly increased with the operation frequency. Aiming for a wideband VCO operating between 3- 6GHz, it is of interest to have the maximum Q at the highest frequencies, since the phase noise increases with frequency and may be reduced with the gain in Q. However, the variations in Q cause unwanted effects on the output amplitude. This issue will be explored in more detail in section 1.7.3.3.

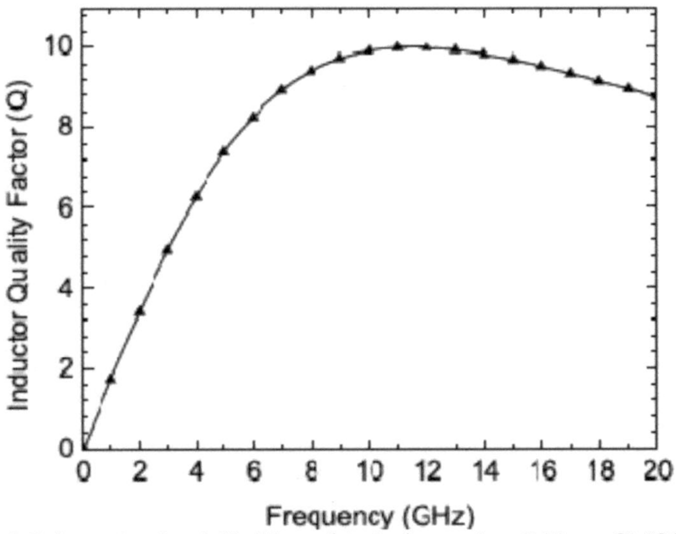

Fig. 9. Simulated Q for a circular 0.45nH on-chip inductor in a 0.18μm CMOS process [2].

1.6 Figure of Merit

Most oscillator designers usually report a figure of merit (FoM) value for their specific design. The most commonly used FoM in the RF community is the power-frequency-tuning-normalized (PFTN) figure of merit (FOM), as defined in [4, 6]:

$$FoM = 10.\,log\left(\frac{KT}{P}\left(\frac{\omega_{o,max}-\omega_{o,min}}{\Delta\omega}\right)\right) - L\{\Delta\omega\} \tag{8}$$

where, $\Delta\omega$ is the frequency offset from the carrier frequency ω_0, P is the power consumed by the VCO core, and $L\{\Delta\omega\}$ is the phase noise measured at an offset $\Delta\omega$ from the carrier. Also, $\omega_{0,max}$ and $\omega_{0,min}$ denote the high-side and the low-side frequencies of the tuning range, respectively.

1.7 Layout of Active and Passive Components

In CMOS VCO circuits, finding the optimal layout for both the passive and active devices is critical to achieving the best possible performance. One reason is the increasing impact of the parasitics in the device layout with technology scaling. Therefore, a well-optimized layout, which minimizes the parasitics and the noise sources, is very important. This section is devoted to these issues, including the integration of spiral inductors with high quality factor, active inductors, capacitors, varactor, resistors, and transistors for realizing the ultimate goal of VCO design.

1.7.1 Resistors

Figures of merit for resistors are sheet resistance, tolerance, parasitic capacitance, and voltage and temperature coefficients. In CMOS technology, resistors can be formed from the implanted well, the gate polysilicon, the source/drain active areas, and metal.

Polysilicon resistors are often used in integrated circuits for their low dependence on voltage and temperature. A low-doped p-type polysilicon resistor is used for applications

requiring high resistance. Despite its good parasitic capacitance, this resistor exhibits a 25% tolerance [8]. On the other hand, highly doped p-type polysilicon resistors are preferred in most cases because of their good matching and low parasitic.
Non-salicide high resistance poly has a sheet resistance between 800 - 1200 ohm/square. Non- salicide P+ (N+) poly resistance has a sheet resistance of 280-455 (95-180) ohm/ square. These non-salicide poly resistors can be used for high-frequency circuits. Salicide P+/N+ poly resistance has a sheet resistance of 2-15 ohm/ square, with small parasitic capacitance.

Diffusion resistors are similar to poly in terms of parasitic capacitance and voltage coefficient. They are typically controlled to a 10% tolerance. Salicide P+/N+ diffusion resistance has a sheet resistance of 2-15 ohm/ square, with large parasitic. Non- salicide P+ (N+) diffusion has a sheet resistance of 110 -190 (60 -100) ohm/ square. Non-salicide diffusion resistors are only suitable for low-frequency circuits, e.g. they are often used for ESD protection.

Well resistors have a large sheet resistance of 300 to 500 ohm/square, with large parasitic capacitance. Because of their strong dependence on voltage, they are usually used to feed a DC bias voltage.

Another high-performance resistor is formed of a thin metal film, further above the substrate in the wiring levels [9]. It has a sheet resistance of 0.025 to 0.115 ohm/square, with several attractive features such as low tolerance, low variation with voltage, and low parasitic.

1.7.2 Capacitors

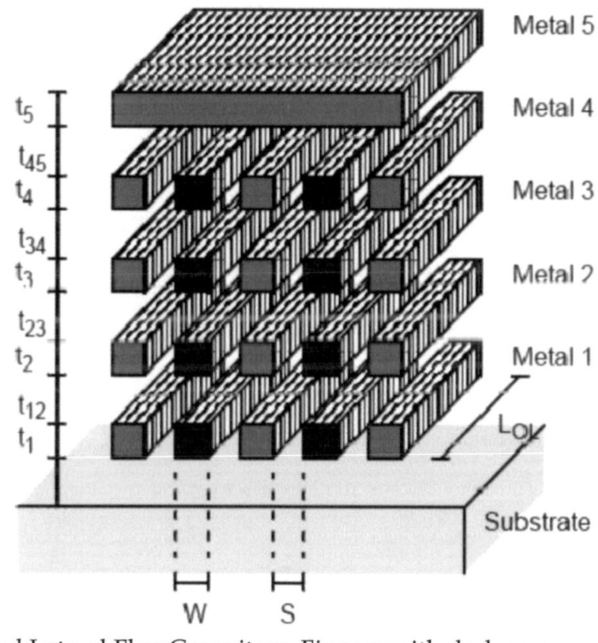

Fig. 10. Four Stacked Lateral Flux Capacitors. Fingers with dark cross-sections are connected to one port. The remaining fingers are connected to the other port [10].

Capacitors can be realized in any IC process using parallel plates from any two different layers (see Figure 10). Much larger capacitance per unit area can be obtained using the polysilicon layer as one or both of the capacitor plates. Nevertheless, a potential problem is that parasitic capacitance from the poly to the substrate may affect the circuit performance.
To achieve large capacitance per unit area, it is common to use several sandwiched-type capacitors and connect them in parallel (Figure 11). In order to obtain two capacitors with a good matching ratio, common-centroid and dummy devices are employed. Matched capacitors should have the same perimeter-area ratio.
Capacitors with relatively high-Q can also be implemented as interdigital, i.e. two conductors on the same plane are terminated in interdigitated fingers. These are used for low capacitance applications (0.05-0.5pF). With more metal layers available in a modern technology, the density of this capacitor tends to improve.

Since polysilicon-based capacitors are lossy, metal-insulator-metal (MIM) capacitors are preferred in RF design. MIM capacitors exhibit high density (e.g. 1-2fF/μm^2) by using an ultra-thin layer of silicon nitride sandwiched along with an intermediate metal layer. Their typical Q exceeds 100 at 1GHz, with a relatively low parasitic capacitance (1% or less) [4].
MIM capacitors and Metal finger capacitors can be simply modeled by equivalent series RC networks, where R represents the series loss from the finite resistance of the metal plates.

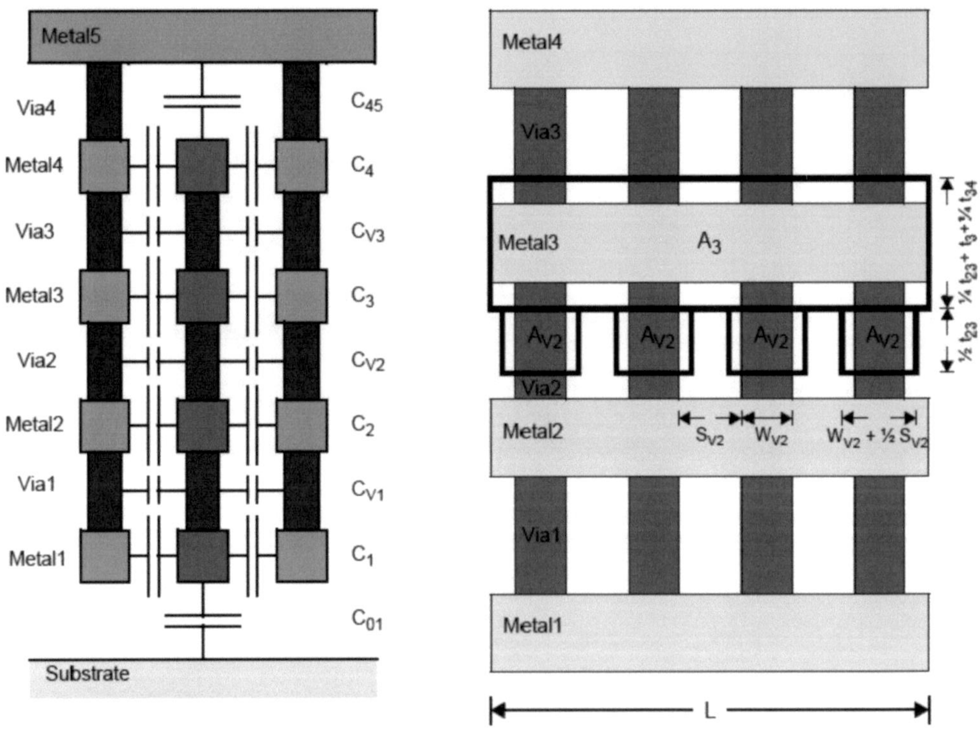

Cross-Section Side View

Fig. 11. Cross-Section of a Vertical Mesh Capacitor (left) and side view (right) [10].

1.7.3 Integrated Passive Inductors

On-chip inductor is by far the most critical component in an LC-tank oscillator, since its Q affects the phase noise performance and determines the power dissipation. As the process technology improves and the number of metal layers is increased, the quality (Q) of the passives is generally enhanced. Typical values of a standard on-chip inductor are in the range of a few nH with a Q ranging from 2-10 (for frequencies below 6GHz), depending on the technology and operating frequency [2].

On-chip inductors often need large loops and they have an area inefficient structure, compared to capacitors and resistors. However, planar inductors are widely implemented due to their flat Q and the ease of fabrication in standard processes. Typical on-chip spiral inductor structures are shown in Figure 12, which consist of multiple squares, octagonal, or circular spiraling turns forming its coils [4].

Making an inductor wider decreases the series resistance, and hence has a positive effect on Q at a particular frequency to a certain extent [12]. However, this would increase the coil capacitance and further reduce the resonant frequency. The maximal width of the metal (usually it is about 15-30 μm) is usually established using an optimization for resonance frequency or Q-factor.

The spiral is generally implemented in the topmost available metal layer because of its larger thickness than lower metal layers which helps reduce resistive losses. Also due to lower parasitic capacitance to the substrate, top metal layers give rise to higher self-resonance frequency. Note that the use of lower metal layers (closer to the substrate) brings down the self-resonance of the inductor. Sometimes two or more levels are connected in parallel to reduce resistance. Again, this technique effectively brings the coil closer to the substrate, which lowers its self-resonance.

The outer diameter of the inductor depends on how wide the inductor wire is, which in turn determines the area the inductor covers. For a given inductor area, one can fill in more turns until the entire space is occupied. Nevertheless, this is not recommended because of loss constraints and the fact that inner turns only slightly increase the overall inductance. Thus, spiral inductors are rarely filled to their maximum number of turns, and increasing the inductance is typically achieved by increasing the coil radius.

The inductance of a spiral is a complicated function of its geometry, and accurate computations require the use of field solvers. However, an approximate estimate, suitable for quick hand calculations as described in [12], gives the result which may deviate about 30% in comparison with field simulator results.

Square spirals offer the largest inductance per area compared to octagonal or circular spiral, whereas circular spirals is known to provide somewhat higher Q factor. The octagonal spirals are used as the next best alternative [4], since often circular geometries are not supported by many layout tools and not permitted in many technologies.

Another popular technique which provides a much more compact layout is to utilize a differential structure, as shown in Figure 13 [4], instead of using two single-ended inductors. In addition, the differential structure suppresses common- or even-mode capacitive parasitics and associated losses [14]. These benefits can also improve the self-resonance frequency and quality factor.

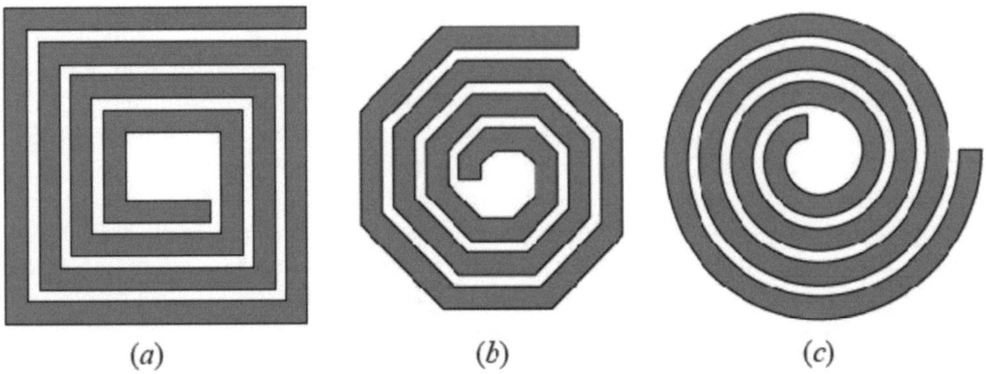

Fig. 12. Typical integrated inductors: (a) square, (b) octagonal, and (c) circular spirals [4].

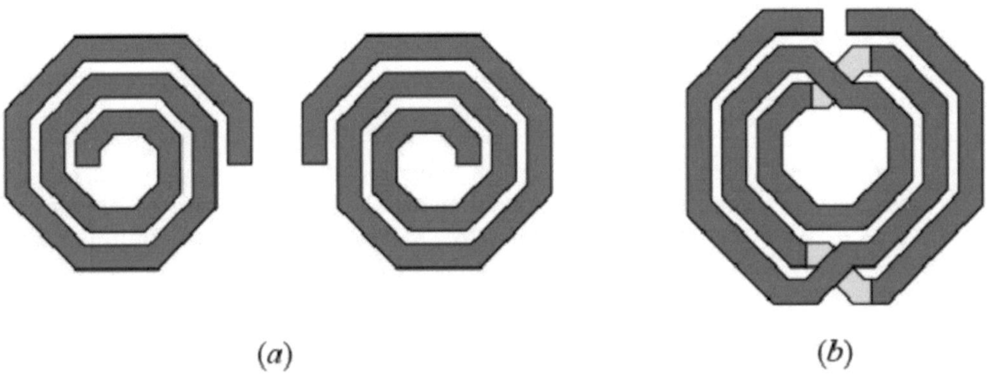

Fig. 13. A pair of single-ended inductors (a) and a differential inductor (b) with similar total inductance [4].

When two or more coils are used on the same chip, the distance between coil centers should be at least two times larger than the coil diameter for each couple of coils.

1.7.3.1 Measures for Q-enhancement

Three technological measures increasing Q are mentioned here. The first measure, which is anticipated to increase Q in two or three times, is using copper (Cu) alloys instead of aluminum (Al) alloys. The second measure is removal of the substrate under the coil (by etching or micromachining). It increases Q in addition by two or three times. The micromachined Cu inductors may have Q's as high as 50, and allow realization of bandpass filters with the insertion loss which is better than -5dB at the frequency about 6GHz.

Third measure is a pattern ground-shield, which has been shown to improve the Q of the inductor, since it reduces the capacitive coupling to the lossy substrate [13]. This technique also reduces the noise coupled from the substrate at the penalty of reduction of the self resonant frequency of the inductor.

Today, such inductors are common in standard available design kits provided by the manufacturers. However, despite these efforts, the inductor Q is still one of the main uncertain parameters in RF circuit design and in many cases the major bottleneck of entire systems.

1.7.3.2 Inductor Modeling

The area of an on-chip inductor can span up to hundreds of µm across and does not scale down with the technology [2]. Aside from their large physical dimensions, integrated inductors are usually described by simple lumped equivalent networks.

Figure 14 (a) shows a lumped π-model for an integrated inductor. L_s describes the series inductance and R_s represents the series resistance of the metal layer. C_p models the interwinding capacitance between the traces. In silicon technology the fairly conductive substrate is close to the spiral, which is essentially creating a parallel plate capacitor (C_{ox}) that resonates with the inductor. R_{sub} model the resistive path in the substrate which also reduces the Q of the inductor. C_{sub} models the capacitive coupling from metal to substrate which reduces the resonant frequency of the inductor.

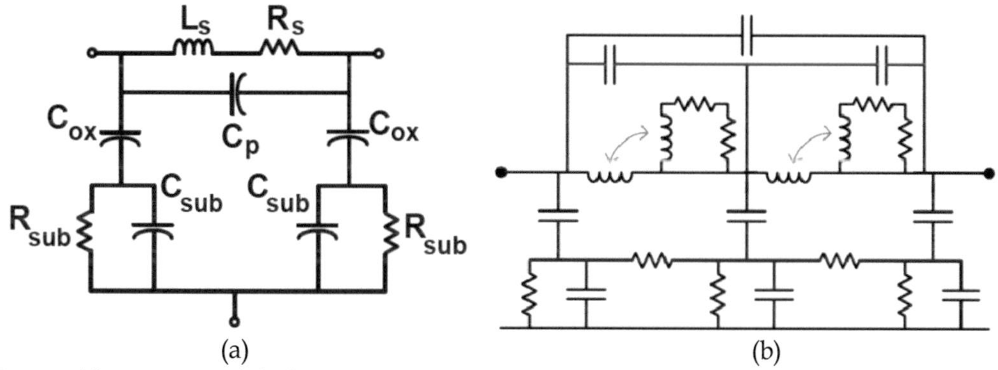

Fig. 14. (a) Basic π-model of an integrated inductor (b) wideband lumped equivalent.

The π-equivalent network is a narrowband model only valid in the close vicinity of that particular frequency and is not suitable in wideband designs [4].

The network shown in Figure 14 (b) approximates the frequency dependence of the most important characteristics of the coil using an expanded lumped equivalent network. As a result, its validity holds over a much wider frequency range and it is better suited for wideband design analysis [4].

1.7.3.3 Effect of frequency

The Q value of ideal inductors is improved with the increase in frequency. This is however not the case for on-chip inductors because the parasitic capacitance and substrate losses show their significance at higher frequencies [12].

The series dc resistance of the inductor is the dominant loss contributor at low frequencies (<1GHz). At higher frequencies, the series resistance rises considerably, due to skin and proximity effects. The skin effect forces the current in the inductor to flow on the outside of the spiral. This makes the inner turns of the spiral less effective than the outer turns and the effective series resistance is increased.

Proximity effects due to fields from adjacent turns result in a similar frequency-dependent non-uniform current distribution and corresponding loss increase. Also, the flow of currents in the substrate translates to additional losses which are a strong function of the substrate resistivity and become significant as frequency increases.

As a result, Q initially rises linearly with frequency since the loss is dominated by the coil's dc series resistance. Eventually, skin and proximity effects as well as substrate losses become dominant. Thus, Q gradually peaks to a maximal value, and beyond which it experiences a fast decline as frequency approaches the coil's self-resonance. Note that the impact of the above effects on the inductor performance is very complicated, and therefore, software tools must be used for its performance optimization.

1.7.4 Active Inductor Design

Active inductors may often be of interest in RF circuits, since passive inductors are not economical in terms of the fabrication technology and die area. An active inductor can be realized by connecting two transconductors with resistive feedback (R_f), as shown in Figure 15 (a) [15-18]. This realization is based on the gyrator-C topology (Figure 15(b)). In Figure 15(a), transistor M2 is employed to reduce the output conductance (g_{ds}), as a result of which the inductance, quality factor, and frequency tuning range are improved. Also, the feedback resistance R_f between M_1 and M_3 significantly increases the inductance [16]. The resistance (R_f) is usually implemented by a passive poly layer.

Due to low-inductance value and narrow frequency range of the above topology, improved cascode structure employing active resistors in the feedback line is also proposed [19]. The fully tunable active inductor (TAI) and its equivalent circuit model are shown in Figure 16(a) and Figure 16(b), respectively. This active inductor exploits a tunable feedback resistance, implemented by connecting the resistor (R_f) in parallel with a transistor. The gate-source voltage (V_{tune}) in this transistor controls the total effective resistance (R_{eff}). This reduces the output conductance and improves the quality factor.

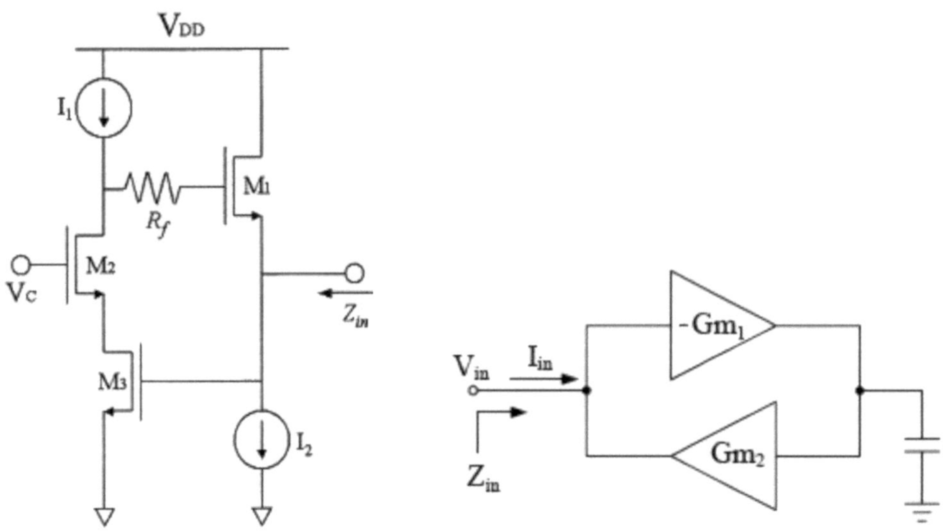

Fig. 15. (a) Schematic of cascode-grounded active inductor with a feedback resistance (b) Gyrator topology

The equivalent capacitance, inductance, and resistors are [19]:

$$C_{eq} = C_{gs3} \tag{9}$$

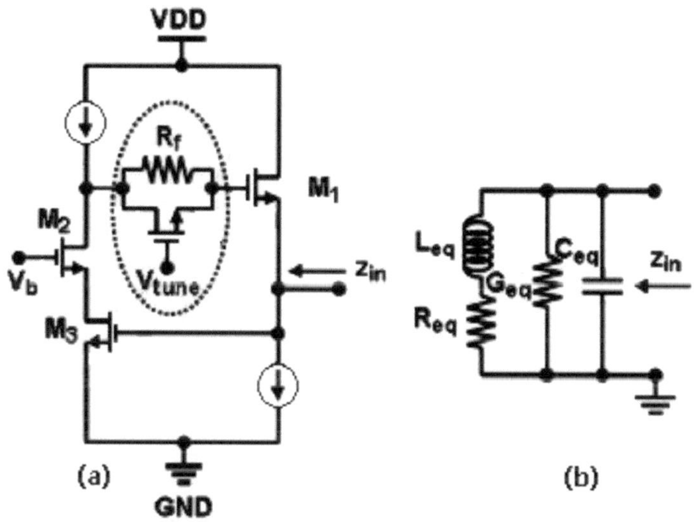

Fig. 16. (a) TAI topology (b) Equivalent circuit model of active inductor

$$L_{eq} = \frac{g_{m1}g_{m2}C_{gs1} + \omega^2 C_{gs1}^2 C_{gs2}(R_f g_{ds2} + 1)}{g_{m1}^2 g_{m3} g_{m3} + \omega^2 g_{m2} g_{m3} C_{gs1}^2} \tag{10}$$

$$R_{eq} = \frac{g_{m1}g_{ds2}g_{ds3} + \omega^2\left[g_{m2}C_{gs1}^2 - g_{m1}C_{gs1}C_{gs2}(R_f g_{ds2} + 1)\right]}{g_{m1}^2 g_{m2} g_{m3} + \omega^2 g_{m2} g_{m3} C_{gs1}^2} \tag{11}$$

$$G_{eq} = \frac{2g_{ds2} + R_f g_{ds2}^2}{R_f g_{ds2} + 1} \tag{12}$$

In (12), the effect of feedback resistor is shown by $(R_f g_{ds2} + 1)$, which is designed for a value greater than unity. Decreasing R_{eq} by the help of R_f results in an increase in L_{eq}. The quality factor and the input impedance of TAI can be obtained from [15]:

$$Q = \left(\frac{\omega L_{eq}}{R_{eq}} \right) \left[\frac{1 - (R_{eq}^2 C_{eq} / L_{eq}) - \omega^2 L_{eq} C_{eq}}{1 + R_{eq} G_{eq} \{1 + (\omega L_{eq} / R_{eq})^2\}} \right] \quad (13)$$

$$z_{in} = \left[\frac{R_{eq} + j\omega L_{eq}}{(1 + R_{eq} G_{eq} - \omega^2 L_{eq} C_{eq}) + j\omega (R_{eq} C_{eq} + L_{eq} G_{eq})} \right] \quad (14)$$

Clearly, with decreasing R_{eq}, the quality factor is improved.
Note that in conventional TAI topology, V_b=constant (see Figure 16 (a)). As can be seen from equations (10), (11), and (13), active resistor has direct effect on increasing L_{eq} and R_{eq}. However, this increase in R_{eq} will degrade the quality factor. To overcome this problem, V_b can be utilized as the extra tuning voltage to control the g_{ds} of transistor M2. Thus, the required inductance and quality factor are achieved by controlling V_{tune} and V_b simultaneously.
For further enhancement of quality factor and inductance, one can utilize the transistor M5 in parallel with feedback resistance R_f, as shown in Figure 17(b) [18]. This transistor, which operates in the cut-off region, exhibits a frequency dependent capacitance as shown in Figure 17(c).
Using a 0.13μm CMOS technology, a tunable resistance from 100Ω to 1.6 kΩ may be achieved [18] for V_{tune}=1.2V to V_{tune}=0.4V, as illustrated in Figure 17(a).

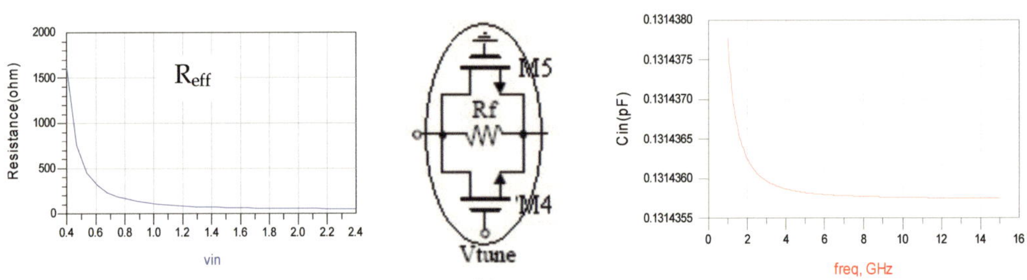

(a) (b) (c)

Fig. 17. (a) Variation of effective resistance versus tuning voltages (b) Proposed active resistance with parallel MOSFET (c) Variation of capacitance in proposed active resistance versus frequency.

The values of each component of equivalent circuit model are expressed below (Cp is equivalent capacitance of M5):

$$C_{eq} = C_{gs3} - \frac{2\omega C_p R_{eff} g_{ds2} (R_{eff} g_{ds2} + 1) - R_{eff} \omega C_p (R_{eff} g_{ds2}^2 + 2 g_{ds2})}{(R_{eff} g_{ds2} + 1)^2 + \omega^2 C_p^2 R_{eff}^2} \quad (15)$$

$$G_{eq}=\frac{2\omega^2 C_p^{\,2} R_{eff}^{\,2} g_{ds2}+\left(R_{eff}g_{ds2}+1\right)\left(R_{eff}g_{ds2}^{\,2}+2g_{ds2}\right)}{\left(R_{eff}g_{ds2}+1\right)^2+\omega^2 C_p^{\,2} R_{eff}^{\,2}} \tag{16}$$

$$R_{eq}=\frac{g_{m1}g_{ds2}g_{ds3}+\omega^2\left[g_{m2}C_{gs1}^{\,2}+\left(C_{gs1}C_{gs2}\right)\left[\frac{g_{m1}C_pC_{gs1}R_{eff}^{\,2}g_{ds2}}{1+\omega^2C_p^{\,2}R_{eff}^{\,2}}-g_{m1}\left(1+\frac{R_{eff}g_{ds2}}{1+\omega^2C_p^{\,2}R_{eff}^{\,2}}\right)\right]\right]}{g_{m1}^{\,2}g_{m2}g_{m3}+\omega^2 g_{m2}g_{m3}C_{gs1}^{\,2}} \tag{17}$$

$$L_{eq}=\frac{g_{m1}g_{m2}C_{gs1}+\omega^2\left(C_{gs1}C_{gs2}\right)\left[\frac{g_{m1}C_pR_{eff}^{\,2}g_{ds2}}{1+\omega^2C_p^{\,2}R_{eff}^{\,2}}+g_{m1}C_{gs1}\left(1+\frac{R_{eff}g_{ds2}}{1+\omega^2C_p^{\,2}R_{eff}^{\,2}}\right)\right]}{g_{m1}^{\,2}g_{m2}g_{m3}+\omega^2 g_{m2}g_{m3}C_{gs1}^{\,2}} \tag{18}$$

In order to have L_{eq} greater and R_{eq} smaller than other conventional inductors, the following relations should be satisfied.

$$C_p>\frac{-g_{ds2}}{\omega^2 C_{gs1}} \tag{19}$$

$$C_p>\frac{C_{gs1}g_{ds2}}{\omega^2} \tag{20}$$

1.7.5 Varactors

Varactors are essential elements of voltage-controlled oscillators (VCOs). The key figures of merit for varactors are tunability (C_{max}/C_{min}), CV linearity for VCO gain variation, quality factor *Q*, tolerance, and capacitance density [8].

In general, two types of varactors have been developed for the RF CMOS processes, MOS accumulation mode capacitor (MOS varactor) and CMOS diode.

CMOS diode varactors are basically reverse-biased p-n junctions which can be implemented using the available p+/n-diffusions and n- or p-wells [4]. These varactors exhibit tunability of about 1.7:1 over a 3-V range, and can be used where fine tuning of capacitance is required. Also, they provide better linearity than MOS varactors.

The MOS varactor can be realized with an *n*-channel MOSFET fabricated in an n-well. Its main advantage is the high intrinsic C_{max}/C_{min} that is much higher than that of p-n junction varactors. This provides an excellent tunability over a wide frequency range and sufficiently high Q factor. The performance of this varactor improves with technology scaling.

Also, a hyper-abrupt (HA) junction varactor has been reported in the literature with a nearly linear *C–V* tuning ratio of 3.1 and a *Q* exceeding 100 at 2 GHz [8].

It should be mentioned that amplitude variations in wideband VCOs may reduce the varactor's capacitive range (C_{max}/C_{min}) and the associated reduction in the overall tuning sensitivity [7].

1.7.6 Transistors

The optimum layout design and biasing of transistors for a voltage-controlled oscillator (VCO) is very essential, since the purity of its output spectral signal is extremely sensitive to device noise. With the reduction in supply voltage, which scales with the transistor features in CMOS technologies, this becomes challenging because of the inherent device noise increase. The appropriate condition for oscillation, for the minimum expected bias current with a reasonable safety margin under worst-case conditions, is set by proper transistor sizing. Moreover, biasing of the transistors, which is anticipated to put an oscillator on the verge of the current-limited and voltage-limited regimes, is critical to achieving the best possible performance.

1.7.6.1 Biasing

Once a MOSFET is biased near characteristic current density [20], e.g. around 0.15mA/μm for n-type transistor, the transistor exhibits a minimum noise figure NF_{MIN}. Interestingly, this property remains invariant over technology nodes, foundries, MOSFET cascodes, as well as the type of transistor. Therefore, it is reasonably expected that circuit topologies realized with combinations of n-type and p-type MOSFETs will behave similarly.

In low noise amplifier (LNA) design, it is often attractive to bias the transistor below the characteristic current density (e.g. about 50% [21]) due to negligible influence on its noise performance and in favorite of reducing the power consumption. It should be noted that in general, the circuit topology in LNA majorly impacts its total noise performance. In other words, when the device NF is minimized, the total noise of the amplifier may not be at the lowest level since the NF concept of device is not necessarily the appropriate indicator for optimizing LNA noise performance. In particular, when NF <3dB, the noise in the circuit is dominated by the thermal noise of the driving source, and reducing the noise of the device cannot have a significant impact on NF. In fact, for optimizing the noise performance in this case, the total noise level and/or signal-noise ratio are more useful.

In VCO, the mechanism of noise to phase noise conversion is very complicated. Since the phase noise is inversely proportional to the power dissipated in the resistive part of the resonant LC tank, the (tail) current through the VCO is set large enough to maximize the voltage swing at the tank. As long as the tail current is below this current level, VCO operates in the current-limited regime. Raising the tail current will cause the VCO to enter in the voltage-limited regime. In this case, further increase of the tail current will increase the phase noise. Based on the author's experience, in the current-limited regime the best phase noise performance is achieved by biasing far below the characteristic current density (e.g., 30% to 50% of this current).

1.7.6.2 Finger Layout

Given the geometry of CMOS devices in oscillator, a multifinger gate structure is the most popular approach to adopt in the layout design. The different gate layout splits induce different parasitic resistance, and the lower noise characteristics result in a lower VCO phase noise performance. When two devices share the same gate length, total gate width, and process, the flicker noise should be similar based on the intrinsic device operation. However, as shown in [22] the parasitic resistances will also contribute to flicker noise.

Thus, reducing the gate width and increasing the finger number in the design of gate configuration can enhance the device noise performance, as long as the gate resistance is decreased [22]. Once the layout structure is determined, the number of contact on the gate is also important. Beside, the design of double-sided gate contacts (two contact holes in both ends of the gate finger) can be utilized to further decrease the resistance.

1.7.6.3 Number of Contacts

Generally speaking, at the expense of increased parasitic capacitance, the more the gate contacts are added, the lower will be the gate resistance. The gate resistances for single-sided and double-sided contacts are given by Equations 21 and 22, respectively [9].

$$R_G = \frac{\frac{R_{CON}}{N_{CON}} + \frac{R_{sq}}{L} / \left[W_{ext} + \frac{W_f}{3}\right]}{N_f} \tag{21}$$

$$R_G = \frac{\frac{R_{CON}}{N_{CON}} + \frac{R_{sq}}{L}\left[W_{ext} + \frac{W_f}{6}\right]}{2N_f} \tag{22}$$

where, R_{CON} is the contact resistance, N_{CON} the number of contacts per gate finger, R_{sq} the gate poly sheet resistance per square, W_{ext} the gate extension beyond the active region, W_f the finger width, N_f the number of gate fingers connected in parallel, and l_{phys} the physical gate length. As a rule of thumb, for the technologies between 180 to 90nm, the optimum finger width appears to be from 1-2μm.

1.7.6.4 Experimental Tests

The 2μm × 36 fingers and 8μm × 9 fingers transistors have been used as a MOS varactor individually in the design of a VCO circuit [22] in a 0.13μm CMOS technology. In both VCO circuits, the rest of the MOS transistors use the same 2μm × 36 fingers gate layout, in order to provide the best noise performance.

The VCO phase noise at 100 kHz offset is as low as -97 and -91 dBc/Hz of 2μm ×36 fingers and 8μm ×9 fingers varactors at 5.2 GHz, respectively, where the dc current is 5 mA at a 1.5-V supply. At 1MHz offset, the respective phase noise is -115 dBc/Hz and -111 dBc//Hz. Thus, the VCO performance is extremely sensitive to device layout. That is because the contribution to the overall noise of the resistance of the gate in an MOSFET is highly layout dependent.
Note that the current density is 0.069mA/μm which is used for the best performance of the VCO [22]. This once again indicates that the transistor biasing in VCO is significantly below characteristic current density.

1.8 Design Considerations for Wideband LC-VCOs

In narrow-band applications, the resonator of the VCO is usually optimized to achieve a maximum Q at the desired operation frequency. This is possible within a limited tuning range, since the transconductance cell can be optimized for a given oscillation amplitude and power dissipation.

In a wide-band design, however, this is not straightforward due to performance variations over the frequency range, e.g. the VCO loop gain, the oscillation amplitude, and the phase noise vary considerably from the low-side to the high-side of the tuning range. In this section, the main design challenges and differences between wide-band and narrow-band VCOs are discussed.

1.8.1 Fundamental Start-Up Constraint

In an LC-VCO, the equivalent parallel tank impedance at resonance R_T is a strong function of the oscillation frequency ω_0 and inductance L, and is given by [4]:

$$R_T(\omega_o) = Q_T.\,\omega_o.\,L = \frac{(\omega_o L)^2}{r_s} \tag{23}$$

where, the overall tank quality factor Q_T is assumed to be dominated by inductor losses characterized here by the physical series resistance r_s of the coil, which eventually becomes a function of frequency due to skin/proximity effects and substrate eddy current induced losses. The above equation is valid as long as the capacitive elements of the tank have a significantly higher Q than the inductor, which may not hold true at very high frequencies.

In any oscillator, the most fundamental design criterion consists of satisfying start-up conditions. In tunable *LC* oscillators, these conditions are themselves a function of frequency [5]. For the generic *LC* oscillator shown in Figure 18, such conditions are satisfied if the pair of complex conjugate poles of the small-signal (initial) loop-gain transfer function lie in the RHP, which occurs when the magnitude of the loop-gain is greater than unity

$$g_m \geq \frac{1}{R_T} = \frac{r_s}{(\omega_o L)^2} \tag{24}$$

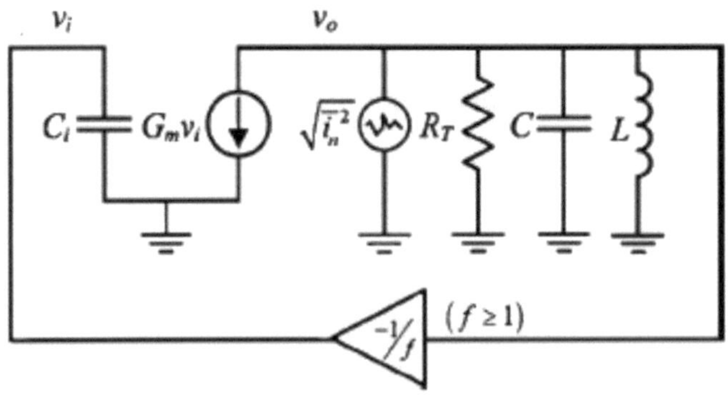

Fig. 18. Generic *LC* oscillator.

Equation (24) indicates a fundamental lower limit on the current consumption for a given transconductor and *LC* tank configuration. In practice, the small-signal transconductance g_m is set to a value that guarantees startup with a reasonable safety margin under worst-case conditions, i.e. at the low-end of the desired frequency range. Thus, wideband VCOs using transconductors fixed at a predetermined critical value feature significant excess of g_m in the upper portion of their frequency range. Raising g_m above this level generally contributes more noise.

1.8.2 Impact of Oscillation Amplitude Variations

As bias current is increased, the VCO's output voltage amplitude also keeps rising. However, the drain cannot exceed the power supply voltage by more than about 0.6 volts before the drain-well diode is turned on, resulting in clipping of the output voltage. As a result, bias current is usually limited by the process.

For the widely used differential cross-coupled *LC* oscillator shown in Figure 19, two such regimes can be identified [6]. In the current-limited regime, the current I_B from the tail current source is periodically commutated between the left and right sides of the tank.

Thus, the resulting fundamental amplitude is directly proportional to I_B and R_T, whereas higher harmonics of the commutated current are attenuated by the bandpass profile of the *LC* tank.

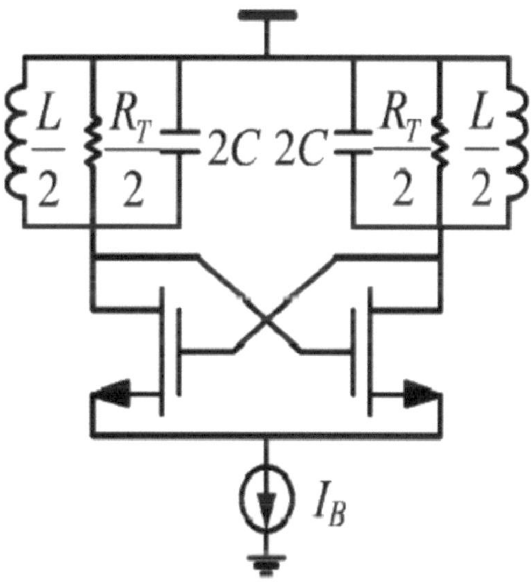

Fig. 19. Differential cross-coupled *LC* oscillator.

As I_B is increased from its minimum value, satisfying start-up conditions, the tank amplitude increases linearly. Eventually, the amplitude saturates by the available headroom from the supply voltage. These two regimes are illustrated in Figure 20(a) [7]. Operating an oscillator in the voltage limited regime is generally undesirable because raising the current will not cause the swing to grow any more, increasing the phase noise [6].

In wideband VCOs, large changes in R_T with frequency can also cause a transition from the current-limited to the voltage-limited regime as frequency increases. Thus, I_B should be reduced as frequency increases in order to prevent such a transition from occurring, otherwise power is wasted.

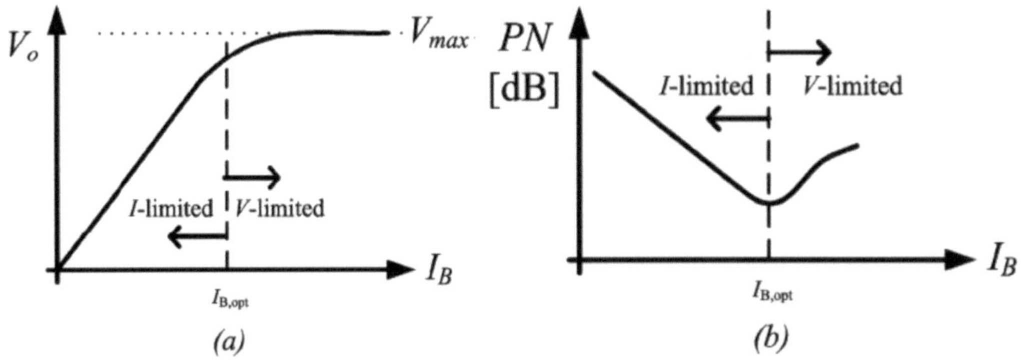

Fig. 20. (a) Steady-state oscillator amplitude versus I_B trend and (b) phase noise versus I_B trend, indicating current- and voltage-limited regimes [7].

1.9 Phase Noise in Wideband Oscillators

To illustrate the impact of oscillation amplitude variations on phase noise, we consider the simplified case of a generic linear time-invariant *LC* oscillator with an equivalent noise generator i_n across its tank, as shown in Figure 18. Solving for the noise to signal power ratio gives [7]:

$$PN \approx \frac{\overline{i_n^2}}{V_o^2} \cdot \frac{R_T^2}{4Q_T^2} \cdot \left(\frac{\omega_o}{\Delta\omega}\right)^2 \propto \frac{(\eta . g_m + 1/R_T)}{V_o^2} \cdot \frac{R_T^2}{Q_T^2} \cdot \left(\frac{\omega_o}{\Delta\omega}\right)^2 \tag{25}$$

where, $(\eta . g_m + 1/R_T)$ has been substituted, implying that noise generators from the energy-restoring transconductor and from the tank loss dominate, as is often the case. V_o is the tank amplitude and $\Delta\omega$ is the frequency offset from the carrier. η is an excess noise factor, which appears to be 2/3 for long-channel devices.

In the current limited regime, (25) can be rewritten as follows [7]:

$$PN \propto \frac{(\eta . g_m + 1/R_T)}{I_B^2} \cdot \frac{1}{Q_T^2} \cdot \left(\frac{\omega_o}{\Delta\omega}\right)^2 \tag{26}$$

For narrowband designs, R_T does not vary appreciably over the tuning range and the phase noise shows a $1/(Q_T^3L)$ dependence. Clearly, there is a direct relationship between bias current and phase noise, which provides the designer with a convenient way to trade power for noise performance.

In the voltage-limited regime, (25) can be rewritten as follows:

$$PN \propto \frac{(\eta . g_m + 1/R_T')}{V_{max}^2} \cdot \left(\frac{\omega_o}{\Delta\omega}\right)^2 \tag{27}$$

where $R'_T<R_T$ due to the excessive signal amplitude bringing the transconductor into its resistive region, which degrades the overall tank quality factor Q_T. In a narrowband design where the voltage-limited regime is reached by increasing I_B, (27) indicates that the phase noise must degrade since the amplitude saturates to V_{max} while the transconductor noise keeps rising.
Figure 20(b) shows a typical scenario of PN versus I_B. The boundary between the two regimes of operation represents the optimum point for achieving lowest phase noise. Increasing I_B beyond this point degrades the performance in terms of both phase noise and power.
While the above observations yield important insights for narrowband designs, frequency dependences must be taken into account in order to assess similar characteristics for wideband VCOs. Here, we restrict the analysis to the current-limited regime since it is the preferred region of operation. Again starting from (25), a phase noise expression highlighting its frequency dependence is derived assuming a fixed current I_B and $V_o \propto I_B \,.\, R_T$.

$$PN(\omega_o) \propto \left[\eta . g_m + \frac{r_s}{(\omega_o L)^2}\right] \cdot \left(\frac{r_s}{L . I_B}\right)^2 \tag{28}$$

Equation (28) reveals that the phase noise tends to improve as frequency increases. Even in cases where r_s grows linearly with frequency, Eq. (28) shows that phase noise is relatively constant with frequency. The reason why phase noise does not degrade with its classical ω_o^2 dependence is that the tank amplitude in this particular topology basically grows with ω_o^2.

However, (28) only applies in the current-limited regime. Wideband designs operated with fixed I_B experience significant amplitude growth as frequency increases, which eventually brings the VCO into the voltage-limited regime where phase noise will degrade. Furthermore, the optimal point for lowest phase noise indicated in Figure 20(b) cannot be held across frequency.

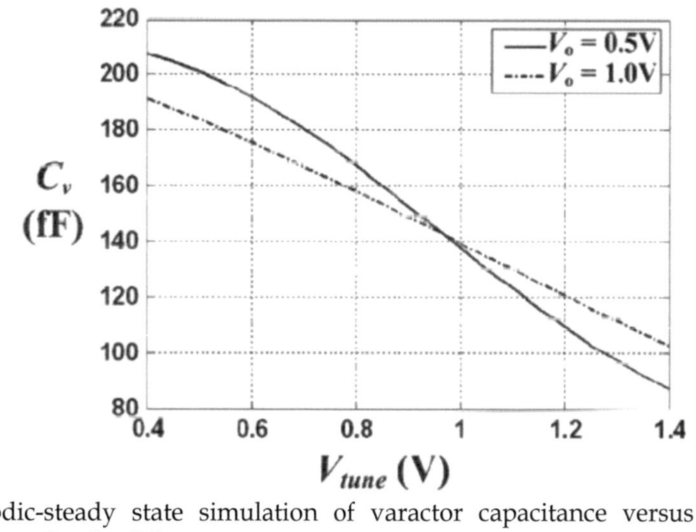

Fig. 21. Periodic-steady state simulation of varactor capacitance versus V_{tune} for two different tank amplitudes [7].

Amplitude variations in wideband VCOs cause several additional second order effects. One such effect is the reduction of the varactor's capacitive range and the associated reduction in the overall tuning sensitivity. Figure 21 shows a typical MOS varactor - curve for different values of oscillation amplitude.
Amplitude variations in wideband VCOs cause variations in the phase noise performance over frequency. Thus, providing a way to control the dependence of oscillation amplitude on frequency is highly desirable.

1.10 Wideband Oscillators

Wide tuning range in the VCO can be obtained by employing a parallel combination of switched binary weighted capacitors and a MOS varactor. However, the VCO loop gain varies considerably over the wide tuning range. Also, the sensitivity of the Q of inductors to operation frequency and varactor nonlinearities and its Q variations cause significant deterioration in phase noise and amplitude variations. These issues complicates the design of wideband (or ultra wideband) VCOs. The objectives of the following sections are to address these issues and provide some guidelines for (ultra) wideband VCO design.

1.10.1 Wideband Tuning

Narrow band *LC*-VCOs have been implemented with optimized performance in the past, since the negative transconductor (g_m) cell can be well designed for a given Q, phase noise, and power consumption. This is due to the fact that in narrow-band VCO the tank Q remains approximately constant over the tuning range. However, the design of (Ultra) Wideband VCOs, e.g. operating between 3-6GHz, is complicated as the equivalent tank impedance at resonance changes considerably along the tuning range. The variations in Q change the output amplitude, as well as the g_m of the transconductor cell, and hence the startup safety margin may not be sufficient over the entire frequency range. Additionally, due to the absence of high and flat Q inductors, the phase noise increases with frequency.

This section gives an overview of various tuning techniques along with the implemented tuning range reported in the literature. Then, it discusses the techniques and issues associated with the design of Ultra Wideband VCOs. Finally, the techniques for phase noise reduction are presented.

1.10.1.1 Tuning with Wieghted Array capacitors

Because the oscillation frequency in an LC-VCO is determined by the tank's resonant frequency, $\omega_0 = 1/\sqrt{LC}$, the tank capacitance may be tuned to adjust the frequency of oscillation. This may be achieved by connecting some combination of MOS capacitors, selected by RF-switches from a weighted array, across a fixed inductor. Each capacitor may be tuned continuously with an analog voltage, and together the array defines the desired piecewise voltage-to-frequency characteristic [23]. In order not to degrade the capacitor Q, the switch must be designed large enough. Consequently, the parasitics associated with the switch may now load the capacitor array when the switch is OFF. This limits the possible tuning frequency.

To alleviate the above problem, the RF switch may be designed using an array of doughnut-shaped sub-FETs, whose gate encloses the drain junction [23]. With this layout, the drain junction capacitance is 20% lower than in a conventional interdigitated FET. The measured tuning range with this array of switched capacitors [23] appears to be 1.34 GHz ±6%. Also, the phase noise remains almost invariant when the RF switch is fully ON or OFF, indicating that the switch resistance does not degrade resonator Q. However, during the switch transition time, the capacitor Q is severely reduced and the phase noise is degraded by 12 dB.

1.10.1.2 Tuning with Inversion mode MOS Varactor

Accumulation MOS (AMOS) varactors cannot achieve their physical maximum and minimum capacitance when the tuning voltage is lower than 1V. For this reason, inversion mode MOS (IMOS) varactors, which provide abrupt gradient of capacitance-voltage curve, can be used for VCO tuning with a low supply voltage [24]. In order to improve the tuning capability further, each IMOS varactor may employ a large resistance in its bulk, isolating the gate to bulk parasitic capacitance of IMOS from the VCO output port. This varactor provides approximately 25% improvement in C_{max}/C_{min} ratio.

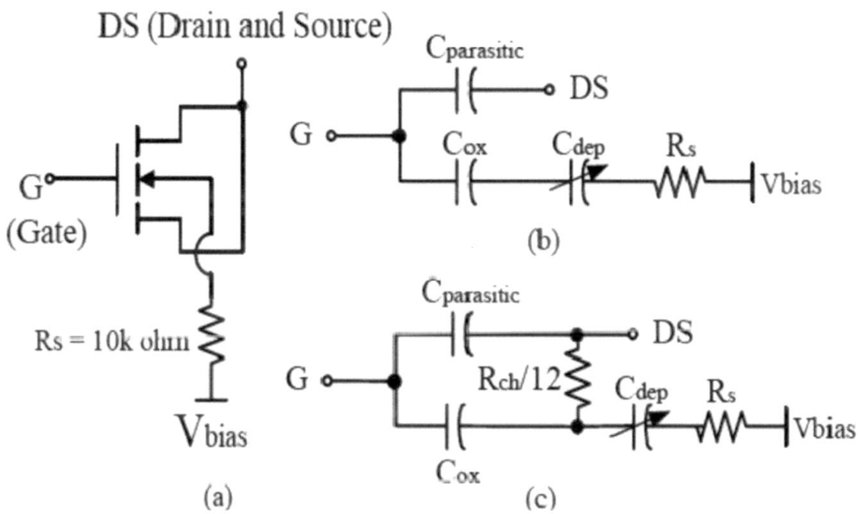

Fig. 22. (a) Circuit schematic of an IMOS varactor with a large bulk resistor Rs (b) The equivalent model in depletion mode (c) The equivalent model in inversion mode [24].

Figure 22 shows the circuit schematic and equivalent models of the IMOS varactors used in the VCO design [24]. In this figure, a large poly resistance Rs (e.g.10kΩ) connects the bulk of the NMOS and the ac ground terminal V_{bias}. When the terminal DS in Figure 22(a) is biased at the positive end voltage, the IMOS is operated in the depletion mode and Figure 22(b) shows the equivalent model. The value of $C_{parasitic}$ is dominated by the gate-source and gate-drain overlap capacitance; C_{ox} is the gate-oxide capacitance and C_{dep} is the depletion capacitance.

However, if the bulk is connected directly to the ac ground, C_{min} will become $(C_{parasitic} + C_{ox} \| C_{dep})$. Thus, C_{min} can be decreased by $(C_{ox} \| C_{dep})$ by using a large resistance R_s in

Figure 22(a). When DS is biased at the negative end, a sheet of electrons accumulates at the surface of the channel and the IMOS is operated in the inversion mode. Figure 22(c) shows the equivalent model. R_{ch} is the channel resistance.

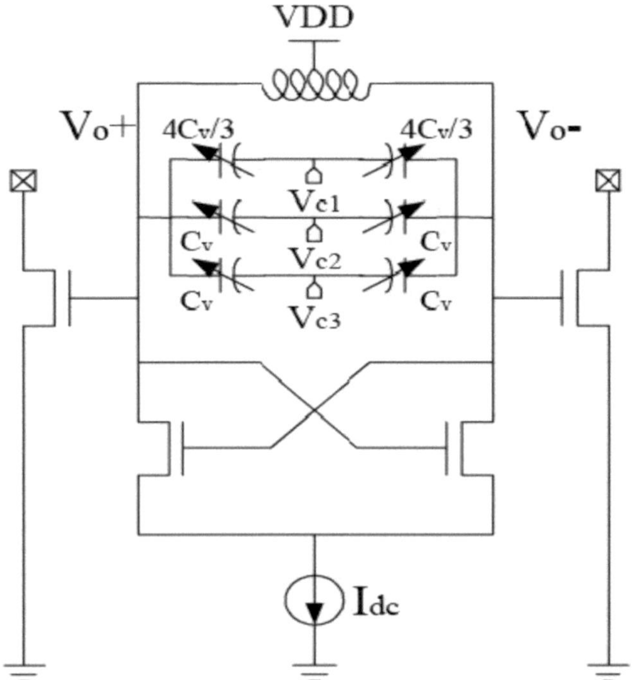

Fig. 23. VCO schematic [24]

The new modified IMOS varactor is utilized in the differential VCO architecture, shown in Figure 23. The simulation results [24] using a 0.18um CMOS technology show that the effective minimal capacitance (C_{min}) is reduced from 775 to 590 fF and the frequency tuning range increases by 500MHz. When the supply voltage is 0.8V, the tuning range of the VCO is from 4.4 to 5.9GHz and the phase noise is -109.65dBc/Hz at 1MHz offset from the carrier at 5.52GHz. The VCO core dissipates 1.2mW of power.

When the supply voltage is reduced to 0.6V, the VCO core consumes only 0.9mW. The tuning range is from 4.7 to 5.9GHz and the phase noise is -105.24dBc/Hz at at the same offset from the carrier.

1.10.1.3 Tuning with Weighted Binary Array

Tuning can be achieved by employing AMOS varactors and a high-Q inductor with a perfectly symmetrical single copper loop [25]. Using an LC cross-coupled differential topology with both PMOS and NMOS latches, fabricated in a 0.13 μm SOI CMOS process, this provides a multi-GHz (3.0-5.6 GHz) wideband VCO. The schematic of the VCO is shown in Figure 24. At a 1 V supply and 1MHz offset, the phase noise is close to -120 dBc/Hz at 3.0 GHz, and -114.5 dBc/Hz at 5.6GHz. The results illustrates that the up-converted flicker noise is reduced in this VCO structure.

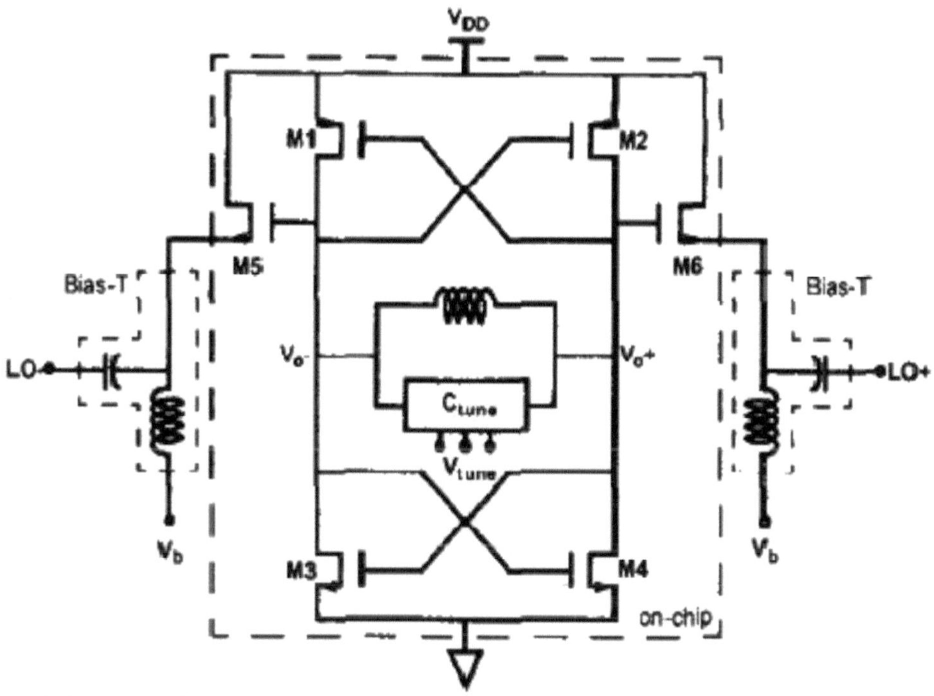

Fig. 24. Schematic of the Band-Switching L-C VCO [25]

1.10.1.4 Tuning with Accumulation-mode MOS Varactors

A very wideband *LC*-VCO in [7], implemented in 0.18μm bulk CMOS, has been described that simultaneously achieves low phase noise and 1.3GHz tuning range around 1.8GHz center frequency. To provide robust operation and stabilize performance over the entire frequency range, the VCO amplitude is controlled using a digital amplitude calibration scheme that does not degrade phase noise and consumes negligible area and power. The proposed calibration-based amplitude control scheme is illustrated in Figure 25.

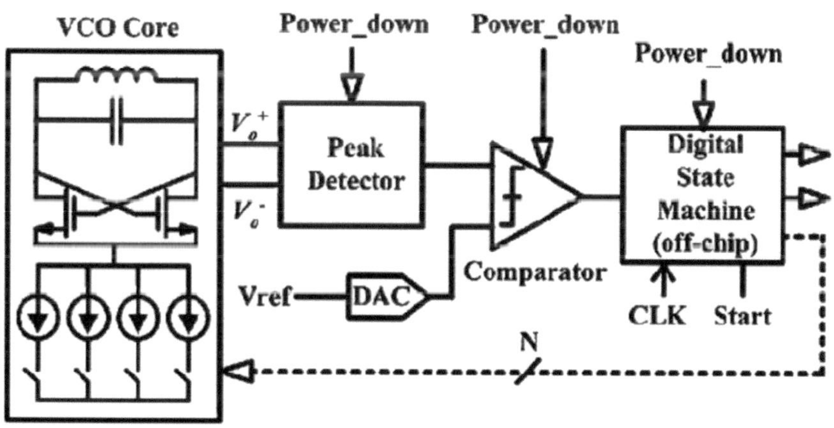

Fig. 25. Proposed calibration-based amplitude control scheme [7].

The VCO core is based on a standard *LC*-tuned cross-coupled NMOS topology. The *LC* tank consists of a single integrated differential spiral inductor, accumulation-mode MOS varactors allowing continuous frequency tuning, and a switched capacitor array providing coarse tuning steps. Figure 26 shows a simplified schematic of the VCO core.
The W/L of the cross-coupled NMOS devices is chosen based on oscillation startup requirements at the low-end (worst-case) of the tuning range.

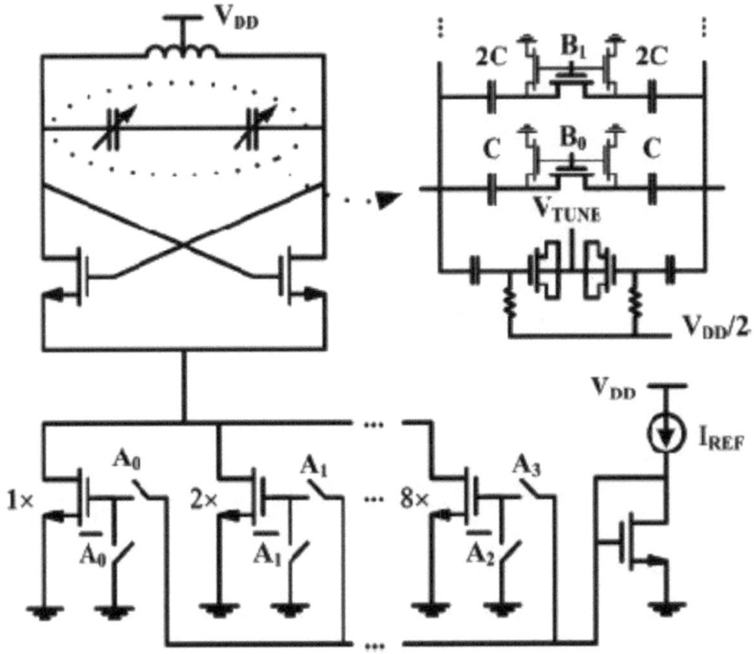

Fig. 26. Simplified VCO core schematic [7].

In order to achieve a large frequency range, the *LC* tank combines a switched capacitor array with a small varactor. The targeted frequency range is split into 16 sub-bands by means of a 4-bit binary-weighted array of switched MIM capacitors. The capacitors are switched in and out of the tank by differential switches.

Suppose a generic binary-weighted band-switching *LC* tank configuration of size *n*, as shown in Figure 27. Assume that:

$$\beta_v = \frac{C_v}{C_{v,min}} \tag{29a}$$

$$\beta_a = \frac{C_a}{C_{a,off}} \tag{29b}$$

$$\beta_v = \frac{C_{total}}{C_p} \tag{29c}$$

where, $C_{v,min}$ is the minimum varactor capacitance for the available tuning voltage range and is reached as the device enters its depletion mode. $C_{a,off}$ represents the effective capacitance of a unit branch of the array in the off state. The MOS switch in a unit branch of the array contributes a parasitic capacitance C_d that is mainly composed of its drain-to-bulk junction and drain-to-gate overlap capacitors, giving $\beta_a=1+C_a/C_d$.
C_p is the total lumped parasitic capacitance and C_{total} equals the total tank capacitance. Hence, (29c) may be equivalently expressed as $\beta_p=1/(\omega_{o,min}{}^2.L.C_p)$. Furthermore, note that according to equations (29a–c), increasing any one of the defined terms increases the achievable tuning range.

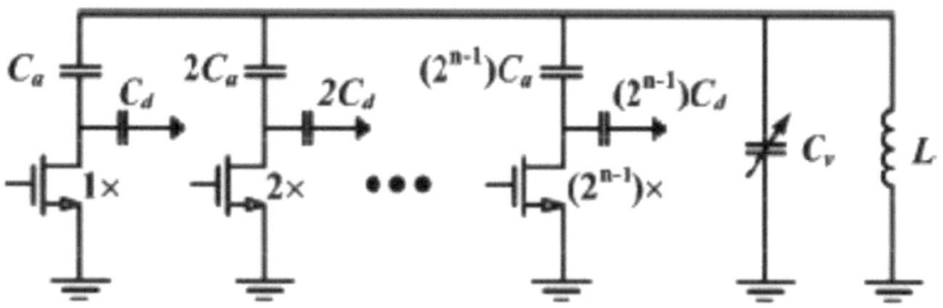

Fig. 27. Generic binary-weighted band-switching LC tank configuration [7].

For a given set of specifications, the tuning range extremities are defined as follows [21]:

$$\omega_{o,min} = [L.(C_v + (2^n - 1).C_a + C_P]^{-1/2} \tag{30a}$$

$$\omega_{o,max} = \left[L.(\frac{C_v}{\beta_v} + (2^n - 1).\frac{C_a}{\beta_a} + C_P\right]^{-1/2} \tag{30b}$$

To guarantee that any two adjacent sub-bands overlap, the following condition must be satisfied:

$$\Delta C_v \geq \Delta C_a \tag{31}$$

where $\Delta C_v = C_v - C_{v,min}$ and $\Delta C_a = C_a - C_{a,off}$. Using (29a) and (29b), (31) can be written as

$$C_v = k.C_a.\frac{\beta_v}{\beta_a}.\frac{(\beta_a - 1)}{(\beta_v - 1)} \tag{32}$$

where k is a chosen overlap safety margin factor and is greater than unity. Equation (32) can be substituted in (30a) to solve for C_a independently of C_v, giving

$$C_a = \frac{\left(L.\omega_{o,min}^2\right)^{-1} - C_p}{k.\frac{\beta_v}{\beta_a}.\frac{(\beta_a - 1)}{(\beta_v - 1)} + 2^n - 1} \quad (33)$$

Thus, having chosen parameters β_a, n, and L, and given design constants $\omega_{o,min}$, k, and β_v, one can solve for C_a and C_v [using (32)]. Taking the ratio of (30b) and (30a) yields the tuning range

$$TR = \frac{\omega_{o,max}}{\omega_{o,min}} \quad (34)$$

To account for the impact of lossy switches, we note that the quality factor of the capacitor array is well approximated as $Q_a=(\omega_o.R_{on}.C_a)^{-1}$, where R_{on} is the resistance of the unit MOS switch. Given that $\beta_a=1+C_a/C_d$, the resulting quality factor of the capacitor array is given by

$$Q_a = \frac{1}{\omega_o.R_{on}.C_d.(\beta_a - 1)} \quad (35)$$

Note that since the MOS switch would generally use the minimum available gate length and $C_d \propto W$, the product is approximately constant for a given technology. Figure 28(a) shows values of TR and Q_a from (34) and (35) plotted versus β_a for a typical scenario, and clearly illustrates the direct trade-off between tuning range and Q_a.

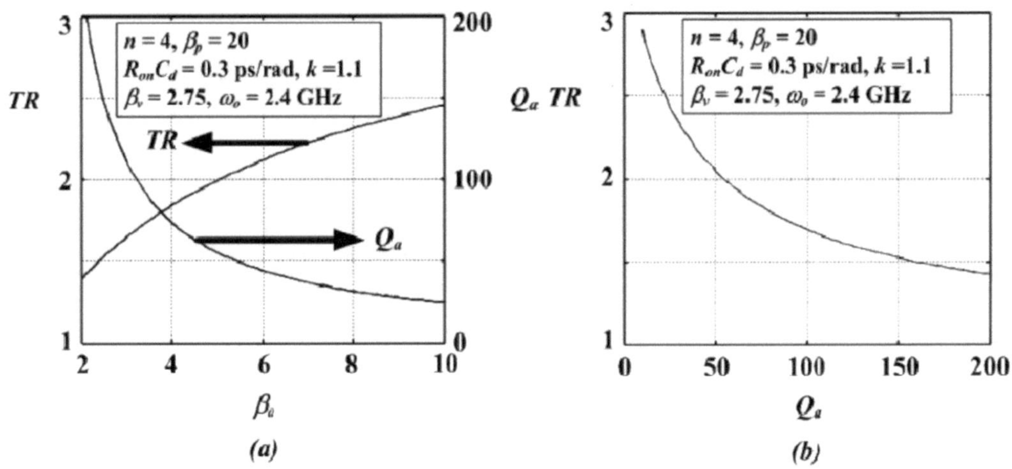

Fig. 28. (a) Tuning range and capacitor array quality factor versus β_a (b) Tuning range versus Q_a [7].

Each switch contributes additional loss to the tank due to its finite resistance, R_{on}. Thus, minimum-length NMOS devices are utilized and made as wide as possible before the resulting parasitic drain-to-bulk capacitance limits the achievable tuning range.

Because the desired tuning range has been divided into several sections, a small accumulation-mode NMOS varactor is sufficient to cover each frequency sub- band.

The tank inductor was realized as a 5.6-nH differential spiral on a 2- μm-thick top metal layer achieving a measured (single-ended) Q ranging from about 7.5 to 9 over the VCO frequency range [7].

Figure 29 shows the measured and simulated phase noise at the lower, middle, and upper ends of the tuning range running at a core power consumption of 10, 4.8, and 2.6 mW, respectively. The measured frequency range is 1.14–2.46 GHz.

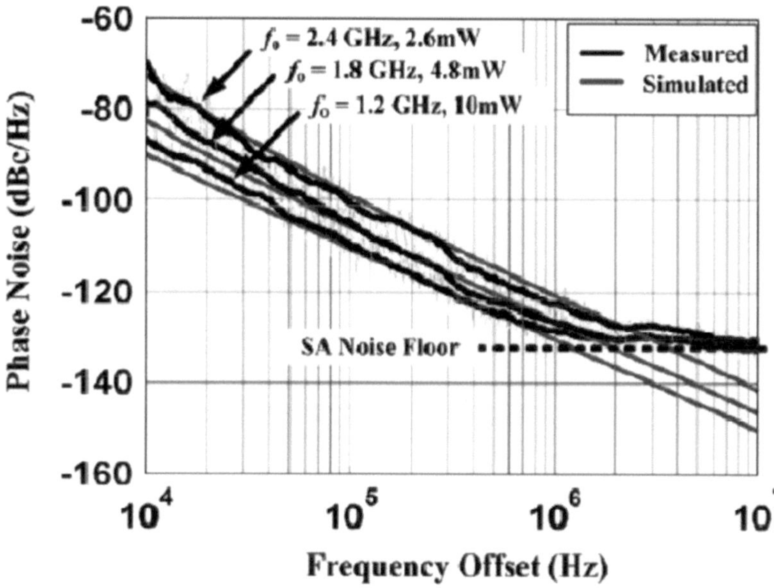

Figu. 29. Phase noise at 1.2, 1.8, and 2.4 GHz for a core power consumption of 10, 4.8, and 2.6 mW, respectively [7].

1.10.1.5 Tuning with Switched-Capacitor Array and Varactors

Weighted array capcitors may also be used for wideband frequency tuning [3]. Although PMOS transistor requires higher current to provide the same transconductance (g_m) as NMOS transistor, PMOS differential pair is used to achive a better phase noise (see Figure 30).

This design uses a switched-capacitor array and varactor together to form the capacitive portion of the tank. As illustrated in Figure 31, the tank capacitance is formed by a varactor diode capacitance that varies from $C_{v,min}$ to $C_{v,max}$, a capacitor array that varies from $C_{a,min}$ to $C_{a,max}$, and a parasitic capacitance C_p. In essence, this structure provides coarse tuning via the capacitor array and fine tuning via the varactor.

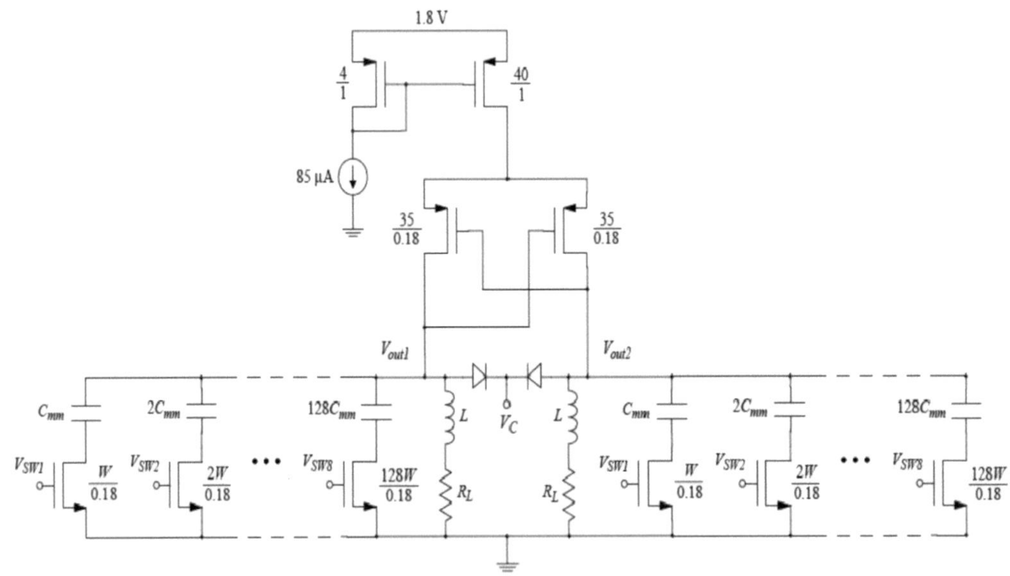

Fig. 30. Complete VCO schematic [3]

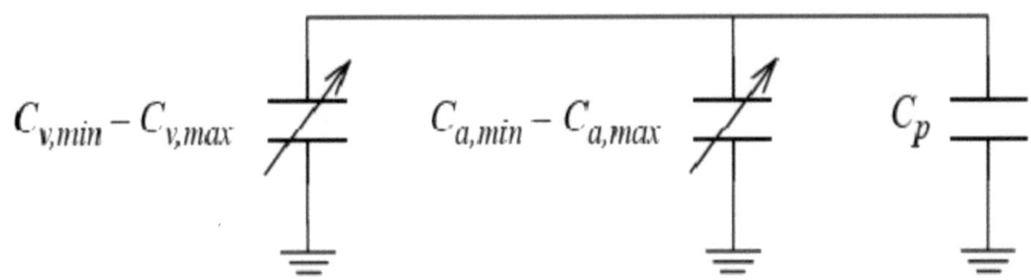

Fig. 31. Tank capacitances [3].

To determine how to size the capacitors, switches, and varactor, one can start with the desired continuous tuning range, f_{min} to f_{max} and inductance range, L_{min} to L_{max}. The widest range of total tank capacitance needed to tune from f_{min} to f_{max} corresponds to the lowest inductance value L_{min}. The minimum and maximum capacitance values that define this range are given by:

$$C_{t,min}^{Lmin} = [(2\pi . f_{max})^2 . L_{min}]^{-1} \tag{36}$$

$$C_{t,max}^{Lmin} = [(2\pi . f_{min})^2 . L_{min}]^{-1} \tag{37}$$

The general binary weighted capacitor array is shown in Figure 32, where C_{mm} represents the capacitance of a metal-metal capacitor and C_{dd} represents parasitic drain capacitance. To maintain a constant *Q* for each switch/capacitor pair when the switches are on, as each capacitor size doubles, the channel on-resistance must halve. Therefore, the NMOS switch widths are also binary-weighted (since channel resistance is inversely proportional to channel width), and consequentially, the parasitic drain capacitances associated with each switch are binary-weighted too.

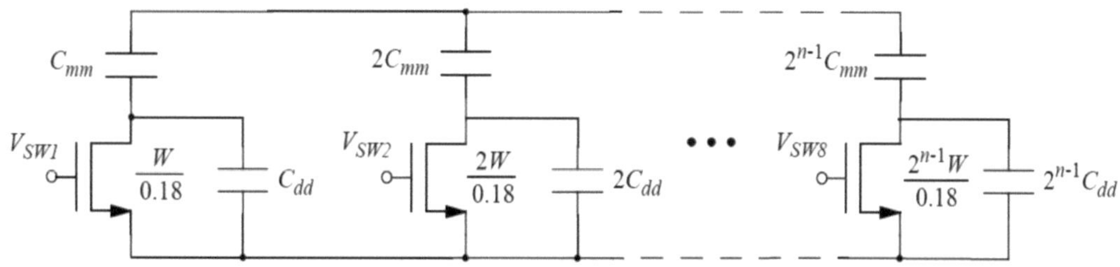

Fig. 32. General binary-weighted capacitor array [3].

Using the above topology, a 2-GHz VCO has been implemented and simulated in a 0.18-μm CMOS process with 1.8V power supply. The resulting tuning range is 1.848 to 2.044 GHz.

1.10.1.6 Tuning with Switched oscillators

In this technique, one of an array of independent oscillators may be selected with a MOSFET switch connected to a common-mode point outside the oscillator loop [23] (Figure 33**).** The inductors which tune each oscillator are sized differently. The outputs combine in buffer FETs with a common drain, one of which is turned **ON** by the selected oscillator. These FETs are of small size so as not to excessively load the resonant circuit in the oscillator core. A larger buffer follows to provide adequate drive to the subsequent circuits. Each oscillator is continuously tuned by a MOS varactor.

With this method, either an array of weighted capacitors may be switched in parallel with a single oscillator core, or one of an array of multiple oscillator cores may be selected, each tuned by inductors of various sizes.

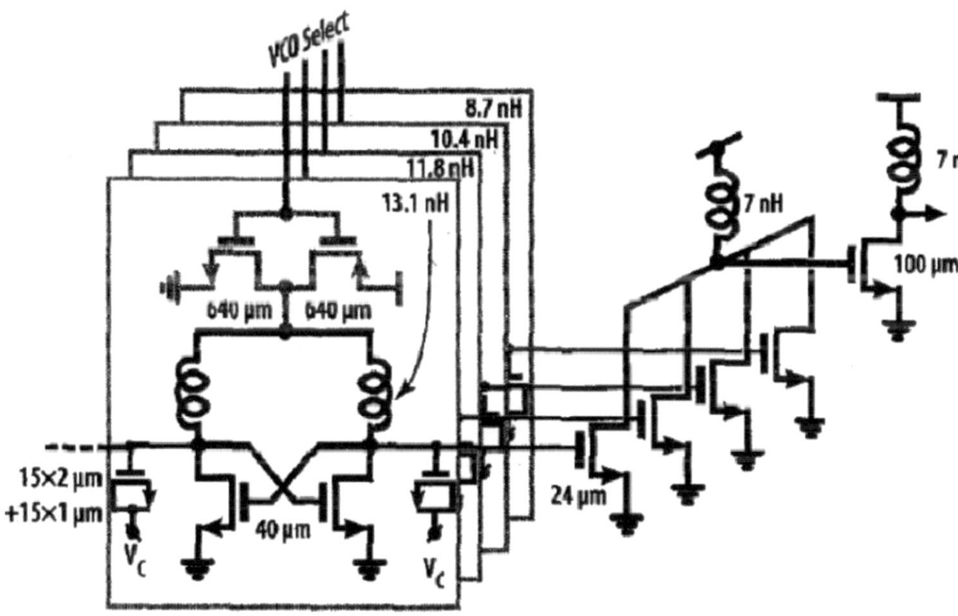

Fig. 33. Switched array of oscillators, with a combined output [23]

Using the above switched tuning methods, RF CMOS oscillators are shown to obtain a wide tuning characteristic, e.g. a frequency range from 1.4 to 1.85GHz with the required overlaps between the switched segments [23].

1.10.1.7 Tuning with Switched Resonator

The switched resonator concept, illustrated in Figure 34, can be utilized to increase the tuning range and to achieve low phase noise over the tuning range at reasonable power consumption [26]. The LC tanks include MOS varactors, inductors, and variable resonator transistors M3 and M4.

In this figure, the inductance seen between ports 1 and 2 is changed by turning M3 on and off. When the transistor is off, the inductance is approximately the sum of L1 and L2. The actual combined inductance is somehow lower due to the effects of C_{GD} in series with C_{GS}, and C_{DB} of M1. These capacitances also affect the capacitance seen from L_1 side (C_{p1}).

When M3 is on, L_2 is shunted out and the inductance is decreased. Furthermore, when M3 is on, C_{p1} is reduced because the transistor capacitances and the capacitances associated with L_1 (partially) and L_2 are shunted to ground by the low on-resistance of M3, thus, leading to simultaneous decreases of inductance and capacitance.

This ability to simultaneously tune L and C provides greater flexibility to trade-off phase noise and power consumption, as well as to achieve given phase noise performance over a larger frequency range compared to using only switched capacitors. In fact the resonators are used for band selection, while varctors provide the tuning within bands. This concept has been implemented for frequencies from 667 to 1156 MHz. The phase noise at a 600 kHz offset versus oscillation frequency is about -123 dBc/Hz.

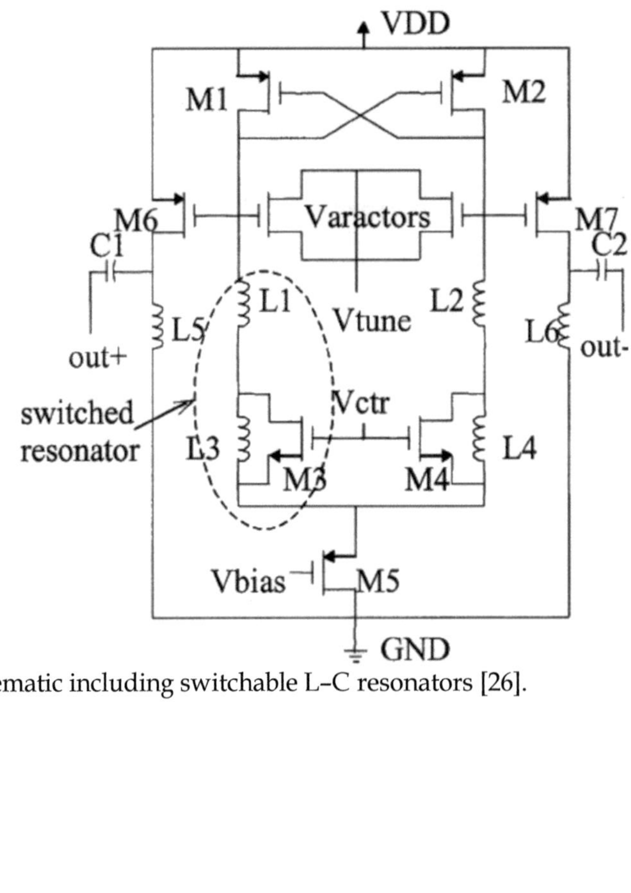

Fig. 34. VCO schematic including switchable L–C resonators [26].

1.10.1.8 Tuning with Variable Inductor

The variable inductor consists of a conventional planar spiral inductor, above which a metal plate is placed such that it can be moved vertically using a MEMS parallel-plate actuator [27]. By generating DC bias between the stationary electrode and the movable electrode (the metal Plate), the metal plate is moved vertically, resulting in the variation of inductance. The bias voltage can control the inductance continuously.

Using the above variable inductor in a LC-VCO (see Fig. 34), fabricated using a 0.35μm CMOS technology, it can be tuned for different frequency ranges [27], e.g. entire tuning is from 2.14GHz to 3.13GHz. The inductance is changed from 3.87nH to 5.98nH, while the respective quality factor changes from 2.98 to 3.87. The typical phase noise at 1MHz offset is -112dBc/Hz, which remains almost constant for the entire tuning range.

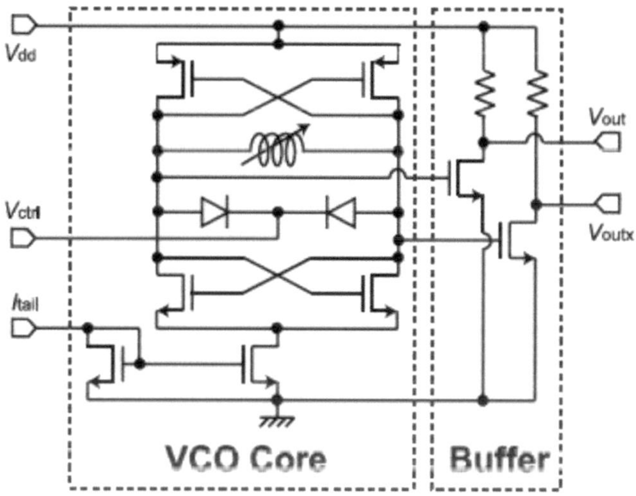

Fig. 35. Schematic of LCVCO [27]

1.11 Phase Noise Improvement Techniques

As explained above, LC-VCO are often designed with sufficiently high phase noise performance. To achieve this, utilizing low-flicker-noise active devices and high-Q resonators are the most commonly techniques. However, with increasing frequnecy tuning range, due to variation in quality factor and ampltitude of oscillation the perfomance may not maintain. In Section 1.7.6 we discussed the techniques of transistor layout design and its biasing to minimize the device noises,which can lead to the design of a high perfomrnace wide tunig VCO. This section presents two simple methods [28, 29] for phase noise reduction which can be incorporated in UWB VCO design.

1.11.1 Harmonic Tuning

Harmonic tuning technique can reduce the phase noise in LC-VCOs [28]. In this technique the output waveform zero crossing points become steeper. As a result, the phase noise is reduced due to increase of the voltage on the resonator.

This is explained using leeson equation for phase noise as follows [28].

$$F = 2 + \frac{8\gamma R I_T}{\pi V_o} + \gamma \frac{8}{9} g_{mbias} R \quad (38)$$

where, I_T is bias current, γ denotes the channel noise coefficient of the FET, and V_0 is the resonator voltage. Clearly, with increasing V_0 due to harmonic tuning, F is reduced. In addition, in this technique the S_{11} parameter is shorted at second harmonic, which improves the phase noise further. Figure 36 illustrates the schematic of the VCO before and after phase noise improvement.

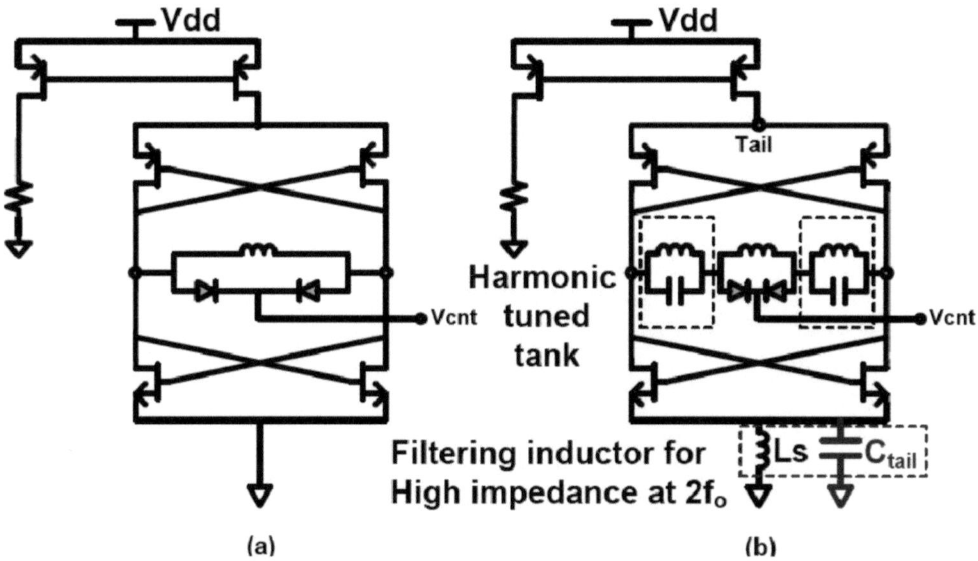

Fig. 36. Schematic of VCO (a) before (b) after phase noise reduction

As can be seen in Figure 36 (b), two series resonators are utilized in addition to main resonator.These resonators are designed such that they are open in fundamental and third harmoics frequencies, while they are shorted at second harmonics. Thus, the output signal attains a rectangle shape instead of a sine wave.This in turn reduces the phase noise due to abrupt switching.

Noise fitering is also exploited in [28]. In top-biased differential oscilators, direct connection of NMOS pair to ground forces one of them to enter the triode region when they turn off. This reduces the quality factor in general . Using LC pair with oscilation frquency at second harmonic gives a high impedance at this harmoic and removes the loading effect of oscillator in triode. This technique may improve the phase noise by 10dB [28].

1.11.2 Feedback method

An alternative technique for noise suppression is given in [29], in which a frequency to current converter (FCC) extracts the noise properties of VCO output signal. This extracted current then passes through an integrator, which converts it to a voltage carrying important noise and frequency properties. This voltage will enter a low pass filter and fed back as an input voltage to the oscillator.

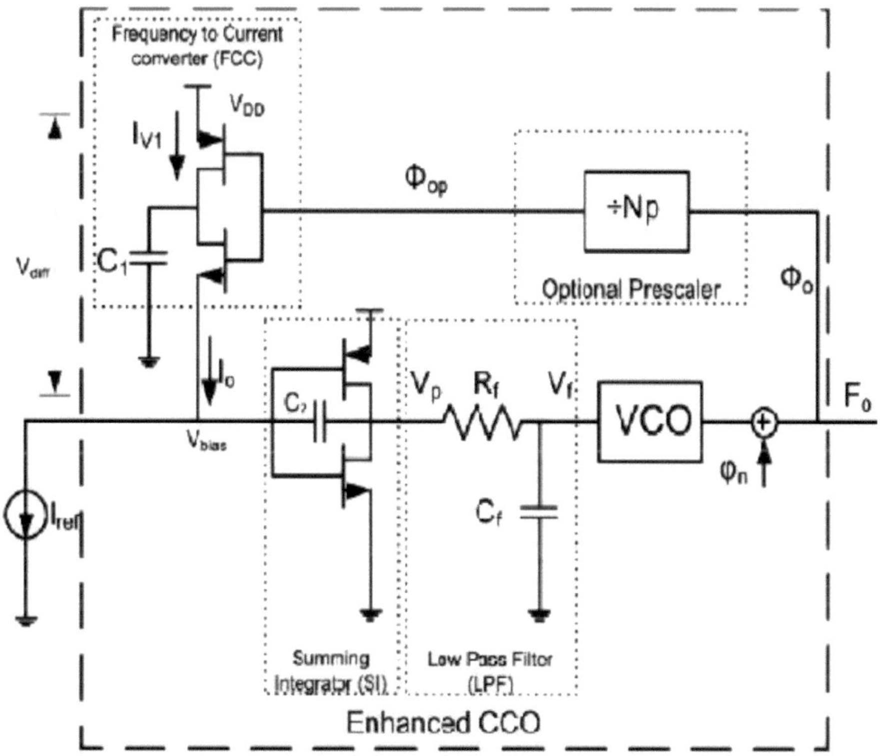

Fig. 37. Schematic of phase noise reduction with feedback [29]

The system in Figure 37 can be interpreted as current controlled oscillator (CCO), which exhibits better noise compared to its initial state. The output capacitance of FCC is charged to VCC in each period and then discharged to V_{bias}. Therefore, the current source in FCC represents the phase noise characteristics of VCO output signal. The difference between this current with I_{ref} is integrated. The output voltage is proportional to signal phase noise. The filter suppresses the high frequency component. This technique can give rise to 10dB phase noise improvement [29].

1.12 Design of Ultra Wideband Oscillators

Design of Ultra wideband (UWB) VCOs demands extending the tunability bandwidth to multi-gigahertz range (i.e. in the range of 3 to 10CHz). A method to achieve this is based on tunable active inductors (TAI) despite their noise and nonlinearity, since they have major advantages over passive inductors in terms of area, tunability, and higher Q factors.

This section describes the design of UWB CMOS VCO, using the tunable active inductor (TAI) presented in section 1.7.4. The transistor sizing, layout issues, and the trade-off between power and bandwidth are discussed. Also, the robustness of the oscillator performance under reduced bias voltage, temperature change, and process variations are examined. Finally, the effect of packaging is investigated.

1.12.1 TAI-Based VCO

In order to incorporate the one-port TAI, the conventional single-ended Colpitts or Hartley topology can be chosen (see Figure 1). The former incorporates a single inductance, and hence replacing it with TAI provides a limited improvement of its tuning range. On the other hand, Hartley topology can incorporate two TAIs, and therefore it provides a wider tuning range [19, 33]. However, the phase noise degradation due to these TAIs is a concern, which demands a technique of phase noise reduction for this structure. These are discussed in the following.

1.12.2 TAI-based Colpitts VCO

A TAI-based VCO may be implemented using the Colpitts topology shown in Figure 1(a). In this implementation, the output has been derived from the drain using a load inductor (L_{load}). This isolates the output port from the resonator and also provides a higher output power. Note that, higher value of the load inductor also helps in harmonic suppression.
The proposed TAI is illustrated in Figure 38(a), and the TAI-based Colpitts oscillator [30] is shown in Figure 38(b). The expressions for the undamped oscillation frequency, as well as the start-up condition for oscillation in terms of the resonator elements and the intrinsic parameters of the transistor M_1 are:

$$\omega_n \approx \sqrt{\frac{(C_1C_2 + C_2C_3 + C_3C_1) + \left(\frac{R_lC_1C_3}{R_{ds}}\right)}{C_1C_2C_3L + \left(\frac{R_lC_1C_2C_3L_{load}}{R_{ds}}\right)}} \tag{39}$$

$$g_m \gg \left[\frac{\omega_n^2LC_1C_3 - (C_1 + C_3) + A}{C_3R_{ds}}\right]$$

$$A = \omega_n^2[L_{load}(C_1C_2 + C_2C_3 + C_3C_1) + RR_{ds}C_1C_2C_3 - \omega_n^2LL_{load}C_1C_2C_3] > 0 \tag{40}$$

C_3 has to be chosen large as compared to C_1 and C_2 such that it has negligible effect on the oscillation frequency. From the denominator in (39), it can be observed that $R_l \ll R_{ds}$ and L_{load} (denoted by Z_{load} in Figure 38(b)) is of the same order as L_1. Thus, L_{load} has a negligible effect on ω_n. However, the use of L_{load} demands a higher g_m for the start -up condition due to the additional positive term A in (40).
Equation (41) gives the dependence of the phase noise on the loaded Q, noise generated, and the signal power on the resonator node.

$$L\{\Delta\omega\} \propto \frac{NKT}{PQ^2}\left(\frac{\omega_o}{\Delta\omega}\right)^2 \tag{41}$$

where, N is the noise factor, P is the signal power at the resonator, Q is the loaded quality factor of the resonator, and $\Delta\omega$ is the deviation from the carrier frequency.
From (39), it is evident that $R_l << R_{ds}$, and hence, has a negligible effect on the oscillation frequency. However, it has a significant effect on the Q of the inductor, as well as the loaded Q of the resonator, which directly affects the phase-noise performance of the oscillator (see (41)).
Although the high Q of the active inductor has a positive effect on the phase-noise performance, the active devices in the inductor generate additional noise that results in a higher noise factor, which degrades the phase noise.

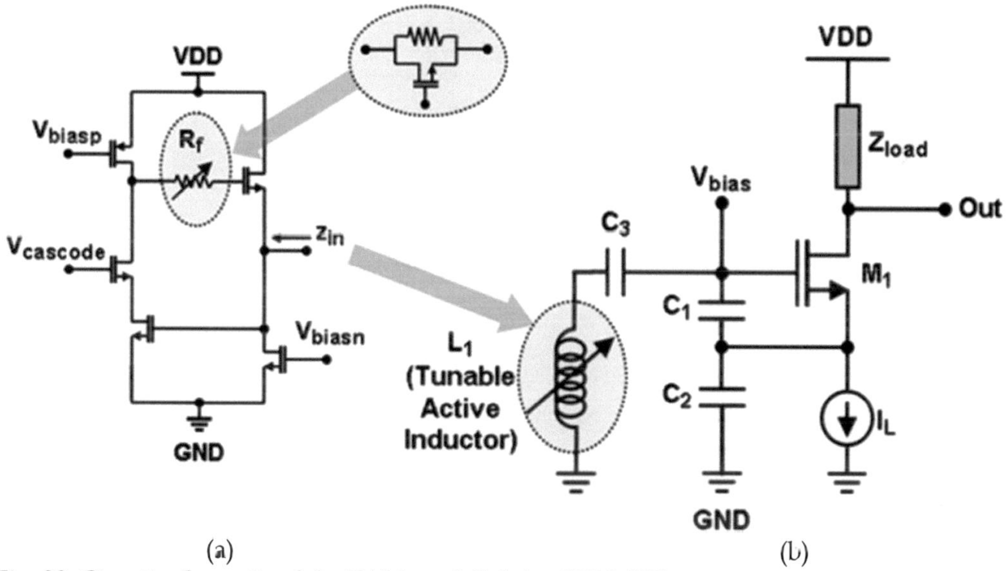

Fig. 38. Circuit schematic of the TAI-based Colpitts VCO [30]

With the above TAI-based VCO implemented in a 0.18µm standard CMOS technology, a frequency range of 500 MHz – 2.0 GHz is achieved [30].The total circuit consumes 13.8 mW of power from a 1.8-V supply. The phase noise varies from -78 to -90 dBc/Hz at 1-MHz offset from the carrier over the tuning range.
In general, phase noise decreases with oscillation frequency. One possible reason for this might be that a lower resistance is required in the active inductor to generate lower inductance, resulting in higher oscillation frequencies.
Moreover, from the trend of the phase-noise variation, it can be found that the noise floor is reached very early, which results in the flat characteristics of the phase noise at offsets higher than 1 MHz. Also, for high output power, the phase noise decreases. However, the variations of the output power and phase noise with the oscillation frequency are not monotonous.

1.12.3 TAI-based Hartley UWB-VCO

The basic structure for Hartley oscillator with a common source amplifier and passive inductors is shown in Figure 39(a). Also, Figure 39(b) illustrates this oscillator using two grounded active inductors in parallel.

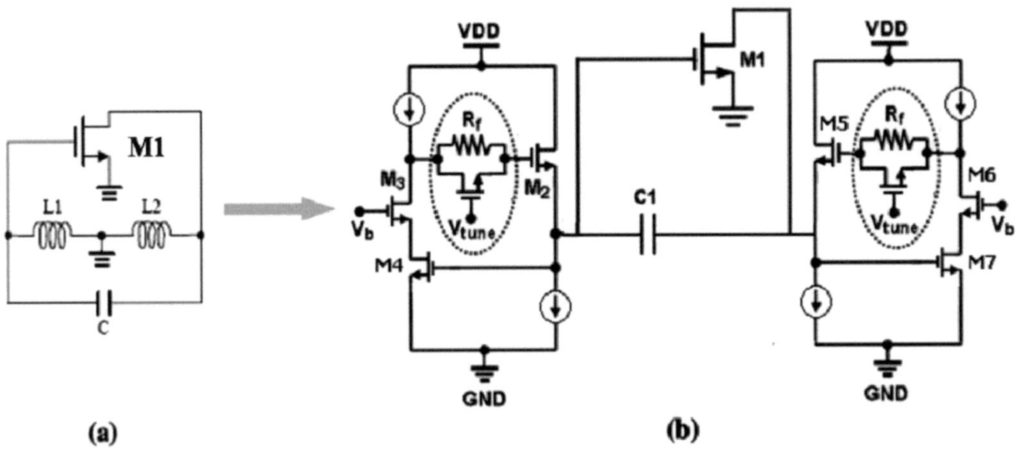

Fig. 39. a) Schematic of Harley Oscillator b) Harley oscillator with active inductors

To prevent the drain of the transistor from any external loading effects and also to suppress the harmonics, the transistor drain can be connected to feedback loop and the supply voltage through a series capacitance and a passive RF choke (see Fig. 40), respectively. Note that, the value of L larger than 5nH will sufficiently suppress the harmonics.

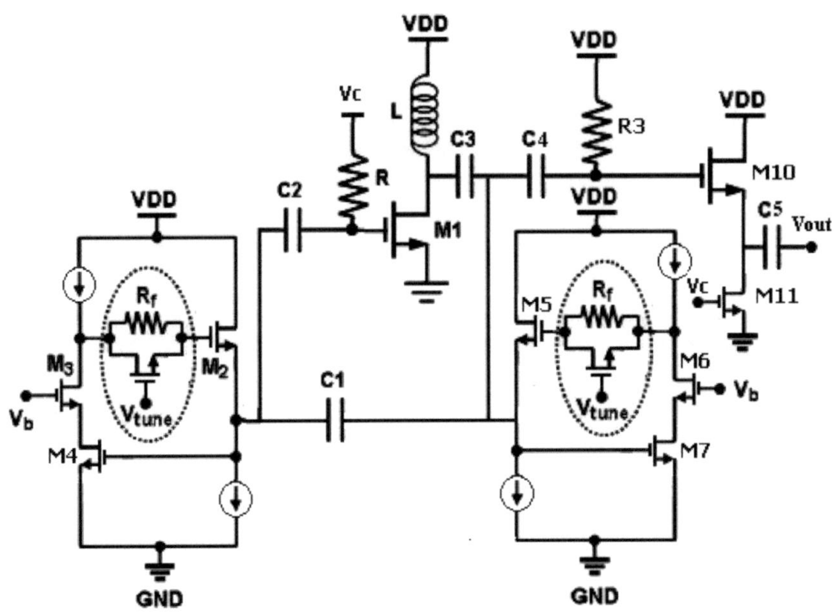

Fig. 40. Proposed schematic of UWB VCO

Assume the inductances associated with the two TAIs are L_1 and L_2. For starting the oscillation, the gain of the feedback system must equal to unity and the phase shift around the loop should be zero. Basically, the frequency of operation is $1/\sqrt{(L_1+L_2)C_1}$. However, in high frequency, the inductance L and the parasitic capacitances of the transistor M1 should also be counted for.

Thus, the size of M1 has an important role in frequency of oscillation, as well as in phase noise and power dissipation. The optimum size of the transistor is obtained when its gate-to-source capacitance (Cgs) is nearly equal to the feedback capacitance [19, 33]. In Fig. 41, the effect of width (W) of M1 on the phase noise and frequency of oscillation is illustrated, using a 0.18μm CMOS technology.

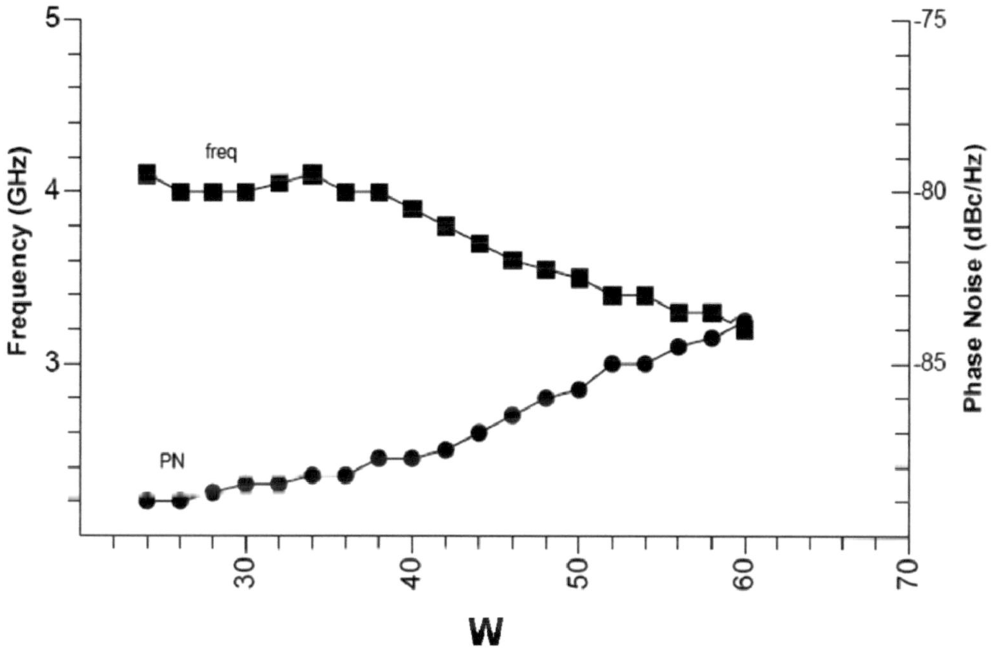

Fig. 41. Frequency and phase noise variation versus width (**W**) of M1

Obviously, when W increases, the frequency reduction is due to increasing parasitic capacitance and hence the total capacitance in the LC tank. The optimum W for 4GHz is achieved for W=38μm which gives rise to -88dBc/Hz of phase noise at 1MHz offset from the carrier.

The value of L also impacts the frequency and phase noise. The reduction of L for increasing the frequency is reasonable as long as it sufficiently suppresses the harmonics. Figure 42 shows the effect of using a relatively small **L** on output harmonics. Note that with decreasing the size of M1, the minimum requirement for **L** is increased because of smaller capacitance associated with M1.

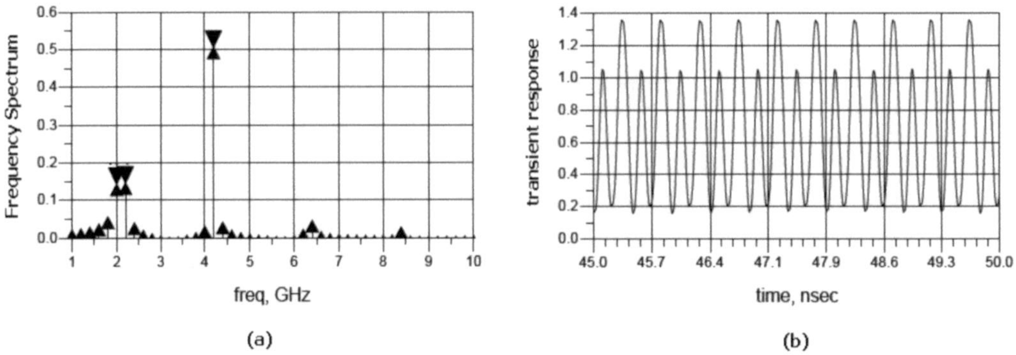

Fig. 42. a) spectrum of output signal b) time domain output signal with harmonics

Also, the value of resistance (R) in the gate of M1 affects the amplitude and bandwidth of oscillation. A typical value of 0.5KΩ can provide 1.3V of amplitude.
The capacitances in the feedback loop determine the phase noise and the frequency. Figure 43 shows the effects of C2, C3, and C4 on frequency. Small variations of the capacitors give rise to limited change in frequency, while the change in phase noise is large.

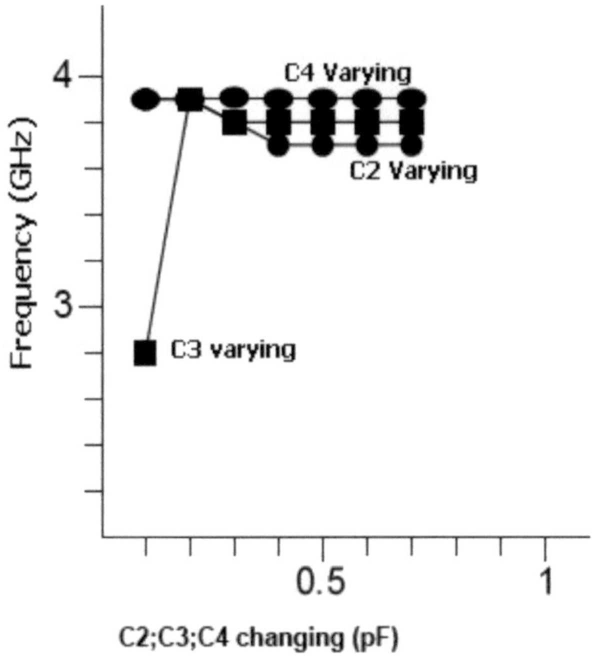

Fig. 43. The effect of capacitors on frequency

The lowest phase noise is achieved when the capacitors are equal. In this case, the optimum noise at 3.8GHz is -92dBc/Hz at 1MHz offset. Based on the results in Figure 41 for transistor sizing, the feedback capacitance C1 is approximately 10fF, i.e. the same size as C_{gs} in M1. The effect of C_1 as the main capacitor in the feedback has a significant impact on oscillation frequency and bandwidth. With decreasing C_1 higher frequency and better phase noise are achieved at the cost of decreasing the tuning bandwidth. Figure 44 shows the frequency as a function of C1.

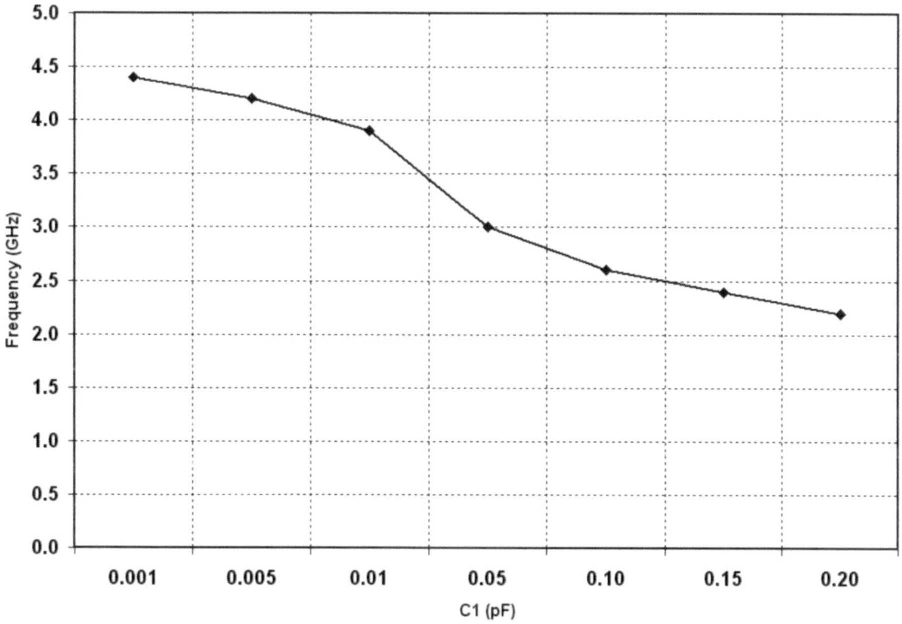

Fig. 44. Frequency as a function of C1.

The tuning of TAI is accomplished by the voltage V_{tune} of the transistor in feedback path (see Fig. 39), as long as its Vgs<Vt. Thus, the sizing of M1 is an important factor for tuning range

By increasing the aspect ratio (W/L) of M1, it needs a smaller gate voltage. As a result, the tuning transistor turns on with smaller voltage values, which in turn reduces the tuning range. By reducing the aspect ratio of M2, the equivalent capacitance of the active inductance is reduced, resulting in a better phase noise. Decreasing g_{ds} of M2 decreases the low-end frequency of the active inductance, and hence provides a wider tuning range.
The g_{ds} of M2 also affects the Q factor, and provides a way of preventing Q degradation. Thus, the active inductance is tuned using both V_{tune} and V_b.
Taking into account the feedback loop, the gain expression for VCO results in the following equation:

$$\left(CC_3LL_1\right)\omega^4-\left(CL_1+C_3L_2+C_3L\right)\omega^2+1=0 \quad (12)$$

Solving (42) for ω, we have:

$$\omega=\frac{\left(CL_1+C_3L_2+C_3L\right)-\sqrt{\left(\left(CL_1+C_2L_2\right)^2+C_2^2L^2+2C_2^2LL_1-2CC_2LL_1\right)}}{2CC_3LL_1} \quad (43)$$

The accuracy of operating frequency obtained from (43) will be compared to that obtained from simulation in the following.
Simulation illustrates that the phase noise is minimized when the sizing of transistor M1 is such that its C_{gs} is the same as C_1. Also, M1 plays a major role in designing the centre frequency of operation. As the aspect ratio (W/L) of M1 is increased, the central frequency will decrease, at the cost of higher total power dissipation. The variation of operating frequency versus Width (W1) of M1 is depicted in Figure 45.

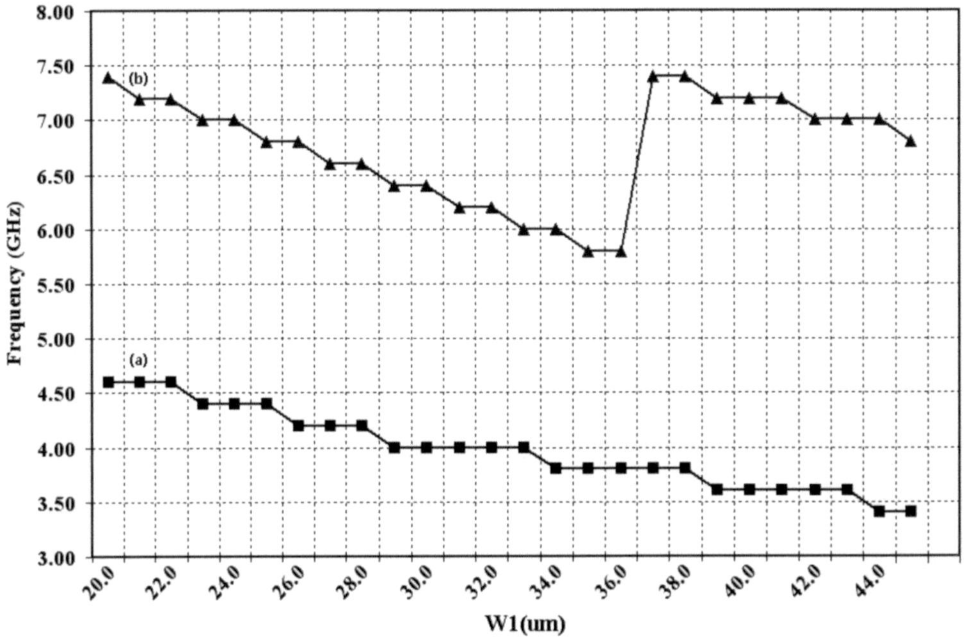

Fig. 45. a) lower frequency variation (b) upper frequency variation

As this figure shows, with decreasing the width of M1 and using the highest V_{tune}, output amplitude tends to reduce while frequency is increased. When the width is 37μm, the oscillator enters non-oscillation mode, forcing to decrease V_{tune} by 0.1V. Consequently, the high-side frequency range is lowered. This will also occur for 20μm width.
On the other hand, enlarging M1 increases the power. Figure 46 illustrates the trade-off between the power and bandwidth.

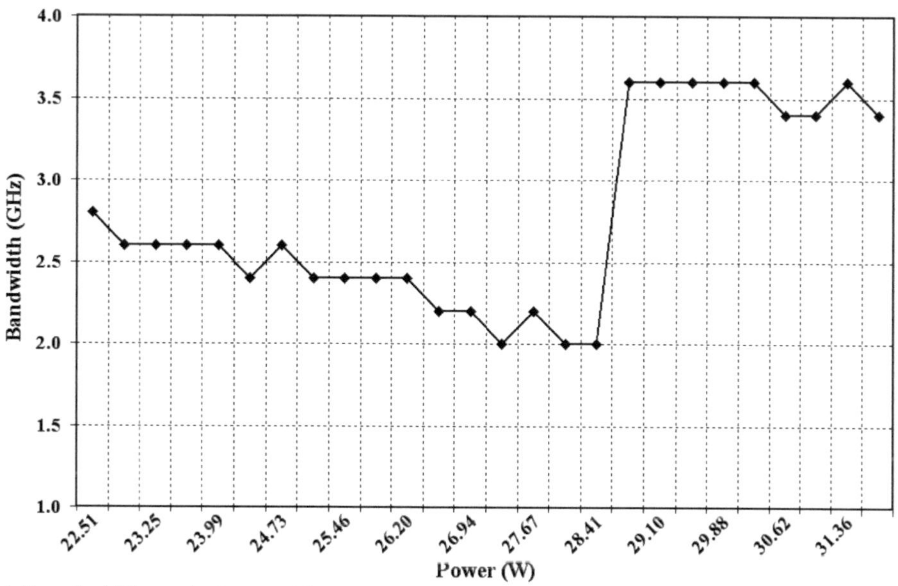

Fig. 46. Bandwidth variations with power

Thus, given the bandwidth and power, Figure 45 and Figure 46 can be used for proper sizing of M1.

Output stage in Figure 40 consists of a source follower amplifier (M10-M11), which in addition to DC cancellation handles the effects of the next stage. In contrast to M1 sizing, W/L ratio of the output stage less likely affects the frequency of oscillation. However, enlarging the size of the output stage improves the phase noise, as shown in Figure 47.

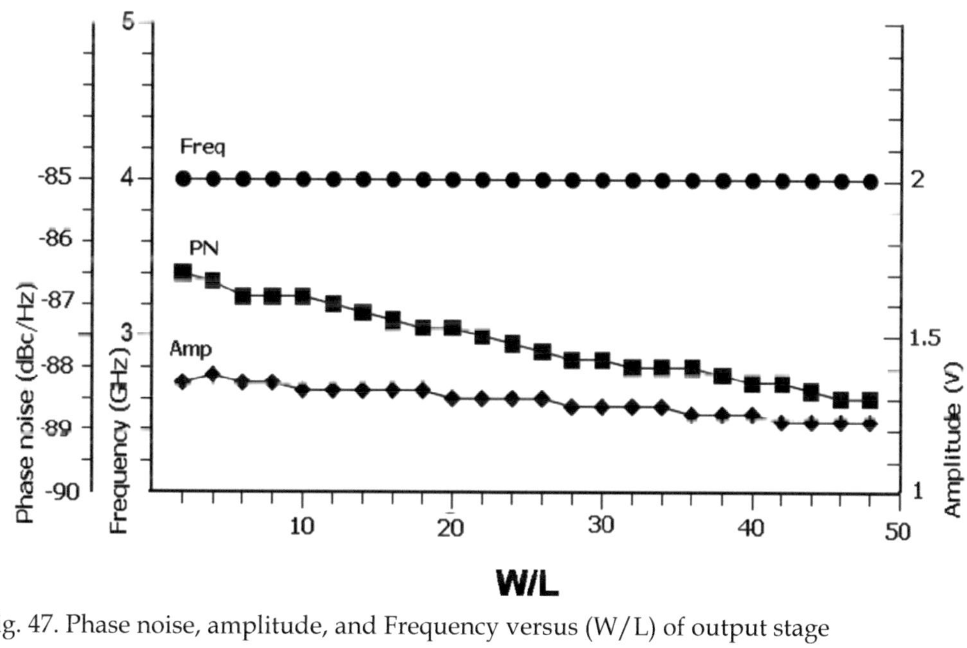

Fig. 47. Phase noise, amplitude, and Frequency versus (W/L) of output stage

1.12.3.1 Comparisons

The circuit in Figure 40 is simulated in a 0.18μm CMOS technology with a power supply of 1.8V. The complete VCO with the values of its elements is shown in Figure 48. The total power is 29.1mW, with dc current of 2mA in active inductor and 17mA in the main core of oscillator. Tuning range of 3.8GHz- 7.4GHz is achieved by varying V_{tune} from 1V to 2.5V, as shown in Figure 49. Maximum quality factor of active inductor is acquired at 3.8GHz with 0.55nH inductance. At 1MHz frequency offset, phase noise varies from -92.05dBc/Hz to -70dBc/Hz.

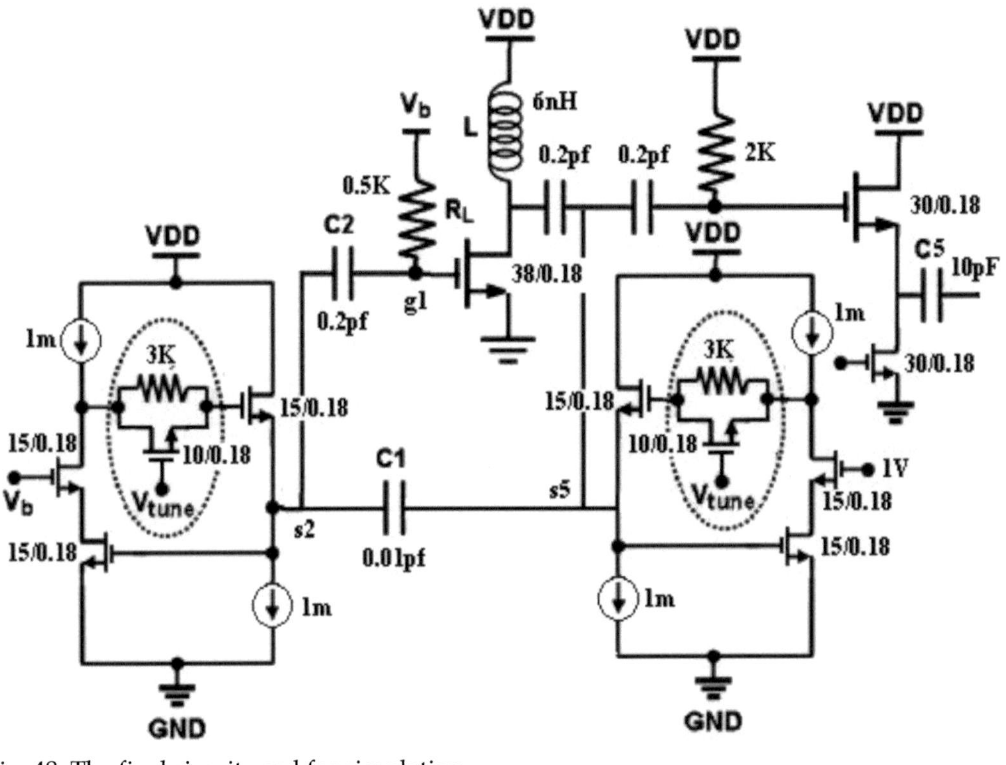

Fig. 48. The final circuit used for simulation

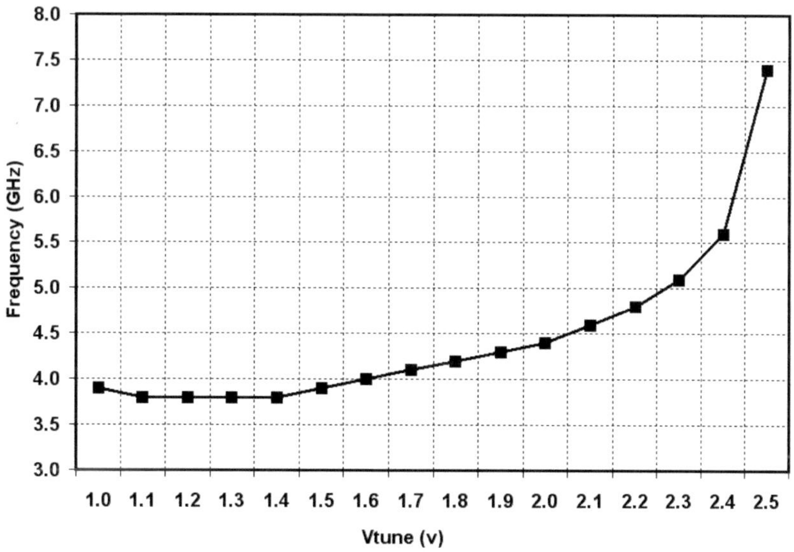

Fig. 49. Frequency variation with V_{tune}

Comparison of the accuracy between frequencies computed from (43) and those obtained from simulation are shown in Figure 50. V_{tune} can be increased until the parallel NMOS in active resistor switches on. As a result, the active inductor can be tuned from 0.34nH to 0.61nH, as depicted in Figure 51.

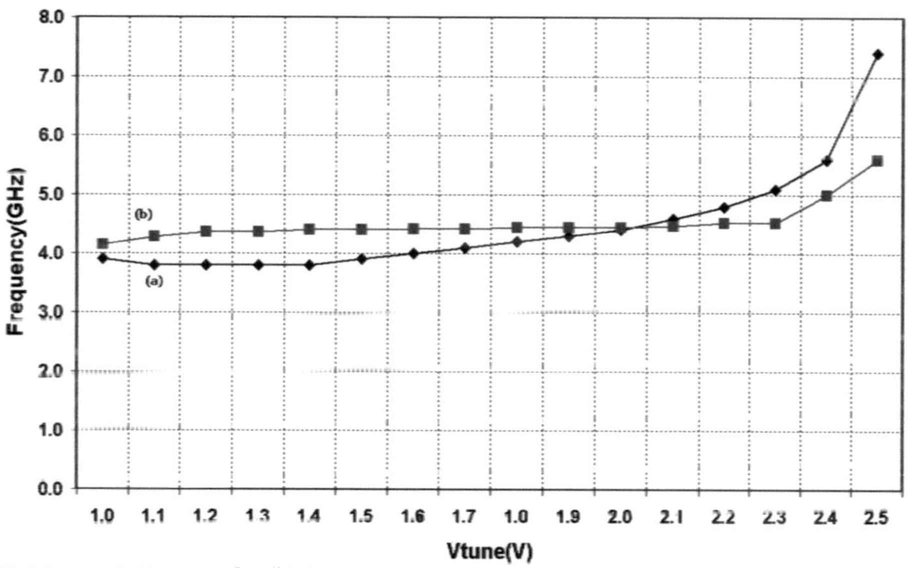

Fig. 50. (a) simulation results (b) frequencies derived from equation (43)

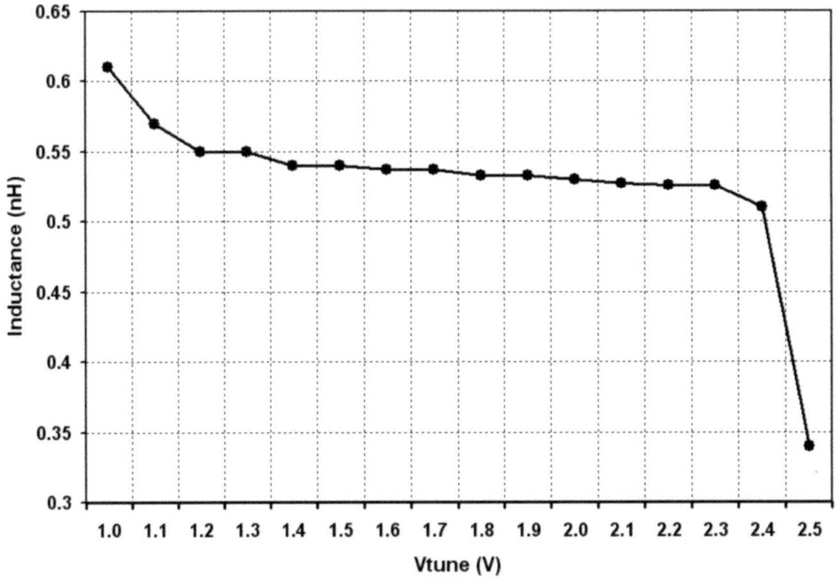

Fig. 51. Inductance variation with Vtune

1.12.3.2 Phase Noise Results

For phase noise simulation, different trade-offs between circuit elements may be examined to estimate the best performance. Simulations show that, when C2, C3 and C4 are equal, the best phase noise performance is achieved. Despite [30], which employs only a single biasing voltage for active load, separate bias voltage, Vc, can be utilized for active load M11 (see Figure 40). This will prevent quality factor degradation due to increasing V_{tune}, and improves the phase noise about 4dBc/Hz, as shown in Figure 52.

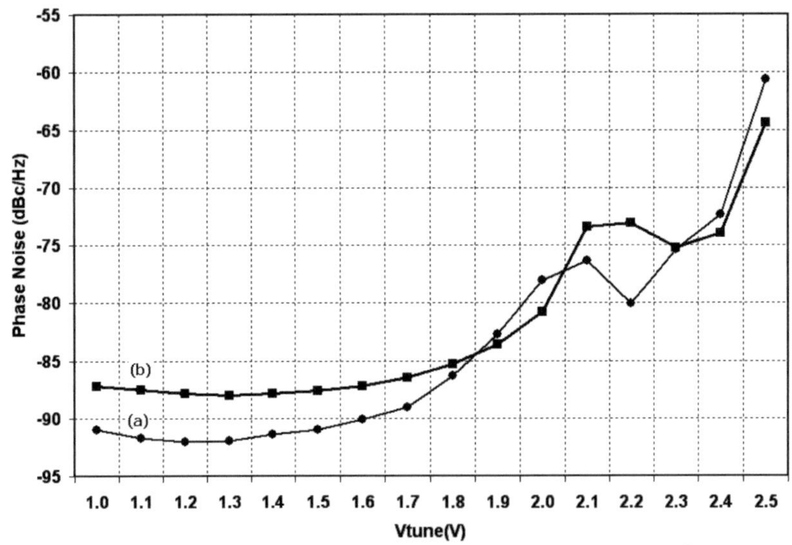

Fig. 52. (a) phase noise variation by tuning V_C (b) phase noise variation for V_C=constant

1.12.3.3 Effect of Bias Voltage Decreasing

The oscillator performance may also be examined by decreasing the supply voltage. Obviously, this will reduce the amplitude of oscillation. In this case, the phase noise quickly wraps up to worse quantity. The results of simulation at 4GHz show that reducing V_{DD} to 1.4V will have negligible effect on phase noise. Nevertheless, further reduction of the supply voltage will significantly degrade the phase noise, such that for V_{DD} =1V phase noise is -82dBc/Hz. Despite this, the frequency range of operation tends to maintain. These are shown in Figure 53 and Figure 54.

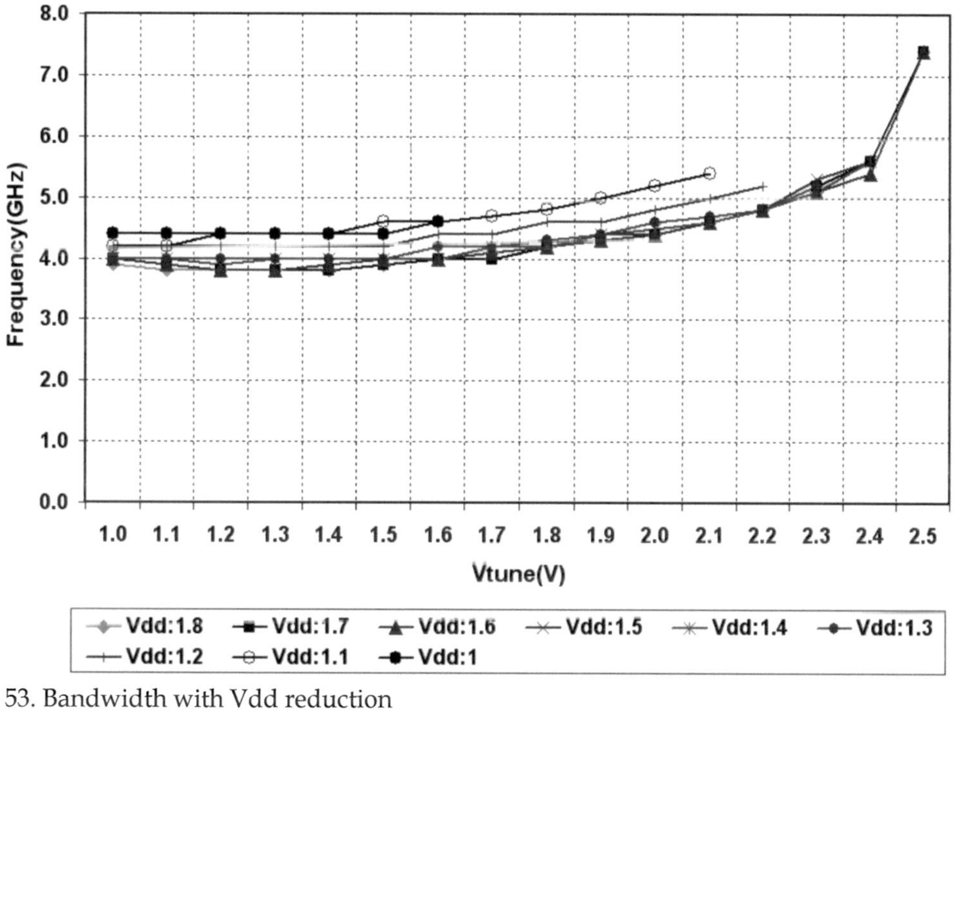

Fig. 53. Bandwidth with Vdd reduction

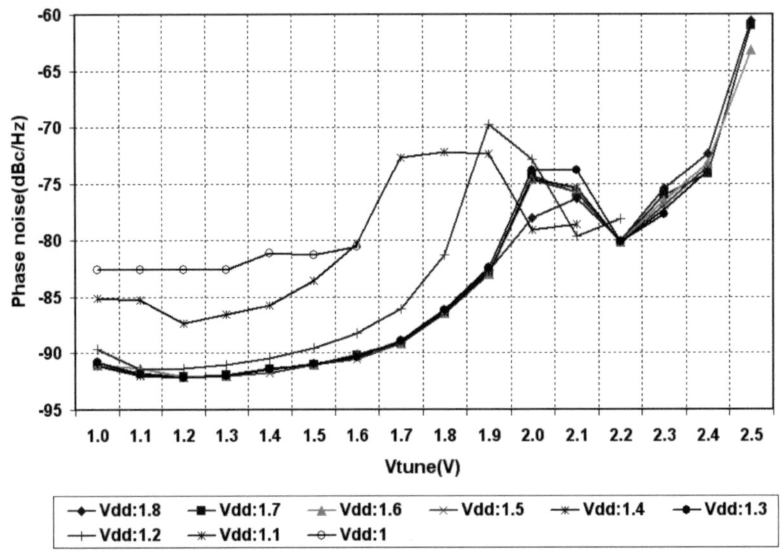

Fig. 54. Phase noise versus Vdd reduction

1.12.3.4 Effect of Process Variations

Simulation results show 2% and 0.1% change in frequency and phase noise, respectively, for 5% variation in bias voltage. For 10% change in temperature, the phase noise is only changed by 0.1% while the frequency is approximately constant.
In addition, mobility variation of NMOS model around 5% shows 0.5% and 1% variations in phase noise and frequency of operation, respectively.

1.12.3.5 Package and Wirebond Modeling

For accurate simulation of the RF circuit, an equivalent model of pad including the bonding wires is required to be tested [11]. Suppose the QFN package with equivalent model of Figure 55 is employed [31].

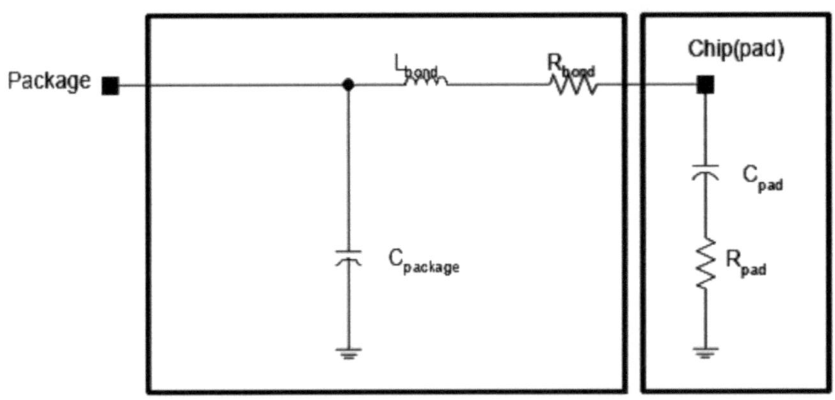

Fig. 55. Wirebonding and pad model [31]

Simulations show that adding the model elements to the circuit reduces the high-end frequency of the tuning range from 7.4GHz to 7.0GHz, while the phase noise will experience slight improvement. Other package models [32] were also tested for 3.8GHz. The results are compared in Table 1.

Package model	Frequency (GHz)	Phase Noise (dBc/Hz)	Equivalent circuit		
			L(nH)	C(pF)	R(Ω)
SOIC-20	3.8	-91.84	5.01	0.71	0.03
SSOP-20	3.8	-92.21	3.49	0.42	0.04
TSSOP-20	3.8	-92.18	2.80	0.31	0.05
TVSOP-20	3.8	-92.11	2.56	0.34	0.04
QFN-20	3.8	-92.25	1.10	0.35	0.05

Table 1. comparison between different package models

1.12.3.6 Oscillator Layout

Layout design can be divided into two parts as of passive and active devices. Capacitors and passive inductor may be designed using different layers of metals [19, 26]. For instance, passive inductor (L in Figure 48) can be implemented with 4 metal layers, which exhibits a very low serial resistor. Nevertheless, it introduces a very large parasitic capacitor, forcing the layout to be changed to one-layer design [19]. Here "L" is designed as square spiral inductor with layer one metal. Total area occupied for the lumped inductor is 157 μm *157 μm. Capacitors of C1 to C4 have been designed using metal layers of one to four, using finger-based architecture [26]. Total area occupied for each capacitor is 20 μm *21 μm. Poly silicon resistors are also utilized with narrow layers of poly silicon shaped in a way to form the desired resistance.

For phase noise reduction and chip size minimization, finger-based layout has been utilized for transistors. Each gate is divided into number of fingers, which are utilized symmetrically between cascade transistors. Using this method with poly silicon resistors, the active inductor layout is designed as shown in Figure 56.

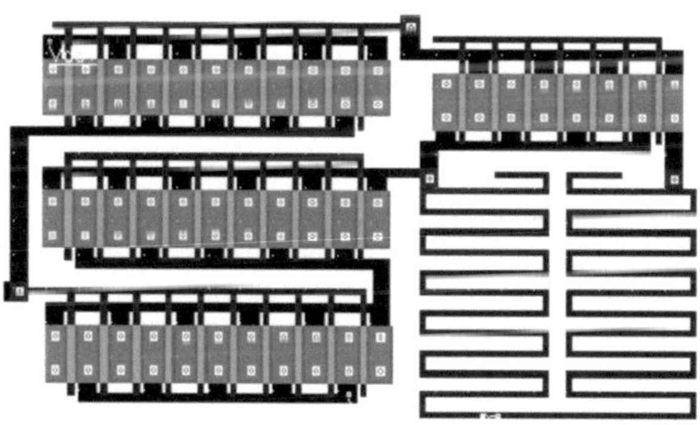

Fig. 56. Active inductor layout

Symmetric finger-based design typically helps in 10% chip size reduction. Total occupied die area is $0.22mm^2$ as shown in Figure 57.

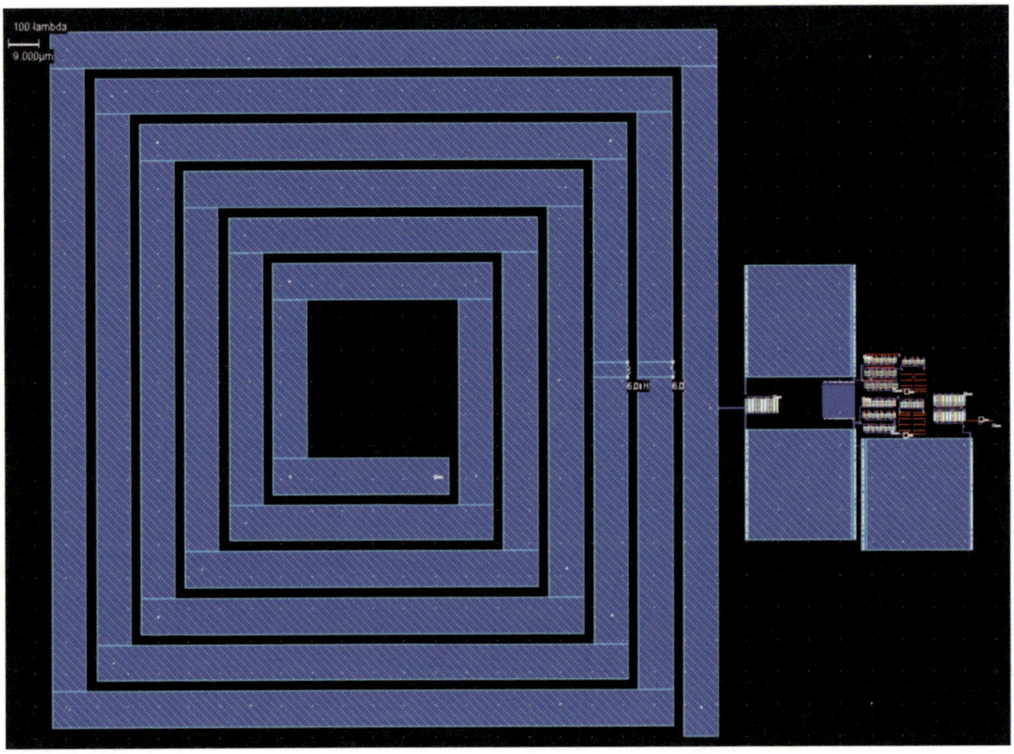

Fig. 57. VCO Circuit layout

1.12.3.7 Phase Noise Reduction

The noise reduction techniques were described in Section 1.11. First, the Noise filtering technique [28] is employed here. This implies LC resonating networks in the sources of M1 and M11, instead of directly connecting them to ground, as shown in Figure 58.

The frequency of oscillation for LC networks is 2GHz. This helps in turning the NMOS off rapidly and having a positive impact on the phase noise. Simulation in this case shows 3dBc/Hz improvement in the phase noise, reducing it to -93.7dBc/Hz from -91.01dBc/Hz at the frequency of 4GHz and the offset of 1-MHz. Although this limits the frequency tuning range, it can be used as a good technique for noise reduction when narrower frequency range is required.

As explained above, another technique for noise suppression is given in [29], in which a frequency to current converter extracts the noise properties of VCO output signal. This extracted current then passes through an integrator, which will converts it to a voltage carrying important noise and frequency properties. This voltage will enter a low pass filter and fed back as an input voltage to the oscillator.

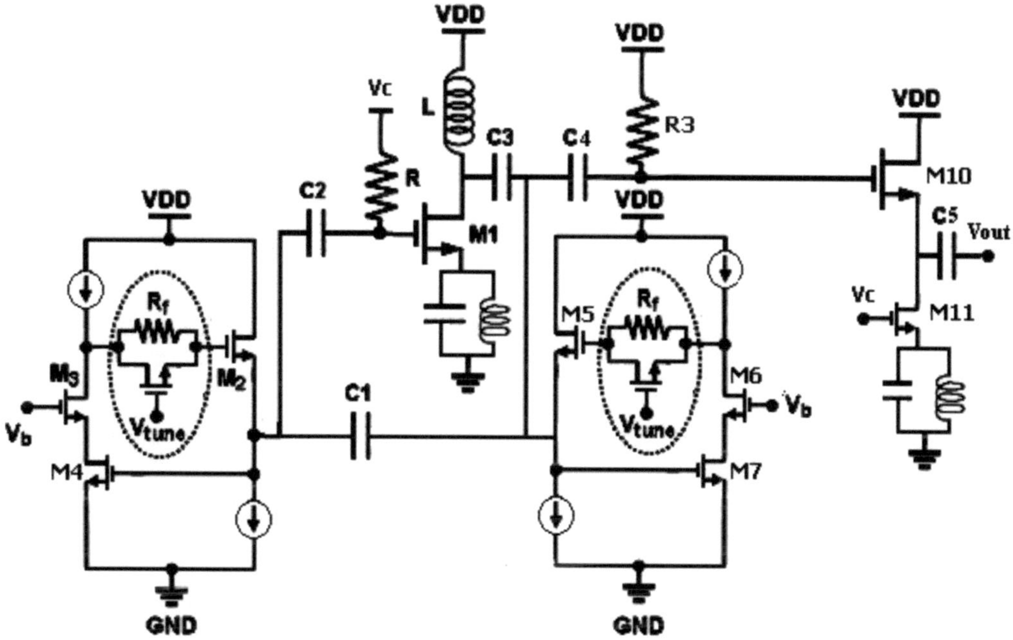

Fig. 58. Noise filtering technique

Although this method has been tested for ring oscillators [34] and shows a significant decrease in phase noise, here we obtain only 1dBC/Hz improvement for UWB oscillator. Characteristics of the proposed VCO and also a number of previously simulated oscillators are shown in Table 2 and Table 3, respectively. Comparison with similar designs illustrates a wider tuning range with better noise performance and gain factor for the UWB oscillator presented in this section.

Technology	0.18 μ m CMOS Technology
Power supply	1.8V
Bias current	17.21mA
Power Dissipation	29.1mW
Frequency Range	3.8GHz ~ 7.4GHz
Phase noise	-92.05 ~ -75.42 dBc/Hz @1MHz

Table 2. brief characteristics of proposed VCO

Year	Freq. range GHz	K_{VCO} (MHz/V)	Process	Ref.
2001	4.20 ~ 5.05	340	0.25um	[35]
2005	2.70 ~ 5.40	1687	0.18um	[30]
2005	0.50 ~ 2.0	500	0.18um	[27]
2005	1.14 ~ 2.46	270	0.18um	[7]
2005	1.90 ~ 2.19	116	0.18um	[34]
2007	3.80 ~ 7.40	2400	0.18um	[19]

Table 3. comparison with Previously simulated VCOs

1.13 Summary

This chapter has explored the techniques for VCO design with wide tuning range. An overview of various wideband tuning solutions proposed in the literature and the associated design challenges have been discussed. Wideband (Ultra Wideband) oscillators can be realized by carefully designing passive and active devices. The techniques for sizing and layout design of active and passive elements are discussed to optimize the phase noise performance of oscillators. The feasibility of CMOS VCO capable of multi-GHz operation has been demonstrated. The performance of the VCOs highlight the higher tuning ranges achieved in the case of inductive tuning. The VCO based on inductive tuning, realized by the tunable active inductor (TAI) using a 0.18μm CMOS technology, can provide a tuning range between 0.5–2.0 GHz and 3.8-7.4GHz using Colpitts and Hartley structures, respectively. Also, it is shown that with phase noise reduction techniques such as PLL-based feedback and harmonic tuning, the phase noise can be improved for 1-3dB.

1.14 References

[1] A. Hajimiri and T. Lee, "Design Issues in CMOS Differential LC Oscillators," IEEE Journal of Solid-State Circuits, vol. 34, no. 5, pp. 717–724, 1999.

[2] Ali Fard, "Analysis and Design of Low-Phase-Noise Integrated Voltage-Controlled Oscillators for Wide-Band RF Front-Ends", PhD Thesis, Department of Computer Science and Electronics, M¨alardalen University Press, 2006.

[3] Nathan Sneed, "A 2-GHz CMOS LC-Tuned VCO using Switched-Capacitors to Compensate for Bond Wire Inductance Variation", University of California, Berkeley, 2001.

[4] Axel Dominique Berny, "Analysis and Design of Wideband LC VCOs," PhD thesis, Electrical Engineering and Computer Sciences, University of Berkeley, 2006.

[5] A. Parssinen, J. Jussila, J. Ryynanen, L. Sumanen, and K. Halonen, "A 2-GHz wide-band direct conversion receiver for WCDMA applications," IEEE Journal of Solid-State Circuits, vol. 34, no. 12, pp. 1893–1903, 1999.

[6] D. Ham and A. Hajimiri, "Concepts and methods of optimization of integrated LC VCOs," IEEE J. Solid-State Circuits, vol. 36, no. 6, pp. 896–909, June 2001.

[7] Axel D. Berny, Ali M. Niknejad and Robert G. Meyer, "A 1.8-GHz LC VCO With 1.3-GHz Tuning Range and Digital Amplitude Calibration," IEEE journal of solid-state circuits, VOL. 40, NO. 4, pp. 909-917, 2005.

[8] J. S. Dunn et.al. "Foundation of RF CMOS and SiGe BiCMOS technologies," IBM J. Res. & Dev., vol. 47, no. 2/3, pp. 101-138, 2003.

[9] Krzysztof Iniewski, Wireless Technologies_Circuits, Systems, and Devices, CRC Press, Taylor& Francis Group, 2008.

[10] K. T. Christensen, "Low Power RF Filtering for CMOS Transceivers," PhD thesis, Electrical Engineering, Technical University of Denmark, 2001.

[11] T. Lee, "The Design of CMOS Radio-Frequency Integrated Circuits," *Cambridge University Press*, 1998.

[12] Junaid Aslam, "Study and Comparison of On-Chip LC Oscillators for Energy Recovery Clocking," Master thesis, Department of Electrical Engineering, Linköping University, 2005.

[13] C. P. Yue and S. S. Wong, "On-Chip Spiral Inductors with Patterned Ground Shields for Si-Based RF IC's," IEEE Journal of Solid-State Circuits, vol. 33, no. 5, pp. 743–752, 1998.

[14] A. Niknejad, R. Meyer, and J. Tham, "Fully-integrated low phase noise bipolar differential VCOs at 2.9 and 4.4 GHz," in Proceedings of the 25th Solid-State Circuits Conference, pp. 198–201, 1999.

[15] Chien-Cheng Wei, Hsien-Chin Chiu and Wu-Shiung Feng "An Ultra-Wideband CMOS VCO with 3-5GHz Tuning Range," *IEEE International Workshop on Radio-Frequency Integration Technology*, 2005

[16] Chao-Chih Hsiao, Chin-Wei Kuo, Chien-Chih Ho and Yi-Jen Chan, "Improved Quality-Factor of 0.18-μm CMOS Active Inductor by a Feedback Resistance Design," *IEEE Microwave and Wireless Components Letters*, vol. 12, no. 12, 2002.

[17] T. Y. K Lin and A. J. Payne, "Design of a Low-Voltage, Low-Power, Wide-Tuning Integrated Oscillator," *IEEE International Symposium on Circuits and Systems*, 2000

[18] S. H. Elahi, A. Nabavi, "A UWB LNA with Interference Rejection Using Enahnced-Q Active Inductor," Japan, IEICE Electronics Express, vol. 6, no. 6, 335 - 340, 2009

[19] M. Mehrabian, A. Nabavi "An Ultra Wide Tuning Range VCO with Active Tunable Inductors," International Review of Electrical Engineering, pp. 931 - 937, 2008.

[20] Timothy O. Dickson, Kenneth H. K. Yau, Theodoros Chalvatzis, Alain M. Mangan, Ekaterina Laskin, Rudy Beerkens, Paul Westergaard, Mihai Tazlauanu, Ming-Ta Yang, Sorin P. Voinigescu, "The Invariance of Characteristic Current Densities in Nanoscale MOSFETs and Its Impact on Algorithmic Design Methodologies and Design Porting of Si(Ge) (Bi)CMOS High-Speed Building Blocks, " IEEE Journal of Solid-State Circuits, vol. 41, no. 8, pp. 1830-1845, 2006.

[21] K. Hadipour, A. Nabavi, "Highly linear mm-wave CMOS low noise amplifier," IEICE Electronics Express, vol. 7, no. 1, pp. 20-26, 2010.

[22] Chien Chih Ho, Gong-Hao Liang, Chi-Feng Huang, Yi-Jen Chan, *Senior Member, IEEE*, Chih-Sheng Chang, and Chih-Ping Chao, "VCO Phase-Noise Improvement by Gate-Finger Configuration of 0.13-μm CMOS Transistors," IEEE Electron Devices Letters, vol. 26, no. 4, pp. 258-260, 2005.

[23] A. Kral, F. Behbahani, and A. A. Abidi, "RF-CMOS Oscillators with Switched Tuning," IEEE Custom Integrated Circuits Conference, pp. 555-556, 1998.

[24] Chung-Yu Wu, Chi-Yao Yu, "A 0.8V 5.9GHz wide tuning range CMOS VCO using inversion-mode band switching varactors," IEEE Conference, pp. 5079-5082, 2005.

[25] Neric Fong, Jean-Olivier Plouchart, Noah Zamdme, Duixian Liu, Lawrence Wagner, Calvin Plett and Gamy Tarr, "A Low-Voltage Multi-GHz VCȮ with 58% Tuning Range in SOI CMOS," IEEE custom integrated circuits conference, pp. 423-426, 2002
[26] Zhenbiao Li and Kenneth O., "A 900-MHz 1.5-V CMOS Voltage-Controlled Oscillator Using Switched Resonators With a Wide Tuning Range," *IEEE Microwave and Wireless Components Letters*, pp. 137-139, 2003.
[27] Yoshiaki Yoshihara, Hirotaka Sugawara, Hiroyuki Ito, Kenichi Okada, and Kazuya Masu, Inductance-Tuned LC-VCO for Reconfigurable RF Circuit Design," IEICE Electronics Express, vol.1, no.7, 156–159, pp. 156-159, 2004.
[28] Jinsung Choi, Seonghan Ryu, Huijung Kim, and Bumman Kim, "A Low Phase Noise 2 GHz VCO using 0.13 μm CMOS process," IEEE APMC2005 Proceedings.
[29] Dimitrios Mavridis and Kostas Efstathiou, "A VCO's Phase-Noise Reduction Technique," IEEE Conference, pp.101-104, 2006.
[30] Rajarshi Mukhopadhyay, John D. Cressler, and Joy Laskar, " Reconfigurable RFICs in Si-Based Technologies for a Compact Intelligent RF Front-End," IEEE Transaction on Microwave Theory and Techniques, vol. 53, no. 1, pp. 81-93, 2005.
[31] Sajay Jose, Design of RF CMOS Power Amplifier for UWB Applications, MS Thesis, Blacksburg, Virginia, 2004.
[32] Frank Mortan, Lans Wright, Quad Flatpack No-Lead Logic Packages, Application Report, Texas Instruments.
[33] M. Mehrabian, A. Nabavi, N.Rashidi, "A 4~7GHz Ultra Wideband VCO with Tunable Active Inductor," *ICUWB 2008*, pp. 21-24, 2008.
[34] Khouzema B. Unchwaniwala, Michael F. Caggiano, "Electrical Analysis of IC Packaging with Emphasis on Different Ball Grid Array Packages," IEEE Electronic Components and Technology Conference, 2001.
[35] C. Sa\mori, S. Levantino, V. Boccuzzi, A -94dBc/Hz@l00kHz, fully-integrated, 5-GHz, CMOS VCO with 18% tuning range for Bluetooth applications, IEEE Custom Integrated Circuits Conference pp. 201-204, 2001.

Design and implementation of ultra-wide-band CMOS LC filter LNA

GAUBERT Jean, BATTISTA Marc, FOURQUIN Olivier and BOURDEL Sylvain
IM2NP Aix-Marseille University & UMR CNRS 6242
FRANCE

1. Introduction

Demand for low cost and high data-rate wireless communication systems is increasing. Since the FCC has authorized communication in the 3.1 GHz to 10.6 GHz frequency band, several technologies have been developed to satisfy the communication market. Typically, Orthogonal Frequency Division Multiplexing (OFDM) technique appears to be good candidate for high speed data communication whereas carrier less Impulse Radio (IR-UWB) is a good solution for low cost systems or positioning systems. The allocated frequency bands for UWB are 3.1–10.6 GHz in North America, 6–8.5 GHz in Europe, and 3.4–4.8 GHz, 7.25–10.25 GHz in Japan.
In integrated UWB systems the LNA must provides a high voltage gain on a high impedance output load given by a digitizer or a pulse detector in Impulse Radio UWB architectures, or by a mixer in OFDM architectures. So the LNA is one of the most important analog bloc of the receiver. To achieve low cost the LNA must be fully integrated and must consume low power and low die area. Ideally the LNA must be broadband matched to a 50Ω antenna, and must provide a high voltage gain on a high impedance value capacitive output load. In addition a constant group delay is required in the signal bandwidth to maintain the signal integrity of the pulsed wideband signal.

2. Review of wide band CMOS low noise amplifiers architectures

Architectures allowing large bandwidths are numerous. The main architectures used in CMOS technology in the frequency ranges considered here are:
(i) Distributed Amplifiers, (ii) Feedback Amplifiers, (iii) Common Gate Amplifier, and (iiii) LC Filter LNA.
These architectures can be combined with techniques allowing a bandwidth enhancement as shunt or series peaking, or with techniques allowing the noise figure reduction as the noise cancelation technique.

2.1 Distributed Amplifiers

Among all the broadband amplifier topologies the distributed amplifier architecture is certainly the most powerful in term of bandwidth which can be obtained with a given technology. The principle of the distributed amplifier is to produce two artificial transmission lines coupled by several elementary amplifiers. The input and output capacitor of the elementary amplifiers are all or part of the capacitors constituting the transmission lines (Ginzton et al., 1948). The inductive part of the artificial transmission lines is synthesized by either inductors or by sections of transmission lines. In this topology the amplifier stages are not cascaded, but in parallel. Therefore distributed amplifiers provide lower gains compared with other architectures, but theirs main advantage is the ability to achieve very large bandwidths. In addition, these amplifiers provide a constant group delay over the entire bandwidth and they can be used in the context of pulse-type signals of very large bandwidth. The main disadvantages are the silicon area used to synthesize artificial transmission lines, and a heavy DC power consumption resulting from the numerous stages commonly required to obtain an high gain value.

Zhang (Zhang & Kinget, 2006) has used a distributed amplifier architecture to design a UWB LNA in a 0.18μm CMOS technology. The strength of this design is the power consumption which is below 10 mW. This low DC power consumption for a distributed amplifier has been obtained by using a low number of stages and also by biasing the MOS transistors in a weak inversion mode. But, as expected, the power gain is low (8dB) and also the silicon area is high (1.16 mm^2) because of the great number of spiral inductors (8).

Heydari (Heydari, 2007) has also used a distributed amplifier architecture in a 0.18μm CMOS technology. The originality of this design is to use bandwidth enhancing inductors. So the full FCC bandwidth is obtained with a good noise figure but with high power consumption (21mW). However the gain is low (8dB) and the number of inductors very high (11 spiral inductors).

2.2 Feedback Amplifiers

Another widely used broadband topology is the feedback architecture. The principle is to exchange gain with bandwidth. A shown in Fig. 1, a simple way to implement a feedback amplifier is to insert a resistor between the input and the output of a voltage amplifier implemented here by a cascode stage.

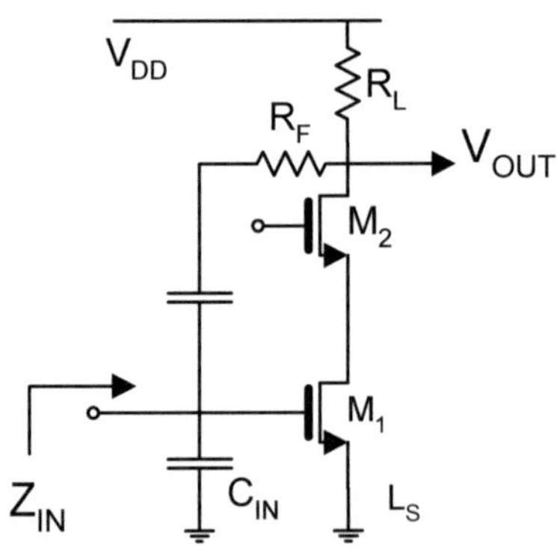

Fig. 1. Resistive feedback amplifier basic topology

C_{IN} is the total amount of input capacitance of the cascode amplifier stage. The voltage amplification in the low frequency range is given by (1) and the input impedance Z_{IN} by (2) and (3). In the low frequency range Z_{IN} is roughly equal to $1/g_{m1}$ if the transconductance value is high.

$$A_v = -\frac{g_{m1}.R_F - 1}{1 + R_F / R_L} \tag{1}$$

$$Z_{IN} = R_{IN} // C_{IN} \tag{2}$$

$$R_{IN} = \frac{R_L + R_F}{1 + g_{m1}.R_L} \tag{3}$$

To obtain a power matching in the low frequency range R_{IN} must be equal to the antenna impedance which has generally a standard value of R_0=50Ω. Consequently the 3 dB cut-off frequency directly depends on the input capacitor C_{IN} by (4).

$$f_C = \frac{1}{\pi.R_0.C_{IN}} \tag{4}$$

Therefore the bandwidth is limited by the input capacitor C_{IN} which is mainly the C_{GS} of the input MOSFET. If a 50Ω input matching is required in a given bandwidth f_{max} the size of the input MOSFET is limited and that leads to poor amplification and noise performances in CMOS technologies. A larger MOS size can be used by adding an inductor at the input but at the expense of a higher silicon area.

Such resistive feedback topology has been used by Kim in a 0.18μm CMOS technology (Kim et al., 2005). This amplifier uses an active load, and a bandwidth enhancing inductor to obtain more gain. It also uses an inductive series peaking in the first and second stage load. The measured power gain is 13.5 dB with 25mW DC power consumption. The noise figure is lower than 7dB in the 2-9 GHz frequency range and this LNA uses 3 inductors.

Reiha has used a feedback topology in a 0.13μm technology (Reiha et Long, 2007). However in this design the feedback is implemented by means of on chip inductive transformers. The full 3.1-10.6 GHz FCC bandwidth is obtained with a high gain (15dB), a low noise figure (less than 2.1dB) and furthermore with a DC power consumption less than 10 mW. Nevertheless this LNA shows a non linear phase response leading to a non constant group delay in the bandwidth which can lead to a distortion of the received pulse. But the main drawback of this design is the use of on chip transformers which are note always available in CMOS technologies.

2.3 Common gate Amplifiers

The common gate topology is also a simple way to obtain a wide band amplifier. Indeed a 50 Ω input matching can be obtained just by setting the g_m of the input MOSFET at the value of 20 mS. The LNA bandwidth is limited by the input capacitor which is mainly the C_{GS} of

the input MOSFET. So, like in the case of the resistive feedback topology, the size of the input MOSFET is limited by the bandwidth. That leads in CMOS technologies to a poor gain performance. So bandwidth extension techniques must generally be used at the expense of silicon area. Another drawback of this topology is that simultaneous power and noise matching is not possible. So if this LNA architecture is used without additional techniques such as noise cancellation the noise figure is very high.
Chen has used the Common Gate topology to design an UWB LNA in a 0.18μm CMOS technology (Chen & Huang, 2007). The first stage is a common gate stage with a bandwidth enhancing inductor, and the second stage is a cascode stage with an inductive series peaking. As expected the noise figure is high especially in the high frequency range (6.5dB@10GHz). The main advantage of this LNA is the low number of spiral inductors.

Liao has used the noise cancellation technique to lower the noise figure of the common gate topology (Liao & Liu., 2007). The noise cancellation principle is to add a second path between the input and the output. For the signal these two paths are in phase, but the noise current generates to opposite voltages at the input of these two paths and so the noise is cancelled at the output. This way this LNA shows a noise figure performance (5dB@10GHz) better than the previous LNA despite they are both designed in the same technology. However the drawbacks of noise cancellation technique are an increase of the DC power consumption and of the silicon area. Indeed this LNA consumes 20mW and uses 5 spiral inductors.

2.4 LC filters Amplifiers

In LC filter amplifier architecture the input matching cell is designed with inductors and capacitors like in a standard band-pass filter. So the LNA frequency response is accurately defined with a given center frequency, a given fractional bandwidth and a given ripple. The input MOSFET is embedded in the LC filter architecture (see Fig. 2). The input MOSFET is sized so its input capacitor matches the series capacitor of a ladder LC filter. The filter resistive termination is synthesized by the inductive degeneration of the input MOS M_1 provided by L_S. The strength of this architecture is to provide a well controlled band-pass response. This band-pass response reduces the noise equivalent bandwidth and so the noise output voltage. The main drawback is to need necessarily inductors and so low silicon area cannot be addressed with this architecture.

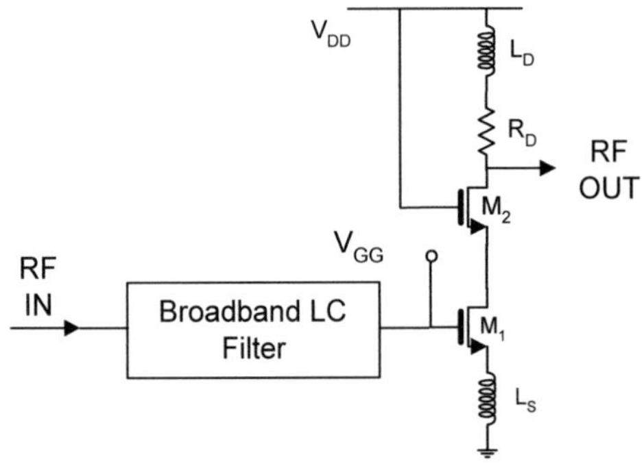

Fig. 2. LC filter amplifier topology

Bevilacqua has implemented a third order Tchehebytcheff band-pass input matching cell in a 0.18μm CMOS technology (Bevilacqua & Nikenejad, 2004). This LNA uses five spiral inductors and consequently consumes a large silicon area. The power consumption is low (9 mW) but the noise figure is high especially in the high frequency range (8dB@9.5GHz). The low noise figure performance is due to the large number of inductors between the input and the first amplification stage. The strength of this design is its high selectivity in comparison to previous architectures.
Battista has implemented a LC filter LNA in a 0.13 μm CMOS technology with a second order Tchehebytcheff band-pass input matching cell (Battista et al., 2008, a). Comparatively to a third order response the number of spiral inductors is reduced in the input matching cell and consequently there are less lossy inductors between the input and the gate of the input MOSFET. So a better noise performance is obtained especially in the high frequency range (4.8dB@10GHz).
Standard LC ladder filter input matching cell cannot address small fractional bandwidth such as 6-8.5 GHz ECC frequency band. These small fractional bandwidths can be addressed by using an input matching cell architecture using passive admittance inverters (Gaubert et al., 2005).

In the following sections we present a design method for these LC filter amplifiers based on our research works in this area published in (Gaubert et al., 2005), (Battista et al., 2008,a), (Battista et al., 2008,b) and (Battista et al., 2010).

3. LC filter input matching cell design

Two different cases have to be considered depending on the fractional bandwidth value of the input filter. The fractional bandwidth is defined by the absolute bandwidth divided by the center frequency.

3.1 Broadband input matching cell for small fractional bandwidths

If the full 3.1-10.6 GHz FCC UWB frequency band or a large bandwidth is used, then the fractional bandwidth b of the LC ladder input matching cell is around unity. In this case the design method proposed in (Bevilacqua & Nikenejad, 2004) leads to inductor values which can be integrated in standard CMOS technologies. On the other hand when b is smaller than about 50%, the inductor values of input matching cell are much dispersed and the integrated inductors have very low self-frequency resonance (SFR) values or low quality factors Q. (Battista et al., 2008,b). For example the ECC 6-8.5 GHz frequency band allows fractional bandwidth b lower than 35%. Such fractional bandwidths lead to large inductor values with self frequency resonance (SFR) lower than the operating LNA frequencies in traditional LC filter LNA architecture. By using admittance inverters, broadband LC filter input matching cell for small fractional bandwidths can be implemented in standard CMOS technologies (Gaubert et al., 2005).
Such input matching cells are obtained from the band-pass filter using admittance inverters shown in Fig. 3.a. which is equivalent to the classical LC ladder filter shown in Fig. 3.b. This filter can be implemented in CMOS technologies with the architecture shown in Fig. 3.c. The corresponding LNA input matching cell is given in Fig. 3.d. In Fig 3.a, 3.b, and 3.c the element values are normalized by the center frequency of the LNA bandwidth f_0 and by R_0 =

50Ω. In the LNA input matching cell given in Fig. 3.d., the terminating resistance of the input filter is synthesized by the inductive source degeneration of the FET M_1. This architecture allows the choice of arbitrarily values for the input matching cell inductors L_{P1} and L_{P2}. This way, practical inductor values leading to high SFR value and high Q factor can be chosen according to the LNA operating bandwidth. Once the values of inductors L_{P1} and L_{P2} are fixed, relations (5)-(13) give the input matching cell element values for a given power consumption and a given value of the degeneration inductance L_S.

$$z_{IN} = \frac{Z_{IN}}{R_0} = \frac{g_{m1} L_S}{R_0 C_{GS1}} + \frac{j\omega L_S}{R_0} + \frac{1}{j\omega R_0 C_{GS1}} = r_{IN} + j\, x_{IN} \tag{5}$$

$$J_1 = \sqrt{\frac{b}{g_1 \lambda_{P1}}} \tag{6}$$

$$J_2 = \frac{b}{\sqrt{g_1 g_2 \lambda_{P1} \lambda_{P2}}} \tag{7}$$

$$J_3 = \sqrt{\frac{b}{g_2 g_3 r_{IN} \lambda_{P2}}} \tag{8}$$

$$\gamma_{J1} = J_1 \left(1 + J_1^2\right) \tag{9}$$

$$\gamma_{J2} = J_2 \tag{10}$$

$$\gamma_{GS1} = J_3 \left(1 + J_3^2 r_{IN}^2\right) \tag{11}$$

$$\gamma_{P1} = \frac{1}{\lambda_{P1}} - J_1 - J_2 \tag{12}$$

$$\gamma_{P2} = \frac{1}{\lambda_{P2}} - J_2 - J_3 \tag{13}$$

In these expressions $b=(f_{P2}-f_{P1})/f_0$ is the fractional bandwidth, f_{P1} and f_{P2} are respectively the lower and higher cut-off frequencies and f_0 the center frequency of the input filter. g_1, g_2, g_3 are the normalized values of the low-pass equivalent filter, and J_1, J_2, J_3 are the normalized values of the admittance inverters (Zverev, 1967). The values of J_1 and J_3 must be low in comparison to unity in order to match an antenna resistor R_{ANT} of 50Ω.

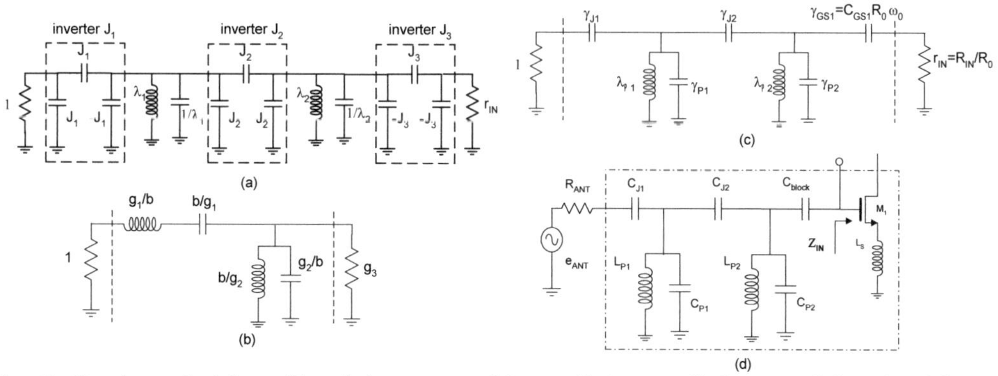

Fig. 3. Single ended broadband input matching cell for small fractional bandwidths. (a) Input matching cell architecture showing the admittance inverters. (b) Equivalent LC ladder filter (c) Input matching cell equivalent circuit. (d) LNA broadband input matching cell architecture.

3.2 Broadband input matching cell for large fractional bandwidths

In the case of large fractional bandwidths such as the full 3.1-10.6 GHz FCC UWB frequency band, the traditional LC filter architecture can be employed (Bevilacqua & Nikenejad, 2004). However a second order input matching cell allows lower number of inductors and consequently less input matching cell losses. The use of a two section LC ladder filter topology with a Tchebycheff second order response allows a noise figure reduction (Battista et al., 2008,a). The corresponding filter topology is shown in Fig. 4.a and the input matching cell of the LNA as shown in Fig. 4.b. In this implementation the series capacitor b/g_2 is synthesized by the MOSFET capacitance C_{GS}, and the series inductor g_2/b is synthesized by L_{G2} in series with L_G.

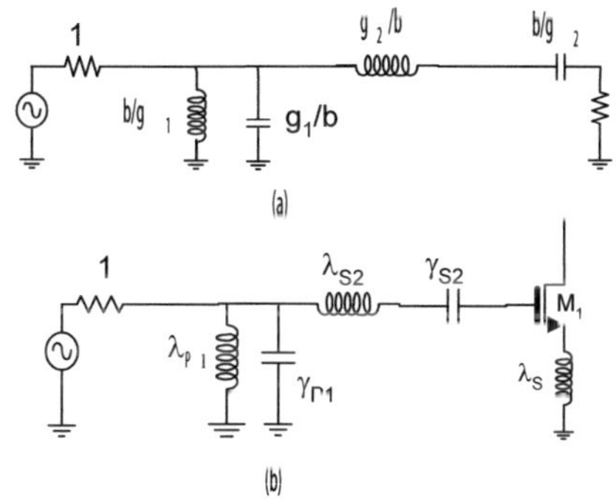

Fig. 4. Input matching cell for large fractional bandwidths. (a) Second order LC ladder filter. (b) Single ended input matching cell implementation.

The element values of the normalized input matching cell are given by relations (14)-(18) where g_i are the normalized values of the second order Tchebycheff Low-Pass ladder filter and b the fractional bandwidth.

$$\gamma_{P1} = \frac{g_1}{b} \tag{14}$$

$$\lambda_{P1} = \frac{b}{g_1} \tag{15}$$

$$\gamma_{GS} = \frac{b}{g_2} \tag{16}$$

$$\lambda_{S2} + \lambda_S = \frac{g_2}{b} \tag{17}$$

$$r_{IN} = \frac{1}{g_3} \tag{18}$$

The overall series inductor value L_{S2} + L_S is reduced by using an even Tchebycheff response. Indeed the normalized value of the corresponding inductor g_2/b is low in such response type. Consequently L_{S2} and L_S are low enough to have good features even in the high range of the UWB frequency band. Comparatively, the use of a third-order response would lead to a series resonator with a normalized inductor value of g_1/b much higher.

4. LC filter LNA architecture analysis

4.1 LNA architecture modeling

The LNA architecture is given in Fig. 5.a. This architecture can be analyzed in the following way (Battista et al., 2008,b).

In the bandwidth the LNA input is power matched to the antenna. Consequently the resistive termination R_{IN} of the input matching cell, provided by the MOSFET M_1 by means of inductive source degeneration, receives an input power equal to the available power P_{AV} at the antenna output given by (19) where e_{ANT} is the open voltage at the antenna and R_{ANT} its radiation resistance.

$$P_{AV} = R_{IN} i_1^2 = \frac{e_{ANT}^2}{4 R_{ANT}} \tag{19}$$

So, in the input filter bandwidth, the magnitude of the current i_1 flowing into the gate of M_1 is given by:

$$i_1 = \frac{e_{ANT}}{\sqrt{4 R_{IN} R_{ANT}}} \tag{20}$$

The equivalent circuits of the first and the second stage are given respectively in Fig. 5.b. and Fig. 5.c. M_2 is loaded by the parallel resonator L_3, C_3, R_3, where C_3 is the overall capacitor at M_2 drain which is given by:

$$c_3 \cong c_{GD2} + c_{DB2} + c_{IN2} \quad (21)$$

where C_{IN2} is the second stage input capacitance. Assuming the effect of C_{GD1}, C_{DB1} and C_{GS2} negligible in the cascode configuration, and neglecting the real part of the input impedance of the second stage, we get:

$$\frac{v_{OUT1}}{\left(e_{ANT}/2\right)} = \frac{L_3}{L_S}\sqrt{\frac{R_{IN}}{R_{ANT}}}\frac{1}{1+\frac{j\omega}{Q_3\omega_{03}}-\left(\frac{\omega}{\omega_{03}}\right)^2} = \frac{A_{V1}}{1+\frac{j\omega}{Q_3\omega_{03}}-\left(\frac{\omega}{\omega_{03}}\right)^2} \quad (22)$$

With

$$Q_3 = \frac{R_3}{L_3\omega_{03}} \qquad \omega_{03} = \frac{1}{\sqrt{L_3C_3}} \quad (23)$$

It should be pointed that (22) is valid only in the LNA bandwidth where the LNA input is power matched to the antenna by the input matching cell. Outside the LNA bandwidth, the input matching cell provides a band-pass response which modifies the output voltage v_{out1}.

The second stage voltage gain A_{V2} can be approximated by (24), where $1/r_{DS3}$ and $1/r_{DS4}$ are the output conductance of M_3 and M_4. R_L and C_L are set by the input impedance of the following stage (see Fig. 5.a).

$$\frac{V_{Out2}}{V_{Out1}} \cong \frac{-g_{m3}r_{EQ}}{1+j\omega/\omega_{C2}} = \frac{A_{V2}}{1+j\omega/\omega_{C2}} \quad (24)$$

where

$$r_{EQ} = r_{DS3} \,//\, r_{DS4} \,//\, R_L \quad (25)$$

$$c_{EQ} = \left(c_{DB3} + c_{GD3} + c_{DB4} + c_{GD4} + c_L\right) \quad (26)$$

$$\omega_{C2} = \frac{1}{r_{EQ}c_{EQ}} = 2\pi f_{C2} \quad (27)$$

Finally the whole LNA voltage amplification in the bandwidth is given by:

$$\frac{v_{OUT2}}{\left(e_{ANT}/2\right)} = \frac{A_{V1}}{1+\dfrac{j\omega}{Q_3\omega_{03}}-\left(\dfrac{\omega}{\omega_{03}}\right)^2}\frac{A_{V2}}{1+\dfrac{j\omega}{\omega_{C2}}} \tag{28}$$

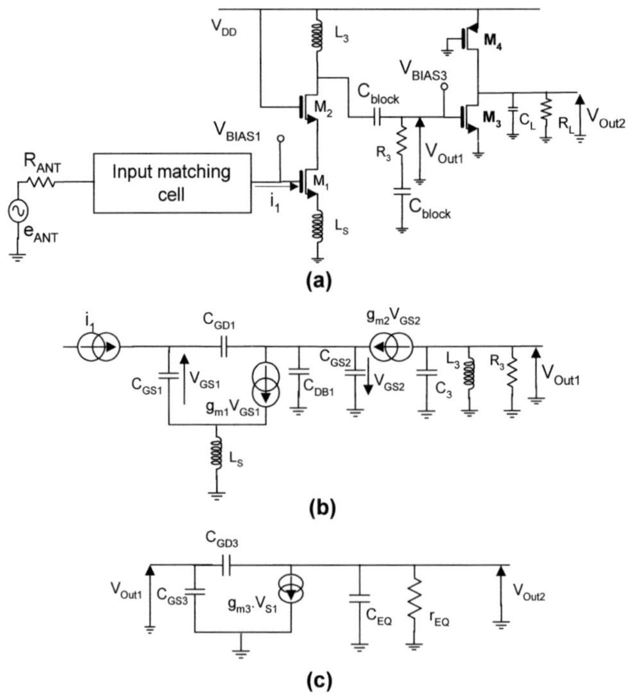

Fig. 5. LNA architecture. (a) LNA architecture. (b) First stage equivalent circuit. (c) Second stage equivalent circuit.

4.2 Noise figure optimization

The goal is to minimize the noise figure at power matching for a given current consumption I_{01} of the LNA first stage.

It is shown in (Nguyen et al., 2004) that the optimum noise impedance Z_{OPT} of the inductively degenerated common source topology is given by:

$$Z_{OPT} = \frac{A}{\omega C_{GS1}} - \frac{B}{j\omega C_{GS1}} - jL_S\omega \tag{29}$$

where A and B are two parameters that only depend on the MOS noise parameters α, δ, γ, c. From (5) and (29) we get:

$$Z_{OPT} - Z_{IN}^{*} = \frac{A}{\omega C_{GS1}} - R_{IN} + \frac{(1-B)}{j\omega C_{GS1}} \tag{30}$$

In order to minimize the noise figure at power matching we can cancel the real part of (30) at a given frequency f by setting M_1 width to fulfil:

$$\gamma_{GS1}\,\Omega = \frac{A}{r_{IN}} \tag{31}$$

In (31) Ω is the normalized frequency f/f_0. It is important to notice that the imaginary part of (30) cannot be cancelled because B is not a design parameter. Indeed B only depends on the used process. From (31) and (5), we obtain the optimal source inductor value:

$$L_{SOPT}\left(\omega\right) = \frac{A}{g_{m1}\omega} \tag{32}$$

For band-pass LNAs the optimal L_S value must be chosen with (32) at the center frequency of the bandwidth f_0. So the discrepancy is less than (b/2)% in the whole LNA bandwidth.

In the case of small fractional bandwidths, an optimal M_1 size can be found to satisfy both (31) for noise minimization and the input matching cell relations (5)-(13). (11) can be approximated by (33) because J_3 must be chosen in order to be low in comparison to unity in the input matching cell design as mentioned above.

$$\gamma_{GS1} \approx J_3 \tag{33}$$

Reporting (33) and (31) in (8) gives (34). (34) gives the optimal MOSFET width as a function of the input filter characteristics (g_1, g_2, g_3, b) and the inductor normalized value λ_{P2}.

$$\gamma_{GS1} = \frac{b\Omega}{g_2 g_3 \lambda_{P2} A} \tag{34}$$

In the case of large fractional bandwidths, the size of the MOSFET M_1 is set by (16). From (16), and (31), with (18) we get (35):

$$b = \frac{A g_2 g_3}{\Omega} \tag{35}$$

(35) shows that the noise minimization cannot be achieved for arbitrarily values of the fractional bandwidth b. This issue can be addressed by using the DC blocking capacitor C_{S2} in Fig. 4.b as a design parameter allowing an increase of the M_1 size. This way (16) becomes:

$$\frac{\gamma_{S2}\cdot\gamma_{GS}}{\gamma_{S2}+\gamma_{GS}} = \frac{b}{g_2} \tag{36}$$

and both the noise minimization and the power matching can be achieved by taking a M_1 width leading to (37):

$$\gamma_{GS} = \frac{A.g_3}{\Omega} \tag{37}$$

Provided (38) is satisfied.

$$\gamma_{GS} = \frac{A.g_3}{\Omega} \geq \frac{b}{g_2} \tag{38}$$

If (38) is not satisfied another way is to use a parallel capacitor between the gate and the source terminals of M_1 in order to decrease the value of C_{GS} while satisfying (16).

4.3 Voltage gain maximization

(28) shows that the voltage amplification in the LNA bandwidth results from the product of a second order low pass response by a first order low pass response given by the second stage. A high r_{EQ} value may be used in order to maximize the second stage gain A_{V2}. However a high r_{EQ} value leads to a second stage cut-off frequency lower than the lower cut-off frequencies of the LNA. To overcome this problem, the drop with the frequency of the second stage voltage gain in the LNA bandwidth is compensated by setting the quality factor Q_3 of the second order response greater than $1/\sqrt{2}$.
To maximize A_{V1}, (22) shows that the value of L_3 must be maximum. However the frequency resonance f_{03} of the parallel resonator must be higher than the highest cut-off frequency of the LNA. So, in order to maximize L_3, C_3 must be minimized. In this way we size M_3 much smaller than M_2. In addition M_2 is set to the minimal value which allows the driving of the DC current of the first stage in order to minimize C_{GD2} and C_{DB2}.
To maximize further A_{V1}, (22) shows that L_S must be minimized. However the value of L_S must satisfy the input matching cell relations.

In the case of small fractional bandwidths the input matching cell relations are given by (5)-(13). Taking into account (33), L_S and g_m values are thus linked by (5) and (9) and must satisfy (39):

$$g_m L_S = \frac{b}{\gamma_{GS} g_2 g_3 \omega_0 \lambda_{P2}} \tag{39}$$

So, in this topology, the voltage gain can be increased for the same current consumption by decreasing L_S and by increasing C_{GS} or L_{P2} in order to maintain (39). Another way to increase the voltage gain by decreasing L_S is to maintain the $g_m L_S$ product at a constant value by increasing the current consumption.

In the case of large fractional bandwidths the input matching cell relations are given by (1) and (14)-(18). (1), (16), (18) give (40):

$$g_m L_S = \frac{b}{g_2 g_3 \omega_0} \tag{40}$$

Additionally the size of M_1 is set by (16). Consequently the only way to increase the voltage gain is to decrease L_S while maintaining the $g_m L_S$ product to a constant value by increasing the current consumption.

5. Differential ended architecture

5.1 Differential ended Input matching cell for small fractional bandwidths

The differential ended input matching cell is deduced from the single ended architecture shown in Fig. 3.a (Battista et al., 2010). In this topology the equivalent differential ended cell shown in Fig. 6.a has the same number of inductors than the single ended cell. In order to achieve higher gain, the differential ended input filter implemented in the LNA could be terminated by two cascode common source amplifier with inductive degeneration as shown in Fig 6.c. The element values of the differential ended input matching cell are given by the relations 5-13 like in the single ended matching cell case.

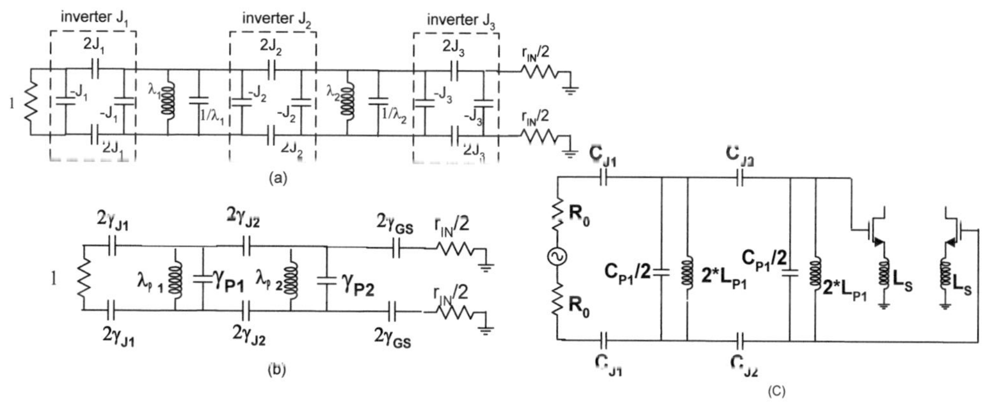

Fig. 6. Differential ended matching cell. (a) Normalized band-pass filter with admittance inverters. (b) Normalized input matching cell. (c) Input matching cell implementation.

5.2 Differential ended Input matching cell for large fractional bandwidths

A differential ended input matching cell implementation, shown in Fig. 7, has been proposed in (Bevilacqua et al., 2006). In order to enhance the amplification performance in the UWB frequency range, two arms, build with common source with inductive degeneration, are preferred to differential transistor pair architecture. Element values of the differential ended input matching cell are deduced from the single ended input matching cell case shown in Fig. 4.b, and can be computed with relations (14) -(18).

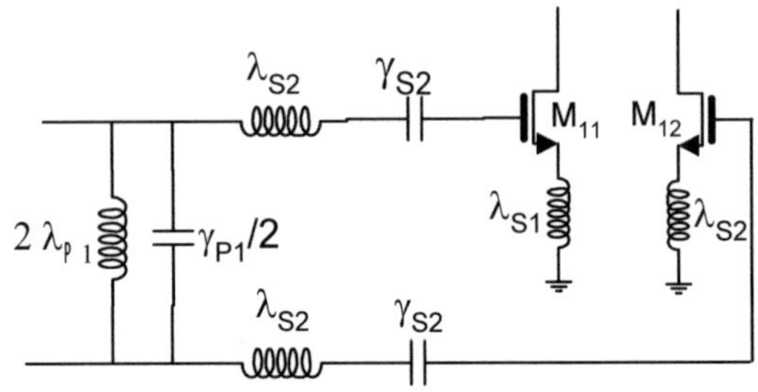

Fig. 7. Input matching cell for large fractional bandwidths. (a) Second order LC ladder filter. (b) Single ended input matching cell implementation. (c) Differential ended input matching cell.

5.3 Differential ended LNA architectures

A fully differential ended LNA architecture is shown in Fig. 8 where the first and the second stage of the single ended architecture have been duplicated. This way the fully differential LNA has similar electrical performances than the single ended LNA at the price of about twice the DC power consumption.

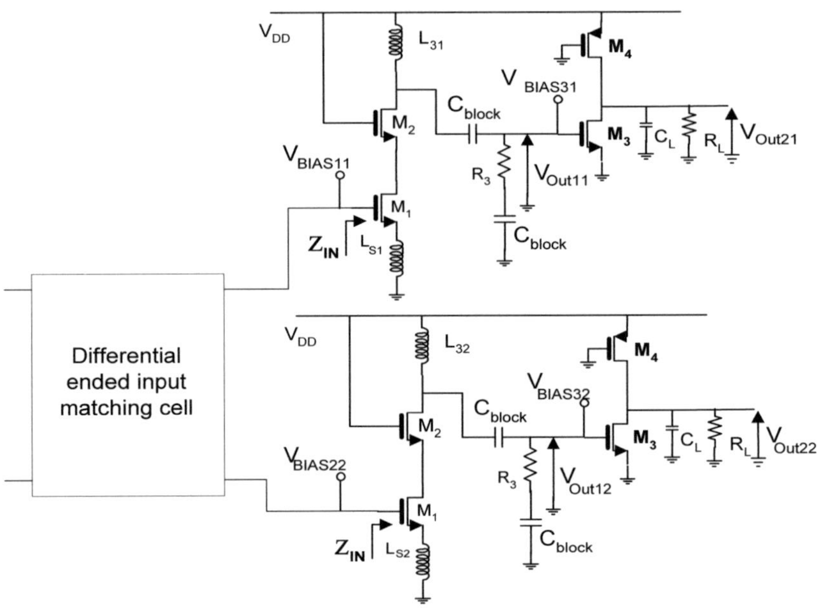

Fig. 8. Fully differential LNA architecture.

A differential ended termination at the LNA output can also be obtained by adding a third stage where a single to differential conversion is made as shown in Fig. 9. This way the inductor number needed is the same than in the single ended architecture and the whole LNA power consumption is nearly unchanged. Like for the second stage, the third stage voltage gain drop with the frequency must be compensated by setting the Q factor Q_3 of the first stage output load to the value that achieves a flat LNA amplification in the whole bandwidth.

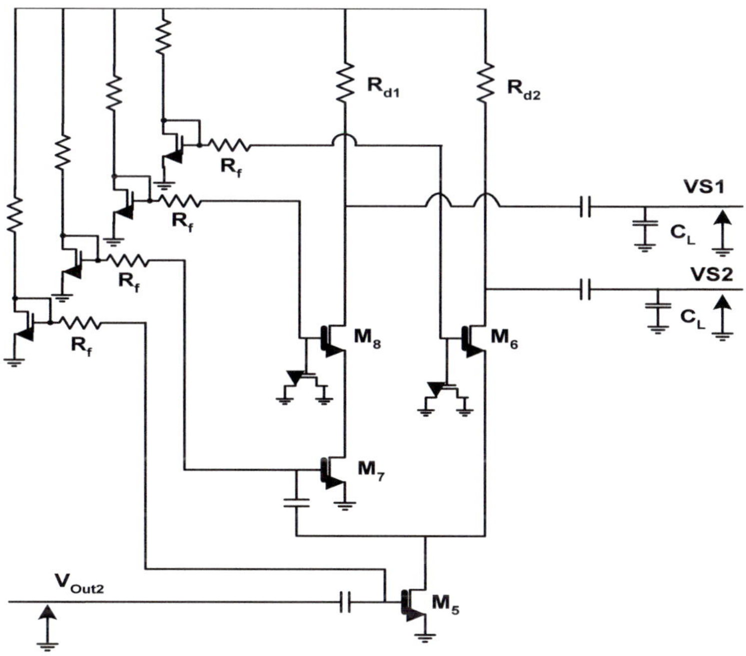

Fig. 9. Single ended to differential ended conversion stage.

6. LNA Implementation in Standard CMOS Technologies

6.1 Layout and simulation methodology

An implementation methodology of LC filter UWB LNA in a 0.13μm standard CMOS technology is given in this section (Battista et al., 2010). The technology consists of a high resistive substrate (about 10 Ωcm) with 6 metal layers, MIM capacitors and spiral inductors with RF models. Fig. 10 shows the microphotograph of a stand alone LNA prototype. Due to the large distances between inductors imposed by the technological design rules, long interconnects as long as 300μm are needed in the input matching cell. In such interconnects both the inductive, capacitive and resistive effects must be taken into account in simulation in order to optimize the layout. Additionally such interconnects must be properly designed to minimize the losses and so the noise figure. For theses purposes we used low characteristic impedance microstrip lines (MSL) designed according to the technological design rules. Generally, for MSL topology realized in CMOS technologies, ground is located on the lowest metal layer and the highest and thickest metal layer is used to design the signal path. CMOS foundry design kits don't usually contain transmission line models. To describe MSL, physical TEM T-Line model available in A.D.S. software has been used. This model provides an electrical description of frequency dependant loss in single mode quasi-TEM wave-guide. All parameters of the model are extracted from full wave Electromagnetic simulations.

The MSL ground plane, which is connected to the HF ground pads, is the local ground at the chip level. The power supply pad (VDD) is decoupled by using several MIM and MOS capacitors in order to get a large on chip capacitor value (a few hundred of pF) leading to a low return path ground impedance at high frequencies.

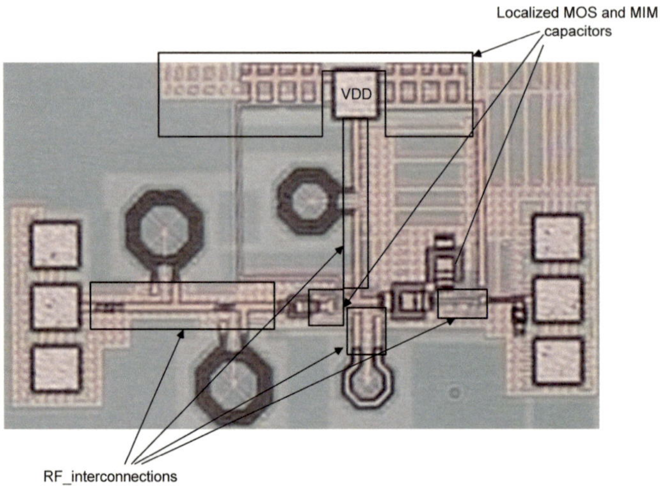

Fig. 10. Microphotograph of a stand alone LNA prototype.

For the LNA electrical simulations, we used the design kit models for active and passive lumped components, and the T-Line model, described above, for the MSL. MSL effects modify LNA performances, particularly the bandwidth and the cut-off frequencies. So to achieve the targeted characteristics, the initial component values must be modified according to the layout, by taking into account the interconnect effects. Fig. 11 shows a comparison between the measured input return loss and the simulation results with and without the MSL model. This comparison clearly shows that interconnects effects shift significantly the input matching cell bandwidth (about 1GHz in this case). By using MSL, both parasitic effects (inductive and capacitive effects) are well modelled and controlled, consequently the simulation results agree well with measurement results. Fig. 12 shows a comparison between measured and simulated results of the voltage gain and the noise figure for a 6.8-8.8 GHz LNA prototype. A good agreement between measured and simulated results is also observed.

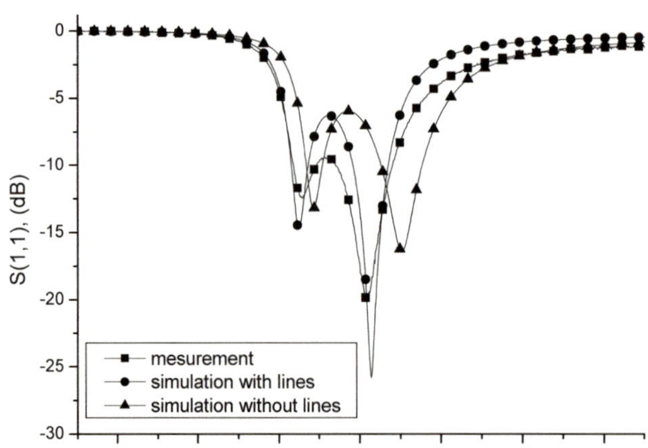

Fig. 11. Simulated and measured input return loss for a 6.8-8.8 GHz LNA.

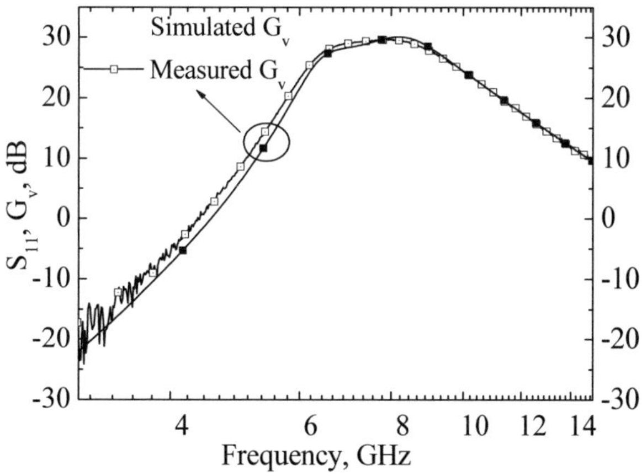

Fig. 12. Simulated and measured voltage gain loss for a 6.8-8.8 GHz LNA.

6.2 LNA implementation in UWB System on Chip

The methodology presented in section 6.1 has been validated on several stand alone LNA for different UWB sub-bands. These results are presented in section 7. Despite of the good agreement observed between simulation and measurement results in the case of simple test structures, UWB LNA can not be integrated into system-on-chip (SoC) without dealing with the substrate coupling effects when analog and digital circuits operate in a same chip. In this section the implementation of a LNA in an Impulse Radio UWB SoC is discussed. Fig. 13 shows a IR-UWB receiver architecture where the LNA is followed by a high speed ADC. In this example the ADC is built of D-latches, oscillators and buffers. Switching noise of such digital circuits generates harmonics that propagate through the silicon substrate and ground network and affect the sensitive analog HF circuits like LNA. Substrate noise effects are particularly important in UWB SoC where lower order harmonics fall in the large bandwidth of sensitive components like the LNA.

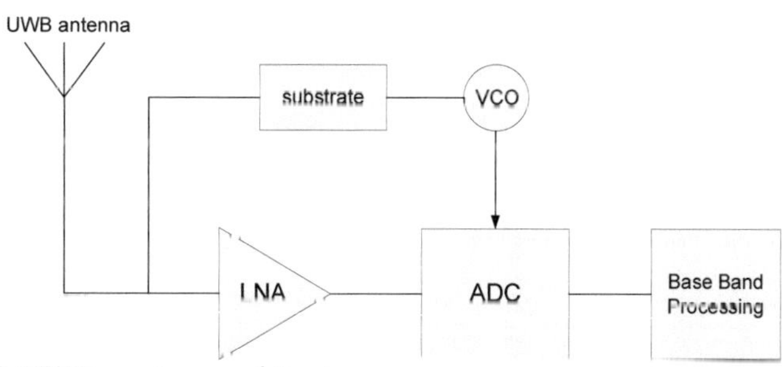

Fig. 13. Typical IR-UWB receiver architecture

Different devices that built the LNA can be affected by substrate noise. The active devices are less influenced thanks to the guard rings placed close to the transistors. However the large surface of ground shield of inductors can modify the path of noise propagation and inject the noise into the ground network of the chip. The noise received at LNA input may degrade significantly the receiver operation. Indeed the substrate noise is amplified by the high voltage gain of the LNA and is sampled by the ADC. When efficient shielding and grounding techniques are not used high substrate noise level may be measured at the LNA input.

Guidelines to reduce the substrate noise in UWB SoC are given in (Fanei et al., 2007). The substrate noise can be decreased by reducing the VCO frequency, introducing a ground plane to protect sensitive interconnects (such in MSL case), or increasing the distance between sensitive analog and digital circuits.

Another way to reduce the substrate noise at the LNA input can be deduced from EM simulations which indicate that patterned ground shields of inductors inject substrate noise into the ground network. By separating the inductor ground shields from the ground circuit of the LNA, the substrate noise can be reduced in the UWB band. Fig. 14 shows the EM models of conventional and modified layouts of the LNA input matching cell and Figure 15 shows a comparison between the power spectrum of the two structures. The noise is injected through a metallic plane instead of a full VCO implementation (Fanei et al., 2007).

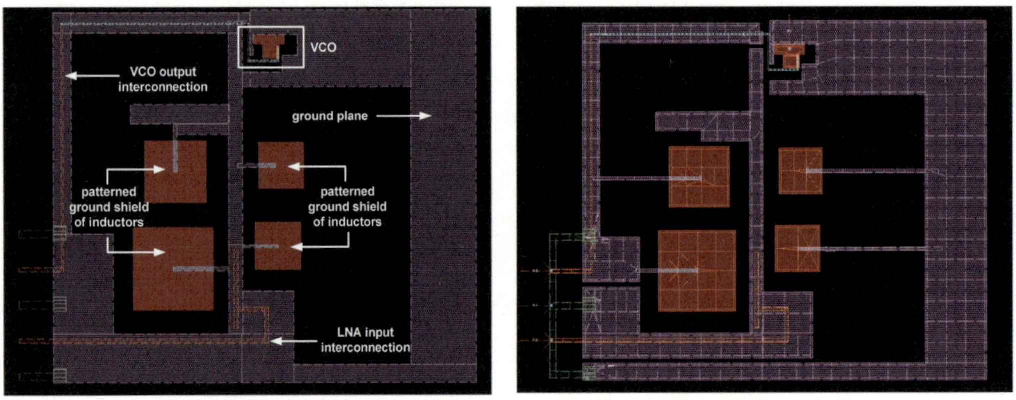

(a) (b)

Fig. 14. (a) EM model of the interconnect of the IR-UWB receiver. (b) EM model of the modified layout.

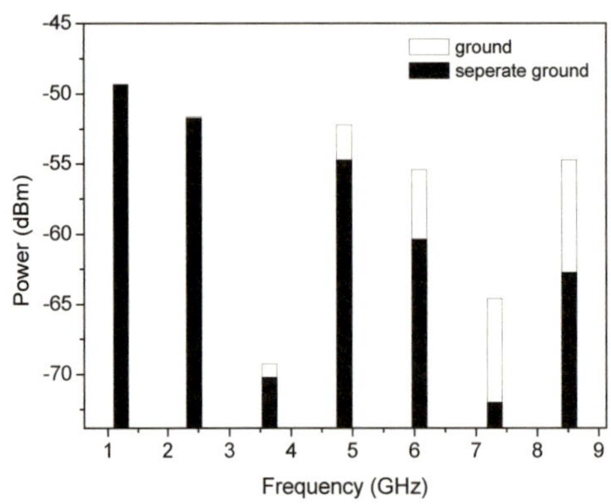

Fig. 15. Injected substrate noise spectrum at LNA input for the conventional and modified LNA layouts.

Simulations show that the LNA ground separation allows an injected substrate noise reduction in the UWB frequency band. The noise level reduction is around 5 to 10 dB in the 6-10 GHz frequency band.

6.3 LNA packaging

Regarding the LNA packaging stringent issues must be overcome to meet the signal integrity for UWB bandwidth and especially in the case of large bandwidth pulses. UWB is generally used for low cost applications and consequently high performance high end packages cannot be used. Low cost packages generally use bond wire interconnects, however the bandwidth of such interconnects is limited by the parasitic inductor coming from bond wire lengths. The schematic description of a high frequency bond wire carrier to die transition is given in Fig. 16.a. The transition generally connects a 50Ω grounded coplanar line on the chip carrier to on chip microstrip line. The transition includes three bond wires. The length of the bond wires with usual technological design rules for the die and package is about 1 mm. Such high frequency bond wire carrier to die transition can be modelled by an equivalent π network between two reference ports P1 and P2 (see Fig. 16.a) (Cubillo et al., 2008). It should be pointed that the bond wire transition model given in Fig.16.b includes the effects of both the signal bond wire and also the two bond wires connecting the carrier ground to the die ground. If a typical value of 15dB Return Loss is targeted in the bandwidth such basic transition cannot meet the 3.1-10.6 GHz UWB bandwidth.

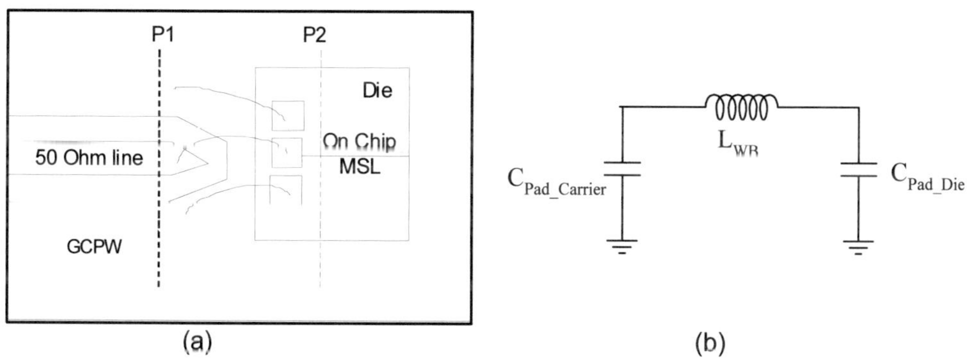

Fig. 16. Bond wire transition. (a) Schematic description. (b) Lumped equivalent π network.

The transition bandwidth can be extended up to 10.6 GHz by designing a third order low pass filter embedding the bond wire transition ensuring a ripple value lower than that of the wire bond transition himself (Cubillo et al., 2008). As shown in Fig. 17 the Low-Pass filter inductor is obtained thanks to the inductor of the π network of the bond wire transition model L_{WB}. The two capacitor of the Low-Pass filter are obtained by adding a distributed capacitor C_1 on the carrier and a MIM capacitor C_2 on the chip.

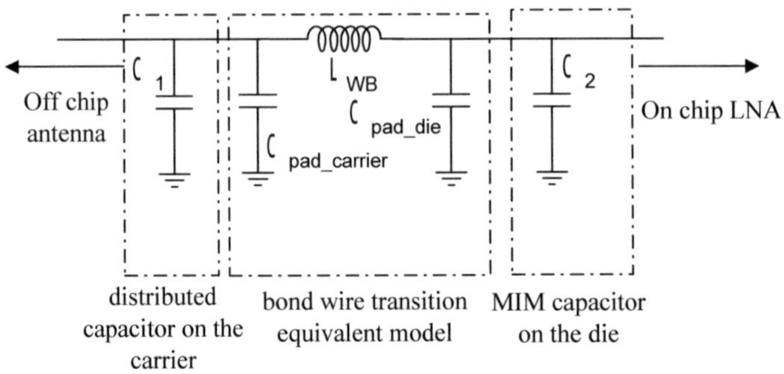

Fig. 17. Third order low pass filter embedding the bond wire transition.

7. Some results

Many LNA prototypes have been implemented in a standard 0.13μm CMOS technology. All the LNA outputs are loaded by a 60fF capacitor in order to emulate an ADC or a pulse detector load. The measurements instruments (spectrum analyser for the noise characterization and network analyser for scattering parameters measurements) are isolated at LNA output by using an on chip capacitance divider. For accurate characterization of the prototypes, the on chip capacitance divider has been also characterized on the same wafer to retrieve the output voltage from S parameters. The noise figure measurements are made with a spectrum analyzer and a noise source taking into account the mismatch at LNA output. The measurement results are summarized in Table 2 and compared to other published UWB LNAs.

	Tech. μm	BW GHz	Area mm^2	P_{DC} mW	Gain dB	NF dB	S_{11} dB	IIP3 dBm
(Yu et al., 2007)	0.18	2.7-9.1	1.57	7	10	3.8-6.9	<-10	+1
(Heydari, 2007)	0.18	0.1-11	0.76	21.6	8	2.9	<-12	-3.5
(Chen, 2007)	0.18	2-11.5	0.33	13.4	14.8	3.1-4	<-10	+3
(Chen & Huang, 2007)	0.18	2.8-7.2	1.63	32	19.1	3-3.8	<-5	-1
(Reiha & Long, 2007)	0.13	3.1-10.6	0.87	9	15.1	2.1-2.8	<-10	-8.5
(Liao & Liu, 2007)	0.18	1.2-11.9	0.59	20	9.7	4.5-5.1	<-11	-6.2
(Shim et al., 2007)	0.18	0.4-10	0.42	12	12.4	4.4-6.5	<-10	-6
(Bevilacqua & Nikenejad, 2007)	0.18	2.9-11	0.98	9.5	16	3.8-4.4	<-10	-
This work	0.13	6.8-8.8 [1]	0.4	15	29.5 [3]	4-5.2	<-10	-8.5 [4]
This work [5]	0.13	6.8-8.8 [1]	0.5	21	30.6 [3]	-	<-7.8	-8 [4]
This work	0.13	6-10 [2]	0.4	21.6	26.5 [3]	3.5- 4.6	<-12	-8 [4]
This work [5]	0.13	6-10 [2]	0.5	22	28 [3]	-	< -8	-8 [4]
This work	0.13	3.1-10.6 [1]	0.4	18	22 [3]	2.8-3.7	<-10	-7 [4]
This work [4]	0.13	6.4-7.8 [1]	0.4	14	31 [3]	3.3-4.7	<-8	- 8
This work [4,5]	0.13	6.4-7.8 [1]	0.5	20	34 [3]	3.4-4.7	<-8	-8
This work [4,6]	0 .13	6.4-7.8 [1]	0.77	28	35 [3]	3.2-4.4	<-7	-

[1]1dB bandwidth ; [2] 0.5dB bandwidth ; [3] voltage gain ; [4] simulated value; [5]differential output, [6] fully differential

Table 2. Summary of several published CMOS UWB LNA

8. Conclusion

The design of Ultra-Wide-Band LC filters LNA has been presented in this chapter. Architectures for both small fractional bandwidths such as the 6-8.5 GHz ECC frequency band and for large fractional bandwidths such as 3.1-10.6 GHz FCC frequency band have been proposed. Based on an analytical modelling of the LC filters LNA architecture, a design methodology allowing the noise figure minimization and the voltage gain maximization has been presented. The LNA implementation in standard CMOS technologies in the context of integrated receivers has been considered. Simple layout rules allowing reliable designs have been proposed. Several LNA prototypes for different fractional bandwidths have been fabricated in a 0.13μm CMOS technology. Measurement results agree well with the simulations and compare favourably with other published LNA.

9. References

Battista M., Gaubert J., Egels M., Bourdel S., Barthélemy H., 6-10 GHz Ultra Wide-Band CMOS LNA, *Electronics Letters*, February 2008, 44, (5), pp. 343-344.

Battista M., Gaubert J., Egels M., Bourdel S., Barthélemy H., High Voltage Gain CMOS LNA For 6-8.5 GHz UWB Receivers, *Transactions on Circuits And Systems – II*, Vol. 55, N° 8, August 2008, pp. 713, 717.

Battista M., Gaubert J., Fanei A., Bachelet Y., Egels M., Pannier Ph., Bourdel S., Barthelemy H., Bas G., Design and implementation of UWB CMOS LC filters LNA for carrier less impulse radio receivers, Analog Integr Circ Sig Process, February 2010, DOI 10.1007/s10470-009-9401-z

Bevilacqua A., Niknejad A. M., An Ultrawideband CMOS Low Noise Amplifier for 3.1-10.6-GHz Wireless Receivers, *IEEE Journal of Solid-State Circuits*, 2004, 39, (12), pp. 2259-2268.

Bevilacqua A., Sandner C., Gerosa A., Neviani A., A Fully Integrated Differential CMOS LNA for 3–5-GHz Ultrawideband Wireless Receivers, *IEEE Microwave and Wireless Components Letters*, 2006, 16, (3) pp. 134-136.

Chen H-K., Chang D-C., Juang Y-Z., Lu S-S., A Compact Wideband CMOS Low-Noise Amplifier Using Shunt Resistive-Feedback and Series Inductive-Peaking Techniques, *IEEE Microwave and Wireless Components letters*, 2007, 17, (8), pp. 616-618.

Chen Y-J E, Huang Y-I, Development of Integrated Broad-Band CMOS Low-Noise Amplifiers, *IEEE Transactions on Circuits and Systems -I: regular papers*, 2007, 54, (10), pp 2120-2127

Cubillo, J. R.; Gaubert, J.; Bourdel, S.; Barthelemy, H.; RF Low-Pass Design Guiding Rules to Improve PCB to Die Transition Applied to Different Types of Low Cost Packages; *Advanced Packaging, IEEE Transactions on*; Volume 31, Issue 3, Aug. 2008, pp 527 - 535.

Fanei A., Pannier Ph., Gaubert J., Battista M., Bachelet Y., Substrate noise in LC-matched ultra wide-band amplifier of UWB systems, *IEEE Conference on Electron Devices and Solid State Circuits, EDSSC 2007*, 20-22 December 2007, pp 469 - 472.

Gaubert J., Egels M., Pannier Ph., Bourdel S., Design Method For broadband CMOS RF LNA, *Electronics Letters*, 2005, 41, (7), pp. 383-384.

Ginzton E. L., Hewlett W. R., Jasberg J. H., and Noe J. D., Distributed amplification, *Proc. IRE*, vol. 36, pp. 956–969, (Aug. 1948).

Heydari P., Design Considerations for Low-Power Ultra Wideband Receivers, *Proceedings of the Sixth International Symposium on Quality Electronic Design (ISQED'05)*, 2005, pp. 668-673.

Heydari P., Design and Analysis of a Performance-Optimized CMOS UWB Distributed LNA, *IEEE Journal of Solid-State Circuits*, 2007, 42, (9), pp. 1892-1905.

Kim, C.-W., Jung, M.-S. Lee, S.-G.: Ultra-wideband CMOS low noise amplifier, *Electronics Letters*, 2005, 41, (7), pp. 384-385.

Liao C-F, Liu S-I, A Broadband Noise-Canceling CMOS LNA for 3.1–10.6-GHz UWB Receivers, *IEEE Journal of Solid-State Circuits*, 2007, 42, (2), pp 329-339.

Nguyen T-K., Kim C-H, Ihm G-J, Yang M-S, Lee S-G, CMOS Low-Noise Amplifier Design Optimization Techniques, *IEEE Transactions on Microwave Theory and Techniques*, 2004, 52, (5), pp 1433-1442.

Reiha M. T., Long J. R., A 1.2 V Reactive-Feedback 3.1–10.6 GHz Low-Noise Amplifier in 0.13 _m CMOS, *IEEE Journal of Solid-State Circuits*, 2007, 42, (5), pp. 1023-1033.

Shim Y., Kim C-W., Lee J., Lee S-G., Design of Full Band UWB Common-Gate LNA, *IEEE Microwave and Wireless Components letters*, 2007, 17, (10), pp 721-723.

Yu Y-H., Emery Chen Y-J., Heo D., A 0.6-V Low Power UWB CMOS LNA, *IEEE Microwave and Wireless Components letters*, 2007, 17, (3), pp. 229-231.

Zhang F. and Kinget P., Low power programmable-gain CMOS distributed LNA for ultra-wideband applications, *Symp. VLSI Circuits Dig. Tech. Papers*, Jun. 2005, pp. 78–81.

Zverev Anatol I., Handbook of Filter Synthesis, *John Willey & Sons* (New York, 1967), chapter. 6.10.

11

CPW ultra-wideband circuits for wireless communications

Mourad Nedil[(1)], Azzeddine Djaiz[(1)], Mohamed Adnane Habib[(1)] and Tayeb Ahmed Denidni[(2)]

[(1)]: UQAT-LRCS, University of Quebec in Abbitibi-Témiscaminque Canada

[(2)]:INRS-EMT, University of Quebec Canada

1. Introduction

Wireless communications represent one of the highest growing markets, especially on the development of mobile communications and wireless local area networks (WLANs), where high capacity transmission systems are required. These concern new wideband RF wireless components such as antennas, filters and so on.

Recently Ultra-Wideband (UWB) radio technology has been getting more popular for high-speed wireless connectivity applications, since the Federal Communications Commission (FCC)'s decision to permit the unlicensed operation band from 3.1 to 10.6 GHz in 2002 (Stutzman et al., 1998). The UWB radio system is very promising, since transmission data rates greater than those of the other wireless LAN systems can be obtainable with less power dissipation. In this area, various studies are under progress, especially in UWB filters, which is one of the key passive components in the design of microwave circuits for UWB systems. The requirements of an UWB filter are: low insertion loss over the operating band, good performances at low frequency and outside the operating band to meet FCC's limits. Moreover, it is necessary to have a good group delay performance, which is strongly important to impulse-radio UWB systems.

The conventional RF circuits design procedures are adequate only for relatively narrowband, but they are not suitable for wideband application. In addition, the most major challenge is to design an ultra-wideband RF circuit with about 110 % percent fractional-bandwidth requirement, which makes some widely used techniques for UWB designs inefficient.

In this chapter, some UWB RF circuits will be presented and detailed. The chapter is organized as follows. After this introduction, the UWB transition and filters will be described in section II and III. In section IV, an analysis and design of a wideband directional coupler will be described. Section V, will present the UWB technique for an antenna. In the section VI, the UWB RF system will be presented. Finally, the last section presents the conclusion.

2. Ultra-wideband Transitions

Planar transmission lines such as microstrip and coplanar waveguide (CPW) have been applied in various microwave and millimeter-wave circuits. In some multilayered structures, these transmission lines coexist and are even combined to develop new circuit components (Nerguezian et al., 2005). For instance, multilayer microwave integrated circuits require more flexibility to use both microstrip and CPW circuit technologies. To ensure the compatibility between these technologies, low-loss, wideband, and compact transitions between microstrip and CPW lines are necessary.

2.1 Microstrip to CB-CPW transition

There are two main techniques for the transition between a microstrip and CPW. One is by electrical contact, and the other electromagnetic coupling (Tanaka et al., 1988; Theodorou et al., 1995). One type uses vias to connect the top layer CPW ground planes with the lower microstrip ground plane and the other does not. The transitions with via holes are compact and broadband, but the vias cause parasitic inductance and are difficult to fabricate. Existing via-less transitions are narrow band and large. Transitions by electromagnetic coupling require no wire bonds or via holes, but most of them suffer from narrow bandwidth and larger size.

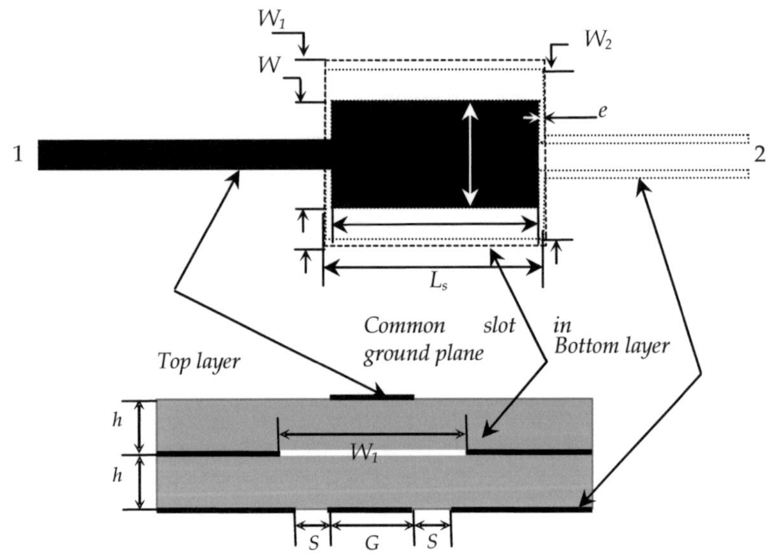

Fig. 1. Layout of the microstrip-to-CB-CPW transition.

Various approaches for transitions between microstrip and CPW lines on separate layers have been introduced such as electromagnetic coupling (Chen et al., 1996; Tran et al., 1993). In practice, additional conducting planes are often present below the substrate in order to electromagnetically separate the circuit from its environment (Tran et al., 1993). Vialess CBCPW-to-MSL transitions using electromagnetic (EM) coupling of three-line couplers have been reported (Burke et al., 1989; Zhu et al., 1999). However, the broadside CB-CPW to microstrip transition has never been proposed.

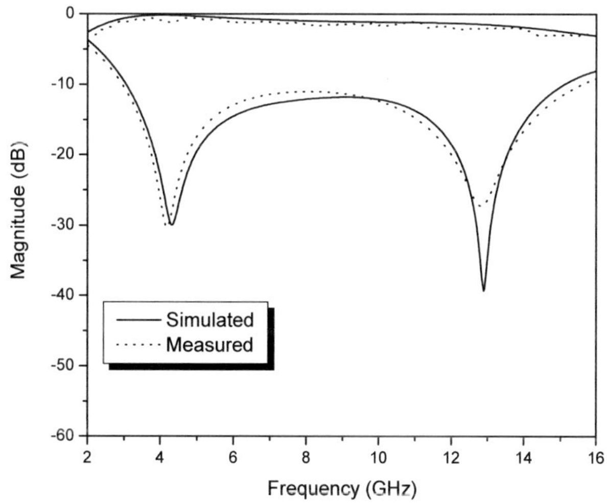

Fig. 2. Simulated and measured results of the UWB transition.

In this section, an ultra-wideband microstrip to a CB-CPW transition using the frequency-dependent behavior of surface-to-surface slot coupling is proposed.

Fig. 1 shows the geometrical layout of the proposed two-port microstrip-to-CB-CPW transition. This transition is characterized by an aperture formed on the common ground plane of the two-layered structures to provide a fed-through coupling between the upper microstrip and the lower CB-CPW lines. In this structure, the upper microstrip conductor is vertically coupled with the central strip conductor of the lower CB-CPW via a slot-coupled located in the common ground plane.

To validate the proposed approach, a prototype circuit was designed, fabricated and measured. Simulation and experimental results of the transition are shown in Fig. 2. From these curves, it can be seen that a good agreement is observed and the microstrip to CB-CPW transition offers a very wide bandwidth of ~ 12 GHz.

2.2 Back-to-Back CB-CPW to CB-CPW Transition

Some applications, such as multilayer microwave integrated circuits, require the flexibility to use the CPW circuits in deferent layers. Therefore, low-loss, wideband, and compact transitions between these layers are necessary to ensure good compatibility. In this area, vertical interconnections between various signal lines in different layers are often needed in a multilayer circuit environment. In this area, printed slots have been suggested to be versatile for vertical transitions. They can be implemented to couple electromagnetic energy from one side of a circuit module to another separated by a common conductor. The conductor backed coplanar waveguide (CBCPW) technology is an attractive option because it provides the benefit of added mechanical support and heat sinking ability compared to conventional CPW. Few works on CBCPW-to-CBCPW transitions have been done. However, these transitions are based only on via connections.

In this subsection, a new type of CBCPW-to-CBCPW transition based on the concept of slot coupling in the common ground plane will be presented. This transition is characterized by an aperture etched on the common ground plane of the two stacked layer CBCPW lines to provide a fed-through coupling between the upper CBCPW line and the lower CB-CPW line. This transition can offer advantages of broad bandwidth, compact size, low fabrication cost, and high reliability.

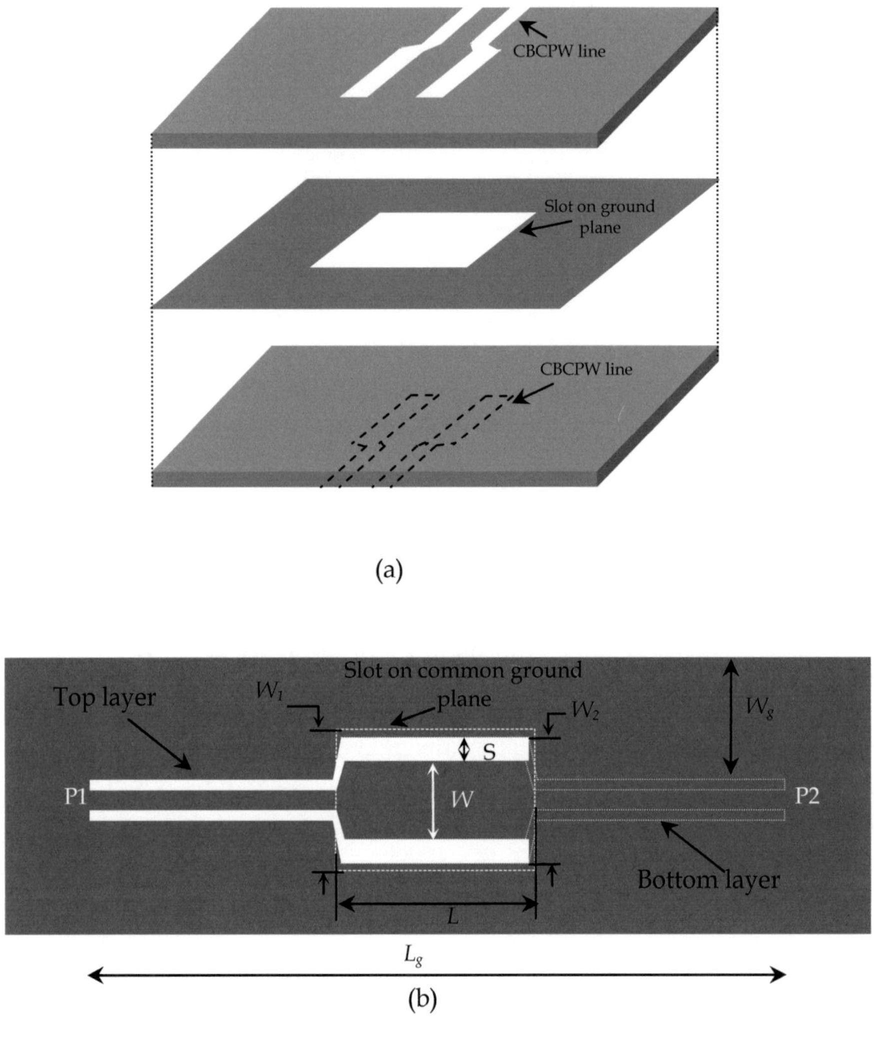

Fig. 3. Layout of the CB-CPW-to-CB-CPW transition.

Fig. 3 shows the geometrical layout of the proposed two-port CBCPW-to-CBCPW transition. This arrangement of the back-to-back CBCPW transition allows the both transmission lines to share a common ground plane. Each CBCPW line is formed by abruptly ending the slots as shown in Fig. 3. As a result, an RF current flows around the end of the slot, and therefore magnetic energy is stored behind the termination. Then, this energy is coupled via a rectangular slot located in the common ground plane from the top layer line to second line located in the bottom layer.

To verify the performances of the proposed design, a back-to-back prototype transition was fabricated, and the scattering parameters were measured. Simulation and experimental results of the transition are shown in Fig. 4. From these curves, it can be seen that the comparison between simulated and experimental data shows a good agreement, and the CBCPW-to-CBCPW transition offers a very wide bandwidth of ~ 12 GHz, which operates well over almost the entire band of 3-15 GHz.

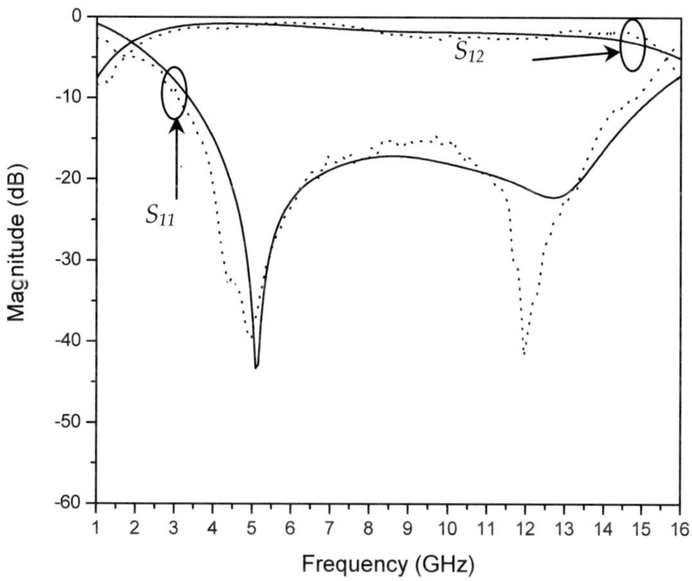

Fig. 4. Simulated and measured results of the CB-CPW transition.

3. Ultra-Wideband Filters

The conventional filter synthesis procedure is adequate only for the relatively narrowband filters, and it is not suitable for the wideband filters. In addition, the most difficult problem is to design ultra-wideband filter with about 110 % percent fractional-bandwidth requirement, which makes some widely used techniques for UWB designs inapplicable.

3.1 Ultra-Wideband Filter Design Based on CPW-to-Microstrip transition

As mentioned, the most challenging problem in the design of UWB filter is the 110 % bandwidth requirement. For this issue, an UWB filter design is introduced. Fig. 5 shows the layout of the proposed filter. The filter structure is based on the back-to-back microstrip-to-CB-CPW transition described in the previous section. The filter is composed of two CBCPW to microstrip transitions and a microstrip line section, which is used as a multiple-mode (MMR) resonator between the two transitions. At the center frequency of the concerned UWB passband, both side sections of this MMR (CBCPW to microstrip transitions) are identical, and they are chosen as one quarter-wavelength ($\lambda_g/4$) while the middle section is set as one half-wavelength ($\lambda_g/2$).

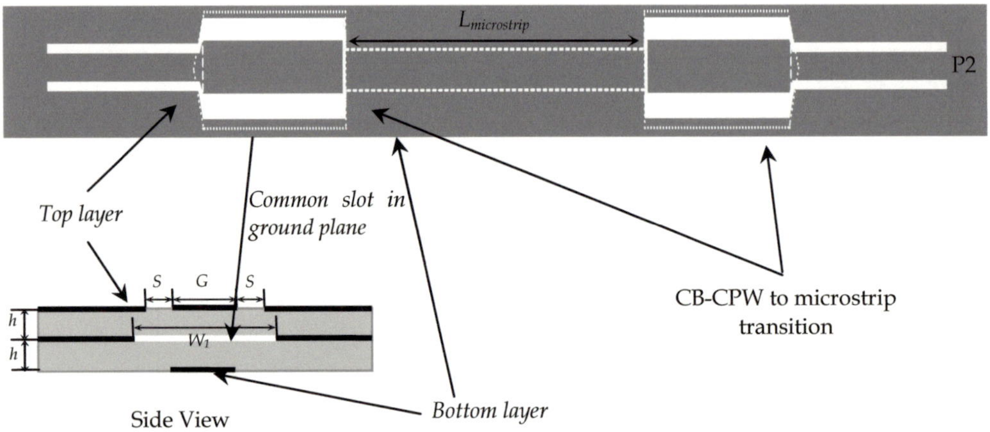

Fig. 5. Layout of the CBCPW fed UWB filter

Numerical simulations on the filter were carried out with the electromagnetic simulator ADS MOMENTUM. In these simulations, it is found that the out-of-band rejection at high frequencies can be improved by optimizing both CB-CPW and microstrip line of the transitions. To optimize the performance of the proposed filter, a parametric study was also performed and the optimal dimensions of the proposed filter are determined, in which $L_{microstrip}$ = 15.5 mm, L = 7.8 mm, L_S = 8.1 mm, W = 1.4 mm, W_1 = 3.13 mm, W_2 = 2.68 mm, G = 1.83 mm, e = 0.15mm.

Fig. 6. Photograph of the fabricated UWB filter.

The fabricated filter was measured using a network analyzer HP8720, and its photograph is shown in Fig. 6. The simulated and measured results are shown in Fig. 7. It can be seen that the measured results agree well with the simulated ones. Both the measured and the simulated results show that, the proposed filter has a small insertion loss.

Fig. 8 shows the simulated and measured results of the group delay. The group delay varies between 0.3 and 0.50 ns with a maximum variation of 0.2 ns, which leads to good linearity of the proposed UWB filter. The group delay of the proposed filter is found to be lower than that of the hybrid microstrip/CPW filter. From these results, it can be concluded that the proposed filter satisfies the requirements of a small and flat group delay over the operating band, which is strongly required for impulse radio systems to minimize the distortion in short pulse transmission system.

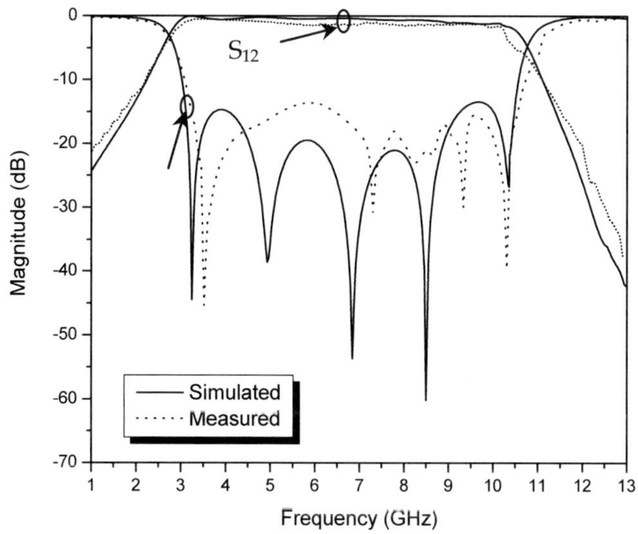

Fig. 7. Simulated and measured results of the UWB filter.

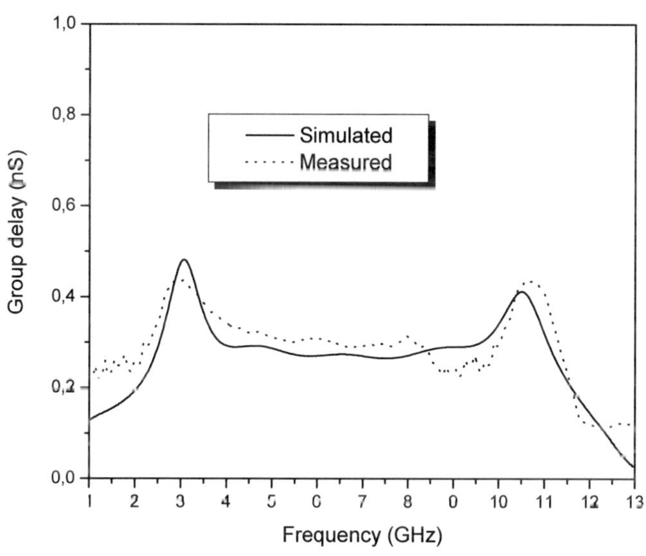

Fig. 8. Simulated and measured results of the group delay of the UWB filter.

3.2 Microstrip fed Ultra-Wideband Filter

Similarly with the UWB filter introduced earlier, the second filter is composed of two microstrip-CBCPW transitions and a section of CBCPW transmission line is designed. The CBCPW feed line and the microstrip line are replaced by microstrip feed line and a section of CBCPW, respectively to generate the multi-mode resonator (MMR). At the central frequency of the concerned UWB passband, the two side sections of this MMR are equally selected as one quarter-wavelength while the central section is set as one half-wavelength ($\lambda g_0/2$) long. As such, the second resonant frequency of this MMR can be readily allocated around 6.85GHz.

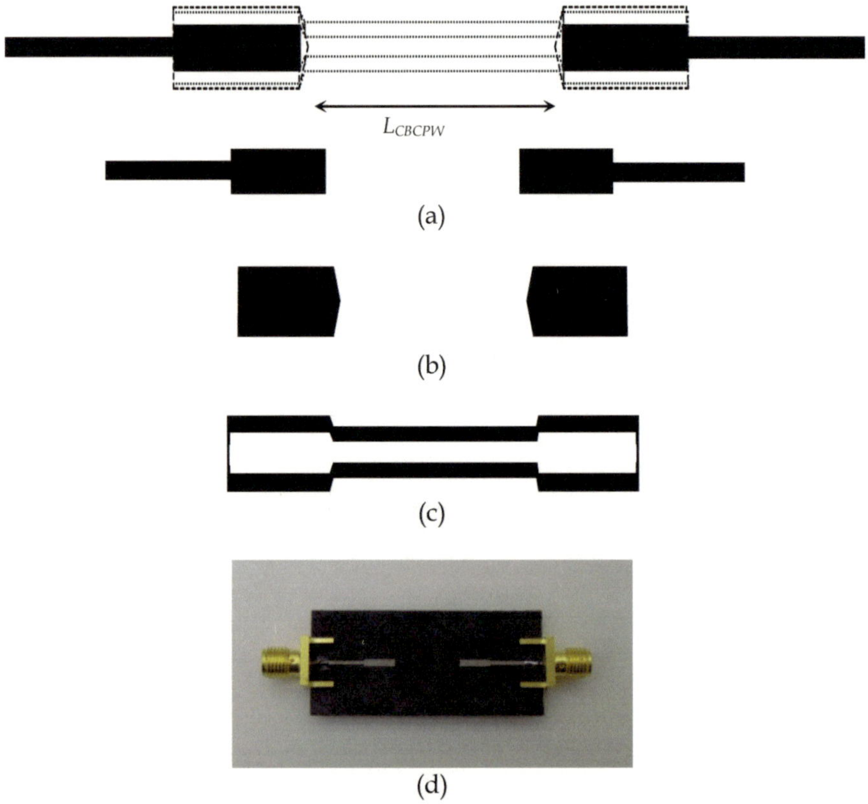

Fig. 9. Layout of the UWB filter (a) Top layer (b) Common slot in ground plane (c) Bottom layer (d) Fabricated filter.

The fabricated filter is illustrated in Fig. 9. The simulated and measured results are shown in Fig. 10. It can be seen that the measured results agree well with the simulated ones. Both the measured and the simulated results show that, in the in-band performance, a small insertion loss. This filter presents a good performance in terms of return loss compared to the first filter design.

Fig. 11 shows the simulated and measured results of the group delay of this filter which is about 0.3 nS. From these results, it may be concluded that this filter is similar to the first UWB filter in terms of small and flat group delay.

It can be seen that for each filter, the optimum out-of-band rejection should be improved especially in low frequencies.

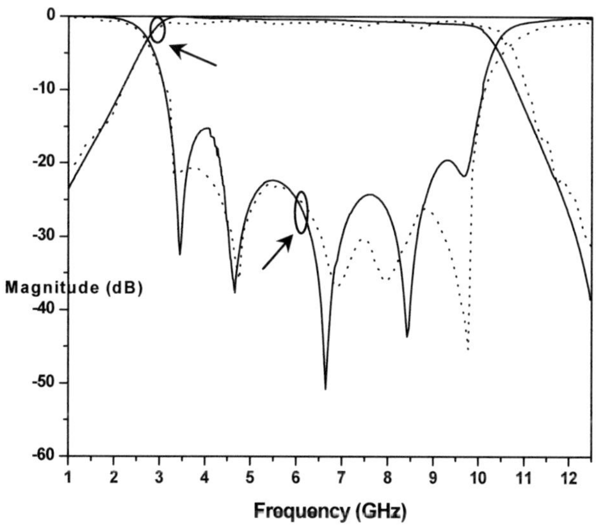

Fig. 10. Simulated and measured results of the proposed UWB filter.

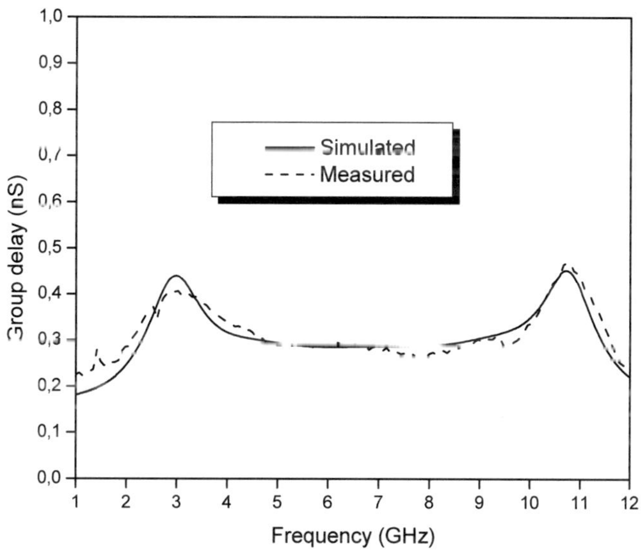

Fig. 11. Simulated and measured results of group delay of the UWB filter.

4. Ultra-Wideband Directional Coupler

Directional couplers are fundamental and indispensable components used in microwave integrated circuits applications. Indeed, these components are often used in microwave systems to combine or divide RF signals, and they are commonly applied in many applications, such as antenna feeds, balanced mixers, modulators and so on.

Tight-coupling directional couplers are often required in the design of various multiport circuits or beamforming networks of antenna arrays. In the practical issue, these couplers should be compact in order to be easily integrated with other components in the same circuit. For instance, the microstrip branch line couplers or hybrid ring couplers have extensively been employed in printed microstrip array feeding networks (Tudosie et al., 2006). However, these couplers have inherently narrow bandwidths.

To overcome this situation, CPW technology has been proposed to implement various couplers. Indeed, CPW technology offers several attractive features: absence of costly and inductive via holes, ease of making shunt and series connections, ease of controlling the characteristics of CPW lines by changing the slot and strip widths, and possible implementability at millimeter-waves applications. Furthermore, directional couplers with CPW structures can also provide a higher directivity. Using this technology, different configurations of CPW directional couplers have been proposed (Lim et al., 1999). Moreover, to improve directional coupler performances, the conductor-backed coplanar waveguide technology was also proposed to reduce the coupler size and to avoid air bridges used to connect ground planes of the conventional CPW technology (Lim et al., 1999). In this area, few works on CB-CPW couplers have been reported in literature [6-9]. A 3-dB CB-CPW coupled-line directional coupler has been used in tunable analog phase shifting [6]. A finite-extent backed conductor on the other side of the substrate is added to the conventional edge-coupled CPW structure has been suggested in [7] to enhance the coupling. Recently, broadside CB-CPW directional coupler has been proposed in [8]. However, this coupler has not been optimized to have the maximum of bandwidth to covers ultra-wideband applications.

In this section, a wideband multilayer directional coupler using slot-coupled technique is proposed.

Fig. 12a shows the layout of the proposed hexagonal slot-coupled directional coupler. It allows coupling two CPW lines placed in different layers through a rectangular slot etched on the common ground plane.

4.1 Quasi-Static Coupler Analysis

For the analysis of this work, it is assumed that the proposed configuration has a ground plane with infinite size and all conductors are perfect. This structure supports both fundamental modes, namely odd and even. The even and odd-mode coupler impedances, Z_{e0} and Z_{o0}, are calculated using conformal mapping techniques to determine the coupler capacitance per unit length for even and odd-modes. These modes are illustrated in Fig. 12b. These modes can be isolated by assuming an electrical wall for the odd mode and a magnetic wall for the even mode. For each mode, the structure is analyzed in a manner similar that reported in [8]. In this section, expressions for the effective dielectric constant as well as the characteristic impedance for the odd and even modes obtained using the quasi-static conformal mapping technique will be presented.

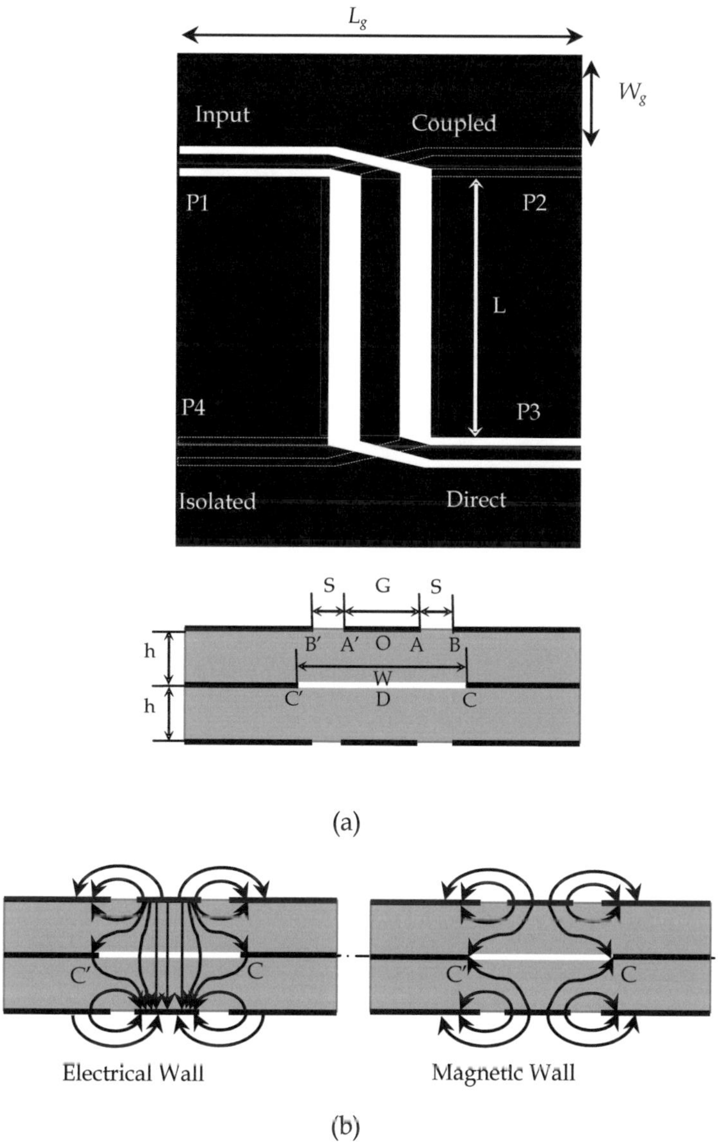

Fig. 12. Broadside directional slot-coupled coupler: (a) Layout (b) Odd and even-mode electric field distribution.

For the odd-mode excitation, an electrical wall is placed in the plane of symmetry (CC′) as shown in Fig. 13. The analysis is then restricted to upper half of the structure. Then, the total odd-mode capacitance per unit length can then be considered as the sum of two components, C_{o1}, C_{o2}, representing the electrical field in the upper region (air) and middle region (dielectric), respectively.

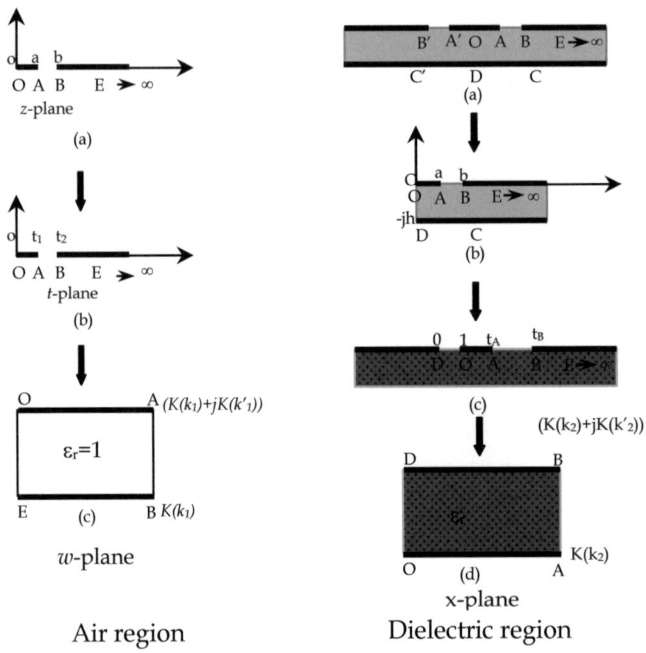

Fig. 13. Conformal mapping transformation of the odd-mode

a) Odd Mode (air)

The Schwarz-Christoffel transformation can be done from the t-plane to the *w*-plane (Fig. 13). The transformation equation for the configuration with only air above the interface is given by

$$t = z^2 \tag{1}$$

The Schwarz-Christoffel integral is then

$$w = \int_{t_0}^{t} \frac{dt}{\sqrt{t(t-t_1)(t-t_2)}} \tag{2}$$

The capacitance per unit length C_{01} is then obtained as

$$C_{o1} = 2\varepsilon_0 \frac{\overline{OA}}{\overline{AB}} = 2\varepsilon_0 \frac{K(k_0)}{K'(k_0)} \tag{3}$$

The argument k_0 is :

$$k_0 = \frac{a}{b} = \frac{G}{G+2S} \tag{4}$$

where $K(k_0)$ and $K(k'_0)$ are the complete elliptical of the first kind and its complement. The accurate expression for the ratio $K(k_0)/K(k'_0)$ have been reported in [9]. These are given below:

$$\frac{K(k)}{K(k')} = \frac{\pi}{\ln\left[\dfrac{2(1+\sqrt{k'_0})}{1-\sqrt{k'_0}}\right]} \qquad \text{if } 0 \le k \le 0.707 \tag{5.a}$$

$$\frac{K(k)}{K(k')} = \frac{1}{\pi}\ln\left[\frac{2(1+\sqrt{k_0})}{1-\sqrt{k_0}}\right] \qquad \text{if } 0.707 \le k \le 1 \tag{5.b}$$

with $k'_0 = \sqrt{1-k_0^{\ 2}}$

These expressions are the same for the even-mode in the air case.

b) Odd Mode (dielectric)

As shown in Fig. 13, an electric wall is assumed to be present at CC′ plane of the structure in the dielectric region. The configuration is first converted into the *t*-plane by the following expression:

$$t = \cosh^2\left(\frac{\pi z}{2h}\right) \tag{6}$$

$$C_{o2} = 2\varepsilon_r \varepsilon_0 \frac{K(k_1)}{K'(k_1)} \tag{7}$$

$$k_1 = \frac{\tanh\left(\dfrac{\pi a_1}{2h}\right)}{\tanh\left(\dfrac{\pi b_1}{2h}\right)} \tag{8}$$

with $a_1 = t_A$ *and* $b_1 = t_B$

The total capacitance C_{oT} is obtained as:

$$C_{oT} = C_{o2} + C_{o1} \tag{9}$$

The odd-mode permittivity $\varepsilon_{o,eff}$ is defined as [9],

$$\varepsilon_{o,eff} = \frac{C_{oT}(\varepsilon_r)}{C_{oT}(\varepsilon_r)} \tag{10}$$

The odd-mode characteristic impedance is given by [9]:

$$Z_{o,0} = \frac{60\pi}{\sqrt{\varepsilon_{o,eff}}\left[\frac{K(k_0)}{K(k'_0)} + \frac{K(k_1)}{K(k'_1)}\right]} \tag{11}$$

c) Even Mode (dielectric)

The even-mode dielectric is assured by considering the magnetic wall in the section (CC'). The electrical field of the coupler in the even-mode show that we can replace the symmetrical half-plane structure with quarter-plane with taken electrical wall (OD) into account (see Fig. 14b).

The analysis of the even-mode is similar to the odd-mode. Fig. 14 shows the progression from the *Z*-plane, to an intermediate stage in the *t*-plane, and finally to a parallel-plate capacitor in the *x*-plane. The configuration in Fig. 14a is first converted into the one shown in Fig. 14b, by mapping expression (6).The asymmetrical line configuration in Fig. 14c is transformed into symmetrical line configuration, as shown in Fig. 14d [11].

$$C_{e2} = 2\varepsilon_r\varepsilon_0 \frac{K(k_4)}{K'(k_4)} \tag{12}$$

$$k_4 = \sqrt{\frac{2a_1(b_1 + b_2)}{(a_1 + b_1)(a_1 + b_2)}} \tag{13}$$

with $a_1 = t_A = \cosh^2(\frac{\pi G}{4h})$, $b_1 = t_B = \cosh^2(\frac{\pi(S + G/2)}{2h})$ and $b_2 = -t_c = \sinh^2(\frac{\pi W}{4h})$

The total capacitance C_{oT} of the odd-mode case is:

$$C_{eT} = C_{o2} + C_{e1} \tag{14}$$

The odd-mode permittivity ε_{oeff} is defined as,

$$\varepsilon_{e,eff} = \frac{C_{eT}(\varepsilon_r)}{C_{eT}(\varepsilon_r)} \tag{15}$$

The odd-mode characteristic impedance is given by

$$Z_{e,0} = \frac{60\pi}{\sqrt{\varepsilon_{e,eff}}\left[\frac{K(k_3)}{K(k'_3)} + \frac{K(k_4)}{K(k'_4)}\right]} \tag{16}$$

The coupling coefficient K expressed as:

$$K = \frac{Z_{0,e} - Z_{0,o}}{Z_{0,e} + Z_{0,o}} \tag{17}$$

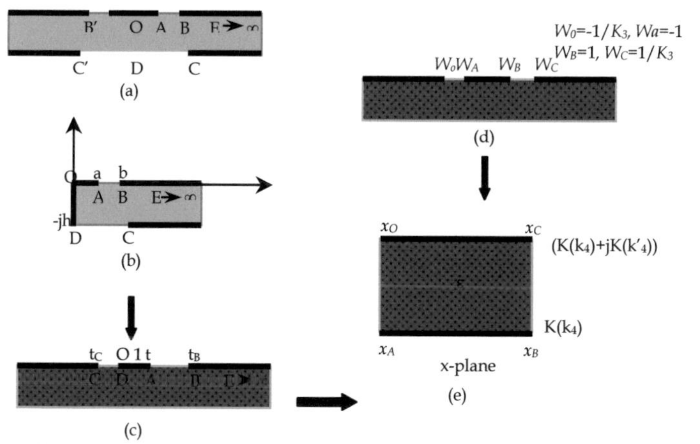

Fig. 14. Conformal mapping transformation of the even-mode in the dielectric region.

4.2 Results and Discussion

Numerical results of odd-mode characteristic impedances of the CPW multilayer slot coupled-coupler are plotted in Fig. 15, versus the normalized gap width *S/h* and normalized strip width *G/h*. It is seen that, for a fixed substrate thickness, as the gap width (*S*) the odd-mode characteristic impedance is increased, whereas those while the strip conductor width (*G*) increases, the odd-mode characteristic impedance $Z_{0,0}$ decrease. In fact, the odd-mode parameters change slowly as the gap width is increased up to a certain limit.

The variation of the even-mode characteristic impedance can be expressed as a function of the normalized gap width *S/h*, the normalized slot-coupled width *W/h* and *W/G* are shown in Fig. 16. As can be seen for a fixed strip conductor and thickness (*G, h*), $Z_{e,0}$ while increases the slot-coupled width (*W*) increases.

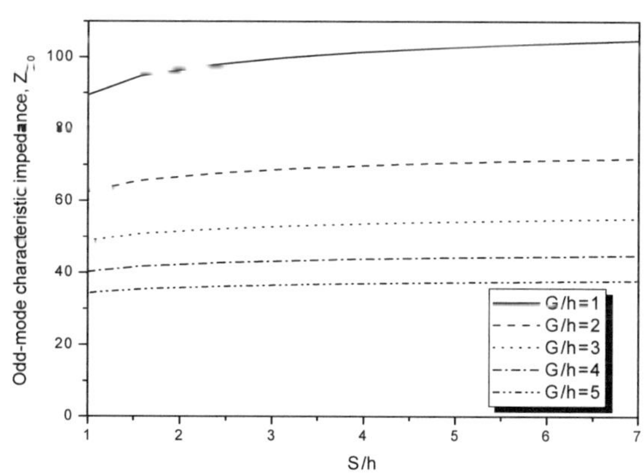

Fig. 15. Odd-mode characteristic impedance

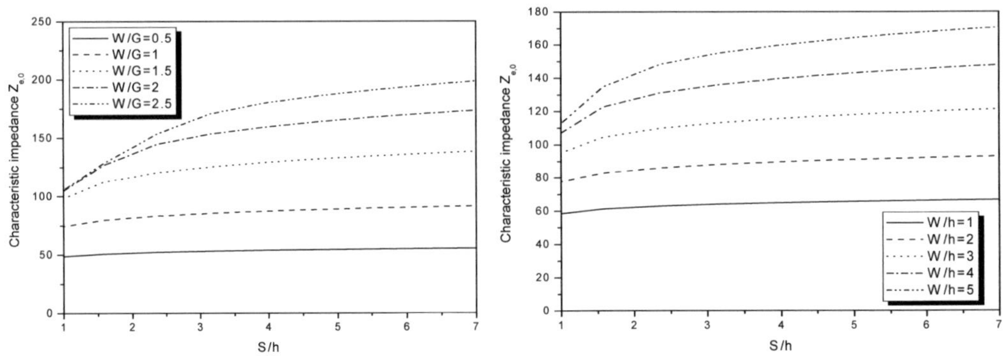

(a) (b)

Fig. 16. Even-mode characteristic impedance as a function of (a) *W/G* (b) *W/h*

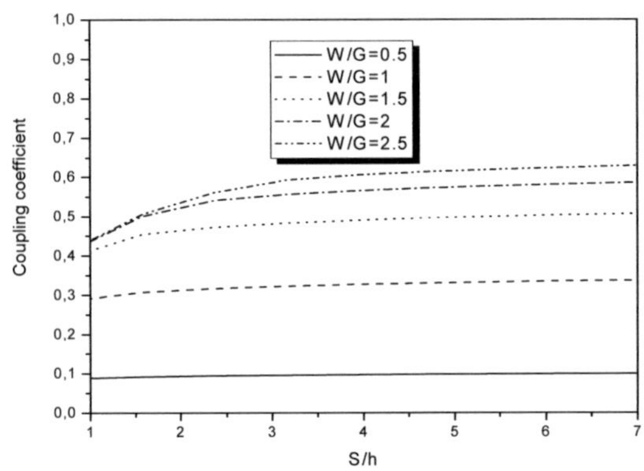

Fig. 17. Coupling coefficient

In addition, it is shown that the slot-coupled width *W* affect considerably the characteristic impedance $Z_{0,e}$ (see Fig. 16). However, the parameter *W* does not affect the odd-mode characteristic impedance, which is forced to be short circuited via an electrical wall.

The computed coupling coefficient *K* is shown in Fig. 17 for both normalized slot-coupled width *W* and normalized slot width *S*. For a fixed strip conductor *(G)*, the coupling increases as *S* and *W* increase. It can be noted that the parameter *W* affects considerably the coupling of the proposed coupler.

Since there are various interactions among the parameters involved in the proposed design, a rigorous analysis is necessary for the optimization of the coupler parameters. A commercial computer software package ADS MOMENTUM [7] is used as a CAD tool to design the proposed coupler. First, the top and bottom 50 Ω transmission lines were designed using a duroid substrate (RT/ Duroid 5880) having a dielectric constant of $\varepsilon_r = 2.2$ and thickness h = 0.254 mm. As CPW characteristic impedance is controlled by changing the slot or the strip width, it was necessary to investigate each parameter in order to obtain the right value for the coupling. It was shown that for a fixed substrate thickness and slot width S, the coupling increases as G increases. Second, the length L of the coupler was designed to be a quarter wavelength at 5 GHz. Third, the coupling slot width was determinated in order to increase the coupling between the CPW lines. Based on this parametric study, the optimum design has the following dimensions: L = 11.9 mm, W = 4.85 mm, S = 1.3 mm, and G = 1.6 mm.

Fig. 18. Photograph of the fabricated circuit prototype

To validate our design, the proposed coupler was fabricated and measured using an HP8772 network analyzer. The photography of the fabricated prototype is shown in Fig. 18. The simulated and measured return loss and the insertion loss are shown in Fig. 19. From these results, it can be concluded that a bandwidth of ~ 4 GHz (~80%) is achieved. The average value of the coupling for the direct port and the coupled port is 3.5 -dB. The return loss and isolation are better than 15 -dB within the operating band. The simulated and measured phase shift between the two ports are plotted in Fig. 20. The phase difference between the direct and coupled ports is approximately 90° across the operating band, which confirms the proposed approach. Furthermore, the comparison between simulated and experimental data shows a good agreement.

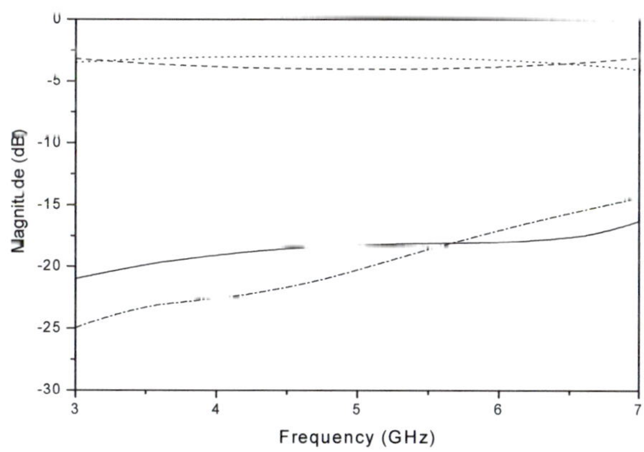

(a)

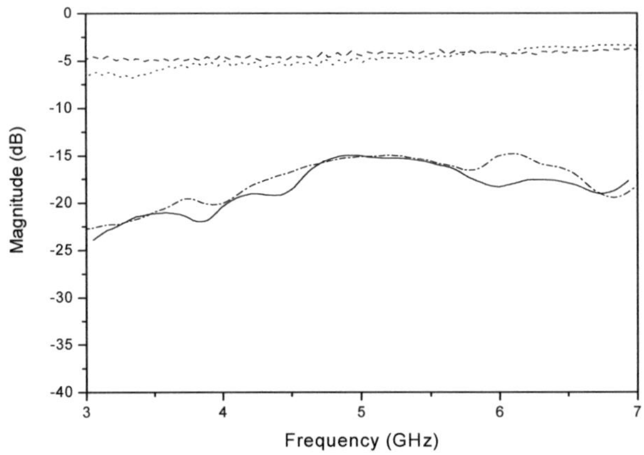

(b)

Fig. 19. Scattering parameters of the proposed coupler.

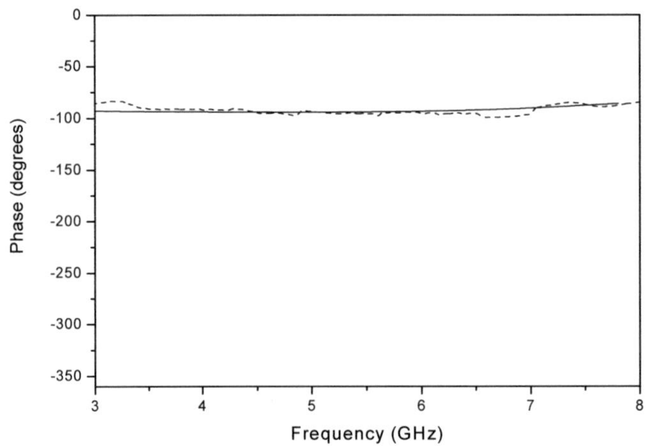

Fig. 20. Simulated and measured phase difference.

5. Ultra-Wideband Antenna

Antenna becomes a part of electrical devices in wireless communication system after late 1888, Heinrich Hertz (1857–1894) were first demonstrated the existence of radio waves. The UWB technology opens new door for wireless communication system, since the current wireless system increasing exponentially. Back from spark-gap impulse to pulse radio, UWB system plays a dominant role in communication system as the antenna is one of the wireless communications components. In general, the antennas for UWB systems should have sufficiently broad operating bandwidth for impedance matching and high-gain radiation in desired directions.

5.1 Ultra-Wideband Monopole

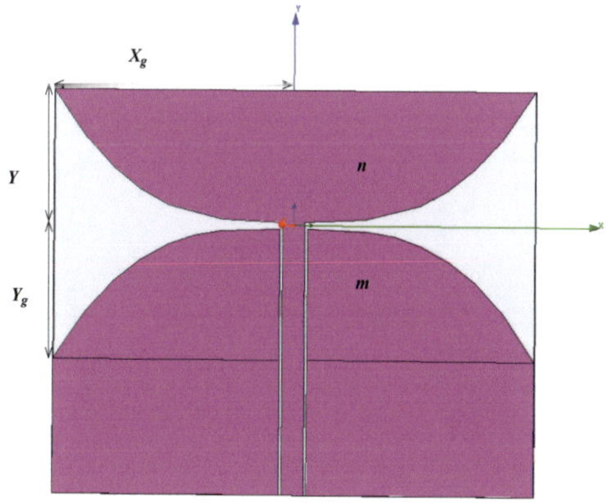

(a)

(b)

Fig. 21. UWB monopole-like antenna. (a): Antenna layout, (b): Antenna photograph

Fig. 21 shows a monopole-like ultra-wideband antenna. The lower metallic surface represents the ground, and the upper arm is a quarter-wavelength radiating element acting as a monopole. The matching over the entire UWB bandwidth is guaranteed by the curved shape of both the monopole and the ground plane.
The antenna is etched on Rogers 5880 substrate with a permittivity of 2.2 and a height of 1.575mm. Since the antenna is realized with coplanar technology, all the metal is removed from one side of the substrate. On the metallic side, a CPW line is etched. The central line has 1.87mm of width and is spaced with 0.2mm from each lateral ground plane side, as showed in Fig. 21a.

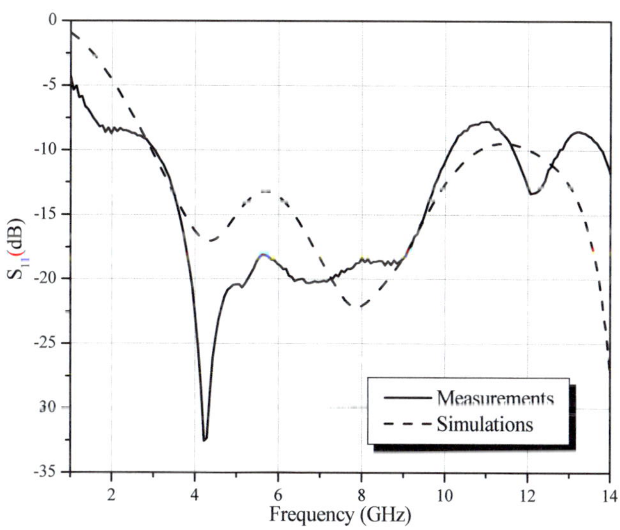

Fig. 22. Antenna return loss

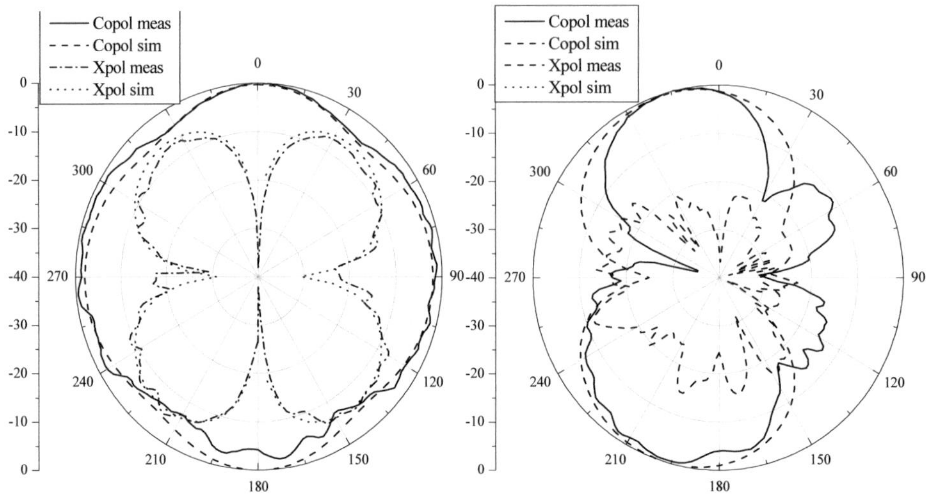

(a) (b)

Fig. 23. Radiation pattern at 7GHz. (a) H-plane. (b) E-Plane

Fig. 22 shows the experimental and simulated antenna return loss. From these curves, it can be concluded that the antenna provides a bandwidth from 3GHz to 10GHz with a return loss below -10dB. Two close resonances can be observed, the first one at 4GHz and the second one around 8GHz. The radiation patterns at 7GHz are plotted in Fig. 23. The radiation patterns in the H-plane are omni-directional; they are similar to classical monopole radiation pattern for the H-plane. For the E-plane however, the radiation patterns shape changes with the frequency. With the help of simulation tool, the antenna efficiency has been recorded to be more than 95% over the entire bandwidth.

5.2 Ultra-Wideband slot antenna

When used in confined areas such as underground communications, UWB systems can coexist with other communication systems, such as WiMax, WLAN, HYPERLAN. which are commonly used for networking; this kind of devices creates interference with UWB systems. In order to avoid this frequency overlapping, it is useful to exclude the undesired frequencies for UWB applications. Instead of burdening systems with filters, one may think of designing UWB antennas with band rejection at the undesired frequency band. One approach is to perturb the radiating element shape (Ma et al., 2007). Other approaches suggest including stubs, slots, or SRR resonators (Abbosh et al., 2008). to the radiating element. Lee (Lee et al, 2006) have chosen to perturb matching impedance and create an open circuit at the undesired frequency.
First, an UWB antenna was designed. The antenna layout is depicted in Fig. 24. A circular patch is fed through a CPW line. This circular patch excites a circular aperture which is etched on the CPW ground plane. The antenna dimensions, defined in Table 1, are set in order to meet frequency bandwidth requirements. Considering a substrate of permittivity ε_r, and thickness h, one can derive a preliminary value of aperture radius with respect to the following equations (Abbosh et al., 2006; Abbosh et al., 2008)

$$R_s \cong \frac{c}{4f}\sqrt{\frac{2}{1+\varepsilon_{reff}}}\,, \tag{18}$$

where ε_{reff} is the effective relative permittivity corrected considering substrate thickness, namely

$$\varepsilon_{reff} = \frac{1+\varepsilon_r}{2} - \frac{1-\varepsilon_r}{2}\left[1+12\,h/d\right]^{-0.5} \tag{19}$$

d is the antenna widest dimension; Equation (2) is simplified to be

$$\varepsilon_{reff} = \frac{1+\varepsilon_r}{2} \tag{20}$$

The circular patch dimension is then considered with respect to the aperture radius as

$$R_p \cong \frac{R_s}{2} \tag{21}$$

The radiating element, namely the aperture, is chosen circular in order to achieve a wide bandwidth feature, so is the shape of the feeding patch.

In order to achieve a design where a certain frequency bandwidth is rejected from the antenna frequency response, the frequency notch is obtained by modifying the radiating element. This modification should not perturb antenna normal behavior over its operating bandwidth but for a considered range of frequency. To do so, a half of ring slot etched on the circular patch is considered (Fig. 24b); its center is kept identical to the circular patch. Its diameter is considered so that the arc length is equal to the half wavelength at the notch frequency (Equation 22).

$$R_n \cong \frac{c}{2\pi f_n}\sqrt{\frac{2}{1+\varepsilon_{reff}}} \tag{22}$$

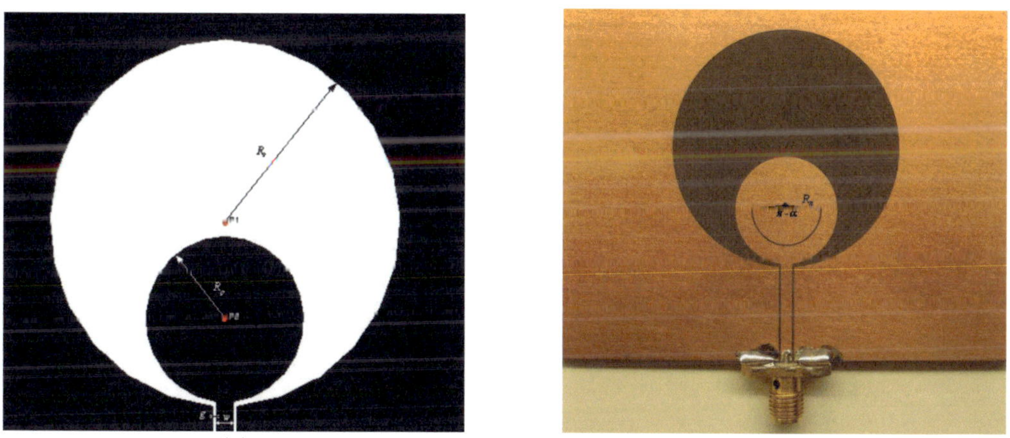

(a) (b)

Fig. 24. Antenna structure (a) UWB Antenna layout, (b) notched UWB antenna photograph.

Variable	R_s	R_p	R_n	$P_1\,P_2$	w	g	w_n
Dimension (mm)	20	9	6	10.5	2	0.35	0.25

Table 1. Antenna dimensions.

Fig. 25a shows that the real part of the antenna impedance fluctuates around 50Ω, while its imaginary part remains with small values and oscillates around zero; this is mainly because a continuous coupling is obtained between the circular patch and the circular ground at different positions, and hence matching is achieved for different frequencies. Antenna parameters are summarized in Table 1.

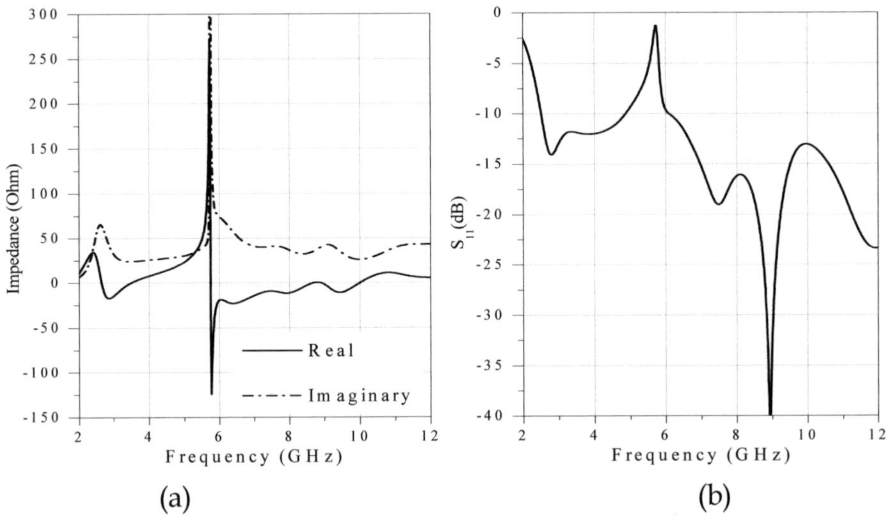

Fig. 25. Notched antenna impedance matching (a) Antenna impedance, (b) return loss.

Radiation patterns for different frequencies over the operating bandwidth in principal planes are shown in Fig. 26; specifically, radiation patterns at the notch frequency are plotted in Fig. 26c,d. It is worth to underline that the antenna keeps somehow an omnidirectional pattern in the H-plane. A good agreement between simulated and measured radiation patterns is observed.

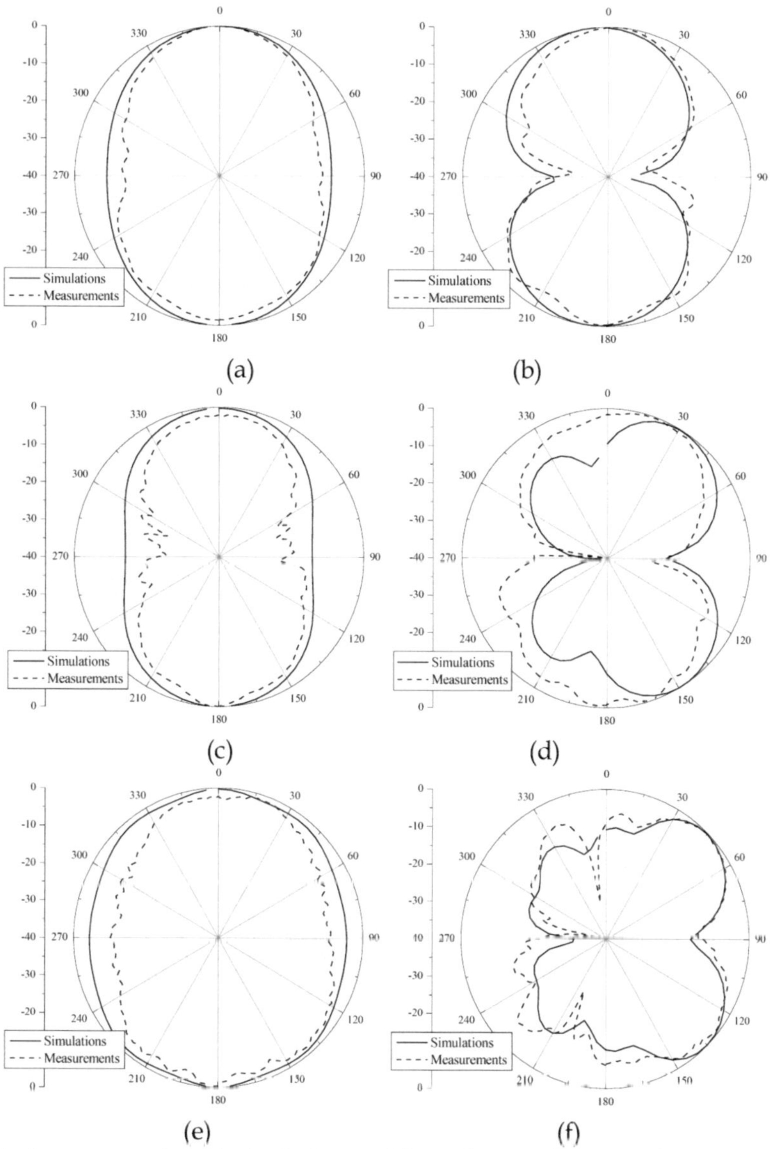

Fig. 26. Radiation pattern in principal planes: (a) H-plane at 3.5GHz, (b) E-plane at 3.5GHz, (c) H-plane at 6GHz, (d) E-plane at 6GHz, (e) H-plane at 9GHz, (f) E-plane at 9GHz.

6. Butler Matrix

The main cause of degradation of communication quality is multipath fading. This multipath phenomenon arises when a transmitted signal undergoes reflection from various obstacles in the propagation environment which degrades the transmission quality and limits the frequency efficiency. Smart antennas are one resolution to overcome this problem. Smart antenna systems are introduced to improve wireless performance and increase system capacity by spatial filtering, which can separate spectrally and temporally overlapping signals from multiple users. Smart antennas systems can be generally categorized into two approaches based on transmit strategy: adaptive arrays and switched beams. Adaptive arrays consist of multiple antenna elements at the transmitting and/or receiving side of the communication link, whose signals are processed adaptively in order to exploit the spatial dimension of the mobile radio channel. This technique allow to steer the main lobe in the desired signal direction and to create pattern nulls in directions of interferences, which results in a better signal-to-interference ratio. However, the physical implementation of these algorithms is more complex and leads to costly systems. On other hand, switched beams systems are referred as antenna array system that forms multiple fixed beams with enhanced sensitivity in a specific area. This antenna system detects signal strength, selects one of the several predetermined fixed beams, and switches from one beam to another as the user moves.

One of the most widely-known of switched beam networks is Butler matrix. It is a passive feeding *NXN* network with beam steering capabilities for phased array antennas with *N* outputs connected to antenna elements and *N* inputs or beam ports. Feeding an *N*-element antenna array using an *NXN* Butler matrix, N orthogonal beams can be generated, and each one has a gain of the whole array.

In this area, it is strategic to have wideband and spatial filtering at the same time to combine the both advantages. However, conventional Butler matrices, which use that a network composed of microwave hybrids and crossovers, have a limited bandwidth. In addition, crossovers add undesired effects such as increased insertion losses, mismatched junctions, additional line cross couplings and poor power handling.

In this section, a design of an ultra-wideband multilayer beamforming network based on a multilayer *4X4* Butler matrix is described. This matrix is advantageously used to offer a very wide bandwidth and to reduce the number of crossing lines. To validate the proposed design, an experimental prototype of the proposed *4X4*-matrix was designed, fabricated and measured. Simulation and experimental results including return loss, insertion loss are presented and discussed. Furthermore, to examine the performance of the proposed matrix in terms of beamforming, a 4 antenna array was built and connected to this matrix to form a multiple beam antenna system.

Fig. 27 shows the proposed Butler matrix. This matrix uses CB-CPW directional coupler, a crossover, and phase shift transmission lines. The multilayer system permits to reduce the number of crossovers as shown in Fig. 28.

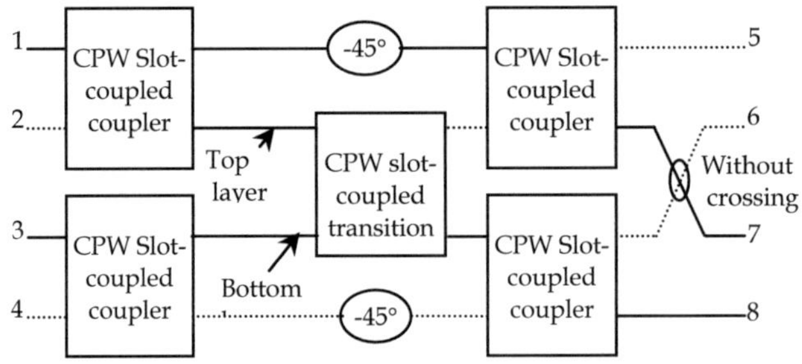

Fig. 27. Block diagram of the UWB Butler matrix.

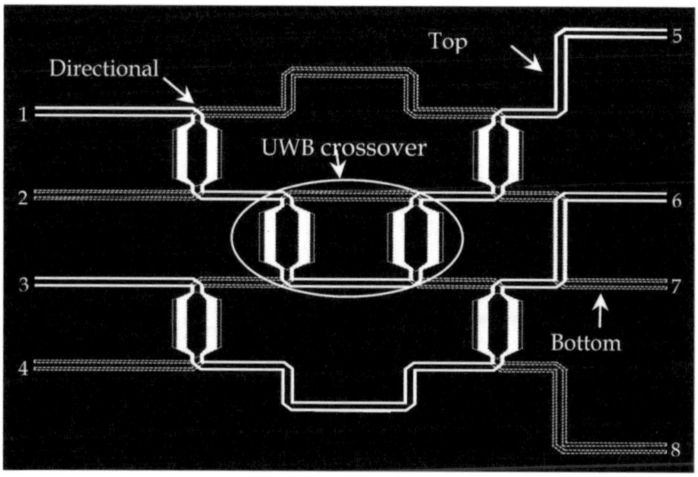

Fig. 28. Layout of UWB *4 X 4* Butler matrix

A signal incident at input ports (#1, #2, #3, or #4) is divided into four output ports (#5, #6, #7, and #8) with equal amplitude and specified relative-phase differences. The phase shift of -45° is designed by using a section of transmission line, which produces a phase shift of $\theta=2\pi l/\lambda_g$.
The Butler matrix is designed for the frequency range from 4 to 8 GHz. Fig. 28 shows the layout of the proposed Butler matrix. Fig. 29 shows simulation results of the insertion and return loss for the port 1 when the other ports are matched. These results demonstrate that the matrix has a good performance in terms of magnitude which is around -7.5 dB. Return loss is better than 15 dB and coupling to the output ports are well equalized (around -7.5 dB). It can be concluded that the obtained results are very promising.

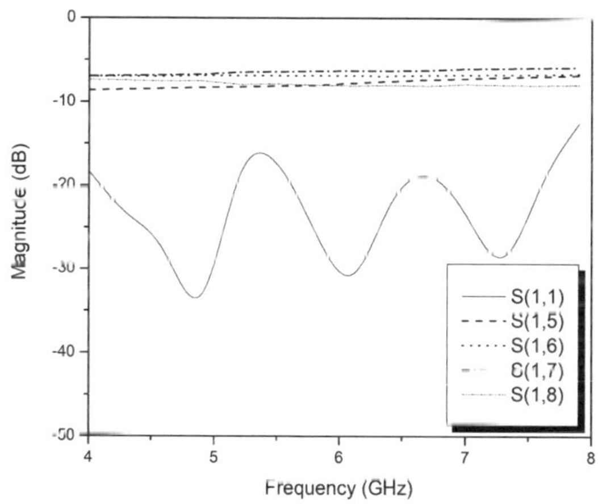

Fig. 29. Simulated results of multilayer Butler matrix.

Using this matrix with four-antenna array, four beams can be produced. Fig. 30 shows theoretical radiation pattern in the H-plane at 5.8 GHz. From this figure, it can be seen that the proposed matrix produces a four orthogonal beams. These features make the proposed matrix suitable for UWB beamforming applications.

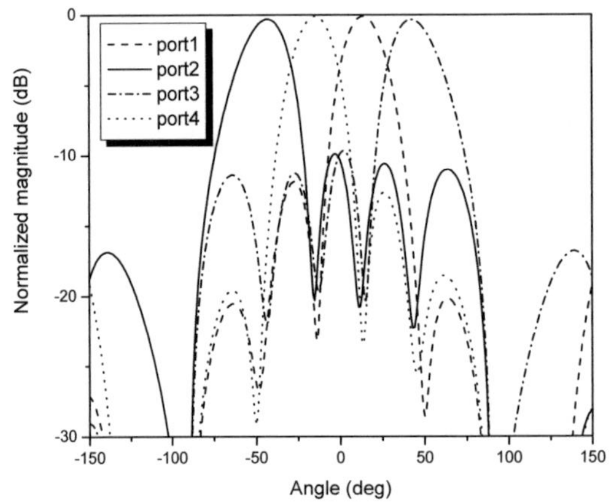

Fig. 30. Simulated results of H-plane radiation pattern at 5.8 GHz.

7. Conclusion

A non exhaustive overview of passive high frequency ultra-wideband devices has been presented. In order to achieve ultra-wideband systems for high data rate transferring and ultra-short time performances, a complete beam-switching antenna system is requested. Ultra-wideband antennas can be obtained through certain techniques such as thick impedance matching planar monopoles or wide radiating aperture slots. A complex feeding system, butler matrix for instance, needs to be combined with antenna array for beam-switching applications. Such a feeding network must present ultra-wideband abilities. An example of ultra-wideband butler matrix has been described based on ultra-wideband couplers and transitions. Other passive devices such as ultra-wideband filters are connected to the antenna system in a complete receiver structure. This interesting filed of research is finding a lucrative applications in industry, specifically with actual high data rate exigencies.

8. References

Abbosh, M. & Bialkowsky, M. E. (2008). Design of Ultrawideband Planar Monopole Antennas of Circular and Elliptical Shape, *IEEE Trans. Antenna and propagat.*, Vol. 56, No. 1, (Jan. 2008) pp. 2473-2479, 0018-926X.

Abbosh, M. & Bialkowsky, M. E. (2006). A Planar UWB Antenna with Signal Rejection Capability in the 4-6GHz Band, *IEEE Microw. Wirel. Comp. Lett.*, Vol. 54, No. 6, (May 2006) pp. 278-280, 1531-1309.

Bona, M.; Manholm, L.; Satarski, J. P. & Svensson, B. (2002). Low-Loss Compact Butler Matrix for a Microstrip Antenna , *IEEE Trans, on Microwave Theory and Tech.*, Vol. 50, No. 9, (Sept 2002) pp. 2069-2075, 0018-9480.

Burke, J. J. & Jackson, R.W. (1989). Surface-to-surface transition via electromagnetic coupling of microstrip and coplanar waveguide, *IEEE Trans. Microwave Theory Tech.*, Vol. 37, No.3, (Mars 1989) pp. 519–525, 0018-9480.

Chao, R.Y. & Chung, K.S. (1994). A low profile antenna array for underground mine communication, *Proceedings of ICCS'94*, pp. 705-7091994, vol. 2, 0-7803-2046-8, Singapore,Nov 1994, IEEE, Singapore.

Chen, A.; Tsai, M. & Alexopoulos, G. (1996). Optimization of aperture transitions for multiport microstrip circuits, *IEEE Trans. Microw. Theory Tech.*, Vol. 44, No. 12, (Dec. 1996) pp. 2457–2465, 0018-9480.

Corona, A. & Lancaster, M. J. (2003). A High-temperature superconducting Butler matrix, *IEEE Trans. On Applied Superconductivity*, Vol. 13, No. 4, (Dec. 2003) pp. 3867-3872, 1051-8223.

Dall'omo C.; Monediere, T.; Jecko, B.; Lamour, F.; Wolk, I. & Elkael, M. (2003). Design and Realization of a 4x4 Microstrip Butler Matrix without Any Crossing in Millimeter-Wave, *Microwave and Optical Technol. Lett.*, Vol. 38, No. 6, (Sept. 2003) pp. 462-465 , 0895-2477.

Denidni, T. A. & T. E. Libar, (2003). Wide band four-port Butler matrix for switched multibeam antenna arrays, *IEEE Proceedings on Personal, Indoor and Mobile Radio Communications*, pp. 2461-2463, 0-7803-7822-9, Beijing, Sept. 2003, IEEE, Beijing.

Dogandzic, A.; Riba, J.; Seco, G. & Swindlehurst, A. L. (2005) Positioning and navigation with applications to communications, *IEEE Signal Proc. Magazine*, Vol. 22, (July 2005) pp.10–11, 1053-5888.

Fakoukakis, F. E.; Diamantis, S. G.; Orfanides, A. P. & Kyriacou, G. A (2006). Development of an Adaptive and a Switched Beam Smart Antenna System for Wireless Communications, *Journal of Electromagnetic Waves and Applications*, Vol. 20, No. 3, (2006) pp. 399-408, 0920-5071.

He, J.; Wang, B.-Z.; He, Q.-Q.; Xing, Y.-X. & Yin, Z.-L. (2007). Wideband X-Band Microstrip Butler Matrix, *Progress In Electromagnetics Research*, Vol. 74, (2007) pp. 131-140, 1559-8985.

Ivanov, T. & Mortazawi, A. (1995). Two stage double layer microstrip spatial amplifiers, *Microwave Symposium Digest, 2006. IEEE MTT S International*, 0-7803-1209-0, pp.589-592, Atlanta, 1995, IEEE, Atlanta.

Lee, W S.; Kim, D-Z.; Kim, K-J. & Yu, J-W (2006). Wideband Planar Monopole Antennas With Dual Band-Notched Characteristics, *IEEE Trans. Antenna and propagat.*, Vol. 54, No. 6, (June 2006) pp. 2800-2806, 0018-926X.

Lim, C & Uysal, S. (1999). Design of a Broadband Directional Coupler Using Microstrip-Like Multilayer Technology, *Microwave and Optical Technol. Lett.*, Vol. 23, No. 5, (Nov. 1999) pp. 273-275, 0895-2477.

Ma, T-G & Wu, S-J. (2007). Ultrawideband Band-Notched Folded Strip Monopole Antenna, *IEEE Trans. Antenna and propagat.*, Vol. 55, No. 9, (Sept. 2007) pp. 2473-2479, 0018-926X.

Macnamara, T.M. (1998). Position and Magnitudes of Fixed Phase Shifters in Butler Matrices Incorporation 90° Hybrids , *IEE Proceedings*, Vol. 135, No 5, (Oct 1988) pp. 359 - 360, 0950-107X.

Ming-Ju, Stuber; G. L. & Austin, M. (1998). Performance of switched-beam smart antennas, for cellular radio systems, *IEEE Trans. Veh. Technol.*, Vol. 47, No. 1, (Feb. 1998) pp. 10-19, 0018-9545.

Nedil, M.; Denidni, A. T & Talbi, L. (2004). Design of a Broadband slot Antenna Fed by CPW for Wireless Application at 5.8 GHz, *IEEE* Vehicular Technology Conf., VTC2004-Spring, pp. 18-21, 0-7803-8255-2, May 2004, IEEE, Roma.

Nedil, M.; Denidni, A. T & Talbi, L. (2006). Novel Butler Matrix Using CPW Multilayer Technology, *IEEE Transactions on Microwave Theory and Techniques*, Vol. 54, No. 1, (Jan. 2006) pp. 499-507, 0018-9480.

Nerguizian, C.; Despins, C.; Affes, S. & Djadel, M. (2005). Radio-channel characterization of an underground mine at 2.4 GHz wireless communication, *IEEE Trans. On Wireless Commun.*, Vol. 4, No. 5, (Sept. 2005) pp. 2441-2453, 1536-1276.

Porcino, D. & Hirt, W. (2003). Ultra-wideband radio technology: Potential and challenges ahead, *IEEE Comm. Mag.*, Vol. 4, No. 7, (July 2003) pp. 66-74, 0163-6804.

Sharma, R.; Chakravarty, T.; Bhooshan, S. & Bhattacharyya, A. B. (2006). Design of a novel 3db microstrip backward wave coupler using defected ground structure, *Progress In Electromagnetics Research*, Vol. 65, (2006) pp. 261-273, 1559-8985.

Stutzman, W. L. & Thiele, G. A. (1998). *Antenna Theory and Design, second edition*, John Wiley & Sons, 978-0-471-02590-0, New York.

Tanaka, T.; Tsunoda, K. & Aikawa, M. (1988). Slot-coupled directional couplers between double-sided substrate microstrip lines and their applications, *IEEE Trans. Microwave Theory Tech.*, Vol. 36, No. 12, (Dec. 1998) pp. 1752-1757, 0018-9480.

Theodorou, A. S. & Uzunoglu, N. K. (1994). Transition properties of a vertical conductor connecting two microstrip lines at different planes, *IEEE Trans. Microw. Theory Tech.*, Vol. 42, No. 12, (Dec. 1994) pp. 1162–1172, 0018-9480.

Tran, A. M. & Itoh, T. (1993). Analysis of Microstrip Lines Coupled Through an Arbitrarily Shaped Aperture in a Thick Common Ground Plane, *Microwave Symposium Digest, 2006. IEEE MTT-S International*, 0-7803-1209-0, pp.819-822, ,Atlanta, 1993, IEEE, Atlanta.

Tudosie, G.; Barth, H. & Vahldieck, R. (2006) A Compact LTCC Butler Matrix Realization for Phased Array Applications, *Microwave Symposium Digest, 2006. IEEE MTT-S International*, pp.441-444, 0-7803-9541-7, San Francisco, CA,June 2006, IEEE, San Francisco.

Warns, C.; Menzel, W., & Schumacher, H. (1998). Transmission lines and passive elements for multilayer coplanar circuits on silicon, *IEEE Trans. Microw. Theory Tech.*, Vol. 46, No. 5, (May 1998) pp. 616–622, 0018-9480.

Watanabe, K.; Ishihara, J. & Yasumoto, K. (1999). Coupled-Mode Analysis of a Gating-Assisted Directional Coupler Using Singular Perturbation Technique," Journal of Electromagnetic Waves and Applications, Vol. 13, No. 12, (1999) pp. 1681-1682, 0920-5071.

Wincza, K. & Gruszczynski, S. (2005) A broadband 4/spl times/4 Butler matrix for modern-day antennas, *European Microwave Conference*, Vol. 2, pp. 4, 2-9600551-2-8, Paris, Oct. 2005, IEEE, Paris.

Winter, J. H. (1998). Smart Antennas for Wireless Systems, *IEEE Personal Communications*, Vol. 1, (Feb. 1998) pp. 23-27, 1070-9916.

Wong, M. F.; Hanna,V. F. ; Picon, O. & Baudrand, H. (1991). A novel coplanar-waveguide directional coupler with finite-extent backed conductor, *IEEE Trans. Microwave Theory Tech.*, Vol. 12, No.12, (Dec. 1991) pp. 2123–2129, 0018-9480.

Wu, J.-J (2008). A Multimode Interference Coupler with Exponentially Tapered Waveguide, *Progress In Electromagnetics Research C*, Vol. 1, (2008) pp. 113-122, 1559-8985.

Zhu, L. & Wu, K. (1999). Ultrabroad-band vertical transition for multilayer integrated circuits, *IEEE Microw. Guided Wave Lett.*, Vol. 9, No. 11, (Nov. 1999) pp. 453–455, 1051-8207.

12

Filter bank transceiver design for ultra wideband

Christian Ibars, Mònica Navarro, Carles Fernández–Prades,
Xavier Artiga, Ana Moragrega and Ciprian George–Gavrincea
Centre Tecnològic de Telecomunicacions de Catalunya - CTTC
Spain

Antonio Mollfulleda
Gigle Networks
Spain

Montse Nájar
Universitat Politècnica de Catalunya
Spain

1. Introduction

Ultra Wideband (UWB) communications are steadily gaining acceptance worldwide, as the regulatory bodies of several countries define its frequency bands and rules of operation. Out of the many technologies available to generate an UWB signal, two of them have been favored, in recent standardization activities, namely Orthogonal Frequency Division Multiplexing (OFDM) and Impulse Radio (IR). On one hand the IEEE 802.15.3a standard defines an UWB signal based on OFDM, which consists of a large number of digitally-generated narrow subcarriers. On the other hand, the IEEE 802.15.4a standard defines an UWB signal based on pulses of short duration, technology known as IR. In addition to these technologies included in standards, other modulation schemes have been proposed for UWB, such as frequency-modulated UWB, or IR transmitting even shorter, sub-nanosecond pulses. The latter has the advantage of providing very accurate ranging and localization estimates based on the time of arrival, which can be measured with high precision thanks to the large signal bandwidth.
In this chapter we will address the challenges encountered in the transmission and detection of an Impulse Radio Ultra Wideband (IR–UWB) signal in environments with multipath propagation. The main problem in such systems is that multipath produces time dispersion resulting in a very large number of resolvable paths at the receiver. We will argue that it is considerably difficult to design receivers that have both high efficiency in capturing the received signal energy and low complexity. The traditional approaches, such as correlating the received signal with a local template, or the RAKE Receiver, suffer from poor performance since they have to lock to a single propagation path, or a small subset of them, respectively. Non-coherent receivers also fail to deliver the full potential of UWB; in particular, they do not provide sufficient ranging accuracy.
Motivated by this challenge, in this chapter we develop a receiver architecture based on a frequency domain filter bank. The receiver consists mainly of a stage of bandpass filters fol-

lowed by intermediate speed analog–to–digital converters (ADCs) that sample each subband at Nyquist rate. This architecture presents two important advantages: it allows a flexible design where the number of branches and the ADC speed can be selected depending on the desired performance; and it can potentially capture all the received signal energy regardless of the severity of multipath propagation. We analyze the Filter Bank Receiver by first developing the underlying theory of time-frequency signal representations, and then deriving its performance in terms of mean square error (MSE) and bit error rate (BER), comparing it to other receiver types.

Another important performance aspect of UWB receivers is their capability to provide accurate time of arrival estimates, and thus accurate ranging and localization. We address this aspect by first analyzing synchronization schemes for UWB and then presenting a time of arrival algorithm in the frequency domain, suitable for the filter bank receiver architecture. Subsequently, we describe algorithms for ranging and localization based on time of arrival.

The last part of this chapter is devoted to describing a real implementation of the filter bank receiver. The architecture consists of an UWB RF front end followed by a digital back end which processes the received samples and implements the signal detection and time of arrival estimation algorithms. Wideband RF design is tackled using wideband low noise amplifiers (LNAs) and downconversion stages to provide lowpass signals to the ADC stage. Gaussian bandpass filters are used, which have very good time and frequency concentration properties. The digital section is implemented with a hybrid architecture consisting of a programmable logic device (PLD) to handle the high aggregate sampling rate, and a digital signal processor (DSP) to implement signal processing algorithms in a flexible and easily reprogrammable fashion.

2. Ultra Wideband Signals and Channel

In impulse radio technology, the transmitted signal consists of a series of low energy, wide bandwidth pulses $p(t)$, with a duration in the order of hundreds of picoseconds. Transmitted pulses are typically shaped so that their power spectrum $|P(f)|^2$ satisfies the power spectral density (PSD) constraints set by regulatory bodies (*Generic Harmonized European Standard for UWB Communications (ETSI EN 302 065)*, 2008; *Revision of part 15 of the Commission's Rules Regarding Ultra-Wideband Transmission Systems*, 2002). Several pulses are sent for each transmission symbol in order to achieve the necessary energy per bit. At the transmitter, bits are grouped in data symbols and transmitted at symbol rate $R_s = 1/T_s$ where T_s is the symbol period. Each symbol interval is divided in N_f equally sized intervals of length T_f, known as frame intervals. In turn, each frame interval is divided in N_c equally spaced time intervals of length T_c known as chip intervals. In each frame interval only one pulse is transmitted, which is located in one of the N_c chip intervals. In case that Pulse Position Modulation of order M (M–PPM) is used, each chip interval is further divided in M modulation intervals of length T_Δ[1]. Typically, time hopping (TH) or direct sequence (DS) spreading is used to determine the pulse position and polarity, respectively, in each frame interval, with the purpose of satisfying the PSD mask. A general expression for a waveform carrying a block of N_b consecutive

[1] Although we define here the division in modulation intervals within the chip interval, it may take place at higher levels. For example, the symbol period may be divided into M modulation intervals and subsequently divided in frame and chip intervals, as in the IEEE 802.15.4a Standard.

symbols can be written as

$$s(t) = \sum_{l=0}^{N_b} \sum_{h=0}^{N_h-1} c_{h,l}^{DS} a_l p \left(t - lT_s - b_l T_\Delta - c_{h,l}^{TH} T_c - hT_f \right) \tag{1}$$

where $c_{h,l}^{DS} \in \{-1, 1\}$ is the DS code chip amplitude for the h–th frame of the l–th symbol, $c_{h,l}^{TH} \in \{0, \cdots, N_c - 1\}$ selects the chip interval of the h–th frame of the l–th symbol, a_l is the amplitude of the l–th symbol and b_l is the time position of the l–th symbol. An example of the resulting transmitted signal is shown in Fig. 1.

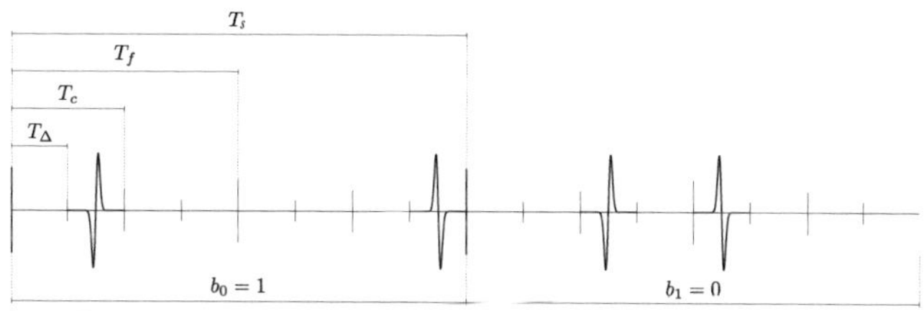

Fig. 1. Example of IR–UWB signal with TH and DS codes. $N_h = 2.N_s = 2$, $N_c = 2$, $BPSK$. Bit sequence $\{b_0 = 0, b_1 = 1\}$.TH Code sequence $\{0, 1, 1, 0\}$.DS Code sequence $\{1, -1, 1, -1\}$.

In order to fully understand the design principles of IR–UWB receivers, it is important to understand the channel propagation effects on the transmitted signal. In order to develop a common channel model, the IEEE 802.15.4a Standards Group considered several possibilities and established a modification of the traditional Saleh-Valenzuela model (Saleh & Valenzuela, 1987) as a statistical channel model for UWB. According to this model, signal paths are grouped into clusters, containing several rays with different gains ($\beta_{q,r}$) and propagation delay ($\tau_{q,r}$) where q and r are cluster index and path index inside each cluster respectively. The resulting baseband channel model is given by

$$h(t) = \sum_q \sum_r \beta_{q,r} \delta(t - \tau_r) \tag{2}$$

The UWB channel has been characterized in IEEE 802.15.4a (Molisch et al., 2004), where several types of channels are described. Among other environments, channel types 3 and 4 model an indoor environment in line of sight (LOS) and non–line of sight (NLOS) configurations respectively. The main challenge in UWB propagation stems from the fact that the receiver is very resolutive in time. Since the transmitted pulse is very short, paths separated by one nanosecond or less may be resolvable by the receiver, resulting in hundreds of paths for typical propagation environments. According to values provided in (Molisch et al., 2004), Table 1 shows the number of paths containing the 85% of the energy and the r.m.s. delay spread of channel models 3 and 4. The first parameter ranges from 22 to 15, while the latter can be up to 13 ns. Therefore, channel dispersion is very challenging for the receiver, both in terms of capturing the received signal energy and in terms of channel estimation, as it is argued in the following sections.

For the sake of simplicity and without loss of generality we will consider a simplified channel model that avoids the differentiation of paths in clusters. In this model each ray is represented by its amplitude (β_r) and delay τ_r, where r is the path index. Then, the baseband channel model can be expressed as

$$h(t) = \sum_r \beta_r \delta(t - \tau_r) \tag{3}$$

Channel Model	*Environment*	*r.m.s. delay spread*	*Avg. no. paths for > 85% energy*	*Avg. no. paths over −10 dB*
3	Indoor (office) LOS	10 ns	22.4	14.4
4	Indoor (office) NLOS	13 ns	45.5	30.4
5	Outdoor LOS	29 ns	35.8	17.3
6	Outdoor NLOS	74 ns	65.1	24.5

Table 1. Time Dispersion of IEEE 802.15.4a Channel Models.

where index r includes information of the number of cluster and the number of ray in each cluster. According to this channel model and assuming the presence of additive white Gaussian noise (AWGN) $\eta(t)$ with variance σ_η^2 the received signal is given by

$$r(t) = \sum_r \beta_r s(t - \tau_r) + \eta(t) \tag{4}$$

In general the maximum excess delay of the channel, $\tau_{max} = max\{\tau_r\}$, can be longer than the modulation interval T_Δ, and even longer than the symbol interval T_s, causing inter–symbol interference (ISI). However, to evaluate the capabilities of capturing the received signal energy on different receiver approaches it is assumed that $\tau_{max} < T_\Delta$. Note that with this assumption all bit energy lies in one of the available modulation intervals. In this case, defining

$$h_p(t) = p(t) \otimes h(t) \tag{5}$$

the received signal can be modeled as

$$r(t) = \sum_l \sqrt{E} h_p\left(t - lT_s - b_l T_\Delta - c_{h,l}^{TH} T_c - hT_f\right) + \eta(t) \tag{6}$$

3. Filter Bank Receiver Architecture

As it can be inferred from the previous section, designing a good receiver for UWB in dispersive channels is a challenging task given the large number of resolvable propagation paths. We begin this section with a brief overview of UWB receivers. As we will see, these receivers, which provide very good performance in traditional narrowband transmission, present several shortcomings when dealing with UWB signals in dispersive channels. This motivates the filter bank architecture, which consists in splitting the UWB signal in several subbands and then sampling them at Nyquist rate. This architecture aims at maximizing the received signal energy while keeping complexity at bay. Moreover, we will see that the presented receivers may be obtained through a generalized filter bank interpretation.

3.1 Overview of Ultra Wideband Receivers

A first approach, referred to as *stored reference (SR) Receiver*, consists in correlating the received signal with a locally generated template $s_{tmp}(t)$ and then sampling the output at rate $F = \frac{1}{T}$, where T is the integration time of the correlation. The stored reference receiver is shown in Fig. 2. The signal template $s_{tmp}(t)$ is generated with the same structure used at the transmitter, that is,

$$s_{tmp}^{sr}(t) = \sum_l \sum_h \sum_{k=0}^{N_{sr}} c_{h,l}^{DS} p\left(t - lT_s - c_{h,l}^{TH} T_c - hT_f - kT - \tau_s\right) \tag{7}$$

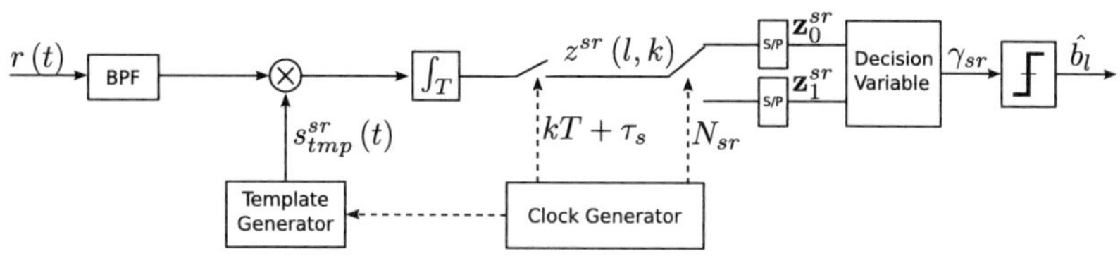

Fig. 2. Stored Reference Receiver.

where $p(t)$ is the transmitted pulse with unit energy, l represents the symbol index and N_{sr} is the number of samples taken in each modulation interval, which is given by $N_{sr} = \frac{T_\Delta}{T}$. The term τ_s represents the sampling offset, which is intentionally modeled to represent the ability of the receiver to modify τ_s to maximize the captured energy, particularly on multipath channels. After the analog correlator, the signal is sampled by an ADC at rate N_{sr}/T, and fed to a bank of correlators operating on decision variables $\mathbf{z}_0^{sr}$ and $\mathbf{z}_1^{sr}$, containing all samples taken at each respective modulation interval. Finally, a decision variable is obtained as

$$\gamma_l = \mathbf{w}^T \left(\mathbf{z}_1^{sr} - \mathbf{z}_0^{sr}\right) \tag{8}$$

where the weights $\mathbf{w}$ correspond to a whitened matched filter for reception with Gaussian noise (Kay, 1998).

Another common approach to receive spread spectrum signals in a multipath propagation environment is the *RAKE Receiver*, shown in Fig. 3. The RAKE receiver uses multiple correlators that lock at different multipath replicas (Zhu et al., 2008). The output of the correlators is sampled and combined before symbol detection. RAKE receivers require accurate estimation of the delay, amplitude, phase and shape (distortion) of the pulses at each individual arrival. When the number of fingers N_{rk} is equal to the number of resolvable paths, this receiver constitutes in fact the matched filter receiver. In practice, given the large number of resolvable UWB paths, the receiver will capture only a fraction of the received signal energy, since increasing N_{rk} has a relevant impact on its complexity.

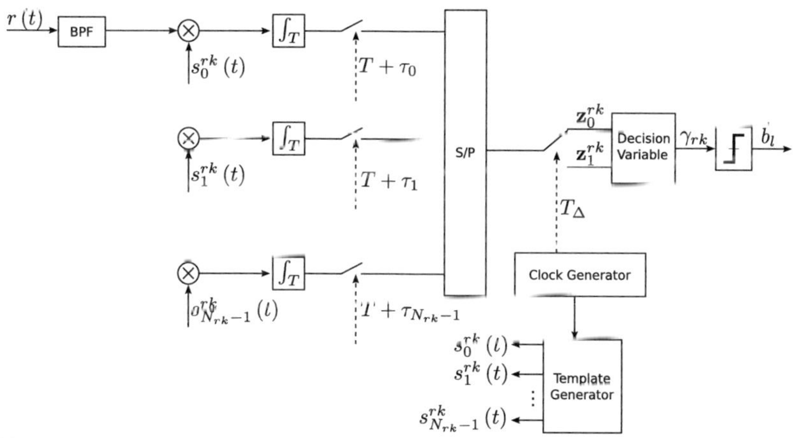

Fig. 3. RAKE Receiver.

Since the received signal is correlated by locally generated replicas of the effective channel impulse response, the analysis of the RAKE receiver is similar to that of the SR receiver. The

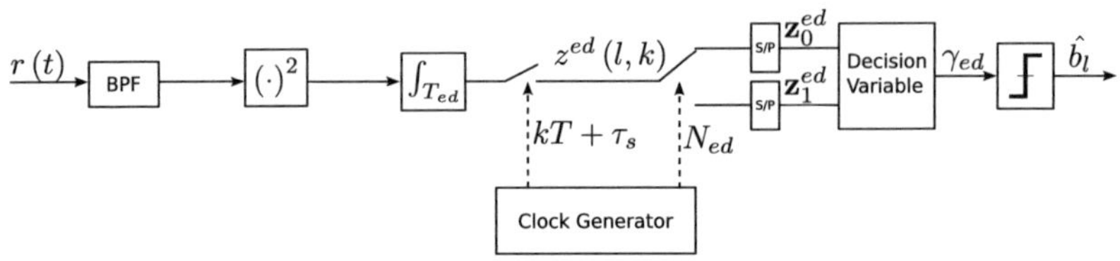

Fig. 4. Energy Detector Receiver.

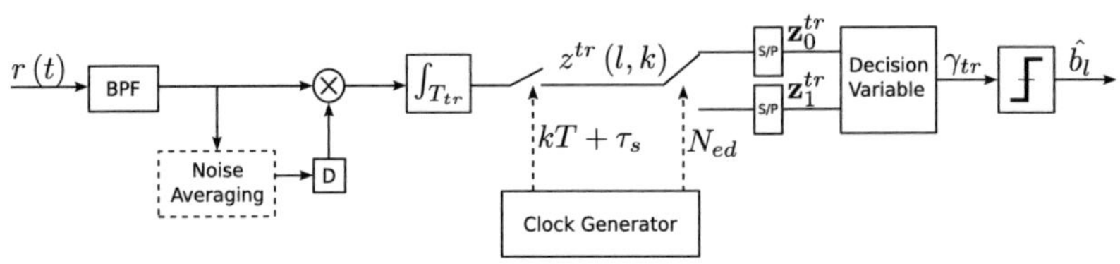

Fig. 5. Transmitted Reference Receiver.

signal template of the k–th finger is constructed in the same way as the transmitted signal and is given by

$$s_k^{rk}(t) = \sum_l \sum_h p\left(t - lT_s - c_l^{TH} T_c - hT_f - \tau_k\right) \tag{9}$$

where $k \in \{0, \cdots, N_{rk} - 1\}$ and τ_k represents the k–th propagation path with largest energy. Note that the RAKE receiver requires N_{rk} ADC converters sampling at symbol rate while SR receiver requires just one converter and an oversampling factor of N_{sr} with respect to the RAKE approach. In both cases the number of samples taken in a modulation interval is a critical parameter.

In the following we discuss two non-coherent approaches, namely the *Energy Detector* and the *Transmitted Reference Receiver*. In contrast to RAKE and SR approaches the energy detector (ED) receiver does not correlate the received signal with a local template. Instead, the analog front-end adds up the received energy in each modulation interval to create the decision variables. Fig. 4 shows the main blocks that constitute the ED receiver.

The Transmitted Reference Receiver was originally created to avoid the local knowledge of the correlation template, which requires a priori knowledge of the carrier to interference ratio (CIR). To this end, the transmitted signal generates a reference pulse for each transmitted pulse. The two pulses are separated an interval that is longer than the maximum excess delay of the channel. The first pulse is used as a correlation template while the second pulse is used for signal detection. The receiver functional block diagram is depicted in Fig. 5. The signal is correlated by a delayed version of itself, integrated and then sampled at rate T. For each modulation interval N_{tr} samples are collected, where $N_{tr} = \frac{T_\Delta}{T}$, and then processed.

3.2 Time-frequency Representations

The coherent receivers described in the previous sections, namely stored reference and RAKE receivers, use analog components to generate a signal template and correlate it with the received signal. This approach places serious complexity constraints on these structures, such as the number of fingers of the RAKE receiver. An interesting alternative is to perform all these operations (template generation and correlation) in the digital domain, where more complex structures can be addressed if enough computing power is available. However, implementing an all-digital receiver (see (Blazquez et al., 2003) for example) requires sampling the received signal at Nyquist rate, which can be very challenging for signals with up to 10 GHz bandwidth. An alternative approach is considered in this section, where sampling is performed in a time-frequency grid rather than in the time domain only.

Representing a signal by a discrete set of samples is a fundamental problem in signal processing. Signal projection onto a set of base functions and series expansion of signals provides an elegant way to represent a broad range of possibilities for signal acquisition. An important step in a series expansion is the choice of an appropriate basis to represent the signal of interest. That is, given a signal $s(t)$ choosing a set of functions $\gamma_k(t)$ and $g_k(t)$ such that the basis coefficients are obtained as

$$s_k = \langle s(t), \gamma_k(t) \rangle = \int_{-\infty}^{+\infty} s(\tau)\,\gamma_k(\tau)\,d\tau \tag{10}$$

while the original signal is reconstructed as

$$s(t) = \sum_k s_k g_k^*(t) \tag{11}$$

where (10) is known as the analysis equation while the linear expansion in (11) is known as the synthesis equation. If $g_k(t) = \gamma_k(t)$, then (11) is known as the orthogonal series expansion of $s(t)$. Otherwise, the functions $\gamma_k(t)$ and $g_k(t)$ are a set of biorthogonal functions with the property

$$\left\langle g_j(t), \gamma_i(t) \right\rangle = \delta_{i-j}(t)$$

where $\delta_{i-j}(t)$ is defined such that $\delta_{i-j}(t) = 0$ unless $i = j$, in which case $\delta_0(t) = \delta(t)$. The idea to take signal samples from its representation in the time–frequency plane was suggested by (Gabor, 1946). Instead of processing the entire signal at once, Gabor proposed to divide the signal into equally sized segments and then perform the Fourier transform of each segment. The result provides local information about the frequency content on each time interval. To perform the two dimensional sampling on $s(t)$ the time axis is divided into N equally sized intervals of length T, which represent the time-domain sampling period. Each segment of $s(t)$ is labeled as $s_n(t)$ and is given by

$$s_n(t) = s(t)\,\Pi\left(\frac{t-nT}{T}\right) \tag{12}$$

where n indexes the number of segments and $\Pi(t)$ represents a square pulse of unit length and amplitude. Since $s_n(t)$ is a time-limited signal, its Fourier transform $S_n(f)$ can be expressed as the sequence of discrete samples

$$S_n(f) = \sum_k S(kB)\,Sinc\left(\frac{f}{B} - k\right) \tag{13}$$

where $B = \frac{1}{T}$ is the sampling interval in the frequency domain. Fig. 6 shows an example of the two-dimensional sampling grid. The product BT defines the density of samples taken from the time–frequency energy distribution of the signal. Nyquist density, defined as the time–frequency product $BT = 1$, provides the minimum set of samples required for perfect signal reconstruction. Lower values of BT imply oversampling the signal, while larger values correspond to subsampling, in which case not all the signal energy is captured.

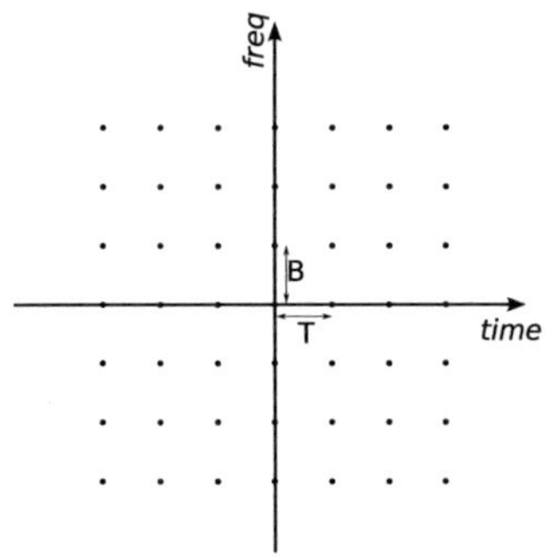

Fig. 6. Example of 2-dimensional sampling grid.

Let us denote by $s_{n,m}$ the two–dimensional samples of $s(t)$. Indexes n and m represent the time and frequency domain sampling, respectively. Denoting $\hat{s}_n(t)$ as the periodic signal obtained by the sampling of $S_n(f)$ it follows that

$$s_{n,m} = S_n(mB) = \int_{-T}^{T} \hat{s}_n(t) e^{-j2\pi mBt} dt \tag{14}$$

$$= \int_{-\infty}^{\infty} s(t) \Pi\left(\frac{t-nT}{T}\right) e^{-j2\pi mBt} dt \tag{15}$$

Therefore, the two–dimensional samples can be expressed as a function of the time-domain signal $s(t)$ as follows

$$s_{n,m} = \int_{-\infty}^{\infty} s(t) \gamma_{n,m}(t) dt \tag{16}$$

where

$$\gamma_{n,m}(t) = \Pi\left(\frac{t-nT}{T}\right) e^{-j2\pi mBt} \tag{17}$$

Using the synthesis equation of the series expansion, the reconstruction of the signal $s(t)$ is given by

$$\hat{s}(t) = \sum_n \sum_m s_{n,m} \gamma^*_{n,m}(t)$$

Assuming that an uncounted number of frequency domain samples are taken on each interval and $BT = 1$, one would provide a perfect signal reconstruction. Limiting the number of samples on each interval to a finite number M leads to the M–th order representation of $s(t)$, which is defined as the truncated series expansion,

$$\tilde{s}(t) = \sum_n \sum_{m=0}^{M-1} s_{n,m} \gamma^*_{n,m}(t)$$

A figure of merit of the quality of signal acquisition can be given in terms of the MSE of the truncated series representation, which is given by

$$\begin{aligned} MSE_{2D} &= \int |s(t) - \sum_n \sum_{m=0}^{M-1} s_{n,m} \gamma^*_{n,m}(t)|^2 dt \\ &= \sum_n \sum_{m=M}^{\infty} |s_{n,m}|^2 \end{aligned}$$

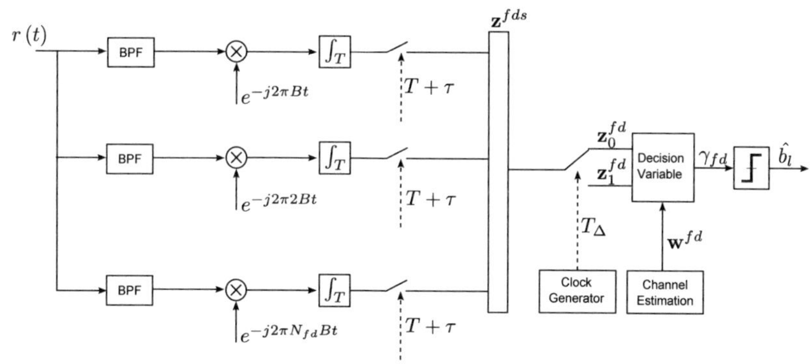

Fig. 7. Block diagram of a Filter Bank Receiver.

Therefore, having the a priori knowledge of the signal bandwidth one can define M to achieve a given MSE on the signal reconstruction.

3.3 Filter Bank Receiver

The fundamental idea behind the filter bank receiver is to provide an implementation that allows us to obtain a highly accurate time-frequency representation of the received UWB signal. Consider an IR signal as described in Section 2, in which 2–Pulse Position Modulation (PPM) modulation is used. The signal length conveying a block of N_p bits is $T_p = N_p T_s$. The channel model is the same one used in (3) where the maximum excess delay of the channel is considered lower than the modulation interval. The noise is assumed to be AWGN with variance σ_η^2. Fig. 7 shows the block diagram of the filter bank receiver. The receiver implements a 2–dimensional sampling stage by splitting the input signal into M paths and correlating it with the basis function

$$\gamma_{n,m}(t) = \Pi\left(\frac{t - nT}{T}\right) e^{-j2\pi mB(t-nT)} \tag{18}$$

In practice, this operation may be carried out with orthogonal, or quasi–orthogonal, bandpass filters. The output of each correlator is sampled at a rate $\frac{1}{T}$, and all samples associated to each modulation interval are arranged in a vector. The captured samples can be expressed as

$$z_{n,m} = \left\langle r(t), \gamma_{n,m(t)} \right\rangle \tag{19}$$

where $m \in (1, ..., M)$ indexes the samples in frequency domain. The collected samples for each symbol form a two–dimensional set of samples. Using (6) and (19) it follows that, when the signal is present on a given interval,

$$z_{n,m} = \left\langle h_p(t), \gamma_{n,m(t)} \right\rangle + \left\langle \eta(t), \gamma_{n,m}(t) \right\rangle \tag{20}$$

Let $\mathbf{z}_0^{fb}(l)$ be the vector gathering all samples in the modulation interval associated to $b_l = 0$ of the l–th symbol, and $\mathbf{z}_1^{fb}(l)$ the vector for the time interval corresponding to $b_l = 1$. The statistics of $\mathbf{z}_0^{fb}(l)$ and $\mathbf{z}_1^{fb}(l)$ are given by

$$\mathbf{z}_0^{fb}(l) = \begin{cases} \mathcal{N}\left(\mathbf{z}_p^{fb}(k), \mathbf{C}_\eta^2\right), & b_l = 0 \\ \mathcal{N}\left(\mathbf{0}, \mathbf{C}_\eta^2\right), & b_l = 1 \end{cases} \tag{21}$$

$$\mathbf{z}_1^{fb}(l) = \begin{cases} \mathcal{N}\left(\mathbf{0}, \mathbf{C}_\eta^2\right), & b_l = 0 \\ \mathcal{N}\left(\mathbf{z}_p^{fb}(k), \mathbf{C}_\eta^2\right), & b_l = 1 \end{cases} \tag{22}$$

where $\mathbf{z}_p^{fb} = [\{\left\langle h_p(t), \gamma_{n,m(t)} \right\rangle\}_{n,m}]^T$ and $\mathbf{C}_\eta$ is the noise covariance matrix. These vectors are combined to make the decision variable. Defining the combining weights as $\mathbf{w} = [w_0, w_1, \cdots, w_{MN_{fb}-1}]^T$, the decision variable is given by

$$\gamma_l = 2\Re\{\mathbf{w}^H\left(\mathbf{z}_1^{fb} - \mathbf{z}_0^{fb}\right)\} \tag{23}$$

The weights that lead to optimal solution for Gaussian noise correspond to the generalized matched filter solution (Kay, 1998), which defines the weights as $\mathbf{w} = [\mathbf{C}_{fb}^{-1}\mathbf{z}_p^{fb}]$. The statistics of the decision variable are given by

$$\gamma_l^{fb} = \begin{cases} \mathcal{N}\left(\mathbf{z}_p^{fb^H}\mathbf{C}_{fb}^{-1}\mathbf{z}_p^{fb}, \mathbf{z}_p^{fb^H}\mathbf{C}_{fb}^{-1}\mathbf{z}_p^{fb}\right), & b_l = 1 \\ \mathcal{N}\left(-\mathbf{z}_p^{fb^H}\mathbf{C}_{fb}^{-1}\mathbf{z}_p^{fb}, \mathbf{z}_p^{fb^H}\mathbf{C}_{fb}^{-1}\mathbf{z}_p^{fb}\right), & b_l = 0 \end{cases} \tag{24}$$

Using (24) it follows that the BER for the filter bank receiver is given by

$$BER_{fb} = Q\left(\sqrt{\mathbf{z}_p^{fb^H}\mathbf{C}_{fb}^{-1}\mathbf{z}_p^{fb}}\right) \tag{25}$$

Provided that the set of functions $\gamma_{n,m}(t)$ constitute an orthogonal basis, and assuming that the noise vector is AWGN, the noise covariance matrix becomes $\mathbf{C}^{fb} = \mathbf{I}\sigma_\eta^2$ and the BER is reduced to

$$BER_{fb} = Q\left(\sqrt{\frac{\mathbf{z}_p^{fb^H}\mathbf{z}_p^{fb}}{2\sigma_\eta^2}}\right) \tag{26}$$

Note that the product $\mathbf{z}_p^{fb^T}\mathbf{z}_p^{fb}$ can be expressed, in terms of the MSE of the M–th order representation of $s(t)$, as

$$\mathbf{z}_p^{fb^T}\mathbf{z}_p^{fb} = \sum_{n=0}^{N}\sum_{k=1}^{M} \|H_n(kB)\|^2 = \tag{27}$$

$$= \sum_{n=0}^{N}\left(1 - \sum_{k=M+1}^{\infty} \|S_n(kB)\|^2\right) = \tag{28}$$

$$= \sum_{n=0}^{N}(1 - MSE_n) = 1 - MSE \tag{29}$$

where $H_n(f)$ is the Fourier transform of $h_p(t)\Pi\left(\frac{t-nT}{T}\right)$. Therefore, the BER of the filter bank receiver may also be expressed in terms of the reconstruction MSE.

At this point it is interesting to look back at the SR and RAKE receivers as implementations of a more general filter bank concept. Both receivers are based on sampling the received signal after correlating with a locally generated template. While the SR Receiver implements a single correlator, the RAKE Receiver uses a multiple correlators in parallel. In both cases, the correlation can be expressed a as signal projection over a particular basis. Therefore, SR and RAKE receivers can be expressed as a generalized class of receiver based on signal projection over a given basis. The complexity of each receiver is determined by the following factors:

- Size of the basis, which is determines the number of sampling units.
- Sampling frequency at each ADC.
- Sampling offset of each ADC.
- Requirement that sampling clock is synchronized with received signal.

This interpretation is useful to compare SR and RAKE receivers to the frequency domain filter bank receiver. In Table 2 we compare these receivers in terms of requirements and complexity. In the table, N stands for the number of samples captured in each modulation interval.

Receiver Type	Basis function	N	Number of sampling units	*Synchronized clock*
SR	$p(t)$	≥ 1	1	No
RAKE-M	$\beta_n p(t-\tau_n)$	1	$M_{rk} > 1$	Yes
Filter bank	$\Pi\left(\frac{t-nT}{T}\right) e^{-j2\pi mBt}$	$\geq M/B$	$\geq B/M$	No

Table 2. Comparison of UWB Receivers as Generalized Filter Banks.

3.4 Performance of the Filter Bank Receiver

We now compare the performance of the filter bank receiver with the other receivers described. In terms of performance, one may look at the reconstruction MSE or the BER, which are related by (29). Regarding the BER, the IEEE channel model type 3 is used, bounding the maximum excess delay to $max\{\tau_r \leq 50ns\}$. The receivers are assumed to be accurately synchronized to the leading edge of the received signal. The receiver settings used in the simulations are summarized in Table 3, which also reports the mean square error for each receiver. It can be seen that a filter bank receiver achieves the lowest MSE if 4 or more filters are used, even compared to a RAKE receiver with 16 fingers. The average BER of the receivers in Table 3 is shown in Fig. 8. As it can be seen, the BER of the filter bank receiver approaches the matched filter bound as the number of filters increases, and is lower than for the other receivers for $M \geq 4$. In the simulations, an ideal basis function with square pulses was used. Such basis may not be used in practice, since it requires each filter to have unlimited bandwidth. The use of different basis functions may deteriorate the performance of the filter bank receiver. Moreover, if the basis functions do not form an orthogonal basis, further receiver processing is necessary. Results in (Mollfulleda et al., 2010) show, however, that the performance of a filter bank receiver using implementable Gaussian filters is still superior to other receiver types.

4. Time of Arrival Estimation and Localization

The wide bandwidth used by UWB radio systems provides two fundamental advantages for localization applications, especially in short–range wireless networks. On the one hand, diversity in frequency components increases the probability that some portion of the signal power can penetrate and go through obstacles. This allows applications such as through–the–wall

Receiver Type	*Sampling Rate*	*No. of ADC*	*samples on each Modulated interval*	MSE (dB)
SR-2G	2 GHz	1	$N_{sr} = 50$	-1.67
SR-4G	4 GHz	1	$N_{sr} = 100$	-2.52
RK-8	20 MHz	8	$N_{rk} = 8$	-3.92
RK-16	20 MHz	16	$N_{rk} = 16$	-5.92
Filter Bank M=2	2 GHz	4	$N_{fb} = 400$	-2.3
Filter Bank M=4	2 GHz	8	$N_{fb} = 800$	-10.59
Filter Bank M=6	2 GHz	12	$N_{fb} = 1200$	-13.8

Table 3. Receiver Settings for BER Simulation.

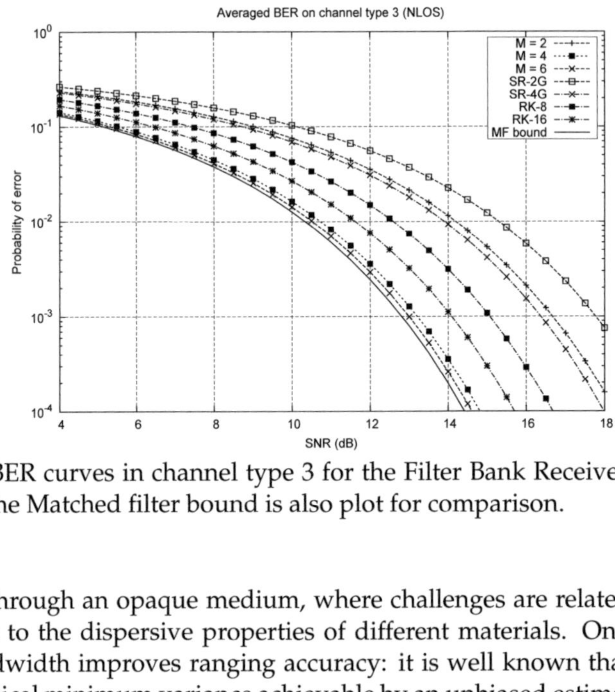

Fig. 8. Averaged BER curves in channel type 3 for the Filter Bank Receiver, SR receiver, and RAKE Receiver. The Matched filter bound is also plot for comparison.

radars, or vision through an opaque medium, where challenges are related to counteracting the distortion due to the dispersive properties of different materials. On the other hand, a large relative bandwidth improves ranging accuracy: it is well known that the Cramér–Rao Bound (the theoretical minimum variance achievable by an unbiased estimator) of time–delay estimator is inversely proportional to the RMS bandwidth, also known as Gabor bandwidth, defined as:

$$B_{RMS} = \sqrt{\frac{\int_{-\infty}^{\infty} f^2 \left|P(f)\right|^2 df}{\int_{-\infty}^{\infty} \left|P(f)\right|^2 df}} \tag{30}$$

where $P(f)$ is the Fourier transform of the pulse waveform. Inspecting equation (30), it is easily seen that we can increase the RMS bandwidth using modulations whose power spectrum concentrates a greater percentage of their power farther from the signal center frequency, because of the weighting term f^2. In that sense, IR–UWB systems exhibit a very large RMS bandwidth due to the short duration of the pulses (less than one nanosecond), which have strong high–frequency components. This implies that the fundamental lower limit of the variance of an IR–UWB timing estimator is dramatically small, and hence this explains the potentiality of this technology for accurate localization or ranging purposes. However, current technology can hardly cope with sampling rates at or above the Nyquist rate, and thus the Cramér–Rao Bound is difficult to attain, notably in dense–multipath indoor environments.

Indeed, one of the most attractive features of UWB systems is their intrinsic potential to allow for very accurate positioning. Due to their large signal bandwidth, UWB signals exhibit very high time resolution. This high time resolution allows receivers to resolve individual components in dense multipath propagation scenarios, which has strong implications to obtain accurate time of arrival (TOA) measurements. In order to measure the TOA between two nodes the receiver needs to identify the first arriving path, which is associated to LOS propagation. In a multipath scenario, the direct path may be masked in a multipath cluster, unless the receiver is able to resolve individual paths within that cluster. Therefore, time–based positioning is the most widely selected technique when implementing localization in UWB systems. This section addresses the estimation of timing measurements and their application to ranging and positioning. We start addressing the more general problem of synchronization for very broadband signal systems and continue with a review of the state–of–the–art on TOA estimation algorithms, which can be broadly classified in two main categories: energy detection and correlator-based.

Special attention is placed to the the filter bank receiver in order to derive suitable algorithms for TOA estimation of the LOS signal, emphasizing some of the main drawbacks linked to the receiver architecture, and arguing for a frequency domain processing for the estimation of the TOA, particularly suitable for the filter–bank receiver, as shown in (Navarro & Nájar, 2007). The filter-bank architecture of the receiver falls very naturally into frequency domain processing since the filters output represents the DFT components of the received UWB signal. Also, well–known high–resolution spectral estimation methods can be applied directly to the frequency domain signal samples achieving very accurate timing estimation. Finally, the section addresses positioning by considering a particular approach based on data fusion algorithms. This technique is particularly attractive for developing global positioning systems that solve the outdoor/indoor transition problem efficiently.

4.1 Synchronization for Wideband Signals

Synchronization is an essential part in every communication system, but it is critical in UWB communication systems, given that small timing errors of the order of the pulse duration can considerably degrade system performance. In general, synchronization involves recovering information at several levels: carrier recovery, symbol timing recovery, and frame synchronization. However, in the case of carrier-less impulse radio UWB, based on PPM modulation, synchronization is reduced to timing synchronization.

The synchronization technique to be developed depends on the receiver architecture and capabilities. A broad classification falls into synchronization for coherent and non–coherent receivers. The coherent reception of IR–UWB signal indicates the recovery of polarity of UWB pulse as well as the position information, while the non–coherent reception can only recover the position information by collecting the energy of the pulses. Most of the research work on IR–UWB implementation focuses on a non–coherent receiver because it has the advantage of avoiding the use of a bank of correlators and pulse matched filter, which leads to simpler implementations.

Nevertheless, we shall review the coherent techniques suitable for PPM modulated IR–UWB signals to provide a benchmark for lower complexity techniques. The basis can be found on the matched filter solutions, see (Oh & Kim, 2008; Oh et al., 2009; Wu et al., 2008), and (Kim et al., 2009). As introduced earlier, the advantages of coherent reception include:

- First, the coherent reception is important for frame acquisition and ranging during the preamble symbol interval. Timing or frame acquisition in a coherent receiver is very accurate compared with a non–coherent receiver, which in turn leads to accurate ranging.
- Second, coherent reception can achieve more channel coding gain since convolutional decoding can be performed during the header and payload intervals.

Research on coherent algorithms for UWB receivers was first conducted by (Lee & Scholtz, 2002), proposing a CLEAN (see (Högbom, 1974)) based iterative correlation algorithm; while high precision can indeed be achieved, the iterative amplitude estimating and adjusting process makes the algorithm extremely computationally burdensome. (Wu et al., 2007) optimized the process of amplitude adjusting, which greatly reduced the computation complexity without harming performance; however, in presence of severe multipath, the algorithm still has to carry out repeated correlations and amplitude estimations. Therefore, some researchers considered detecting the direct path directly from the match–filtering output of the received signal. In the work by (Chung & Ha, 2003), the peak of match–filtering output was considered as the location of the direct path, but this is only applicable for LOS situations with transceiver antennas being omnidirectional. Threshold detection was conducted in (Low et al., 2005) and (Lee & Yoo, 2006), but presenting some difficulties for a practical implementation. Traditional tracking loops were implemented based on phase–locked loops (PLLs) and baseband code tracking delay–locked loops (DLLs). However, because of the extremely low duty cycle and significantly large bandwidth in IR–UWB, it is no longer valid to use the traditional sampling and interpolation method, see (Gardner, 1986). This challenge motivates us to draw on conventional PLL, delay locked loop, and code tracking loop theories to design appropriate equivalent timing locked loop for tracking of ultra–short IR–UWB impulses.

4.1.1 Synchronization in UWB Systems with Dirty Templates

The Timing with Dirty Templates (TDT) approach applied to PPM was presented in (Yang, 2006). The derivation is as follows: first, we reformulate the integrate–and–dump operation for PPM signals:

$$x(k;t) = \int_0^{T_s} r_{2k+1}(t;\tau)\check{r}_{2k}(t;\tau)dt \qquad \forall\tau \in [0, T_s), \tag{31}$$

where

$$\check{r}_k(t;\tau) = r_k(t+\Delta;\tau) - r_k(t-\Delta;\tau), \tag{32}$$

and $\Delta = b_l T_\Delta$ is the PPM modulation index in (1). To see how (31) enables TDT, let us first consider its noise–free part

$$\chi(k;\tau) = \int_0^{T_s} \rho_{2k+1}(t;\tau)\check{\rho}(t;\tau)dt, \tag{33}$$

where $\rho_k(t;\tau)$ and $\check{\rho}(t;\tau)$ represent the noise–free parts of $r_k(t;\tau)$ and $\check{r}(t;\tau)$, respectively. By definition, and since waveform $p_r(t)$ has a nonzero support upper bounded by the symbol duration T_s, we have

$$\rho_k(t;\tau) = \sqrt{E}\sum_{m=0}^{1} p_r(t + mT_s - \check{\tau}_0 - s_{k-k_{\tau_0}-m}\Delta), \tag{34}$$

$$\check{\rho}_k(t;\tau) = \rho_k(t+\Delta;\tau) - \rho_k(t-\Delta;\tau), \qquad \forall t,\tau \in [0, T_s) \tag{35}$$

where $\check{\tau}_0 = [\tau_0 - \tau]_{\text{ mod } T_s}$ and $k_{\tau_0} = \left\lfloor \frac{\tau_0 - \tau}{T_s} \right\rfloor \in \{0, -1\}$. Although k_{τ_0} can induce demodulation delay, it does not affect the τ_0 estimation. For notational brevity, we will henceforth omit k_{τ_0}. Using (34), Appendix I of (Yang, 2006) shows that, when the PPM modulation index satisfies $\Delta \ll T_f$, the noise–free part of $x(k;\tau)$ in (31) simplifies to

$$\chi(k;\tau) \approx (s_{2k-1} - s_{2k})E_A(\check{\tau}_0) + (s_{2k} - s_{2K+1})E_B(\check{\tau}_0) \tag{36}$$

where we have used the definitions

$$E_A(\check{\tau}_0) = E \int_{T_s - \check{\tau}_0}^{T_s} p_r^2(t)dt \tag{37}$$

$$E_B(\check{\tau}_0) = E \int_0^{T_s - \check{\tau}_0} p_r^2(t)dt \tag{38}$$

Non–data–aided TDT

Averaging with respect to the random symbols $\{s_k\}$, the mean–square of $\chi(k;\tau)$ is

$$E_s\left\{\chi^2(k;\tau)\right\} \approx \frac{1}{2}\left(E_R^2 - 3E_A(\check{\tau}_0)E_B(\check{\tau}_0)\right) \tag{39}$$

which contains the energy product $E_A(\check{\tau}_0)E_B(\check{\tau}_0))$ and is uniquely maximized at $\check{\tau}_0 = 0$, that is, at the correct timing $\tau = \tau_0$. In (39), $E_R = E_A(\check{\tau}_0) + E_B(\check{\tau}_0) = E\int_0^{T_s} p_r^2(t)dt$ is the constant energy of the unknown aggregate template at the receiver.
When we take into account the bandpass–filtered zero–mean additive Gaussian noise $\eta(t)$, the symbol–rate samples obtained by integrating and dumping the products of adjacent "dirty templates" become

$$x(k;\tau) = (s_{2k-1} - s_{2k})\, E_A(\check{\tau}_0) + (s_{2k} - s_{2k+1})\, E_B(\check{\tau}_0) + \zeta(k;\tau) \tag{40}$$

where the noise term $\xi(k;\tau)$ can be expressed as

$$\xi(k;\tau) = \xi_1(k;\tau) + \xi_2(k;\tau) + \xi_3(k;\tau) \tag{41}$$

$$\xi_1(k;\tau) = \int_0^{T_s} \check{\rho}_{2k}(t;\tau)\eta_{2k+1}(t;\tau)dt \tag{42}$$

$$\xi_2(k;\tau) = \int_0^{T_s} \rho_{2k+1}(t;\tau)\left(\eta_{2k}(t+\Delta;\tau) - \eta_{2k}(t-\Delta;\tau)\right)dt \tag{43}$$

$$\xi_3(k;\tau) = \int_0^{T_s} \eta_{2k+1}(t;\tau)\left(\eta_{2k}(t+\Delta;\tau) - \eta_{2k}(t-\Delta;\tau)\right)dt \tag{44}$$

with $\eta_k(t;\tau) = \eta(t + kT_s + \tau), \forall t \in [0, T_s)$. Appendix II of (Yang, 2006) shows that the noise term $\xi(k;\tau)$ can be well approximated as white Gaussian noise with zero mean and variance $\sigma_\xi^2 \approx 2E_R N_0 + BT_s N_0^2$. Then, the mean square of the samples of $x(k;\tau)$ can be found as

$$E_{s,\xi}\{x^2(k;\tau)\} = E_s\{\chi^2(k;\tau)\} + E_{xi}\{\xi^2(k;\tau)\} \tag{45}$$

$$\approx \frac{1}{2}\left(E_R^2 - 3E_A(\check{\tau}_0)E_B(\check{\tau}_0) + 2\sigma_{xi}^2\right) \tag{46}$$

which is uniquely maximized when $\check{\tau} = 0$, that is, when $\tau = \tau_0$. Then, the non–data–aided TDT is:

$$\tau_0 = \arg \max_{\tau \in [0, T_s)} E_{s,\xi}\{x^2(k;\tau)\} \tag{47}$$

Replacing the ensemble mean with its sample mean estimator, we have the following timing algorithm:

$$\hat{\tau}_0 = \arg \max_{\tau \in [0, T_s)} \frac{1}{K} \sum_{k=1}^{K} \left(\int_0^{T_s} r_{2k}(t;\tau) \check{r}_{2k-1}(t;\tau) dt \right)^2 \tag{48}$$

This estimator is a blind (non–data–aided) unbiased and consistent estimator in the mean–square sense, as can be seen from the mean and variance of the cost function:

$$m(K,\tau) = E\left\{ \frac{1}{K} \sum_{k=1}^{K} \left(\int_0^{T_s} r_{2k}(t;\tau) \check{r}_{2k-1}(t;\tau) dt \right)^2 \right\} = \tag{49}$$

$$= \frac{1}{2}\left(E_R^2 - 3E_A(\check{\tau}_0)E_B(\check{\tau}_0) + 2\sigma_\xi^2 \right) \tag{50}$$

and

$$\sigma^2(K,\tau) = \text{var}\left\{ \frac{1}{K} \sum_{k=1}^{K} \left(\int_0^{T_s} r_{2k}(t;\tau) \check{r}_{2k-1}(t;\tau) dt \right)^2 \right\} = \tag{51}$$

$$= \frac{2\sigma_\xi^2}{K}\left(E_R^2 - 3E_A E_B + \sigma_\xi^2 \right) + \frac{1}{4K}\left(E_R^2 - 3E_A E_B \right)^2 \tag{52}$$

It is worth emphasizing that the basic idea behind our TDT estimator is that $E_A(\check{\tau}_0)E_B(\check{\tau}_0)$ is minimized when $\check{\tau}_0 = 0$ and thus $\tau = \tau_0$. Although terms E_R and σ_ξ are unknown because $p_r(t)$ is unknown, they remain constant $\forall \tau$, and thus do not affect the peak–picking operation in finding $\hat{\tau}_0$.

Data–aided TDT

From (40), we observe that: 1) when $\check{\tau}_0 \neq 0$, then $x(k;\tau)$ only contributes noise if $s_{2k-1} = s_{2k} = s_{2k+1}$ and 2) when $\check{\tau}_0 = 0$, then $x(k;\tau)$ only contributes noise if $s_{2k} = s_{2k+1}$. To avoid these noise–only contributions that do not contain any timing information, the training sequence $\{s_k\}$ should be designed such that no successive symbols are the same. Hence, the training sequence for data–aided TDT is designed to comprise a repeated pattern $(1,0)$; that is

$$s_k = \{k+1\}_2 \tag{53}$$

It can be easily verified that this pattern simplifies (40) to

$$x(k;\tau) = E_B(\check{\tau}_0) - E_A(\check{\tau}_0) + \xi(k;\tau) \tag{54}$$

Then, its mean–square becomes

$$E_\xi\left\{ x^2(k;\tau) \right\} = E_R^2 - 4E_A(\check{\tau}_0)E_B(\check{\tau}_0) + \sigma_\xi^2 \tag{55}$$

Notice that the estimator (48) relies on three major steps: correlation, averaging, and squaring. The training sequence in (48) allows us to swap the order of these steps and alleviate the noise effects. Specifically, in the data–aided mode, it follows from (54) that

$$E_{\xi}^{2}\{x(k;\tau)\} = E_{R}^{2} - 4E_{A}(\breve{\tau}_0)E_{B}(\breve{\tau}_0) \tag{56}$$

In other words, by taking the *squared–mean* instead of *mean–square*, the noise variance term in (55) is eliminated. This observation leads us to the following result of a timing algorithm tailored for our carefully designed training sequence:

$$\hat{\tau}_0 = \arg \max_{\tau\in[0,T_s)} \left(\frac{1}{K}\sum_{k=1}^{K}\int_0^{T_s} r_{2k}(t;\tau)\breve{r}_{2k-1}(t;\tau)dt\right)^2 \tag{57}$$

The mean and variance of this cost function can be obtained as

$$m(K;\tau) = E_{R}^{2} - 4E_{A}(\breve{\tau}_0)E_{B}(\breve{\tau}_0) + \frac{\sigma_{\xi}^{2}}{K} \tag{58}$$

$$\sigma^2(K;\tau) = \frac{2\sigma_{\xi}^{2}}{K}\left(E_{R}^{2} - 4E_{A}(\breve{\tau}_0)E_{B}(\breve{\tau}_0) + \frac{\sigma_{\xi}^{2}}{K}\right) \tag{59}$$

4.1.2 Time of Arrival Estimation

One can view the estimation of TOA as a particular case of the timing acquisition problem. Synchronization is seen as the timing information required for data demodulation while TOA is linked to identify the first arriving path, but in essence both require similar techniques. In the case of IR–UWB the maximum likelihood (ML) solution is known (Lottici & Mengali, 2003) but has strong practical limitations due to the requirement of very high sampling rates and complexity. Although different ML approaches have appeared in the literature that manage to reduce complexity considerably López–Salcedo & Vázquez (2005); Yang & Giannakis (2005) there still exist practical limitations for their use in positioning applications. Efforts have been steered towards near optimum less complex solutions, most of them based on time domain approaches.

The majority of practical solutions for TOA estimation found in the literature can be broadly classified in energy-based and correlation-based approaches. A simplified representation of the receiver block diagram is depicted in Fig.9 for an scheme based on a correlator/matched–filter and energy detection, respectively. Energy based TOA estimators received considerable attention as a viable alternative to correlation-based methods (Cheong et al., 2005; Rabbachin et al., 2005) which require the estimation of the pulse shape. Indeed, energy detectors do not require expensive pulse-shape estimation algorithms and represent a good solution for low–power and low–complexity systems. The estimation scheme proposed and analyzed in (Rabbachin et al., 2005) is representative of a large class of energy based TOA estimation algorithms, where the incoming signal is squared and integrated over time intervals comparable with the pulse width. The integration time intervals defines in fact the time resolution of the algorithm and is also strongly related to its latency. These schemes also consider additional processing to improve signal quality. For instance, in (Rabbachin et al., 2005) the energies within non–overlapping adjacent windows are collected over several symbol periods to reduce the effects of background noise. The location of the direct path is computed as the index of the first interval where the energy overcomes a suitable threshold.

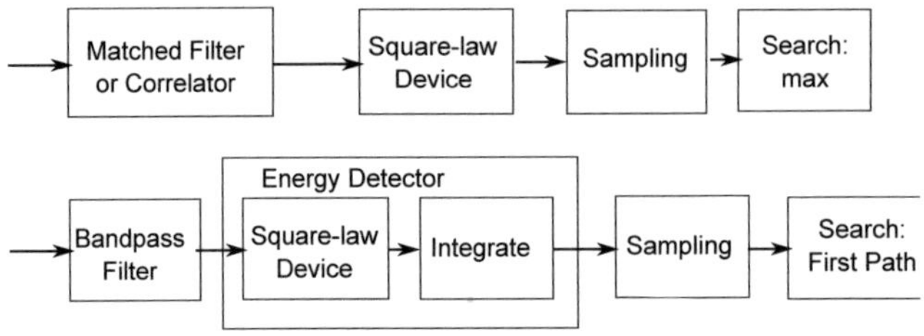

Fig. 9. Correlator (top) vs energy detector (bottom) approaches for TOA estimation.

Motivated by reducing sampling constraints and complexity, the estimation of the TOA in UWB is typically implemented in a two step approach. It consists on a first coarse estimation stage that provides symbol synchronization with coarse resolution, followed by a fine estimation stage that fully exploits the high time resolution capabilities of UWB signals and aims to achieve timing synchronization close to the theoretical bounds (of the order of pulse duration). The typical lower bound for timing synchronization accuracy is given by the Cramér–Rao bound, which has been found for multipath scenarios (Gezici et al., 2005; Navarro & Nájar, 2009; Shen & Win, 2008; Zhang et al., 2005). However this bound is not tight for low to medium signal–to–noise ratio (SNR) values. For low SNR ranges other bounds like the improved Ziv–Zakai bound has been found (Dardari et al., 2006).
An example of a two stage approach for a low cost non-coherent receiver based on an energy detection can be found in (Guvenc & Sahinoglu, 2005a;b). The basic principle is based on integration windows which time resolution changes between the two stages. The estimation accuracy depends on the window resolution which in turn will impact on the searching time. Acquisition time is strongly dependent on the search algorithm. Aiming at reducing the search time, (Ibrahim & Buehrer, 2006) proposes to exploit the statistical knowledge (derived from first phase "coarse estimation") and clustered nature of arriving paths to improve the performance on the fine acquisition stage reducing the acquisition time in dense multipath environment. Further work on the development of advanced search strategies to reduce the mean acquisition time involved in the synchronization process appears in (Gezici et al., 2003; Renzo et al., 2008; Suwansantisuk & Win, 2007; Suwansantisuk et al., 2005).
Therefore, important aspects to evaluate performance/complexity trade-offs are:

- Timing acquisition window duration. That is, the minimum data window required to perform acquisition.
- Computational complexity associated to the signal processing algorithm for timing estimation.
- Latency: involves signal acquisition window, search time, and processing time. The latter is typically negligible in comparison with the others.

For the UWB receiver implementation described in this chapter, a two stage approach has been found particularly suitable for timing synchronization. Next we outline the basis of the proposed TOA estimator. In order to define the ranging problem and develop the framework for a ranging system, let the received signal be described by (6), which we reproduce and expand here to represent channel multipath explicitly:

$$r^{sr}(t) = \sum_{m}\sum_{l} \sqrt{E}p\left(t - lT_s - c_l^{TH}T_c - b_lT_\Delta - \tau_m\right) + \eta(t) \tag{60}$$

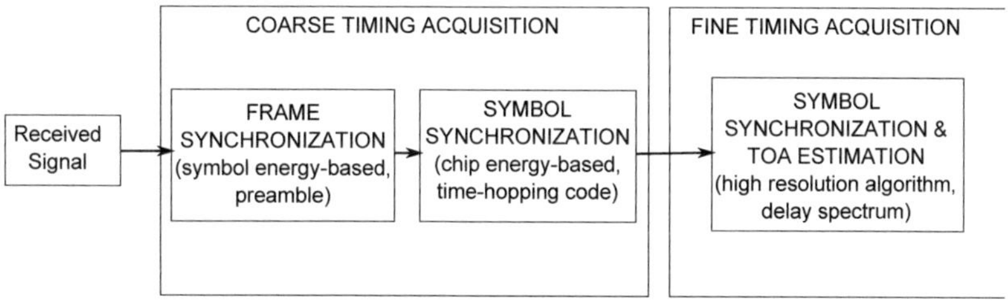

Fig. 10. Block diagram of the proposed two stage TOA estimator.

With no loss of generality the multipath delays are assumed $\tau_0 < \tau_1 < \ldots \tau_{max}$. Thus, the TOA estimation problem results in the estimation of τ_0. The TOA estimator operates without knowledge of the specific pulse waveform $p(t)$ or the channel. It requires though, the knowledge of the preamble in the data frame structure to provide the initial frame synchronization. Fig. 10 shows the block diagram of the synchronization scheme and TOA estimator. First, the coarse estimation stage performs the frame synchronization which identifies the position of the preamble within the data frame[2]. This requires a minimum acquisition window equivalent to the duration of two frames to ensure the preamble is captured as a whole. Once the preamble position is identified, the algorithm applies a low complexity coarse timing estimator based on a minimum distance criterion that exploits the signal temporal structure associated with the time-hopping code.

Let us define $\mathbf{c} = \left[c_0^{TH} \ldots c_{N_f-1}^{TH}\right]$ as the time–hopping sequence vector, with integer elements $c_i^{TH} \in \{0, 1, \ldots, N_c - 1\}$ and $\boldsymbol{\Gamma}$ as the circulant matrix that contains the relative delays in number of chip intervals between consecutive pulses within a symbol period for all possible sequence shifts. More specifically, defining $\rho_c(n)$, as the number of chips between two consecutive transmitted monocycles,

$$\rho_c(n) \triangleq \begin{cases} N_c - c_{n-1}^{TH} + c_n^{TH} & n = 0, 1, \ldots, N_f - 1 \\ N_c + c_{N_{f-1}}^{TH} - c_0^{TH} & n = N_f \end{cases}$$

the circulant matrix $\boldsymbol{\Gamma}$ is given by,

$$\boldsymbol{\Gamma} = \begin{bmatrix} \rho_c(1) & \rho_c(2) & \ldots & \rho_c(N_f - 1) & \rho_c(N_f) \\ \rho_c(2) & \rho_c(3) & \ldots & \rho_c(N_f) & \rho_c(1) \\ \vdots & & & \ddots & \vdots \\ \rho_c(N_f) & \rho_c(1) & \ldots & \rho_c(N_f - 2) & \rho_c(N_f - 1) \end{bmatrix}$$

where each row is a shifted version of the previous one. Hence, the relative distance between the N_f estimated positions of the monocycle pulses conforms the following vector,

$$\boldsymbol{\delta} = \begin{bmatrix} \alpha_1 - \alpha_0 & \ldots & \alpha_j - \alpha_{j-1} & \ldots & \alpha_{N_f-1} - \alpha_{N_f-2} \end{bmatrix}$$

The estimation of the frame number $v \in \{1, \ldots, N_f\}$ which the first detected pulse belongs to is obtained applying a minimum distance criterion. More specifically,

$$v = \arg \min_{j=1,\ldots,N_f} \left\| \boldsymbol{\delta} - \boldsymbol{\Gamma}_j \right\|^2 \tag{61}$$

[2] Here frame refers to the data packet structure.

where $\mathbf{\Gamma}_j \equiv \mathbf{\Gamma}(j, 1 : N_f - 1)$ denotes the $N_f - 1$ first j–th row elements of the matrix $\mathbf{\Gamma}$. The search process reduces to identify the closest shifted time-hopping sequence to the estimated $\boldsymbol{\delta}$, which involves a fixed number of vector norm operations that only depends on the time–hopping sequence length with typical values of the order of a few tens. From the estimated v and the time–hopping sequence known by the receiver, the TOA coarse estimation can be directly identified as,

$$\hat{\tau}_0^c = \left(\alpha_0 + N_c - c_v + (N_f - v)N_c\right) T_c \tag{62}$$

Once the beginning of the symbol is coarsely estimated, fine estimation of the time delay is performed on a symbol by symbol basis. This process is illustrated in Fig. 11. The filter–bank architecture conveniently fits into a frequency domain TOA estimation, since the filters output results in equivalent discrete Fourier transform (DFT) samples of the received signal (Mollfulleda et al., 2006; Vetterli & Herley, 1992) that can be directly processed by the fine TOA estimator. The motivation for using the frequency domain approach is twofold: on the one hand it is known that super–resolution methods, which operate in the frequency domain, have proven to provide high resolution for the estimation of the time of arrival; on the other hand the signal frequency samples are provided for free by the filter–bank receiver.
The fine time delay estimation and demodulation comprises the following steps:

1. Estimation of the correlation matrix from the filter bank output, which are equivalent to the frequency domain samples, corresponding to the k–th symbol, by averaging over the properly arranged frame signals in the symbol. That is, given the time-hopping sequence knowledge the monocycles are aligned for the estimation of the correlation matrix.
2. Calculation of the periodogram from the correlation matrix. In this case, the periodogram represents the signal energy distribution over time.
3. Search for the first peak in the periodogram that exceeds a predetermined threshold.

These steps provide a fine time of arrival estimation which may be used for ranging and localization, as explained in the following section.

4.2 Ranging and Localization

Ranging is a process or method to determine the distance from one location or position to another location or position. Locating is a process used to determine the location of one position relative to other defined positions, using estimated ranges as inputs. In this section we briefly outline techniques that can be applied to UWB systems.

4.2.1 Ranging

Ranging applications require the transceiver to be able to perform accurate TOA measurements but also a ranging protocol is needed in order to deliver the ranging measurement. Consider two nodes, where each transceiver is able to send, receive and process UWB packets. Ranging can be accomplished by measuring the round trip time of flight (TOF) between the two transceivers.Transceiver 1 (TXR1) sends an UWB packet to transceiver 2 (TXR2) that processes the packet and sends an answer back. Then TRX1 computes the distance between transceivers as

$$d = \frac{c(T_{\text{round}} - T_{\text{process}})}{2} \tag{63}$$

is the elapsed time between the instant TRX1 sent the first pulse and the instant it received an answer, T_{process} is the processing time in TRX2, and c is the speed of light. This is the basic

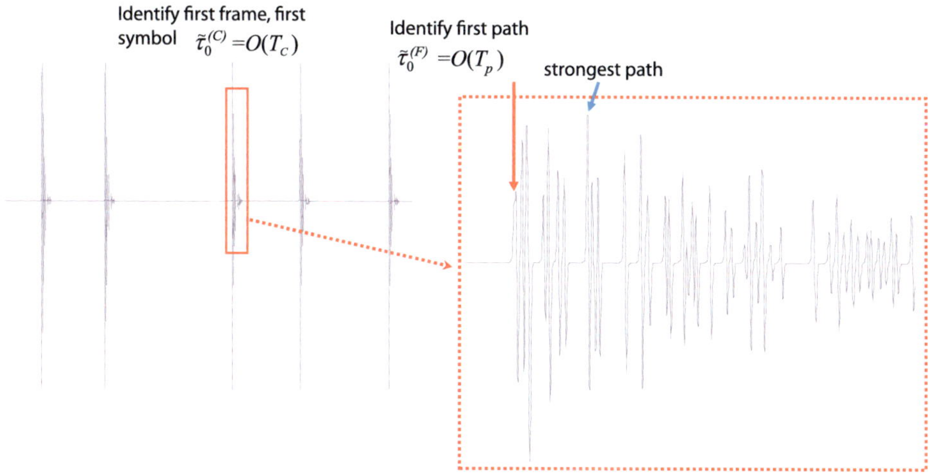

Fig. 11. Illustration of coarse and fine estimates in a typical multipath environment (CM3 IEEE 802.15.4a channel model). The coarse estimate is resolved with chip period accuracy, while the fine estimate is of the order of the pulse duration.

principle behind the 2–way ranging protocol adopted by the standard 802.15.4a. This standard also proposes a 4–way protocol, based on concatenating two phases of the 2–way protocol in order cancel the effect of clock drifts. Note that the distance estimation is strongly dependent on the precision of the clocks used in the two transceivers to measure the corresponding times. Besides the errors associated with multipath propagation, that degrades TOA estimation accuracy and introduces bias if LOS is blocked or strongly attenuated, clock drifts also constitute a technological problem. IR–UWB receivers require synchronization blocks with the accuracy of tens of picoseconds, which are very difficult (and expensive) to implement in analog circuits, see (Zhen et al., 2006). An evaluation of the impact an eventual clock offset on the ranging system, according to (Saito & Sanada, 2008), points towards the reduction of received pulse energy, thus affecting range. The mitigation of this effect can be done via the ranging protocol, see (Ahmed & Heidari-Bateni, 2006; Xing et al., 2007) and (Oh & Kim, 2008). Other examples of works related to UWB–based ranging include (Ko et al., 2008; Nam et al., 2008; Sahinoglu & Gezici, 2006; Zhen et al., 2006; 2007), and (Kim, 2009).

4.2.2 Localization Algorithms

The equations relating measurements to target's position depend on whether the time of transmission t_{Tx} is known or unknown. When the system consists of several beacons emitting from known locations at known instants (*i.e.* a synchronized beacon network), we speak of spherical positioning. The estimated travel time or receiving power is converted to range. Each range measurement defines a sphere centered at the beacon, on which the receiver must lie. The intersection of several spheres (corresponding to several beacons) defines the position of the receiver.

If t_{Tx} is not known, we can measure differences in travel times and convert them into differences in ranges to the beacons, in order to cancel the unknown. The locus of all points at the same distance of two given points in a 3D space is a hyperboloid, which is defined by a range difference. Again, the intersection of several hyperboloids indicates the receiver's position. A review on the localization equations can be found in (Sayed et al., 2005). Possible approaches are:

- **Localization from Time of Arrival or Received Signal Strength (RSS)**: A TOA (or a RSS) measurement specifies the range between a reference node and a target node, which defines a circle for the possible positions of the target node. Therefore, in the presence of three measurements, the position of the target node can be determined by the intersection of three circles via trilateration (see Fig. 12).
- **Localization from Time Difference of Arrival (TDOA)**: Each time difference of arrival (TDOA) parameter defines a hyperbola for the position of the target node. Hence, in the presence of three reference nodes, two TDOA measurements can be obtained with respect to one of the reference nodes. Then, the intersection of two hyperbolas, corresponding to two TDOA measurements, determines the position of the target node (see Fig. 12).
- **Localization from Angle of Arrival (AOA)**: Two AOA measurements between a target node and two reference nodes can be used to determine the position of the target node via triangulation (see Fig. 12).
- **Statistical approaches**: Estimation of the most likely position of the target node based on the reliability of each parameter estimate, which is determined by the characteristics of the noise corrupting measurements.

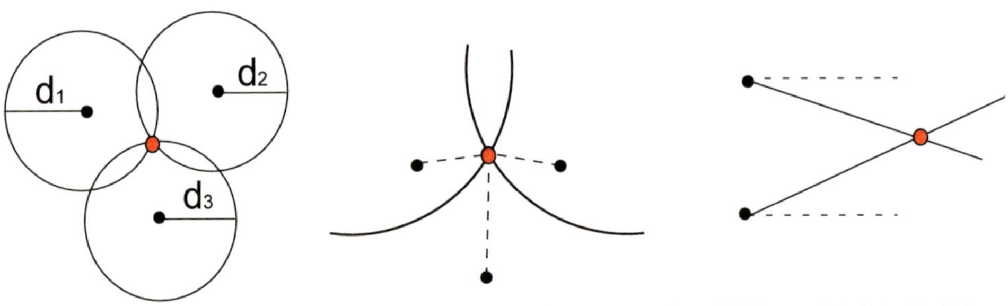

Fig. 12. Position estimation via TOA or RSS (left), TDOA (middle), and AOA (right).

References of recent works in UWB–based localization can be found in (Gezici et al., 2005), (Rahmatollahi et al., 2008), (Sahinoglu et al., 2008), and (Gezici & Poor, 2009).

5. Implementation Challenges

The current and future trend in UWB transceiver development is the use of radio frequency (RF) complementary metal–oxide–semiconductor (CMOS) (RF/CMOS) technology since it allows a drastic reduction in size and power consumption (Mahfouz et al., 2009). It also provides a seamless integration of the RF front-end and the digital back–end leading to System–on–chip (SOC) solutions. A good commercial example of that is the low power, 802.15.4a standard compliant UWB transceiver developed by Decawave (Decawave, 2009). However, commercial solutions using multiple chips in separate substrates like the tags in the Sapphire DART system (Zebra Enterprise Solutions, 2009) are also being successfully used. In this section,

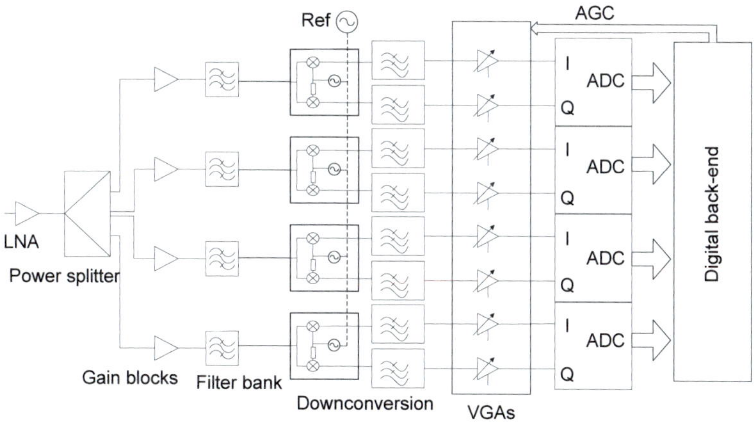

Fig. 13. Block diagram of filter bank receiver implementation.

the implementation of a filter bank receiver using low cost commercial-off-the-shelf (COTS) components, combined by microstrip structures, is addressed. While we focus on COTS technology, most of the basic requirements discussed apply also to CMOS technology.

5.1 RF Front-end

The major benefit of the filter bank architecture with respect to all-digital receivers is that it allows the use of low cost, low speed, and low power consumption ADC. It is achieved splitting the received signal in several branches and filtering it by a set of bandpass filters that cover the entire band of interest. The reduced bandwidth of each filter permits the use of low speed ADCs to perform an RF sampling in terms of sampling frequency. However, the input analog bandwidth requirement for the band from 3.1 GHz to 10.6 GHz, the designated Federal Communications Commission (FCC) band, is well over the features of commercial devices that typically reach only values under 2.5 GHz. Thus a direct down conversion stage can be implemented to shift the filtered pulses to baseband enabling a baseband sampling. Fig. 13 shows a the implementation details of a filter bank receiver with four branches. In the figure, the first stage is a LNA, followed by a power splitter. Then, on each branch an additional gain block and the corresponding bandpass filters follow. Each filtered signal is in turn downconverted to baseband and low-pass filtered. Finally, an automatic gain control (AGC) stage adjusts the signal gain for the ADC stage, which provides the digital signal.
The LNA limits the receiver noise figure (NF) improving its sensitivity. Its role is very important in UWB receivers since the transmitted power is very limited and the only ways to increase the link margin is averaging consecutive pulses and reducing noise to the minimum. Besides the basic requirements for the LNA of low NF and high gain, considering that filter bank receivers are intended to exploit most of the bandwidth allowed for UWB transmissions, a flat response of the gain and NF over frequency ranges of several GHz is also desired. This is the most challenging requirement since input and output matching must be reached over a wide bandwidth. To that end there are commercially available monolithic microwave integrated circuitss (MMICs) that present NF under 3 dB and gains greater than 15 dB over the entire FCC allowed bandwidth.
Typical operating ranges for low data rate UWB systems reach up to 100 m, which require a receiver dynamic range of 40 dB, since the path loss attenuation increases 20 dB each

Fig. 14. 4 stages 2-way Wilkinson divider (left), 3-stage, 4-way Wilkinson divider (middle), and single stage, 4-way Wilkinson divider (right).

decade. This dynamic range can be obtained through the AGC stage built with variable gain amplifiers (VGAs). The AGC should be implemented in baseband because a 40 dB VGA in a wide bandwidth is hard to achieve. Moreover, current COTS devices allow controlling baseband VGAs directly from the digital back-end, simplifying the AGC implementation, since the required detection and reference comparison can be done in the digital domain. Finally, the amplification chain is completed by a set of gain blocks that provide the necessary gain for longer ranges. They can be set in the RF part between the power splitter and the filter bank, or after the downconversion. In RF they act also as buffers attenuating the undesired reflections produced at the filter inputs due to their high reverse isolation. However, the overall gain must be well distributed between RF and baseband in order to minimize the possibility of instabilities caused by high gains over wide bandwidths.

The next component after the initial LNA is the power divider, which must be designed to operate in a very wide bandwidth. Resistive dividers have several advantages like naturally wide bandwidth and compact sizes since they are made of lumped resistors, though they do not suit UWB receivers well because of their inherent losses. Wilkinson power splitters have instead no losses, all ports matched, output ports isolated, and can be easy implemented in microstrip technology. Using multistage dividers the required wide bandwidths can be achieved. The main idea behind their design is that the width of each $\lambda/4$ transmission line section can be determined using optimum multi-section quarter wave transformer theory and the value of the isolation resistors can be determined following singly terminated filter design theory (Lee et al., 2001). N–way dividers can be easily implemented concatenating canonical 2–way splitters if N is a power of 2. Fig. 14 shows different Wilkinson power dividers.

The bank of filters can be implemented with microstrip technology using well known parallel-coupled line half-wavelength resonators. The strip thickness and the open-effect of microstrip lines has to be taken into account in their design to adjust center frequency and bandwidth (Hong & Lancaster, 2001). Moreover, modifications in the even mode impedance of the central sections can be performed to calibrate the delay introduced by each filter, which has to be equal to avoid pulse distortion and SNR degradation.

In each receiver branch the downconversion consists of a quadrature mixer, a voltage controlled oscillator (VCO) acting as a local oscillator (LO) and a low pass filter. This is the most demanding part of the receiver in terms of number of components and power consumption, since mixers have to be driven by rather high LO powers. The use of quadrature mixers allows the extraction of the in-phase and quadrature components of the filtered pulses, needed for coherent processing. LOs have to oscillate at the center frequencies of the bandpass filters to perform direct downconversion, and these frequencies have to be an integer multiple of the pulse repetition frequency used in the transmitter. As a consequence the VCOs must be locked to a precise reference. In fact, all the VCOs have to be locked to the same reference in order to

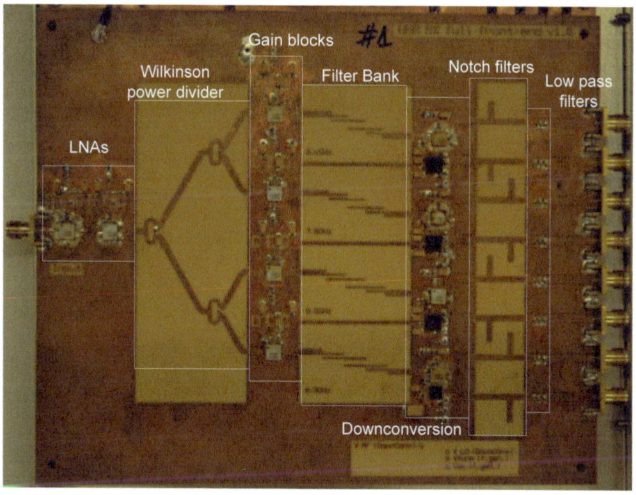

Fig. 15. Filter bank RF front-end.

minimize the jitter and phase noise contribution to the overall SNR. One possible way to lock all the LO to the same reference is to use a PLL or a direct direct digital synthesizer (DDS) to generate a lower frequency and then use a comb generator to produce harmonics at the desired frequencies. Comb generators can be implemented driving amplifiers in the saturation region. In the downconversion stage, the signal bandwidth has been reduced by a factor equal to the number of branches, and COTS components can be found for the mixers and VCOs, and low pass filters can be implemented using lumped elements. Note that these filters have to be rather smooth, otherwise their time response would be too long.
Fig. 15 shows a picture of a four branches filter bank RF front-end that operates in the European UWB band, from 6 GHz to 8.5 GHz. It does not include the AGC circuits and the circuits needed to lock the four VCOs to the same reference. Note that a set of notch filters implemented by microstrip single stubs are used to eliminate the leakage of the LO frequencies in the baseband outputs.

5.2 Digital Back-end

Programmable digital electronics devices are a very common solution for digital signal processing due to their reconfigurability and low production cost. UWB transceivers make no exception in using digital solutions for the processing part, solutions that can consist in the use of DSPs or PLDs. Moreover, control of the RF Front–end can be done digitally so the digital part will not only implement the processing algorithms but will also manage the whole system. DSPs are a good solution when processing power is needed, while PLDs are a suitable solution for interfacing and controlling applications. Implementing an UWB transceiver poses a number of challenges, and by far the most critical one is due to the high bandwidth nature of the signal. The filter bank architecture splits the bandwidth of the received signal into M branches, each one corresponding to a different frequency sub band of the original signal. It relaxes the constraints imposed by the high bandwidth and allows the signal processing tasks to be performed at lower speed. Following this approach, UWB processing modules can be designed to operate at less than 500 MHz which makes their implementation feasible using low cost PLDs. In contrast with this advantage, the processing module will need to be

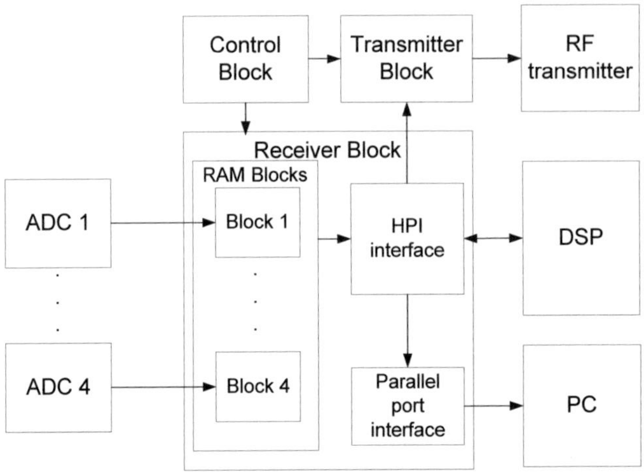

Fig. 16. Hybrid architecture for the digital back end of a filter bank receiver.

able to handle a bigger number of inputs. Generally, the data inputs of the digital back end coming from the ADCs consist of different lines with I and Q components. The number of simultaneous input data bits may expressed as

$$M \times N \times 2 \times 2 \tag{64}$$

where M is the number of branches of the filter bank and N is the number of bits of the I and Q differential components (2 samples for each component). On the other hand, another constraint of a communication system is the processing time that can be limited by the data interchange protocol between the systems. Implementation of the processing module using a DSP is not an optimum solution for the case of filter bank architecture because the most common DSP are not able to handle a big number of inputs and the frequency performance of the DSP is not fully utilized. In the case of the PLDs, the processing module will need to have a parallel architecture with multiple processing units corresponding to each branch of the system which will lead to a high resource utilization of the device.

A hybrid architecture, consisting of a PLD, used to manage the inputs and to control the RF part, and a DSP used to implement the processing algorithms, is an interesting compromise solution. It takes advantage of the processing speed and easy reprogramming features of the DSPs by implementing the processing algorithm using a serial architecture; and of the flexibility and parallelization of PLDs to handle high data rates. In Fig. 16 an example of a hybrid architecture using an field–programmable gate array (FPGA) and a DSP is illustrated (George et al., 2009).

This solution implements the digital back–end of an UWB transceiver using low cost COTS components, and can be used as a testbed for testing the performance of different processing algorithms for the case of filter bank architecture. The reprogrammable feature of the DSP section allows easy testing and prototyping of new signal processing algorithms, while the PLD allows the system to handle the very high data rates generated by the ADCs following the RF filter bank.

6. Conclusion

In this chapter we described an UWB receiver based on a frequency domain filter bank. We first defined the signal model and propagation environment for UWB, from which it was seen that an efficient UWB receiver needs to deal with the large time dispersion of the channel. After reviewing the alternatives, namely the SR Receiver, RAKE Receiver, and non-coherent receivers, and after providing the theoretical basis of time-frequency representations of signals, we presented the filter bank receiver. This receiver, consisting of several bandpass filters followed by Nyquist sampling, was shown to outperform other types of receivers in typical dispersive environments. The next section of this chapter was devoted to the description of algorithms for UWB synchronization, time of arrival estimation, and localization. For UWB synchronization, both data-aided and non-data-aided schemes were reviewed. Turning then our attention to time of arrival estimation, a frequency domain algorithm, suitable for the filter bank receiver, was presented. The algorithm consists of an initial coarse timing acquisition phase followed by a fine timing estimation. Time of arrival estimation is a fundamental parameter for different localization algorithms, as it is also shown. Finally, we addressed a hardware implementation of filter bank receivers for UWB. The main challenges of this architecture are the design of wideband components in the RF front end, and the high aggregate sampling rate at the digital back end. The hardware solutions presented effectively dealt with both problems.

7. References

Ahmed, K. I. & Heidari-Bateni, G. (2006). Improving two-way ranging precision with phase-offset measurements, *Proceedings of the IEEE Global Telecommunications Conference, GLOBECOM'06*, San Francisco, California.

Blazquez, R., Lee, F. S., Wentzloff, D. D., Newaskar, P., Powell, J. D. & Chandrakasan, A. P. (2003). Digital architecture for ultra-wideband radio receiver, *IEEE Vehicular Technology Conference*, pp. 1303–1307.

Cheong, P., Rabbachin, A., Montillet, J., Yu, K. & Oppermann, I. (2005). Synchronization, TOA and position estimation for low-complexity LDR-UWB devices, *IEEE International Conference on Ultra-Wideband*, Zurich, Switzerland, pp. 480–Ű484.

Chung, W. C. & Ha, D. S. (2003). An accurate ultra wideband (UWB) ranging for precision asset location, *Proceedings of the IEEE Conference on Ultra Wideband Systems and Technologies*, Reston, Virginia, pp. 389–393.

Dardari, D., Chong, C.-C. & Win, M. Z. (2006). Improved lower bounds on Time–of–Arrival estimation error in realistic UWB channels, *IEEE International Conference on Ultra-Wideband*, Waltham, MA, USA, pp. 531–537.

Decawave (2009). Scensor advance product information, www.decawave.com/downloads.html.

Gabor, D. (1946). Theory of communication, *Journal if the Institute of Electrical Engineers* **93**: 429–457.

Gardner, F (1986). A BPSK/QPSK timing-error detector for sampled receivers, *IEEE Transactions on Communications* **34**(5): 423–429.

Generic Harmonized European Standard for UWB Communications (ETSI EN 302 065) (2008). *Technical report*, European Telecommunications Standards Institute (ETSI).

George, G., Artiga, X., Moragrega, A., Ibars, C. & di Renzo, M. (2009). Flexible FPGA-DSP solution for an IR-UWB testbed, *Ultra-Wideband, 2009. ICUWB 2009. IEEE International Conference on*, pp. 413 –417.

Gezici, S., Fishler, E., Kobayashi, H., Poor, H. V. & Molisch, A. F. (2003). A rapid acquisition technique for impulse radio, *Proc. IEEE Pacific Rim Conf. on Communication, Computers and Signal Processing*, Vol. 2, Victoria, BC, Canada, pp. 627–630.

Gezici, S. & Poor, H. V. (2009). Position estimation via Ultra-Wide-Band signals, *Proceedings of the IEEE* **97**(2): 386–403.

Gezici, S., Tian, Z., Giannakis, G. B., Kobayashi, H., Molisch, A. F., Poor, H. V. & Sahinoglu, Z. (2005). Localization via ultra-wideband radios, *IEEE Signal Processing Magazine* **22**(4): 70–84.

Guvenc, I. & Sahinoglu, Z. (2005a). Low complexity TOA estimation for Impulse Radio UWB systems, *Technical report*, Mitsubishi Electric Research Laboratories, Dec.

Guvenc, I. & Sahinoglu, Z. (2005b). Threshold selection for UWB TOA estimation based on kurtosis analysis, *IEEE Commun. Lett.* **9**(12): 1025–1027.

Högbom, J. (1974). Aperture synthesis with a non-regular distribution of interferometer baselines, *Astronomy and Astrophysics Supplement Series* **15**: 417–426.

Hong, J.-S. & Lancaster, J. (2001). *Microstrip Filters for RF/Microwave Applications*, John Wiley & Sons Inc.

Ibrahim, J. & Buehrer, R. (2006). Two–stage acquisition for UWB in dense multipath, *IEEE J. Selected Areas Commun.* **24**(4): 801–807.

Kay, S. K. (1998). *Fundamentals of Statistical Signal Processing Volume II: Detection Theory*, Prentice Hall PTR.

Kim, H. (2009). A ranging scheme for asynchronous location positioning systems, *Proceedings of the 6th Workshop on Positioning, Navigation and Communication, WPNC'09*, Hannover, Germany, pp. 89–94.

Kim, J., Roh, D.-S. & Shin, Y. (2009). Pulse repetition based selective detection scheme for coherent IR-UWB systems, *Proceedings of the 6th IEEE Consumer Communications and Networking Conference,CCNC'09*, Las Vegas, Nevada.

Ko, S., Takayama, J. & Ohyama, S. (2008). A novel RF symmetric double sided two way range finder based on Vernier effect, *Proceedings of the International Conference on Control, Automation and Systems, ICCAS'08*, Seoul, Korea, pp. 1802–1807.

Lee, J.-Y. & Scholtz, R. A. (2002). Ranging in a dense multipath environment using an UWB radio link, *IEEE Journal on Selected Areas in Communications* **20**(9): 1677–1683.

Lee, J.-Y. & Yoo, S. (2006). Large error performance of UWB ranging in multipath and multiuser environments, *IEEE Transactions on Microwave Theory and Techniques* **54**(4): 1887–1895.

Lee, S., Kim, C., Choi, K., Park, J. & Ahn, D. (2001). A general design formula of multi-section power divider based on singly terminated filter design theory, *Microwave Symposium Digest, 2001 IEEE MTT-S International*, pp. 1297–1300.

López–Salcedo, J. & Vázquez, G. (2005). NDA maximum–likelihood timing acquisition of UWB signals, *IEEE Workshop on Signal Processing Advances in Wireless Communications (SPAWC'05)*, New York, USA.

Lottici, A. D. V. & Mengali, U. (2003). Channel estimation for ultra-wideband communications, *IEEE J. Selected Areas Commun.* **20**(9): 1638–1645.

Low, Z. N., Cheong, J. H., Law, C. L., Ng, W. T. & Lee, Y. J. (2005). Pulse detection algorithm for line-of-sight (LOS) UWB ranging applications, *IEEE Antennas and Wireless Propagation Letters* **4**: 63–67.

Mahfouz, M., Fathy, A., Kuhn, M. & Wang, Y. (2009). Recent trends and advances in uwb positioning, *Wireless Sensing, Local Positioning, and RFID, 2009. IMWS 2009. IEEE MTT-S International Microwave Workshop on*, pp. 1 –4.

Molisch, A., Balakrishnan, K., Chang, C.-C., Emami, S., Fort, A., Karedal, J., Kunisch, J., Schantz, H., Schuster, U. & Simiak, K. (2004). IEEE 802.15.4a channel model - final report, *IEEE 802.15 Task Group 4*.

Mollfulleda, A., Ibars, C., Leyva, J. A. & Berenguer, L. (2006). Practical demonstration of filter-bank receiver for ultra-wideband radios, *European Conference on Wireless Technology*, Manchester, UK.

Mollfulleda, A., Ibars, C. & Mateu, J. (2010). Ultra-wideband receiver based on microwave filterbbank, *IEEE International Conference on UltraWideband (ICUWB)*.

Nam, Y., Lee, H., Kim, J. & Park, K. (2008). Two-way ranging algorithms using estimated frequency offsets in WPAN and WBAN, *Proceedings of the 3rd International Conference on Convergence and Hybrid Information Technology, ICCIT '08*, Busan, Korea, pp. 842–847.

Navarro, M. & Nájar, M. (2007). TOA and DOA Estimation for Positioning and Tracking in IR-UWB, *Proceedings of the International Conference on Ultra Wideband*, Singapore.

Navarro, M. & Nájar, M. (2009). Frequency domain joint TOA and DOA estimation in IR-UWB, *IEEE Transactions on Wireless Communications* . Under review.

Oh, M.-K. . & Kim, J.-Y. (2008). Ranging implementation for IEEE 802.15.4a IR-UWB systems, *Proceedings of the IEEE Vehicular Technology Conference, VTC'08*, Singapore.

Oh, M.-K. ., Park, J.-H. & Kim, J.-Y. (2009). IR-UWB packet-based precise ranging system for u-Home networks, *IEEE Transactions on Consumer Electronics* **55**(1): 119–125.

Rabbachin, A., Montillet, J., Cheong, P., de Abreu, G. & Oppermann, I. (2005). Non-coherent energy collection approach for ToA estimation in UWB systems, *IST Mobile & Wireless Communications Summit*, Dresden, Germany.

Rahmatollahi, G., Pérez Guirao, M. D., Galler, S. & Kaiser, T. (2008). Position estimation in IR-UWB autonomous wireless sensor networks, *Proceedings of the 5th Workshop on Positioning, Navigation and Communication, WPNC'08*, Hannover, Germany.

Renzo, M. D., Annoni, L. A., Graziosi, F. & Santucci, F. (2008). A novel class of algorithms for timing acquisition for differential transmitted reference (DTR) ultra wide band (UWB) receivers architecture, performance analysis and system design, *EEE Trans. Wireless Commun.* **7**(6): 2368–2387.

Revision of part 15 of the Commission's Rules Regarding Ultra-Wideband Transmission Systems (2002). *Technical report*, Federal Communications Commission (FCC).

Sahinoglu, Z. & Gezici, S. (2006). Ranging in the IEEE 802.15.4a standard, *Proceedings of the IEEE Annual Wireless and Microwave Technology Conference, WAMICON'06*, Clearwater, Florida.

Sahinoglu, Z., Gezici, S. & Güvenc, I. (2008). *Ultra-wideband Positioning Systems: Theoretical Limits, Ranging Algorithms, and Protocols*, Cambridge University Press.

Saito, Y. & Sanada, Y. (2008). Effect of clock offset on an IR-UWB ranging system with comparators, *Proceedings of the IEEE International Conference on Ultra-Wideband, ICUWB'08*, Hannover, Germany.

Saleh, A. & Valenzuela, R. (1987). A statistical model for indoor multipath propagation, *IEEE Journal on Selected Areas on Communications* **5**(2): 128–137.

Sayed, A. H., Tarighat, A. & Khajehnouri, N. (2005). Network–based wireless location, *IEEE Signal Processing Magazine* **22**(4): 24–40.

Shen, Y. & Win, M. (2008). Effect of path-overlap on localization accuracy in dense multipath environments, *IEEE International Conference on Communication (ICC'08)*, Beijing, China.

Suwansantisuk, W. & Win, M. Z. (2007). Multipath aided rapid acquisition: Optimal search strategies, *IEEE Trans. Inform. Theory* **53**(1): 174–193.

Suwansantisuk, W., Win, M. Z. & Shepp, L. A. (2005). On the performance of wide-bandwidth signal acquisition in dense multipath channels, *IEEE Trans. Veh. Technol.* **54**(5): 1584–1594.

Vetterli, M. & Herley, C. (1992). Wavelets and filter banks: Theory and design, *IEEE Trans. Signal Processing* **40**(9): 2207–Ű2232.

Wu, S., Ma, Y., Zhang, Q. & Zhang, N. (2007). NLOS error mitigation for UWB ranging in dense multipath environments, *Proceedings of the Wireless Communications and Networking Conference, WCNC'07*, Hong Kong.

Wu, S., Zhang, Q., Fan, R. & Zhang, N. (2008). Match-filtering based TOA estimation for IR-UWB ranging systems, *Proceedings of the International Wireless Communications and Mobile Computing Conference, IWCMC'08*, Crete, Greece.

Xing, L. J., Zhiwei, L. & Shin, F. C. P. (2007). Symmetric double side two way ranging with unequal reply time, *Proceedings of the IEEE 66th Vehicular Technology Conference, VTC'07 Fall*, Baltimore, MD, pp. 1980–1983.

Yang, L. (2006). Timing PPM-UWB signals in ad hoc multiaccess, *IEEE Journal on Selected Areas in Communications* **24**(4): 794–800.

Yang, L. & Giannakis, G. B. (2005). Timing ultra–wideband signals with dirty templates, *IEEE Transactions on Communications* **53**(11): 1952–1963.

Zebra Enterprise Solutions (2009). Sapphire dart product data sheet, zes.zebra.com/pdf/product-datasheets/ds_app_dart.pdf.

Zhang, J., Kennedy, R. & Abhayapala, T. (2005). Crámer-rao lower bounds for the synchronization of UWB signals, *EURASIP Journal on Applied Signal Processing* **3**: 426–438.

Zhen, B., Li, H.-B. & Kohno, R. (2006). UWB ranging and crystal offset, *Proceedings of the IEEE 63rd Vehicular Technology Conference, VTC'06-Spring*, Melbourne, Australia, pp. 1445–1449.

Zhen, B., Li, H.-B. & Kohno, R. (2007). Clock management in ultra-wideband ranging, *Proceedings of the 16th IST Mobile and Wireless Communications Summit*, Budapest, Hungary.

Zhu, X., Yong-qiang, H., Fu-wei, J. & Ke-chu, Y. (2008). Performance analysis of RC-SRake receiver in Ultra-Wideband communication under IEEE 802.15.4a channel, *Proceedings of the 11th IEEE International Conference on Communication Technology, ICCT'08*, Hangzhou, China, pp. 268–271.

Passive devices for UWB systems

Fermín Mira[1], Antonio Mollfulleda[3], Pavel Miškovský[1],
Jordi Mateu[1,2] and José M. González-Arbesú[2]
[1]*Centre Tecnològic de Telecomunicacions de Catalunya*
[2]*Universitat Politècnica de Catalunya*
[3]*Gigle Networks*
Spain

1. Introduction

The release from the U.S. Federal Communication Commission (FCC) of the unlicensed use of the Ultra-Wide-Band (UWB) frequency range of 3.1-10.6 GHz, fed the interest for developing communication systems to be used on applications requiring high data rate transmission. The complete success and spreading of these novel applications requires inexpensive and reliable UWB communication systems and devices. The set of passive components included in these systems is definitely a key point on their full development. To this end, many efforts have been done by both the academic and industrial sectors, focusing their research activities on the development of UWB passive components. Although the design of passive components for microwave narrow band applications follows well-established procedures or even mathematical description, the development and design of UWB passive components is a challenge, and most of the procedures used on the synthesis of narrow band component, circuit models and design procedures are not applicable for such wideband frequency ranges. In this book chapter we present the design, fabrication and measurement of most of the key passive components playing a role on an UWB communication system. To illustrate so, the following figures, Fig.1a and Fig.1b, outline the transmitter and receiver architecture of the constructed demonstrator at CTTC (Mollfulleda et al., 2006). Although we will not go into details on the design of the whole transmitter and receiver it would allow us to identify the passive components and their role and requirements from a system perspective.
In both, transmitter and receiver architectures we identify as a first and second component of the system chain an antenna and an UWB frontend preselected filter (Mira et al., 2009). The following passive component is a power combiner/splitter for the transmitter/receiver, respectively. The transmitter side also includes a pulse shaping network in the pulse generator box (see Fig.1a) and a pulse inverter necessary in certain modulation schemes. Finally as can be seen in the receiver outlined in Fig. 1b a filter bank will be used on the signal detection.

2. Antennas for Optimum UWB System Performance

According to the definition of the FCC (FCC, 2002) an "UWB antenna" is an antenna that potentially uses all its bandwidth all the time, and its properties are stable across the operational band: impedance match, radiation pattern, gain, polarization, etc. Several types of UWB antennas have thoroughly been described in literature. Generally they have smooth shapes such

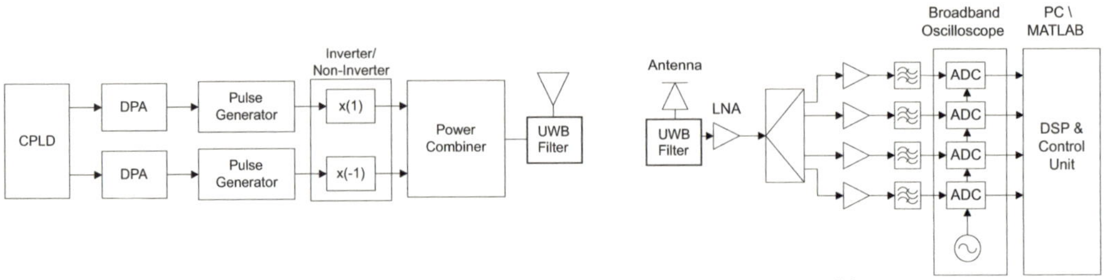

a) b)

Fig. 1. Outline of the transmitter a) and the receiver b).

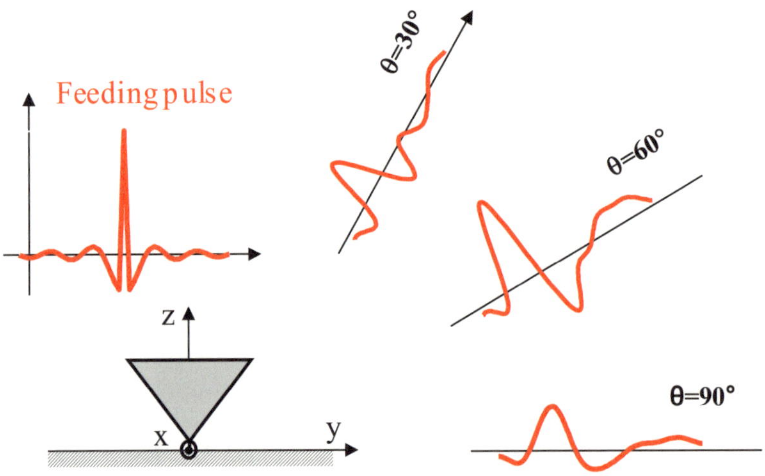

Fig. 2. Spatially dependent distortion of the UWB pulse radiated by triangular UWB monopole.

as the Lindeblad's coaxial horn (Lindeblad, 1941), Kraus "volcano smoke" antenna (Paulsen et al., 2003) or Barnes UWB slot antenna (Barnes, 2000). Usually their performance is assessed in terms of input impedance Z_{in}, gain G, radiation efficiency, etc, independently. In wide frequency ranges this assessment can be a very laborious process because antenna parameters tend to vary significantly across the operational bandwidth, and for some of the aforementioned parameters even with the spatial direction. Due to the wideband nature of UWB signals, the radiated signal distortion, as illustrated on Fig. 2, is an inherent UWB antenna issue that can deteriorate the overall system performance.

For UWB pulse radiation (Montoya & Smith, 1996), transmitting antennas should ideally have low reflected voltage at the feeding port, they should radiate a waveform similar to the feeding pulse (no distortion) or its derivative (known distortion), but they also should have high radiation efficiency. Various antenna impedance loading schemes that potentially could attain these characteristics have been proposed by different authors. Among others, Wu (Wu & King, 1965) intended to extend the bandwidth of the antenna, Kanda (Kanda, 1978) preserved the radiated pulse shape, Rao (Rao et al., 1969) improved the far-field pattern over a range of frequencies, making them potentially interesting in the context of antenna design for UWB systems. Fig. 3 shows how the losses distributed along the antenna can be used to im-

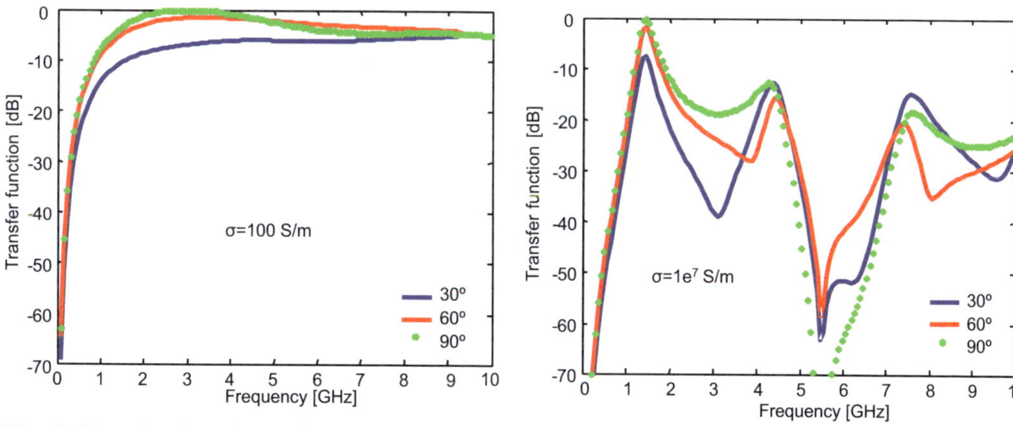

Fig. 3. Transfer functions of a tx-rx system using linear monopoles of different conductivities (left $\sigma = 100$ S/m, right $\sigma = 1e7$ S/m). The receiver antenna is placed in different relative positions $\theta = 30°, 60°, 90°$ with respect to the transmitter. Dotted line represents the spectrum of the transmitter antenna feeding pulse.

prove the antenna performance in terms of radiated pulse distortion. The transfer functions between the transmitter and the receiver load using linear monopoles are shown for two different monopole conductivities. High antenna losses ($\sigma = 100$ S/m) induce less variation in transfer function which is the origin of the low transmitted pulse distortion.
Inspired by the work of Wu, Rao and Kanda, the design of a progressively loaded monopole for an UWB system will be illustrated in the following paragraphs. Specifically resistively loaded monopoles, and to overcome the reduction of radiation efficiency capacitively loaded monopole antennas will be considered. Both types of monopole loadings have been previously reported in the literature (Kanda, 1978), (Rao et al., 1969) and an analytical equation for the loading profiles has been derived in order to achieve a traveling wave (Wu & King, 1965). However in the following paragraphs the design procedure for both types of monopoles uses an evolutionary technique in order to optimize the performance of the monopoles in the sense of radiation efficiency and Spatially Averaged Fidelity (*SAF*), (Miskovsky et al., 2006), (Miskovsky, 2010). Almost identical figure of merit called Pattern Stability Factor (PSF) was proposed by Dissanayake (Dissanayake & Esselle, 2006).

2.1 Resistively Loaded Monopole

Several optimization techniques can be used to achieve an optimum performance of a resistively loaded monopole in terms of a given set of constraints. Evolutionary techniques, such as genetic algorithms (Johnson & Rahmat-Samii, 1997), particle swarm optimization (Robinson & Rahmat-Samii, 2004) or ant colony optimization (Rajo-Iglesias & Quevedo-Teruel, 2007) are usually used when the degrees of freedom of the problem and the constraints are not connected through equations that allow a gradient optimization. In this particular optimization problem of a resistively loaded monopole a Particle Swarm Optimization technique (PSO) has been used. A wire monopole of height h is considered (Fig. 4a), divided into N segments and having a purely resistive impedance R_i in each segment (being i the segment number). The optimization technique should find the specific set of N resistors to be used along the monopole to achieve both a maximum averaged fidelity SAF and a maximum mean radiation efficiency e_{rad}. Both constraints are used to define a fitness function F to be maximized by the algorithm, that is:

$$F = \omega_1 \cdot SAF + \omega_2 \cdot e_{rad} \tag{1}$$

In equation (1), ω_1 and ω_2 are weighting coefficients used to stress one of the physical parameters representing the performance of the antenna. In the following explanations SAF and e_{rad} are scaled between 0 and 1 and the coefficients ω_1 and ω_2 are considered equal to 0.5. In order to reduce the time required for the optimization technique to find a solution in the solution space, three considerations have been done:

- To use a commercial set of resistors. This means that a resistor R_i can only take values from a previously selected resistor series (e.g., E12) within the range from 0 Ω to 1 MΩ. A series with a total of 86 resistor values was used.
- To reduce the number of problem unknowns (e.g. problem dimension) instead of solving for a random combination of N resistors. An increasing loading profile is assumed being in accordance with the literature. However some degrees of freedom are added to allow exploring decreasing and decreasing plus increasing profiles. Specifically, the resistive loading profile is considered to follow a parabolic function, quite similar to the one derived by Wu (Wu & King, 1965)

$$R(z_i) = R_0(z_i - z_0)^2 \tag{2}$$

  the monopole being placed along the z-axis and fed at $z = 0$. Then, R_0 represents the aperture of the parabola, z_0 is the position of the parabola minimum with respect to the origin, and z_i the coordinate center of segment i.
- The tolerance of the resistor values for the chosen resistor series (10%) has not been accounted for.

Such proceeding reduces the number of optimization variables from N (number of resistors) to 2 (number of variables in equation 2). The goal of the optimization is to find the loading profile specified by the values of R_0 and z_0 that maximizes the desired antenna performance objective F. The optimization of the loaded monopole was realized in Matlab® using a method of moments based code named Numerical Electromagnetics Code (NEC) as electromagnetic simulator (Burke & Poggio, 1981). The set of solutions obtained during the optimization procedure (or Pareto front) of 3 monopoles with lengths 11.5 mm, 30 mm and 40 mm and having a radius of 0.8mm is shown in Fig. 4b. The Pareto front shows what performance can be expected from such resistively loaded monopole in terms of radiation efficiency and averaged fidelity SAF. The optimization needed 70 iterations using a swarm of 40 particles. The monopole feeding pulse is considered to have an ideal planar spectrum within the frequency range from 2.5 GHz to 10.5 GHz. As a reference, the unloaded monopoles performance having the same wire radius and lengths should be assessed in terms of fidelity SAF and e_{rad}. In Fig. 4b those can be found on the Pareto fronts as points with the highest possible radiation efficiency. From Pareto fronts shown on Figure 2.4 it can be concluded that by resistively loading a linear monopole there is always a trade-off between the mean radiation efficiency and the spatially averaged fidelity which means that maximum SAF of 1 and maximum mean efficiency of 1 can never be reached simultaneously. The solution having the best fitness F for each monopole is also shown in Fig. 4b.

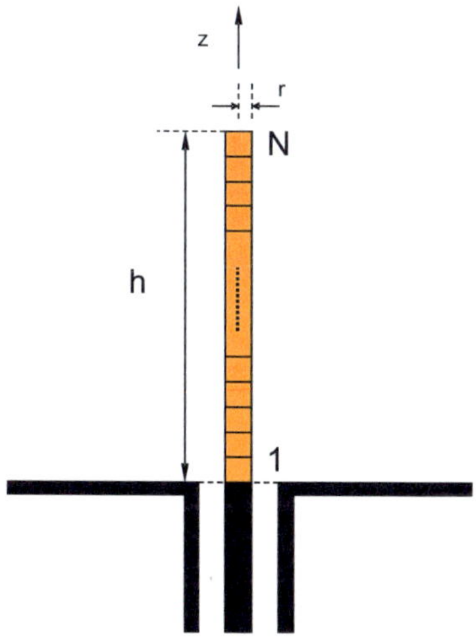

(a) Scheme of the monopole.

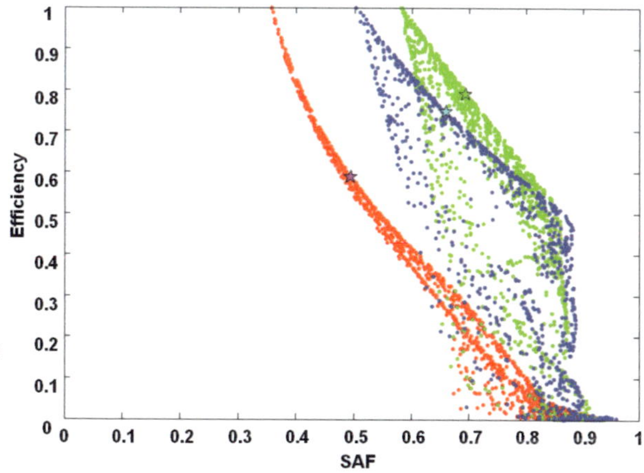

(b) Pareto fronts for three monopole lengths red $h = 11.5$ mm, green $h = 30$ mm, and blue $h = 40$ mm (Miskovsky et al., 2007). Stars represent the solutions with the best fitness for each monopole.

Fig. 4. Monopole with loaded segments.

The overall 3D representation of the radiated pulses at 5.31 m from the 30 mm long monopole (oriented along z-axis) between $\theta = 0°$ and $\theta = 90°$ are shown in Fig. 5. This representation confirms the stable time position of the main peak. The radiated pulses are very similar to the template (ideal pulse feeding the monopole with a planar spectrum in the operating frequency band) for the range $\theta = 60°$ to $\theta = 90°$. However, for the range from $\theta = 10°$ and $\theta = 30°$ the pulse distortion is important compared to the template, but still the major peak position agrees pretty well with the position of the template maximum. The average fidelity SAF is 69%, which means that the transfer function of the obtained antenna is highly wideband. Nevertheless the mean radiation efficiency is 79% which is considerably high value.
The influence of E12 series resistors tolerances was assessed by simulation. The 10% tolerance of resistor value induces a mean radiation efficiency and SAF variation lower than ± 0.5. This is considered acceptable for the monopole fabrication. Unfortunately, the parasitics effects of the discrete component package could influence seriously the monopole performance. Thus for the monopole fabrication some method without the need of considering the parasitics should be used.

2.2 Capacitively Loaded Monopole

To overcome the reduced radiation efficiency of a resistively loaded monopole (due to ohmic losses in the loading resistors) capacitive loading can be used. A capacitively loaded antenna has also been optimized using PSO with the fitness function F defined in terms of SAF and in this case in terms of reflected energy at the feeding point of the antenna. The radiation efficiency was not considered in the optimization because capacitively loaded monopoles are practically 100% radiation efficient. A wire monopole oriented along z-axis with the same physical dimensions as the resistively loaded monopole ($h = 30$ mm, $r = 0,8$ mm) was used as a basic structure. The capacitive loading profile, optimized on such wire monopole follows

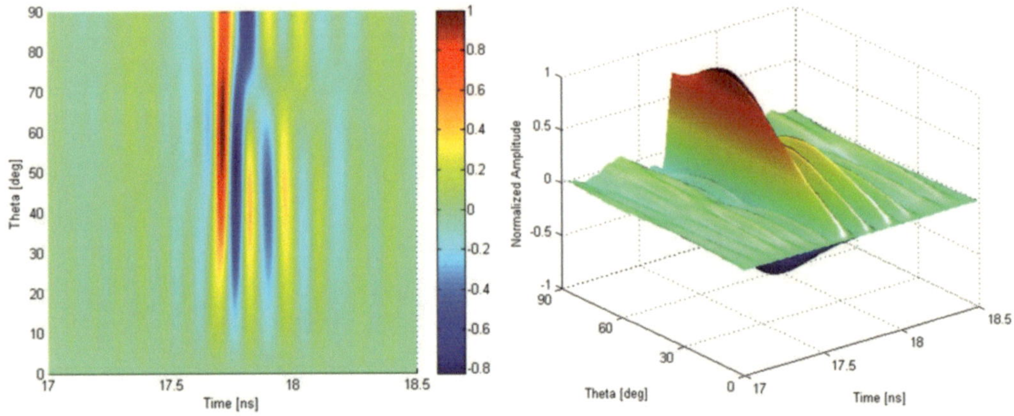

Fig. 5. 3D representation of the pulses radiated by the 30 mm long resistively loaded monopole.

an exponential distribution (3), as defined by Rao (Rao et al., 1969), with capacity decreasing towards the end of the monopole. The capacities are computed for the centers of the monopole segments z_i according to equation (3).

$$C(z_i) = C_0(e^{\alpha z_i} - 1)^{-1} \tag{3}$$

The solution space of the optimization was defined by the parameters that are to be optimized: C_0 and α. The capacity for each segment is chosen from the closest value from *muRata* capacitor kit series, GRM18-KIT-B with values between 0.5 pF and 10 μF . The pulses radiated by the optimized ($C_0 = 1.5e^{-12}$ and $\alpha = 10$) capacitively loaded monopole at 5.31 m and at all angular directions between $\theta = 0°$ and $\theta = 90°$ are shown in Fig. 6. The figure shows that the pulse peak position is stable with direction, and that the pulse shape is quite similar to the pulse fed to the antenna. Fidelity SAF for the best solution is 57% and the reflected energy is 30%. In comparison with the optimized resistively loaded monopole, the amount of reflected energy is practically the same (31% for optimum resistively loaded monopole from previous section). When capacitive loading is used the radiation efficiency is close to 100% within the entire frequency band. The difference in fidelity SAF values is not significant here, due to the different definition of fitness function combining the fidelity SAF with reflected energy instead with radiation efficiency.

2.3 Summary

The radiated signal distortion dependence with spatial direction is an inherent UWB antenna issue, usually assessed qualitatively. Recently proposed compact frequency and direction-independent antenna distortion descriptors such as spatially averaged fidelity can be used to assess the UWB antenna performance in terms of radiated signal distortion. As shown by several authors, the impedance loading distributed along the antenna can be used to improve the antenna distortion performance. Impedance loading of linear monopoles can be optimized by means of antenna descriptors yielding optimum UWB system performance in terms of radiated pulse distortion, radiation efficiency, etc. The evolutionary optimization techniques can

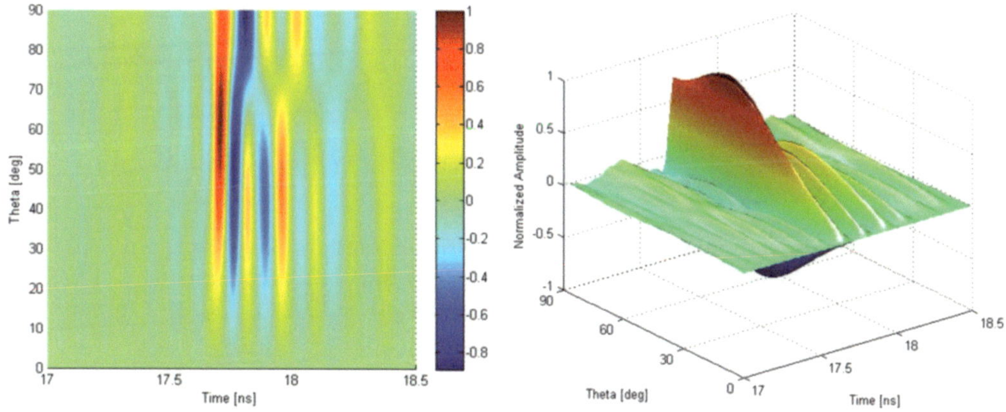

Fig. 6. 3D representation of the pulses radiated by the 30 mm long capacitively loaded monopole.

significantly reduce such optimization problem complexity and consequently the computational load. The performances of the optimum capacitively loaded monopole and optimum resistively loaded monopole of the same length were compared in terms of spatially averaged fidelity, mean radiation efficiency e_{rad} and input port accepted energy. The resistively loaded monopole attains better performance than the monopole with capacitive loading in terms of spatially averaged fidelity, however its radiation efficiency is obviously lower that the efficiency of the capacitive monopole. The performances of both monopoles in terms of the input accepted energy are almost the same. In both cases, the Pareto fronts show what performance can be expected from such loaded monopoles in terms of spatially averaged fidelity, radiation efficiency and amount of energy reflected at the input port.

3. UWB SIW Filter

There is an increasing demand on communication systems which require stringent selective filters with low insertion loss, easy manufacturing and integration into RF circuits. Filters implemented in standard waveguide technology exhibit good performance, but they are bulky, heavy and not suitable for low-cost mass production techniques. On the other hand, microstrip filters present low Q-factors and high radiation losses, especially at millimeter-wave frequencies. Substrate integrated waveguide (SIW) is a recently emerged technology that has attracted much interest because of its low-profile, ease of fabrication with conventional planar circuit processes, such as PCB and LTCC, and achievable high Q-factors. The SIW structure consists of a dielectric substrate comprised between a pair of metal plates which are connected through via holes. This configuration confines the field inside the structure, and therefore does not exhibit undesired couplings between resonators, thus allowing a fine control of the couplings (Tang et al., 2007).

Filters covering a whole microwave band are frequently required in modern transceivers, such as those used in ultra-wideband (UWB) applications. However, few examples of such filters can be found in SIW technology (Zhang et al., 2005)-(Chen et al., 2007), with typical bandwidths between 10 – 20% and responses without any transmission zero. In (Chuang et al., 2007), a dual-mode SIW filter with a bandwidth of 8.5% and transmission zeros is proposed.

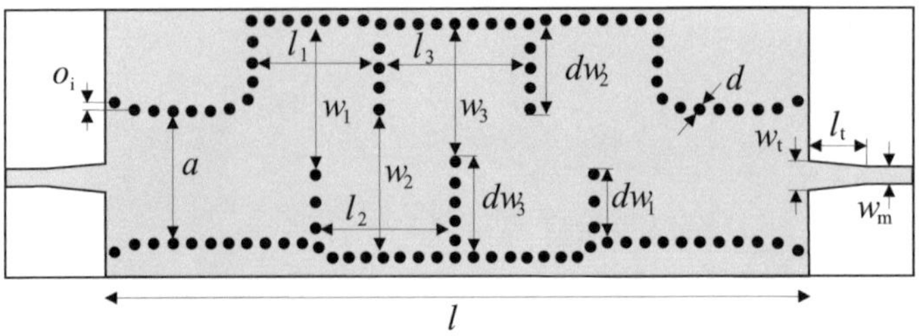

Fig. 7. Design of a seven-pole SIW filter in zigzag meandered topology, where $o_i = 0.9$ mm, $a = 12.80$ mm, $l = 76.62$ mm, $l_1 = 12.74$ mm, $l_2 = 14.11$ mm, $l_3 = 15.40$ mm, $w_1 = 17.23$ mm, $w_2 = 14.43$ mm, $w_3 = 15.64$ mm, $dw_1 = 7.13$ mm, $dw_2 = 9.35$ mm, $dw_3 = 7.76$ mm, $w_t = 2.8$ mm, $l_t = 7.0$ mm, $w_m = 1.85$ mm and $d = 1.05$ mm.

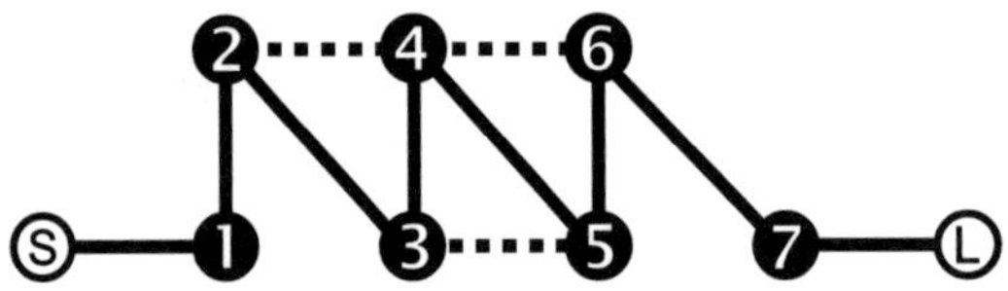

Fig. 8. Coupling topology of the proposed SIW filter.

Bandwidths around 60% are obtained in (Hao et al., 2005) by combining SIW technology with periodic structures.

This section proposes a zigzag filter topology, which includes additional controllable cross-couplings in order to perform sharper responses and a more flexible tuning of the transmission zeros. Therefore, this novel topology has been successfully used for the design of a 28% filter bandwidth for European UWB applications (EU, 2007).

3.1 Design of a SIW Filter in Zigzag Topology

The UWB SIW filter is designed following a zigzag meandered topology (see Fig. 7), originally proposed in (Guglielmi et al., 1995) for waveguide technology. This configuration provides a more compact filter compared to the classical inline topology, and also allows the location of transmission zeros in the upper band due to existing cross couplings between non-adjacent resonators (see the scheme in Fig. 8). These transmission zeros are especially relevant for ultra-wideband applications, since they allow to increase the near upper side out-of-band rejection level of the filter responses. In order to design this novel SIW filter topology, the CAD tool described in (Mira et al., 2007) has been used, since it provides very accurate full-wave responses for SIW filters in CPU times of the order of few seconds.

The SIW filter has been designed using a Rogers RO4003C substrate with thickness 0.813 mm, dielectric constant $\epsilon_r = 3.60$ (the manufacturer recommends $\epsilon_r = 3.55 \pm 0.05$ for circuit design purposes), and loss tangent $\tan\delta = 0.0027$ at 10 GHz. This low-cost substrate, widely employed for manufacturing printed circuits, allows an easy metallization of the vias holes without initial special treatment.

The symmetric configuration shown in Fig. 7 provides a seven-pole electrical response, due to the inner five SIW resonant cavities coupled following a zigzag shape, and to the input and output SIW sections that are connected to the feeding lines through waveguide to microstrip transitions (Deslandes & Wu, 2001). The width a of the input and output sections defines the sharpness at the band-edge in the lower side band, due to the transmission zero introduced by

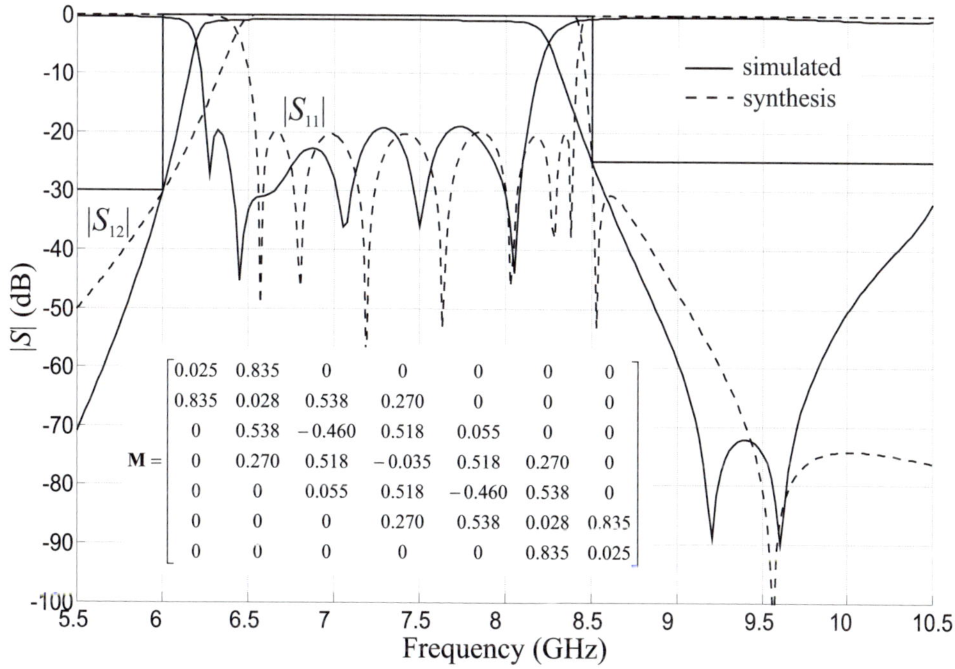

Fig. 9. S-parameters provided by the synthesized coupling matrix related to the scheme in Fig. 8 ($R_S = R_L = 0.9898$), and simulated data for the SIW filter of Fig. 7.

the finite cut-off frequency of the waveguide. Additionally, the parameter o_i is used to adjust the level of the return losses. Finally, each cavity is bounded by decoupling walls dw_i, whose lengths l_i and widths w_i are found to set the resonant frequencies of the cavities and recover the required couplings between them.

The SIW filter has been designed to comply with the European UWB mask, that imposes $|S_{12}| = -30$ dB at 6 GHz and $|S_{12}| = -25$ dB at 8.5 GHz (see Fig. 9). Our aim is to comply with the proposed mask for frequencies up to 10.5 GHz. In Fig. 9, we include the goal synthesized response for the scheme of Fig. 8, considering a bandwidth of 1.84 GHz and two transmission zeros in the upper band for satisfying the restrictive UWB requirements (synthesis). At the same time, we found the dimensions for the initial SIW filter structure of Fig. 7 that best fits the UWB mask, whose response is also included in Fig. 9. As it can be observed, the simulated response of the SIW filter has a return loss level greater than 19 dB (achievable because of the displacement o_i introduced in the first via holes), a very selective upper side of the out-of-band response due to the two synthesized transmission zeros, and a more pronounced fall in the lower side band attributed to the higher cut-off frequency of the input and output sections.

3.2 Introduction of Flexible Cross-couplings

Although the two transmission zeros placed at the upper band edge of the previous filter give rise to an improved selectivity response, its zigzag meandered topology only allows for achieving moderate cross-couplings between non adjacent cavities, and therefore a limited control on the location of the transmission zeros. As it can be observed in the synthesized response of Fig. 9, the filter selectivity can be improved when the first transmission zero is placed closer to the pass-band. For such purpose, it is required to have a higher degree of

control of the cross-couplings, which can be obtained through the opening of the decoupling walls (dw_i with $i = 1, 2, 3$ in Fig. 7) by removing one of the via holes as shown in Fig. 10.
Fig. 11 outlines the effect of opening the decoupling walls dw_1, dw_2, and dw_3, respectively. In doing so, the spacing between transmission zeros and their position can be controlled, pushing the first spurious response toward higher frequencies. In Fig. 11, we see that by opening the first decoupling wall dw_1 the first transmission zeros are brought closer to the band edge, which improves the selectivity and reduces the transmission zero spacings. A similar effect over the selectivity is observed by opening the second decoupling wall dw_2, now increasing the space between the two transmission zeros. Finally, by opening the third decoupling wall, the transmission zero spacing increases and the out of band response improves, although the pass-band is slightly reduced.

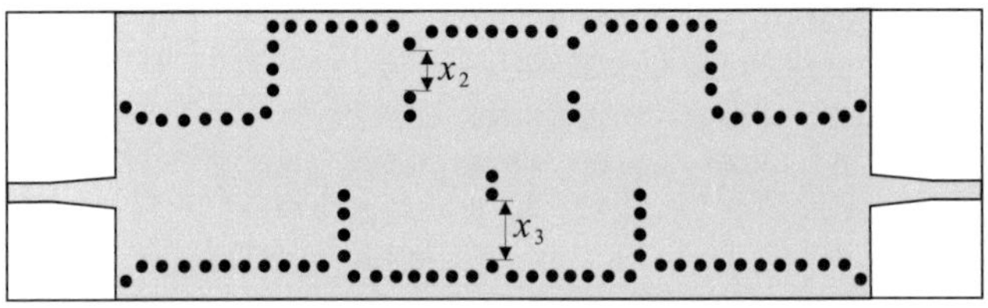

Fig. 10. Design of a seven-pole zigzag SIW filter topology with more flexible cross couplings, where $o_i = 1.3$ mm, $a = 12.79$ mm, $l = 76.62$ mm, $l_1 = 12.33$ mm, $l_2 = 13.35$ mm, $l_3 = 14.90$ mm, $w_1 = 14.89$ mm, $w_2 = 14.09$ mm, $w_3 = 12.61$ mm, $dw_1 = 6.62$ mm, $dw_2 = 8.43$ mm, $dw_3 = 9.41$ mm, $x_2 = 4.02$ mm and $x_3 = 5.76$ mm, $w_t = 2.8$ mm, $l_t = 7.0$ mm, $w_m = 1.85$ mm and $d = 1.05$ mm.

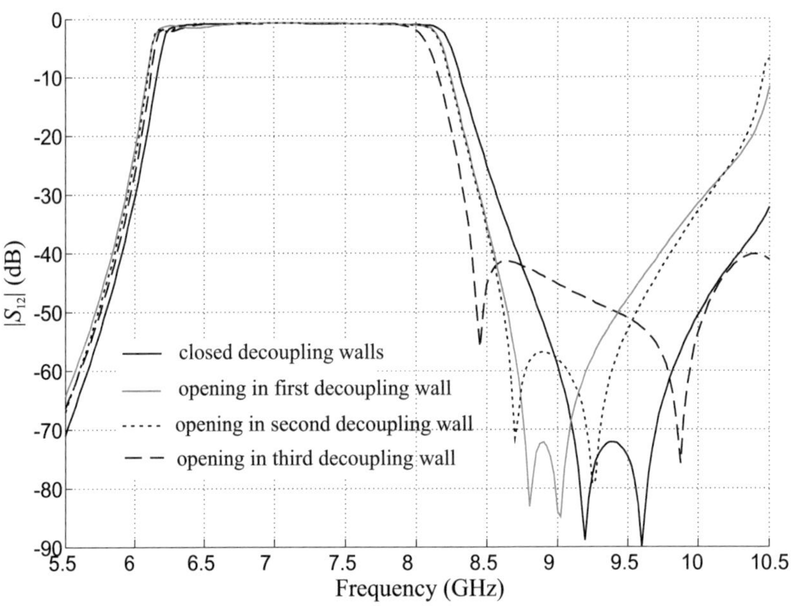

Fig. 11. S-parameters of the novel SIW filter topologies.

Thus, making use of the additional degree of flexibility provided by the novel SIW structure shown in Fig. 10, we may obtain the synthesized values of the goal coupling matrix to get a more selective response (synthesis of Fig. 9). Using this information, a new SIW filter has been designed by opening the second and third decoupling walls. These changes in the filter topology improve the selectivity, and move the first spurious response towards higher frequencies. The layout of this new filter is shown in Fig. 12, and its simulated response is outlined in Fig. 13 with grey solid lines. In the same figure, we also show the simulated response for the first SIW filter displayed in Fig. 7 with grey dashed lines. It can be concluded that the new SIW filter exhibits a better selectivity, due to the proximity of the first transmission zero to the pass-band, while also preserving a good out-of-band performance with $|S_{12}| < -25$ dB from 8.5 GHz to 10.5 GHz.

Finally, two prototypes of the designed filters have been manufactured in order to validate the simulated results. Measurements of the two filters are overlapped with the simulated results in Fig. 13, showing a very good agreement with numerical data and compliance with the UWB proposed mask (EU, 2007). The measurements have been performed by means of a universal test fixture with 1.85 mm connectors. The connectors are not included in the calibration procedure, and the associated insertion losses have been estimated about 0.30 dB. Although both designed and measured filters satisfy the UWB mask, the second one exhibits a better fitting into the mask due to the placement of transmission zeros closer to the band edges. According to the measurements, the transmission response for the first filter falls to -30 dB at 5.9928 GHz and -25 dB at 8.4985 GHz, whereas for the filter with more flexible cross-couplings it falls to -30 dB at 5.9967 GHz and -25 dB at 8.4904 GHz. With regard to the return losses, the first filter has a minimum value of 19 dB, whereas for the second case it slightly decreases to 17 dB.

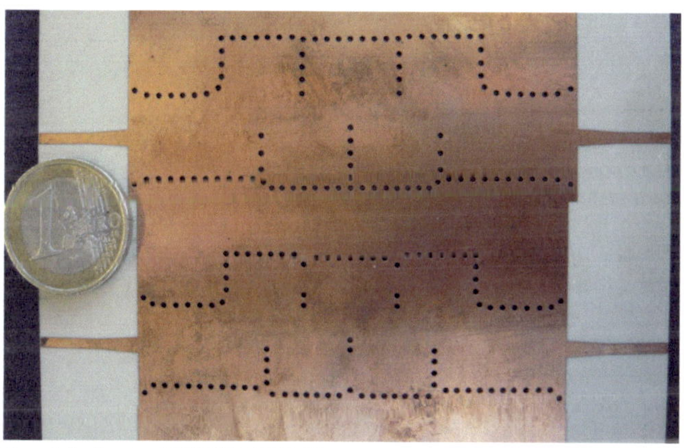

Fig. 12. Layout of the fabricated UWB SIW filters

The insertion losses for the second SIW filter are presented in Fig. 14, where they are compared with the results provided by the commercial software Ansoft HFSS (v 11.1). The simulation data have been obtained by assuming several values for the metal conductivity, which in practice is lower than the nominal one (Tang et al., 2007), (Bozzi et al., 2007). Taking into account that the connector losses are around 0.3 dB, in our case an equivalent conductivity of $\upsilon = 1.6 \cdot 10^7$ S/m compares rather well with the experimental results. Removing the connector losses, the complete filter (including the microstrip to SIW transitions) has an insertion loss level of 1.18 dB, which reduces to 1 dB if the transitions are not considered. Such results provides an estimated Q-factor of around 220 for the rectangular SIW resonator at 7.5 GHz.

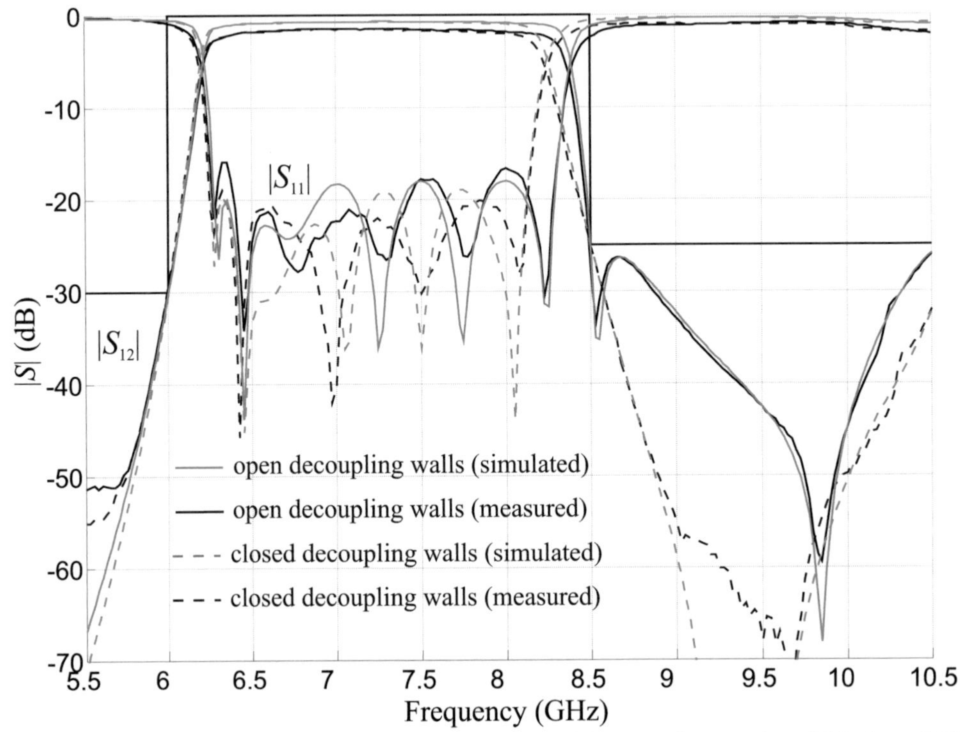

Fig. 13. Comparison between the electrical responses of the two designed and fabricated UWB SIW filters.

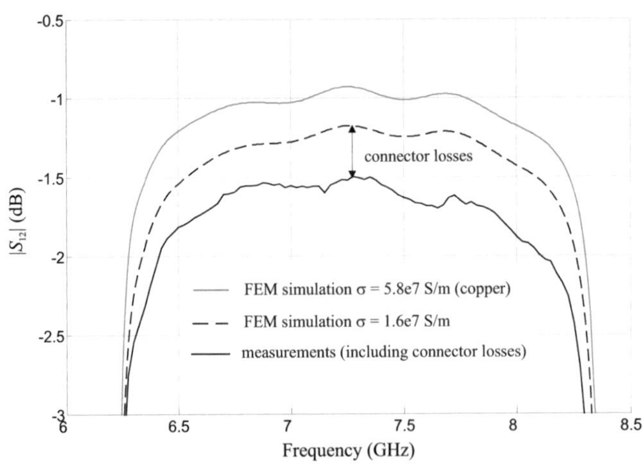

Fig. 14. Insertion losses for the UWB SIW filter shown in Fig. 10 and Fig. 12.

4. Filter Bank for UWB Systems

A microwave filter-bank has been designed for the development of an all-digital Impulse Radio (IR) Ultra-Wide-Band (UWB) receiver. The receiver is based on a frequency domain sampling technique, where each filter precedes one sampling unit, taking the energy for a given frequency band. Therefore, each band is digitalized in a parallel scheme by a set of relaxed sampling speed Analog-to-digital converters (ADC) (see Fig. 1b). Note that its real time sampling scheme counterpart would impose stringent demand on sampling speed, which for FCC compliance would be 20 Gsps, resulting unfeasible for most practical implementations.
To implement an optimal receiver the set of filters requires covering the whole spectrum of the received signal energy in a set of orthogonal frequency bands. The complexity of the receiver is determined by the number sampling units, that is the number of filters, and the sampling rate, which essentially relates with the bandwidth of each filter. A reduced number of filters results in wider bandwidth and larger ADC sampling rates, whereas a large number of filters results in lower ADC sampling rates. Therefore, a tradeoff exists between the number of filters and the sampling rate of the ADCs to be used in the receiver implementation.
The microwave filter bank presented in this work consists of a total of four filters with equal bandwidth in order to cover the frequency range inside the FCC UWB spectrum (3.1GHz - 10.0GHz). This results in four filters 1.57GHz equally spaced in frequency. The bandwidth and shape of the filter frequency responses are essentially related in the way the energy is obtained at each frequency band and therefore determining the signal reconstruction procedure, which is assumed to be implemented on the DSP & Control Unit of Fig. 1b. A set of quasi-orthogonal basis of filter frequency responses and yet capture the whole signal energy, could be performed by means of filters with very sharp selectivity and flat in-band frequency response. This in practice needs of high order filters implemented with very high Q resonators, which might be unfeasible for consumable UWB equipment.
This work bases the signal reconstruction procedure on the frame theory techniques (Daubechies, 1990). This theory essentially provides the mathematical tools for signal reconstruction when the set of frequency samplers (filters) does not constitute an orthogonal set of functions. Note that this is very interesting from a practical point of view, since may account for the technological limitation and even for the manufacturing imperfections of the RF components. From the theory of frames we may conclude that any type of filter could be used for the signal reconstruction (Daubechies, 1990). However it can be also demonstrated that an IR signal a Gaussian like filter type response is the one producing the best mean squared error of the signal reconstruction for a given scheme complexity (Mollfulleda et al., 2010). At this point is also worth to mention that the bandwidth of the Gaussian filter for the signal reconstruction has been defined down to -10dB.
A Gaussian like filter type exhibits a frequency response with no flat in-band performance, rounded band edges and poor selectivity. Note that those characteristics are common in any lossy low order filter (Hong & Lancaster, 2001). Therefore, in addition of synthesizing a Gaussian filter response which would result in an asymmetric topology and an increased the number of couplings to be designed, a Gaussian like response can be implemented by means synthesizing a conventional low order Butterworth or Chebyshev responses, using low Q resonators. We choose to design four Butterworth bandpass filters of order 3. The designing parameters (central frequency F_0, bandwidth B_w and fractional bandwidth FBW) of each filter are detailed in Table 1.
Since the four filters have the same B_w and are centered at different frequencies, the fractional bandwidths ranges from 17.4% to 39.2%. The FBW is a critical parameter on the filter design,

	Filter 1	Filter 2	Filter 3	Filter 4
F_0 (GHz)	4.0	5.6	7.3	9.0
B_w (GHz)	1.57	1.57	1.57	1.57
FBW	39.2%	28.0%	21.4%	17.4%

Table 1. Design parameters the filter-bank.

since it sets the coupling strength between resonators, and may therefore set the technology to be used for the filter implementation as well as the filter topology. For instance, in planar technology, filters with very small fractional bandwidth could be implemented with end coupled resonators, since the coupling between resonators have to be very weak. In contrast, this topology cannot be used for the design of wider band filter and one usually needs to go for parallel coupled resonator configurations (Hong & Lancaster, 2001).

We desired to use the same topology for the design of the four filters. The target is to specify a single filter configuration properly scaled in size in order to be mapped at the corresponding frequency band. In practice this results in filters with the same electrical length which in conjunction with the filter bandwidths (equal for all filters, see Table 1) will give filters with the same group delay. Although this condition is not essential for the signal reconstruction it facilitates the reconstruction procedure.

We used planar technology for the design of the filters and the proposed filter configuration is outlined in Fig. 15. This topology consists on a double-sided configuration to combine microstrip and coplanar resonant modes coupled by means of wideband couplings. The wideband couplings have been performed by elliptical patches, which allow us to control the coupling according to the size of the patch. Fig. 15 shows the top and bottom layers of a single filter. The top layer (Fig. 15a) is formed by the 50Ω feeding lines connected to an elliptic patch. The elliptic patch is then coupled to a resonator in the bottom layer (Fig. 15b).

The resonator in the bottom layer consists on a high impedance resonant transmission line with elliptic patches at both ends. The high impedance transmission line results in a resonator with low Q which helps to round the filter shape on the edges and therefore resembling into a Gaussian filter. The function of the elliptic patches connected at the ends of the resonator is twofold. These elliptic patches help to control the coupling between the resonators and the input/output port as well as between the other resonators. Note that this coupling will be very different depending on the filter designed (filter 1, filter 2, filter 3 or filter 4 of Table 1). The elliptic patches are also loading capacitively the resonator and therefore reducing its physical length for a given resonant frequency (Abbosh, 2007).

The resonator in the bottom layer is then coupled to the resonator at the top layer. The resonator at the top layer consists of a 50Ω resonant transmission line, again capacitively loaded at both end by means of an elliptic patch. As in the resonator in the bottom layer the function of the elliptic patch is to reduce the length on the resonator and to control the coupling between the resonator of the top and bottom layer.

Note that the presented topology is functioning like an end coupled filter where the resonators are conveniently distributed in two layers and the end of the resonators is properly designed to control the wider range of required couplings. Note that if we would instead be used a single layer for the filter designs, the couplings between resonators would required to set the coupling very close, probably resulting in unfeasible for conventional planar technology.

Once decided the filter topology and shape of the resonators to be used, the dimensions of the layout, this is width and length of the transmission lines, and dimensions of the elliptic

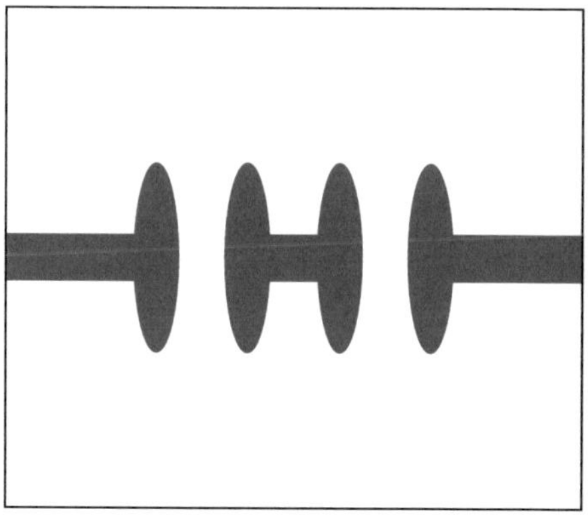

(a) Top layer

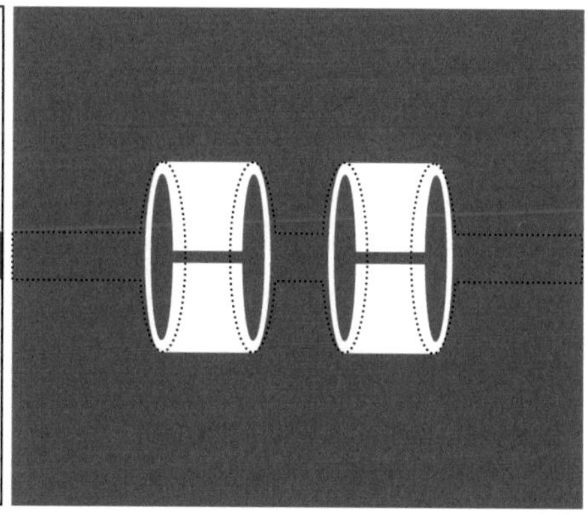

(b) Bottom layer. Dotted line is the top layer outline.

Fig. 15. Layout of the designed fitler.

patches, have been designed using conventional techniques for the design of coupled filters (Hong & Lancaster, 2001). The material used for the design of the four filters is Rogers 4003 with 3.38 of dielectric permittivity, the thickness of the dielectric is 0.5 mm and with 17 μm of cooper metallization at both sides. The loss tangent of the dielectric over the whole frequency range is assumed to be constant to 0.002.

Finally the designed filters have been fabricated and measured. In Fig. 16 we show the picture of the bottom and top layer of the filter at lower frequency (Filter 1 of Table 1). Fig. 16 also shows the measured and simulated response of Filter 1, showing both very good agreements over the whole frequency range. Fig. 16 shows the top-view of the whole filter bank, showing the compactness of the filters. Also in Fig. 16 we can see the frequency response of the whole filter bank. The frequency responses cover the whole frequency range and consecutive filter cross-over at the defined bandwidth of -10 dB, as expected from the design.

5. Shaping Networks

The shaping network is a passive component included in the pulse generator device on the transmitter side and it is essentially used to adjust the generated pulse into the UWB mask. In this section we will present two different approaches for the pulse shaping implementation. Both circuit approaches have been designed, fabricated, measured and tested.

The first approach uses the concept of a transmission line connected to a short-circuited stub. The transmission line is then fed by stepped signal, which due to the reflection and sign inversion occurring in the short-circuited stub generates a Gaussian monopulse which spectrum fits the UWB mask. In the proposed topology this idea is implemented by means of a balanced network following a hybrid configuration. This new configuration compensates the unbalanced effects due to the T-junction between the transmission line and the short-circuited stub (Mollfulleda et al., 2005). We refer to this approach as Hybrid configuration.

In contrast with the previous approach, the second one presents a shaping network which needs to be fed by a very narrow impulse whose frequency response it is almost flat in frequency. Then the function of the proposed shaping network is fitting such a response into the UWB mask. To this end we proposed a very compact topology which consist of two coupled

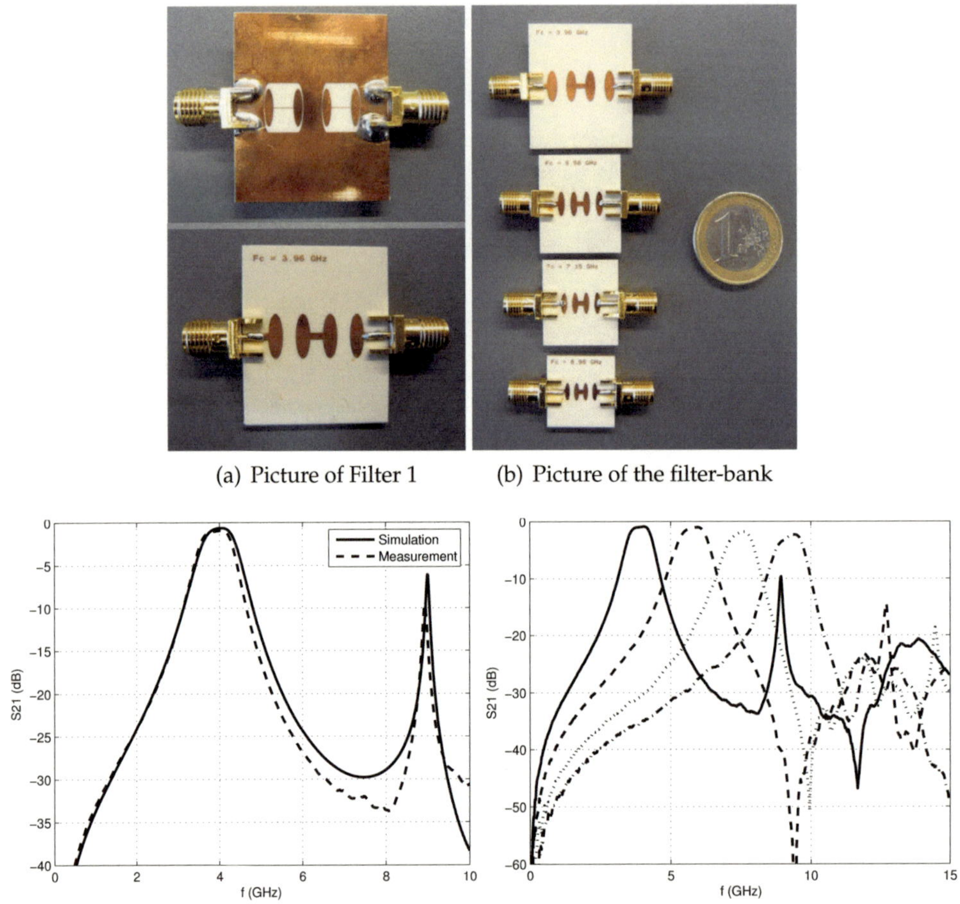

(a) Picture of Filter 1 (b) Picture of the filter-bank

(c) Measured S21 on Filter 1 (d) Measured S21 on Filter-bank

Fig. 16. Picture and frequency response of fabricated filter-bank.

lines in the top layer and increases its bandwidth by introducing a coupling slot on the ground plane. We refer to this approach as Coupled line configuration.

5.1 Hybrid Configuration

The concept of a transmission line connected to a short-circuited stub can be illustrated as in Fig. 17, where a Z_0 impedance transmission line is loaded with a $Z_0/2$ impedance short circuit stub. Then the Guassian pulse results from the summation of the travelling wave through the main transmission line and the reflected signal coming from the stub, when an step signal is driven in port 1.

The connection between the transmission line and the stub is typically performed by means of a T-junction. In practice, the T-junction introduces unbalanced response in the rising and falling edge of the output pulse, i.e., the step propagated towards the stub and the step propagated towards the load have different amplitude (Ross, 1965). As a consequence a degraded impulse response is obtained. In other words, when the circuit is fed with and impulse ($\delta(t)$)

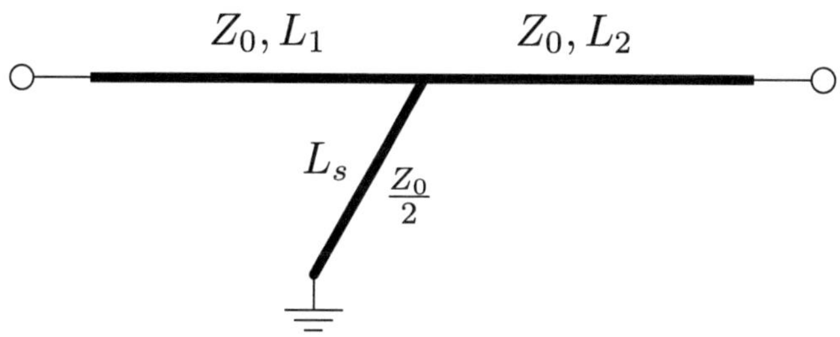

Fig. 17. Single short-circuit stub pulse shaping network.

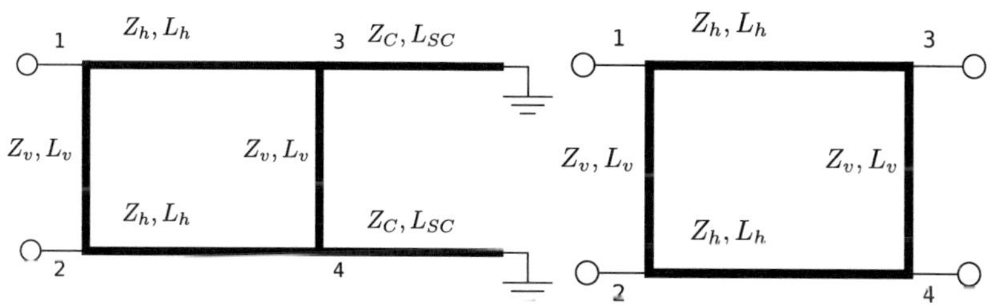

(a) Hybrid shaping network loaded with short-circuited stubs.

(b) unloaded 4-port hybrid symmetric-topology.

Fig. 18. Robust shaping network based on hybrid topology.

the response of the circuit can be written

$$h_{DLSN}(t) = k_1 \delta(t - \tau_1) - k_2 \delta(t - \tau_2) \tag{4}$$

where τ_1 and τ_2 represent the delays of the output impulses and depend on the dimension of network (see L_1, L_2 and L_s of Fig. 17 The scaling factors k_1 and k_2 represent their corresponding amplitudes.

The unbalanced response of the T-junction makes k_1 different than k_2. Ideally, one would like to obtain a balanced response ($k_1 = k_2$). To do that we might tune the impedances of the circuit of Fig. 17, at the expense of introducing further significant delayed versions of the input signal (Smith, 2002).

The work reported in (Mollfulleda et al., 2005) is described, whose network topology is shown in Fig. 18a. The hybrid-symmetric topology of this structure allows to compensate the effects introduced by the T-junction. The values Z_v, Z_h, and L_h, L_v, $L_{S}C$, are respectively the impedances and length of the corresponding transmission lines.

To analyze the proposed structure, we start considering the 4-port network of Fig. 18b. When the port 1 is excited with an impulse signal $\delta(t)$, it produces a train of impulses at ports 2, 3 and 4. These responses can be expressed as:

$$h_{1i}(t) = k_{1i}\delta(t - \tau_{1i}) + \sum_j k_{ij}\delta\left(t - \tau_{ij}\right) \tag{5}$$

where $h_{1i}(t)$ is the signal at port i, k_{1i} and τ_{1i} are the amplitude and delay of the first signal reaching port i, respectively. k_{ij} and τ_{ij} are the amplitude and delay of the impulses that appears at point i caused by further internal reflections on the structure.

The design of the structure must be performed so as to consider negligible the additional terms in (5). From now on, we will assume that $h_{1i}(t)$ is only composed of the first reaching impulse.
When the ports 3 and 4 are loaded with the short circuit stubs (as shown in Fig. 18a), the corresponding impulses are reflected back signed inverted. By considering the symmetric topology of the network the resulting impulse response results:

$$h_{12} \approx k_+ \delta(t - \tau_{12}) - k_- \delta(t - \tau_{13} - \tau_{14} - \tau_{SC}) \tag{6}$$

$$k_+ = k_{12}, \quad k_- = 2k_{13}k_{14} \tag{7}$$

where τ_{SC} is the one way propagation delay of the short circuit stub. Note that the length of the stubs in ports 3 and 4 may be used to determine the pulse width. However, also note that the minimum pulse width depends on the values of τ_{12}, τ_{14} and τ_{13}, which in turn depend on the dimension of the network (L_v, L_h). Since this topology has more parameters to be adjusted (Z_v, Z_h, L_h, L_v, L_{SC}) it offers a better control on the desired amplitude and delay of the outcoming impulses, i.e, k_+, k_- and τ_{1i} in (6), and even on the amplitude of the undesired delayed versions of the input impulse.
The design process consists of adjusting the parameters Z_v, Z_h, L_h, L_v, L_{SC} to get an impulse response as (4) with $k_1 = k_2 = 0.5$. Given the symmetric topology of the network, it is just required to adjust one of the impedances (Z_v or Z_h) and one of the line lengths (L_h or L_v).
We start the design we start fixing L_v and Z_v. The length L_v determines the signal delay of the shaping network, τ_{12} in (6). For this design we fix $\tau_{12} = 110$ ps. The input and output impedance as well as Z_v have been set to $Z_1 = Z_2 = Z_v = 50\Omega\frac{1}{2}$.
Under the assumptions above, the values of k_+ and k_- in (6) mostly depend on Z_h. In addition the length of the lines is straightly related to the technology and permittivity of the material to be used. In this case we assume microstrip technology with a dielectric constant of 3.
The design process is divided in two steps. In the first step Z_h is set so to achieve $k_+ \approx k_- \approx 0.5$. To do that ports 2, 3 and 4 are loaded to match 50Ω. By simulating the device response we asses k_+ and k_- as a function of the impedance Z_h. Simulation results provide $Z_h = 70.71\Omega$.
The second step takes the simulation model of Fig. 18a and the value of k_- is evaluated as a function of L_h. By simulation we obtain a length $L_h = 2.2$ mm giving a value of $k_- = -0.496$.
To test the procedure described so far we have built and measured an Hybrid-Symmetric pulse shaping circuits. The structure had been implemented in microstrip technology. The substrate had 1.52 mm thickness and a dielectric permittivity of 3. Fig. 19a shows a picture of the design.
The resulting topology had been measured using a E8361A Vector Network Analyzer from Agilent Technologies. This instrument allows to measure the frequency response of the device and to compute its time domain impulse response by means of an inverse Fourier transform. As well-known from signal processing theory, the resolution in the time response is inversely proportional to the window frequency. The result presented below has been obtained with a wide-band measurement up to 30 GHz.
Fig. 19 shows the measured and simulated time response. The simulated performances had been modified to account the delay introduce by the SMA connectors and the out-of-layout commercial short circuit. The results presented at Fig. 19 exhibit a very symmetric response, i.e. k_+ and k_- in (6) are nearly equal. As expected from the analysis above, this circuit configuration compensates the effects introduce by the T-junction, so that the two main reflected impulses reach the output port at the same time.

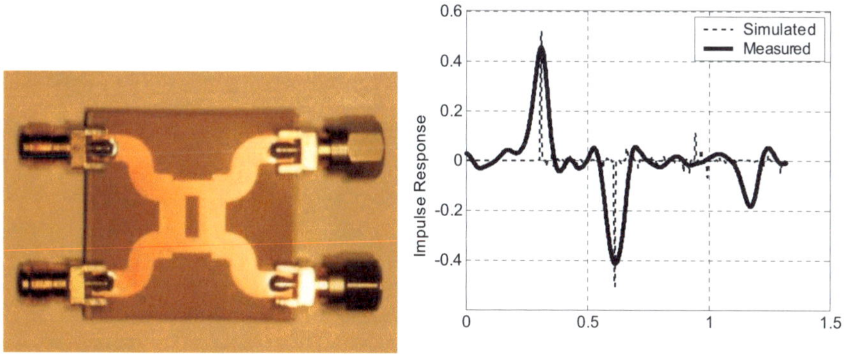

(a) Fabricated shaping network. (b) Measured and simulated Results.

Fig. 19. Impulse response of fabricated shaping network.

5.2 Coupled line Configuration

The shaping network topology presented in this section consists on a pair of parallel coupled transmission lines, being the aim of the design to coupled energy only in the band where the UWB is defined. The proposed design uses the idea presented in (Li, 2006)]. Figure 20 outlines the layout of the designed shaping network, where in the top layer it can be identified the input and output 50Ω transmission lines connected to a narrower transmission lines which are coupled to each other. In a conventional coupled transmission line structure the strength of the coupling is essentially set by the proximity between the two transmission lines and the line width (Gupta, 1996). In this case a wideband strong coupling is required to meet the specifications of the UWB system. To achieve so, an slot aperture is introduced in the ground plane of the topology. The layout of the aperture is represented in Fig. 20b. By introducing the aperture in the ground plane the field distribution changes, removing part of the field going from the strips of the top layer to the ground plane, and enhancing the fringing field between the two strips, hence making their coupling stronger. As usually done in couplers based on transmission line topologies the confronted area of the coupled lines it is a quarter wavelength at the central operating frequency.

Following this idea we have designed a pulse shaper that fits to the UWB mask, where the bandwidth of the frequency response is defined at −10 dB insertion losses. The material use for the design has a 0.508 mm thick substrate with dielectric permittivity of 3.38, with a 0.0027 loss tangent and the cooper on both sides has a thickness of 17 μm.

Fig. 21 shows the fabricated shaping network following the parallel coupled concept described above. The picture of the top layer with the two coupled transmission line reflects the compactness of the topology. The bottom layer includes the ground plane and the aperture used for enhancing the coupling strength between the two coupled lines.

The fabricated device has then been measured using a broadband network analyzer. Fig. 22a illustrates the shaping network frequency response from *DC* to 15 GHz. The frequency response is centered at 6.2 GHz and exhibit transmission zeros at *DC* and at 12.2 GHz. The results of the frequency response are then used to obtain the impulse response of the network. The results are depicted in Fig. 22. In this case the impulse response coincides with the intended output pulse since this network is proposed to be fed with a very narrow pulse.

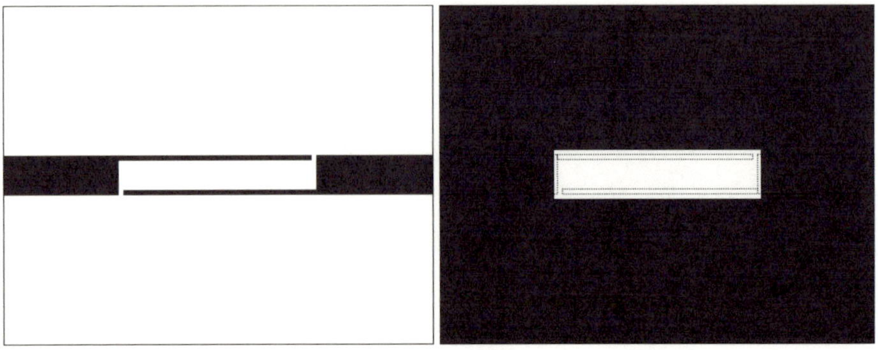

(a) Top layer (b) Bottom layer. Dotted line is the top layer outline.

Fig. 20. Outline of the topology of the proposed shaping network.

(a) Top layer (b) Bottom layer.

Fig. 21. Picture of fabricated shaping network.

Note as well, that such structure can be interpreted as a two order filter where the resonant frequencies are set by the length of the quarter wavelength transmission lines. Another interpretation would be a lumped series capacitor blocking the low frequency signals, where the cutting frequency at the lower band edge is set by the value capacitor (i.e; the coupling strength), and the open circuit quarter-wavelength stubs are producing a transmission zeros at twice of the central frequency.

6. Pulse Inverter/Non-Inverter

The pulse inverter is used in the present architecture (Fig. 23) because of the use of CDMA Direct Sequence Spread Spectrum. The key point of the inverter block lies in the transitions between balanced and unbalanced propagation modes. The pulse inversion is achieved by introducing a transition between unbalanced to balanced mode and, subsequently, a transition from balanced to unbalance but changing the reference plane at the output. This idea was introduced in (Gupta, 1996) using transitions between microstrip and coplanar slotlines.
The Inverter/Non-Inverter circuit has two different paths: one performs the pulse inversion whereas the other does not change the pulse sign. In Fig. 11 is depicted the final layout of this stage including the top and bottom layers. The Non-Inverter branch line has the same length as the Inverter branch. This is necessary to maintain both ways synchronized and same strip losses.

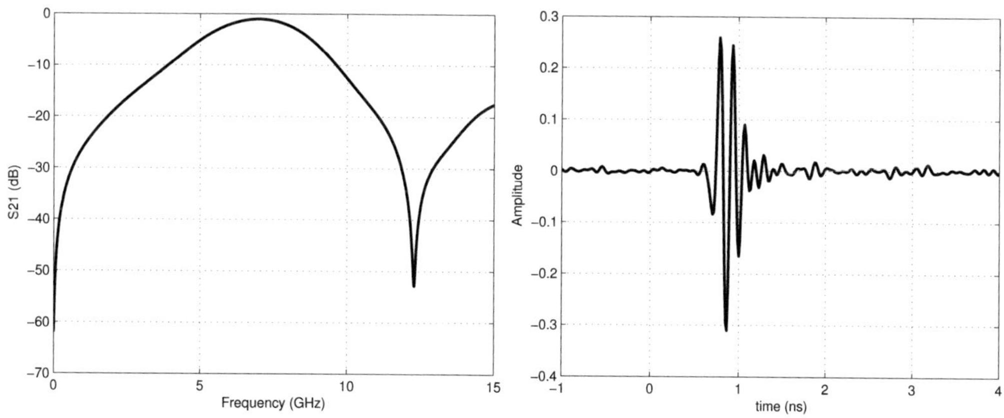

(a) Frequency domain. (b) Time domain.

Fig. 22. Measured time and frequency response of fabricated shaping network.

In Fig. 24 a measurement of the positive and negative pulses is depicted. The pulse width is 185ps, whereas the peak-to-peak amplitude is 2.2V. The generated pulses is caused by the inductive effect of the SRD package (Mollfulleda et al., 2006).

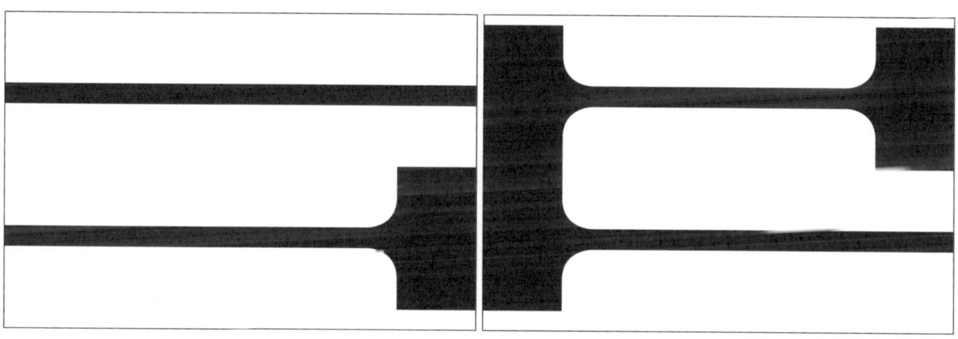

(a) Top Layer. (b) Bottom Layer. Dotted line represents the outline of the top layer

Fig. 23. Layout of implemented pulse inverter.

7. Power Combiner/Splitter

The power splitter/combiner is an essential device in both the transmitter and receiver chain (see Fig 1). This section will present the design of a two-output/inputs power splitter/combiner. This design follows the concept of a coupled line configuration, where in the top-layer now three coupled lines are used to distribute the signal, whereas the required wide bandwidth performance is achieved by means of a coupling slot on the bottom layer.
To illustrate the functioning of the following approach, Fig. 25 shows the cross-section of a three coupled transmission lines, where in a power splitter case the line in the middle acts as a feeding strip, whose power is then distributed into the adjacent strips by means of fringing

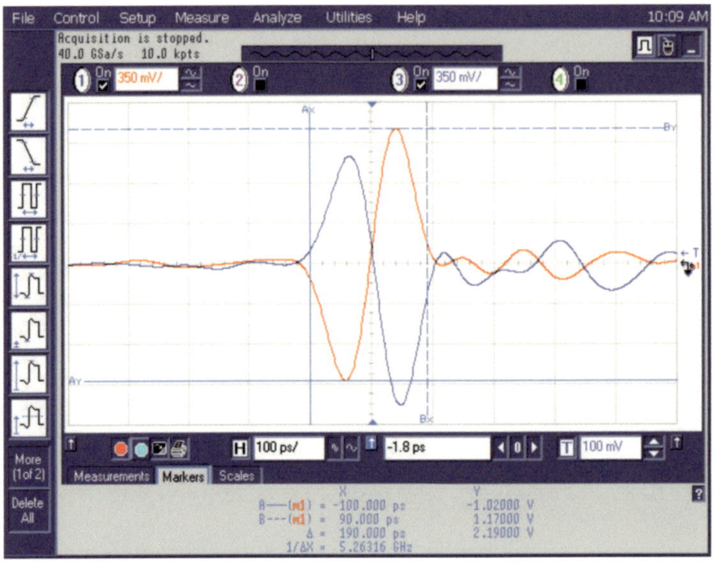

Fig. 24. Measurement of pulse inverted and non-inverted pulse.

field. In Fig. 25 we also outline the existing capacitances between the strips. In particular Fig. 25a outlines the capacitance between each strip and the ground plane (C_{ii}), and the capacitance between the strips C_{ij}. The capacitance between the strips set actually the strength of their couplings. As occurring in section 5.2 by removing the ground plane below the strips, the C_{ii} become negligible and the coupling between the strips (C_{ij}) increases, thus achieving a wider bandwidth response.

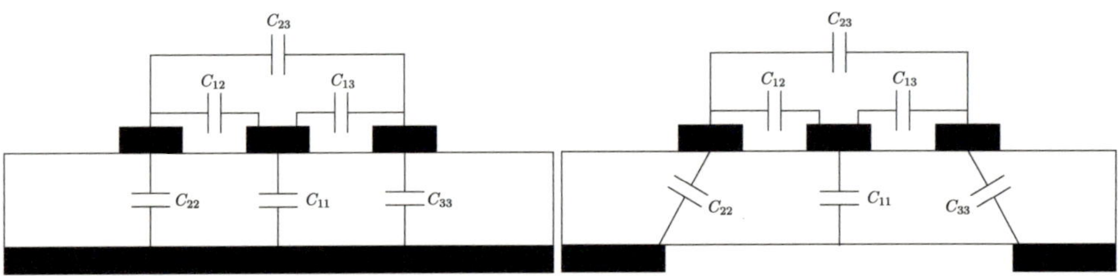

(a) Microstrip configuration. (b) Microstrip with apperture in ground plane

Fig. 25. Coss-section of a three coupled line structure.

Using this concept we have evaluated two topologies, which are outlined in Fig. 26. Both topologies have been designed in planar technology using a substrate with a dielectric permittivity of 3.38 and 0.508 mm of thickness, with 17 μm thickness of cooper metallization on both sides. Fig. 26a shows the topology of a wideband power splitter when no aperture exists in the ground plane, hence the equivalent circuit of an elemental section (i.e. the equivalent circuit of a cross-section), would correspond to the one of Fig. 25a. In order to improve the operation bandwidth we introduce an aperture slot in the ground plane (see Fig. 26b). By doing so the distributed capacitance on a cross-section of the three coupled lines follows the pattern outlined in Fig. 25b.

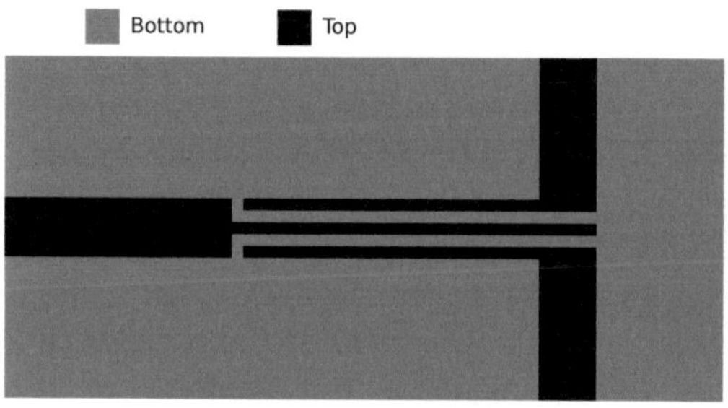

(a) Microstrip configuration.

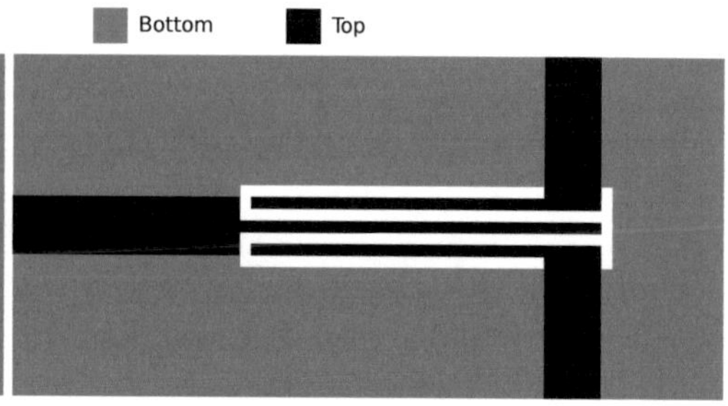

(b) Microstrip with apperture in ground plane

Fig. 26. Layout of power based on a three coupled line structure.

Both topology can be explained with the equivalent circuit model described in Fig. 27. This circuit model consists on a quarter-wavelength input transmission line modeling the center strip of the three coupled lines. The input strip is then coupled to two quarter-wavelength transmission lines, by means of two admittance inverters. These two lines are also coupled to each other by another admittance inverter. Being therefore this structure also interpreted as filtering structure with one input port and two output ports (diplexer), with identical response at both output ports.

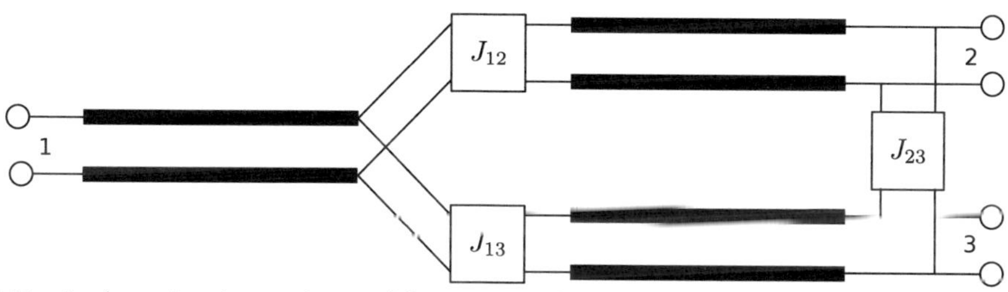

Fig. 27. Equivalent circuit topology of the proposed power splitter.

The designed power splitter of Fig. 26b had then been fabricated and measured. A picture of the top and bottom view of the fabricated devices is shown in Fig. 28a, where it can be observed the compactness of the design. The measured results of the transmission coefficient of the implemented filter are outlined in Fig. 28b, exhibiting the expected wideband response.

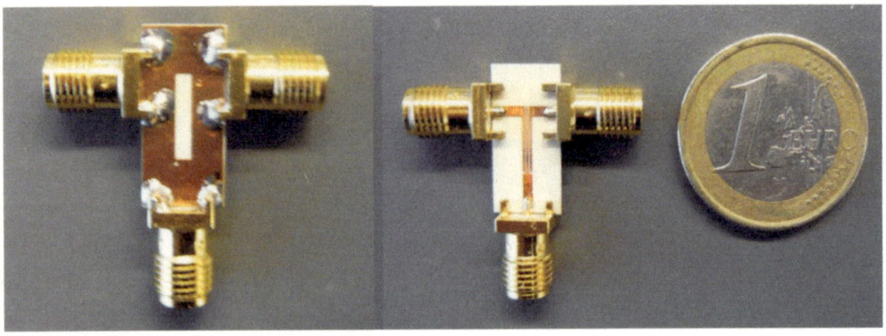

(a) Picture of implemented power splitter.

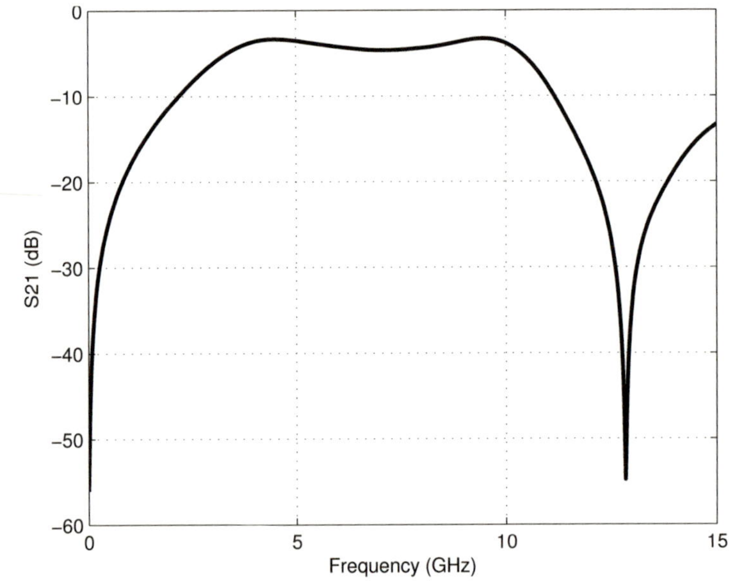

(b) Measured S21 of implemented power splitter

Fig. 28. Fabricated power splitter and measured response.

8. References

A., M., Najar, M., Miskovsky, P., Leyva, J. A., Berenguer, L., Ibars, C. & Navarro, M. (2006). Quetzal: Qualified ultra-wideband testbed for reduced data-rates and location, *IEEE International Conference on Testbeds and Research Infrastructures for the Development of Networks and Communities*, pp. 191–197.

Abbosh, A. M. (2007). Planar bandpass filters for ultra-wideband applications, *IEEE Trans. on Microwave Theory and Techniques* **55**(10): 2262–2269.

Barnes, M. A. (2000). *Ultra-Wideband Magnetic Antenna*, US Patent 6,091,374.

Bozzi, M., Pasian, M., Perregrini, L. & Wu, K. (2007). On the losses in substrate integrated waveguides, *Proceedings of 37th European Microw. Conf.*, Munich, pp. 384–387.

Burke, G. J. & Poggio, A. J. (1981). *Numerical Electromagnetics Code (NEC) - Method of Moments*, Rep. UCID18834, Lawrence Livermore Lab., Livermore, CA.

Chen, X., Drolet, D. & Wu, K. (2007). Substrate integrated waveguide filters for airborne and satellite system applications, *Proceedings of Canadian Conference on Eletrical and Computer Enginnering CCECE*, pp. 659–662.

Chuang, C., Lin, H. & Wang, C. (2007). Design of dual-mode siw cavity filters, *Proceedings of IEEE TENCON*, pp. 1–4.

Daubechies, I. (1990). The wavelet transform, time-frequency localization and signal analysis, *IEEE Trans. On Information Theory* **36**(5): 961–1005.

Deslandes, D. & Wu, K. (2001). Integrated microstrip and rectangular waveguide in planar form, *IEEE Microwave Wireless Comp. Lett.* **11**(2): 68–70.

Dissanayake, T. & Esselle, K. P. (2006). Correlation-based pattern stability analysis and a figure of merit for uwb antennas, *IEEE Trans. Antennas Propag.* **54**(11): 3184–3191.

EU (2007). 21 february 2007 - commission decision 2007/131/ec on allowing the use of the radio spectrum for equipment using ultra-wideband technology in a harmonised manner in the community, *Official Journal of the European Union* (L55): 33–36.

FCC (2002). Revision of part 15 of the commission's rules regarding ultra-wideband transmission systems, *Technical report*, Federal Communications Commission (FCC). `http://www.wireless.fcc.gov/rules.html`.

Guglielmi, M., Montauni, F., Pellegrini, L. & Arcioni, P. (1995). Implementing transmission zeros in inductive-window bandpass filters, *IEEE Trans. Microwave Theory Tech.* **43**(8): 1911–1915.

Gupta, K. C. (1996). *Microstrip Lines and Slotlines*, Artech House, Boston.

Hao, Z., Hong, W., Chen, J., Chen, X. & Wu, K. (2005). Compact super-wide bandpass substrate integrated waveguide (siw) filters, *IEEE Trans. Microwave Theory Tech.* **53**(9): 2968–2977.

Hong, H.-S. & Lancaster, M. J. (2001). *Microstrip Filters For RF/Microwave Applications*, John Wiley & Sons Inc.

Johnson, J. & Rahmat-Samii, Y. (1997). Genetic algorithms in engineering electromagnetic, *IEEE Antennas and Propagation Magazine* **39**(4): 7–21.

Kanda, M. (1978). A relatively short cylindrical broadband antenna with tapered resistive loading for picosecond pulse measurements, *IEEE Trans. Antennas Propag.* **26**(3): 369–373.

Li, K. (2006). Experimental study on uwb pulse generation using uwb bandpass filters, *IEEE International Conference on UltraWideband*, ICU, pp. 103–108.

Lindeblad, N. E. (1941). *Wideband Antenna*, US Patent 2,239,724.

Mira, F., Blas, A. S., Boria, V. & Gimeno, B. (2007). Fast and accurate analysis and design of substrate integrated waveguide (siw) filters, *Proceedings of 37th European Microw. Conf.*, Munich, pp. 170–173.

Mira, F., Mateu, J., Cogollos, S. & Boria, V. (2009). Design of ultra-wideband substrate integrated waveguide (siw) filters in zigzag topology, *IEEE Microwave Wireless Comp. Lett.* **19**(5): 281–283.

Miskovsky, P. (2010). *UWB antenna design for communication system performance optimization*, Ph.D. dissertation, Universitat Polytecnica de Catalunya-TSC.

Miskovsky, P., Arbesu, J. M. G. & Romeu, J. (2006). Application of uwb antenna descriptors to lossy dipole performance assessment, *Proceedings of IEEE Antennas Propag. Soc. Int. Symp.*, Albuquerque NM, pp. 175–178.

Miskovsky, P., Arbesu, J. M. G. & Romeu, J. (2007). What can we expect from a continuously tapered, resistivelay loaded monopole, for uwb applications, *Proceedings of IEEE Antennas Propag. Soc. Int. Symp.*, Honolulu HI, pp. 1421–1424.

Mollfulleda, A., Ibars, C. & Mateu, J. (2010). Ultra-wideband receiver based on microwave filterbbank, *IEEE International Conference on UltraWideband*, ICU.

Mollfulleda, A., Leyva, J. & Berenguer, L. (2006). Impulse radio transmitter using time hopping and direct sequence spread spectrum codes for uwb communications, *Proceeding of International Symposium on Advanced Radio Technologies, ISART*, NTIA, pp. 49–57.

Mollfulleda, A., Miskovsky, P. & J.Mateu (2005). Robust passive shaping network for impulse radio and uwb signal generator, *IEEE International Microwave Symposiumn*, pp. 1339–1342.

Montoya, T. P. & Smith, G. S. (1996). A study of pulse radiation from several broad-band loaded monopoles, *IEEE Trans. Antennas Propag.* **44**(8): 1172–1182.

Paulsen, L., West, J. B., Perger, W. F. & Kraus, J. (2003). Recent investigations on the volcano smoke antenna, *Proceedings of IEEE Antennas Propag. Soc. Int. Symp.*, vol. 3, pp. 845–848.

Rajo-Iglesias, E. & Quevedo-Teruel, O. (2007). Linear array synthesis using an ant-colony-optimization-based algorithm, *IEEE Antennas and Propagation Magazine* **49**(2): 70–79.

Rao, B., Ferris, J. & Zimmerian, W. (1969). Broadband characteristics of cylindrical antennas with exponentially tapered capacitive loading, *IEEE Trans. Antennas Propag.* **17**(2): 145–151.

Robinson, J. & Rahmat-Samii, Y. (2004). Particle swarm optimization in electromagnetics, *IEEE Trans. Antennas Propag.* **52**(2): 397–407.

Ross, G. (1965). The synthetic generation of phase coherent microwave signals for transient behaviour measurements, *IEEE Trans. on Microwave Theory and Techniques* **13**(5): 704–706.

Smith, P. W. (2002). *Transient Electronics, Pulsed Circuit Technology*, John Willey & Sons.

Tang, H., Hong, W., Chen, J., Luo, G. & Wu, K. (2007). Development of millimeter-wave planar diplexers based on complementary characters of dual-mode substrate integrated waveguide filters with circular and elliptic cavities, *IEEE Trans. Microwave Theory Tech.* **55**(4): 776–782.

Wu, T. T. & King, R. W. P. (1965). The cylindrical antenna with non-reflecting resistive loading, *IEEE Trans. Antennas Propag.* **13**(3): 369–373.

Zhang, Y., Hong, W., Wu, K., Chen, J. & Hao, Z. C. (2005). Development of compact bandpass filters with siw triangular cavities, *Proceedings of Asia-Pacific Micro. Conf. APMC.*

14

UWB radar for detection and localization of trapped people

Egor Zaikov and Juergen Sachs
Electronic Measurement Research Lab, TU Ilmenau
Germany

1. Motivation and literature survey

The problem of rescuing people from beneath the collapsed buildings does not have an ultimate technical solution that would guarantee efficient detection and localization of victims. The main techniques in use are:

- Cameras with long optical fibers that are injected into the holes or fissures in the collapsed buildings (the usability of such devices and their efficiency depend on the structure of collapsed building and besides, when the victim is detected it is difficult in the most cases to determine its actual position).
- Sledge hammers are used to give a signal to potential victims, and rescuers with microphones are waiting for hearing the response (obvious limitation of this method is that unconscious people cannot be detected. Localization of victims is a problem as well)
- Search dogs are deployed in the disaster area. They detect presence of victims efficiently by smell, but information about their actual positions or quantity cannot be indicated. Moreover, dog is likely to indicate the presence of dead person which distracts rescuers from locations where living people can still be found.

Due to the ability of electromagnetic waves to penetrate through typical building materials and its significant (in order of centimetres) spatial resolution, UWB radar was considered as a prospective tool for detection and localization of people trapped beneath the collapsed building within the European project RADIOTECT (Ultra Wideband Radio application for localization of hidden people and detection of unauthorized objects). In particular, the aim was to develop a radar system that can detect person by his/her breathing through thick layer of rubble (1-2 meters of reinforced concrete). In short main RADIOTECT results related to breathing detection were presented in (Zaikov, 2010). Evidently, detection of person by respiratory activity has an added value in comparison with methods in use (listed above), since new possibilities for detection and localization of multiple unconscious victims arise.
Ability to detect respiratory and cardiac motion by means of UWB radar is reported in numerous articles and field studies. To name a few:

- In (Chernyak, 2006) basic algorithm for breathing detection in the absence of non-stationary clutter is developed and analyzed with respect to radar theory. Pulse radar is considered.
- In (Ossberger et al., 2004) algorithm for through-wall breathing detection that compensates for dilation of emitted waveform due to the wall is presented. Algorithm is

based on Continuous Wavelet Transform. Pulse radar is considered. Besides, ability to detect breathing through 20 cm- thick brick wall is demonstrated.

- In (Narayanan, 2008) noise radar is used for breathing detection. Breathing signature is separated from unwanted signal components by means of Hilbert-Huang transform. Finally, breathing is clearly detected through 30 cm- thick concrete wall (useful signal is 3 dB higher then highest noise peak)
- In (Levitas, & Matuzas, 2006) and (Levitas et al., 2008) two algorithms for breathing detection are proposed by group from Geozondas Inc. In (Levitas, & Matuzas, 2006) breathing is detected as a strong variation in the spectrum of received radar response. However, this approach doesn't differentiate between breathing and any other motion in radar cross-section. Algorithm in (Levitas et al., 2008) detects breathing as a periodical variation of some waveform. Neither in (Levitas, & Matuzas, 2006) nor in (Levitas et al., 2008) this waveform is considered to be known a priori in contrast to (Chernyak, 2006) and (Ossberger et al., 2004). In (Levitas et al., 2008) breathing was clearly detected through 16-cm thick brick wall by means of impulse radar. Importantly, ability to detect two breathing persons simultaneously is demonstrated. Breathing rate of two persons was deliberately different, but this difference is not the only distinction between two persons in received signal since it can be seen that two breathing signatures arrive at different distances to antennas.

Historically, UWB radars were extensively applied as Ground Penetrating Radars (GPR) in the fields of geophysics, archaeology and for the detection of buried mines prior to using them for the problem described in this chapter. No surprise though that some investigations were carried out in order to determine the efficiency of GPRs for the detection of people buried beneath the rubble:

- Thorough test of GPR as a detector of living person is described in (Bechtel Special Technologies Laboratory Ground Penetrating Radar, 2003). The GPR was originally developed under the sponsorship of the U.S. Department of Energy's Special Technologies Program for other applications (unfortunately, no details about antenna type/bandwidth is given in the report). This Operational Test and Evaluation was conducted by personnel of Virginia Task Force 1 (VATF1), Urban Search and Rescue (US&R) Team and the California Task Force 2 (CATF2) US&R Team. Test was conducted on November 5, 2003, at the rubble pile of Fairfax County. To cite from the report, 'In general, the system has the capability to penetrate 1-2 feet of rubble and an associated airspace of up to 6 feet. In some scenarios, the system detected breathing of victims up to 9 feet through one or two thicknesses of concrete and airspace'
- More results about using commercial GPR (SIR-3000 by Geophysical Survey Systems, Inc.) are presented in (Geophysical Survey Systems, Inc., 2005). Importantly, antennas recommended for breathing detection are 270 MHz or 400 MHz antennas (lower frequencies then in the most of other studies). To cite from the report, 'GPR can easily penetrate the concrete debris and "bend around" the metal reinforcing bars. Tests have also shown that GPR can note the presence/absence of a live person behind an intact 50 cm heavily reinforced (2 mats of rebar) wall.'
- Last but not least, there is a commercially available device for detecting people beneath the rubble: LifeLocator™ by UltraVision Security Systems, Inc. Citation from (UltraVision Security Systems, Inc.): 'Detection Distance through Debris Pile: Up to 15' (4.6 meters) for breathing , up to 20' (6.4 meters) for motion '. Rubble type is not specified.

Separately I should briefly mention the use of narrowband radars for the problem under investigation.

- In (Arai, 2001) breathing person was detected through more then 2 meters of diverse debris.
- Commercial Bioradar BR402 by BOS - Sondermaschinenbau GmbH is a narrowband device with operating frequency 1 299 MHz. Remarkable penetration depth is mentioned (however, without specifying material type and airspace size): 'The coverage depends on the antenna shape and the material to be penetrated, and can be up to 8 meters', (BOS - Sondermaschinenbau GmbH).

Finally, the contents of previous research in the area determined the direction of our approach to breathing detection considerably. Below relevant points related to our effort in connection to earlier studies are summarized:

- It can be seen that reported depth were breathing is detected with narrowband radar is higher then that for UWB radars. Obviously, this can be explained by notion that radar electronics in the case of narrowband device is able to treat signals of higher power. However, narrowband radars have poor resolution capacity and that is, they do not provide sufficient abilities to detect multiple persons or, most importantly, to determine the position of trapped victim. Besides, there are much more possibilities for cancellation of clutter arising from moving surrounding in UWB radar. Our aim was to utilize unique abovementioned properties of UWB radar.
- Previously reported research in breathing detection with UWB radar was mainly concentrated on detection and enhancement of useful signal. While viable data processing methods proposed are diverse, according to (Yarovoy & Ligthart, 2007), the fact that UWB radar allows for positioning of trapped victim have not yet been proven experimentally. The problems of multiple victims and clutter did not receive much attention as well.

2. Hardware for breathing-detecting radar system

Prototype radar developed for through-rubble detection of human being is a M-sequence radar with one transmitting and two receiving channels (Zaikov et al., 2008). Its structure is shown if figure 1.

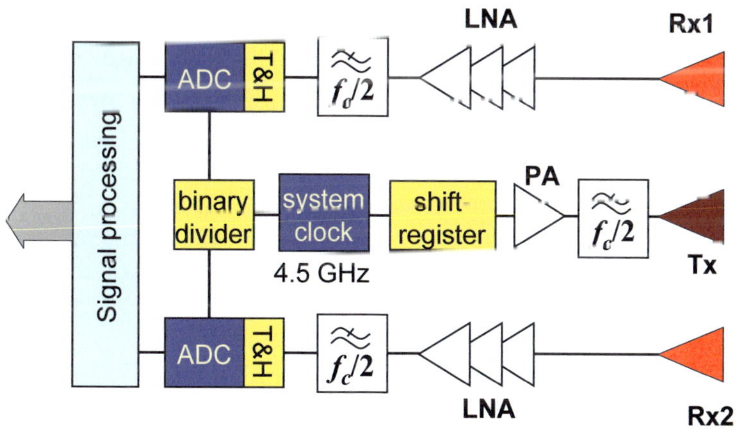

Fig. 1. System structure an M-Sequence radar with one transmitter and two receivers.

Fig. 2. Radar device and antennas used in prototype system. Courtesy to MEODAT, Ilmenau and IRK, Dresden.

The shift-register, pulsed by the RF-clock, provides the M-sequence, which is a stimulus signal transmitted by the Tx-antenna. Further, on the receiver side signal is converted into the digital domain via sub-sampling controlled by binary divider. Obviously, the received signal is a pseudo-random one, and it cannot be further used directly. Thus, the time-domain radar signal is reconstructed by means of a correlation procedure. After that, the signal is available for further processing in the form similar to that of the impulse radar signals.
The system clock frequency for the device is about 4.5 GHz, which results in the operational bandwidth of about DC−2.25 GHz. The M-sequence order is 9, i.e. the impulse response covers 511 samples regularly spread over 114 ns. This corresponds to an observation window of 114 ns leading to an unambiguous range of about 16 m in free space. 256 hardware averages are always computed within FPGA of the radar head to provide a reasonable data throughput and to improve the SNR by 24 dB. Additional software averaging can be completed by main computer, if required.
Advantages of using M-sequence radar module as related to the topic of this chapter are briefly summarized below:

- Low jitter due to the stability of shift register and binary divider. Importance of this point for breathing detection is explained in part 3 of this chapter.

- Fast data acquisition. The system works reliably while collecting 32 A-scans per second which is certainly fast enough to catch the fastest human breathing. Moreover, this acquisition rate gives us good possibilities to discriminate breathing response from unwanted clutter like drift of electronics and reflection from moving surrounding.

- Lowest frequency in radar response is a few MHz. Although motion associated with respiratory activity is minor, frequencies below 300 MHz are still useful for breathing detection in many cases(less efficient then higher frequencies if we do not take rubble attenuation into account though due to the minor magnitude of breathing in comparison with wavelength). Ability of electromagnetic waves to penetrate typical building materials is higher for low frequencies. Measurement example in support of this point in the case of breathing is given in figure 3.

The last point about frequency range was crucial for constructing the antennas to be used in radar prototype. One important requirement for the total system is that it has to be efficient under diverse conditions on different types of rubble, including moist rubble. In practice that means retaining low frequencies well below 300 MHz in the measured data. On another hand the lower the frequencies the larger the antennas to be used. As a compromise between the size of antennas (smaller antennas mean less deployment time, they are more convenient) and the need to catch low frequencies, planar spiral antennas 70 cm in diameter were chosen (figure 2). Transmitting and receiving antennas have different polarization in order to minimize the crosstalk between antennas and increase the transmitted power which gives us possibility to penetrate more rubble. Antennas are functional in the frequency range from 0.15 GHz to 1.1 GHz.

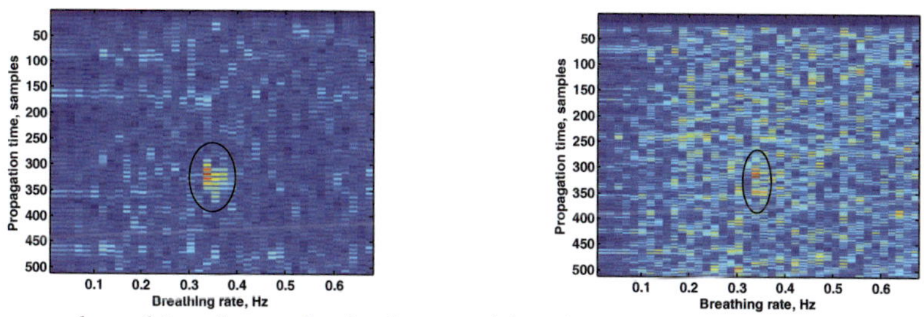

Fig. 3. Person, breathing beneath the heap of bricks inside the pipe, made of reinforced concrete. Data is filtered with upper cutoff frequency of 300 MHz (on the left, person is detected as bright red point and marked) and 700 MHz (on the right, location of person is marked, but it is not distinguishable from noise peaks).

3. Statement of the problem and breathing detection

Breathing signature in radar response is caused by the minor (in comparison to walking) shift of body parts. The physical problem of detecting such minor motion is illustrated in figure 4.
It can be observed that minor motion, like breathing, is felt mainly on the flank of the measured signal, since the slight shift of the waveform from its incipient state produces the largest variation of waveform at the steepest slope. This is described by the following relation:

$$\Delta V = a\frac{2\Delta d}{c} \quad (1),$$

where a is the slope and c is speed of light.
Therefore, the smallest displacement Δd which can be observed depends on the rise time of the backscattered signal and the smallest detectable voltage variation ΔV . The rise time of the waveform is typically limited by the test object (i.e. the rubble or the wall) if the radar bandwidth is sufficiently high as it is in our case. The voltage resolution is limited by random noise caused by the radar device or external interferer. In what follow, we suppose that no external interferer is present.
In that case, the total noise on the flank results from additive noise and jitter which can be expressed by following equation:

$$\sigma = \sqrt{\sigma_a^2 + a^2 t^2} \quad (2),$$

where σ_a is additive noise, t_j is rms jitter and a is the slope the signal interval of interest.

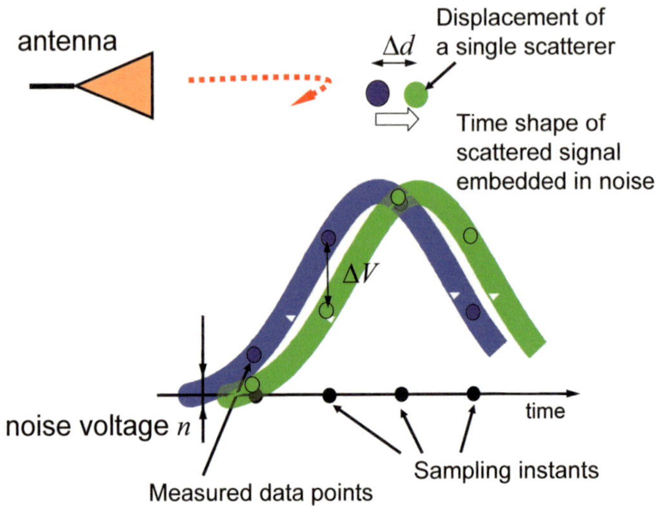

Fig. 4. Principle of detecting minor motions by means of UWB radar

That is, the jitter performance of the radar device is crucial for this particular task, since both jitter and minor motion caused by breathing are originated at the flank of the radar signal. However, measurements were carried out to estimate the jitter in M-sequence radar and only additive noise could be observed. As it was mentioned above, for our problem this is one of the most important advantages of an M-Sequence conception compared to other ultra-wideband principles.

Breathing manifests itself in the radar response as a very specific signal. Below, its features are summarized that were taken into account during development of detecting processing methods (see figure 5 for illustration of these points):

1. The geometrical variations of the chest caused by breathing will be quite less than the range resolution of the radar. This can be observed in figure 5, where response from breathing person is shown at different phases of respiratory activity.
2. Distance from antennas to breathing person does not change during the measurement (otherwise, the change is indicated by strong motion). That is, breathing typically appears at the certain moments of propagation time (see figure 5).
3. Breathing can be considered as periodical motion over a certain interval of time. The frequency of breathing can change slowly with the time, but it is always within the frequency window, which is known a priori (0.2—0.5 Hz). In figure 5 the periodical patterns, produced by breathing are shown.
4. Breathing appears as correlated motion in several neighbouring cells in radar response. The size of the breathing-related segment of radar cross-section is determined by antenna, physical size of the body which is moved during the respiration activity, position of the body, by rubble type, thickness and structure.
5. The response from breathing person can be extremely weak, since the victims of interest are buried beneath the rubble which strongly attenuates the sounding waves.

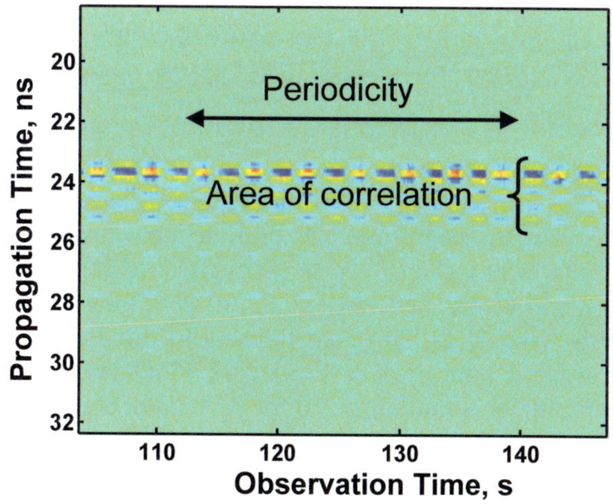

Fig. 5. Person, breathing 2 meters away from the antennas.

Second and third point lead to the idea of using time-frequency representations (in slow-time) for breathing detection similar to how it is done in (Narayanan, 2008) and (BOS - Sondermaschinenbau GmbH) in order to discriminate breathing from any other signal component. However, in this work we mainly concentrate on the situation when point four from the list is valid. In this case instantaneous amplitude of breathing is small in comparison with noise and it is not well detected in time-frequency representation while it is good visible in frequency after appropriate signal processing.

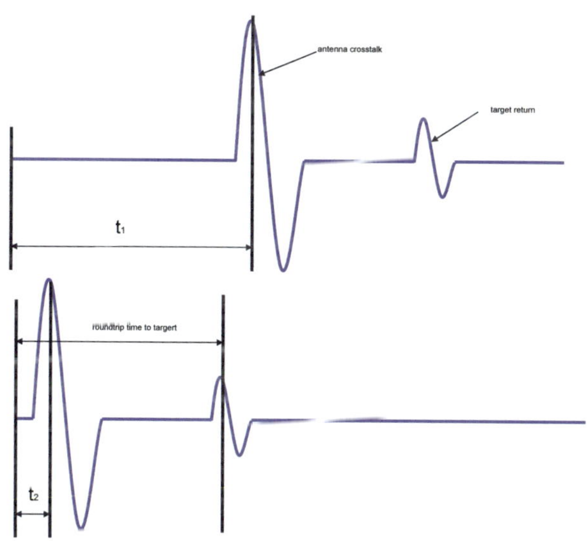

Fig. 6. Shift of IRF to time-zero estimate.

In M-sequence radar used IRFs are shifted by random value in propagation time every time the device is switched on. That is, information about distance from antennas to object is not related to propagation time where the motion is seen in the raw data. To avoid this effect,

IRF can be circularly shifted left by $t_1 - t_2$ (see figure 6), where t_1 is a time instant where maximal value of IRF arises (it is supposed to be related to antenna crosstalk) and $t_2 = \sqrt{\varepsilon}d/c$, where ε is a dielectric constant of rubble and d is a distance between the centres of transmitting and receiving antennas.

Antenna cross-talk and multiple responses from stationary background typically dominate the radargram, hampering straightforward motion detection. That is, the stage of background removal algorithm should be implemented within the software for motion detection. Due to our a priori knowledge about breathing frequencies, the task of background removal is reduced to high-pass filtering in the direction of observation time without taking into account relocation of the target. However, in one of the algorithms proposed in the chapter for non-stationary clutter reduction, signal variation that is slower then lowest breathing rate possible is used for estimating clutter. That is, the cut-off frequency used for high-pass filtering at this stage should be quite lower then 0.2 Hz. In addition, vertical (fast-time) filtering should be carried out to limit the bandwidth to the actual bandwidth of received signal. In our case that means bandpass FIR filtering in the range from 150 MHz to 1.1 GHz (this corresponds to antenna bandwidth)

3.1 Localization of useful signal in the observation time direction

If the signal after pre-processing (shifting to time zero and band pass filtering) is denoted as $h(t,\tau)$, it is convenient to transform the signal into frequency domain $H(t,f)$. This allows us to operate over the signal in the domain, where breathing is localized most compactly due to its periodicity, although breathing is still spread over a certain range in propagation time (see figure 5). From the point of view of detection theory, the absolute value of $H(t,f)$ computed via FFT is the optimal statistics for detecting the sine component with frequency f and uniformly distributed phase appearing at the distance, corresponding to propagation time t. Besides, phase of $H(t,f)$ is also important for the target signature enhancement (see next chapter). In practice, (t,f) is the most convenient domain both for signal enhancement and for final decision about whether the person is present.

Experiments prove that for considerable time interval signal from breathing person can be approximated by sine quite precisely. However, sine is not perfect and some part of energy is spread over the bandwidth and besides, the frequency of breathing can change with the observation time going. One example when breathing is not detected via FFT due to its non-stationarity is given in figure 7.

In order to get more consistent estimate of quasi-periodical breathing response we used method similar to well-known Welch technique (given below). The main difference of our approach from this classical method is that we do not average periodograms of data segments. Instead, we use FFTs of each segment for calculating estimates via cross-correlation method described in the next part and then average results. Another important aspect is the size of segments for computing FFT. Our chose is to use one--two minute-segments: this is close to the time of data acquisition for breathing detection as a periodical signal via FFT given in literature. Of course, nobody can say in advance how breathing signal of particular person will change over time, but this value seems to produce good results in our measurements (figure 7).

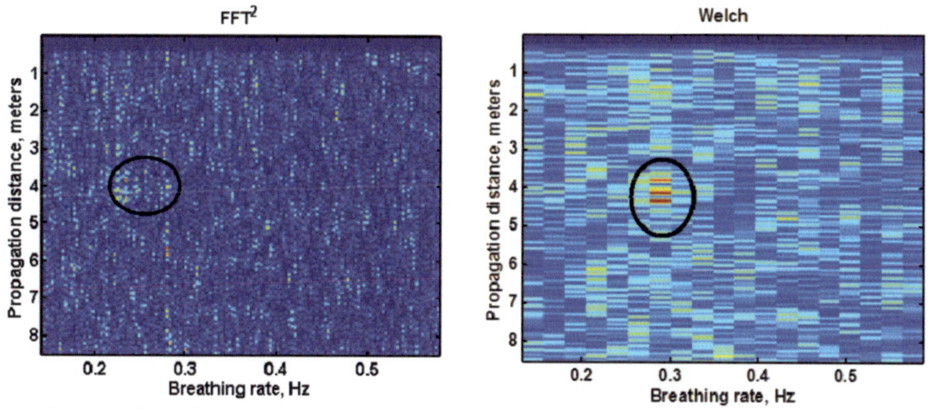

Fig. 7. Person breathing about 1 meter deep beneath moist rubble as detected by two methods.

Welch algorithm:

1. Each signal $h(t_i, \tau)$ is divided into the number of overlapping signals.
2. Periodogram of each segment is calculated as $S_{i,k}(e^{j\omega}) = \frac{1}{n}\left|\sum_{l=1}^{n} w_l h(t_i, \tau_l) e^{-j\omega l}\right| / \frac{1}{n}\sum_{l=1}^{n}|w_l|$, where n is length of the segment and k is its number, w is a windowing function.
3. The set of periodograms is averaged over k in order to calculate PSD estimate $S_{WELCH}(e^{j\omega})$

3.2 Enhancement of useful signal in the propagation time direction

As it was mentioned above, any motion caused by breathing arrives at several neighbouring instants in propagation time. However, backscattered waveform is not known a priori, since it depends on antennas, the size of the body during breathing, body position, rubble thickness, structure and its dielectric properties.

Similarity between two signals can be measured by means of cross-correlation. Thus, since both coherence and energy of signals increases this measure, cross-correlation can be used for breathing detection in a way, described below.

In slow-time direction cross-correlation of two datasets with different fast time t_λ indices at frequencies f_k is easily calculated in (t, f) domain:

$$R_{i,j,k} = real(H(t_i, f_k) H^*(t_j, f_k)) \qquad (3)$$

For the given absolute values of $H(t_i, f_k)$ and $H(t_j, f_k)$, absolute value of $R_{i,j,k}$ is maximal when the phase-shift between periodicals, represented by $H(t_i, f_k)$ and $H(t_j, f_k)$ is either zero or π (that is, periodicals are either in phase or maximum of the first periodical corresponds to the minimum of the second one). These two kinds of phase-shifts exist between breathing-related signal of two distinct types (see figure 5). Breathing response can be enhanced by averaging k maximal absolute values of cross-correlation terms within the n consecutive cells in the direction of propagation time.

4. Non-stationary clutter reduction

Electromagnetic waves are radiated by UWB antennas in all directions. Of course, most of the energy is directed towards rubble heap under investigation, but given the weakness of useful signal due to the rubble attenuation reflections from non-stationary background can hamper detection of breathing victims significantly. In general, this is valid for any scenario where moving objects are present in the vicinity of antennas (distance of few meters in our case). Typical sources of non-stationary clutter are: trees and shrubs or metallic rebars when the weather is windy; people passing by the place of operation, trucks working in the area.

Fig. 8. Sources of non-stationary clutter at measurement place

Evidently, some steps can be carried out to prevent clutter from handicapping the measured data by removing all its sources from the area, but this requires significant time and manpower. Besides, some measures can be taken with using metal covering and absorbing materials in order to alleviate the problem. This helps to a certain extent, but none absorber is ideal and the lower the frequency we are working with the more it is difficult to shield it, especially given that as such system should be mobile and easy to handle. That is, the problem of reducing the non-stationary clutter with appropriate software methods had to be addressed. The problem of clutter removal is complex from algorithmic point of view because there is not much a priori information about it which could serve as a basis for solution. Clutter can overlap with breathing signature in distance, appearing in the same frequency range. The problem is similar to characterizing moving environment for video cameras and in both these problems there seems to be no ideal solution and diverse algorithms are being developed in this field. Further in this chapter we consider two strategies we used to solve the problem and ideas behind them.

4.1 Signal-Clutter separation with Principal component analysis (PCA)

Principal component analysis (PCA) is a data processing tool, frequently used in image processing, data compressing and data visualization. PCA reveals the orthogonal basis of vectors (principal components) with a specific property, that projection of original observations on the first principal component contains the largest variance possible (first vector is chosen in such a way, that the variance in the projection is maximal). The most popular task for using PCA is dimensionality reduction in a data set by retaining those characteristics of the dataset that contribute most to its variance, by keeping lower-order principal components and ignoring higher-order ones.

Mathematically, the basic operation for computing PCA is singular value decomposition (SVD) of the data matrix:

$$H = UDT^{T} = \sum_{i=1}^{N} u_i D_{i,j} v_i^T \qquad (4),$$

where $V = [v_1, v_2, ..., v_N]$ and $U = [u_1, u_2, ..., u_N]$. SVD calculates N uncorrelated sequences, PCs $y_i = D_{i,i} v_i$. D is a diagonal matrix of singular values, and $D_{i,i}$ decrease for larger i. Both PCs y_i and eigenvectors u_i often have simple graphical interpretation, depending on the nature of input data. For instance, in GPR data first PCs often represent clutter component, since largest variance in observations comes from the ground return which is slightly different for the data acquired at different points. In this case, there are strong peaks in first y_i at the distance of ground return and first y_i shows how ground return changes with the position of measurement.

With respect to our problem we can expect that after applying SVD to $h(t,\tau)$ breathing will be confined to different PCs than clutter, since breathing and clutter are uncorrelated types of motion. Notably, this is the only a priori assumption about the measured data used in this method. Further processing is reduced to projecting the measured data onto selected

PCs y_i that contribute significant portion of energy into measured dataset and making decision, whether some of them represent breathing (this decision can be made on periodicity of useful signal). In case only noise is present in the measured data (no non-stationary clutter) ideally breathing should be confined to the PC responsible for largest variance y_1. In the cluttered media first few PCs typically represent clutter, which is stronger then attenuated breathing signature.

In practice, PCA yields remarkable separation between signal and clutter for many scenarios. However, the more frequently clutter motion arises in the data, the less it seems to be 'uncorrelated' with breathing and the worse they are separated.

4.2 Estimating the clutter from low-frequency variation

As it was mentioned before, we can assume that breathing signal cannot have rate less then certain value (we use $f_l = 0.2$ Hz). On another hand, in practice we do not have clutter sources fluctuating so fast that data content with rates slower then f_l is not disturbed, any response from walking person or wavering plants has strong low-frequency component. Based on this a priori assumption following simple algorithm for clutter cancellation can be used:

1. Two datasets are calculated: $h_{fast}(t,\tau)$ and $h_{slow}(t,\tau)$ from original $h(t,\tau)$ by means of high-pass filtering and low-pass filtering accordingly. Cut-off frequency equals f_l
2. If at certain instant $h_{slow}(t_i,\tau_j) > k\sigma_{slow}$, then $h_{fast}(t_i,\tau_j)$ is considered to be cluttered and it is cancelled. σ_{slow} is a standard deviation of $h_{slow}(t,\tau)$ measured in clutter-free environment. Typical value for k is in the range 3–3.5. That is, the clutter is detected when in $h_{slow}(t,\tau)$ we receive value which is unlikely to be generated by noise.

Obvious advantage of this algorithm is that separation of clutter from useful data is not blind, since clutter is detected in $h_{slow}(t,\tau)$ where breathing signal cannot appear.

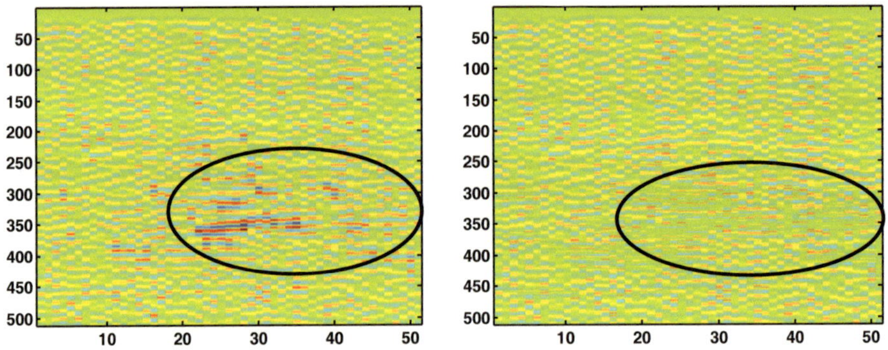

Fig. 9. $h_{fast}(t,\tau)$ before and after clutter cancellation Few results for clutter cancellation are shown below.

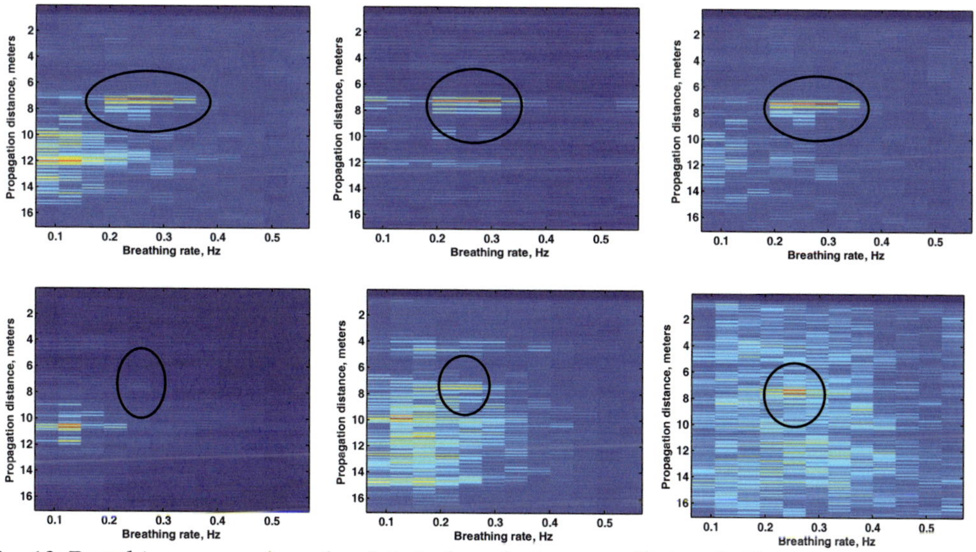

Fig. 10. Breathing person in radar data before clutter cancellation (left), after processing with PCA (the number of components to represent breathing s chosen as a best feat by operator) and after clutter cancellation from low-frequency variation (right) for two different scenarios

However, it should be noted that although both algorithms described are functional, there are much more strategies possible due to the complexity of the problem.

5. Localization of breathing person

Localization of breathing person is the final stage of data processing applied to the problem under discussion. This stage incorporates most of the added value of system in total, since while there are multiple methods for detecting trapped victims (search dogs is probably most successful one), finding out the position of person is much more difficult with present techniques.

With one transmitter, number of receiving antennas necessary to localize a person is three. However, it is convenient to consider main aspects of the problem for 2d space, two receiving antennas as it is shown in figure 11 and then extend it to 3d and three receivers. Antenna configuration shown in figure 11 reflects antenna system of radar prototype created in RADIOTECT project and most of the data was collected with person right beneath the antennas. For 3d localization additional measurement with relocating receiving antenna from initial position was carried out.

In radar response electromagnetic waves reflected from different points in space arrive at different moments in fast time, which is related to distance passed by waves. We consider rubble as a homogeneous media, since no information about its internal structure is available. Although in our experiments on real rubble no significant effects of its heterogeneity spoiled localization results, this is likely to limit system performance for some scenarios. In homogeneous media distance passed by electromagnetic waves between transmitter, i -th receiver and reflected from some object equals

$$l_i = \frac{ct}{\sqrt{\varepsilon}} \tag{5}$$

Set of possible Cartesian coordinates for an object appearing in radar at such distance for scenario in figure 11 is given by following equations:

$$l_1 = \sqrt{x^2 + y^2} + \sqrt{(x-d)^2 + y^2} \tag{6}$$

$$l_2 = \sqrt{x^2 + y^2} + \sqrt{(x+d)^2 + y^2} \tag{7}$$

Each equation describes elliptical curve around antennas different for each point in radar response. When we find a point beneath antennas where two ellipses corresponding to one object cross, we estimate position of this object via calculating Time of Arrival (TOA) of electromagnetic waves.

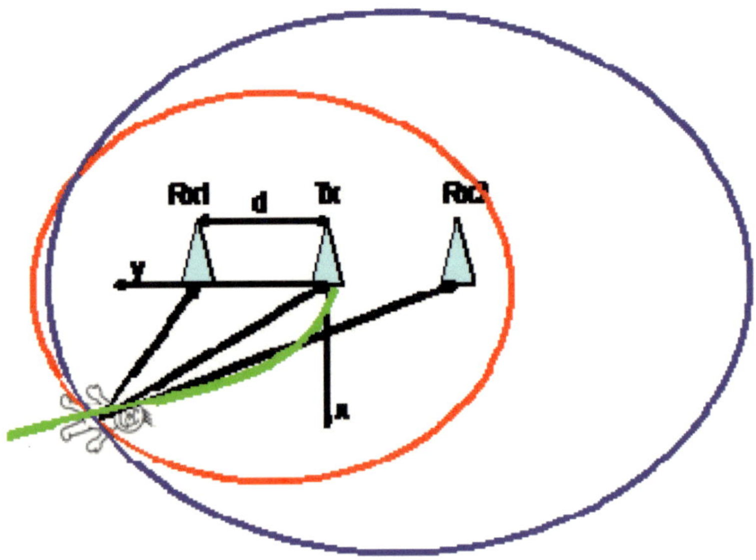

Fig. 11. Localization principle

Another possible way is to calculate Time Difference of Arrival (TDOA) of the object response in two receiving channels via

$$l_{1,2} = \sqrt{(x+d)^2 + y^2} - \sqrt{(x-d)^2 + y^2} \tag{8}$$

It can be seen in figure 12 that there is certain shift of breathing response in one channel relative to the second one in fast time. For each such shift there is a hyperbolic curve in the space (shown green in figure 11), representing all possible points where reflecting object can be situated. Equation (8) determines this hyperbola. Finally, for given antenna configuration it is possible to calculate position of the object using combined TOA/TDOA estimate (finding crossing of ellipse and hyperbola). In this case, for calculating the size of this shift maximizing the average cross correlation (as in 3.2) from dataset composed of both receiving channels with respect to size of the shift was carried out. Often using combined TOA/TDOA estimate gives less angular error in localization rather then pure TOA (it can be seen in figure 13 that crossing of ellipse and hyperbola is less blurred around the antennas). Another interesting point in figure 12 is that waveforms associated with breathing look pretty different for two identical receiving antennas even though they are not separated by rubble heap from breathing person.

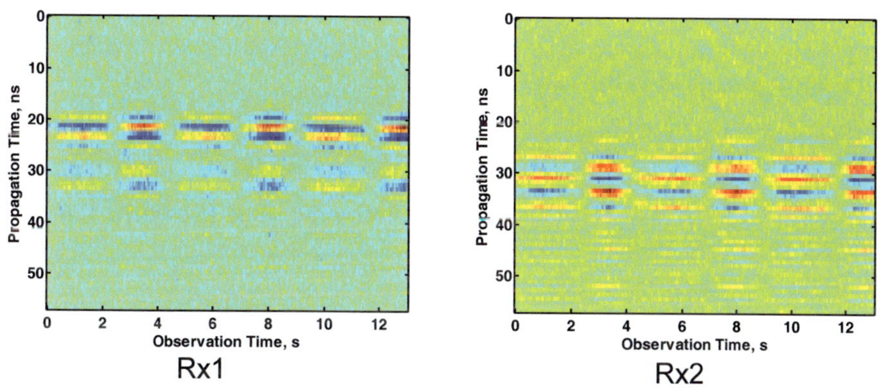

Fig. 12. Breathing person as seen by 2 radar receivers.

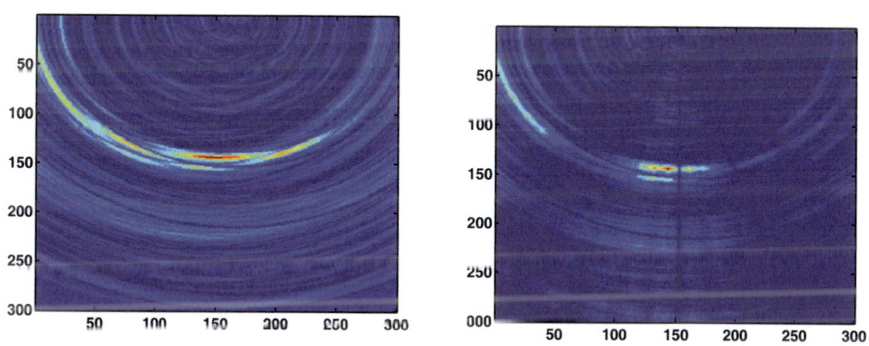

Fig. 13. Object seen by radar localized via TOA method (left) and combined TOA/TDOA approach (right)

Finally, algorithm used localization of breathing person is described below:

1. Detecting breathing signature and its rate in input data $H(t,f)$ by average cross-correlation method. For both receiving channels vectors $H(l_i, f_j)$ are calculated.

2. Calculating "geometry" matrices, containing possible distances were breathing person can be situated. Matrices contain all possible distances correspondent to TOA and TDOA estimates.

3. Interpolation of each $H(l_i, f_j)$ and their local average cross-correlations onto appropriate 2d "geometry" matrix and addition (multiplication) of the results to receive image $I(x, y)$.

For 3d localization and three receiving antennas almost identical approach was used with TOA estimates. The only modification is extension of "geometry" matrices to 3d.

Algorithm has following limitations:

- Heterogeneity of rubble can cause serious mistakes in some scenarios
- Imprecise value of ε for rubble material under real conditions can cause some error in localization.
- In the case of two or more victims if they are situated at almost identical distances to antennas ghost target can appear (this happens because ellipses related to different victims cross). However, all victims in this case will be shown.

6. Experimental results

In this part measurement results are summarized excluding those presented above in order to clarify some aspects of signal processing.

6.1 Breathing detection in intact building

Any can assume that after building is collapsed in some places thickness of ruins to penetrate will be less then in other locations. However, in average detection capacity is expected to be better in collapsed building, since due to the smaller distance between antennas and person propagation losses decrease. In figure 14 breathing person is detected as a yellow spot through three floors of intact building.

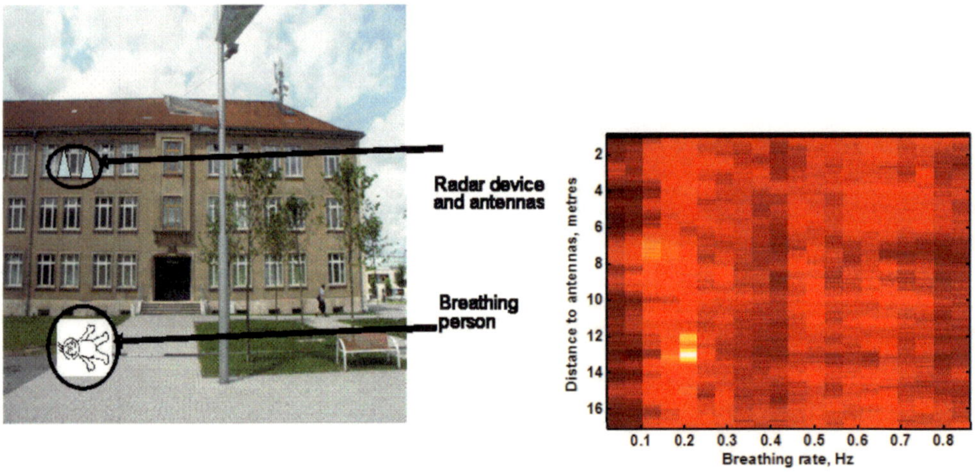

Fig. 14. Detection of breathing person in intact building. Person was lying on the floor in the basement, while radar device and antennas were on the second floor

6.2 Breathing detection through the heap of rubble

Most of other measurements were carried out on the pile of diverse rubble (mainly composed of reinforced concrete). During measurements campaign thickness of rubble was increased from 1.2--1.3 up to 1.6—1.7 meters, which depth (as it can be seen in figures below) produced result on the limit of our detecting capabilities. Detection through 1.2—1.3 meters is evident (although as it can be seen some positions and people produce better result then others). Besides, tests with multiple persons (up to three) were carried out.
Detection methods described above are online and they were implemented inside GUI, operating the radar device. Thus, all experimental results in this part represent screenshots taken from the measurement software immediately at the test area. Breathing is detected as a bright point in the left part of the screen which shows data in (t, f)-domain. Right part of the screen represents preprocessed data in (t, f) and can be used for detecting strong motion.

Fig. 15. Detection area

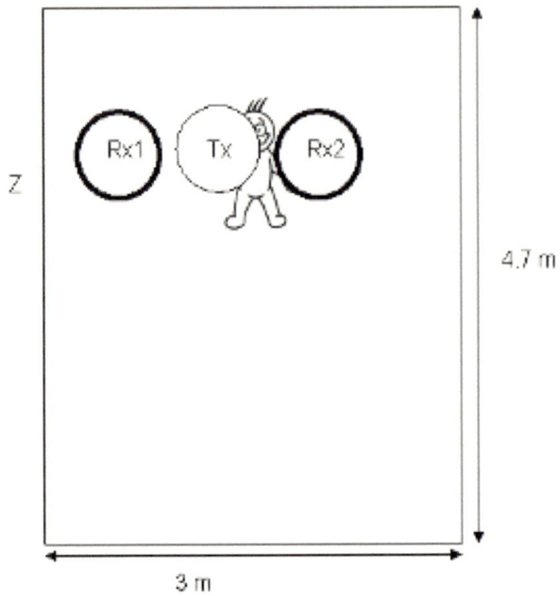

Fig. 16. Scenario for establishing penetration capabilities of the radar, view from above

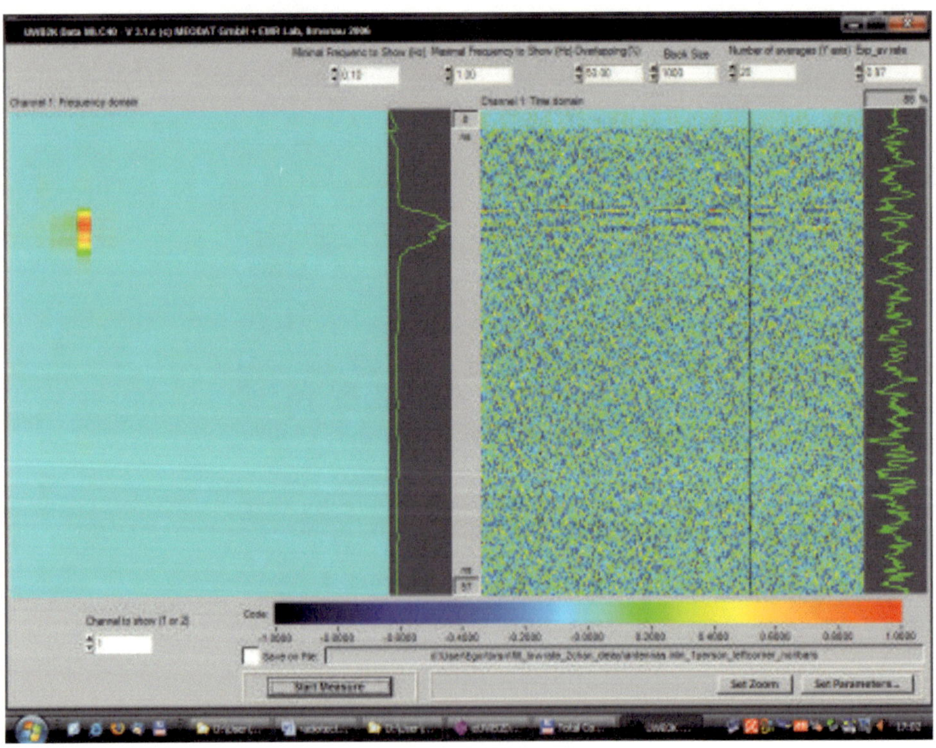

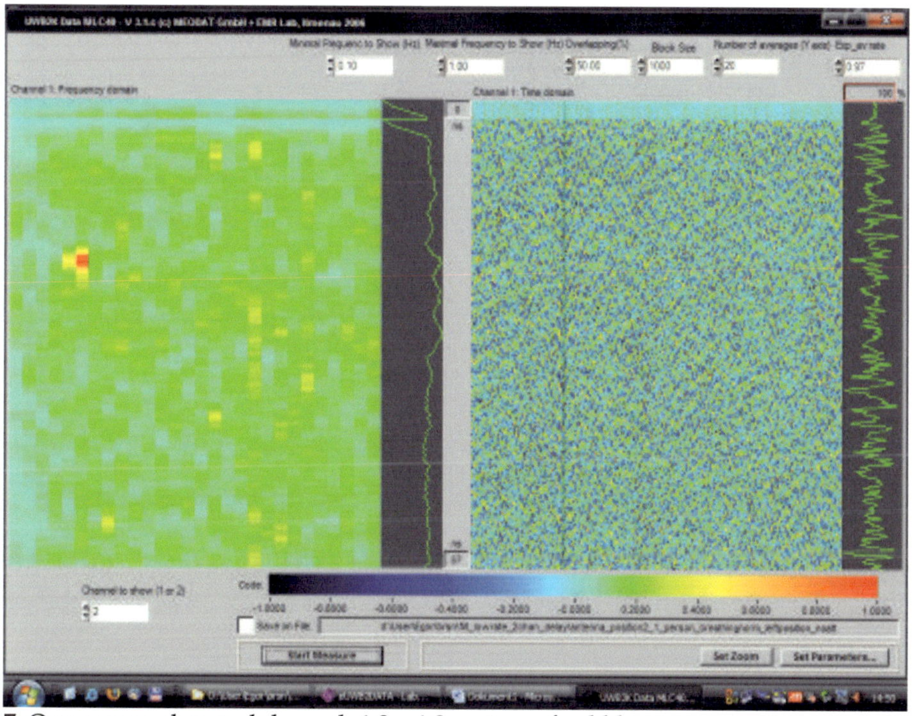

Fig. 17. One person detected through 1.2 – 1.3 meters of rubble

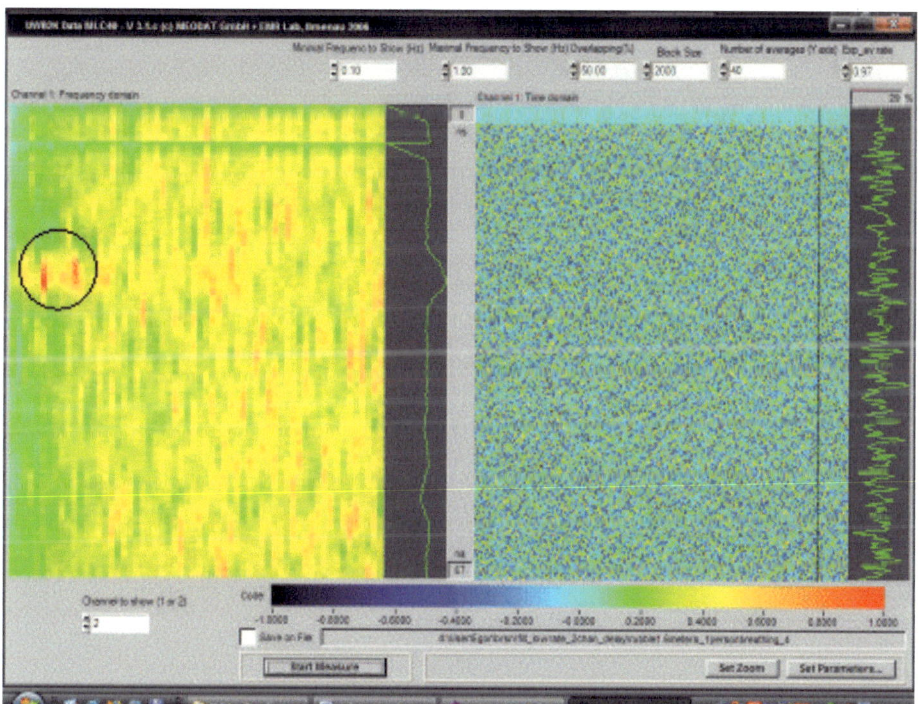

Fig. 18. One person detected through 1.6 – 1.7 meters of rubble

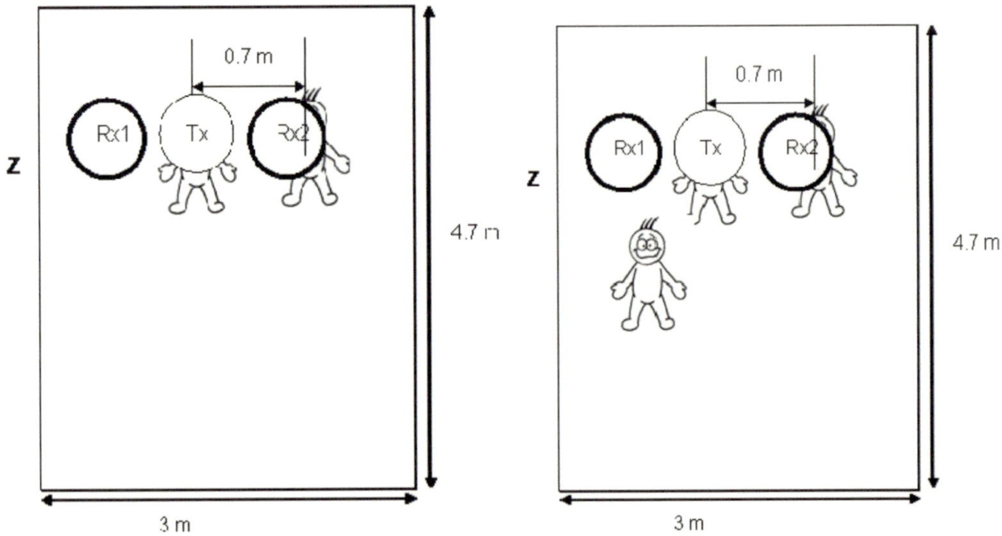

Fig. 19. Detection of multiple people through rubble pile, view from above. Identical positions as in scenario with two persons were used for 2d localization in the next chapter.

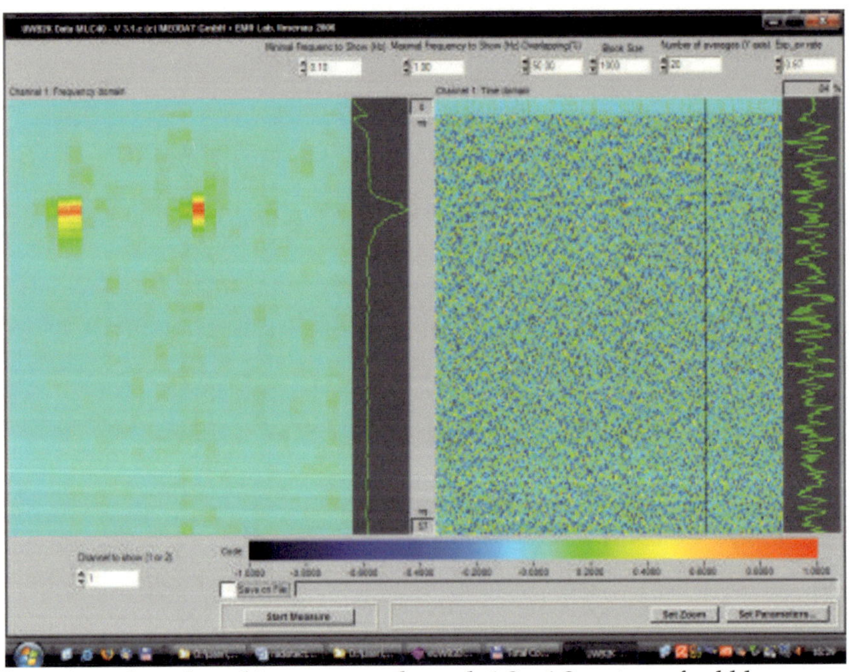

Fig. 20. Detection of two breathing persons through 1.2—1.3 meters of rubble

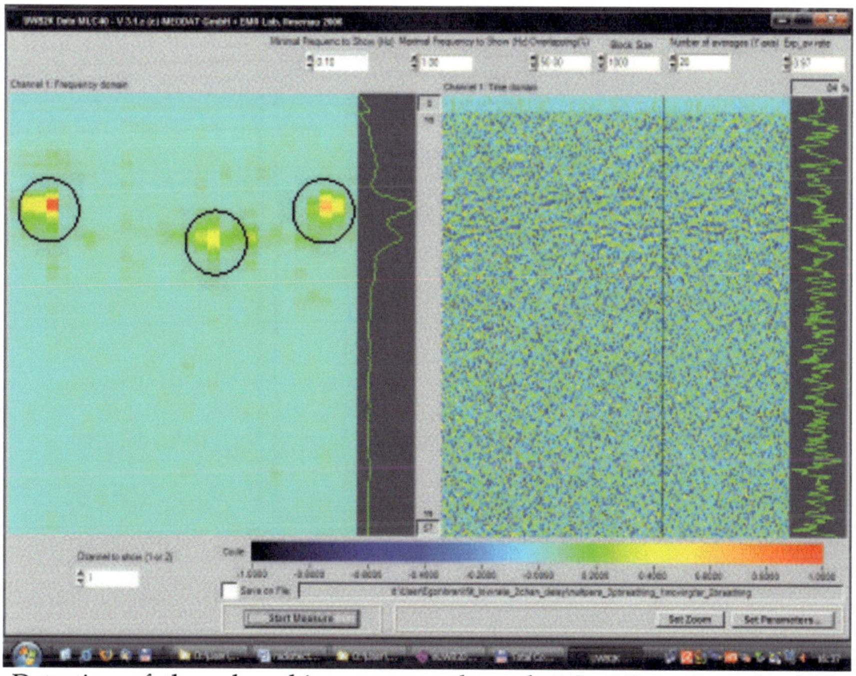

Fig. 21. Detection of three breathing persons through 1.2—1.3 meters of rubble. Person outside the plane containing antennas and other people is moving strongly with his hands.

6.3 Victim localization

Data collection for localization of victims was accomplished at the same heap of rubble as in the previous chapter. Two types of localization were successfully applied to measured data: 2d localization when person is situated in the same plane as three antennas with combined TOA/TDOA method and 3d localization of person with TOA when additional measurement after relocating antenna was carries out.

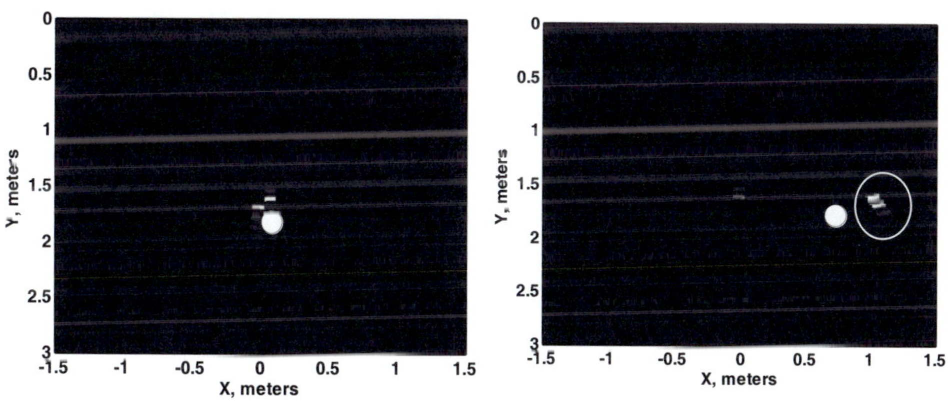

Fig. 22. Detection and 2d localization of two persons breathing at different positions one after another (positions of persons and antennas are shown in figure 19). Pictures here represent vertical plane containing antennas and person. Zero of each axis corresponds to the centre of transmitting antenna. Actual positions of victims are shown as white circles.

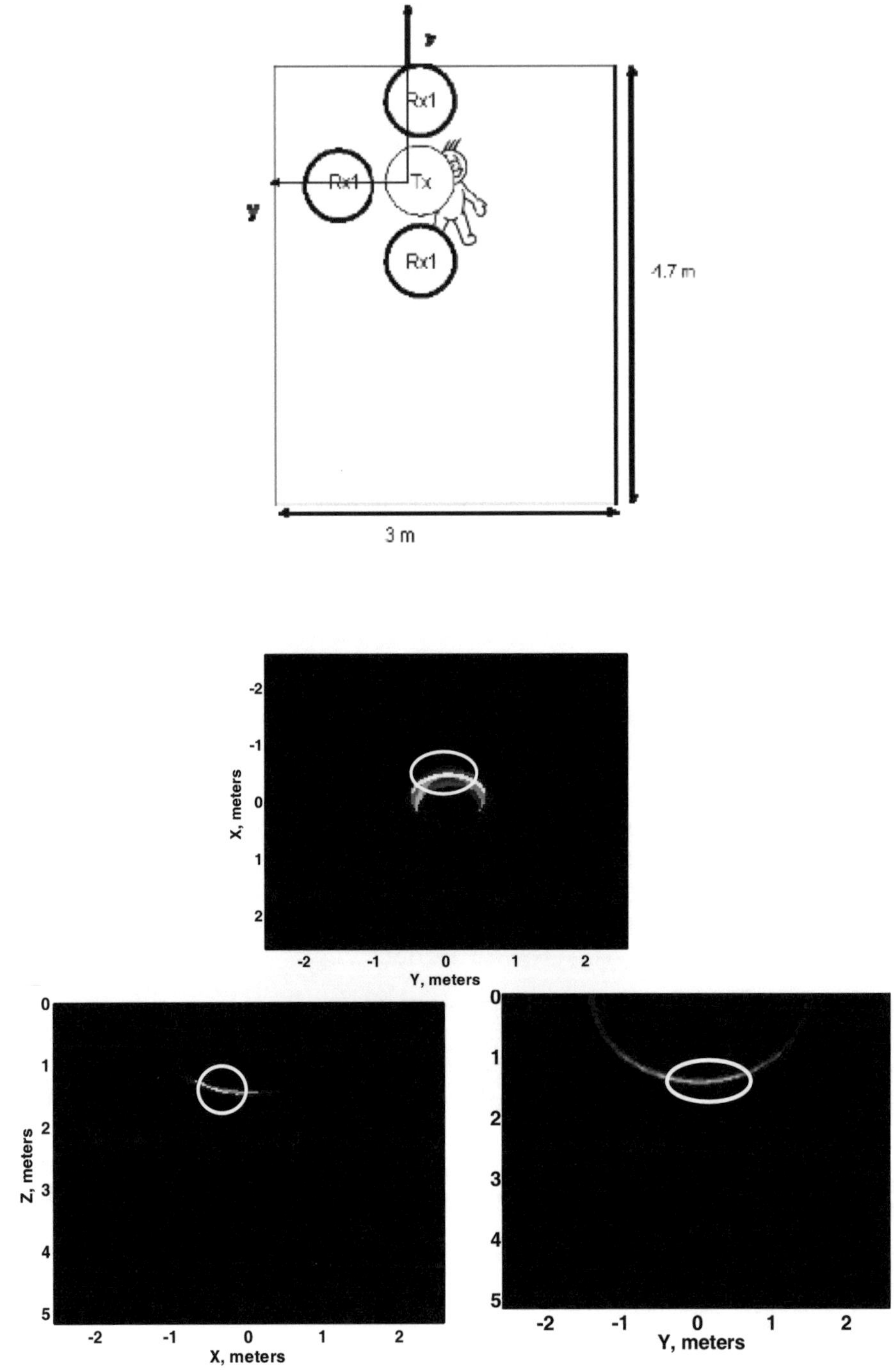

Fig. 23. Detection and 3d localization of breathing person. Breathing is detected as maximum in 3d array (marked). Zero of each axis corresponds to the centre of transmitting antenna. Actual position of victim is right beneath transmitting antenna.

7. Conclusions and future work

Finally, we summarize the most important points of this chapter in relation to the possibilities of improving breathing-detecting radar further.

- In general, breathing enhancement is well developed from algorithmic point of view and results are reported in numerous papers. With our hardware and algorithms detection of breathing without any additional motion was possible through the maximum of 1.5–1.6 meters of concrete rubble with reinforcements. Besides, ability to detect multiple victims is also shown. However, important target for future research is development of reliable detecting algorithm that provides information about victim presence automatically without operator.
- The problem of clutter removal is complex from algorithmic point of view because there is not much a priori information about unwanted signals that could serve as a basis for the solution. That is, cutter can overlap with breathing signature in distance, appearing in the same frequency range. Two approaches are demonstrated it this paper, but much more methods can be applied to this problem.
- Open questions in localization are 'ghost targets' as well as rubble heterogeneity. However, the problem of 'ghost targets' is not absolutely critical (it appears only when multiple victims are present at similar distance to antennas, and multiple victims can still be detected together with additional target). Furthermore, when victims have different breathing rates, this information can be used for separating real targets from 'ghosts'. Rubble heterogeneity can possibly be taken into account if some information about rubble structure is available (whether it is received by means of radar or any other method).

8. References

Arai, I. (2001). Survivor search radar system for persons trapped under earthquake rubble, *Proceedings of APMC 2001*, pp 663-668 vol.2, ISBN: 0-7803-7138-0, Taipei, Taiwan, December 2001

Bechtel Special Technologies Laboratory Ground Penetrating Radar (STL GPR) (2003). Operational Test and Evaluation Report of Ground Penetrating Radar for Casualty Location in Rubble, November 2003

BOS - Sondermaschinenbau GmbH. Locate to Live — Save of Live (Bioradar BR402)

Chernyak, V. (2006). Signal Processing in Multisite UWB Radar Devices for Searching Survivors in Rubble, *Proceedings of EuRAD 2006*, pp. 190 - 193, ISBN: 2-9600551-7-9, Manchester, September 2006

Geophysical Survey Systems, Inc. (2005). Technical Note 103: Using the SIR-3000 as a Breathing Detector with the "Breathe" Setup, February 2005

Levitas, B. & Matuzas, J. (2006). UWB Radar for Human Being Detection Behind the Wall, *Proceedings of IRS 2006*, pp. 1 - 3, ISBN: 978-83-7207-621-2, Krakow, Poland, May 2006

Levitas, B. Matuzas, J. & Drozdov, M. (2008). Detection and separation of several human beings behind the wall with UWB Radar, *Proceedings of IRS 2008*, pp. 1 - 4, ISBN: 978-83-7207-757-8, Wroclaw, Poland, May 2008

Narayanan, R.M. (2008). Through wall radar imaging using UWB noise waveforms, *Proceedings of ICASSP 2008*, pp. 5185 - 5188, ISBN: 978-1-4244-1483-3, Las Vegas, NV, April 2008

Ossberger, G.; Buchegger, T.; Schimback, E.; Stelzer, A. & Weigel, R., Non-Invasive Respiratory Movement Detection and Monitoring of Hidden Humans Using Ultra Wideband Pulse Radar, *Proceedings of the International Workshop on Ultrawideband Systems and Technologies*, pp. 395-399, ISBN: 0-7803-8373-7, May 2004

UltraVision Security Systems, Inc. Product Backgrounder: LifeLocator™

Yarovoy, A.G. & Ligthart, L.P. (2007). UWB Radars: Recent Technological Advances and Applications, *Proceedings of Radar Conference, 2007 IEEE*, pp. 43 - 48, ISBN: 1-4244-0284-0, Boston, MA, April 2007

Zaikov, E.; Sachs, J.; Aftanas, M.; & Rovnakova J. (2008). Detection of trapped people by UWB radar, *German Microwave Conference, GeMiC 2008*, pp 240-243, ISBN: 978-3-8007-3086-5, Hamburg, Germany, March 2008

Zaikov, E.; (2010). UWB radar for detection and localization of trapped people, *Proceedings of 11th International Radar Symposium IRS-2010*, June 16-18, Vilnus, Lithuania, June 2010

15

Design and characterization of microstrip UWB antennas

Djamel ABED[1] and Hocine KIMOUCHE[2]

[1]*Telecommunication Laboratory, University of Guelma*

[2]*Microwave and Radar Laboratory, Military Polytechnic School*

Algeria

1. Introduction

Ultra–WideBand (UWB) technology was approved by the Federal Communications Commission (FCC) in February 2002 (FCC, 2002). According to the FCC regulations, the frequency band from 3.1 to 10.6 GHz can be used for short–range and high speed wireless communications systems. This recent allocation of a very wide spectrum of frequencies for the devices uses, with effective isotropic radiated power (EIRP) less than - 41dBm/MHz has presented numerous exciting opportunities and challenges for antenna designers. UWB antennas should be effective in transmitting, compact, non dispersive, and have a good wide impedance bandwidth properties, these features are desirable for both indoor and outdoor hand–held UWB applications. In practical UWB applications, microstrip antennas that can be directly printed onto printed circuit boards (PCBs) are the most promising candidates. Such a PCB antenna has a low profile, a low manufacturing cost and can easily be integrated with other parts of monolithic microwave integrate circuit (MMIC) for a transceiver or any other UWB system. To satisfy such requirements, various types of planar antennas have been developed for UWB communications over the last few years. Also, several bandwidth enhancement techniques have been reported, to improve the impedance bandwidth of these antennas. Microstrip UWB antennas are usually constructed by etching a radiator onto the dielectric substrate of a piece of the PCB and a partial ground plane onto the opposite side if the antenna is fed by microstrip transmission line or on the same side in the case of coplanar waveguide (CPW) feeding. In the literature, many different microstrip UWB antennas with circular, elliptical, triangular, rectangular, hexagonal, and so on patches are currently being considered for UWB applications.

This chapter presents an overview of UWB antennas design an characterization, some novel designs were investigated and presented. The first class of studied UWB antennas is microstrip monopole antennas including the microstrip/CPW–fed modified – elliptical monopole antennas. The second class is for UWB slot antennas, where a novel stepped inverted cone slot antenna with different stub shapes is proposed for UWB applications. In the third class a notched band UWB antenna is presented; the proposed UWB have been developed to notch–band UWB antenna by inserting a U–shape slot into patch. The advantage of this approach is that the stop–band filter (slot) can directly integrated in antenna structure. The study includes detailed parametric analysis of the antennas performances with relation to the desirable properties for UWB antennas.

2. Microstrip UWB Monopole Antennas

Microstrip UWB monopole antennas are usually constructed by etching the radiator element with a microstrip/CPW feeding structure and the partial ground plane on dielectric substrate. In this section we present two novel microstrip UWB monopole antennas.

Printed Modified Elliptical Monopole (PMEM) Antenna

The printed modified elliptical monopole (PMEM) antenna (Kimouche, 2009) shown in figure 1 is designed to cover the UWB band from 3.1 GHz to 10.6 GHz. The antenna consists of modified−elliptic shaped radiator etched on a top side of PCB (FR4, $\varepsilon_r = 4.32$, loss tang of 0.017 and 1.59 mm in thickness) and fed by 50−Ohms microstrip−line of width $W_f =$ 3 mm. The modified semicircular−shaped ground with a rectangular notch defined by $(W_n \times L_n)$ mm is printed in the bottom side. A parametric study of microstrip−fed PMEM antenna on the main parameters of the patch radiator, and the partial modified−semicircular ground plane (on the back of substrate) has been optimized by using electromagnetic software simulator. The patch radiator connected to the microstrip−line is the result of two identical 1/4 ellipse spaced by a distance d fixed at 3 mm and placed in the part of circular-shaped base. Each 1/4 ellipse is defined by the radius of the major axe R_1 and the radius of the minor axe R_2. The base is define by the height D, the major radius and the minor radius r_1 and r_2, respectively. The minor radius R_2 is fixed by the value of the parameter D. The elliptical ratio (ER) defined by $ER = R_2/R_1$ has been optimized for five values of the parameter D.

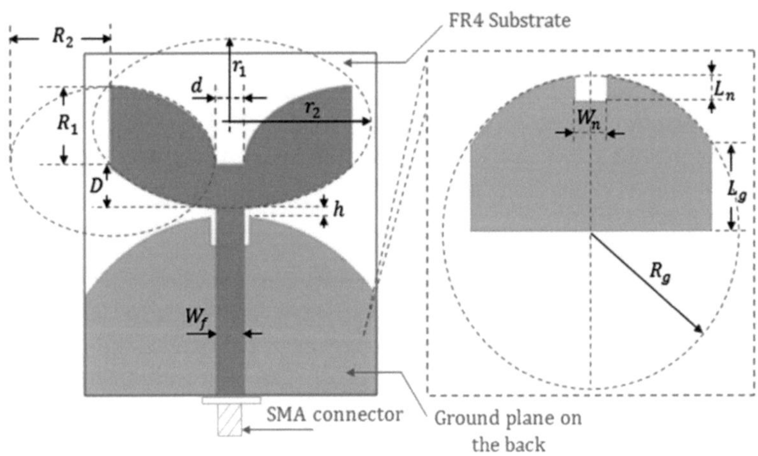

Fig. 1. Geometry of the Microstrip-fed PMEM Antenna

The simulated return losses as function of frequency for the five different values of D and ER are illustrated in figure 2. The optimal values of the patch radiator are found to be $D = 4.45$ mm, $R_1 = 8$ mm, $R_2 = 8.8$ mm, $r_1 = 9.25$ mm, and $r_2 = 11.1$ mm. The effect of the distance h between the modified elliptical patch radiator and the ground plane called feed gap is simulated for return loss as function of frequency. As shown in figure 3, the return loss characteristics for the microstrip−fed PMEM antenna was simulated for different feed gaps ($h = 0.3$, 0.5, 0.7, 1.5, and 3)mm. It is shown that the −10 dB operating bandwidth of the antenna varies remarkably with the variation of the feed gap h, but the return loss

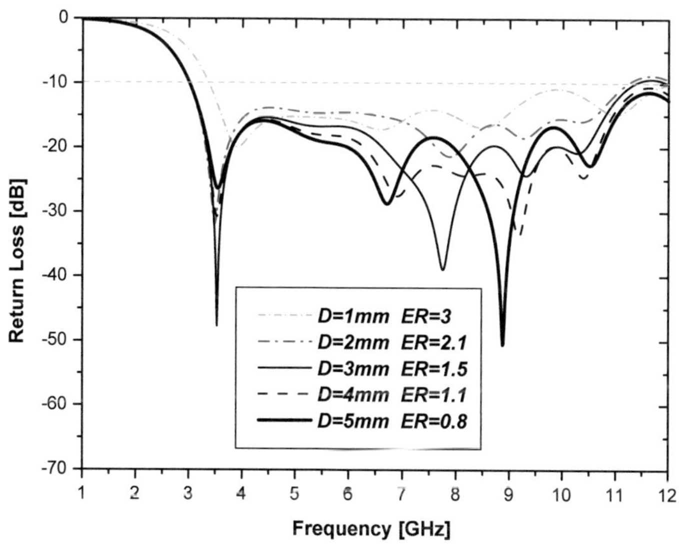

Fig. 2. The Effect of the Parameter *D* and the Elliptical Ratio *ER*

curves have similar shapes for the different feed gaps. The optimal feed gap is found to be at $h = 0.3$ mm. The shape of the ground plane is chosen to be a modified semi−circular with a rectangular notch. The ground plane size is defined by the radius R_g and the length L_g. Figure 4 shows the simulated return loss curves with the optimal values $h = 0.3$ mm and the previous optimal patch radiator parameters for different radius values R_g. It can be seen that the variation of the ground plane width shifts all the resonance modes across the spectrum. We noticed that the lower−edge frequency will decrease when the radius R_g increase. Also, it is clear that most of the values of R_g can achieve an ultra−wideband, for example the value $R_g = 20$ mm achieve a bandwidth of 13.34 GHz (2.85 − 16.19 GHz).
Also, it is seen that the antenna bandwidth is sensitive to the variation of the parameter L_g. Figure 5 illustrates the return loss for different values of L_g. The optimized value was found to be $L_g = 10.5$ mm.
The notch introduced in the ground plane is used to miniaturize the proposed microstrip−fed PMEM antenna and to improve its impedance matching. This technique is introduced in (Bao, 2007) to improve the impedance bandwidth of rectangular patch antenna and in (Kobayashi, 2007) to compact circular disc antenna. Figure 6 illustrates the simulated return loss curves of the proposed microstrip−fed PMEM antenna with and without the rectangular notch in the ground plane. It is observed that the ground plane with an optimal rectangular notch of (3.5×3)mm improves significantly the impedance bandwidth and creates other resonant frequencies.

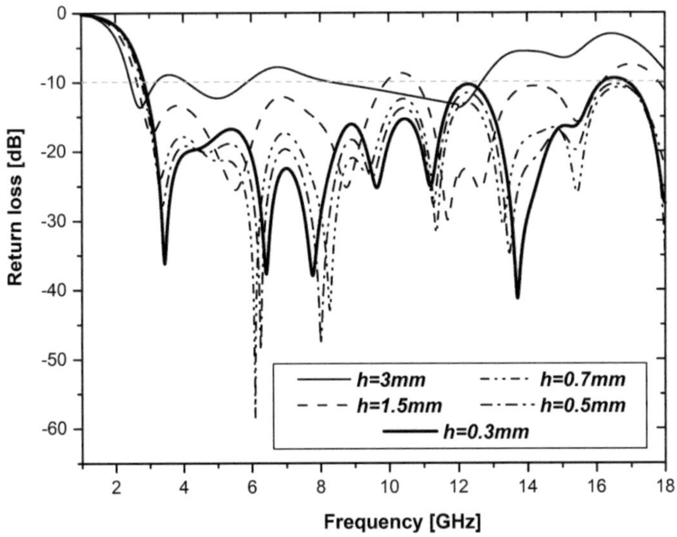

Fig. 3. The Effect of the Feed Gap *h* of the Microstrip-fed PMEM Antenna

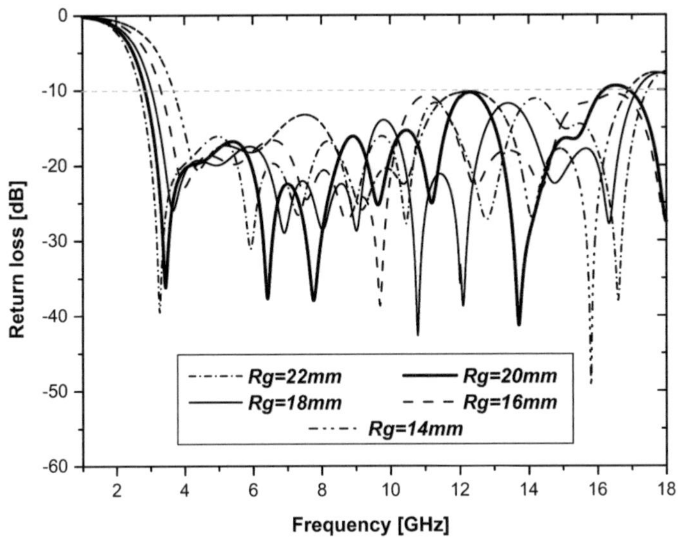

Fig. 4. The Effect of the Radius *Rg* of the Microstrip-fed PMEM Antenna

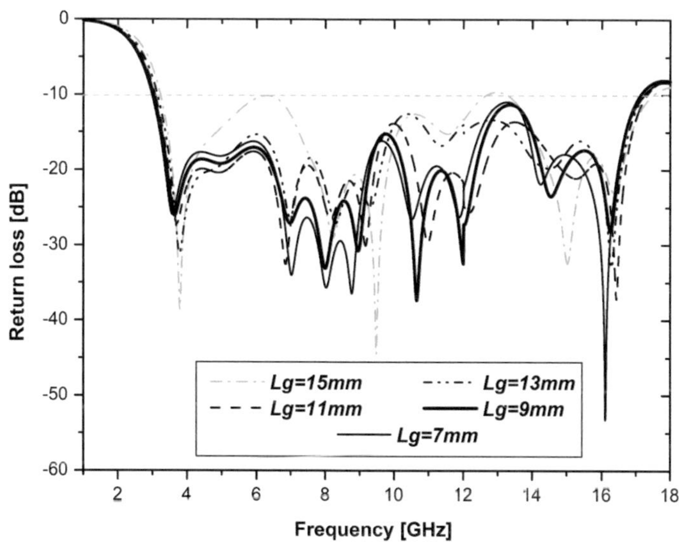

Fig. 5. The Effect of the Parameter *Lg* of the Microstrip-fed PMEM Antenna

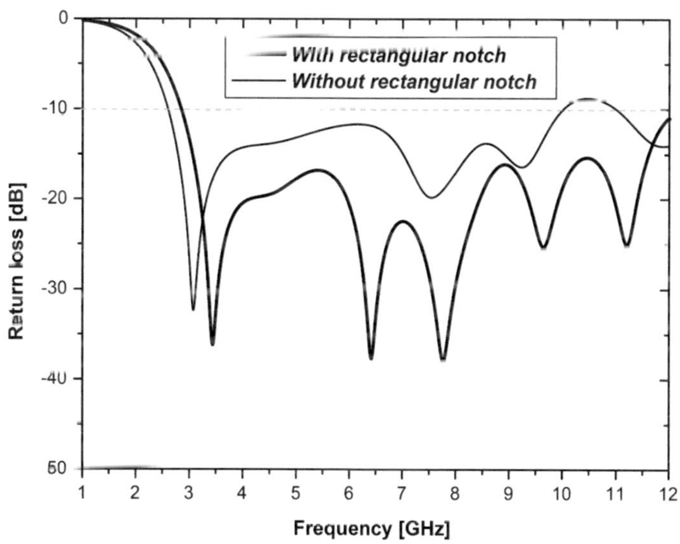

Fig. 6. The Effect of the Rectangular Notch in the Groundplane of the Microstrip-fed PMEM Antenna

A prototype of the microstrip−fed PMEM antenna with optimal design, i.e. $h = 0.3$mm, $D = 4.45$mm, $R_1 = 8$mm , $R_2 = 8.8$mm, $r_1 = 9.25$mm, $r_2 = 11.1$mm, $d = 3$mm, $R_g = 20$mm, and $L_g = 10.5$mm, was fabricated and tested. Figures (7.*a*) and (7.*b*) present photographs of top side and bottom side of microstrip−fed PMEM antenna, respectively.

(a)

(b)

Fig. 7. Photographs of the Microstrip-fed PMEM Antenna. *(a) Top Side, (b) Back Side*

A Comparison between simulated return loss and measured return loss obtained by using an Agilent HP 8719ES vector network analyzer (VNA) is shown in figure 8. It is shown that the measured bandwidth of the proposed microstrip−fed antenna covers the FCC commercial UWB band with a fractional bandwidth of 113%.

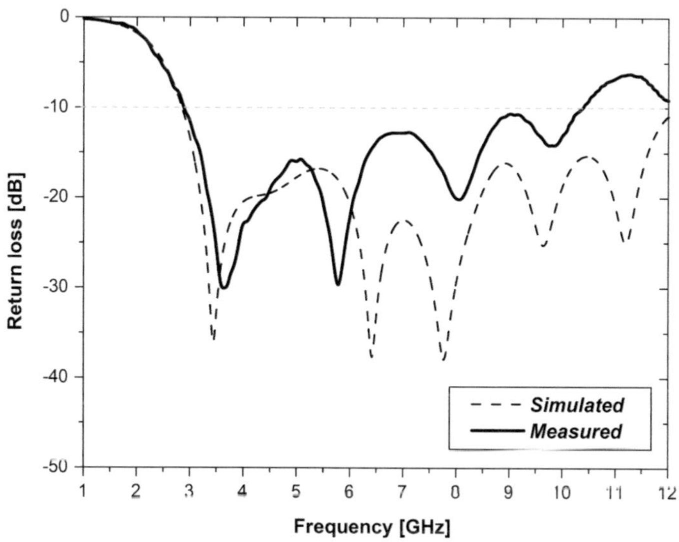

Fig. 8. Comparison between Simulated and Measured Return Loss Curves of the Microstrip-fed PMEM Antenna

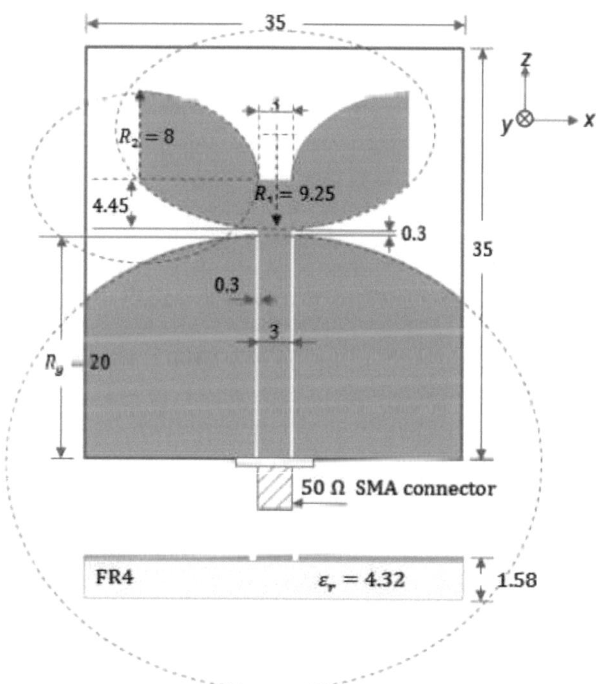

Fig. 9. Geometry of the Proposed CPW-fed PMEM Antenna

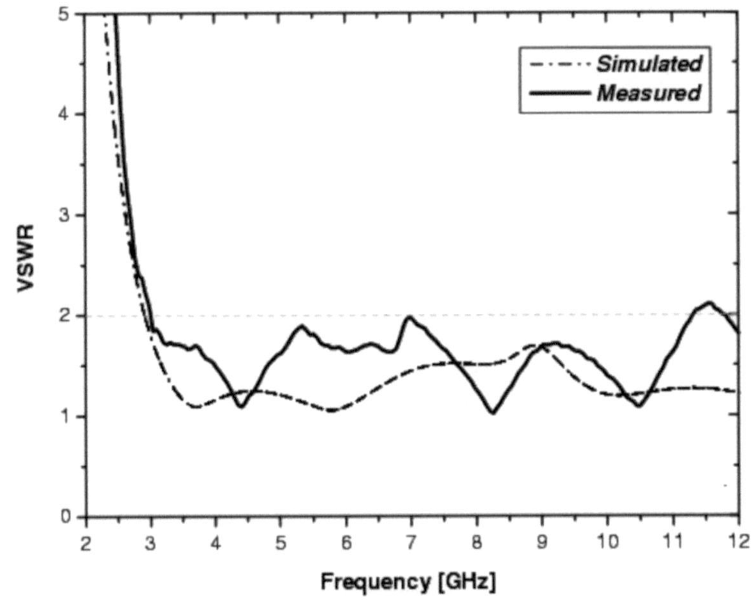

Fig. 10. Comparison between Simulated and Measured VSWR Curves of the CPW-fed PMEM Antenna

The previous proposed PMEM antenna can also fed by coplanar waveguide (CPW), in view of UWB applications. Figure 9 illustrates the configuration of the proposed CPW−fed PMEM antenna (Abed, 2008) with the optimal parameters, where an FR4 substrate with relative permittivity of 4.32 and thickness of 1.58mm is used.

The CPW−fed PMEM antenna with the optimal geometrical parameters was fabricated. Measured and simulated VSWR (Voltage Standing Wave Ratio) are shown in figure 10. The measured bandwidth defined by VSWR$\leq$ 2 of the proposed antenna with a feed gap of 0.3mm is from 3GHz to 11.3GHz, which covers the entire UWB band.

The far−field ($2D$) radiation patterns for the proposed CPW−PMEM antenna are also carried out at three frequencies. Figures ($11.a$) and ($11.b$) show the radiation pattern at azimuthal and elevation planes, respectively. As it can be seen from the figures, omnidirectional patterns can be observed for the $H-$plane. These patterns are comparable to those reported for a conventional dipole antenna. It is very important to note that at the higher frequency there is an obvious deviation from the omnidirectional shape in the $H-$plane radiation patterns. Also, the $E-$plane patterns have large back lobes at low frequency and with increasing frequency they become smaller, splitting into many minor ones. For the antenna gain, it is found that the proposed microstrip−fed PMEM antenna has a simulated maximum gain which varies between 0.18 dBi and 3.61 dBi within the UWB band.

By comparison with the microstrip−fed PMEM antenna, the CPW−fed PMEM antenna presents a less gain inside the UWB band with a peak gain of 2.98 dBi at the frequency 5.6 GHz.

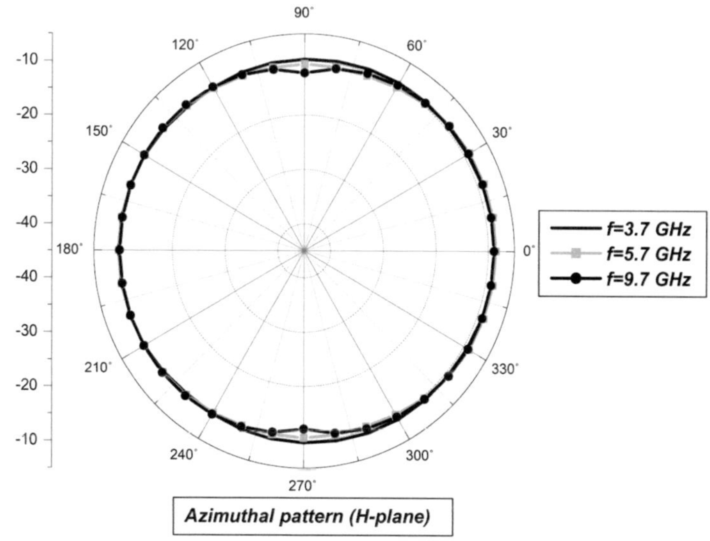

(a)

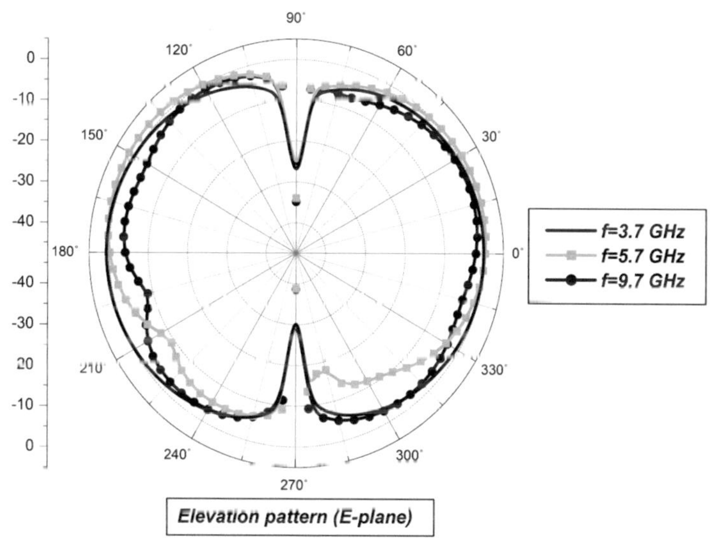

(b)

Fig. 11. Radiation Pattern of the CPW-fed PMEM Antenna. *(a) Azimuthal Pattern (H-plane)*, *(b) Elevation Pattern (E-plane)*

3. Microstrip Slot UWB Antennas

Various printed slot antenna configurations such as rectangle (Jang, 2000), (Chiou, 2003), (Chen, 2003) and (Liu, 2004), triangle (Chen, 2004) and (Chen, 2003), circle (Soliman, 1999) and (Sze, 2006), arc−shape (Chen, 2005), annular−ring (Chen, 2000) and others are proposed for narrowband and wideband application. In (Lee, 2002), a round corner rectangular wide slot antenna which is etched on a substrate with dimension of (68×50)mm, the measure -10dB bandwidth can achieve 6.17GHz (2.08GHz to 8.25GHz). In (Chen, 2003), a CPW square slot antenna feed with a widened tuning stub can yield a wide impedance bandwidth of 60%. The antenna has a dimension of (72×72)mm and its gain ranges from 3.75dBi to 4.88dBi within the operational band. It is shown that the achieved bandwidths of these antennas cannot cover the whole FCC defined UWB frequency band from 3.1 GHz to 10.6GHz. However, only a few microstrip / CPW−fed slot antennas with features suitable for UWB applications have been demonstrated in the literature. In (Chair, 2004), a CPW−fed rectangular slot antenna with a U−shaped tuning stub can provide a bandwidth of 110% with gain varying from 1.9dBi to 5.1dBi. Nevertheless, the antenna size is big (100×100)mm. The same for (Angelopoulos, 2006), where a microstrip−fed circular slot can operate over the entire UWB band, but with a slot diameter of 65.2 mm. In (Denidni, 2006) and (Sorbello, 2005) UWB circular /elliptical CPW−fed slot and microstrip−fed antennas designs targeting the $3.1 - 10.6$GHz band. The antennas are comprised of elliptical or circular stubs that excite similar−shaped slot apertures. The same slots shapes were excited by a U−shaped tuning stub in (Liang, 2006), where an empirical formula is introduced to approximately determine the lower edge of the -10dB operating bandwidth. Others UWB slots antenna are proposed in (Sadat, 2007) and (Cheng, 2007). In this section, the microstrip−fed PSICS antenna configuration is investigated for UWB communications.

Stepped Inverted Cone Slot Antennas

The configuration of the proposed printed stepped inverted cone slot (PSICS) antenna is shown in figure 12. The proposed antenna with different feeding stubs is designed to cover the entire UWB band. The PSICS antenna consists of stepped inverted−cone shaped stub on the top side of (50×52)mm(FR4, $\varepsilon_r = 4.32$, loss tang of 0.017 and $H = 1.59$ mm in thickness) fed by 50−Ohms microstrip−line of width $W_f = 3$mm. The ground plane with the inverted stepped cone slot is printed on the bottom side.

A parametric study of the proposed PSICS UWB antenna on the main parameters of the stepped inverted−cone slot in the ground plane and the feeding stub structure are optimized by using an electromagnetic simulator based on the Method of Moment (MoM).

The effect of the parameters R_s, L_{s1}, L_{s2}, W_{s1}, W_{s2} and W_{s3} which define the inverted−cone shaped slot was carried out. The good frequency bandwidth (2.21GHz − 11.5GHz) was found for a radius $R_s = 20$mm and the optimal values of the parameters L_{s1}, L_{s2}, W_{s1}, W_{s2} and W_{s3}. These values are presented in the table below.

Parameter	L_{s1}	L_{s2}	W_{s1}	W_{s2}	W_{s3}
Optimal value (mm)	2	6	4.5	3.5	21.5

Table 1. Optimal Values of the Stepped Inverted-Cone Slot Parameters

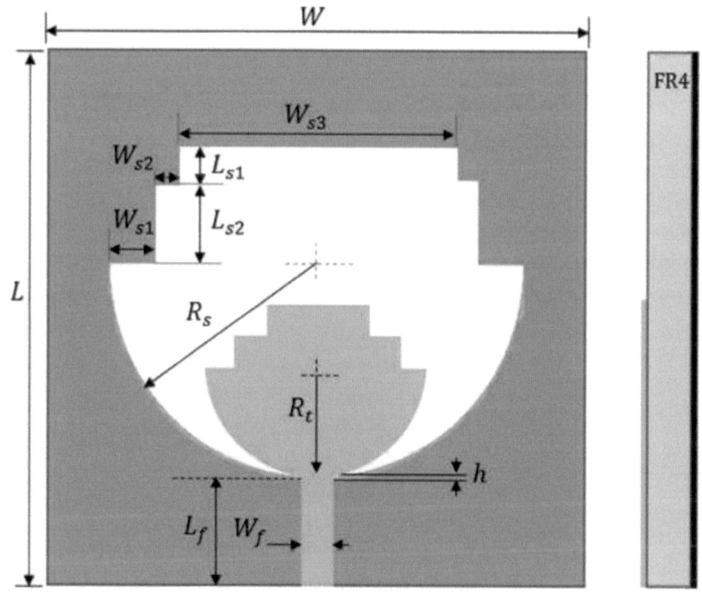

Fig. 12. Geometry of the Microstrip-fed PSICS UWB Antenna

The tuning stub of the PSICS antenna has the same shape as the slot. It is also, defined by the radius R_t and the parameters L_{t1}, L_{t1}, W_{t1}, W_{t2} and W_{t3}, as shown in figure13.

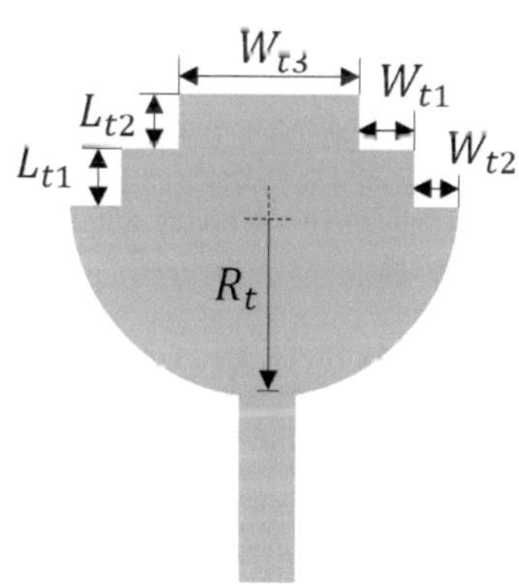

Fig. 13 The Parameters of the Stepped Inverted-Cone Stub

The optimal feed tuning stub radius is found to be at $R_t = 10$mm, with an extremely bandwidth range from 2.21GHz to 11.5 GHz. Also, it seems that when the value of the parameters L_{t1}, L_{t2} and L_{t3} decrease, the first resonance shift to the low frequency but the antenna bandwidth decrease. The optimal values of the stepped–inverted cone stub parameters are presented in the table 2.

Parameter	L_{t1}	L_{t2}	W_{t1}	W_{t2}	W_{t3}
Optimal value (mm)	2	4.5	6	3	4

Table 2. Optimal Values of the Stepped Inverted-Cone Stub Parameters

In order to optimize the coupling between the microstrip−line and the stepped inverted−cone slot. The stepped inverted−cone stub was compared with two different stubs as shown in figure 14. The first one is an inverted-cone and the second stub has a circular shape.

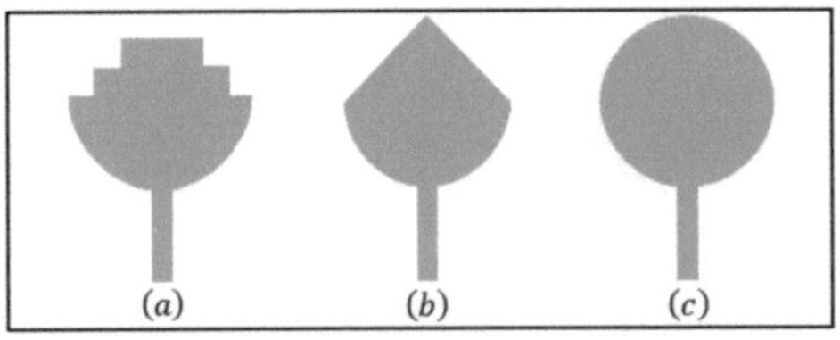

Fig. 14. Different Stub Shapes Studied for the Microstrip-fed PSICS UWB Antenna

The return loss of the microstrip−fed PSICS antenna was simulated for the three proposed stubs. Figure 15 illustrates a comparison between simulated return loss curves.
It shown that all the proposed antenna stubs have similar return loss curves, with an ex-

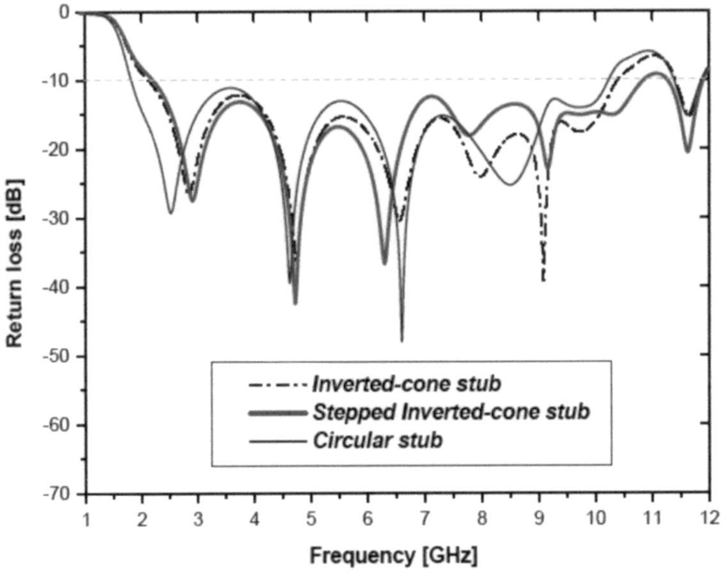

Fig. 15. Return Loss Curves of the Microstrip-fed PSICS Antenna for Different Stubs

tremely −10dB bandwidth which can covers the FCC UWB band. It is notice that the stepped inverted-cone slot increase significantly the possibility of the antenna feeding.

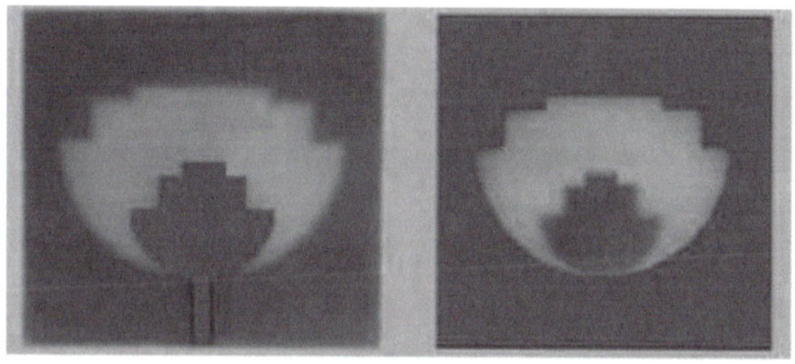

(*a*)

(*b*)

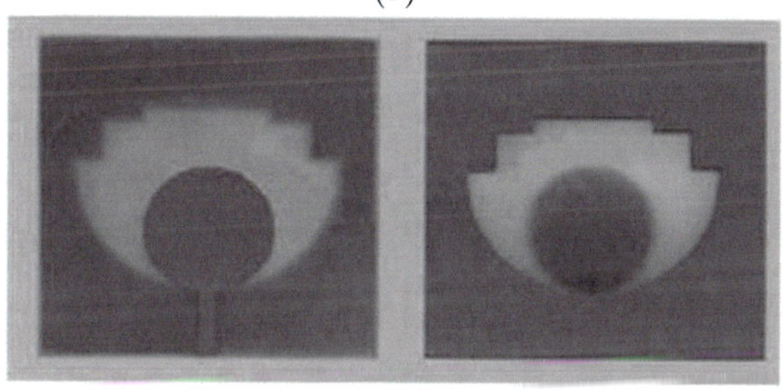

(*c*)

Fig. 16. Photographs of Realized Microstrip-fed PSICS Antennas. *(a) with Stepped Inverted-Cone Stub, (b) with Inverted-Cone Stub, (c) with Circular Stub*

Three prototypes of the microstrip−fed PSICS antenna with three different stubs in optimal design, was fabricated and tested. Figures (16.*a*), (16.*b*) and (16.*c*) present photos of PSICS antenna with stepped inverted−cone stub, inverted−cone stub and circular stub, respectively.

The return losses were measured by using vectorial network analyzer. Figures (17.*a*), (17.*b*) and (17.*c*) illustrate a comparison between simulated and measured return loss curves of the PSICS antenna with stepped inverted-cone stub, inverted-cone stub and circular stub, respectively. Generally speaking, as illustrated in figure(17.*a*), the measured return loss curve agrees with the simulated one in most range of the low frequencies band.

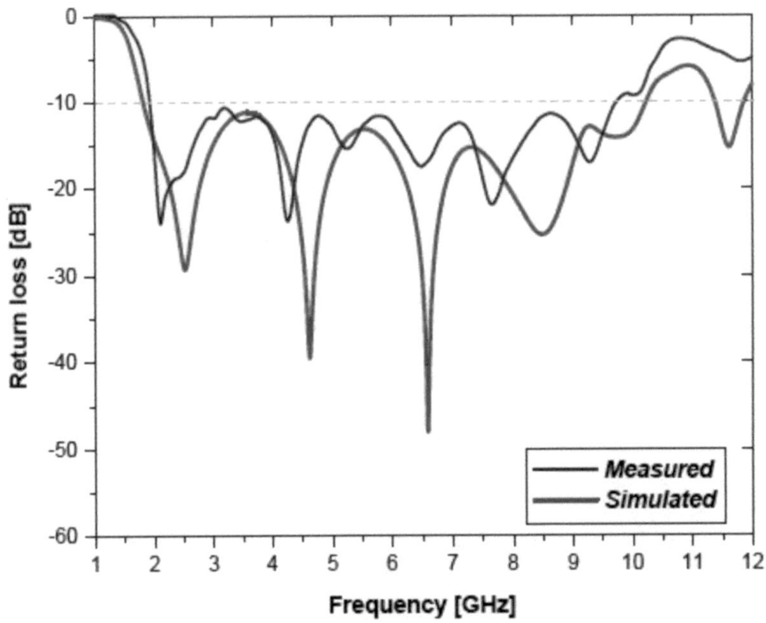
Return loss [dB]
Frequency [GHz]
Measured
Simulated

(*a*)

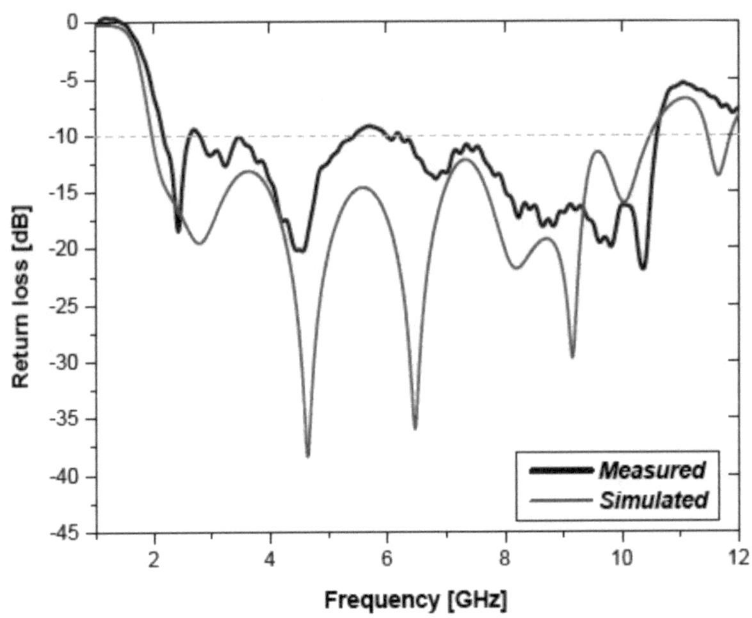
Return loss [dB]
Frequency [GHz]
Measured
Simulated

(*b*)

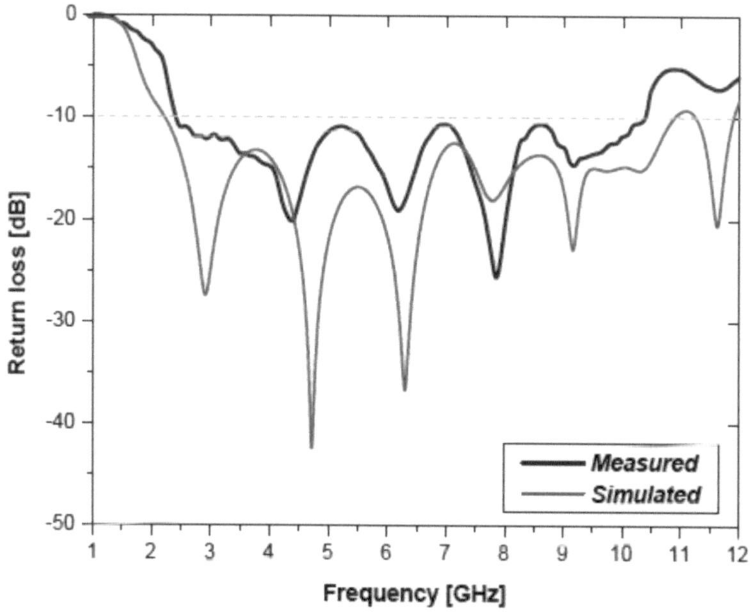

(c)

Fig. 17. Comparison between Simulated and Measured Return loss Curves of the Microstrip-fed PSICS UWB Antennas. *(a) with Stepped Inverted-Cone Stub, (b) with Inverted-Cone Stub, (c) with Circular Stub*

The −10dB bandwidth covers an extremely wide frequency range in both simulation and measurement. In figure(17.*b*), the UWB characteristic of the microstrip−fed PSICS antenna with a circular stub is confirmed in the measurement. It is shown that there is a good agreement between simulated and measured lower edge frequencies. However, there is significant difference between simulated and measured high edge frequencies.
The far−field radiation patterns of the PSICS antennas were also simulated at three frequencies. Figure 18 shows the radiation pattern of PSICS antenna with the inverted−cone stub at azimuthal and elevation planes. It is very important to note that the PSICS antenna with the different feeding structures can provide similar radiation patterns. As can be seen from the figure, omnidirectional patterns can be observed for the H−plane.

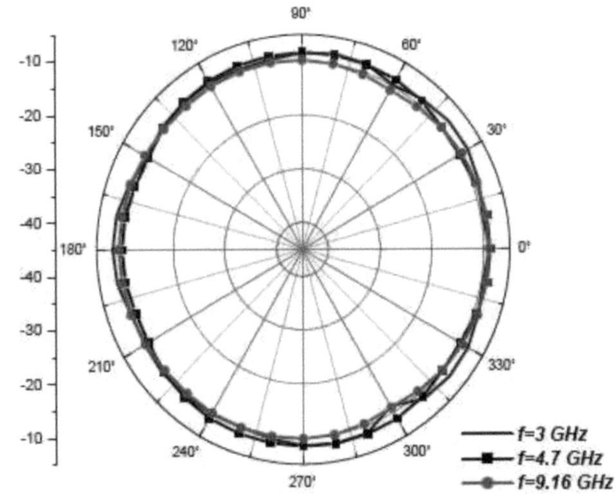

(a)

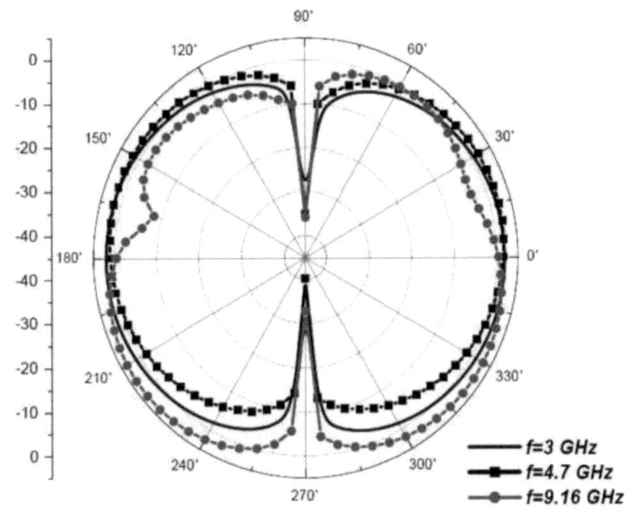

(b)

Fig. 18. Radiation Pattern of the Microstrip-fed PSICS Antenna with Steped-Inverted Cone Stub. *(a) Azimuthal Pattern (H-plane), (b) Elevation Pattern (E-plane)*

4. Microstrip Frequency Notched UWB Antennas

UWB technology is becoming an attractive solution for wireless communications, particularly for short and medium-range applications. UWB systems operate over extremely wide frequency bands (wider than 500MHz), according to the FCC regulations, the unlicensed usage of UWB systems for the indoor communications has been allocated to the spectrum from 3.1 to 10.6GHz. Within this UWB band, various narrowband technologies also operate with much higher power levels, as illustrated in figure 19. It is clear, that there is frequency-band sharing between the FCC's UWB band and the IEEE 802.11a. (5.15 – 5.825GHz) frequency band and the wireless local area networks bands: HiperLAN (5.150 – 5.350GHz) and WLAN (5.725 – 5.825GHz). Therefore, it may be necessary to have a notch for this band in order to avoid interferences. Recently, various suppression techniques have been developed for UWB communications to improve the performance, the capacity and the range. Some techniques are used at the receiver stage, including notch filtering (Choi et al, 1997), linear and nonlinear predictive techniques (Rusch, 1994), (Rusch, 1995), (Proakis, 1995), (Carlemalm, 2002) and (Azmi, 2002), adaptive methods (Lim et al., 1996) and (Fathallah et al., 1996), MMSE detectors (Poor, 1997) and (Buzzi, 1996), and transform domain techniques (Buzzi et al., 1996), (Medley, 1997), (Weaver, 2003) and (Kasparis, 1991). Another approach for interference suppression is used at the antenna. Based on this approach various frequency-notched UWB antennas have been developed by inserting diffident slot shapes (Chen, 2006), (Hong, 2007), (Yan, 2007), (Yuan, 2008) and (Wang, 2008).

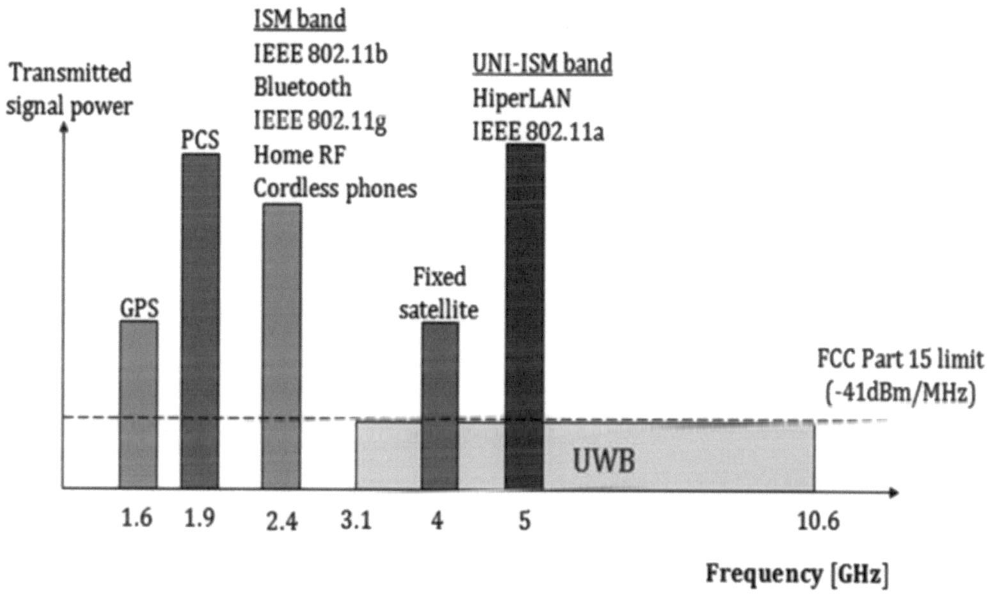

Fig. 19. The Coexistence of the UWB System and the Others Narrowband Systems

The advantage of this approach is that the stop-band filter (slot) is integrated directly in the antenna structure, and this is very important for communication devices which become smaller and more compact. In this section, we present the ability to achieve frequency notching characteristics in the previous proposed PMEM antenna by using the U–slot technique. The geometry of the notched-band PMEM antenna is shown in figure 20. The U–shaped slot introduced in the patch radiator is designed to notch the WLAN band.

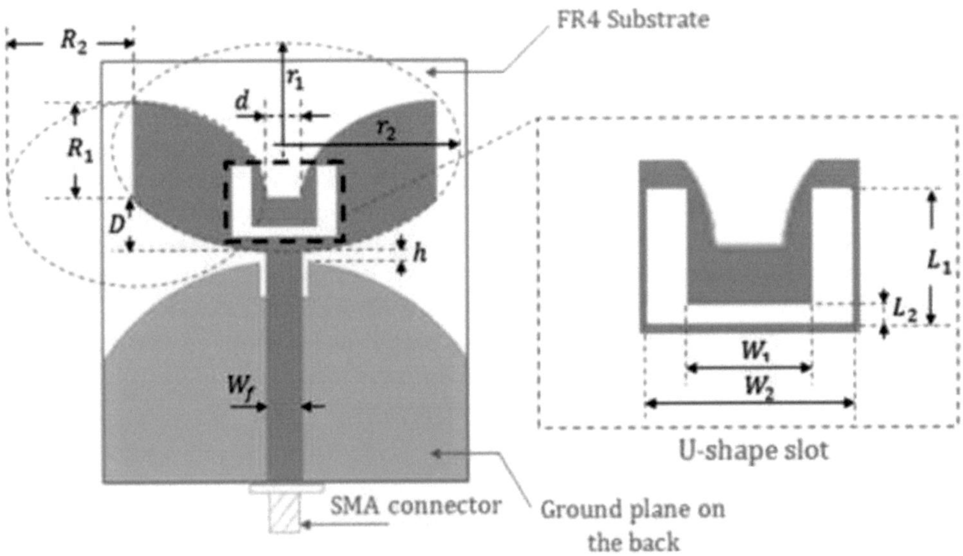

Fig. 20. Geometry of the Notched-Band Microstrip-fed PMEM UWB Antenna

The optimal values (in mm) of the patch radiator and the ground plane are presented in the table 3.

Parameter	L_{t1}	L_{t2}	W_{t1}	W_{t2}	W_{t3}
Optimal value (mm)	2	4.5	6	3	4

Table 3. Optimal Values of the U-Shape Slot

Band-notch function study

The influence of the parameters $L_1, L_2, W_1,$ and W_2 of the U-shaped slot introduced in the patch radiator are studied. To see the influences on the performance of the antenna an EM simulator is used. It is seen that by embedding the U$-$slot on the radiation patch, band-notched characteristic is obtained.

Figure (21.a), shows the VSWR of the antenna with different L_1 of the slot location as the length L_2 are fixed at 0.75mm. It is seen that when L_1 is between 4.1mm and 4.3mm , the antenna has a band-notch function at the WLAN band.

Figure (21.b) shows the VSWR of the antenna for different values of L_2. It is seen that the length of the slot determines the frequency range of the notched band. As L_2 increases, the notched band shifts toward the higher frequency. It is found that by adjusting the length of slot to be about 0.75mm a notched frequency band of about 5.6 $-$ 5.95GHz is obtained.

Figures (22.a) and (22.b) show the VSWR of the antenna with different slot widths W_1 and W_2, respectively. It is seen that when W_1 is smaller than 2mm, the antenna has a band-notch function at the WLAN band.

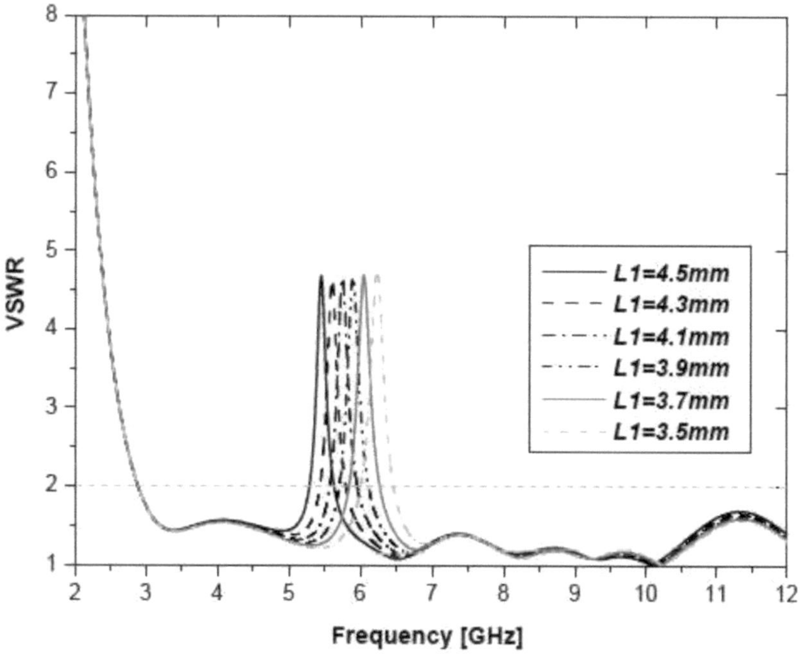

(*a*)

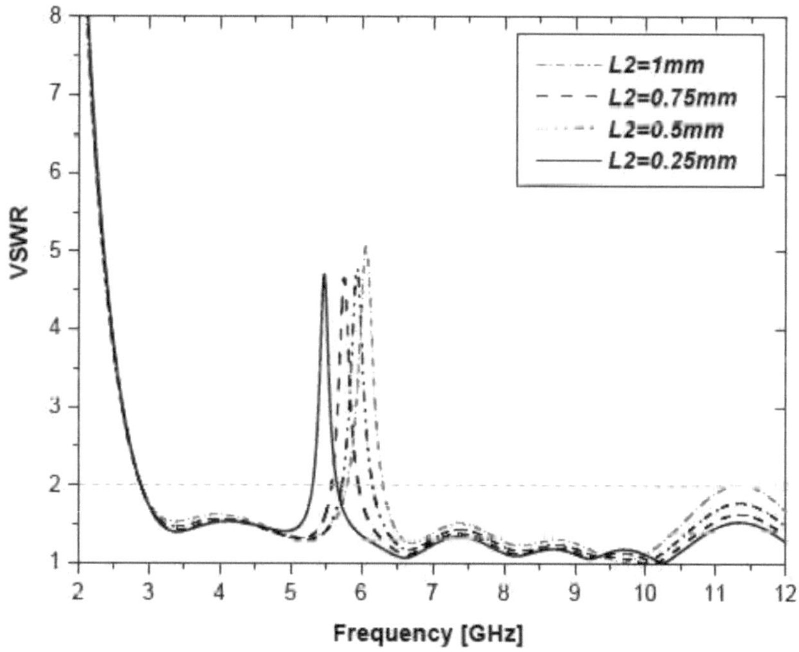

(*b*)

Fig. 21. VSWR versus U-Shape Slot Parameters. *(a) The Effect of L1, (b) The Effect of L2*

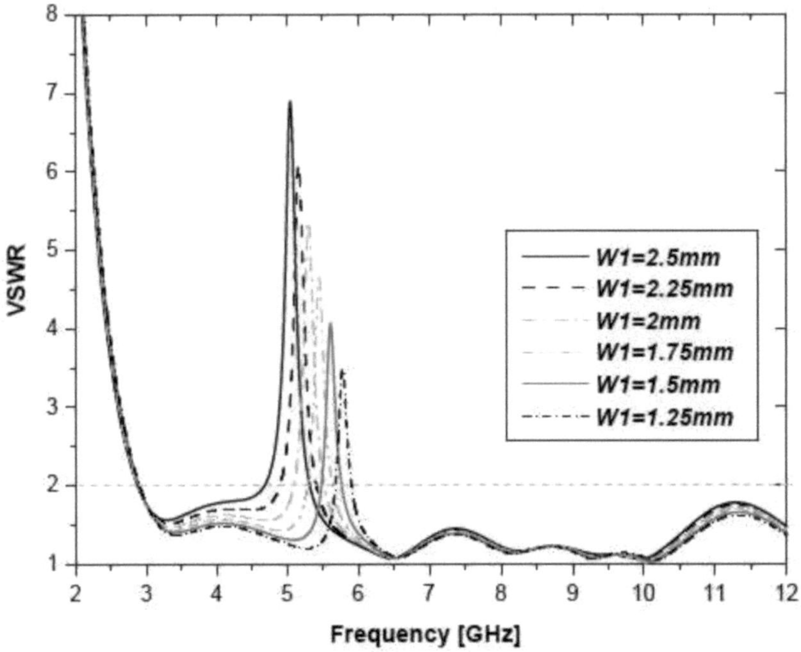

(a)

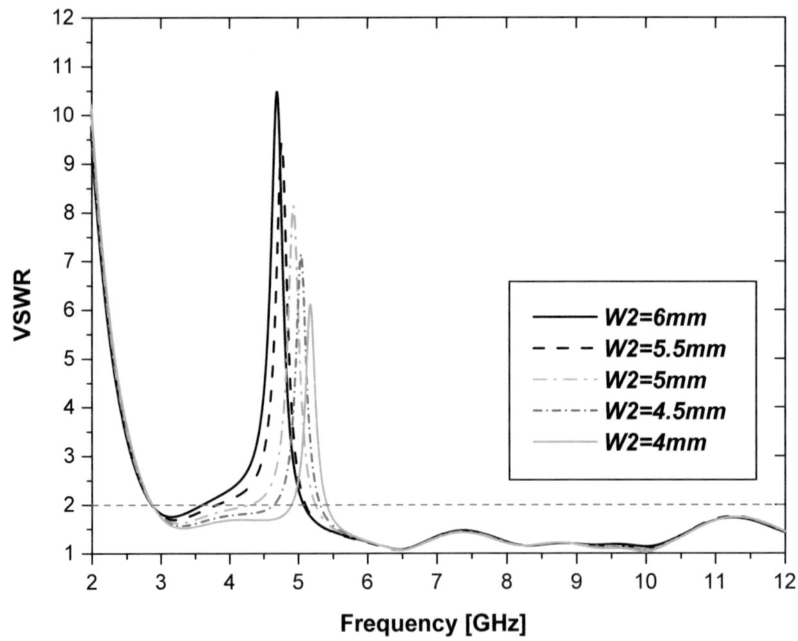

(b)

Fig. 22. VSWR versus U-Shape Slot Parameters. *(a) The Effect of W1, (b) The Effect of W2*

A prototype of the microstrip-fed notched-band PMEM antenna with optimal design, was fabricated as shown in figure 10. A comparison between simulated return loss and measured return loss obtained by using a VNA is shown in figure 24.

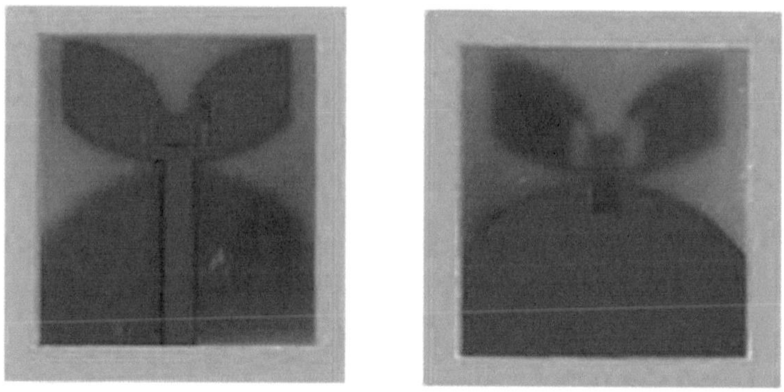

(a) (b)

Fig. 23. Photographs of Realized Notched-Band PMEM UWB Antenna. *(a) Top Side, (b) Back Side*

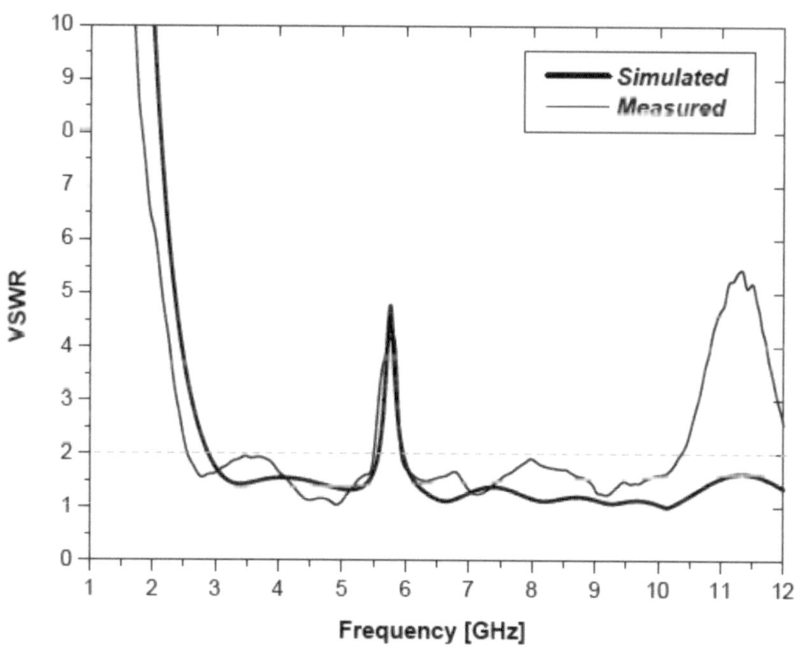

Fig. 24. Comparison between Simulated and Measured VSWR Curves of the Notched-Band Microstrip-fed PMEM UWB Antenna

It is shown that there is a good agreement between simulated and measured VSWR curves at the most range. However, after the frequency 10.4GHz the measured VSWR will be greater than 2, where the simulated one remains less than 2. In other words a frequency-notch function at WLAN band is investigated. This characteristic is very attractive for UWB applications.

5. Acknowledgement

The authors acknowledge Dr. Attrouz, B. chief of Microwave and radar laboratory at Military Polytechnic School (EMP) in Algeria for his help in antenna prototypes realization/measurement and his very useful discussions and motivation.

6. References

Abed, D. Kimouche, H. and Atrouz, B. (2008). Small-size printed CPW-fed antenna for ultra-wideband communications. *IEE Electronics Letter*, Vol. 44, No. 17, (August 2008) 3 (1246 - 1248)

Akansu, A., Tazebay, M. Medley, M. and Das, P. (1997). Wavelet and subband transforms: fundamentals and communication applications. *IEEE Commun. Mag.*, Vol. 35, (December 1997) 11 (104-115)

Angelopoulos, E. S., Anastopoulos, A.Z. Kaklamani, A. A. Alexandridis, F.L. and Dangakis, K. (2006). Circular and Elliptical CPW-fed Slot and Microstrip-fed Antennas for Ultra-wideband Applications. *IEEE Antennas and Wireless Propagation Letters*, Vol. 5 (2006) 4 (294-297)

Azmi, P. and Nasiri-Kenari, M. (2002). Narrow-band interference suppression in CDMA spreadspectrum communication systems based on sub-optimum unitary transforms. *IEICE Trans. Commun.*, Vol. E85-B, No. 1, (January 2002) 8 (239-246)

Bao, X.L. and Ammann, M. J. (2007). Investigation on UWB printed monopole antenna with rectangular slitted ground plane. *Microwave and Optical Technology Letter*, Vol. 49, (2007) 3 (1585 - 1587)

Buzzi, S., Lops, M. & Tulino, A. (1996). Time-varying mmse interference suppression in asynchronous DS/CDMA systems over multipath fading channels, *Proceedings of IEEE Int. Symp. on Personal, Indoor and Mobile Radio Communications*, pp. 518-522, September, 1998

Carlemalm, C. Poor, H. V. and Logothetis, A. (1996). Suppression of multiple narrowband interferers in a spread-spectrum communication system. *IEEE J. Select. Areas Commun.*, Vol. 18, No. 8, (August 2000) 10 (1365-1374)

Chair, R., Kishk, A.A. and Lee, K.F. (2004). Ultrawide-band Coplanar Waveguide-fed Rectangular Slot Antenna. *IEEE Antennas and Wireless Propagation Letters*, Vol. 7, No. 12 (2004) 3 (227-229)

Chen,W.-S, Huang, C.-C. and Wong, K.-L. (2000). A novel microstrip-line-fed printed semicircular slot antenna for broadband operation. *Microwave and Optical Technology Letters*, Vol. 26, No. 4, (August 2000) 3 (237-239)

Chen, H. D. (2003). Broadband CPW-fed Square Slot Antennas with A Widened Tuning Stub. *IEEE Transactions on Antennas and Propagation*, Vol. 51, No. 8, (August 2003) 5 (1982-1986)

Chen, W.-S. and Hsieh, F.-M. (2004). Broadband design of the printed triangular slot antenna. *IEEE Antennas and Propagation Society International Symposium*, Vol. 4, (June 2004) 4 (3733-3736)

Chen, J.-S. (2006). Dual-frequency annular-ring slot antennas fed by CPW feed and microstrip line feed. *IEEE Transactions on Antennas and Propagation*, Vol. 53, No. 1, (January 2005) 2 (569-571)

Chen, H.-D., Li, J.-N. and Huang, Y.-F. (2006). Band-notched ultra-wideband square slot antenna. *Microwave and Optical Technology Letters*, Vol. 48, No. 12, (December 2006) 3 (2427-2429)

Cheng, P. and Rydberg, A. (2008). Printed Slot Inverted Cone Antenna for Ultra Wideband applications. *IEEE Antennas and Wireless Propagation Letters*, Vol. 7 (2008) 4 (18-21)

Jang, Y.W. (2003). A Broad-Band CPW-Fed Strip- Loaded Square Slot Antenna. *IEEE Transactions on Antennas and Propagation*, Vol. 51, No. 4, (April 2003) 3 (719-721)

Choi, J. & Choi, N. (1997). Narrow-band interference suppression in direct sequence spread spectrum systems using a lattice IIR notch filter, *Proceedings of IEEE Int. Conf. Acoustics, Speech, Signal Processing (ICASSP)*, pp. 1881-1884, Munich, Germany, April 1997

Denidni, T.A., and Habib, M.A. (2006). Broadband Printed CPW-fed Slot Antenna. *IEE Electronics Letters*, Vol. 42, No. 3 (February 2006)

Fathallah, H. & Rusch, L. (1996). Enhanced blind adaptive narrowband interference suppression in dsss, *Proceedings of IIEEE Global Telecommun. Conf.(GLOBECOM)*, pp. 545-549, London, November, 1996

Report and Order in the CommissionŠs Rules Regarding Ultra-Wideband Transmission Systems, *Released by Federal Communications Commission(FCC)*, (April 2002).

Hong, S., Shin, J. Park, H. and Huang, J. (2007). Analysis of the band-stop techniques for ultra wideband antenna. *Microwave and Optical Technology Letters*, Vol. 49, No. 5, (May 2007) 5 (1058-1062)

Jang, Y.W. (2000). Broadband cross-shaped microstrip-fed slot antenna. *IEE Electronics Letters*, Vol. 36, No. 25, (December 2000) 3

Kasparis, T. (1991). Frequency independent sinusoidal suppression using median filters. *IEEE Int. Conf. Acoustics, Speech, Signal Processing (ICASSP)*, pp. 612-615, Toronto, April, 1991

Kimouche, H.; Abed, D. & Atrouz, B. (2009). Investigation on Microstrip-fed Modified Elliptical Monopole Antenna for UWB communication, *Proceedings of 3rd European Conference on Antennas and Propagation (EuCAP)*, pp. 1450 - 1454, Berlin, Germany, March 23-27, 2009

Kobayashi, H. sasamori, T. Tobana, T. and Abe, K. (2007). A Study on Miniaturization of Printed Disc Monopole Antenna for UWB Applications Using Notched Ground Plane. *IEICE Trans. Commun.*, Vol.E90-B, No.09, (September 2007)

Lee, H.-L., Lee, H.-J., Yook, J. -G. and Park, H. K. (2002). Broadband Planar Antenna having Round Corner Rectangular Wide Slot. Antennas and Propagation Society International Symposium, Vol. 2, (June 2002) 4 (460-463)

Liang, P.Li. and Chen,X. (2006). Study of Printed Elliptical/Circular Slot Antennas for Ultrawideband Applications Communication. *IEEE Transaction on Antennas and Propagation*, Vol. 54, No. 6 (June 2006) 6 (1670-1675)

Lim, T. J. & Rasmussen, L. K. (1996). Adaptive cancelation of narrowband signal sin overlaid CDMA systems, *Proceedings of IEEE Int. Workshop Intelligent Signal Processing and Communication Systems*, pp. 1648-1652, Singapore, November, 1996

Liu, Y.F., Lau, K. L., Xue, Q. and Chan, C. H. (2004). Experimental studies of printed wide-slot antenna for wide-band applications. *IEEE Antennas and Wireless Propagation Letters*, Vol. 3, (December 2004) 3 (273-275)

Medley, M. (1997). Narrow-band interference excision in spread spectrum systems using lapped transforms. *IEEE Trans. Commun.*, Vol. 45, No. 9, (November 1997) 11 (1444-1455)

Poor, H., V. and Wang, X. (1997). Code-aided interference suppression in DS/CDMA spread spectrum communications. *IEEE Trans. Commun.*, Vol. 45, No. 9, (September 1997) 11 (1101-1111)

Proakis, J. (1996). Interference suppression in spread spectrum systems. *IEEE Int. Symp. on Spread Spectrum Techniques and Applications*, Vol. 1, (September 1996) 8 (259-266)

Rusch, L. and Poor, H. (1994). Narrowband interference suppression in CDMA spread spectrum communications. *IEEE Personal Commun. Mag.*, Vol. 42, (April 1994) 11 (1969-1979)

Rusch, L. and Poor, H. (1995). Multiuser detection techniques for narrowband interference suppression in spread spectrum communications. *IEEE Trans. Commun.*, Vol. 42, (April 1995) 11 (1727-1737)

Sadat, S., Fardis, M., Geran, F. and Dadashzadeh, G. (2007). A Campact Microstrip Square Ring Slot Antenna for UWB Aplications. *Progress In Electromagnetic Research (PIER)*, Vol. 67 (June 2007) 7 (173-179)

Soliman, E. A. Brebels, S. Beyne, E. and Vandenbosch, G. A. E. (1999). CPW-fed cusp antenna. *Microwave and Optical Technology Letters*, Vol. 22, No. 4, (August 1999) 2 (12056-12057)

Sorbello, G., Consoli, F. and Barbarino, S. (2002). Numerical and Experimental Analysis of a Circular Slot Antenna for UWB Communication. *Microwave and Optical Technical Letters*, Vol. 44, No. 5 (June 2005) 6 (465-470)

Sze, J.-Y., Hsu, C.-I.G. and Jiao, J.-J. (2006). CPW-fed circular slot antenna with slit back-patch for 2.4/5 GHz dual-band operation. *IEE Electronics Letters*, Vol. 42, No. 10, (May 2006)

Wang, F.-J., Yang, X.-X., Zhang, J.-S., Gao, G.-P. and Xiao, J.-X. (2008). A band-notched ring monoplole antenna. *Microwave and Optical Technology Letters*, Vol.50, No.7, (July 2008) 3 (1882-1884)

Weaver, R. D. (1997). Frequency domain processing of ultra-wideband signals. *IEEE Asilomar Conf. Signals, Systems Computers*, pp. 1221-1224,Pacific Grove, CA, November, 2003

Hong, S., Shin, J. Park, H. and Huang, J. (2007). The band-notch function for a compact coplanar waveguide fed super-wideband printed monopole. *Microwave and Optical Technology Letters*, Vol. 49, No. 11, (November 2007) 3 (2769-2771)

Yuan, T., Qiu, C.-W., Li, L.-W., Leong, M. S. and Zhang, Q. (2008). Elliptically shaped ultra wideband patch antenna with band-notch features. *Microwave and Optical Technology Letters*, Vol. 50, No. 3, (March 2008) 3 (736-738)

16

UWB antennas: design and modeling

Yvan Duroc and Ali-Imran Najam
Grenoble Institute of Technology
France

1. Introduction

1.1 Brief history of antennas and their evolution

The antenna is an essential part of any wireless system as it is the component providing transition between a guided wave and a free-space wave. According to the IEEE standard definitions of terms for antennas (IEEE, 1993), an antenna is defined as a means for radiating or receiving radio waves. During the period 1885-1900, some pioneers invented the antennas and the wireless systems. The wire antennas were inaugurated in 1842 by the inventor of telegraphy, Joseph Henry who had also discovered electromagnetic waves and had even formulated the idea that light waves were of this type. About forty years later, the antennas and the first wireless systems emerged. In 1885, Edison patented a communication system using vertical, top-loaded and grounded antennas. In 1887, Hertz launched, processed and received radio using a balanced or dipole antenna as a transmitter and a one-turn loop containing a spark gap as a receiver. The invention of antenna is credited to Popov who proposed a device capable of detecting electromagnetic waves in the atmosphere and introduced the concept of antenna in 1895. The initial concepts of phase arrays were proposed in 1889. Several advances in antennas were patented in 1897 by Lodge and these contributions yielded matching, tuning, and addition of the word "impedance" to the language. Finally, the first most significant application was the telegraph of Marconi patented in 1900.

Many decades after these early investigations, the antenna has drawn a lot of attention over the years and has remained a subject of numerous challenges. Although dipole and loop antennas are still widely used for various radio systems, yet the antennas have been evolved remarkably with respect to both their topologies and usages. Research conducted on antennas is driven by several factors. The first factor deals with the increase of the bandwidth and shift of operational frequency to the higher bands. With the ever-increasing need for mobile communication and the emergence of many systems, it has become important to design broadband antennas to cover a wide frequency range. Modern wireless applications require the processing of more and more data in different forms, higher data rates, higher capacity and multi-standard abilities. There are numerous well-known methods to increase the bandwidth of antennas including designs with log-periodic profile, travelling-wave topologies, increase of the substrate thickness and the use of a low dielectric substrate, various impedance matching and feeding techniques, multiple resonators and slot antenna geometry (Walter, 1990; Agrawal et al., 1997; Amman & Chen, 2003a; Islam, 2009).

The second factor deals with field pattern and the ways to control it. One method is to use a multitude of identical radiating elements to form an array. The elementary antennas are fed from a single source through a network of transmission line and/or waveguides. In such systems, the shape of the radiation pattern is governed by the field pattern of the elementary antenna (which is chosen to be as simple as possible), the power distribution among the elements and geometric details of their arrangement. Many examples are available in the literature (Chang, 1997). Even if the arrays were initially designed for high power purposes using bulk antennas, but their developments in planar and integrated forms using microstrip patches are more attractive (Munson, 1974). The third factor deals with isotropic behavior, i.e., the ability of antennas to radiate equally in all directions. Indeed in the context of wireless sensor networks, radio frequency identification or millimetre-length communications, the random and time-varying orientations of the devices with respect to each other cause strong variations of the transmitted signal due to the radiation anisotropy and polarization mismatches of antennas. Ad-hoc sensor networks for human motion capture systems based on wearable sensors as well as the localization of mobile objects are typical upcoming applications requiring quite constant received power whatever be the orientations of devices relative to each other (Puccinelli & Haenggi, 2005). Directions of departure and arrival of a beam can totally change while in use and fall into antenna radiating null. Polarization mismatches can also cause fading of the transmitted power. It is therefore difficult to maintain the quality of service. Isotropic antenna is a hypothetical idealized device that does not exist in reality (Mathis, 1951). A close approximation can be a stack of two pairs of crossed dipole antennas driven in quadrature. When space has to be covered in all directions, smart antennas with pattern and polarization agility are required. However, for many applications, generalizations of adaptive smart antenna are still far away due to their high cost or power consumption or because of size and integration issues. Consequently, there is a need for small antennas with optimized radiation pattern and polarization to provide wide coverage. One method to obtain quasi-isotropy behavior is to associate several elementary antennas in complementary way in terms of fields and polarization. The concept of spatial coverage factor as well as its application to a quasi-isotropic antenna has been introduced (Huchard et al., 2005). According to wireless applications and the associated devices, the type of antennas can be very different. For example, the main requirements for an antenna of a cellular mobile radio phone will be small type, low profile and broad/multi bandwidth.

Last but not least, in modern wireless communication systems, complex signal processing techniques and digital routines are considered in order to build a device which is flexible enough to run every possible waveform without any restrictions on carrier frequency, bandwidth, modulation format, date rate, etc. This is the philosophy of future radio systems such as Software Defined Radio (SDR) and cognitive radio firstly introduced by Mitola (Mitola, 1995; Mitola and Maguire, 1999). In this context, the antenna becomes not only one of the most important parts in a wireless system but it is also flexible and "intelligent" enough to perform processing function that can be realized by any other device. The antennas are becoming increasingly linked to other components (e.g., system-on-chip) and to other subject areas (such as digital signal processing or propagation channels). To accurately integrate the antenna performance into the design of the overall wireless system, specific models compatible with standard languages are highly desired. Such modeling allows the right design and optimization of wireless RF front-ends including antennas.

1.2 Ultra Wideband technology

Ultra Wideband (UWB) is an emerging technology for future short-range wireless communications with high data rates as well as radar and geolocation (Yang & Giannakis, 2004). Indeed, the use of large bandwidths offers multiple benefits including high date rates, robustness to propagation fading, accurate ranging and geolocation, superior obstacle penetration, resistance to jamming, interference rejection, and coexistence with narrow bandwidth systems. It should be noted that the first UWB signals were generated in experiments by Hertz who radiated sparks via wideband loaded dipoles. However, this type of communication was abandoned at that time due to non-availability of resources to recover the wideband energy effectively. Later during the 1960s and 1970s, impulse radio technologies were being used to develop radar, sensing, military communications and niche applications. A landmark patent in UWB communications was submitted by Ross in 1973. However, it was in 1989 that the term "Ultra Wideband" appeared in a publication of department of defense in the United States (U.S.) and the first patent with the exact phrase "UWB antenna" was filed on behalf of Hughes in 1993. Thus, interest in UWB was revived in the 1990s thanks to the improvements in digital signal processing and notably the investigation on Impulse Radio (IR) by Win and Scholtz (Win & Scholtz, 1998). Finally, it was in 2002 when the interest for UWB systems was greatly magnified by the decision of the United States frequency regulating body, the Federal Communications Commission (FCC), who released a report approving the use of UWB devices operating in several unlicensed frequency bands [0-960 MHz], [3.1-10.6 GHz], and [22-29 GHz]. Since then, regulations were defined through notably emission spectral masks around the world,. In Europe, the Electronic Communications Committee (ECC) has proposed its most recent proposal in April 2009. In contrast to the FCC's single emission mask level over the entire UWB band, this report proposed two sub-bands with the low band ranging from 3.1 GHz to 4.8 GHz (authorized until 2011 with mitigation techniques included to ensure coexistence) and the high band from 6 GHz to 8.5 GHz. The upper bound for Effective Isotropic Radiation Power (EIRP) is common and has been set out to be - 41.3 dBm/MHz. Even if the authorized frequency bands are different according to the world regions, the definition of UWB is universal. UWB describes wireless physical layer technology which uses a bandwidth of at least 500 MHz or a bandwidth which is at least 20% of the central frequency in use. Two approaches have been developed for UWB systems: pulsed operation and multiple narrow bands. Among these techniques, the original approach is based on IR concept. Impulse Radio refers to the use of a series of very short duration pulses, which are modulated in position or/and amplitude. As signals are carrier-less, i.e., only baseband signals exist; therefore no intermediate frequency processing is needed. Alternative schemes are Multi-Band Orthogonal Frequency Division Multiplexing (MB-OFDM) and Multi-Carrier Code Division Multiple Access (MC-CDMA).

To guarantee the coexistence of UWB with other communication standards, the authorized transmitted power is always very low which limits the development of UWB communication systems with very high data rates and/or the coverage of larger distances. The association of Multiple Input Multiple Output (MIMO) systems (which exploit rich scattering environments by the use of multiple antennas) with UWB technology is more and more studied. It seems to be a very potential approach for enhancing capacity, increasing range, raising link reliability and improving interference cancellation (Siriwongpairat et al., 2004; Yang & Giannakis, 2004; Kaiser et al., 2006). Recent works have also shown the

prospects of using the UWB technology into the next generation RFID (Radio Frequency Identification) systems. Indeed, promises have been highlighted in order to achieve larger operating range, accurate localization, robustness to interference and more security in multiple access systems (Zou et al., 2007; Hu et al., 2007; Dardari & D'Errico, 2008). Further, when the wireless systems that are potential candidates for cognitive radio are considered, UWB seems to be one of the tempting choices because it has an inherent potential to fulfill some of the key requirements of cognitive radio (Manteuffel et al.; 2009). These requirements include no spurious interference to licensed systems, adjustable pulse shape, bandwidth and transmitted power, support of various throughputs, provision of adaptive multiple access, and security of information. However, it is not claimed that a cognitive wireless system using only the UWB technology can handle all the requirements of an ideal cognitive radio. Advances in reconfigurability of RF front-ends, particularly reconfigurable (multiple) antennas, afford a new "hardware" dimension for optimizing the performance of wireless communication systems (Sayeed & Raghavan, 2007).
The prospects of UWB are always growing, however, the future wireless systems using UWB technology involve many new challenges, especially, related to the design and modeling of UWB antennas. Section 2 presents an overview of different categories of UWB (single and multiple) antennas emphasizing their main properties. Section 3 focuses on the approaches for the characterization and modeling of UWB antennas. Conclusions and perspectives are presented in the last section.

2. Design of Ultra Wideband Antennas

2.1 UWB antenna properties

An antenna is a device that converts a signal transmitted from a source to a transmission line into electromagnetic waves to be broadcasted into free space and vice versa. An antenna is usually required to optimize or concentrate the radiation energy in some directions and to suppress it in the others at certain frequencies. A good design of the antenna can relax system requirements and improve overall system performance. In practice, to describe the performance of an antenna, there are several commonly used antenna parameters, such as impedance bandwidth, radiation pattern, directivity, gain, input impedance, and so on.
Particularly, a UWB antenna is defined as an antenna having a fractional bandwidth greater than 0.2 and a minimum bandwidth of 500 MHz.

$$BW = 2\frac{f_H - f_L}{f_H + f_L} \geq 0.2 \quad \text{and} \quad f_H - f_L \geq 500\,\text{MHz} \tag{1}$$

where f_L and f_H are the frequencies defining the antenna's operational band. For example, an IR-UWB system, which would comply with the emission mask and operate within the 3.1-10.6 GHz frequency range allocated in U.S, needs an antenna achieving almost a decade of impedance bandwidth spanning 7.5 GHz.
However, UWB antennas are firstly antennas! As a consequence, UWB antennas try to achieve the same goals, and are subjected to the same physical constraints (e.g., low cost, small size, integration capability, etc.) and the same electrical constraints (e.g., impedance matching, radiation pattern, directivity, efficiency, polarization, etc.) as in the case of narrowband antennas. Further, due to the large bandwidth, the electrical parameters

become frequency dependent complicating the design and analysis. In addition to the conventional characterization parameters, some specific parameters must be examined in order to take into account the distortion effects, notably, critical for IR applications. These specific parameters include group delay, phase response and impulse response. The radiation pattern is desired to be constant within the overall operating frequency in order to guarantee the pulse properties to be same in any direction. The group delay is given by the derivative of the unwrapped phase of an antenna. If the phase is linear throughout the frequency range, the group delay will be constant for the frequency range. This is an important characteristic because it helps to indicate how well a UWB pulse will be transmitted and to what degree it may be distorted or dispersed.
The specifications of the antenna design will be a trade-off of these parameters taking into account not only the expected application but also the technique of transmission (multiple narrow bands or pulsed operation) to be used. Some parameters have to be declared more important than others. Two types of requirements can be distinguished. The physical constraints arise when one strives to develop antennas of small size, low profile and low cost (materials, maintenance and fabrication), and with embeddable capability. The electrical constraints arise while designing antennas with wideband impedance bandwidth covering all sub-bands (for MB-OFDM) or the bandwidth where most of the energy of the source pulse is concentrated (for IR), steady directional or omni-directional radiation patterns, constant gain at directions of interest, constant desired polarization, high radiation efficiency and linear phase response (for IR).

2.2 UWB antenna characteristics

In 2003, a history of UWB antennas is presented by H.G. Schantz who emphasizes the relevant past works on UWB antennas and their important wide variety (Schantz, 2003): *"Ultra-Wideband has its roots in the original spark-gap transmitters that pioneered radio technology. This history is well known and has been well documented in both professional histories and in popular treatments. The development of UWB antennas has not been subjected to similar scrutiny. As a consequence, designs have been forgotten and then re-discovered by later investigators"*.
Thus, in the recent years, a lot of UWB antenna designs have been reported and presented in the academic literature (Schantz, 2005; Wiesbeck & Adamiuk, 2007; Chang, 2008) and in some patents (Akdagli et al., 2008). The main challenge to design a UWB antenna comes from the coverage of large bandwidth because the matching and energy transmission require to be verified for the entire bandwidth. However, the traditional trade-offs such as size vs. efficiency and size vs. bandwidth (Chu-Harrington limit) still influence the characteristics and performance of antennas.
UWB antennas may be categorized into different types according to their radiating characteristics: frequency independent antennas, multi-resonant antennas, travelling wave antennas and small element antennas.

2.2.1 Frequency independent antennas

Frequency independent antennas, such as biconical, spiral, conical spiral and log periodic antennas are classic broadband and UWB antennas. They can offer real constant impedances and consistent pattern properties over a frequency bandwidth greater than 10:1. There are two principles for achieving frequency independent characteristics.

The first one was introduced by Rumsey in the 1950s. Rumsey's principle suggests that the pattern properties of an antenna will be frequency independent if the antenna shape is specified only in terms of angles. Infinite biconical and spiral antennas are good examples whose shapes are completely described by angles. For the log periodic antennas, the entire shape is not solely specified by angles rather it is also dependent on the length from the origin to any point on the structure. However, the log periodic antennas can still exhibit frequency independent characteristics. Fig. 1 illustrates the geometry of spiral, log periodic and conical spiral antennas.

The second principle accounting for frequency independent characteristics is self-complementarities, which was introduced by Mushiake in the 1940s derived from the Babinet's principle in optics. Mushiake discovered that the product of input impedances of a planar electric current antenna (plate) and its corresponding "magnetic current" antenna was the real constant $\eta^2/4$, where η is the intrinsic impedance. Hence, if an antenna is its own complement, the frequency independent impedance behavior is obtained. In Fig. 1 (a), if the lengths W and S are the same, i.e., the metal and the air regions of the antenna are equal; the spiral antenna is self-complementary. Fig. 1 (d) shows the geometry of a logarithmic spiral antenna.

Although the frequency independent antennas can operate over an extremely wide frequency range, they still have some limitations. Firstly, to satisfy Rumsey's requirement, the antenna configuration needs to be infinite in principle but, in practice, it is usually truncated in size. This requirement makes the frequency independent antennas quite large in terms of wavelength. Secondly, the frequency independent antennas tend to be dispersive because they radiate different frequency components from different parts of the antenna, i.e., the smaller-scale part contributes higher frequencies while the large-scale part accounts for lower frequencies. Consequently, the received signal suffers from severe ringing effects and distortions. Due to this drawback, the frequency independent antennas can be used only when the waveform dispersion may be tolerated.

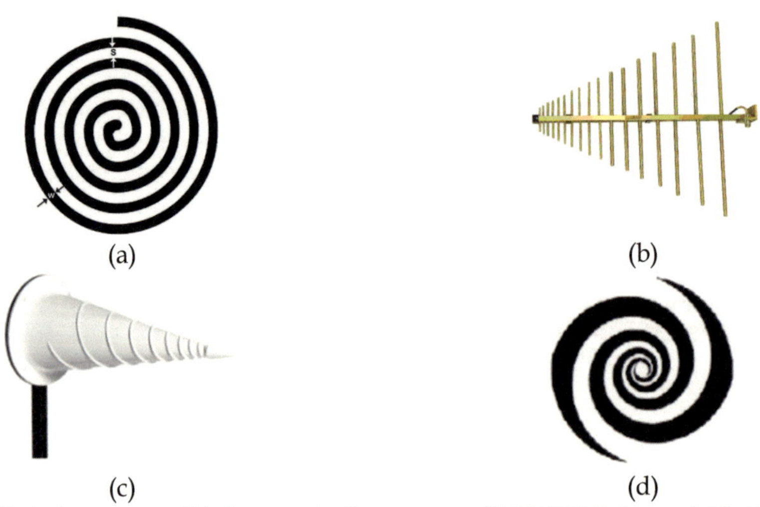

Fig. 1. (a) Spiral antenna; (b) Log periodic antenna (SAS 510-7 from A.H. Systems Inc); (c) Conical spiral antenna; (d) Logarithmic spiral antenna.

2.2.2 Multi-resonant antennas

Multi-resonant antennas are composed of an arrangement of multiple narrowband radiating elements. This type of antenna includes log periodic antennas or Yagi antennas (Fig. 1(b)). Planar versions of these antennas also exist. Although these antennas are UWB, yet they are not convenient for IR-UWB systems because their phase centers are not fixed in frequency and therefore exhibit dispersion.

2.2.3 Travelling wave antennas

Travelling wave antennas include horn antennas, tapered slot antennas and dielectric rod antennas. These antennas feature a smooth and gradual transition between a guided wave and a radiated wave, and have good properties for UWB.

Horn antennas constitute a major class of UWB directional antennas and these are commonly used for measuring radiation patterns or for ground penetrating radar applications. They consist of rectangular or circular waveguides which are inherently broadband. Their bandwidth is relatively large, i.e., 50% - 180%. These antennas present very good polarization, very low dispersion and very low variation in phase center versus frequency. Fig. 2 (a) shows a double ridge horn antenna as an example.

The Tapered Slot Antenna (TSA) is another important class of UWB directional antennas. A typical TSA consists of a tapered slot that has been etched in the metallization on a dielectric substrate. The profile of tapering may take different forms: linear tapered slot antenna (LTSA), constant width slot antenna (CWSA), broken linearly tapered slot antenna (BLTSA) or exponentially tapered slot antenna (Vivaldi) as shown in Fig. 2 (b). The TSAs are adapted to a wide bandwidth of 125% - 170%. Their radiation pattern is unidirectional in the plane of the substrate and has a low level of cross-polarization. The directivity increases with frequency and the gains achieved by these antennas can go up to 10 dBi depending on the type of profile.

(a)

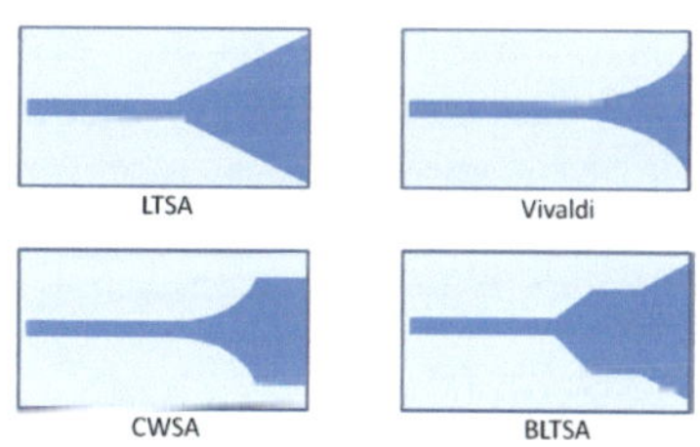

(b)

Fig. 2. (a) Horn Antenna - SA S571 A.H. Sys. Inc; (b) Tapered slot antennas.

2.2.4 Small element antennas

Small-element antennas include Lodge's biconical and bow-tie antennas, Mater's diamond dipole, Stohr's spherical and ellipsoidal antennas, and Thomas's circular dipole. These antennas are direct evolution of monopole and the basic dipole (doublet of Hertz). Antenna engineers discovered that, starting from a dipole or monopole antenna, thickening the arms results in an increased bandwidth. Thus, for a thick dipole or monopole antenna, the current distribution is no longer sinusoidal and where this phenomenon hardly affects the radiation pattern of the antenna, there this strongly influences the input impedance too. This band-widening effect is even more severe if the thick dipole takes the shape of a biconical antenna.

Fig. 3 (a) and Fig. 3 (b) show the evolution from a thin-wire dipole antenna towards a biconical antenna, which presents a frequency independent impedance response. Further evolution may be found in dipole and monopole antennas formed by spheres and ellipsoids (Schantz, 2005). The biconical antenna evolved towards a single cone (Fig. 3 (c)) which presents a limited well-matched impedance bandwidth but a stable phase center within the bandwidth. Thanks to these qualities, the discone antennas are applied for UWB channel measurements and UWB system testing. Fig. 3 (d) and Fig. 3 (e) show alternative possible asymmetrical structures. Another evolution of the biconical antenna is the bow-tie antenna, the flat version of the biconical antenna (Fig. 3 (f)). One of the poles can be transformed into a ground plane (i.e., an electrically large conducting plate) as shown in Fig. 3 (g).

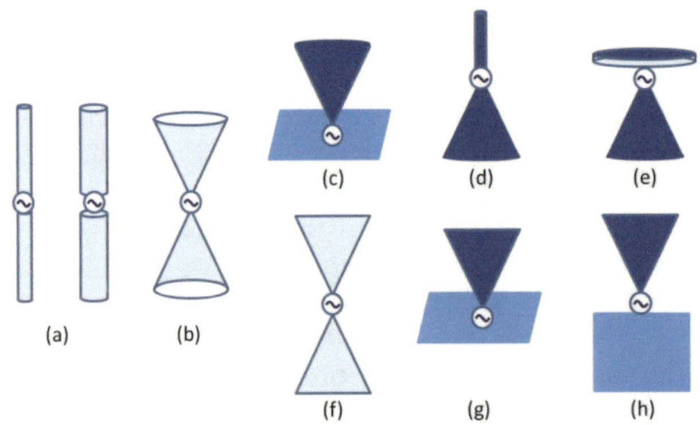

Fig. 3. Evolution of dipole, conical and planar antennas.

Fig. 3 (g) can be also considered as the evolution of the conventional monopole having a straight wire configuration against a ground plane. The monopole is one of the most widely used antennas for wireless communication systems due to its simple structure, low cost, omni-directional radiation patterns and ease for matching to 50 Ω (Balanis, 2005). Besides, it is unbalanced, thus it eliminates the need for a balun, which may have a limited bandwidth. The bandwidth of a straight wire monopole is typically around 10% - 20%, depending on the radius-to-length ratio of the monopole. When the monopole radius is too large related to the feeding line, the impedance mismatch between them becomes significant and the bandwidth cannot be further increased. Finally, a method to obtain bandwidth enhancement is to replace the wire element with a plate which is obviously much "fatter". This plate can take various configurations, such as triangle, circular, square, trapezoid, pentagonal, hexagonal, elliptical and so on (Fig. 4.). Circular and elliptical shapes present especially good broadband characteristics due to the smooth transition between the radiator and the feeding strip.

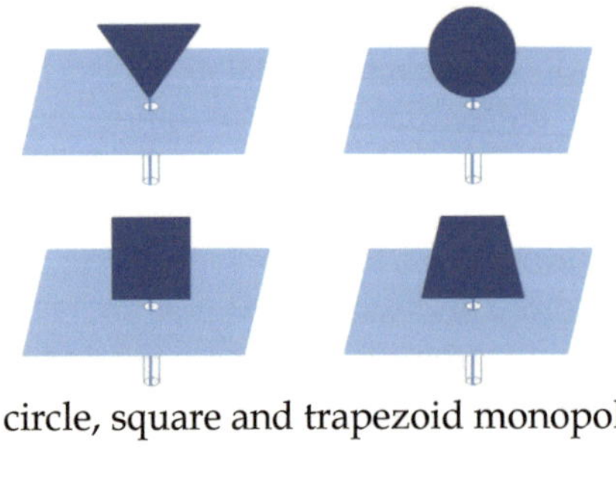

Fig. 4. Examples of triangle, circle, square and trapezoid monopoles.

These broadband monopoles feature wide operating bandwidths, satisfactory radiation properties, simple structures and ease of fabrication. Several techniques have also been proposed to improve the antenna bandwidth, for example, the use of a beveling plate (Ammann & Chen, 2003b), a double feed (Antonino-Daviu et al., 2003) or an asymmetrical feed arrangement (Ammann & Chen, 2003c), a trident-shaped feeding strip (Wong et al., 2005), etc. However, they are not planar structures because their ground planes are perpendicular to the radiators. This drawback limits their practical applications due to their large area.
Research focuses on antennas that can be easily integrated into other RF circuits as well as can be embedded in UWB devices. From 2004, works are intensified on planar and printed UWB antennas. The printed monopole antennas present wideband matching characteristic, omnidirectional radiation patterns, high radiation efficiency and compact size. Many microstrip UWB antenna designs were proposed. The planar radiators are etched onto the dielectric substrate of the printed circuit boards (PCBs). The ground plane may be either coplanar with the radiators or under the substrate. The radiators can be fed by a microstrip line and coaxial cable. Some examples of geometry of such antennas are given in Fig. 4. A printed planar circular disc monopole fed by a microstrip line is presented in Fig. 4 (a) (Liang et al., 2004). A printed planar elliptic patch presenting an impedance matching technique of creating a notch at the ground plane opposite to the microstrip line is illustrated in Fig. 4 (b) (Huang & Hsia, 2005). A rectangular patch with two steps and a slot to improve the impedance matching especially at high frequencies is shown in Fig. 4 (c) (Choi et al., 2004).

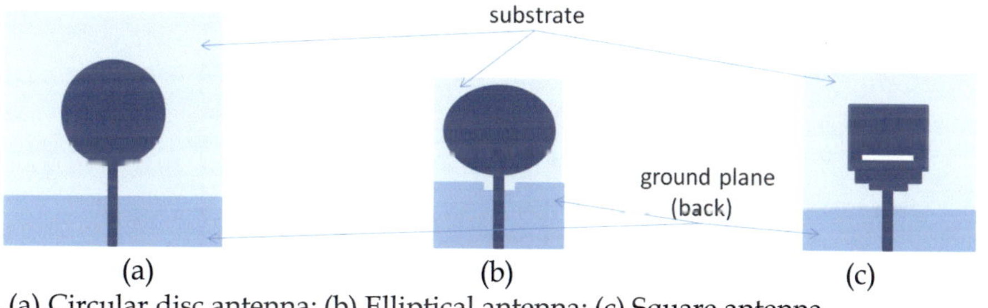

Fig. 4. (a) Circular disc antenna; (b) Elliptical antenna; (c) Square antenna.

2.3 Frequency notched UWB antennas

To prevent interference with existing wireless networks with standards, such as IEEE 802.11a wireless LAN in USA (5.15 GHz - 5.35 GHz, 5.725 GHz - 5.825 GHZ) and HIPERLAN/2 in Europe (5.15 GHz - 5.35 GHz, 5.47 GHz - 5.725 GHz), stopband characteristics of UWB systems are required. However, the use of an additional filter would increase the complexity of UWB systems. To tackle this problem, several novel UWB antennas with band-notched characteristic have been presented. The most popular and the easiest technique is to embed a narrow slot into the radiating patch in order to change the current flow on the metallic parts of the antenna. The slot may have different shapes, such as V-shaped (Kim & Kwon, 2004), U-shaped (Vuong at al., 2007), C-shaped (Lin & Hung, 2006), H-shapped (Bao & Amman, 2007), etc. Other possibilities in order to create a band-notched function are the insertion of strips in the patch (Lin & Hung, 2006), and the insertion of a function of filtering in or before the feed line of the antenna (Visser, 2007; Djaiz et al. 2009).

The compact band-rejected U-slotted planar antenna for IR-UWB presented below illustrates the concept of co-design approach, i.e., antenna and filter. This design is inspired from the planar UWB antenna proposed by Choi (Choi et al., 2004). Fig. 5 shows the geometry of the antenna. A U-Slot filter was added to reject the undesired frequency bandwidth. The antenna is fed by a 50 Ω microstrip line printed on a substrate with partial ground plane.

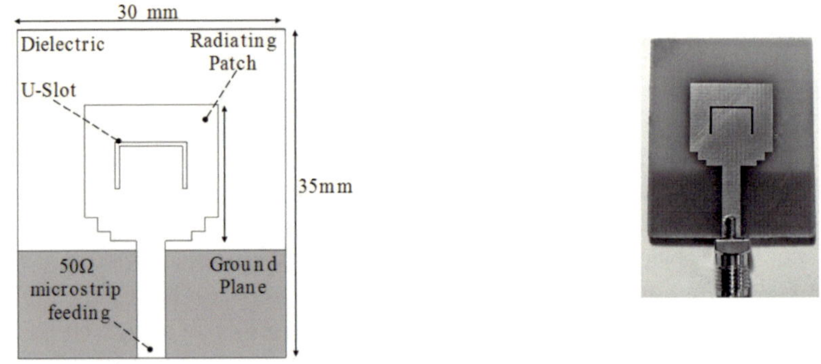

Fig. 5. UWB compact planar monopole antenna (Vuong et al., 2007).

Techniques applied to match the antenna over the UWB frequency band are: the use of two steps and a partial ground plane. The antenna was first studied without the U-Slot filter to operate in the overall UWB frequency band. Once the antenna was designed for operation within the overall UWB frequency band, the U-Slot filter is added to reject the undesirable 5.15 GHz to 5.825 GHz frequency band (Fig. 6).

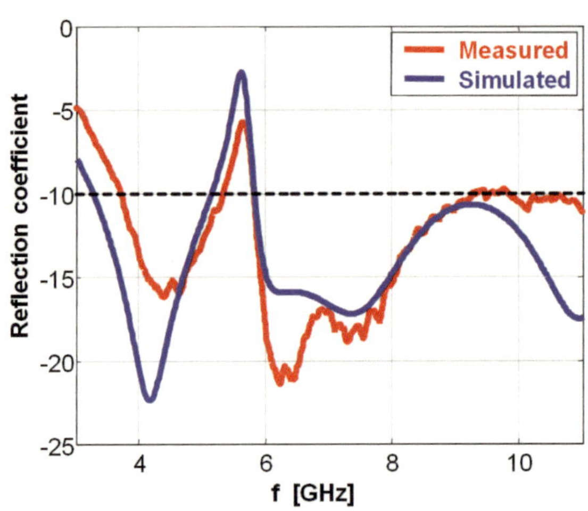

Fig. 6. Measured and simulated reflection coefficient.

Fig. 7 shows the surface current distribution at different frequencies. It can be observed on Fig. 7 (a) that the current concentrated on the edges of the interior and exterior of the U-Slot are opposed at 5.5 GHz. The rejected frequency occurs where the total U-slot length is equal to half the wavelength. Consequently, the antenna impedance changes at this frequency due to the resonant properties of the U-Slot. This leads to a high attenuation of the undesired frequencies. For other frequencies, the addition of the U-Slot filter has few effects.

(a) (b)

Fig. 7. Simulated current distributions. (a) 5.5GHz. (b) 7GHz.

Finally, it should be noted that frequency-notched UWB antennas can also be used in multi-band systems, where the use of a single antenna that can function at potentially widely separated narrow bands of interest, is relevant for economic and cosmetic reasons (Schantz et al., 2003).

2.4 MIMO UWB antennas

Recent studies have demonstrated several advantages of using multiple antenna techniques in UWB wireless communications. Two main kinds of applications have been considered. First, instead of using one radiation element to cover the entire bandwidth, an approach is to use an antenna array in order to improve the global characteristics. The antenna array is made of several radiation elements, each covering a relatively narrow bandwidth, and the sum of their bandwidths fulfils the UWB requirements. The second application is the well-known MIMO technique for the narrowband systems: beamforming, spatial multiplexing and diversity coding techniques. Beamforming techniques use switched-beam smart antennas, adaptive beamformers (adaptive array smart antennas) or phased arrays in order to achieve beam-steering and to increase the signal gain by constructive interference, and finally to reduce the multipath fading effect. Spatial multiplexing exploits MIMO antenna configuration in order to increase the channel capacity; high data rates are achieved by transmitting parallel data streams in the same frequency spectrum. Diversity coding techniques emit a signal from each of the transmit antenna using a space-time coding. It provides signal diversity by exploiting the independent fading in the multiple antenna links. This section focuses on multi-antenna system composed of more than two UWB antennas operating over the same band to achieve the targets of high transmission speed and channel capacity by mitigating the effects of multipath, small-scale fading and co-channel interference. Like single antenna design, multiple-antenna systems are also ideally designed targeting planar geometry and compact size for the reason that it is easy to integrate with the radio devices. However, when the distance between antennas in the system decreases, mutual coupling between them increases causing a degradation of diversity performance. In this context, the main challenge in the design of MIMO antenna is to obtain the independence of each element from the others keeping their size as compact as possible. Research on MIMO antennas has always been carried out for the last several years and is still in progress. A number of MIMO antennas for portable devices have been presented in the literature. These antennas are of multimode, multi-polarized and/or array types exploiting pattern, polarization and/or spatial diversity respectively. The UWB-MIMO antennas have gained popularity very recently. Several strategies have been identified in order to enhance the port isolations of the UWB multi-antenna systems: spatial and angular variations (Wong et al. 2008; Lin & Huang, 2008; Najam et al., 2009), diversity polarization (Mtumbuka et al., 2005; Adamiuk et al., 2009), vector antennas (Rajagopalan et al. 2007), use of stepped ground plane (Cheng et al., 2008), and insertion of stubs (Hong et al., 2008). Moreover, in these applications, it is generally desired to achieve quasi omni-directional radiating patterns and flat gain variations in the operating frequency bands.

From circular disc monopole antenna, the MIMO-UWB antenna, presented below (Fig. 8), has been designed and optimized to match the bandwidth defined by the FCC (i.e. 3.1–10.6 GHz), to achieve a reduced mutual coupling and enhanced isolation, and also to have a compact size. This antenna exploits the approach of using stubs on the ground plane in order to enhance isolation between the radiators.

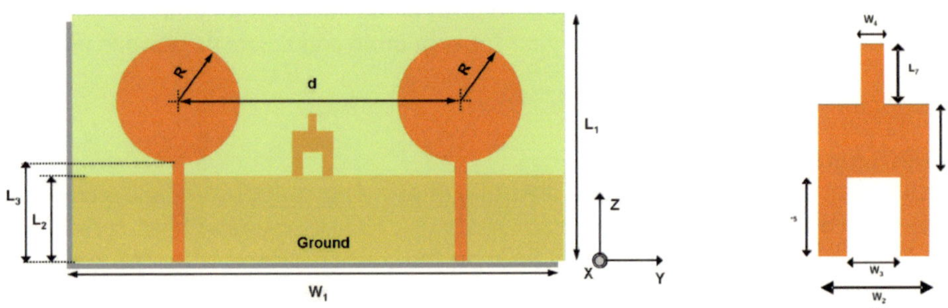

(a) (b)

Fig. 8. (a) Layout of UWB MIMO antenna: global view (L_1 = 40 mm; W_1 = 68 mm); (b) Layout of inverted-Y shaped stub.

The simulated reflection coefficients (S_{11} and S_{22}) for both radiating elements of antenna in decibels are shown in Fig. 9 (a). Due to the symmetry in the structure, S_{11} and S_{22} are the same. Fig. 9 (a) also presents the reflection coefficients of the antenna when there is no stub. It is noticed that the return loss is significantly changed at lower side of the operating band after adding the stub. Thus, it can be said that the return loss is sensitive to the insertion of stub on the ground, yet an impedance bandwidth of 3.2-10.6 GHz is available.

Fig. 9 (b) represents the simulated isolation between the antenna elements considering the case in which one antenna is excited and the other is terminated with matched impedance. Due to symmetry and reciprocity, S_{21} and S_{12} are the same. It is clear from the results that mutual coupling is always less than -11 dB in the frequency range of interest when there is no stub. The addition of the stub reduces mutual coupling significantly, i.e., less than -20 dB in the band of 3.2 - 4.0 GHz, less than -15 dB in the band of 4.0 - 6.8 GHz and less than -20 dB in the band of 6.8 - 10.6 GHz.

To elaborate further, the degree of isolation in the proposed antenna can also be determined by observing surface current distributions. Fig. 10 shows the current distributions with and without stubs at two frequencies 3.5 GHz and 7 GHz when port 1 (left radiating element) is excited and port 2 (right element) is terminated with a load impedance of 50 Ω. The effects of the stub can clearly be noticed by comparing with those without stub. The current is absorbed by stub and thus it reduces the mutual coupling between the two monopoles.

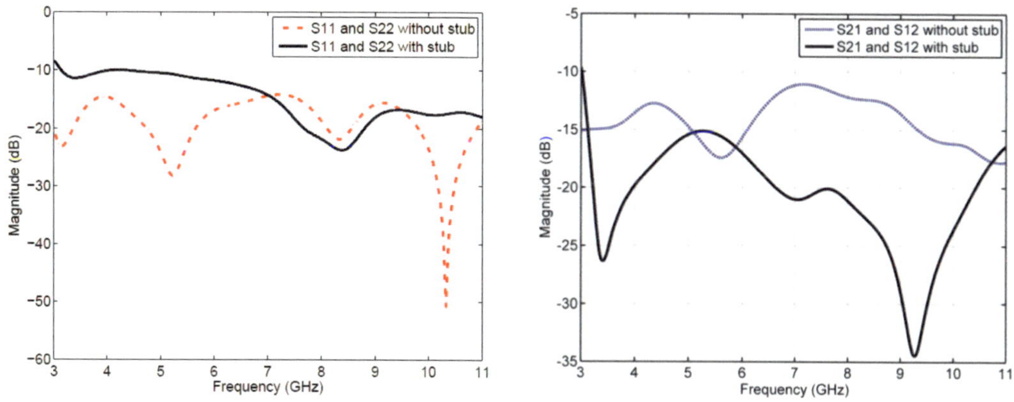

(a) (b)

Fig. 9. (a) Simulated reflection coefficient; (b) Simulated isolation.

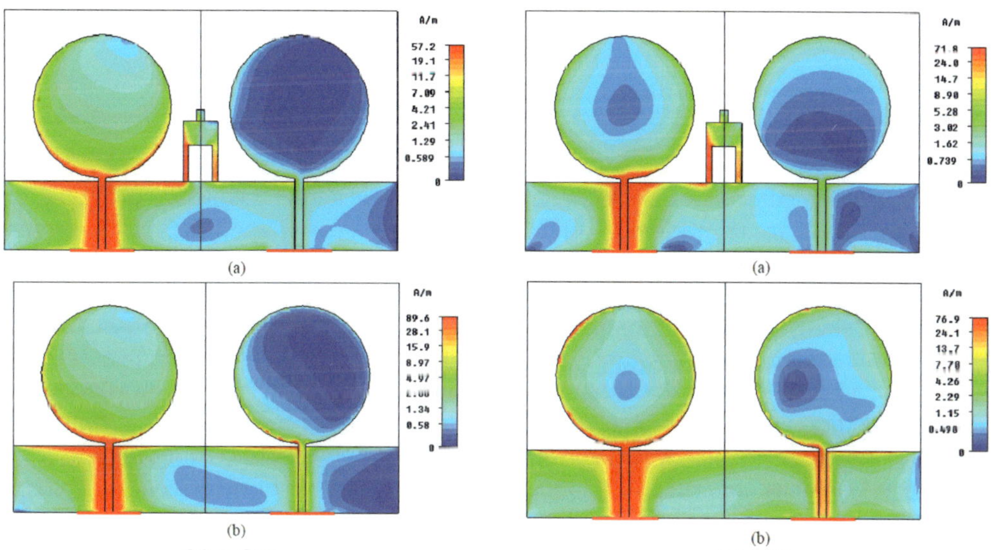

@3.5 GHz @7 GHz

Fig. 10. Surface current distributions of antenna (a) with and (b) without stub.

2.5 Conclusions

UWB antennas make an old but developing subject. Many designs have been developed and new designs are emerging all the time. Future works will focus on the improvement of actual antenna structures and the integration of reconfiguring abilities. For example, concerning the coexistence of UWB systems with the wireless services at 5 GHz, recent studies have shown the interests to use composite right\left handed (CRLH) metamaterials for designing a very small notch filter (Kahng et al., 2009), and to use either PIN diodes or microelectromechanical system (MEMS) switches for achieving reconfigurable UWB antennas with band-notched characteristics (Nikolaou et al., 2009). On the other hand, reconfigurable antennas based on the use of active components with low frequency tuning and switchable UWB band have also been proposed recently (Loizeau & Sibille, 2009). These antennas offer the frequency agility of the RF stages as needed by multi-standard radios. Further in terms of reconfigurability, future antennas should enable to modify their radiation patterns, frequency, polarization, etc.

Another future axe of development resides in flexible, wearable and/or textile antennas. Thus, new applications have been imagined where people will carry a range of devices and sensors including medical or positioning sensors which will enable them to communicate with each other. In this context, UWB systems are the potential candidates. UWB antennas will then be fabricated on flexible organic substrates and integrated into clothing. In the same time, their performance must gain robustness against the deformations.

Finally, it should also be noticed that as analytical solutions to antenna problems (e.g., optimization of the geometry) are very difficult (near to impossible), therefore computer numerical simulation has become the major antenna design tool, especially after the publication of Harrington's book on method of moment in 1968. Significant improvements and advancements have been made in the antenna software industry over the past 15 years. Many fine software packages are now available in the market as an essential aid for antenna analysis and design.

3. Modeling of Ultra Wideband Antennas

3.1 Overview

Considering an antenna as an electromagnetic radiator, a Radio Frequency (RF) engineer will be interested in its radiation pattern, directivity, gain, aperture, efficiency and polarization. However, considering an antenna as a circuit element, an RF circuit designer will be more interested in its input impedance, reflection coefficient and voltage standing wave ratio. Taking account of narrowband systems, all of these characteristics can be considered as frequency independent, i.e., constant for the frequency band in use. Whilst in wideband systems, conventional properties become strongly frequency dependent. Consequently, one important feature of UWB antennas is that they introduce some pulse dispersion due to its frequency sensitive characteristics. Notably concerning impulse radio applications, antennas are critical components since the emitted and received pulse shapes are distorted.

New parameters have been introduced to take into consideration the transient radiations and to reveal phase variation effects. The antenna effective lengths can be considered to specify impulse radiation and reception characteristics of antennas (Shlivinski, 1997). More recently, with the emergence of UWB technology, the frequency domain transfer functions and the associated time domain impulse response derived from antenna effective lengths, have been preferred to describe these characteristics. The antenna is then modeled as a Linear Time Invariant (LTI) system for which the performance will affect the overall performance of the wireless communication system. Different definitions of the parameters involved in obtaining transmit and receive transfer functions have been proposed (Mohammadian et al., 2003; Qing et al., 2005; Duroc et al., 2007). In practice, the transfer functions are deduced from the simulated or measured complex scattering parameter, i.e., transmission coefficient, S_{21}. A Vector Network Analyzer (VNA) is generally used in the frequency domain and a post-treatment allows the assessment of time domain measures (Hines & Stinehelfer, 1974). It should be noticed that the time domain measurement is

possible but the corresponding calibration is not always well established, however the two approaches were demonstrated to be quasi-equivalent (Sörgel et al., 2003). In the literature, the papers which present new UWB antennas propose not only the design aspects and conventional characteristics but also, more and more, a time domain characterization in order to validate the antenna's ability to transmit short pulses and to receive these pulses with low distortion. Moreover, performance parameters (e.g., the fidelity factor and the full width at half maximum), issued to transfer function or impulse response, were introduced to quantify and analyze the pulse-preserving performance of UWB antennas (Sörgel & Wiesbeck, 2005; Kwon, 2006). One issue with many published propagation measurements was that the antenna effect is implicitly included in the measurement but not explicitly allowed for in the channel analysis, e.g., the IEEE 802.15.3a standard model. Thus, the consideration of the antenna effects in order to analyze or evaluate the performance of a UWB system also implied the introduction of antenna models based on transfer function or pulse response (Zhang & Brown, 2006; Timmerman et al., 2007). On the other hand, a lot of research is dedicated to the approaches for the modeling of UWB antennas directly in RF circuit simulators in order to simulate the performance of circuit with the antennas included. A transient model using cascaded ideal transmission lines has been proposed for UWB antennas (Su & Brazil, 2007). Demirkan and Spence have presented a general method for the modeling of arbitrary UWB antennas directly in RF circuit simulators. The antenna modeling approach is also based on the measurements of S-parameters (Demirkan & Spencer, 2007). Finally, recent studies have shown that a parametric modeling could improve the modeling (Licul & Davis, 2005; Duroc et al., 2006; Roblin, 2006). Analytical and compact expressions of transfer functions and impulse responses can be computed from simulations or measurements. The parametric methods are based on the Singularity Expansion Method (SEM) which provides a set of poles and residues.
About MIMO antennas, in the case of narrowband, different parameters can be used to characterize physical effects: the scattering parameters, the envelope correlation, and the total active reflection coefficient. However, these descriptions are not fully adequate when UWB systems are studied. Several works have proposed additional measures dedicated to MIMO-UWB antenna systems in order to improve the effect of the mutual coupling. The effects of UWB array coupling have been investigated using the general expressions for the time domain active array factor and active element factor. The interaction between radiators in a UWB biconical array has been analyzed (D'Errico & Sibille, 2008). Scattering and coupling are discriminated, and a scattering coefficient is introduced neglecting the incident wave curvature and near field effects but allowing the prediction of the multiple antennas performance. A method to compare dual-antenna systems by introducing a referenced diversity gain has been presented (Dreina et al. 2009). A model of coupled antennas, in order to integrate the effects of the coupling between antennas in a model of the propagation channel obtained from ray-tracing or asymptotic methods, has been studied (Pereira et al., 2009). From scattering parameters, a coupling matrix is being introduced, and this approach is validated for the case of canonical antennas and UWB antennas.

In the following part, the prospects of the use of parametric models are shown through several examples.

3.2 Prospects of the use of parametric models

The following applications of the use of parametric models are presented using the small U-slotted planar antenna discussed earlier (§2.3).

3.2.1 Preamble: brief summary of the Singularity Expansion Method

Two of the most popular linear methods are: the polynomial method (first developed by Prony in 1795), and the Matrix Pencil Method which is more recent and computationally more efficient because the determination of the poles is a one-step process (Sarkar & Pereira, 1995). These methods use the same projection in a base of exponential functions. The model is given by:

$$x(t)=\sum_{i=1}^{N} R_i \exp(s_i t) \tag{2}$$

where $\{R_i\}$ are the residues (complex amplitudes), $\{s_i\}$ are the poles and N is the order of the model. Then after sampling, and with the poles defined in the z-plane as $z_i = \exp(s_i T_e)$, the sequence can be written as

$$x(k)=\sum_{i=1}^{N} R_i z_i^k \tag{3}$$

The knowledge of the poles and the residues allows the direct determination of the impulse response and the transfer function. The frequency representation is also a direct function of the poles and residues and can be written in the Fourier plane and z-plane in the equations as follows

$$X(f)=FT[x(t)]=\sum_{i=1}^{N} \frac{R_i}{2\pi jf - s_i} \tag{4}$$

$$X(z)=zT\{x(k)\}=\sum_{i=1}^{N} \frac{R_i}{1-z_i z^{-1}}=\sum_{i=1}^{N} \frac{R_i z}{z-z_i} \tag{5}$$

where the operator "FT" corresponds to the Fourier transform and the operator "zT" corresponds to the z-transform. Using an inverse Fourier transform, the impulse response x(t) of the antenna is determined from the transfer function X(f).

From time domain responses (i.e., impulse responses) characterizing the antennas, the parametric modeling allows the calculation of poles and residues. Hence, a compact and analytical time-frequency model can be deduced.

The quality of the modeling is a compromise between accuracy and complexity, i.e., the order of the model N. Generally, this parameter is not known and it is necessary to estimate it, but there is no straightforward method. It is possible to choose the most significant residues. However, in the presence of noise or considering an on-dimensioned system, the use of singular value decomposition is more relevant. The accuracy of the fit model can then be achieved by calculating the "mean square error" of the difference between the model and the measured or simulated impulse responses or transfer functions (Duroc et al. 2007). In the following analysis, the Signal to Noise Ratio (SNR) is deduced from the power of the obtained error.

3.2.2 Directional time-frequency parametric model of the antenna response

In UWB, as explained previously, additional characteristics of antenna must be introduced to take into account the transient radiation and to reveal phase variation effects. Thus, UWB antennas are considered as linear time invariant systems defined in the frequency domain and the time domain by a complex transfer function and the associated impulse response respectively. The antenna characteristics also depend on the signal propagation direction. As a result, transfer functions and impulse responses characterizing UWB antennas are spatial vectors. Such a characterization provides especially the radiated and received transient waveforms of any arbitrary waveform excitation and antenna orientation. In this context, the presented method provides a compact and analytical time-frequency model of the directional antenna response from a parametric modeling.

A common approach for determining the transfer function and the associated impulse response of a UWB antenna is to exploit the simulated or measured two-port S-parameters of a two-element antenna system. Supposing that the impulse response of a reference antenna is known, then the parametric model of the antenna under consideration can easily be deduced using the previously presented methods. The modeling can be applied for several orientations of the antenna to obtain a directional model. However, whatever is the considered directional impulse response, the dominant poles are the same and only residues need to be adapted (Licul & Davis, 2005). Thus, the complete model can be reduced even further.

For example, the antenna radiation characteristics in the time domain can be represented by the impulse response vs. azimuth angle. For the antenna under test, the model contains only 30 complex pole pairs and 30 associated complex residue sets for any orientation. Moreover, due to the symmetry of the antenna geometry, the models for the considered symmetric orientations (θ = – 45° and 45°) are the same. In consequence, the antenna model complexity is divided by two. Fig. 11 presents the antenna radiation characteristics in the time domain for four orientations of the azimuth plane. The measured and modeled curves match with a very good accuracy (SNR = 54 dB).

.

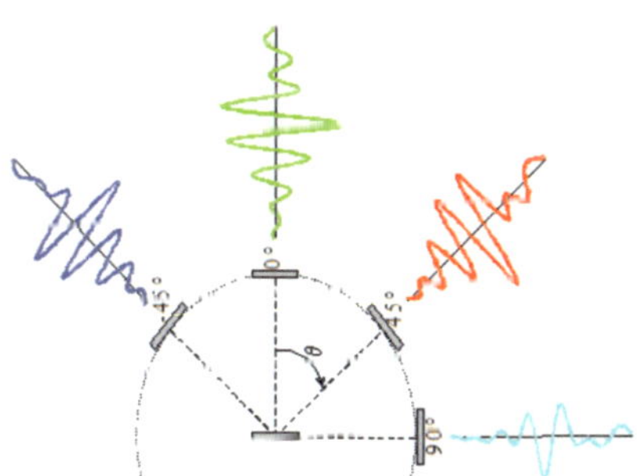

Fig. 11. Antenna radiation characterization in the time domain.

3.2.3 Equivalent circuit of UWB antenna input impedance

In circuit design, antennas are considered as loaded impedances. In narrowband systems, an antenna is simply represented by a 50 Ω resistor or an RLC parallel circuit to consider mismatching. However, when UWB antennas are considered, the circuit modeling becomes more complex as several adjacent resonances have to be taken into account. An efficient method, also based on a parametric approach, can obtain an equivalent circuit of antenna input impedances. Indeed, the parametric approach can also be applied to the antenna input impedance and associated to the Foster's passive filter synthesis method allowing the determination of an equivalent circuit of this impedance.
Firstly the antenna input impedance Z_a is deduced from the reflection coefficient Γ by the equation written as

$$Z_a = Z_0(1+\Gamma)/(1-\Gamma) \tag{6}$$

where Z_0 is the reference impedance (generally Z0=50Ω). As previously mentioned, a parametric model of Z_a can be determined. The achieved model can then be identified as the impedance of the Foster's filter given by

$$Z(p) = \sum_j \frac{A_j p + B_j}{p^2 + 2\alpha_j p + \omega_j^2} \tag{7}$$

Finally, the parametric model of the studied antenna input impedance possesses 12 complex and conjugate couples of poles and residues. The equivalent circuit model is represented in Fig. 12. It should be noted that some resistors have negative values and hence are unphysical electrical components. However, the electric circuit behaves as the antenna input impedance.

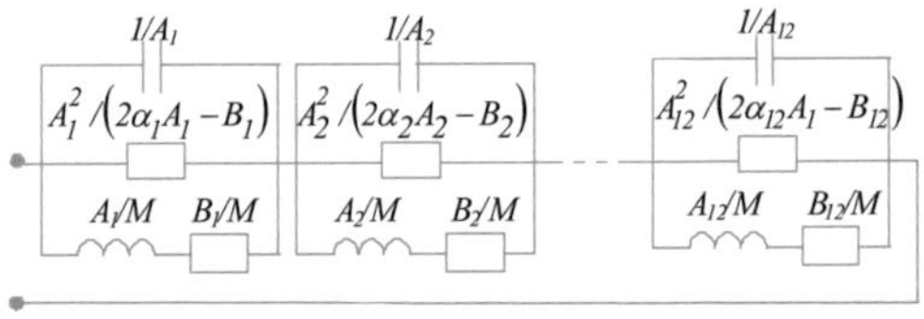

Fig. 12. Equivalent electric circuit of antenna input impedance.

Fig. 13 shows the measured real and imaginary parts of the antenna input impedance compared to the results from the parametric model and the circuit equivalent model simulated with the software SPICE. The model could be improved by increasing the order of the parametric model and the precision of the values allotted to components.

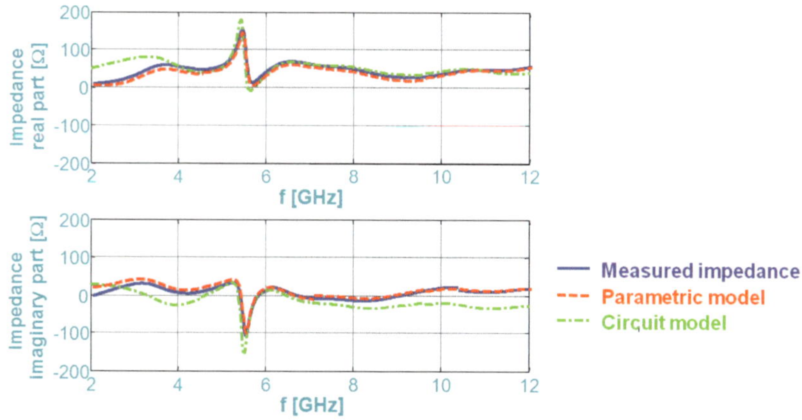

Fig. 13. Real and imaginary parts of antenna input impedance.

3.2.4 VHDL-AMS modeling of an UWB radio link including antennas

A new interesting way to model UWB antennas is to consider them as a part of the radio link in order to design or to optimize a complete UWB transceiver. Such transceivers are generally complex RF, analog and mixed-signal systems. They need an analog and mixed simulation environment for RF, analog and digital simulations. For high level system simulation, Matlab is the traditionally used tool but its use is generally limited to functional exploration. When the circuit design level is needed, every "design community" has its own simulation tools: digital designers work with event-driven simulators, analog designers use SPICE-like simulators, and Radio Frequency Integrated Circuits (RFIC) designers need specific frequency/time domain analysis tools. This large number of simulators makes the design time expensive and generates many compatibility problems. Recently, two major environments have made possible the combination of the three mentioned simulation families in order to suit hybrid system designers needs; the newly released Advance MS RF (ADMS RF) from Mentor Graphics, the RFDE design flow from Cadence/Agilent permit multi-abstraction and mixed-signal simulation and multilingual modeling (VHDL-AMS and SPICE). Some works have shown the usefulness of such an approach for complex mixed-signal system design. None of these works has included the antennas within their models. However, the UWB radio link model including antennas can be written in VHDL-AMS (Very high speed integrated circuit Hardware Description Language - Analog and Mixed Signal) from the parametric model of the transmission parameter S_{21} (Khouri at al., 2007). In order to illustrate the approach, the complete UWB communication chain based on a simple architecture with a non-coherent reception technique is simulated and illustrated in Fig. 14. In the transmission chain, a Rayleigh pulse generator controlled by a clock is used. Consequently, digital data is modulated using OOK (On-Off Keying) which is the classical modulation technique used for UWB energy detection receivers. The reception chain consists of a square-law device used for energy detection of the received signal, a comparator and a monostable circuit.

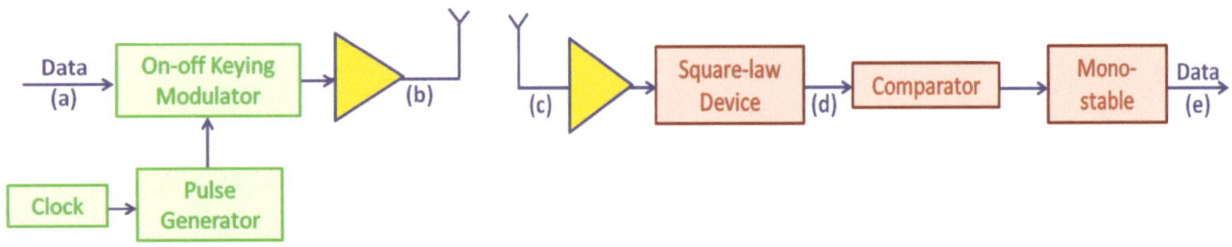

Fig. 14. Simulated UWB communication chain.

Fig. 15 is a UWB transmission chronogram and illustrates the obtained signals. Fig. 15 (a) is a random digital data flow representing the information to be sent. Fig. 15 (b) is the impulse radio OOK signal where pulses are easily modeled in VHDL-AMS by the Rayleigh monocycle. After propagation, the received signal shown in Fig. 15 (c) indicates the attenuation, propagation delay, and antenna's filtering effects. These effects can be better observed by taking the zoom as given in Fig. 16. Then, Fig. 15 (d) represents the extracted energy from which the digital signal in Fig. 15 (e) is recovered.

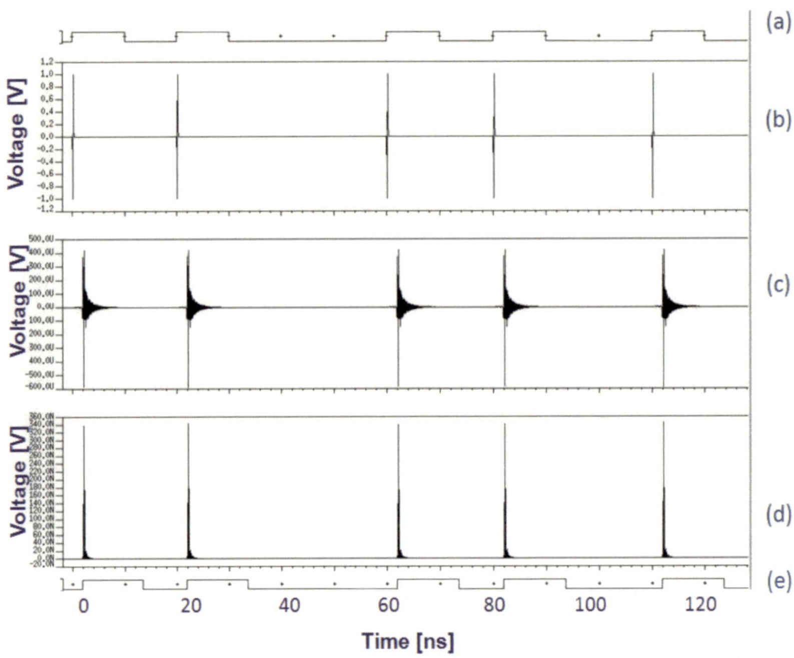

Fig. 15. (a) Random digital flow representing the information to be sent; (b) Impulse radio OOK signal (Ralyleigh monocycle); (c) Received signal (delayed, attenuated and distorted); (d) Extracted energy; (e) Recovered digital signal.

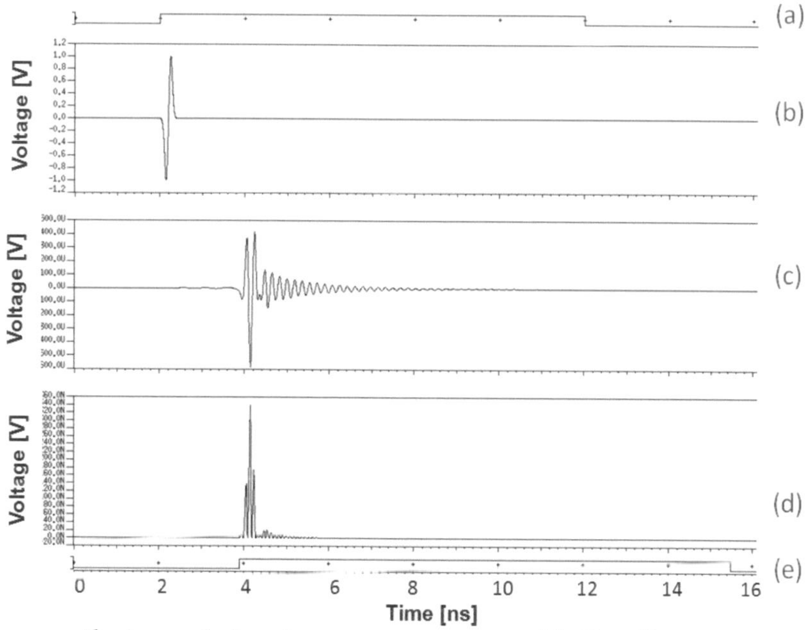

Fig. 16. Zoom on the transmission chronogram represented in Fig. 15.

4. Conclusions and Perspectives

The wide bandwidths of UWB systems present new challenges for the design and modeling of antennas. Familiar antenna architectures like patches and slots have been modified to meet the extension of the bandwidths; the familiar techniques like arrays have been expanded to UWB applications as well as more recent concepts like antenna spectral filtering. The antennas are no more considered as simple loads of 50 Ω or simple energy detectors but as fundamental parts of RF systems providing filtering properties.

UWB systems also appear as very promising solutions for future RF systems. Their next development will imply the need of UWB antennas integrated with new functionalities. The functions of antenna, more particularly the multi-antenna, will evolve and accommodate new technology aspects, such as diversity, reconfigurability and cognition. Obviously, the multi-antenna is not only an association of two or several radiating elements but it will also be integrated with sensors and electronic circuits. Under this evolution, embedded signal processing will be an obligatory stage. The future UWB antennas will be able to scan the environment, to harvest ambient energy, and to reconfigure spatially and spectrally themselves while maintaining the basic communication functions in transmission and reception. Moreover, in a long term perspective, integration of the whole antenna function into a chip would be a significant and strategic added value. In addition, the physical implementation of the "intelligence" with the antenna is also a real challenge. It is a fundamental reason behind the existence of few real physical smart antennas. Furthermore, when wideband systems are envisaged, the design considerations and guidelines for antennas are of the utmost importance. Some works have already presented promising original solutions in order to physically realize analog and digital processing, thanks to

microwave analogue FIR (Finite Impulse Response) filters and FPGA (Field Programmable Gate Array) architectures, respectively.
New UWB antennas models must be developed being radically different from those currently available, and this implies the development of original and innovative approaches. New models should allow the intrinsic characterization of antennas and also the evaluation of their performance in given situations. These models will be able to take into account different functions, such as microwave, signal processing and radiated elements. They must be scalable, generic and adaptive. Taking into account the long term vision of silicon integration of smart antennas, these models must be compliant with classical silicon integrated circuit design tools. Several levels of abstraction must be envisaged, notably with a co-design orientation. Further, the suggested models must give new ways to improve the current structures of antennas and to associate them with new control laws.

5. References

Adamiuk, G.; Beer, S.; Wiesbeck, W. & Zwick, T. (2009). Dual-Orthogonal Polarized Antenna for UWB-IR Technology. *IEEE Antennas and Wireless Propagation Letters*, Vol. 8, (2009) 4 (981-984), ISSN: 1536-1225

Agrawal, P.; Kumar, G.; Ray & K.P. (1997). New Wide-Band Monopole Antennas, *Proceedings of IEEE International Symposium on Antennas and Propagation*, pp. 248-251, ISBN: 0-7803-4178-3, Montréal, Québec, July 1997, IEEE, Piscataway

Akdagli, A.; Ozdemir, C.; Yamacli, S. (2008). A Review of Recent Patents on Ultra Wide Band (UWB) Antennas. *Recents Patents on Electrical Engineering*, Vol. 1, No. 1, (January 2008) 8 (68-75), ISSN: 1874-4761

Ammann, M.J. & Chen, Z.J. (2003). Wideband monopole antennas for multiband wireless systems. *IEEE Antennas and Propagation Magazine*, Vol. 45, (April 2003) 5 (146-150), ISSN: 1045-9243

Ammann, M.J. & Chen, Z.J. (2003). A Wide Band Shorted Planar Monopole with Bevel. *IEEE Transactions on Antennas and Propagation*, Vol. 51, No. 4, (April 2003) 4 (901-903), ISSN: 0018-926X

Ammann, M.J. & Chen, Z.J. (2003). An asymmetrical feed arrangement for improved impedance bandwidth of planar monopole antennas. *Microwave and Optical Technology Letters*, Vol. 40, No. 2, (December 2003) 3 (156-158), ISSN: 0895-2477

Antonino-Daviu, E.; Cabedo-Fabres, M.; Ferrando-Battaler, M. & Valero-Nogueira, A. (2003). Wideband Double-fed Planar Monopole Antennas. *Electronics Letters*, Vol. 39, No. 23, (November 2003) 2 (1635-1636), ISSN: 0013-5194

Balanis, C.A. (2005). *Antenna Theory: Analysis and Design*, Wiley, ISBN: 978-0-471-66782-7, USA

Bao, X.L. & Amman, M.J. (2007). Printed Band-Rejection UWB Antenna with H-Shaped Slot, *Proceedings of International Workshop on Antenna Technology: Small and Smart Antennas Metamaterials and Applications*, pp. 319-322, ISBN: 1-4244-1088-6, Cambridge, UK, March 2007

Chang, D.C. (2008). UWB Antennas and Their Applications, *Proceedings of International Workshop on Antenna Technology: Small Antennas and Novel Metamaterials*, pp. 14-19, ISBN: 978-1-4244-1522-9, Chiba, Japan, May 2008

Chang, K. (1997). *Handbook of microwave and optical components*, Wiley, ISBN: 0471613665, USA

Cheng, Y.; Lu, W.J.; Cheng, C.H.; Cao, W. & Li, Y. (2008). Printed Diversity Antenna with Cross Shape for Ultra-Wideband Applications, *Proceedings of International Conference on Communications Systems*, pp. 813-816, Guangzhou, China, November 2008

Choi, S.H.; Park, J.K.; Kim, S.K. & Park, Y.K. (2004). A new ultra-wideband antenna for UWB applications. *Microwave and optical technology letters*, Vol. 40, No. 5, (March 2004) 3 (399-401), ISSN 0895-2477

Dardari, D. & D'Errico, R. (2008). Passive Ultrawide Bandwidth RFID, *Proceedings of Conference Global Telecommunications*, pp. 3947-3952, ISBN: 978-1-4244-2324-8, New Orleans, November-December 2008, USA.

Demirkan, M. & Spencer, R.R. (2007). Antenna Characterization Method for Front-End Design of Pulse-Based Ultrawideband Transceivers. *IEEE Transactions on Antennas and Propagation*, Vol. 55, No. 10, (October 2007) 12 (2888-2899), ISSN: 0018-926X

D'Errico, R. & Sibille, A. (2008). Single and Multiple Scaterring in UWB Bicone Arrays. *International Journal of Antennas and Propagation*, Vol. 2008, (2008) 11 (1-11), ISSN: 1687-5869

Djaiz, A; Habib, M.A.; Nedil, M. & Denidni, T.A. Design of UWB Filter-Antenna with Notched Band at 5.8 GHz, *Proceedings of IEEE International Symposium Antennas and Propagation*, ISBN: 978-1-4244-3647-7, Charleston, USA, June 2009, IEEE, Piscataway

Dreina, E.; Pons, M.; Vuong, T.P. & S. Tedjini. (2009). Comparison of UWB Dual-Antenna Systems using Diversity, *Proceedings of European Conference on Antennas and Propagation*, pp. 2558-2561, ISBN: 978-3-8007-3152-7, Berlin, Germany, March 2009

Duroc, Y.; Vuong, T.P. & Tedjini, S. (2006). Realistic Modeling of Antennas for Ultra-Wideband, *Proceedings of IEEE Radio and Wireless Symposium*, pp. 347-350, ISBN: 0-7803-9413-5, San Diego, USA, January 2006, IEEE

Duroc, Y.; Ghiotto, A.; Vuong, T.P. & Tedjini, S. (2007). UWB Antennas: Systems with Transfer Function and Impulse Response. *IEEE Transactions on Antennas and Propagation*, Vol. 55, No. 5, (May 2007) 4 (1449-1451), ISSN: 0018-926X

Duroc, Y; Vuong, T.P. & Tedjini, S. (2007). A Time/Frequency Model of Ultra-Wideband Antennas. *IEEE Transactions on Antennas and Propagation*, Vol. 55, No. 8, (August 2007) 9 (2342-2350), ISSN: 0018-926X

Hong, S.; Lee, J. & Choi, J. (2008). Design of UWB diversity antenna for PDA applications, *Proceedings of International Conference on Advanced Communication Technology*, pp. 583-585, Phoenix Park, Republic of Korea, February 2008

Huchard, M.; Delaveaud, C. & Tedjini, S. (2005). Characterization of the coverage uniformity of an antenna based on its far-field, *Proceedings of IEEE International Symposium Antennas and Propagation*, pp. 500-503, ISBN: 0-7803-8883-6, Washington, USA, July 2005, IEEE, Piscataway

IEEE (1993). *IEEE Standard Definitions of Terms for Antennas*, IEEE Std 145-1993, ISBN: 1-55937-317-2, USA

Islam, M.T.; Shakib, M.N.; Misran, N. & Sun, T.S. (2009). Broadband Microstrip Patch Antenna. *European Journal of Scientific Research*, Vol. 27, No. 2, (2009) 7 (174-180), ISSN: 1450-216X

Kahng, S.; Shin, E.C.; Jang, G.H.; Anguera, J; Ju, J.H & Choi, J. (2009). A UWB Combined with the CRLH Metamaterial UWB Bandpass Filter having the Bandstop at the 5 GHz Band WLAN, *Proceedings of IEEE International Symposium on Antennas and Propagation*, ISBN: 978-1-4244-3647-7, Charleston, USA, June 2009, IEEE

Kaiser, T.; Arlan, H.; Chen, Z.N. & Di Benedetto, M.G. (2006). *MIMO and UWB in Ultra Wideband Wireless Communication*, Wiley, ISBN: 9780471715214, USA

Khouri, R.; Duroc, Y; Beroulle, V. & Tedjini, S. (2007). VHDL-AMS Modeling of an UWB Radio Link Including Antennas, *Proceedings of IEEE International Conference on Electronics, Circuits and Systems*, ISBN: 978-1-4244-1377-5, Marrakech, Maroc, December 2007, IEEE

Kim, Y & Kwon, D.H. (2004). CPW-Fed Planar Ultra Wideband Antenna Having a Frequency Band Notch Function. *Electronics Letters*, Vol. 40, No. 7, (April 2004) 3 (403-405), ISSN: 0013-5194

Kwon, D.H. (2006). Effect of Antenna Gain and Group Delay Variations on Pulse-Preserving Capabilities of Ultrawideband Antennas. *IEEE Transactions on Antennas and Propagation*, Vol. 54, No. 8, (August 2006) 8 (2208-2215), ISSN: 0018-926X

Hines, M.E. & Stinehelfer, H.E. (1974). Time-Domain Oscillographic Microwave Network Analysis using Frequency-Domain Data. *IEEE Transactions on Microwave Theory and Techniques*, Vol. 22, No. 3 (March 1974) 7 (276-282), ISSN: 0018-9480

Hu, S.; Chen, H.; Law, C.L.; Chen, Z.; Zhu, L.; Zhang, W. & Dou, W. (2007). Backscattering Cross Section of Ultrawideband Antennas. *IEEE Antennas and Wireless Propagation Letters*, Vol. 6, (2007) 4 (70-73), ISSN: 1536-1225

Huang, C.Y. & Hsia, W.C. (2005). Planar Elliptical Antenna for Ultrawideband Communications. *Electronics Letters*, Vol. 41, No. 6, (March 2005) 2 (296-297), ISSN: 0013-5194

Liang, J.; Chiau, C.C. ; Chen, X. & Parini, C.G. (2004). Printed circular disc monopole antenna for ultra-wideband applications. *Electronics Letters*, Vol. 40, No. 20, (September 2004) 3 (1246-1248), ISSN: 0013-5194

Licul, S. & Davis, W.A. (2005). Unified Frequency and Time-Domain Antenna Modeling and Characterization. *IEEE Transactions on Antennas and Propagation*, Vol. 53, No. 9, (September 2005) 7 (2282-2288), ISSN: 0018-926X

Lin, S.Y. & Huang, H.R. (2008). Ultra-Wideband MIMO Antenna with Enhanced Isolation. *Microwave and Optical Technology Letters*, Vol. 51, No. 2, (December 2008) 4 (570-573), ISSN: 0895-2477

Lin, Y.C. & Hung, K.J. (2006). Compact Ultrawideband Rectangular Aperture Antenna and Band-Notched Designs. *IEEE Transactions on Antennas and Propagation*, Vol. 54, No. 11, (November 2006) 7 (3075-3081), ISSN: 0018-926X

Loizeau, S. & Sibille, A. (2009). A Novel Reconfigurable Antenna with Low Frequency Tuning and Switchable UWB Band, *Proceedings of European Conference on Antennas and Propagation*, pp. 1627-1631, ISBN: 978-3-8007-3152-7, Berlin, Germany, March 2009

Mathis, H.F. (1951). A Short Proof that an Isotropic Antenna is Impossible. *Proceedings of Institute Radio Engineers*, Vol. 39, No. 8, (August 1951) 1 (970)

Manteuffel, D.; Arnold, M.; Makris, Y. & Chen, Z.N. (2009). Concepts for Future Multistandards and Ultra Wideband Mobile Terminal Antennas using Multilayer LTCC Technology, *Proceedings of IEEE International Workshop on Antenna Technology*, ISBN: 978-1-4244-4395-6, Santa Monica, USA, March 2009

Mitola, J. (1995). The Software Radio Architecture. *IEEE Communications Magazine*, Vol. 33, No. 5, (May 1995) 13 (26-38), ISSN: 0163-6804

Mitola, J. & Maguire, G.Q. (1999). Cognitive Radio: Making Software Radios More Personal. *IEEE Personal Communications*, Vol. 6, No. 4, (August 1999) 6 (13-18), ISSN: 1070-9916

Mohammadian, A.H.; Rajkotia, A. & Soliman, S.S. (2003). Characterization of UWB Transmit-Receive Antenna System, *Proceedings of IEEE International Confence on Ultra-Wideband Systems and Technology*, pp. 157-161, ISBN: 0-7803-8187-4, Virginia, USA, November 2003, IEEE

Munson, R.E. (1974). Conformal Microstrip Antennas and Microstrip Phased Array. *IEEE Transactions on Antennas and Propagation*, Vol. 22, (January 1974) 5 (74-78), ISSN: 0018-926X

Mtumbuka, M.C.; Malik, W.Q.; Stevens, C.J. & Edwards, D.J. (2005). A Tri-Polarized Ultra-Wideband MIMO System, *Proceedings of International Symposium on Advances in Wired and Wireless Communication*, pp. 98-101, ISBN: , Princeton, USA, April 2005

Najam, A.I.; Duroc, Y; Leao, J.F.A & Tedjini, S. (2009). A Novel Co-located Antennas System for UWB-MIMO Applications, *Proceedings of IEEE Radio and Wireless Symposium*, pp. 368-371, ISBN: 978-1-4244-2698-0, San Diego, USA, January 2009, IEEE

Nikolaou, S; Kingsley, N.D; Ponchak, G.E; Papapolymerou, J & Tentzeris, M.M. (2009). UWB Elliptical Monopoles with a Reconfigurable Band Notch using MEMS Switches Actuated without Bias Lines. *IEEE Transactions on Antennas and Propagation*, Vol. 57, No. 8, (August 2009) 10 (2242-2251), ISSN: 0018-926X

Pereira, C.; Pousset, Y.; Vauzelle, R. & Combeau, P. (2009). Sensitivity of the MIMO Channel Characterization to the Modeling of the Environment. *IEEE Transactions on Antennas and Propagation*, Vol. 57, No. 4, (April 2009) 10 (1218-1227), ISSN: 0018-926X

Puccinelli, D. & Haenggi, M. (2005). Wireless Sensor Networks: Applications and Challenges of Ubiquitous Sensing. *IEEE Circuits and Systems Magazine*, Vol. 5, No. 3, (September 2005) 13 (19-31), ISSN: 1531-636X

Qing, X.; Chen, Z.N. & Chia, M.Y.W. (2005). Network Approach to UWB Antenna Transfer Function Characterization, *Proceedings of European Microwave Conference*, Vol. 3, ISBN: 2-9600551-2-8, Paris, France, October 2005

Rajagopalan, A.; Gupta, G.; Konanur, A.; Hughes, B & Lazzi, G. (2007). Increasing Channel Capacity of an Ultrawideband MIMO System Using Vector Antennas. *IEEE Transactions on Antennas and Propagation*, Vol. 55, No. 10, (October 2007) 8 (2880-2887), ISSN: 0018-926X

Roblin, C. (2006). Ultra Compressed Parametric Modeling of UWB Antenna Measurements, *Proceedings of European Conference on Antennas and Propagation*, ISBN: 92-9092-9375, Nice, France, November 2006.

Sarkar, T.K. & Pereira, O. Using the matrix pencil method to estimate the parameters of a sum of complex exponentials. *IEEE Antennas and Propagation Magazine*, Vol. 37, No. 1, (February 1995) 8 (48-55), ISSN: 1045-9243

Sayeed, A.M. & Raghavan, V. (2007). On the Impact of Reconfigurable Antenna Arrays in Cognitive Radio, *Proceedings of IEEE International Conference on Acoustics, Speech and Signal Processing*, pp. 1353-1356, ISBN: 1-4244-0727-3, Honolulu, USA, April 2007, IEEE, Piscataway

Schantz, H.G. (2003). A Brief History of UWB antennas, *Proceedings of IEEE Ultra Wideband Systems and Technologies Conference*, pp. 209-213, ISBN: 0-7803-8187-4, Virginia, USA, November 2003, IEEE, Piscataway

Schantz, H.G.; Wolenec, G. & Myszka, E.M. (2003). Frequency Notched UWB Antennas, *Proceedings of IEEE Ultra Wideband Systems and Technologies Conference*, pp. 214-218, ISBN: 0-7803-8187-4, Virginia, USA, November 2003, IEEE, Piscataway

Schantz, H.G. (2005). *The Art and Science of Ultra-Wideband Antennas*, Artech House Publisher, ISBN: 1-5805-3888-6, England

Shlivinski, A.; Heyman, E. & Kastner, R. (1997). Antenna Characterization in the Time Domain. *IEEE Transactions on Antennas and Propagation*, Vol. 45, No. 7, (July 1997) 8 (1140-1147), ISSN: 0018-926X

Siriwongpairat, W.; Olfat, M. & Ray, L.K.J. (2004). On the performance evaluation of TH and DS UWB MIMO systems. *Proceedings of International Conference Wireless Communications and Networking*, pp. 1800-1805, ISBN: 0-7803-8344-3, Atlanta, USA, March 2004, IEEE, Piscataway

Sörgel, W.; Pivit, E. & Wiesbeck, W. (2003). Comparison of Frequency Domain and Time Domain Measurement Procedures for Ultra Wideband Antennas, *Proceedings of Conference on Antenna Measurement and Techniques Association*, pp. 72-76, Irvine, USA, October 2003

Sörgel, W. & Wiesbeck, W. (2005). Influence of the Antennas on the Ultra-Wideband Transmission. *Eurasip Journal on Applied Signal Processing*, Vol. 2005, No. 3, (2005) 10 (296-305), ISSN: 1110-8657

Su, Z. & Brazil, T.J. (2007). Transient Model Using Cascaded Ideal Transmission Lines for UWB Antennas for Co-Simulation with Circuits, *Proceedings of IEEE International Symposium on Microwave*, pp. 2035-2038, Hawai, USA, June 2007

Timmermann, J.; Porebska, M.; Sturm, C. & Wiesbeck, W. (2007). Comparing UWB Freespace Propagation and Indoor Propagation Including Non-Ideal Antennas, *Proceedings of IEEE International Conference on Electromagnetics in Advanced Applications*, pp. 37-40, ISBN: 978-1-4244-0767-5, Torino, Italy, September 2007, IEEE

Visser, H.J. (2007). Low-Cost, Compact UWB Antenna with Frequency Band-Notch Function, *Proceedings of European Conference on Antennas and Propagation*, ISBN: 978-0-86341-842-6, Edinburgh, UK, November 2007

Vuong, T.P.; Ghiotto, A.; Duroc, Y. & Tedjini S. (2007). Design and Characteristics of a Small U-Slotted Planar Antenna for IR-UWB. *Microwave and Optical Technology Letters Wiley*, Vol. 49, No. 7, (July 2007) 5 (1727-1731), ISSN: 0895-2477

Walter, C.H. (1990). *Traveling Wave Antennas*, Peninsula Pub, ISBN: 0-9321-4651-1

Wiesbeck, W. & Adamiuk, G. (2007). Antennas for UWB Systems, *Proceedings of International ITG Conference on Antennas*, pp. 66-71, ISBN: 978-3-00-021643-5, Munich, Germany, March 2007

Win, M.Z. & Scholtz, R.A. (1998). Impulse Radio: How it works. *IEEE Communications Letters*, Vol. 2, No. 2, (February 1998) 3 (36-38), ISSN: 1089-7798

Wong, K.L; Wu, C.H. & Su, S.W. (2005). Ultrawide-band square planar metal-plate monopole antenna with a trident-shaped feeding strip. *IEEE Transactions on Antennas and Propagation*, Vol. 53, No. 4, (April 2005) 8 (1662-1669), ISSN: 0018-926X

Wong, K.L.; Su, S.W. & Kuo, Y.L. (2003). A Printed Ultra-Wideband Diversity Monopole Antenna. *Microwave and Optical Technology Letters*, Vol. 38, No. 4, (June 2003) 3 (257-259), ISSN: 0895-2477

Yang, L. & Giannakis, G.B. (2004). Ultrawideband Communcations: an idea whose time has come. *IEEE Signal Processing Magazine*, Vol. 26, No. 6, (November 2004) 29 (26-54), ISSN: 1053-5888

Yang, L. & Giannakis, G.B. (2004). Analog Space-time coding for multiantenna Ultra-Wideband transmissions. *IEEE Transactions on Communications*, Vol. 52, No. 3, (March 2004) 11 (507-517), ISSN: 0090-6778

Yang, T.; Suh, S.Y.; Nealy, R.; Davis, W.A. & Stutzman, W.L. (2004). Compact Antennas for UWB Applications. *IEEE Aerospace and Electronic Systems Magazine*, Vol. 15, No. 5, (May 2004) 5 (16-20), ISSN: 0885-8985

Zhang, Y. & Brown, A.K. (2006). The Discone Antenna in a BPSK Direct-Sequence Indoor UWB Communication System. *IEEE Transactions on Microwave Theory and Techniques*, Vol. 54, No. 4, (April 2006) 6 (1675-1680), ISSN: 0018-9480

Zou, Z.; Baghaei Nejad, M.; Tenhunen, H. & Zheng, L.R. (2007). An efficient passive RFID system for ubiquitous identification and sensing using impulse UWB radio. *Elektrotechnik and Informationstechnick Journal, Special Issue by Springer Wien*, Vol. 124, (December 2007) 7 (397-403), ISSN: 0932-383X

17

On the Design of a Super Wide Band Antenna

D. Tran, P. Aubry, A. Szilagyi*, I.E. Lager, O. Yarovyi and L.P. Ligthart
International Research Centre for Telecommunication and Radar,
Delft University of Technology, the Netherlands
**Military Equipment and Technologies Research Agency, Romania*

1. Introduction

The adopted term *ultra wideband* (UWB) technology in 1989 by the U.S. Department of Defense, is a technology also known as impulse, baseband or carrier-free radio technology, this technology had a relatively long history, rooted deeply in the *spark-gap* experiment that Heinrich Hertz pioneered radio waves in 1886. Hertz was the first to prove experimentally that energy could be transported through space at the velocity of light by action of electric- and magnetic-waves waves, which was theoretically predicted by James Clerk Maxwell in 1873. Hertz's spark-gap apparatus with an end-loaded half-wave dipole as transmitting antenna and a resonant square loop antenna as receiver could describe as a complete UWB radio system, this famous experiment laid a fundamental concept for wireless transmission and reception of *radio-waves*, at the time more common called *Hertzian-waves* (Kraus, 1985).
Gugleilmo Marconi took Hertz's spark-gap out of the academic laboratory and successfully applied this pulse-communication to wireless telegraphy, he improved the distance between transmitter and receiver by 2 miles in 1895, 15 miles in 1897 and successful sent a Morse code of an "S" letter over the Atlantic ocean in 1901, since then the spark technology dominated the world's wireless technology with its golden period 1901-1915 (Belrose, 1995). Nevertheless, the spark gap technology development was disrupted because: a) the spectral efficiency of the signals generated by the spark-gap transmitters was low, b) as more people was trying to transmit Morse code, the interference between different transmissions were becoming so serious that receiving of the wireless telegraphy became impossible, c) research works in wireless telephony pioneered by Reginald Fessenden and others (Brodsky, 2008) had altered research interests from wideband to narrowband communications, which allowed frequency division multiplexing, offered an easy way of transmitting multiple signals in a finite bandwidth (Molisch, 2007), d) a set-back of impulse communication had been a fact when the U.S. government began banning spark transmitters in 1924 (Brodsky op cit.).
Ultra-wideband radio technology (UWB-RT) inherited a potential of extremely high rate of data communications, Claude Shannon discovered this in 1948 and derived the later-called-as Shannon-Hartley's *channel capacity laws*. This famous theoretical law however was not able to substantiate in practice until the development of the sampling oscilloscope by Hewlett-Packard in 1962, which, in accordance with the Nyquist-Shannon *sampling theorem*, was then capable to reconstruct at-that-time rather large UWB signals (Wilson, 2002).

The needs of sensors that can identify camouflaged and buried objects, and the low probability of intercept and high ranging resolution accredited from research on "time-domain electromagnetic" in the 60s, was attractive to military and radar applications, these attractions brought pulse communication back to business (Razavi et al., 2005).
UWB-RT, thus far, has been around for half a centuries but most research confined only in military applications and systems. The release of the 7.5 GHz of unlicensed spectrum by the US Federal Communications Commission (FCC, 2002) for commercial usages and applications in 2002 sparked a renewed interest in R&D of UWB-RT in industries, universities and governments. Today "ultra-wideband" usually refers UWB-RT where the electronic systems should be able to coexist with other electronic users (FCC, 2004). The UWB-RT has gained strong foothold in many applications in the areas of communications, in industries, health monitoring, law-enforcement, defense and public security, etc., The UWB-RT has established indeed as an inevitable technology in the fabric of our everyday life, however, there remains significant number of challenges for the technology to become ubiquitous, especially in the safety and security issues.
Enhanced by the decision on choosing millimeter wave-based airport security passenger screening sensors by the Transportation Security Administration, new research directives in public security domain are the search for sensors with higher channel capacity, and screening with higher resolution. To compromise both range and Doppler-resolution (Thor, 1962), sensors which support super-wideband (SWB) signaling could be the solution for the problem at hand. Super-wideband radio technology (SWB-RT) could possibly be a potential approach enables high-resolution sensing in free space and in matter including ground-penetrating radar and through-wall sensing. SWB-RT has unique advantages as compared to narrowband technology, and also comprised all UWB-RT's advanced features but with more channel capacity, higher precision and super resolution in communication, ranging and screening, respectively.
One of the challenges in the realization of SWB radio systems is the development of a suitable antenna that sustains SWB-signaling. To obtain wider bandwidth, several bandwidth enhancement techniques have been studied such as: using log periodic arrays in which the different elements are deduced from an homothetic ratio (Rahim & Gardner, 2004), introducing a capacitive coupling between the radiating element and the ground plane (Rmili & Floc'h, 2008), using microstrip-line feed and notching the ground plane (Tourette et al., 2006), using symmetrical notch in the CPW-feeding (Zhang et al., 2009), asymmetrical feeding by micro-strip line together with reduced ground plane and appropriate gap-patch distance (Karoui et al., 2010), adding T-slots for both patch and feeding strip (Rahayu et al., 2008), using cross-lot in the truncated circular patch with tapered microstrip feed line (Kshetrimayum et al., 2008). All these techniques are based on the modification of the surface current distribution to broaden the antenna's impedance bandwidth.
We report here a new SWB antenna architecture (SWBA), whose structure is purposely designed to support the functional section design approach (FSD, i.e. dividing the antenna structure into functional sections). The FSD in turn was utilized to accelerate the bandwidth optimization process; the SWBA and FSD together have conclusively enabled the designer to obtain antennas with SWB performances by optimization of just a most-significant-parameter. It is noted here that in our SWB antenna, hereafter-named prototype 4,

modifications were made at not only the feed-section but also the transition section and the radiation-section as well.

Anticipating and combining of all the advantages of its predecessors (prototypes 1, 2, 3), our new SWP-prototype 4 has been designed, fabricated and evaluated. Measurement results revealed that its SWP-performances are superior to other SWP-radiators reported in open-literature.

It is also worth noting here that our SWB antenna was one of the successful results of the long cooperation between the International Research Centre for Tele-communications and Radar (IRCTR) in the Netherlands and the Military Equipment and Technologies Research Agency (METRA) in Romania.

This chapter is organized as follow: First, in §2 we discussed briefly the wire-version-antennas that all planar UWB and SWB antennas were derived thereof, the concepts of quasi-electric and quasi-magnetic for planar antennas are typically discussed, also definitions pertaining to qualitatively expressing the SWB antenna's impedance bandwidth were considered. In §3, the SWBA and the FSD are proposed and discussed. In §4, we briefly examine the performance of radiator prototype 1 as a "proof of concept" and provide a methodological procedure for simplifying the multivariate optimization (MVO) process, which were intensively used in the design of other prototypes 2, 3, 4, also parametric investigations and numerical simulations of the proposed SWB radiator are shown in this section. Technical issues related to the practical consideration of the design and fabrication are discussed in §5. Measurements of impedance bandwidth, reception patterns and pulse characteristics in both frequency- and time-domain are reported in §6. Acknowledgements are expressed in §7, and final conclusions are summarized in §8.

2. Fundamentals

In designing mw- and mm-wave antennas and components, planar technology offered numerous advantages in comparison to wire- and waveguide-technologies, such as planar, light weight, small volume, low profile, low cost, compatible with integrated- or with active-circuits, easy integrate into passive or active phased arrays and communication systems.

The planar technology facilitates the designers much flexibility in creating a myriad of different UWB and SWB antennas, the architectures of these antennas may different but their topology mainly resembles the traditional wire-version of monopole- or dipole-antennas. The nomenclatural names of planar antennas are confusingly taken over from the wire-version with similar topology. Topological similarities may support such borrowed name, nevertheless it is incorrect—as discussed in the next subsections—regarding to electromagnetic-properties point of view. To avoid such inconsistent idealizations new names and definitions, which support both topological and electromagnetic point of views, will be introduced in this section. We briefly start with recalling the traditional wire-version dipole and monopole antennas in §2.1, then the correct nomenclatures—for the planar version magnetic and electric antennas—are introduced in §2.2, and end with their similarities: quasi-electric and quasi-magnetic antennas in §2.3.

2.1 Dipole and Monopole Antennas

The *Dipole* antenna is one of the oldest radiators with theoretical expressions for the radiation fields being readily available (Balanis, 1997, p.135). The shapes of their radiation

patterns are also well-known [ibis., p.154]. The antenna first used by Hertz in his early RF experiments in the late 19th century, as an example, was a half-wave dipole (Krauss, op. cit.) and the shapes of its 3D-radiation pattern had a similar appearance to a full-doughnut or figure-eight (Balanis op. cit. p.163).
The *Monopole* antenna is formed by replacing one half of the dipole antenna with the ground plane, when the ground plane is large enough the monopole behaves like the dipole, except that its radiation pattern is just one half of the dipole, its gain is twice, while its length is one half of the dipole.
Magnetic dipole and *electric dipole* are standardized and well documented in [IEEE STD 145-1983, p.11-16]. The terms magnetic antenna and electric antenna were logically defined but occasionally used in literature, the first term used to describe radiators which posses radiation properties resembling those of thin wire loop (Balanis, op. cit., p.217), while the second is for those resembling of thin wire linear antennas.

2.2 Electric and Magnetic Antennas

Planar UWB and SWB antennas which geometrically resemble its counterpart (wire)-monopole antennas are widely called monopole. However, this topological naming for the planar radiators is incorrect and confused, because the radiation pattern of all the so-called (planar)-monopole antennas have not the shaped of the monopole but of the dipole antenna i.e., having the shape of the full-doughnut.
To avoid ambiguities, formal definitions for planar antennas are hereafter provided.
The definitions planar-magnetic antenna and planar-electric antenna were constructed by means of an analogy to the wire-loop antenna and the wire-electric dipole which are documented in (IEEE Std, op. cit.; Schantz et al., 2003, 2004; and Tanyer et al. 2009a), to keep this chapter self-content and avoid cross-reference, we summarize them here:
As a first step, let the *base plane* $\boldsymbol{B}$, be the plane comprises the antenna's effective radiating/ receiving aperture, and let $\mathbf{n}$ be the unit normal vector to this plane, with reference to figure 1, $\boldsymbol{B}$ can be assimilated into xOy, while $\mathbf{n} = \mathbf{i}_z$.
Assume that the field has a transverse electromagnetic (TEM) distribution propagating along the base plane. Then the following cases can be distinguished:

1. In the case when the base plane *magnetic field* $\mathbf{H}(\mathbf{r})$, with $\mathbf{r} \in \boldsymbol{B}$, is directed along $\mathbf{n}$, the radiator is referred as *magnetic antenna*.
2. In the case when the base plane *electric field* $\mathbf{E}(\mathbf{r})$, with $\mathbf{r} \in \boldsymbol{B}$, is directed along $\mathbf{n}$,the radiator is referred as *electric antenna*.

The above definitions are strictly applied to structures that support propagating-and-non-rezo TEM- field distributions only, so that the waveguide case is automatically excluded by this TEM regard.
We note here that the above definition have not taken in to account the diffraction effects at the edges/vertexes/corners of the metallic/dielectric material that constituent the transmitting/receiving aperture.

2.3 Quasi-Electric and Quasi-Magnetic Antennas

Most of the cases, particularly in planar antenna configuration, the topology of the radiating apertures may prevent the above-indicated conditions from being rigorously satisfied. Even in such cases, either one or the other of the two situations may prevail, thus correctly

determine the type of the antenna. For instant, a radiator for which the magnetic field strength **H**(**r**) or the electric field strength **E**(**r**) is parallel to **n** over most of the effective aperture will be denoted as *quasi-magnetic* antenna, or *quasi-electric* antenna, respectively. Obviously, planar antennas fed by microstrip-line or co-planar-waveguide can be classified as quasi-electric or quasi-magnetic antennas, respectively.
As will be demonstrated hereby, our prototypes fall in the class of quasi-magnetic antennas, whilst for all patch antennas fed by micro-strip line, as an example, the RAD-NAV antenna (Tran et al., 2010) belongs to the class of quasi-electric antennas.

2.4 Bandwidth Definitions

There are several definitions of bandwidth circulated among our antennas and propagation society; those frequently met are octave-, decade-, ratio-, fractional-, percent-, and ratio-bandwidths. The two definitions, that most frequently used, are the percent bandwidth and the ratio bandwidth. They are defined respectively as follows:

$$B_P = 100\% \times BW / f_C \quad (1)$$

$$B_R = BW / f_L \quad (2)$$

Where:

f_H, f_L are the maximum and minimum frequency at -10 dB, respectively.
BW is the nominal bandwidth defined by $BW = f_H - f_L$
f_C is the central frequency defined by $f_C = (f_H + f_L)/2$
B_P is the percent bandwidth and,
B_R is the ratio bandwidth, commonly noted as B_R = R : 1, where R is the ratio defined as R= f_H/f_L

The *percent bandwidth* (1) has originally been used to describe the narrow-bandwidth of conventional antennas and microwave-devices. Its usage is quite popular and often considered as a standard in many textbooks, nevertheless, it is mathematically not a solid definition because it possesses a defect when f_L approaching zero. For example, suppose that the nominal bandwidth of antennas #1 is 2GHz (0-2GHz), and antenna #2 is 20GHz (0-20GHz). It is clearly that the nominal bandwidth BW of the second antenna is 10 times wider than the first one; however, formula (1) indicates that both antennas have the same percent bandwidth. Another weak point is the percent bandwidth of formula (1) is always less than or equal to 200% irrespective of how wide the antenna's nominal bandwidth was. Note also that formula (1) is often mistakenly called as *fractional bandwidth*, indeed the formula (1) consolidates its meaning "fractional bandwidth" only when the factor 100% is removed.
Alternatively, the *ratio bandwidth* (2) can also be used for expressing the bandwidth of UWB and SWB antennas and devices. The defect at zero- frequency point still lurks there but the 200%-limit is lifted. The use of the ratio bandwidth is more adequate to envision the wideband characteristics of devices under investigation. We choose for the second formula (2) for describing the bandwidth for the SWB-prototype discussed in this chapter.
How to choose two formulas, although no official consent however, the first formula is often used for cases that the bandwidths are less than 100%, whilst the second is for UWB and SWB antennas/devices.

Traditional communications systems typically used signals having a percent bandwidth of less than 1%, while standard CDMA has an approximately of 2%. Early definition in the radar and communications fields considered signals with percent bandwidth of 25% or greater (measured at the *-3 dB points*) to be ultra-wideband. The recent FCC regulations (IEEE Std, 2004), which will be used as a standard throughout this text, defined UWB devices/signals as having an nominal bandwidth which exceeds 500 MHz or percent bandwidth of over 20%, measured at *-10 dB points*.
The term SWB has been often used to indicate bandwidth, which is greater than a decade bandwidth. Since the percent bandwidth confused and failed to envision the SWB property adequately as discussed in §2.4, the "ratio bandwidth" is more suitable and often be used for describing bandwidth of 10:1 or larger, we adopt this convention throughout this report.

3. Antenna Topology, Architecture and the FSD Methodology

Since the release of the license-free band and the regulation of the emission spectra by the FCC in 2002, a myriad of UWB antennas have been created and invented by both industry and academia, most of them are limited to the FCC-band, this 7.5GHz bandwidth corresponds to a moderately short pulse in order of nanoseconds, these short pulses are good enough for high capacity communication, accurate ranging and imaging but not enough for the more stringent needs of precise localization, high resolution screening, sensitive sensing. To satisfy such stringent requirements, challenges are placed on the design of sensors that support signaling of extreme short pulse in the order of hundreds of picoseconds or less. Sensors in the terahertz region support such short pulse and unarguably provide sharpest images, nonetheless the detection range is too short and the sensors are very costly. Note that in the terahertz region, a radiator with only 5% is capable to support, for example, a Gaussian pulse of 20 Ps (assumed unity time bandwidth product), while in the RF-region one must have a SWB radiator of over 11:1 (or 167%, by a lowest frequency of 5GHz) for signaling such a short pulse.
There existed broadside and end-fire UWB antennas with different topologies, which comprised of many configurations are available in open literature. The pattern stability of several antenna's topologies and architectures had been thoroughly investigated and reported by (Messey, 2007, p.163-196). It seemed that there was no broadside antenna architecture could exhibit stable patterns within a bandwidth wider than 10 GHz, and most of them are UWB-radiators with ratio bandwidth much less than 10 : 1.
We propose here an SWB antenna architecture which possessed not only SWB bandwidth lager than 10:1 but also exhibited a much stable patterns in its SWB bandwidth than all those which have been studied and reviewed by (Messey, op. cit.). The SWB prototype 4, and all other prototypes reported in this chapter had been designed, fabricated and evaluated at our IRCTR.
The SWB radiator reports in this chapter, was indeed a revolutionary improved version from IRCTR's previous developed prototypes. All the developed prototypes, shown together in fig. 4, shared the same topology and architecture as depicted in Fig. 1a. The kernel of this topology is its simplicity, and the essence of the antenna's architecture is the logicalness of dividing the antenna into functional sections that enables simplifying the MVO process into a sequence of single-variable optimization (SVO) one.

The merits of the topology, architecture and logical functional blocks, and optimization process will be discussed in §3.1, 3.2 and 3.3, respectively.

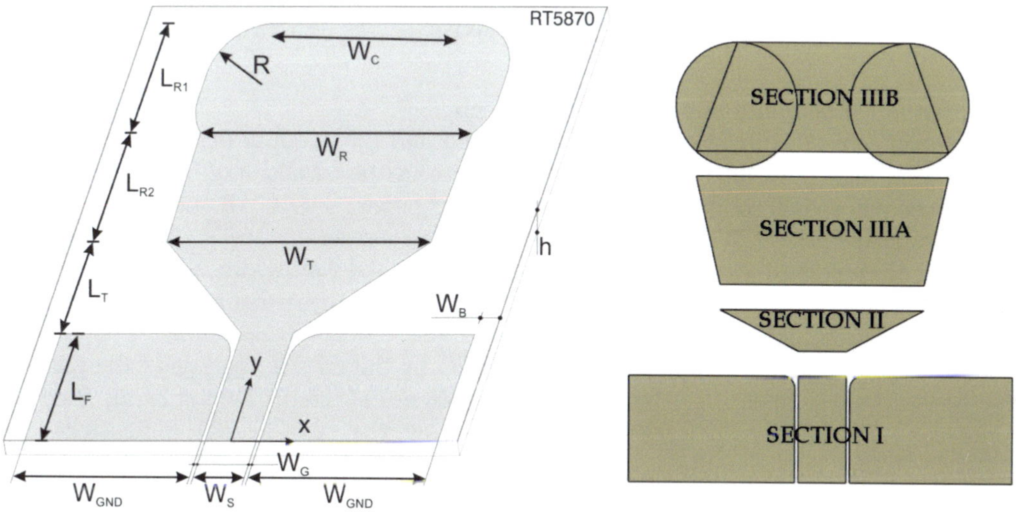

Fig. 1. Proposed configuration: a) Architecture and parameters, b) logical functional sections.

The original antenna topology and architecture of prototype 1 leaved many flexible possibilities for adjusting parameters or scaling dimensions to meet new requirements or applications without much entangled in complicated MVO process. These possibilities have been exploited to double the antenna's bandwidth of prototype 1 (Tran et al, 2007) from 2:1 to 4:1 by (Tanyer et al., 2009a), and further broaden to 9:1 (Tanyer et al., 2009b), and scaled down to the FCC-band for IR-applications (Tanyer et al., 2010).

The prototype 4 is a proof of concept in proving viability of the design of radiators, which are capable of supporting such extreme short-pulse in RF/mw-region. The proposed antenna's topology, architecture and the FSD approach, as will be discussed in subsequence sections, were objectively aimed at two main goals:

- Choosing an antenna topology whose shape is kept simple regarding ease of fabrication, prevent diffractions, easy to scale up/down to meet designer's requirements in size and performance (§3.1).
- Creating an architecture that providing a basis platform for implementing the "FSD approach", and deploying the conceptual "thumb-rules" for effective simplifying the MVO process in to SVO, a much simpler one (§3.2).

3.1 Antenna Topology

The starting point in the design of the SWB antenna reports in this section is mainly credited to the original radiator (Tran et al., op. cit.), whose topology is planar, as sketched in Fig. 1a, with structural topology comprised of following stack-ups:

- Single dielectric layer to provide structural rigidity.
- CPW feeding structure on top of the structure.
- An antenna patch is directly connected to the CPW-feeding, so that they together formed a single planar pattern run on top of the structure.

The CPW feeding structure has been chosen because of it well-behaved properties: such as negligible radiation, low loss, the effective dielectric is constant over a sustained wide frequency range, where the later property is more suitable for super-wide-band feeding a SWB-radiator than the micro-strip line (Simons, 2001).

3.2 Antenna Architecture and the FSD Approach

In antenna design if dimensions are unconstrained and by a proper design, antenna will behave as a high pass filter, and if its dimensions are physically large enough then all frequencies will pass through. Research of published papers over UWB and SWB antennas reveals that most of the UWB and SWB antennas had a considerable larger size, mostly lager than $\lambda_L/2$ of the lowest frequency f_L, and on broadening the bandwidth, a first option, was to resort to stochastic optimization methods, nevertheless, these methods are known for carrying extremely high computational load.

A more feasible alternative approach was provided by the critical analysis of the relation ship between the geometrical parameters and the physics of the problem at hand. The FSD approach was intentionally created in such a way that the overall dimensions are constrained, kept small and the process of optimization can also be simplified.

The logical architecture together with its parameter and FSD-blocks are sketched in fig. 1.

The FSD approach follows the bottom-up strategy, i.e.:

- Starting from the feed section—its CPW feed supports the required impedance bandwidth for SWB signaling.
- Then to the internal transition section—this section is intentionally inserted between the feed and the patch for the purpose of impedance matching, its shape was logically chosen so that it able to serve the design-properties: resonance shifting, impedance matching, and also enable parameter to serve as independent optimized parameter.
- In addition to the radiating section, we divided it in to two sub-sections, which are the patch section and the external transition. The patch section creates an extra degree of freedom to ease the optimization process, and the radiating section provides parameter for shaping radiation patterns. Two round areas had been added to the top corners of the patch for the purpose of 1) diminishing of diffraction at the antenna's top vertices (deformation of sharp corner in to circular edge) and, 2) controlling and retaining the shaped of the radiation patterns at high frequency band of the spectrum, and, 3) subduing the number of parameters to accelerate the optimization process. These four sections are orderly numerated as I, II, IIIA, and IIIB in Fig. 1b.

In summary, the FSD approach assumes the following steps:

- Keep the antenna's overall dimension small and fixed;
- Start orderly from section I, II, IIIA and IIIB (this bottom-up strategy prefers matching impedance bandwidth in prior of pattern bandwidth);
- Separate and understand the role of each section;
- Identify the parameters associate with that section; select the parameter that predominantly influences the function of that section.
- Isolate the effect of that parameter so that an optimization only on that parameter can be undergone, without affecting too much the performance of other sections.

Based on the FSD approach the prototype 1 was first designed and evaluated. Its designed parameters are used as start values for the optimization process of all the later prototypes.

Four prototypes (1, 2, 3, 4 shown in fig. 4) were successful designed and evaluated, the prototype 4 proved to be a radiator which is superior to the others in that both of its impedance bandwidth and radiation pattern are SWB-sustainable.

4. Parameter identification and optimizations

The prototype 1, elaborated by (Tran et al. 2007), formed a basis for the designs of the later prototypes. Its 10GHz impedance bandwidth and designed parameters are plotted in fig. 5 and listed in table 1, respectively. For the detailed works and the measurement results, the reader should refer to (Tran et al., op. cit). The other prototypes all took the designed parameters of prototype 1 as start-values, and used the FSD to identify the significant parameter for its SVO process of bandwidth broadening.

The prototype 2 was obtained by taking the start values of the prototype 1, and using FSD to identify the L_T as its significant parameter for SVO process. The resulting designed parameters and the impedance bandwidth are listed in 2nd column of table 1, and Fig. 5, respectively. The SVO demonstrated the solidity of the FSD approach that the bandwidth can be doubled (from 10GH to 20 GHz) by optimization of just a single parameter L_T. For details of the elaborated work, please refer to (Tanyer et al., 2009a, op cit.)

By keeping L_T fixed, the prototype 3 is obtained by optimizing the lower part of the radiation section which comprised of two parameters L_{R2} and W_T, the first make the total length of the radiator shorter (thus affects the higher frequency), whist the second parameter provide an better match (i.e., lower reflection coefficient). By doing two SVO sequentially (first with parameters L_{R2}, then W_T) we again doubled the nominal BW (form 20GHz to 45GHz), in term of ratio bandwidth it is of B_R = 9:1 as shown in Fig. 5. The resulting parameters are listed in column 3rd table1. Further details of measurements and other properties of this prototype 3, are detailed in (Tanyer et al., 2009b, op. cit).

Prototype 4 is obtained by the combined optimization of the FSD-indentified parameters W_T and W_C, By keeping the optimized parameters of the previous optimization steps (L_T of prototype 3, all others of prototype 1) fixed, and doing 2 SVO sequences, we obtain the SWB impedance bandwidth of B_R greater than 30:1, the result is plotted in Fig. 2. The design parameters are listed in table 1. We noted here that by controlling radii-separation distance W_C we are able to keep the radiation pattern of this prototype less distorted till 50GHz as shown in Fig. 3

The created parameters, their functions, their effects and their usages are discussed in greater details in the next sub-sections The FSD is detailed in §4.1-4.3, the resulted SWB-performances are given in §4.4 and in §4.5 the optimizations of all the prototypes are discussed in details.

4.1 Section I: The feed section

Planar antennas and arrays have been used for micro-wave and millimeter-wave applications for decades, especially in mobile communications where system design requires low profile, lightweight, and high directivity. The two most used feeding methods are micro-strip line (MS) and coplanar waveguide (CPW), they both carried signal excellently in narrow-band and UWB antennas and devices. Many planar antenna arrays have been designed by using MS, however, until recently, only a few works so far have used CPW to feed the array. The CPW has gained increasing popularity in recent years, since it has several advantages over the MS, such as low radiation losses, less dispersion, easier integration with solid-state active devices, and the possibility of connecting series and shunt elements, and suitable for SMD-technology, also for SWB- antennas/devices CPW feeding provides better match and performs better than the MS line (Simons, 2001).

In search for the SWB radiator, both radiator and the feed must be super wide band. Since the SWB-signal first must able to pass through the feeding-line before reaching the antenna, obviously that the feed must be considered first in advance of other sections, we conduct the work with bottom-up approach, i.e., the feed is consider first, because if the feeding mechanism fail to be SWB, then there is no SWB radiator exists no matter how good the radiator will be. The coplanar waveguide is the first choice for feeding the signal to the radiator, because the CPW's effective dielectric is constant, (this property is a key feature in wide band matching the antenna), over a wider BW than micro-strip line, another advantage is, in contrast with MS line, one of the parameter pair (W_S, W_G) can be varied in size and shape, whilst the other is correspondingly changes to keep the characteristic impedance stays unchanged, furthermore CPW is low-loss, and the signal width can be chosen width enough to support characteristic impedance from 30Ohm and higher (Simons, 2001, p.52),

The CPW would be a better choice for SWB-feeding because of it considered features, summarized as follows:

- SWB behavior: the effective dielectric constant is almost independent of frequency (Simon op cit.), this feature is a priori condition for super wide band feeding and matching.
- Dimensional flexibility: the width of the signal line, and hence the corresponding gaps, can be freely designed to accordingly support the physical dimension of the transition region and the antenna.
- The dielectric thickness exerts negligible weight on the economy of the CPW-impedance.

4.2 Section II: The Tapered Transition

The tapered transition has been inserted between the CPW-feed and the radiating patch, this section responsible for a smooth transition between the feed and the antenna, and because the current distribution is denser in this region than the others, this property indicated that this section must have strongest influence in matching the impedance bandwidth. This section has two parameters (L_T, W_T), which are described in details in §4.2.1 and §4.2.2 below

4.2.1 The Internal Transition Length L_T

The length L_T of the tapered transition (section II) is responsible for the smooth transition between the feed and antenna, and proved to be the most sensitive parameter in the design of our prototypes. Anticipation from the theory and design of micro-strip antenna (MSA), it is well-known that the length of the MSA determines the resonance frequency (by lengthen or shorten this parameter, one can shift the resonance frequency to lower or higher band, respectively).

The antenna's resonance is affected by its length, this length is composed by $L_T + L_{R1} + L_{R2}$, when this composed length is changed, and the resonance will presumably change accordingly.
It is observed, from the results plotted in Fig. 5, that when L_T is longer the resonance will shift to lower frequency (as shown by prototype 1, $L_T = 6.4$, Fig. 5), and when L_T is shorter the radiator's resonance will shift to higher frequency (prototype 2, $L_T = 1.64$, Fig. 5)

4.2.2 The Internal Transition Width W_T

The width W_T of the taper transition section (section II), is also a "share-parameter" with lower radiating section (section IIIA); this width provides, as similar role as the width in microstrip patch antenna, a fine-tune mechanism for impedance matching as its nominal value varies. This enhanced matching mechanism are numerically demonstrated with the reflection coefficients of the prototypes 3 and 4 as plotted in Fig. 5, in which they shown a lower reflection coefficient, i.e., a better match.

4.3 Section III: The radiation section

This section comprise of six parameters L_{R1}, L_{R2}, W_T, W_R, W_C, and R_C, in which W_T is the share parameter described in §4.2.2, we divided this section into sub-sections IIA and IIB as sectioned in Fig. 1b. The parameter set of the internal sub-section (IIIA) and the external parameter sub-section (IIIB) are $\{W_T, W_R, L_{R2}\}$ and $\{W_R, L_{R1}, W_C, R_C\}$, respectively.

4.3.1 The Internal Radiating Matching Section

Two parameters, which identified to be key player for this subsection, are $\{W_T, L_{R2}\}$ (the W_R is not touched because it is share parameter of these two sub-sections), by first optimize the width parameter W_T, and by keeping this optimized parameter fixed, and continuing to optimize the other parameter L_{R2}. By this token, (Tanyer et al., 2009b, op cit.) obtained a huge enhancement in ratio bandwidth reported as 9:1. The design parameters are listed in table.1, the result is plotted in fig. 5. More detailed works and measurement results, the reader should refer to (Tanyer et al., op cit.).

4.3.2 The External Radiating Transition Section

This sub-section was often neglected by the designers due to the fact that the current distribution is weak along the edges of this section. However, we observed that it plays an important role in maintaining the shape of radiation pattern in a wide range of frequencies, as will be numerically proved in §4.4

The sub-section IIIB consists of a set of parameters $\{W_R, L_{R1}, W_C, R_C\}$; W_R is a share parameter so we keep it intact. From fig. 1 it is seen that W_{R1} is suppressed and covered by varying the radii-distance W_C, we can also single L_{R1} out because it contribution to the length of the radiator can already be economized by L_T and L_{R2}, so W_C is the only parameter left that we may use to fine-tune the radiator for both SWB performance and radiation pattern characteristics. Prototype 4 utilized this philosophy by varying L_{R2} (instead of L_{R1}) and W_C to obtain the super wideband performance plotted in Fig. 2. It is observed that variation of W_C had no significant impact on reflection coefficient (current distribution along the antenna circle edges are rather week compared with those close to the tapering transition region). Nevertheless, by properly controlling W_C we are able to maintain the usable shape of the radiation patterns up to 50 GHz as shown in Fig. 3. So, W_C is clearly to be the parameter to control the interference of the edge/corner scattering and diffraction of the radiator. In transforming the vertex-diffraction to edge-diffraction, we advocate the use of circular shape; nevertheless, other researchers suggested the shapes (elliptical, football cape, etc.). To answer the question which shape would serve best, we need a further in depth study about all possible pattern sensitive shapes before providing a final conclusive appraisal.

4.4 The prototype 4 and its Super Wide Band Performances

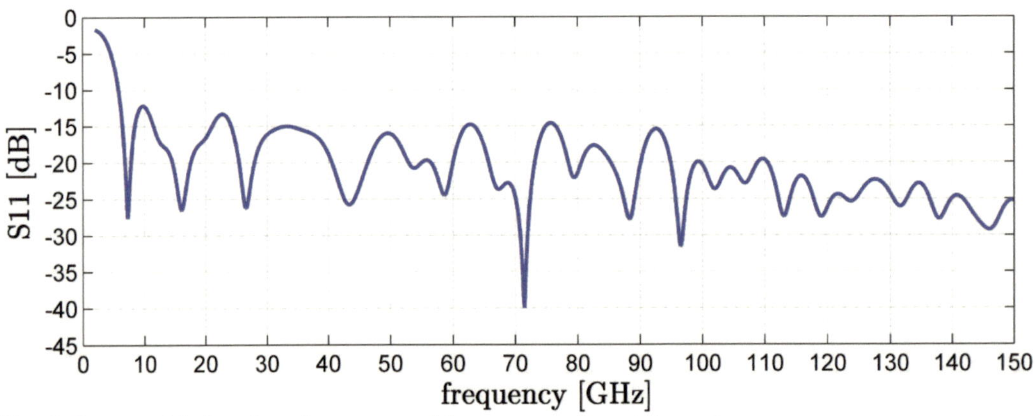

Fig. 2. Super wide band performance of the proposed prototype 4.

Fig. 2 shows the simulated result of the magnitude of the reflection coefficient of our SWB prototype 4. We computed and shown here only up to 150GHz. By close inspection of the reflection coefficient, the reader could observe that the prototype 4 shows a trend and exhibits the behavior of an all-high-pass antenna; its impedance bandwidth could be much wider than shown here.

The numerical results were computed with the following practical assumptions:

- The relative dielectric constant and the loss are assumed constant over the computational bandwidth.
- The commercial Duroid RT5870 high frequency laminated material we used, in deed could practically support up to 77 GHz only (Huang, 2008, p.64); beyond this frequency we may have to look for other dielectric material.

Figure 3 shows the simulated 3D radiation patterns of prototypes 4; the plot indicated that the radiator exhibits a super wide band pattern characteristics, the usable spherical patterns are sustained in a bandwidth wider than 10:1. The SWB properties displayed in fig. 2 and fig. 3 shown that prototype 4 is a true SWB radiator in both impedance and radiation aspects, and its SWB-behavior is superior to antennas reviewed by (Massey, 2007, pp. 163-196). We emphasize here that this radiator is termed as quasi-magnetic antenna, because it is clearly seen that this antenna possessed radiation patterns similar to that of a dipole, therefore calling it monopole reflects wrongly the EM-characteristics that it possesses and exhibits.

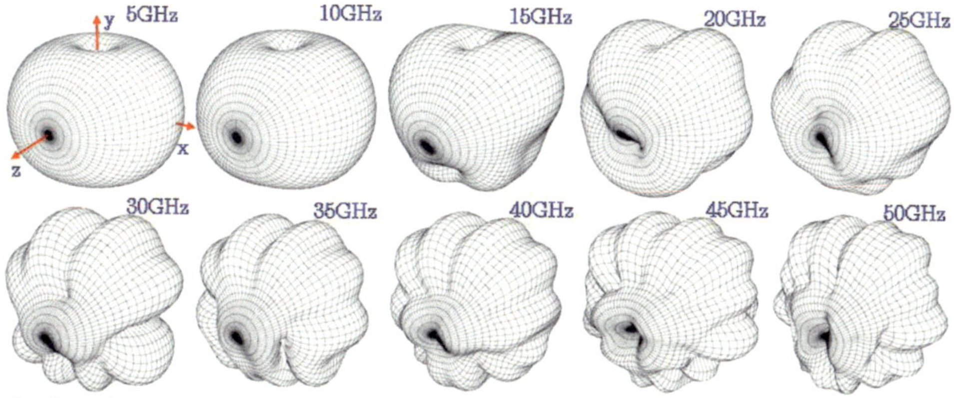

Fig. 3. Complete spectra of 3D-farfield co-polar radiation patterns from 5 to 50 GHz with increment step of 5GHz.

4.5 Optimization Process and Development of Prototypes

Although the proposed topology and architecture is simple, however with a total of 14 parameters it would be an impossible task for the multivariate optimization process.

This section reports in details of how to delimit the variables and how to reduce the number of variables for simplifying the MVO process to a SVO one. In addition, some pragmatic rules are also given for identifying the key parameters, and for weighting the priority of those parameters in the sequentially SVO processes.

To keep the optimization process controllable en less entangled in multivariate-optimization process, efforts have been done in the following steps:

Step 1—Topology and architecture: this step is important in that it had to form a basis for the FSD, and had to keep the antenna topology as simple as possible, but not simplest as (Al Sharkawy et al., 2004), Although all efforts has been carried out to ensure a minimum amount of the created parameters, the structure (fig. 1a) still have a considerable set of parameters { ε_r, h, t; L_F, W_S, W_{GND}, W_G; L_T, W_T; L_{R2}, W_R; L_{R1}, W_C, R }.

Step 2—The FSD: dividing the radiator into sections depending on their main function. Inspection of the radiator's current distribution and the radiator's topology shown in fig. 1a revealed that the radiator could presumably be divided into functional sections as depicted in fig. 1b. The analyzing and optimizing process are conducted following the bottom-up approach that always started from the feed (section I) and ended at the last radiation-section (section III.B). The analysis, optimization and development of the prototypes all should start and avoid as much as possible the *share-parameters* between sections (W_T, W_R); if impasse is met then, as a thumb-rule, the section on top has priority on taking the share parameter.

Step 3—Excluding of fixed parameters: The numbers of parameters of the radiator have been reduced by singling out the non-optimizable parameters. The first three material-parameters { ε_r, h, t}, because their nominal values were already fixed by the manufacturers, are not quite suitable for optimization process as continuous-parameters, so the parameters of the feed section (section I) are kept fixed and excluded in the optimization process.

Step 4– Setting boundaries: in order to accelerate the optimization process and avoiding the problem of unbounded optimization, we put geometrical restrictions on the total width ($2W_{GND} + 2W_G + W_S$) and length ($L_F + L_T + L_{R2} + L_{R1}$) of the antennas fixed to $\lambda_b/2$, where λ_b is wavelength at the design-frequency, and force all the internal parameters and their combination to be constrained inside this antenna's boundary $\lambda_b/2$.

Step 5—Reduction of parameters: in this step, we did further reduction of the number of parameters involved. Exploiting the fact that the feed-section's parameters have no significant added values to the total performance once its optimum values are founded, and the following prior measures have been set, 1) for impedance-matching it is fixedly set to 50 Ω and, 2) for field-matching the impedance-parameter-pair (W_S, W_G) has been chosen such that it is wide enough to support the currents to separately flow along the edges of the signal line W_S, and the feed length L_F must be long enough to support the transformation from coax's TEM to quasi-TEM of the CPW line, so the feed's parameters can ruled out for optimization, and set to be fixed with values as listed in table.1.

Step 6—Start values: This step initiated the start values for the set of parameter listed in step 1. The initialization of the start values was elaborately detailed in (Tran et al., 2007). Prototype 1 (Fig. 4) with the start values as listed in table.1, obtained a BW of 10GHz (fig. 5). Detailed discussions and simulated, measured results can be found in (Tran et al., op. cit.).

Step 7—Simplified process: The 7th step is the simplification of the optimization process by breaking the MVO process down into series of SVO one. It was observed that the current intensity is mainly distributed along the edges of the transition region, this suggested that : a) small variation of the transition parameter in this section (L_T, W_T) would have a strong influence on the flow of the signal current and hence play a large impact on the impedance bandwidth, and exploiting the fact, as similarly in microstrip antenna, that b) the length of the radiator defines the *shifting-property* of the resonance, whilst c) the width of the radiator effectuates the *matching-property*, and d) another *independent-property* is that they can be separately optimized.
So by keeping W_T, the share-parameter between sections II and III.A (fig. 1b), fixed and took just a single-variable-optimization (L_T), the impedance bandwidth was double to 20GHz as obtained by prototype 2, which is plotted in fig. 5. The parameters of prototype 2 are listed in table.1, more details of the electromagnetic properties and measurements regarding the performances of this prototype can be found in (Tanyer et al., op. cit.).

Step 8—BW enhancement: Prototype 3 (fig. 4) was obtained by analyzing and optimization the lower part of radiation section IIIA (fig. 1b). This section has three parameters (W_T, L_{R2}, W_R); first, following the rules discussed in step 2 we left out the parameter W_R since it is the share-parameter between section IIIA and IIIB; next, in order to avoid multivariate-optimization, anticipating the shifting-property and matching-properties discussed as (b) and (c), respectively, in step 7; then two SVO sweepings were carried out, first W_T (property c) and then L_{R1}(property b); the order of W_T or L_{R1} can be chosen freely according to independent-property (d, in step 7). The design parameters of prototype 3 are listed in table.1 in which the parameters of the previous optimized prototype are kept fixed, only the two parameters (W_T and L_{R1}) belonged to section IIIA are investigated and optimized.

Step 9: The design of prototype 4 is aimed at two SWB-compliances: 1) SWB impedance bandwidth, and 2) SWB radiation pattern. The radiation section consists of the following set of parameters (W_T; L_{R2}, W_R; L_{R1}, W_C, R), the length parameters of this set can be keep fixed, because L_{R2} and L_{R1} are resonance-shifting parameters, and the antenna architecture allows us to use other length of the antenna to control the resonance, this was already done by L_T of the lower section, so these two parameters can be singled out of the optimization process; the share parameter W_R can also be neglected because it matching-property is covered by the set {W_C, R}, so by keeping R fixed the parameter set of section III was left with only two parameters left {W_C, W_T}. The procedure followed: fist, keeping the parameters of prototype 1 with the optimized L_T = 1.64mm, then two SVOs were carried out first for W_T and then W_C. The reason that W_T was chosen first is twofold, 1) W_T is more sensitive on matching because the current distribution is denser at the lower part, 2) W_C is the share parameter that mainly located in section IIIA where the matching effect is week, and it is purposely inserted to control the radiation patterns in stead of wideband matching the radiator. The optimized parameters of prototype 4 are listed in table.1. The impedance bandwidth of the prototype 4 is plotted in fig. 2, and fig. 5; also, its SWB radiation patterns were in fig. 3.

4.6 Comparison of the prototypes

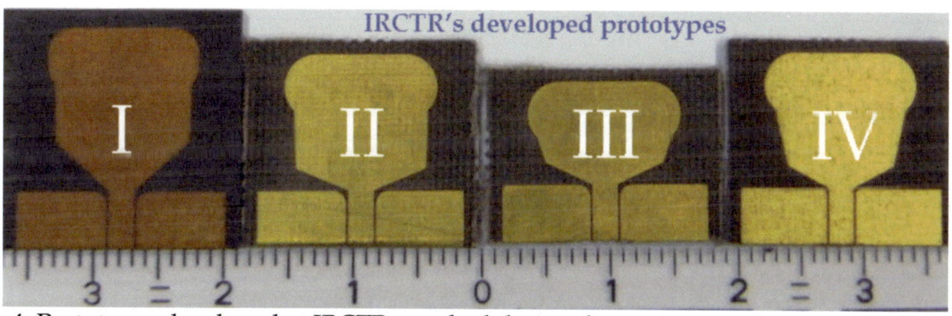

Fig. 4. Prototypes developed at IRCTR, resulted design dimensions are listed in table 1.

Prototypes 1, 2, 3, 4 have been design, fabricated, measured and evaluated, photographs of them are shown in fig 4. At first sign, they seemingly looked different, however they all shared the same topology and architecture as depicted in fig. 1a, only one or two parameters is slightly changed to obtained difference desired performances. For comparison, their correspond impedance bandwidths are plotted together in figure 5. The impedance bandwidth enhancement is improved from 10 GHz, to 20 GHz, 40 GHz and beyond 150 GHz as shown by fig. 5 and fig. 2

The design parameters of prototype 4 and all other prototypes are listed in table.1, so that, the reader, could independently recheck, or reproduce them without much difficulty.

These are results of the FSD methodology and SVO steps described in previous sub-section (§4.4). Note that the SVO should be carried out orderly by A, B and C. (bold and capitalized in table.1), A is dedicated as the first to be optimized, keep that optimized parameter fixed, and goes on with B, then continue with C. For example, the prototype 4, (A) first fixing the taper's height L_{R2} to 4.335mm, then (B) optimizing the taper width W_T, and then (C) adjust the W_C for the radiation-characteristics. The optimized results showed an SWB impedance bandwidth of at least over 150GHz. In fact the result of prototype 4 (with parameters listed in column 4 of Table.1) shown the downtrend of reflection coefficient for increasing frequency (Fig. 2), we expect that prototype 4 will well-behave beyond 150GHz as well.

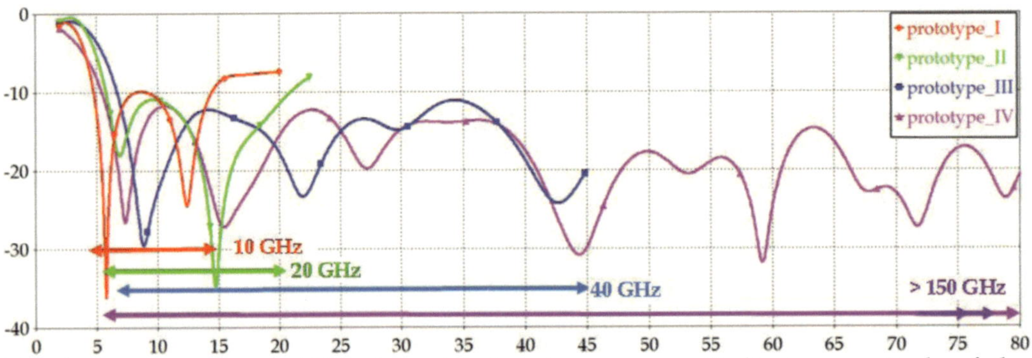

Fig. 5. Impedance bandwidth of the developed prototypes. Ordinate: magnitude of the reflection coefficient [dB]; Abscissa: frequency [GHz].

Parameter (mm)	Prototype 1	Prototype 2	Prototype 3	Prototype 4	Description
L_F	4.25	4.25	4.25	4.25	Length of the feed section
R_F	0.5	0.5	0.5	0.5	Blending radius in the feed section
W_{GND}	6.86	6.86	6.86	6.86	Width of the ground
W_S	2	2	2	2	Width of the signal line
W_G	0.14	0.14	0.14	0.14	Width of the CPW's gap
L_T	3.64	**1.64**	1.64	1.64	Tapering length in the transition region
W_T	10.2	10.2	**9.2 A**	**8.5 B**	Upper tapering in the transition region
L_{R1}	4.33	4.33	4.33	4.33	Resonator length in the radiating region
L_{R2}	4.335	4.335	**1.835 B**	4.335 **A**	Resonator length in the matched radiating region
W_R	10.5	10.5	10.5	10.5	Resonator width in the radiating region
W_C	7	7	7	7.2 C	Circle's separation width
R	2.5	2.5	2.5	2.5	Radius of the top circle area
Bandwidth	4-14GHz	5-25GHz	6.5-45GHz	5-150GHz	Bandwidth enhancement

Table 1. Parameters of the prototypes (all dimensions are in mm), the alphabetical order A, B, C indicates the priority-order of parameters in the SVO process.

5. Design and Fabrication

5.1 Design

All prototypes depicted in Fig. 4, with their design dimensions listed in table.1, have been fabricated on Duroid RT 5880 high frequency laminate with substrate height h=0.787mm, copper cladding thickness t=17μm, relative dielectric constant ε_r=2.2, electric and magnetic loss tangents are given by tan δ_E=0.0027 and tan δ_H=0, respectively. The foremost reason of choosing this material is that it could relatively afford SWB frequency range up to 77 GHz (Huang et al., 2008, p.64). Other reasons are assessments related to temperature, moisture, corrosion and stability, which were investigated in details by (Brown et al., 1980).

5.2 Feed Elongation

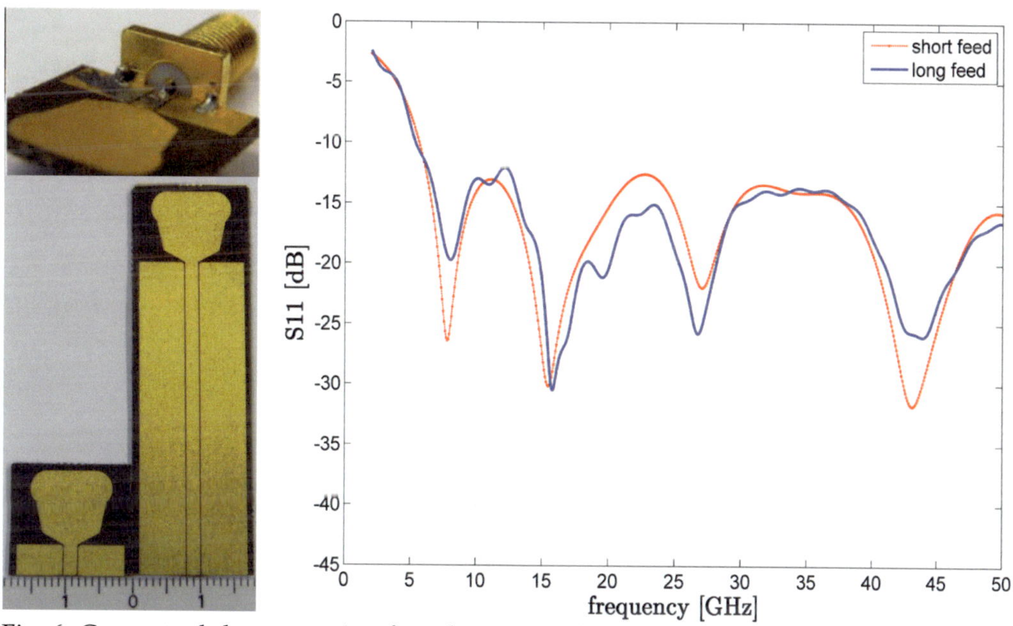

Fig. 6. Conceptual demonstration for advocating of CPW feed elongation, a) radiator with SMA connector, b) radiators with short and elongated feed, b) simulated reflection coefficient magnitudes of antenna with short and long feed.

Since the dimension of the SMA connector's flange is considerably large in comparison with the antenna dimension (see Fig. 6a), this comparable size exerts a huge impact on the antenna's electromagnetic-properties in particularly to the transmission, scattering and radiation mechanism. In order to reduce this obstruction and to measure the antenna's scattering parameters and radiation patterns adequately, it is necessary to elongate the antenna as show in Fig. 6b. To back up the advocating of this elongation, we exploited the facts that the co planar waveguide has negligible radiation, low-loss and constant effective dielectric constant in rather wide range of application from DC to above 50GHz. we decided to elongate the CPW feed L_F to 40mm, and carried out numerical simulations of the same SWB radiators with short and long feed. The magnitudes of the reflection coefficient are compared and plotted in Fig. 6c. As expected, the numerical results exposed a negligible differences as theoretically has predicted (Simons, 2001, p.240). Note that these theoretical properties (negligible radiation and low-loss) were also experimentally consolidated by (Tanyer et al, op cit.).

6. Measurements

The prototype 4 is measured with the Agilent E8364B PNA vector network analyzer, the electronic calibration kit N4693A 2-port ECal-module was used for full-range calibration of the PNA (50GHz).

6.1 Reflection Coefficient

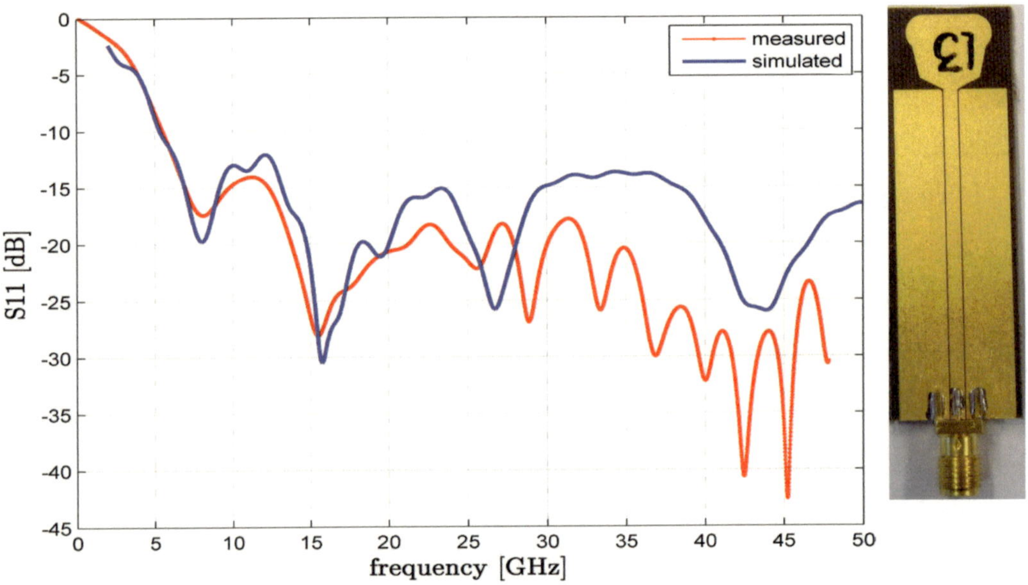

Fig. 7. SWB-performance: simulated and measured results.

The reflection coefficient magnitude of prototype 4 is measured and shown in fig. 7, the measurement agreed well with predicted value. Small deviation as frequency higher than 26 GHz, this defect is inherently caused by the failure of the 3.5mm SMA-connector, whose HF-range is cataloged as 18GHz max. The result indicated that the prototype 4 is a SWB-radiator because its measured ratio-bandwidth B_R is certainly greater than 10:1.

6.2 Far-field Radiation patterns

The far field radiation patterns are measured in the Delft University Chamber for Antenna Test (DUCAT); the anechoic chamber DUCAT (Fig. 8a) is fully screened, its walls, floor and ceiling are shielded with quality copper plate of 0.4 mm thick. All these aimed to create a Faraday cage of internal dimension of 6 x 3.5 x 3.5 m^3, which will prevent any external signal from entering the chamber and interfering with the measurements. The shielding of the chamber is for frequencies above 2 GHz up to 18 GHz at least 120 dB all around (Ligthart, 2006). All sides are covered with Pressey PFT-18 and PFT-6 absorbers for the small walls and long walls, respectively. It is found that one side reflects less than -36 dB. All these measures were taken together in order to provide sufficient shielding from other radiation coming from high power marine radars in the nearby areas.

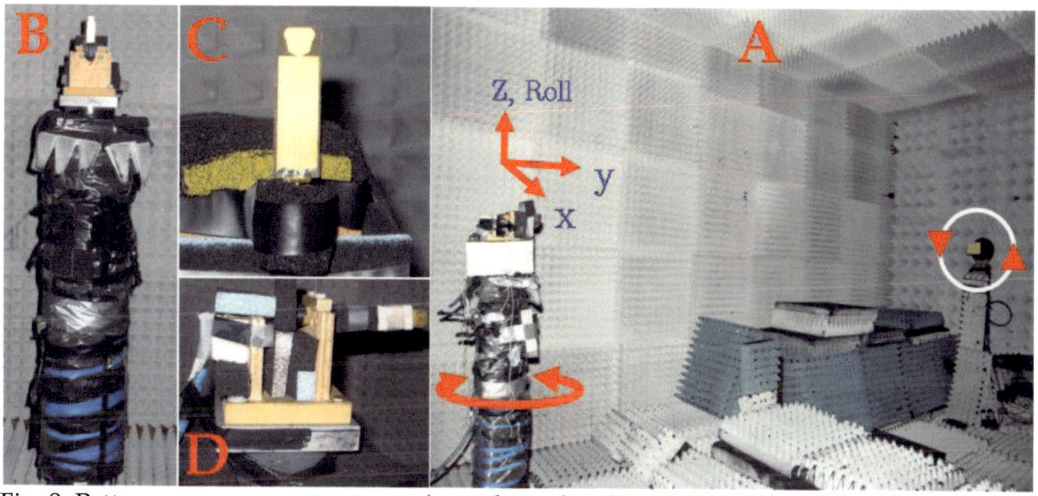

Fig. 8. Patterns measurement set up: a) anechoic chamber DUCAT, b) AUT on the rotatable column, c) Vertical configuration and d) Horizontal configuration.

TX: Single polarization standard horn is used as transmitter, which can rotate in yaw-y-direction to provide V, H polarizations and all possible slant polarizations. The choice of the single polarization horn above the dual polarization one as calibrator is two-folds: 1) keeps the unwanted cross-polarization to the lowest possible level, 2) and also voids the phase center interference and keeps the phase center deviation to the lowest level.

RX: Prototype 4 is put as antenna under test (AUT) on the roll-z-rotatable column (Fig. 8b). For the measurements of polarimetric components (VV, HV, VH, HH, the first letter denotes transmission's polarization state, the second is for the reception), two measurement setups are configured, the 1st is the vertical reception setup (VRS, Fig. 8c) for VV, VH and the 2nd is the horizontal reception setup (HRS, Fig. 8d) for HH, HV. Combination of the two setups and the TX's two polarizations provide full polarimetric patterns of the AUT.

Calibration: the HF-ranges of the Sucoflex-cable, T-adapters and connectors used in this measurement set up all cataloged as 18GHz max, owing to this limitation, we calibrated the PNA with Agilent N4691B cal-kit (1-26GHz).

6.2.1 Co-polar VV radiation patterns

The VV co-polar patterns are acquired with the VRS configuration in which TX-polarization is zenith-oriented. Fig. 9 showed the measured patterns in full calibrated range (§6.2). As predicted, the patterns were symmetrical- and omni-directional in the equipments' dynamic range. Fig. 10 shows the measured VV co-polar patterns for the in-band range (7-15GHz, 1GHz increment). The patterns consolidated the symmetrical receiving/transmitting mechanism of the AUT. Also observed is that all EIRP are less than -42dBm.

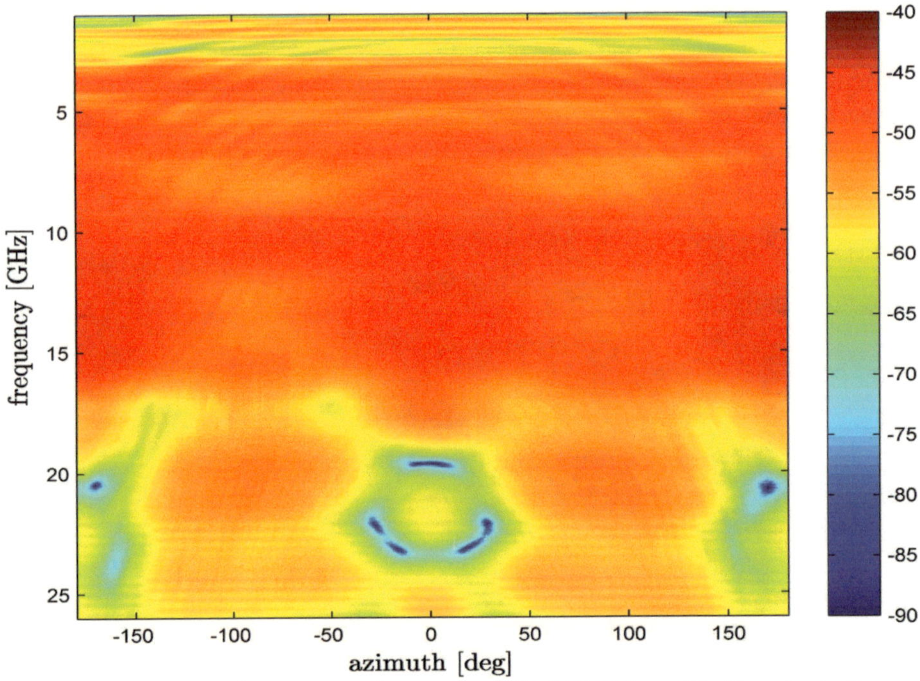

Fig. 9. Full-band VV co-polar measured patterns; RX: VRS; TX: zenithally oriented.

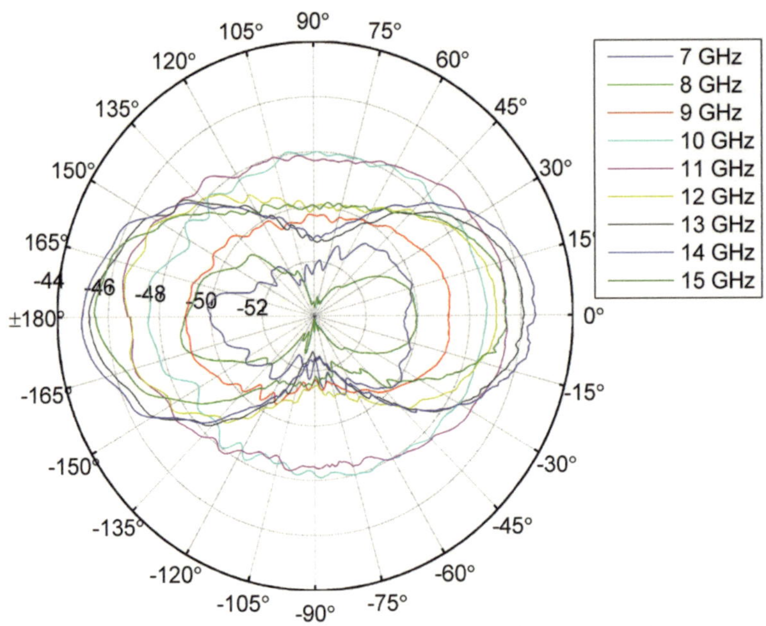

Fig. 10. In-band VV co-polar measured patterns; RX: VRS; Tx: zenithally oriented.

6.2.2 Cx-polar HV radiation patterns

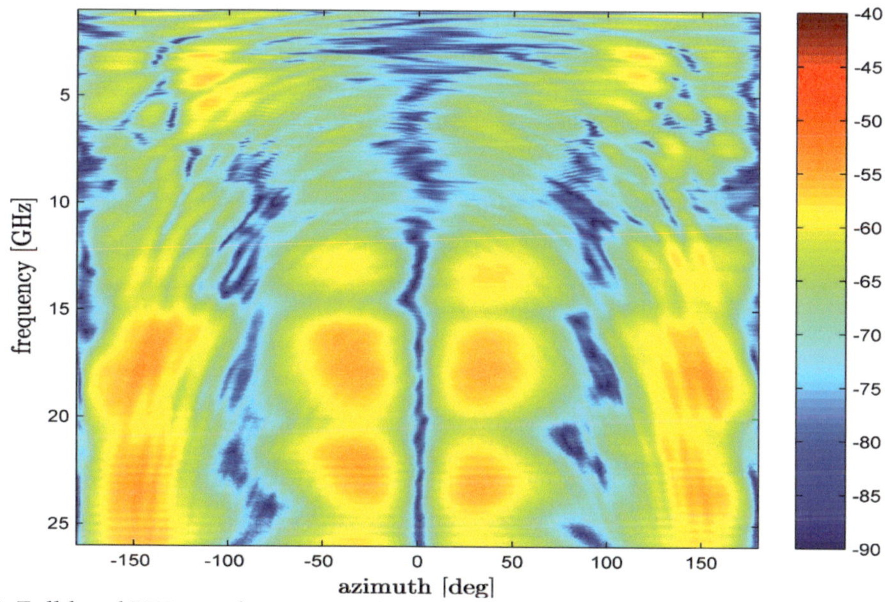

Fig. 11. Full-band HV cx-polar measured patterns; RX: VRS; Tx: azimuthally oriented.

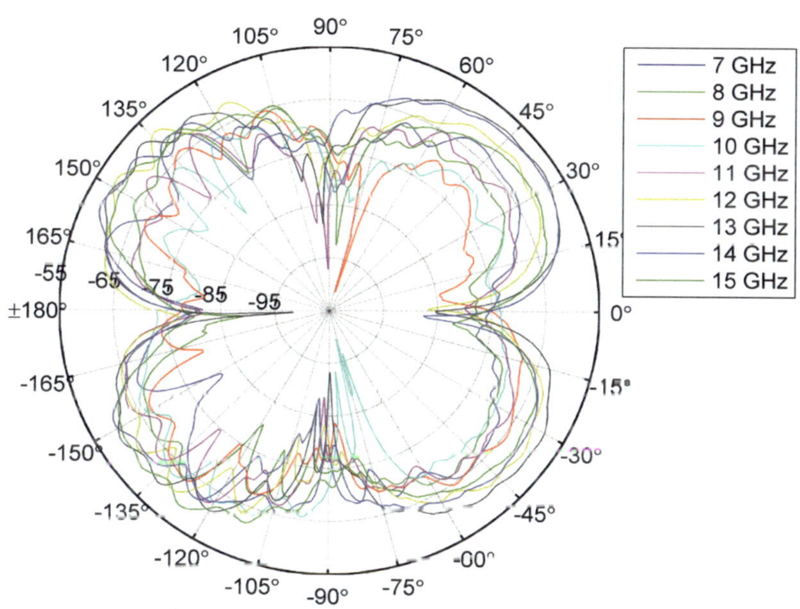

Fig. 12. In-band HV cx-polar measured patterns; RX: VRS; TX: azimuthally oriented.

The HV cx-polar patterns are obtained with the VRS configuration in which TX-polarization in Fig. 8a is 90^0-rotated. Plotted in Fig. 11 are the HV cx-polar patterns. As expected, perfect symmetrical and repeatable patterns can be observed in full-calibrated range (1-26GHz). Fig. 12 showed the measured HV cx-polar patterns for the in-band range (7-15GHz, 1GHz increment). The patterns consolidated the repeatable symmetrical receiving/transmitting mechanism of the prototype 4. Also observed is that all EIRP are less than -65dBm, this revealed that a greater than -20dBm XPD is obtained. Note, in the yoz−plane, theoretically no cx-polar components are expected as all cross polar components cancel each other in the $0^0 - 180^0$ and $-90^0 - 90^0$ direction. In a real case scenario, some cx-polar components are observed, their level being, nonetheless, extremely low (~ -90dBm)

6.2.3 Co-polarized HH radiation patterns

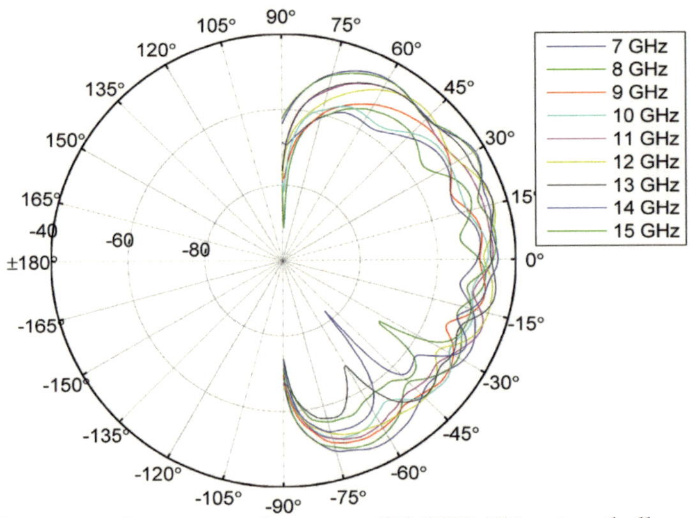

Fig. 13. In-band HH co-polar measured patterns; RX: HRS; TX: azimuthally oriented.

6.2.4 Cx-polarized VH radiation patterns

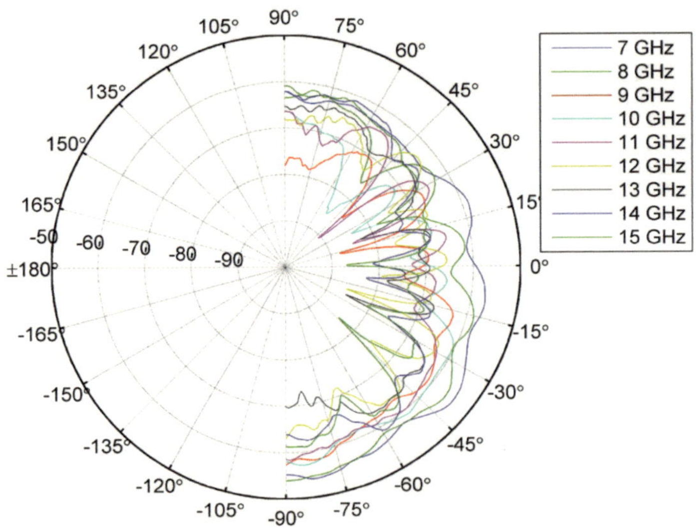

Fig. 14. In-band VH cx-polar measured patterns; RX: HRS; TX: zenithally oriented.

The co-polar (HH) and cx-polar (VH) radiation patterns can be acquired by the HRS with two polarization states of the TX, respectively. However, due to the mounting of the antenna (shown in Fig. 8d) it was not possible to measure the backside of the antenna, thus for the only half of the co-polar and cx-polar patterns were measured. Owing to the frequency limitations of used components (cables, adapters, connectors, absorbents), the DUCAT anechoic chamber specifications (Ligthart, 2006, op. cit.) and the WISE desired band the in-band range is chosen from 7-15GHz.
Fig. 13 showed the measured co-polar HH in-band radiation patterns. The patterns are symmetrical and repeatable with all EIRP less than -42dBm. The measured in-band cx-polar patterns for the VH configuration are plotted in Fig. 14, all peak powers have the EIRP in the order of -60dBm. The XPD of between HH and VH of the HRS displays the same discrimination dynamic as that of VV and HV of the VRS.

6.3 Time Domain Measurements

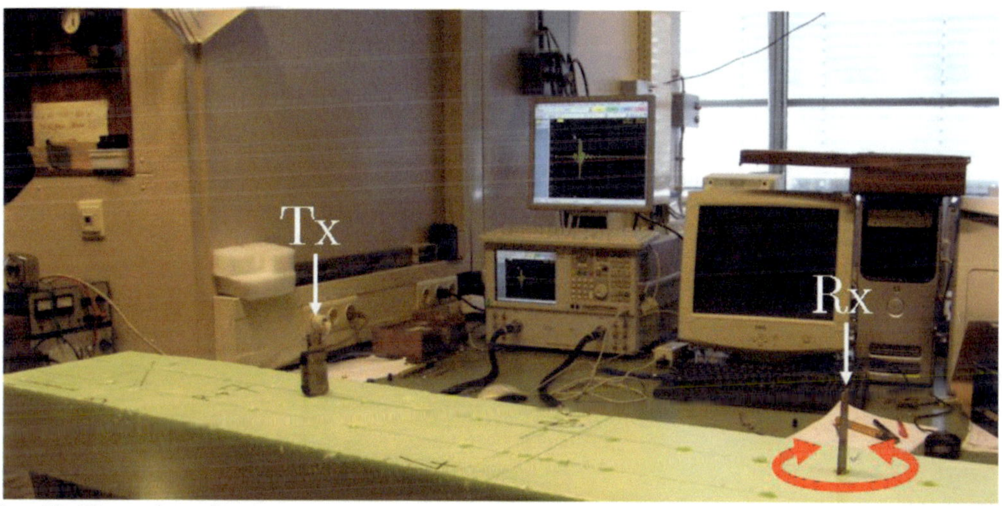

Fig. 15. Time domain measurement setups, equipment: Agilent VNA E8364B; Calibration kit: Agilent N4691B, calibrated method: 2-port 3.5 mm, TRL (SOLT), 300 KHz - 26 GHz

Fig. 15 shows the time domain set up for measurement and evaluation of: 1) pulse deformation, 2) the omni-radiation characteristics of the AUT. The same prototype 4 are used for TX (left) and RX (right), they stand on a horizontal foam bar which situated 1.20m above the floor.

6.3.1 Pulse Measurements

Pulse spreading and deformation: Fig. 16a shows the time-synchronization between the calculated transmit pulse (CTS) and the measured receive pulse (MRP) (for comparison, the CTS has been normalized, time-shifted and compared with the MRP), qualitative inspection shows that the synchronization-timing between transmitted and received pulses is very good, there is no pulse spreading took place, these measured features proved that the device is suitable for accurate ranging/sensing-applications, the small deviation at the beginning of the received pulse is due to RF-leakage (Agilent, AN1287-12, p.38), and at the end of the received pulse are from environments and late-time returns (Agilent, ibid., p.38), Note that the measurements are carried out in true EM-polluted environment as shows in fig. 15, and no gating applied).

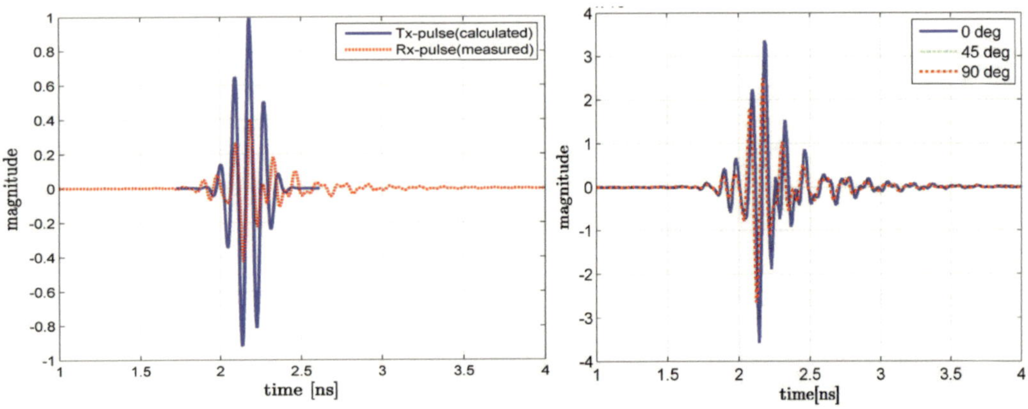

Fig. 16. co-polar transmission results of VRS-configuration; a) face-to-face: calculated vs. measured; b) oblique facing: measured results with RX 0-, 45- and 90-degree rotated.

Omni-radiation characteristics: To correctly evaluate the omni-directional property of the AUT, both quantitative characteristics (spatial) and qualitative characteristics (temporal) are carried out, the spatial-properties of prototype 4 are already tested and evaluated in frequency-domain (as depicted in fig. 9), and only the temporal-characteristic is left to be evaluated. To evaluated temporal-omni-radiation characteristics, three principal cuts are sufficiently represent the temporal-omni-radiation characteristics of the AUT in the time domain. Due to the editorial limitation, we report here only the most representative case (omni-directional in the azimuthal plane, i.e. co-polar VRS, which represents the most of all realistic reception scenarios). Fig. 16b shows three MRPs of the measurement configuration pictured in Fig. 15 with RX 0^0, 45^0, and 90^0 rotated. The results show a perfectly identical in timing, there is no time-deviation or spreading detected between the three cases. Furthermore, although the radiator is planar, it still exhibits a remarkable azimuth-independent property of 3D-symmetric radiators (for the 90^0 configuration, the projection of the receiving aperture vanished, however the prototype still able to receive 90% power as compare to the face-to-face case), this TD-measured results pertained the omni-directional property of the radiator, and this is also in agreement with, and as well consolidate the validity of the measured results carried out in the FD.

6.3.2 Transmission Amplitude Dispersion

To evaluate the amplitude spectral dispersion of the prototype 4, the measured time-domain transmission scattering coefficients of the three co-polar configurations (0^0, 45^0, and 90^0 configurations displayed in figure 15) were Fourier-transformed in to frequency domain. The measured magnitudes are plotted in fig. 17a, the measured results show a smooth and flat amplitude distribution in the designated band, and all are lower than -42dBm.

6.3.3 Transmission Phase Delay and Group delay

The measured phase responses of the transmission parameter for the three co-polar configurations are plotted in Fig. 17b. In narrowband technology, the phase delay defined as $\tau_P = -\theta/\omega$, is a metric for judging the quality of the transmission is the phase delay between the input and output signals of the system at a given frequency. In wideband technology, however, group delay is a more precise and useful measure of phase linearity of the phase response (Chen, 2007). The transmission group delays for the three above-mentioned configurations are plotted in Fig. 17c. The plots show an excellent and negligible group delays in the order of sub-nanosecond, this is no surprise because the phase responses of the prototype are almost linear (fig. 17b), thus the group delay, which is defined as the slope of the phase with respect to frequency $\tau_G = - d\theta/d\omega$, resulted accordingly. Note: although the group delay (fig. 17c) is mathematically defined as a constituent directly related to the phase, but it was impossible to visually observe directly from the phase plot (fig. 17b), but well from the magnitude plot (fig. 17a).

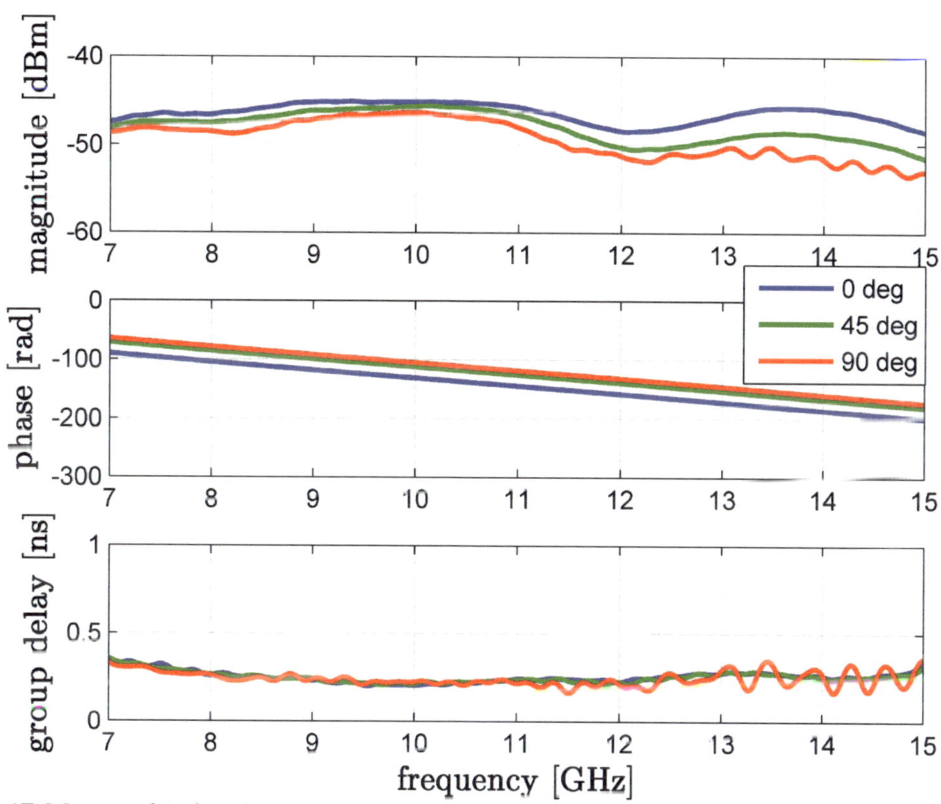

Fig. 17. Measured in-band transmission coefficients a) magnitude, b) phase, c) group delay

7. Acknowledgements

The research reported in this work was effectuated with in the frame of the "Wise Band Sparse Element Array Antennas" WiSE project, a scientific undergone financed by the Dutch

Technology Foundation (Stichting Technische Wetenschapen - STW). This support is hereby gratefully acknowledged.

8. Conclusions

The intent message of this report is not the mathematical formulation, nor the numerical aspects related to the design of proposed prototypes, but focusing on the concept, the design methodology and the pragmatic simplification of MVO process in to a SVO one.
Distinct concepts and definitions are defused and corrected. An SWB-antenna topology with simplest structure is proposed. The single layer topology paved the way for the creating of the obtained SWB antenna architecture. The antenna architecture supported, in turn, the FSD. The introduced design methodology and conceptual concept are consolidated by the developed prototypes.
The antenna architecture provides powerful isolated-parameters to control the antenna characteristics, such as resonance-shifting, resonance matching, bandwidth broadening, diffraction reduction, and SWB pattern maintaining.
The FSD approach is introduced to obtain the required performance, whilst keeping the overall dimension of the radiator fixed, the separated sections provide engineering insights, and can be designed or optimized almost independently.
Parameter order and SVO methodology are elaborated in details, the priority and role of separable parameters are identified, and so, instead of multivariable-optimization, the optimization process can be accelerated by carry out sequence of SVOs. The proposed design, optimization procedure can possibly be used as a gauging-process for designing or optimizing similar SWB structures.
Although the prototype 4 comprised a simplest structure and shape, however superior SWB impedance bandwidth is obtained and stable SWB-patterns are uniquely preserved.
This structure, although, can be modified to obtain huge frequency bandwidth, but cannot be one-size-fit-all for gain-size requirement. However, the architecture is flexible enough for scaling up/down its dimensions to match customer's gain-size requirement.
SWB prototype is designed, fabricated and evaluated for the super wideband impasse, and could possibly used as an alternative radiator for the sub-millimeter-wave regime.
Performances of the prototype are tested and evaluated. Good agreements between numerical predictions and measurements are obtained.
The SWB-prototype has been fabricated years ago but not published elsewhere; due to editorial limits, we exclusively report here only the design methodology and conceptual approach; detailed mathematical formulation and numerical aspects related to this SWB prototype will be published in another occurrence.

9. References

Agilent technologies (2007). Time Domain Analysis Using a Network Analyzer, Application Note 1287-12, 2007.

Al Sharkawy, M. H., Eldek, A. A., Elsherbeni, A. Z., and Smith, C. E. (2004). Design of wideband printed monopole antenna using WIPL-D". 20th *Annual Review of Progress in Applied Computational Electromagnetics*, NY, Syracuse, USA, Apr. 2004.

Balanis, C. A. (1997). *Antenna theory analysis and design*, John Wiley & Sons, Inc, second edition, New York, 1997.

Belrose, J. S. (1995). Fessenden and Marconi: Their Differing Technologies and Transatlantic Experiments During the First Decade of this Century, International *conference on 100 years of Radio*, 5-7 Sept. 1995.

Brodsky, I. (2008). How Reginald Fessenden Put Wireless on the Right Technological Footing, *Proceedings of the Global Communications Conference*, GLOBECOM 2008, New Orleans, LA, USA, 30 Nov.-4 Dec. 2008. pp.3577-81.

Brown, D., Fiscus, T. E, Meierbachtol, C. J (1980). Results of a study using RT 5880 material for a missile radome, In: *Symposium on Electromagnetic Windows*, 15th, Atlanta, GA, June 18-20, Proceeding (A82-2645, 11-32), Georgia Institute of Technology, p.7-12.

Chen Z.N. (2007). Antenna Elements for Impulse Radio, In: *Ultra-wideband Antennas and Propagation for Communications, Radar and Imaging*, Allen B. et al. (Ed.), John Wiley & Sons, 2007.

FCC (2002). Federal Communications Commission, FCC 02-48, ET-Docket 98-153, "*First Report and Order*", Apr. 2002.

FCC (2004), Federal Communications Commission, FCC 04-285, ET-Docket 98-153, "*Second Report and Order and Second Memorandum Opinion and Order*", Dec. 2004.

Huang, Y. & Boyle, K. (2008). *Antennas from Theory to Practice*, John Willey and Sons, Singapore, 2008, pp.64.

IEEE STD 145-1983. *IEEE Standard Definitions of Terms for Antennas*, New York, IEEE Press, 1983, pp.11-16.

Karoui, M. S., Ghariani, H., Samet, M., Ramadi, M., Pedriau, R. (2010). Bandwidth Enhancement of the Square Rectangular Patch Antenna for Biotelemetry applications, *International journal of information systems and telecommunication engineering*, v.1, 2010, iss.1, pp.12-18.

Kraus, J. D. (1985). Antennas since Hertz and Marconi, *IEEE Trans*. AP-33, No. 2, Feb.1985, pp.131-137.

Kshetrimayum, R. S., Pillalamarri, R. (2008). Novel UWB printed monopole antenna with triangular tapered feed lines, *IEICE Electronics express*, vol.5, No. 8, pp. 242-247.

Ligthart, LP (2006). Antennas and propagation measurement techniques for UWB radio, *Wireless personal communications*, 37(3-4), pp.329-360.

Massey, P. (2007). Planar Dipole-like for Consumer Products, In: *Ultra-wideband Antennas and Propagation for Communications, Radar and Imaging*, Allen, B. et al., John Wiley & Sons, West Sussex, England, 2007, pp.163-196.

Molisch, A. F., (2007). Introduction to UWB signals and system, In: *Ultra-wideband antennas and propagation for communications, radar and ranging*, Allen, B. et al., (Ed.), pp.1-17, John Willey and sons, West Sussex, England.

Rahayu, H., Rahman, T. A., Ngah, R., Hall, P. S. (2008). Slotted ultra wideband antenna for bandwidth enhancement, 2008, *Loughborough Antennas & Propagation Conference* 17-18, Mar. 2008, Loughborough, UK.

Rahim, M. K. A. & Gardner, P. (2004). The design of nine element quasi microstrip log periodic antenna, *RF and microwave conference*, 2004. RFM 2004, 5-6 Oct. 2004, Selangor, Malaysia, pp.132–135.

Razavi, B. et al. (2005). A UWB CMOS Tranceiver, *IEEE journal of solid-state circuit*, vol.40, no.12, dec. 2005, pp.2555-2562.

Rmili, H. & Floc'h, J. M. (2008). Design and analysis of wideband double-sided printed spiral dipole antenna with capacitive coupling, *Microwave and optical technology letters,* Vol. 50, No.5, pp. 312-1317.

Schantz, H. G and Barnes, M. (2003). UWB magnetic antenna, *IEEE International Symposium on Antennas and Propagation Digest*, 3, 2003, pp.604-607.

Schantz, H. G. (2004). A brief history of UWB antennas, *IEEE Aerospace and Electronic Systems Magazine*, vol .19(4), pp.22-26, 2004.

Simons, R. N. (2001). *Coplanar Waveguide Circuits, Components, and Systems,* John Wiley & Sons, New York, 2001.

Tanyer-Tigrek, F. M, Tran, D., Lager, I. E., Ligthart, L. P. (2009a). CPW-fed Quasi-Magnetic Printed Antenna for Ultra-Wideband Application, *IEEE Antennas and Propagation Magazine*, Vol.51, No.2, April 2009, 1, pp.61-70.

________, (2009b). Over 150% bandwidth, quasi-magnetic printed antennas, *Antennas and Prop. Society International Symposium,* AP-S, 2009.

________, (2010). *Printed antenna elements with attested ultra wideband array capability,* dissertation, ISBN-978-90-9024664-2, 2010, p.113-135.

Thor, R. C. (1962). A Large Time-Bandwidth Product Pulse-Compression Technique, *IRE Transaction on military electronics*, Vol. MIl-6, No.2, Apr. 1962, pp.169-173.

Tourette, S., Fortino, N., Kossiavas, G. (2006). Compact UWB printed antennas for low frequency applications matched to different transmission lines, *Microwave and optical technology letters*, Vol. 49, No.6, pp.1282-1287.

Tran, D., Tanyer-Tigrek, F. M., Vorobyov, A., Lager, I. E. & Ligthart, L. P. (2007). A Novel CPW-fed Optimized UWB printed Antenna, In: *Proceedings of the 10th European conference on wireless technology,* pp.40-43, Munich, Germany, October 8-10, 2007, Horizon House Publications Ltd, London.

Tran, D. P., Coman, C. I., Tanyer-Tigrek, F. M., Szilagyi, A., Simeoni, M., Lager, I. E., Ligthart, L. P. & van Genderen, P.(2010).The relativity of bandwidth – the pursuit of truly ultra wideband radiators, In: *Antennas for Ubiquitous Radio Services in a Wireless Information Society*, Lager, I. E (Ed.), pp.55-74, IOS Press, 2010, Amsterdam.

Wilson, J. M (2002). Ultra-wideband a disruptive RF technology?, Intel Research and Development, Version 1.3, Sept. 10, 2002.

Zhang, X., Wu, W., Yan, Z. H., Jiang, J. B. & Song, Y. (2009). Design of CPW-Fed monopole UWB antenna with a novel notched ground, *Microwave and optical technology letters,* Vol. 51, No.1, pp. 88-91.

A small novel ultra wideband antenna with slotted ground plane

[1]Yusnita Rahayu , [2]Razali Ngah and [2]Tharek Abd. Rahman
[1]Faculty of Mechanical Engineering, Universiti Malaysia Pahang, Kuantan, Pahang
[2]Wireless Communication Centre (WCC), Faculty of Electrical Engineering, Universiti Teknologi Malaysia, Johor Bahru, Johor
Malaysia

1. Introduction

A few years after the early investigation on ultra wideband (UWB) wireless system, considerable research efforts have been put into the design of UWB antennas and systems for communications. The UWB technology brings the convenience and mobility of wireless communications with higher data rates. Designed for short range, wireless personal area networks (WPANs), UWB is the leading technology for freeing people from wires, enabling wireless connection of multiple devices for transmission of video, audio and other high bandwidth data. UWB short-range radio technology complements other longer-range radio technologies such as WiFi, WiMAX, and cellular wide area communications. Freescale Semiconductor was the first company to produce UWB chips in the world (L. Jianxin, 2006). Its XS110 solution has been commercialized to the market. It provides full wireless connectivity delivering more than 110 Mbps data transfer rate supporting applications such as streaming video, streaming audio, and high rate data transfer at very low levels of power consumption.

Through literature survey, there are two vital design considerations in UWB radio systems. One is radiated power density spectrum shaping must comply with certain emission limit mask for coexistence with other electronic system (FCC, 2002). Another is that the design source pulses and transmitting/receiving antennas should be optimal for performance of overall systems (Z.N. Chen et al., 2004). Emission limits will be crucial considerations for the design of source pulses and antennas in UWB systems. The FCC regulated the spectral shape and maximum power spectral density (-41.3 dBm/MHz) of the UWB radiation in order to limit the interference with other communication systems.

Even though the UWB technology has experienced many significant developments in recent years, however, there are still challengers in making this technology live up to its full potential. The main challenge in UWB antenna design is achieving the extremely wide impedance bandwidth while still maintaining high radiation efficiency. By definition, an UWB antenna must be operable over the entire 3.1 GHz – 10.6 GHz frequency range (FCC, 2002). Therefore, the UWB antenna must achieve almost a decade of impedance bandwidth, spanning 7.5 GHz. The high radiation efficiency is also required especially for UWB applications to ensure the transmit power spectral density requirement achieved. Conductor and dielectric losses should be minimized in order to maximize radiation efficiency. High radiation efficiency is imperative for an UWB antenna because the transmit power spectral density is excessively low. Therefore, any excessive losses incurred by the antenna could potentially compromise the functionality of the system.

In addition, a nearly omni-directional radiation pattern is also desirable in that it enables freedom in the receiver and transmitter location. This implies maximizing the half power beam-width and minimizing directivity. It is also highly desirable that the antenna feature low profile and compatibility for integration with Printed Circuit Board (PCB) (L. Jianxin, 2006).

2. UWB Antenna Design Consideration

Antennas play a critical role in the UWB communication systems and the choice of a specific UWB antenna design has to be based on the application main requirements. Currently, modern telecommunication systems require antennas with wider bandwidth and smaller dimensions than conventionally possible. This has initiated antenna research in various directions, one of which is by using UWB antennas.

Today the state of the art of UWB antennas focuses in the microstrip, slot and planar monopole antennas with different matching techniques to improve the bandwidth ratio without loss of its radiation pattern properties (M.A. Peyrot Solis et al., 2005). The expected antennas are small size, omni-directional patterns, and simple structure that produce low distortion but can provide large bandwidth.

In the past, one serious limitation of microstrip antennas was the narrow bandwidth characteristic, being 15% to 50% that of commonly used antenna elements such as dipoles, and slots (J.F. Zurcher & F.E. Gardiol, 1995). This limitation was successfully removed achieving a matching impedance bandwidth of up to 90%. To increase the matching impedance bandwidth ratio it was necessary to increase the size, height, volume or feeding and matching techniques (R. Garg et al., 2001). Variety of matching techniques have been proposed in the literature reviews, such as the use of slot (Albert K,Y. Lai et al., 1992), (Seok H. Choi et al., 2004), bevel or taper at the bottom of patch (E. Guillanton et al., 1998), notch and partial ground plane (Seok H. Choi et al., 2004) and dual feed (Z.N. Chen et al., 2006), (S. Boris et al., 2005), (H. Ghannoum et al., 2006). Radiators may be slotted to improve the impedance matching, especially at higher frequency (Z.N. Chen et al., 2006). Fractal antenna may also be used to obtain low VSWR UWB performance (Khan, S. N. et al., 2008).

The planar monopole antennas are promising antennas for UWB applications due to their simple structure, low profile, easy to fabricate and UWB characteristics with nearly omni-directional radiation patterns (L. Jianxin, 2006), (N.P. Agrawall et al., 1998), (Chun Y. Wu et al., 2005). Planar monopole antennas feature broad impedance bandwidth but somewhat suffer high cross polarization radiation levels. The large lateral size or asymmetric geometry of the planar radiator causes the cross-polarized radiation. Fortunately, the purity of the polarization issue is not critical, particularly for the antennas used for portable devices (Z.N. Chen, 2006). There are several UWB planar antenna designs, including planar half disk antenna (T. Yang & W. A. Davis, 2004), planar horn antenna (S. H. Lee et al., 2005), and metal plate antenna (K. L. Wong et al., 2004), have been reported.

The critical issue in this UWB antenna design is the size of the antenna for portable devices. The reduction in antenna size presents various problems due to the performance penalties in antenna characteristics, such as impedance, efficiency, and bandwidth. Therefore, to miniaturize the antennas capable of providing ultra wide bandwidth for impedance matching and acceptable gain will be a challenging task. Small antennas are defined as those which have smallness in terms of size, wavelength, and function, and they are divided into four categories (K. Hirasawa & M. Haneishi, 1992). The first is electrically small antennas, which have a very small size compared to the wave length (λ). The second is physically constrained small antennas, which are not necessary electrically small, but are shaped in such a way that considerable size reduction is achieved in one plane. The third is physically small antennas, which have dimensions regarded as small in a relative sense. The last is functionally small antennas, which are antenna systems that achieved additional functions without increasing size. This proposed antenna meets those four categories as a small antenna. Its size is less than a wavelength, compact size in one plane, considerable smaller size compared to the antennas sizes in the references listed (Z.N. Chen et al., 2006), (Giuseppe R. & Max J. Ammann, 2006), (Seok H. Choi et al., 2004), (A. A. Eldek, 2006), (S. Boris et al., 2005), (H. Ghannoum et al., 2006), (T. Huynh & K. F. Lee, 1995), (Mayhew Ridgers, G., 2004), (Y.X. Guo et al., 1998) and suitable for many UWB applications. The T slot for both patch and feeding strip is as a novelty design in terms of slot type.
The theory characteristic modes are also used to design and optimise the proposed UWB antenna. From the study of the behavior of characteristic modes, important information about resonant frequency and the bandwidth of an antenna can be obtained. The current behavior of the antenna are investigated in order to obtain new slotted UWB antenna.

3. T Slotted UWB Antenna

In order to obtain the ultra wide bandwidth, omni-directional radiation pattern, and small size antenna, four matching techniques are applied to the proposed UWB antennas, such as the use of slots, the use of notches at the bottom of patch, the truncation ground plane, and the slotted ground plane. All these techniques are applied to the small UWB antenna without degrading the required UWB antenna's performance. The size of slots and notches are critically affect to the impedance bandwidth. The distance between truncation ground plane to the bottom of the patch is as matching point, where it determines the resonance frequency. To ensure the broad badwidth can be obtained, the proper designs on those parameters are required. The effect of notches, slot, truncation and slotted ground plane to the antenna's performance will be discussed in next section in order to develop a design methodology to control the matching bandwidth of antenna.

3.1 Antenna Geometry

This proposed antenna, shown in Figure 1, originates from conventional rectangular monopole and is realized by adding 'T' slot for both patch and feeding strip. The antenna has a compact dimension of 30 mm x 30 mm (W_{sub} x L_{sub}), designed on FR4 substrate with thickness of 1.6 mm and relative dielectric constant (ε_r) of 4.7.

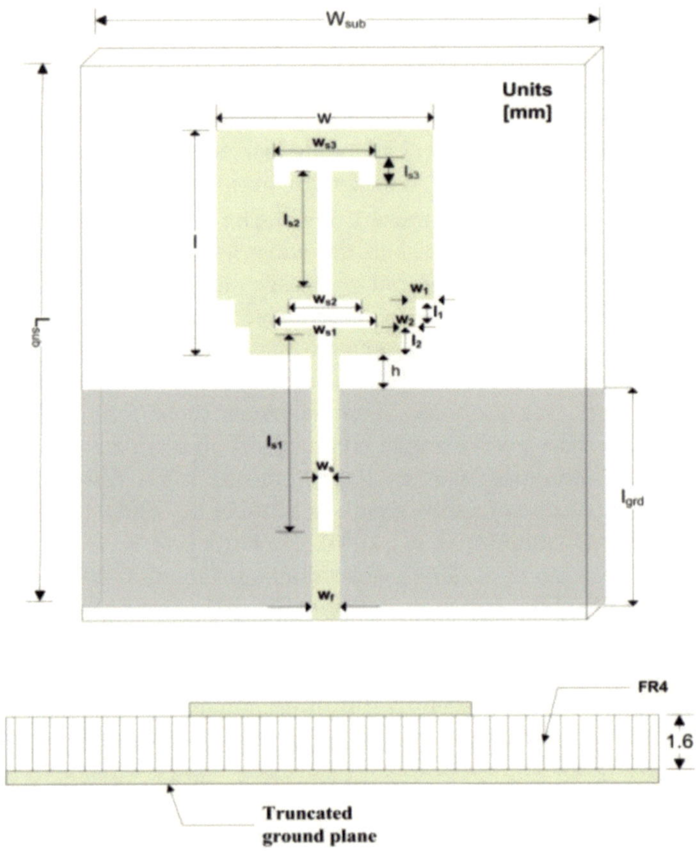

Fig. 1. Geometry of T slotted UWB antenna

The radiator is fed by a microstrip line of 3 mm width (w_f). On the front surface of the substrate, a rectangular patch with size of 15 mm x 12 mm (w x l) is printed. The two notches size of 1.5 mm x 12 mm (w_1 x l_1) and 1 mm x 9 mm (w_2 x l_2) are at the two lower corners of radiating patch. The distance of h between the rectangular patch to ground plane printed on the back surface substrate is 1 mm, and the length (l_{grd}) of truncated ground plane of 11.5 mm. The excitation is a 50 Ω microstrip line printed on the partial grounded substrate. The slot size of w_s, w_{s1}, w_{s2}, w_{s3}, l_{s1}, l_{s2}, l_{s3} are 1, 5, 3, 6, 11, 7, 2 mm, respectively. The main objective in this antenna design is to reduce the size. Obviously, it is difficult to do this without degrading the antenna performance but the main question is whether this degradation is acceptable or not for a given application.

3.1.1 Effect of notches at the bottom of patch radiator

Figure 2 shows the rectangular monopole antenna with various steps notches cutting at the bottom edge. The feed width (w_f) is set to be 3 mm and the feed length (f_l) is set to be 12.5 mm. The first and third notch dimensions are (1 x 1) mm^2 and the second notch is (1 x 1.5) mm^2. Cutting notches at the bottom techniques are aimed to change the distance between the lower part of the planar monopole antenna and the ground plane in order to tune the capacitive coupling between the antenna and the ground plane, thereby wider impedance bandwidth can be achieved. This technique is confirmed by the simulation result shown in Figure 3.

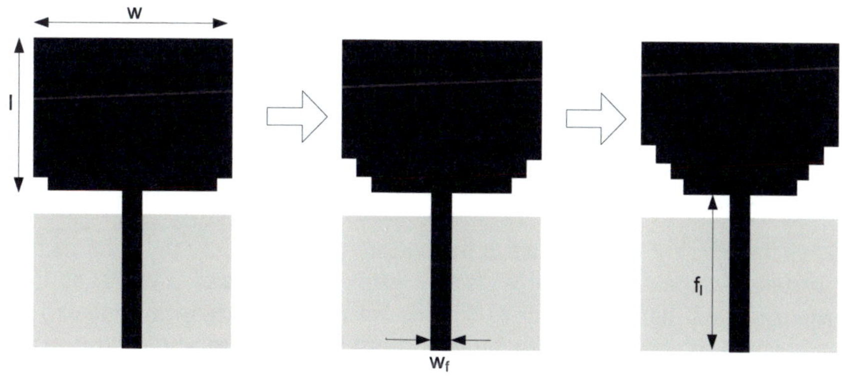

Fig. 2. Various steps notches cutting at the bottom of patch radiator

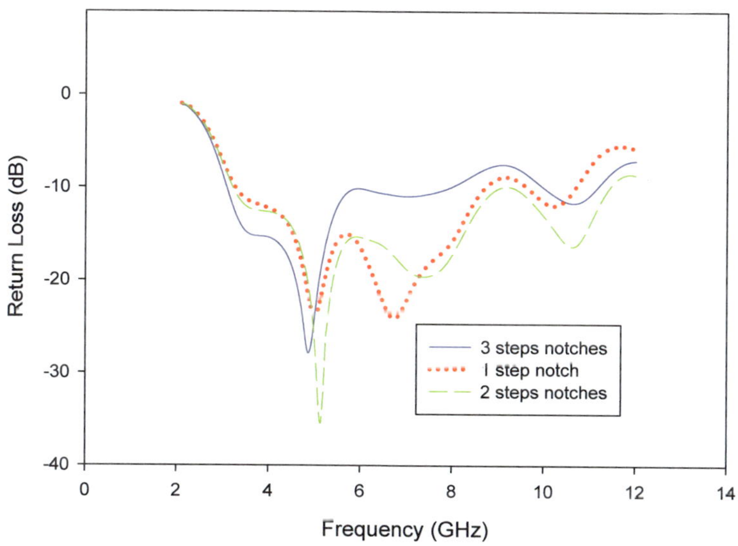

Fig. 3. Simulated return loss of various steps notches cutting at the bottom of patch radiator

As shown in Figure 3, the return loss of antenna with three steps notches cutting at the bottom edge is the worst curve with respect to -10 dB. This is due to its notch variation is more abrupt, thus the bandwidth is smaller. For the two steps notches, the return loss curve is the best, covering 3.17 GHz to 11.5 GHz of frequency ranges. While one step notch at the bottom provides a good matching bandwidth at below 9 GHz and start degrading at higher frequencies.

There is an important phenomenon in Figure 3 at the first resonance occurs at 5.2 GHz for the patch with two notches at the bottom. When the antenna has only one and three notches at the bottom, the first resonances are 4.9 GHz and 5.1 GHz, respectively. Both first resonances are shifted slightly, but still not far from 5.2 GHz. In fact, the quarter wavelength at this first resonant frequency (5.2 GHz) just equals to the length of the antenna and optimized by the simulation software.

Notches	f_L (GHz)	f_U (GHz)	Absolute BW (GHz)	Fractional BW (%)
0	3.56	9.05	5.49	87
1	3.27	8.7	5.43	90
2	3.17	11.5	8.33	113
3	3.07	7.98	4.91	88

Table 1. The effect of notches to the simulated -10dB bandwidths of the proposed antenna

Table 1 shows the effect of two notches at the bottom of the patch to the antenna bandwidth. The basic rectangular patch antenna with a length of 12 mm and a width of 15 mm only provides the fractional bandwidth of 87%. This fractional bandwidth increases to 90% by cutting one notch at the bottom, while the maximum fractional bandwidth reach to 113% by applying two notches at the bottom of the patch antenna. Then, the fractional bandwidth decreases again by cutting three notches. Hence, the proper selections in the size of notches lead to the UWB characteristic.

3.1.2 Effect of Feed Gap and Slotted Ground Plane

The feed gap between ground plane to the bottom of patch is known given crucial effect to the impedance bandwidth. The modified truncated ground plane acts as an impedance matching element to control the impedance bandwidth of a rectangular patch. This is because the truncation creates a capacitive load that neutralizes the inductive nature of the patch to produce nearly-pure resistive input impedance.

Slotted or notched ground plane is also taken into consideration. The size of notches should be properly designed while still maintaining the antenna's performance. The efficient technique to determine the size of notches in the ground plane is by calculating the optimum feed gap between the ground plane and the bottom patch required without adding the notches. Then, the size of notches can be adjusted with respect to the optimum distance.

Figure 4 illustrates the simulated return loss curves for different feed gaps to the ground plane of T slotted antenna. It is shown in Figure 4 and Table 2 that the -10 dB operating bandwidth of the antenna varies with the variation of the feed gap (h) and the dimension of the ground plane. The optimal feed gap is found to be 1 mm with the fractional bandwidth of 116%.

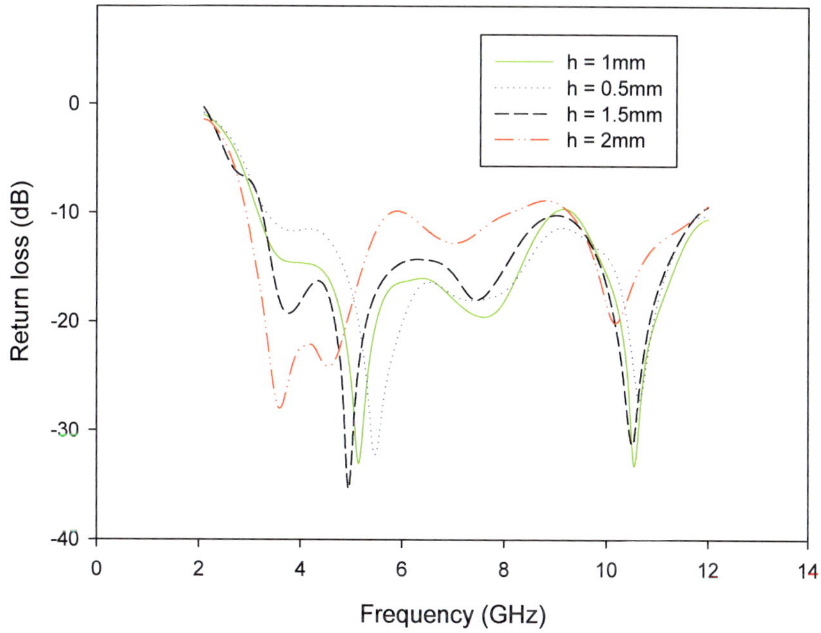

Fig. 4. Simulated return loss curves of T slotted antenna for different feed gaps

h (mm)	f_L (GHz)	f_U (GHz)	Absolute BW (GHz)	Fractional BW (%)
0.5	3.27	12	8.73	114
1.0	3.17	12	8.83	116
1.5	3.27	11.8	8.53	113
2.0	2.98	8.17	5.19	93

Table 2. Simulated -10dB bandwidths of the T slotted antenna for different feed gaps

It can be seen in Table 2 that the -10 dB bandwidth of T slotted antenna does not change much with the variation of the feed gap of the ground plane below 1.5 mm. But beyond this ranges, it will degrade the impedance bandwidth performance. These simulated results indicate that the antenna bandwidth is dependent on the feed gap of the ground plane, since the ground plane serves as an impedance matching circuit.

As shown in Figure 5(a), the return loss < -10 dB always occurs over the frequency range when the input impedance is matched to 50 ohm. The real part (R_e) is close to 50 Ω while the imaginary part (I_m), as shown in Figure 5(b), is not far from zero for the four different feed gaps. When h is 1mm and 1.5 mm, R_e varies tardily at the level of 50 Ω whilst I_m remains small across wide frequency range, leading to a UWB characteristic. However, when h rises to 2 mm, R_e varies more widely and I_m also fluctuates significantly across the frequency range, thus resulting in impedance mismatch at the antenna and hence the decrease of the operating bandwidth. The peak value of resistance is as high as 100 ohms, while the maximum reactance is around 35 ohms.

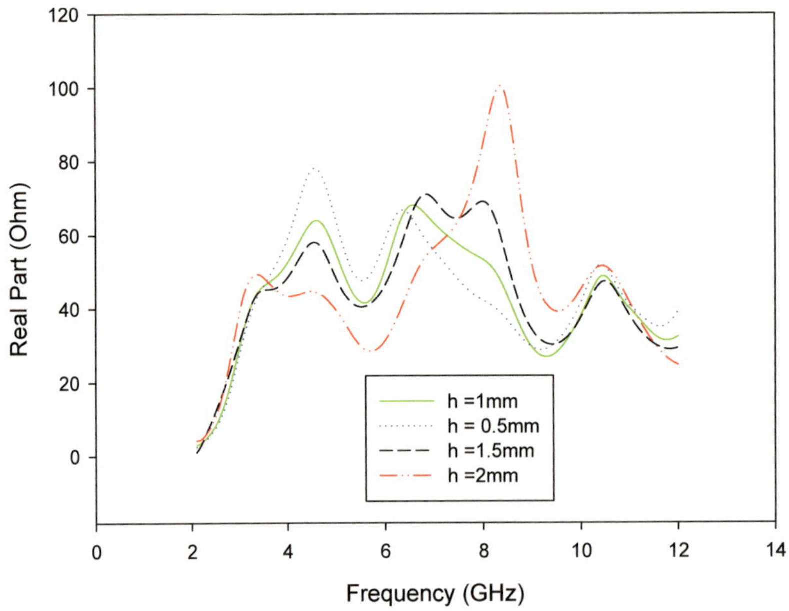

(a)

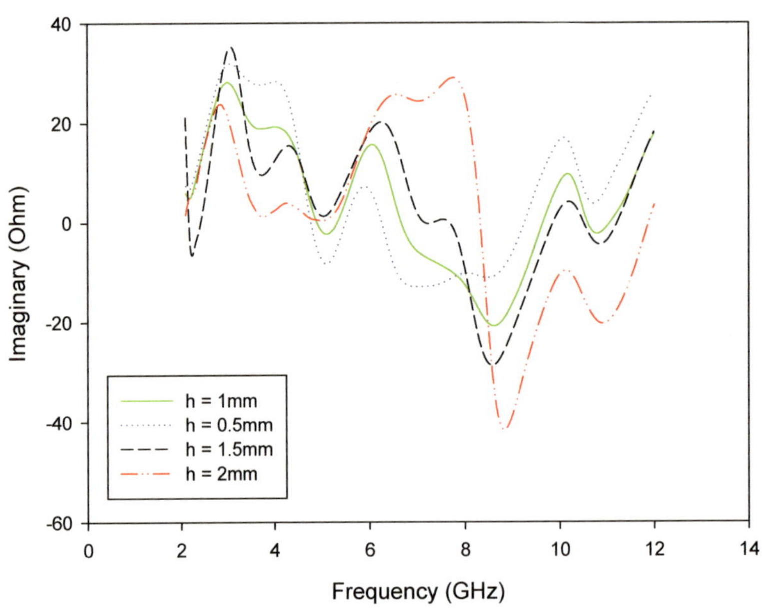

(b)

Fig. 5. Simulated input impedance curves of T slotted antenna for different feed gaps: (a) real part and (b) imaginary part

As mentioned previously, the ground plane acts as impedance matching of the antenna. Modify the partial ground plane to staircase slotted ground plane has improved the return loss of antenna, especially at higher frequency. The geometry of staircase slotted ground plane is shown in Figure 6.

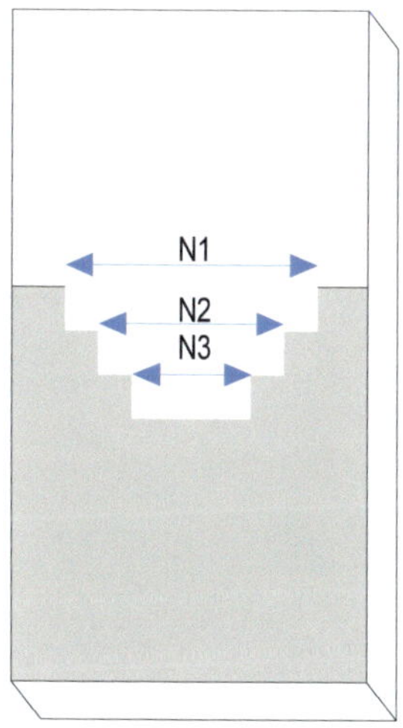

Fig. 6. Geometry of staircase slotted ground plane

Figure 6 shows the geometry of staircase slotted ground plane. By varying the lengths and the widths of slots of ground plane, it is possible to tune the impedance matching as shown in Figure 7.

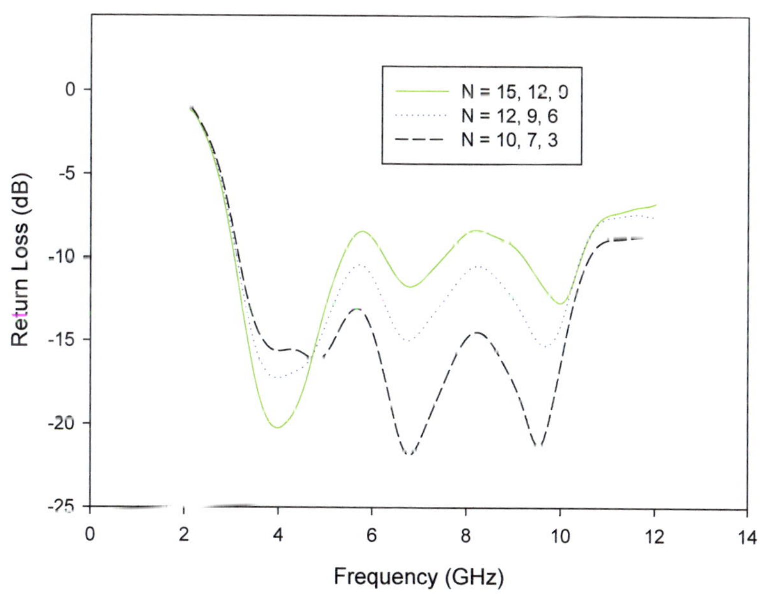

Fig. 7. The effect of various length slotted ground plane to the antenna performance

The width of this slotted ground plane is set to 0.5 mm. The optimum feed gap for T slotted antenna is found to be 0.5 mm above the slotted ground plane. The gap of patch radiator to ground plane is critically effect to the input impedance of antenna. From the simulation, the lengths of slots of N_1, N_2, N_3 of 10, 7, 3 mm give the best return loss for both slotted antennas. It is shown that by increasing the length of slotted ground plane caused degrading the impedance bandwidth of antenna performance.

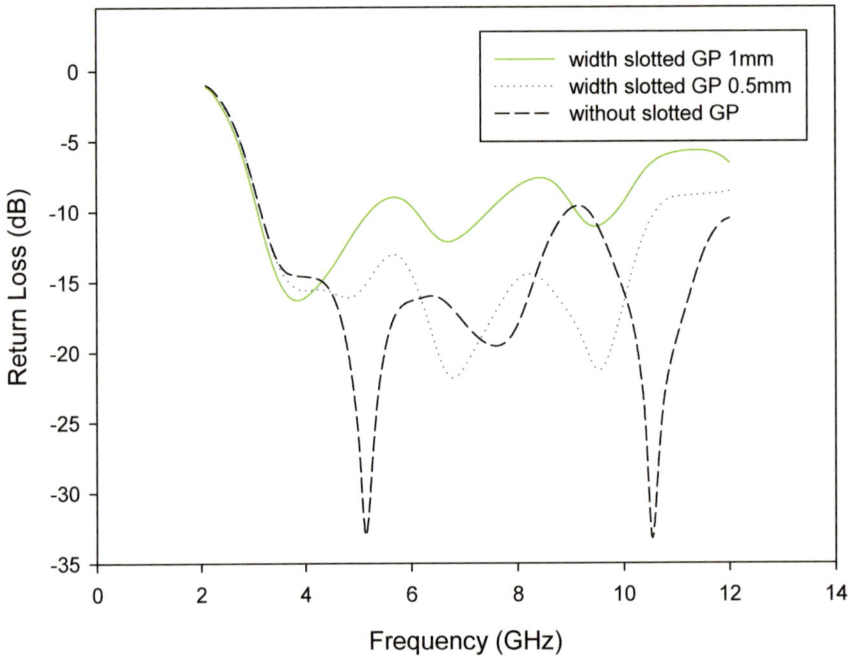

Fig. 8. The effect of various width slotted ground plane to the antenna performance

Figure 8 presents the effect of various width slotted ground plane to the antenna performance. The width slotted ground plane of 1 mm has degraded the antenna return loss above -10 dB. This is due to the width slot has brought the antenna to much more capacitive and far away from the resonance point. The staircase slotted ground plane has improved the return loss around at 9 GHz for T slotted antenna with the width slot of 0.5 mm. It is also shown that the staircase slotted ground plane has removed the lower and upper dip resonances for slotted antenna. The return loss curves fluctuate around -15 dB. The T slotted with slotted ground plane antenna cover frequency range of 3.17 GHz to 10.6 GHz with fractional bandwidth of 108%.

The simulated return loss curve for various number of slotted ground plane for antenna is depicted in Figure 9. It is clearly shown that by increasing the number of slotted ground plane has degraded the antenna performance and led the antenna to much more capacitive especially at higher frequency range.

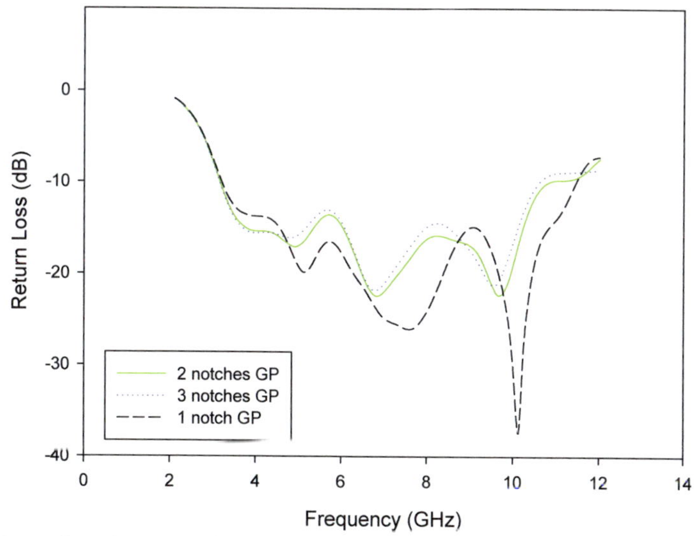

Fig. 9. The effect of various number slotted ground plane to the antenna performance

3.1.3 Effect of Various T slot

The simulated return loss for various T slots antennas is shown in Figure 10. It shows that the T slots have improved the return loss at mid frequencies range, while slightly shifted the upper edge resonance. The return loss provides a very broad bandwidth below -15 dB.

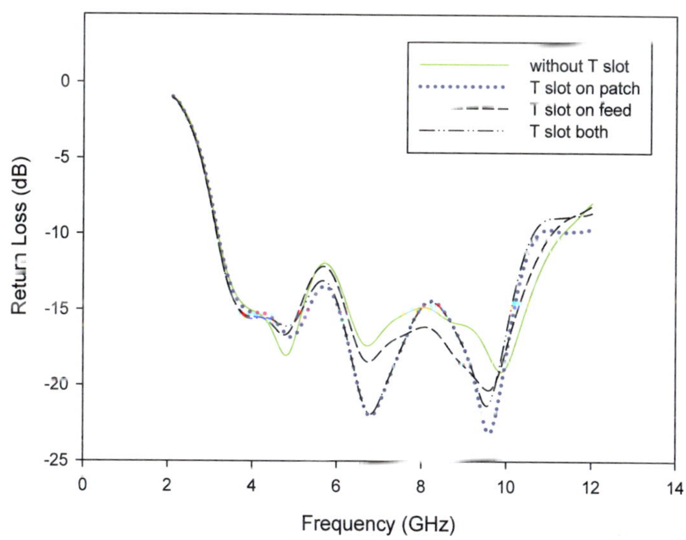

Fig. 10. The simulated return loss of various T slots design for antenna with slotted ground plane

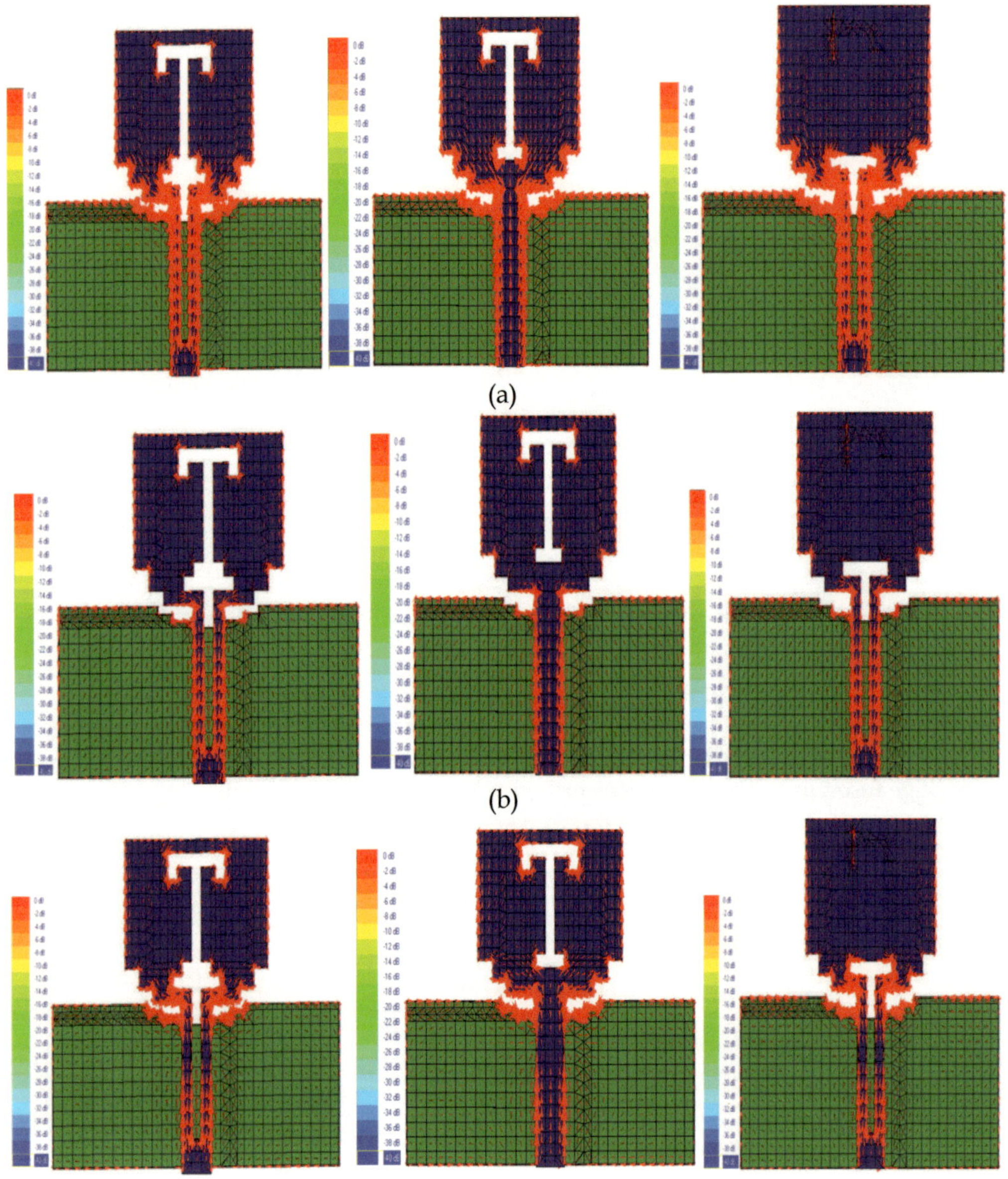

Fig. 11. The simulated current distribution for T slotted antenna with slotted ground plane: (a) 3 GHz, (b) 5.5 GHz, (c) 9 GHz

Figure 11 shows various modified of T slotted antenna with their current distribution at 3, 5.5 and 9 GHz, respectively. Figure 11(a) presents the current distribution of antenna with both T slot on patch and feed, T slot on patch only, and T slot on feed only at 3 GHz. The T slot has resulted much more vertical current through antenna radiator. Most vertical electrical current is distributed near the T slot edges and lead to impedance matching at 3

GHz. The vertical current is most concentrated near the patch edges and slots rather than distributed on the antenna surface at 5.5 GHz and this cause the decrement of the intensity of vertical electrical current on antenna surface. For the antenna's current distribution at 9 GHz, the horizontal current mode occurs on the antenna surface. And it is also shown that some vertical current start flowing down to the base.

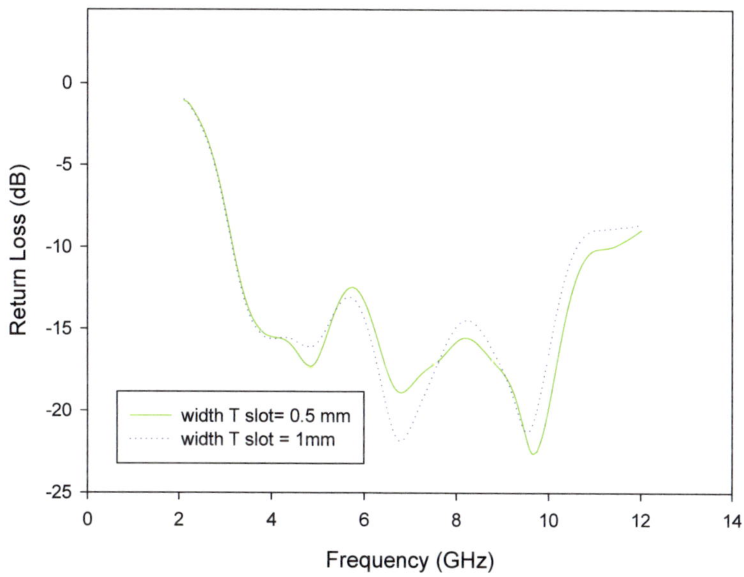

Fig. 12. The simulated return loss for various width of T slots design

Figure 12 shows the return loss of T slots with 0.5 mm and 1 mm width, respectively. From the results, there is not a significant effect to the antenna's return loss performance by decreasing the slot width. The optimum width is found to 1 mm.

3.2 Prototype and Measurement Results

The photograph of T slotted UWB antenna has been developed and shown in Figure 13. In this prototype, measurements are done by using a 50-Ω SMA connecter which is soldered at the bottom edge of microstrip line and connected to network analyzer by an RF cable. The RF cable significantly affects the performance of antenna under test. However, some differences in the simulated and measured results are expected, since in the simulation model the mismatch due to the adapter and connector used are not taken into consideration. In reality the coaxial cable has a considerable effect, especially the length of its inner conductor, which is connected to the input of the antenna, creating an additional inductance. In addition, since the antenna is fed by a microstrip line, misalignment can result because etching is required on both sides of the dielectric substrate. The alignment error results degradation to the antenna performance.

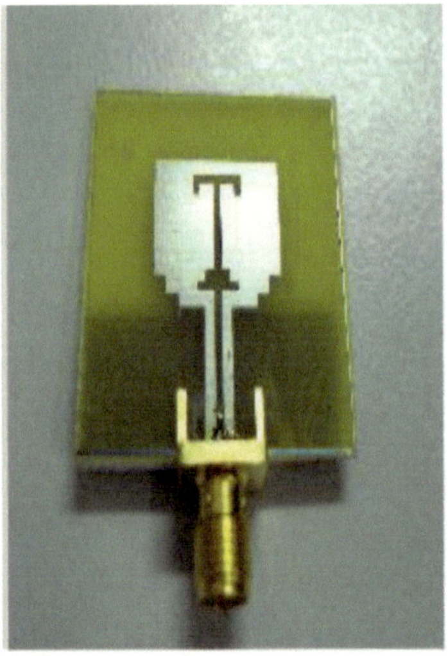

Fig. 13. Prototype of T slotted UWB antenna

As shown in Figure 14, the measured return loss curves for both T slotted antennas with and without slotted ground plane are reasonably close to the simulated results. It is shown that both results have produced multiple resonances frequencies, which shifted from the simulated resonances, but they are still covering the UWB bandwidth requirement. For T slotted antenna with slotted ground plane as shown in Figure 14(a), the frequency ranges cover 3 GHz to 10.23 GHz with respect to -10 dB of return loss. While the second antenna without slotted ground plane as shown in Figure 14(b), the return loss covers 2.3 GHz to 10.4 GHz. From this measured results, the antenna without slotted ground plane is better than the antenna with slotted ground plane in terms of the impedance bandwidth. This is due to the antenna with slotted ground plane need very accuracy in alignment between the slotted ground plane and patch on both sided of substrate during fabrication. The distance of patch to the ground plane is also very small of 0.5 mm. The misalignment occurred affects the impedance bandwidth. The measurements confirm the UWB characteristic of the proposed slotted UWB antennas, as predicted in the simulations.

From experimental experiences, the multiple resonances of return loss occurred on the proposed antennas are due to these antennas printed in the front of FR4 substrate. It has been investigated during the return loss measurement of many wideband antennas that have been developed. In addition, the FR4 substrate quality needs to be taken into consideration. It should be used within six months after purchased in order to avoid the oxidation process. The poor quality of FR4 substrate used produces a poor measured return loss and need longer time during etching process. Thus, perfect impedance match is not easily obtainable. These fabrication processes are important, because a slight error could result in major degradation in antenna performance.

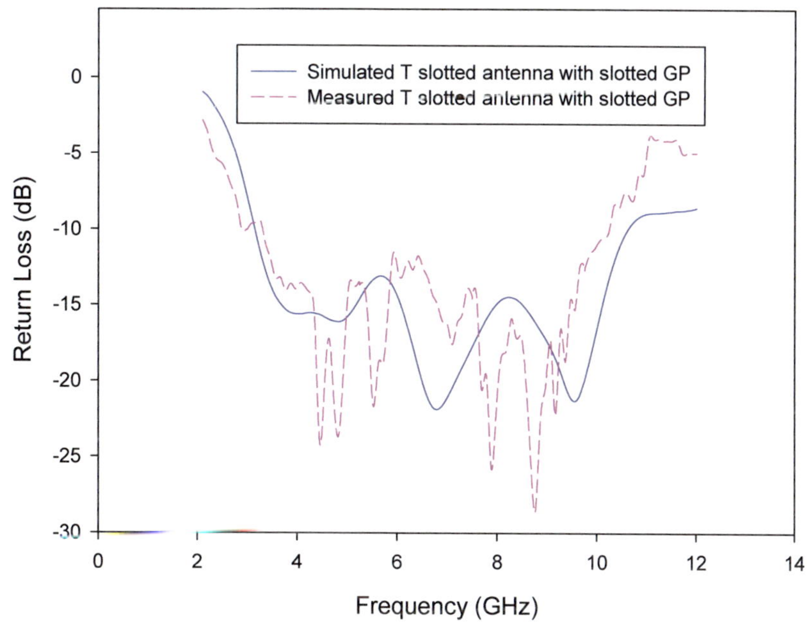

(a)

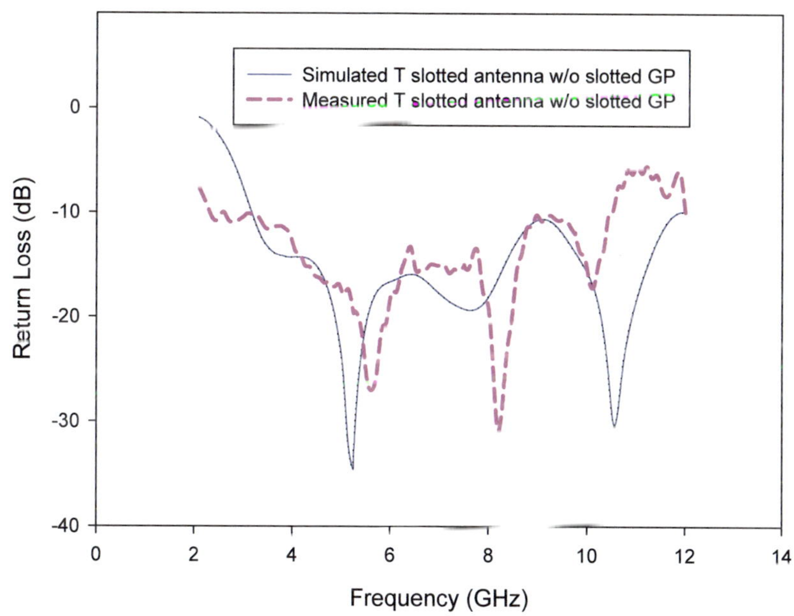

(b)

Fig. 14. The measured and simulated return loss for T slotted antenna: (a) with slotted ground plane and (b) without slotted ground plane

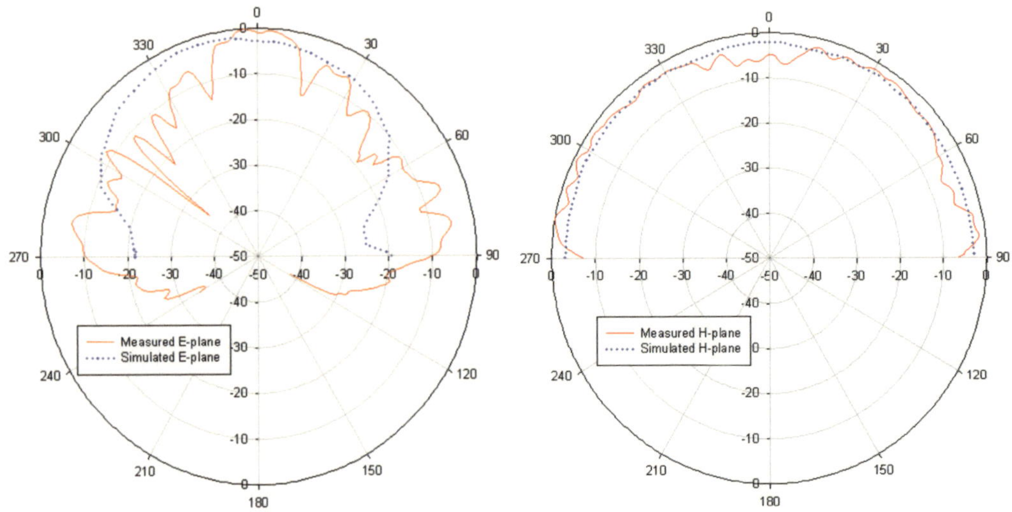

E-Plane H-Plane

(a)

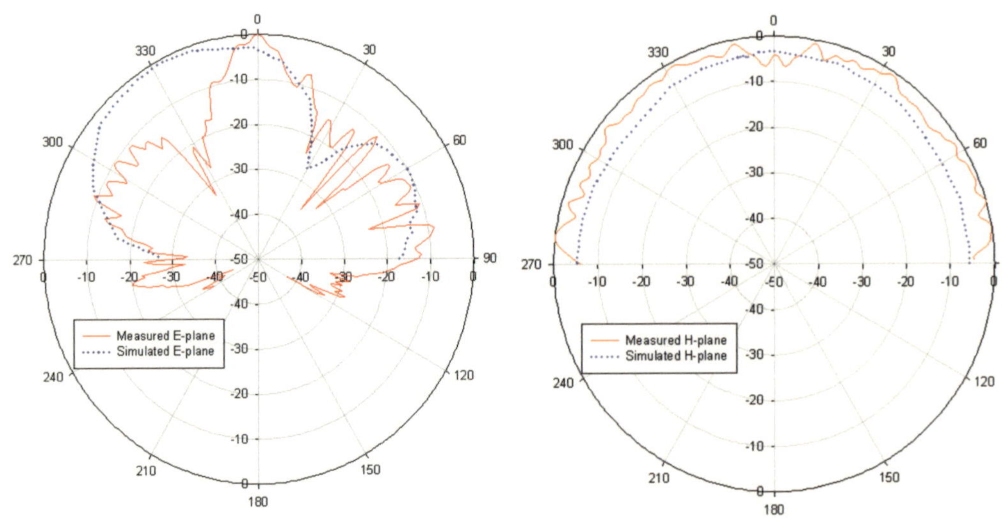

(b)

Fig. 15. The measured and simulated E and H planes (a) 4 GHz, (b) 5.8 GHz

The elevation patterns for the antennas are simulated at the H-plane ($\varphi = 0^0$, yz-plane) and E-plane ($\varphi = 90^0$, xy-plane). The E-plane pattern is the radiation pattern measured in a plane containing feed, and the H-plane pattern is the radiation pattern in a plane orthogonal to the E-plane. These both simulated results are compared to the measured H-plane and E-plane for 4 GHz and 5.8 GHz, as shown in Figure 15. The results show that the radiation patterns are changing as the frequency increases. The measured H-planes show omni-directional radiation pattern over the frequencies. The patterns resulted from the measurements have many ripples in amplitude due to many reflections into the field between the AUT and probe. The reflections may come from the room (floor and ceiling), chamber scattering, antenna holder itself and track inside the anechoic chamber. Various types of leakage occur are also considered as pattern degradation. The most significantly is probably from improper cable connectors allowing excitation of the outside surface (Gary E. Evans, 1990). Leakage will be added to the measured pattern as degradation.

It is also noted from Figure 15 that with increasing frequency to 5.8 GHz, the E-plane patterns become smaller. Many ripples occurred in this frequency. The dips also present for various different angles. Even though the measured radiation patterns are slightly difference to the simulated ones, since their patterns are nearly omni-directional and their return losses are less than -10 dB, this proposed antenna meets the UWB requirements.

4. Conclusion

This chapter presents the design and development of T slotted UWB antenna with slotted ground plane. Four matching techniques have been applied in order to meet the UWB requirements such as T slots for patch and feeding strip, truncation ground plane, slotted ground plane and cutting notches at the bottom of patch radiator. The T slot for both patch and feeding strip is as a novelty design in terms of slot type. Performance analysis in simulation software has been done before the actual prototype developed. The effect of various cutting notches at the bottom of patch radiator, the effect of truncation and slotted ground plane, and the effect of various T slots design with current distribution behavior to antenna performance have been evaluated.

The T slotted antenna with slotted ground plane has shown the return loss varies from -15 dB to -20 dB. However, during fabrication process, the slightly shifted impedance bandwidth has occurred. This is due to the antenna with slotted ground plane need very accuracy in alignment between the slotted ground plane and patch on both sided of substrate. The distance of patch to the ground plane is also very small of 0.5 mm, where is this distance as the impedance matching.

5. References

A. A. Eldek, (2006). Numerical analysis of a small ultra wideband microstrip-fed tap monopole antenna. *Progress In Electromagnetic Research*, PIER 65, pp.59-69.

Albert K. Y. Lai et al. (1992). A novel antenna for ultra-wideband application. *IEEE Transactions on Antennas and Propagation*. Vol. 40(7). July, 1992.

E. Guillanton et al. (1998). A new design tapered slot antenna for ultra-wideband applications. *Microwave Opt. Technol. Lett.* Vol. 19: 286-289.

Federal Communications Commission (FCC), (2002). *Revision of part 15 of the commission's rules regarding ultra-wideband transmission systems*. First Report and Order, ET Docket 98-153, FCC 02-48. April, 2002. http://www.fcc.gov.

Giuseppe R. and Max J Ammann, (2006). A novel small wideband monopole antenna. *Loughborough Antennas & Propagation Conference (LAPC)*, Loughborough University, UK, 11-12th April 2006.

Gary E. Evans. *Antenna Measurement Techniques*. Boston, London: Artech House. 1990.

Hassan Ghannoum, Serge Bories, and Raffaele D'Errico, (2006). Small-size UWB planar antenna and its behaviour in WBAN/WPAN applications. *IET seminar on Ultra wideband System, Technologies and Applications*, April 2006.

J. F. Zurcher and F. E. Gardiol, (1995). *Broadband Patch Antenna*. Norwood, MA: Artech House.

Kazuhiro Hirasawa and Misao Haneishi, (1992). *Analysis, design, and measurement of small and low profile antennas*. Artech House, Boston, London.

Liang Jianxin, (2006). *Antenna Study and Design for Ultra Wideband Communication Applications. PhD Thesis*. Queen Mary, University of London.

M. A. Peyrot Solis, G. M. Galvan Tejada, and H. Jardon Aguilar, (2005). State of the Art in Ultra-Wideband Antennas. *2nd International Conference on Electrical and Electronics Engineering (ICEEE) and XI Conference on Electrical Engineering (CIE 2005)*. Mexico City, Mexico. 101 - 105. September 7-9, 2005.

Mayhew Ridgers, G. (2004). Wideband Probe-feed microstrip patch antennas and modeling techniques. *Thesis PhD*, University of Pretoria, Electrical, Electronic and Computer Engineering.

N. P. Agrawall, G. Kumar, and K. P. Ray, (1998). Wide-Band Planar Monopole Antennas. *IEEE Transactions on Antennas and Propagation*. Vol. 46(2): 294-295. Feb, 1998.

R. Garg et al. (2001). *Microstrip Antenna Design Handbook*. Artech House.

Serge Boris, Christophe Roblin, and Alan Sibille, (2005). Dual stripline fed metal sheet monopoles for UWB terminal applications. *ANTEM*, Saint Malo, France, 15-17th June 2005.

Seok H. Choi, et al, (2004). A new ultra-wideband antenna for UWB applications. *Microwave and Optical Technology Letters*, Vol. 40, No.5, pp. 399-401, 5th March 2004.

T. Huynh and K. F. Lee, (1995). Single-layer single-patch wideband microstrip antenna. *Electronics Letters*, Vol. 31, No. 16, 3rd August 1995.

Y.X. Guo, K.M. Luk, K.F. Lee and Y.L. Chow, (1998). Double U-slot rectangular patch antenna. *Electronics Letters*, Vol. 34, No. 19, 17th September 1998.

Zhi Ning Chen, et al, (2006). Planar antennas. *IEEE Microwave Magazine*, Vol. 7, No. 6, Page(s): 63-73, December 2006.

Zhi Ning Chen et al, (2004). Considerations for Source Pulses and Antennas in UWB Radio Systems. *IEEE Transactions on Antennas and Propagation*. July, 2004. Vol. 52(7).

19

Slotted ultra wideband antenna for bandwidth enhancement

[1]Yusnita Rahayu , [2]Razali Ngah and [2]Tharek Abd. Rahman
[1]Faculty of Mechanical Engineering, Universiti Malaysia Pahang, Kuantan, Pahang
[2]Wireless Communication Centre (WCC), Faculty of Electrical Engineering, Universiti Teknologi Malaysia, Johor Bahru, Johor
Malaysia

1. Introduction

In choosing an antenna topology for ultra wideband (UWB) design, several factors must be taken into account including physical profile, compatibility, impedance bandwidth, radiation efficiency, and radiation pattern. The main challenge in UWB antenna design is achieving the very broad bandwidth with high radiation efficiency and small in size. Accordingly, many techniques to broaden the impedance bandwidth of small antennas and to optimize the characteristics of broadband antennas have been widely investigated in many published papers as listed in references. Some examples of the techniques used to improve the impedance bandwidth of the planar monopole antenna include the use of beveling technique (Z.N. Chen[a] et al., 2006), (Giuseppe R. & Max J. Ammann, 2006), (M.C Fabres[a] et al.,2005), semi-circular base (X.N. Qiu et al., 2005), cutting notches at bottom (Seok H. Choi, et al., 2004), (H. Ghannoum et al., 2006), an offset feeding (Z.N. Chen[a] et al., 2006), (Giuseppe R. & Max J. Ammann, 2006), (M. J. Ammann & Z. N. Chen, 2004), a shorting pin (Z.N. Chen[a] et al., 2006), (E. Lee et al., 1999), and a dual/triple feed (Z.N. Chen[a] et al., 2006), (S. Boris et al., 2005), (K.L. Wong et al., 2005), (H. Ghannoum et al., 2006), (E. Antonio-Daviu et al., 2003), magnetic coupling (N. Behdad & K. Sarabandi, 2005), folded-plate (D. Valderas et al.,2006), (Z.N. Chen et al., 2003), hidden stripline feed (E. Gueguen et al., 2005). The radiators may be slotted to improve the impedance matching, especially at higher frequency (Z.N. Chen[a] et al., 2006), (Z.N. Chen[b] et al., 2006). Planar monopole antennas are good candidates owing to their wide impedance bandwidth, omni-directional radiation pattern, compact and simple structure, low cost and ease of construction. Further detail on various bandwidth enhancement techniques will be discussed in section 2.

2. Various Bandwidth Enhancements

In order to fulfill the UWB antenna requirements, various bandwidth enhancement techniques for planar monopole antennas have been developed during last two decades. The recent trends in improving the impedance bandwidth of small antennas can be broadly divided into the following categories (T. Huynh & K. F. Lee, 1995), (Z.N. Chen[a] et al., 2006), (L. Jianxin, 2006), the first category is the leading of all categories in numbers and varieties. By varying the physical dimensions of the antenna, the frequency and bandwidth characteristics of the resulting UWB pulse could be adjusted (R. J. Fontana, 2004).

2.1 Various Geometry and Perturbations

Planar monopoles with a huge number of different geometries have been numerically characterized (Z.N. Chen[a] et al.,2006). Many techniques to broaden the impedance bandwidth of planar monopole antennas and to optimize the characteristics of these antennas have been widely investigated. Among all these techniques, the beveling technique was reported to yield maximum bandwidth. Various geometries and perturbations are used to introduce multiple resonances as well as input impedance matching. The input impedance is also extremely dependent on the feeding gap configuration (M.C. Fabres[b] et al., 2005). An example of beveling technique most currently used in literature review is shown in Figure 1.

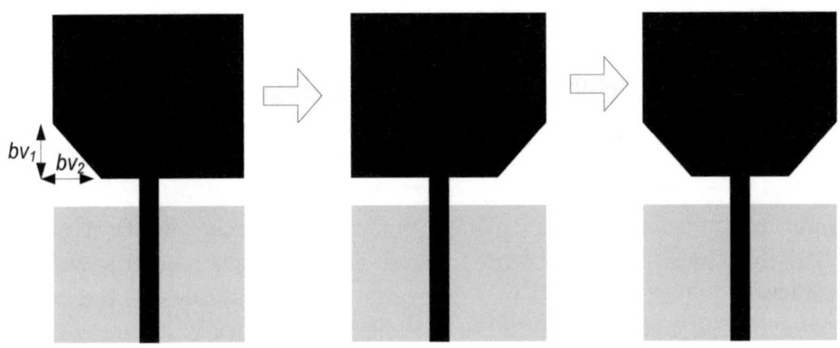

Fig. 1. An example of beveling technique

Beveling the bottom edge of the radiating element has been demonstrated to shift upward significantly the upper edge frequency when properly designed (Giuseppe R. & Max J. Ammann, 2006), (Z.N. Chen[b] et al.,2006), (M. J. Ammann & Z. N. Chen, 2003), (M. J. Ammann, 2001). The optimization of the shape of the planar antenna especially the shape of the bottom portion of the antenna, improve the impedance bandwidth by achieving smooth impedance transition (Z.N. Chen[a] et al., 2006). In fact, this part of the radiator results to be very critical for governing the capacitive coupling with the ground plane. Any reshaping of this area strongly affects the current path (Giuseppe R. & Max J. Ammann, 2006). The election and beveling angle is critical, as it determines the matching of the mode.

The patch radiator may be slotted to improve the impedance matching, especially at higher frequency. The slots cut from the radiators change the current distribution at the radiators so that the impedance at the input point and current path change (Z.N. Chen[a]et al., 2006). A notch is cut from radiator to reduce the size of the planar antenna (Z.N. Chen[b] et al., 2006). Adding a strip asymmetrically at the top of the radiator can also reduce the height of the antenna and improve impedance matching (A. Chai et al., 2005). An offset feeding point has been used in order to excite more modes and consequently improving the impedance bandwidth (M. J. Ammann & Z. N. Chen, 2004). By optimizing the location of the feed point, the impedance bandwidth of the antenna will be further widened because the input impedance is varied with the location of the feed point.

Moreover, other strategies to improve the impedance bandwidth which do not involve a modification of the geometry of the planar antenna have been investigated. Basically, these strategies consist of adding a shorting post to the structure or using two feeding points to excite the antenna (M.C. Fabres(b) et al., 2005). A shorting pin is also used to reduce the height of the antenna (E. Lee et al.,1999). In (Giuseppe R. & Max J. Ammann, 2006), the shorting pin inserted to the antenna that provides a broad bandwidth has been investigated. A dual feed structure greatly enhanced the bandwidth particularly at higher frequencies (E. Antonio-Daviu et al., 2003). By means of electromagnetic coupling (EMC) between the radiator and feeding strip, good impedance matching can be achieved over a broad bandwidth (Z.N. Chen(b) et al., 2003).

The use of double feeding configuration to the antenna structure is to enforce the vertical current mode, whereas it prevents other modes such as horizontal and asymmetrical current modes from being excited, which degrade the polarization properties and the impedance bandwidth performance of the antenna (H. Ghannoum et al., 2006), (Christophe Roblin et al., 2004), (E. Antonino-Daviu et al., 2003), (Eva Antonino et al., 2004). The double feeding gives a significant improvement of the vertical current distribution resulting in better matching notably over the upper-band part (S. Boris et al., 2005). The matching of this upper frequency band is mainly governed by two parameters: the distance between the two monopole ports and the height between the monopole and the ground plane (H. Ghannoum et al., 2006). In (E. Antonino-Daviu et al., 2003), a square monopole antenna with a double feed has been proposed. This feed configuration has shown the improvement on radiation pattern and impedance bandwidth. This is due to a pure and intense vertical current distribution generated in the whole structure.

The hidden feed-line technique on printed circular dipole antenna has been investigated in (E. Gueguen et al., 2005). The specific feeding has shown remove any radiation pattern disturbance generally met with this kind of antenna when fed with a coaxial or a microstrip line. It was also shown a wide frequency bandwidth.

Due to the radiation from planar antenna may not be omni-directional at all operating frequencies because they are not structurally rotationally symmetrical. Roll monopoles is a choice to feature broad impedance bandwidth with omni-directional characteristics (Z.N. Chen(a) et al., 2003). With the roll structure, the antenna becomes more compact and rotationally symmetrical in the horizontal plane. However, the roll monopoles are not easy to fabricate with high accuracy (Z.N. Chen(a) et al., 2006). The folded antenna was also presented in (Daniel Valderas et al., 2006) in order to improve radiation pattern maintaining the broadband behavior. In (Daniel Valderas et al., 2006), the antenna was analyzed employing transmission line model (TLM).

In (A.A. Eldek, 2006), various combinations of bandwidth enhancement techniques was successfully applied in UWB antenna design such as adding slit in one side of the monopole, tapered transition between the monopole and the feed line, and adding notched ground plane.

2.2 Genetic Algorithm (GA)

Optimization of patch geometry is an ideal technique to have single or more optimized figures of merit like, impedance bandwidth. The GA has been successfully applied by a number of researchers to improve the impedance bandwidth (Z.N. Chen et al., 2004), (A. J. Kerkhoff, 2001), (R. Holtzman et al., 2001), (A. J. Kerkhoff et al., 2004), (S. Xiao et al., 2003), (H. Choo & H. Ling, 2003). The optimized shape however is too much irregular and unconventional and this can only be fabricated using the pattern produced in true scale by the GA code.

Electromagnetic optimization problems generally involve a large number of parameters. The parameters can be either continuous, discrete, or both, and often include constraints in allowable values. The goal of the optimization is to find a solution that represents a global maximum or minimum. For example, the application of GA optimization is used to solve the problem of design a broadband patch antenna (Z.N. Chen et al., 2004). Parameters that are usually included in this type of optimization problem include the location of the feed probe, the width and length of the patch, and the height of the patch above the ground plane. In addition, it may be desirable to include constraints on the available dielectric materials, both in terms of thickness and dielectric constants; tolerance limits on the patch size and probe location; constraints on the weight of the final design; and possibly even cost constraints for the final production model. Given the large number of parameters, and the unavoidable mixture of discrete and continuous parameters involved in this problem, it is virtually impossible to use traditional optimization methods. GA optimizers, on the other hand, can readily handle such a disparate set of optimization parameters (Z.N. Chen et al., 2004).

The use of the GA approach in the design of UWB antennas has been proposed in (A. J. Kerkhoff, 2001), (R. Holtzman et al., 2001). The planar fully-metal monopole (PFMM) of bow tie (BT) and reverse bow tie (RBT) have been demonstrated in (A. J. Kerkhoff, 2001), (A. J. Kerkhoff et al., 2004) have an ultra wide bandwidth. The element height, the feed height, and the element flare angle were the parameters that used in optimization. The height essentially determines the operating mode and the lower frequency limit of the antenna, while the flare angle and the feed height control the variation of the input impedance over frequency, the high frequency impedance value, as well as the resonance bandwidth (A. J. Kerkhoff, 2001). In this paper, the GA was used to determine the optimal dimensions of the selected element shape in order to fulfill the given bandwidth requirement. As a result, the RBT antenna can achieve a much wider impedance bandwidth than the BT with significantly reduced sizes.

In (R. Holtzman et al., 2001), the semi-conical UWB antenna was optimized by using the Green's Function Method (GFM) Absorbing Boundary Condition (ABC) with GA. The goal of this optimization is to have significant reduction in the size of the white space, due to the unique capability of the GFM to model arbitrarily shaped boundaries in close proximity to the antenna. The white space is defined as the region between the antenna and the absorbing boundary.

The GA optimizer is also used to reconfigure the radiation characteristics of antenna over an extremely wide-band (S. Xiao et al., 2003). The design results indicate that the antenna can obtain the required goals over an ultra-wide band through reconfiguring the states of the switch array installed in shared aperture when it operates with the higher order modes (S.

Xiao et al., 2003). Optimization of broadband and dual-band microstrip antennas on a high-dielectric substrate by using GA was also proposed in (H. Choo & H. Ling, 2003).

2.3 Resonance Overlapping

Normally, the bandwidth of a resonant antenna is not very broad because it has only one resonance. But if there are two or more resonant parts available with each one operating at its own resonance, the overlapping of these multiple resonances may lead to multi-band or broadband performance.

Theoretically, an ultra wide bandwidth can be obtained if there are a sufficient number of resonant parts and their resonances can overlap each other well. However, in practice, it is more difficult to achieve impedance matching over the entire frequency range when there are more resonant parts. Also, it will make the antenna structure more complicated and more expensive to fabricate. Besides, it is more difficult to achieve constant radiation properties since there are more different radiating elements.

3. Slotted UWB Antenna Design and Development

From various bandwidth enhancement techniques, there are three techniques adopted for this proposed UWB antennas design. The three techniques are the use of slots, truncation ground plane, and cutting notches at the bottom which can lead to a good impedance bandwidth. By selecting these parameters, the proposed antenna can be tuned to operate in UWB frequency range. The performance optimization is done by studying their current distribution. The photograph and current distribution behavior of proposed slotted UWB antenna is shown in Figure 2.

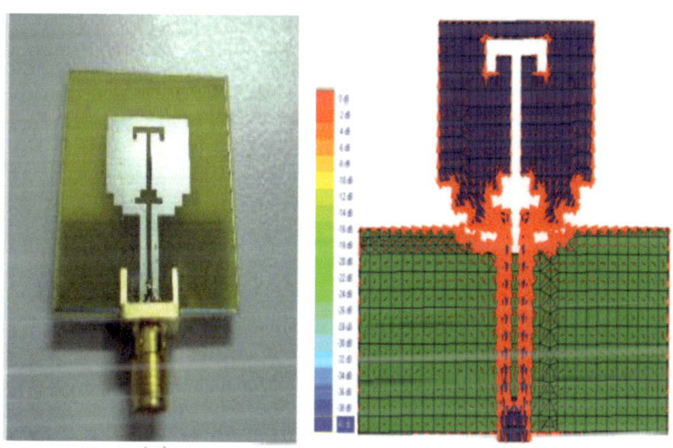

(a) (b)

Fig. 2. (a) Photograph, (b) current distribution with slot

The geometry of antenna originates from conventional rectangular monopole and is realized by adding T slot for both patch and feeding strip. This geometry is taken as initial geometry due to the flexibility of this geometry to be modified. The T slot cutting on patch and feeding strip has disturbed the current direction thus provide a broad bandwidth. This is due to the geometry of an antenna implies the current courses, as shown in Figure 2(b), and make it

possible to identify active and neutral zones in the antenna. Therefore, it will be possible to fix which elements will act on each characteristic. The active zone is the matching and radiator zone. Zone closed to feeding point is the active zone. As shown in Figure 2(b), much current density occurs closed to the feeding edge, while at the top of antenna; the current levels are not too strong. The neutral zones where geometry modifications are useless because neither the radiation pattern nor the matching bandwidth is much influenced.
To better control an antenna behavior, it is necessary to identify neutral zones. The neutral zone can be used to simplify the antenna structure and integrate other function of the systems such as antenna circuits. This investigation has been proposed in (Pele I. et al., (2004), but not much explanation given particularly determine the neutral zone.
The antenna has a compact dimension of 30 mm x 30 mm (W_{sub} x L_{sub}), designed on FR4 substrate with thickness of 1.6 mm and relative dielectric constant (ε_r) of 4.7. The radiator is fed by a microstrip line of 3 mm width (w_f). On the front surface of the substrate, a rectangular patch with size of 15 mm x 12 mm (w x l) is printed. The two notches size of 1.5 mm x 12 mm (w_1 x l_1) and 1 mm x 9 mm (w_2 x l_2) are at the two lower corners of radiating patch. The distance of h between the rectangular patch to ground plane printed on the back surface substrate is 1 mm, and the length (l_{grd}) of truncated ground plane of 11.5 mm. The excitation is a 50 Ω microstrip line printed on the partial grounded substrate. The slot size of w_s, w_{s1}, w_{s2}, w_{s3}, l_{s1}, l_{s2}, l_{s3} are 1, 5, 3, 6, 11, 7, 2 mm, respectively.

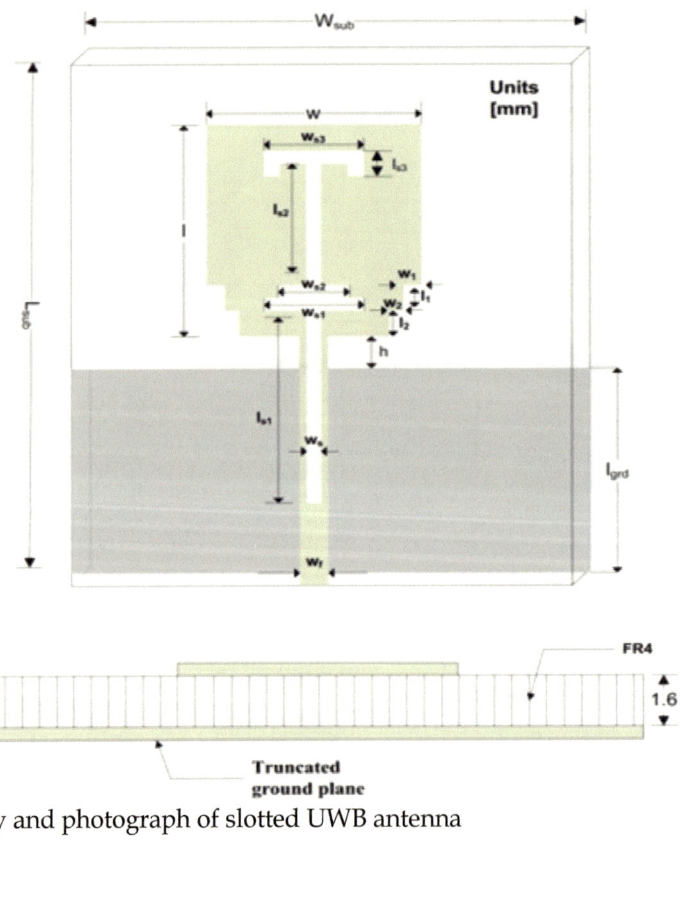

Fig. 3. Geometry and photograph of slotted UWB antenna

Figure 3 shows the geometry of proposed UWB antenna. The slot shapes are designed very carefully by studying the current flow distribution. The discontinuity occurred from cutting notches at the bottom side of a rectangular antenna has enforced the excitation of vertical current mode in the structure. The T slot on the feeding strip produces more vertical current thus improve the matching impedance performance at higher frequencies. The length of the T slot on the feeding strip is designed approximately equal to at 10.5 GHz. While the T slot cutting on the patch provides return loss improvement at 5.2 GHz. Thus, the slot wideband behavior is due to the fact that the current along the edges of the slot introduce the same resonance frequencies, which, in conjunction with resonance of the main patch, produce an overall broadband frequency response characteristic. The effect of T slots to the return loss of antenna is shown in Figure 4.

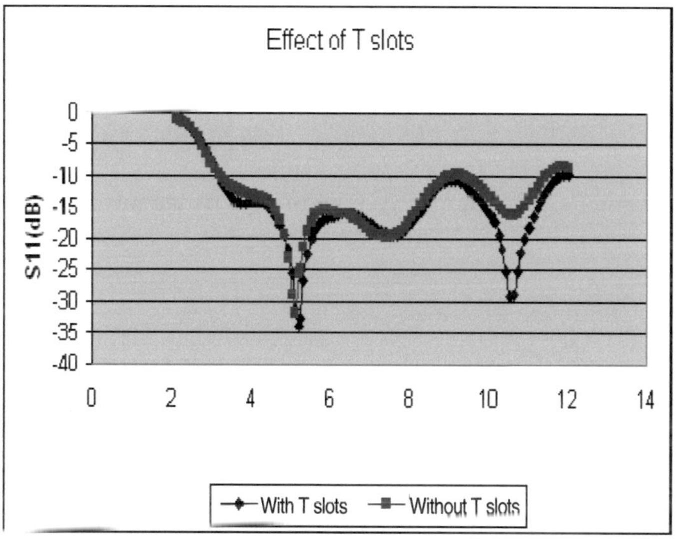

Fig. 4. The effect of T slots to the return loss of antenna

Figure 4 shows the effect of T slots to the antenna performance. From the graph, at upper frequency of 10.5 GHz, the $|S_{11}|$ reaches -30 dB. The bandwidth enhancement is due to much more vertical electrical current achieved in the patch through the T slots resulting in much regular distribution of the magnetic current in the slots. The use of slot embedded on the microstrip patch shows as the most successful technique utilized a coupled resonator approach, in which the microstrip patch acts as one of the resonator and slot as the second resonator near its resonance. In this case, the bandwidth broadening comes from the patch and T-slots, coupled together to form two resonances.

Matching bandwidth is due to the shape of the antenna closed to the feeding point, where currents are strongest. The field supported by these currents would be mainly confined between the bottom part of the rectangular antenna and the ground plane; this is due to the small distance, a small fraction of wavelength, of this edge to the ground plane (D. Valderas et al., 2006). Thereby, this part acts as a matching element.

The study of the current flow on a planar monopole antenna reveals that it is mostly concentrated in the vertical and horizontal edges, as shown in Figure 5. It is observed that the horizontal currents distributions are focused on the bottom edge of rectangular patch. Besides, the horizontal component is also greater than the vertical on this part of the antenna. From Figure 5, it shows that two types current distribution modes occurred on patch radiator and feeding strip such as vertical current mode and horizontal current mode.

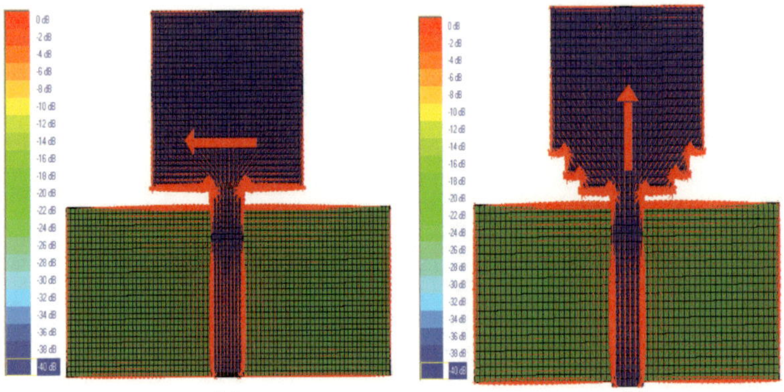

(a) (b)

Fig. 5. Simulated current distribution (a) rectangular, (b) rectangular with two notches at the bottom

Cutting notches at the bottom techniques are aimed to change the distance between the lower part of the planar monopole antenna and the ground plane. The simulated return loss, as shown in Figure 6, covers 3.17 GHz to 11.5 GHz of frequency ranges. The slot also appears to introduce a capacitive reactance which counteracts the inductive reactance of the feed.

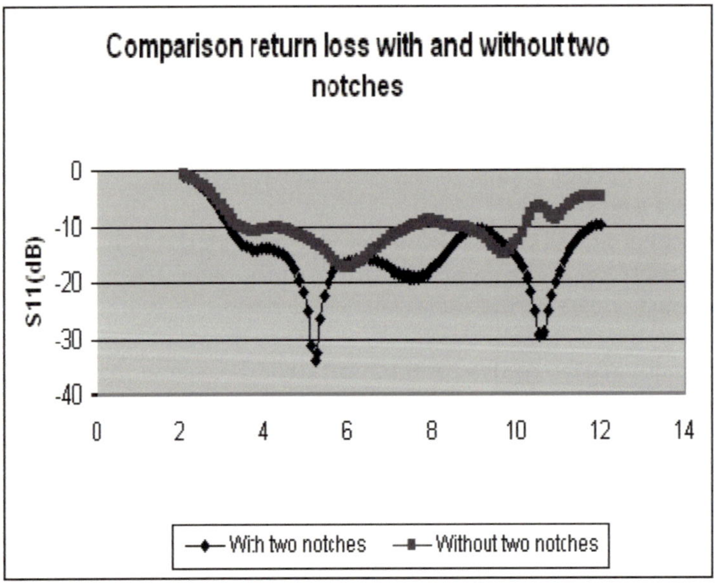

Fig. 6. Comparison of return loss for antenna with and without two notches at the bottom

Figure 6 shows the simulated return loss for both antennas with and without two notches cutting at the bottom edges. Figure 6 shows that the return loss performance of antenna without two notches at the bottom starts degrading its performance at 7.5 GHz, this is due to more horizontal current mode occurs in the whole structure which degrade the polarization properties and the impedance bandwidth performance of the antenna, as shown in Figure 5. In order to modify the equivalent characteristic impedance on the antenna, the distance of the bottom edge to the ground plane and the bottom profile of the monopole should be varied. By varying the edges closed to the feeding point means modifying the current path on the antenna.

The simulated input impedance for antenna with one notch, two notches, and three notches cutting at the bottom edges are also performed and shown in Figure 7. It shows that the loops around matching impedance (50 ohm), which is located at the centre of smith chart. It also shows that the one step and three steps notches cutting at the bottom give more capacitive to the antenna than the two steps notches especially at higher frequency ranges. The ground plane as an impedance matching circuit and also it tunes the resonant frequencies.

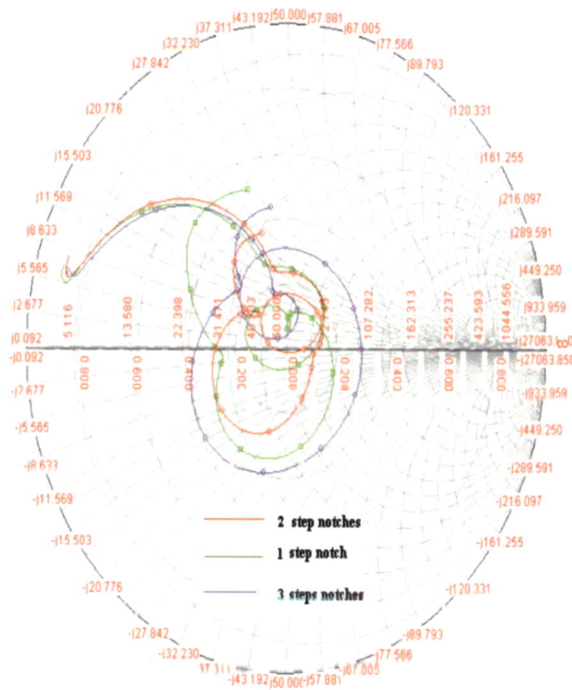

Fig. 7. Simulated input impedance for various notches

Figure 8 shows the simulated current distribution of the proposed antenna at three different frequencies. It shows that the current density decreasing by increasing the frequency. Most vertical electrical current is distributed near to T slot edges rather than distributed on the antenna surface.

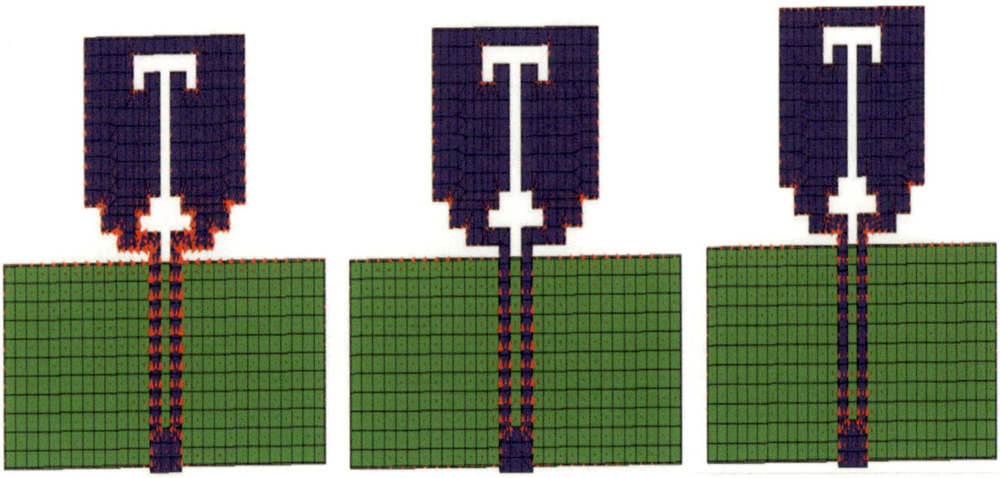

(a) (b) (c)

Fig. 8. Simulated current distribution at (a) 3GHz, (b) 6.5 GHz, (c) 10.5 GHz

To validate the simulation results, an antenna prototype was fabricated and tested. In this prototype, measurements are done by using a coaxial port which is soldered at the bottom edge of microstrip line. However, some differences in the simulated and measured results are expected, since in the simulation model discrete and not coaxial port is used. In reality the coaxial cable has a considerable effect, especially the length of its inner conductor, which is connected to the input of the antenna, creating an additional inductance.

The simulated and measured return losses are plotted in Figure 9. The resonance frequencies are shifted from the simulated result but they are still covering the UWB bandwidth requirement. The return loss curves of frequency ranges above 10.5 GHz are getting worst. In addition, since the antenna is fed by microstrip line, misalignment can result because etching is required on both sides of the dielectric substrate. The alignment eroror results degradation to the antenna performance.

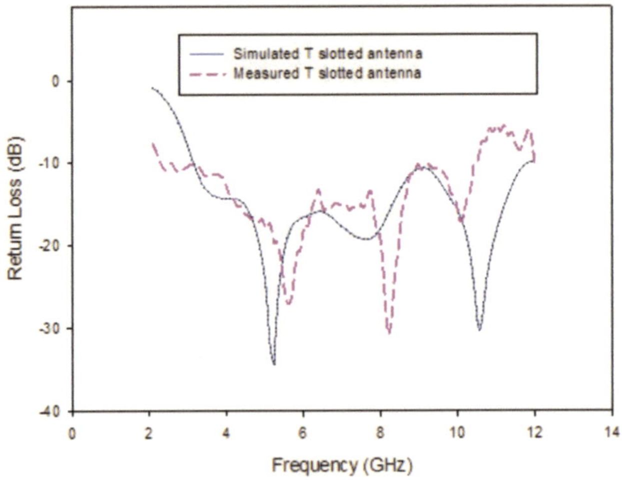

Fig. 9. The simulated and measured return loss

Once the resonance frequencies were identified, principal radiation patterns were taken to characterize the operational performance of antenna. These measurements were obtained using indoor anechoic chamber room. Several requirements are needed to take into consideration during the measurement process. Obtaining true patterns depends primarily on accurately positioning the probe, accurately measuring the field, and eliminating distortions in the field introduced by the room, track, or probe itself. The room reflections must be lower than the basic side-lobe level, the probe itself must have low reflections and accurate position.

The measured radiation patterns were plotted into horizontal (H) and vertical (V) cuts. The H-cut is cut for the azimuth plane with fixed elevation angle at 0^0 and vary the azimuth angle. The V-cut is cut for the elevation plane with fixed azimuth angle at 0^0 and vary the elevation angle.

The existing chamber employed the spherical near field measurement as shown in Figure 10. By definition, near field tests are done by sampling the field very close to the antenna on a known surface. From the phase and amplitude data collected, the far field pattern must be computed in much the same fashion that theoretical patterns are computed from theoretical field distributions. The transformation used in the computation depends on the shape of the surface over which the measurements are taken with the scanning probe (Gary E. Evans, 1990).

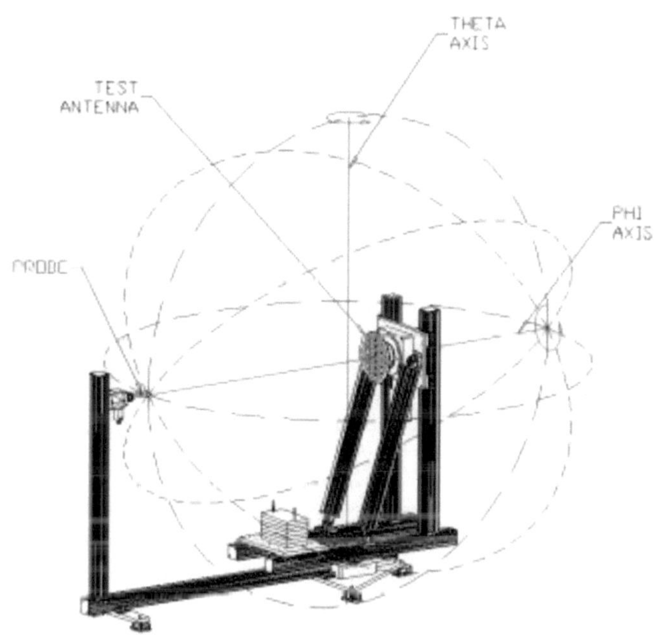

Fig. 10. Coordinate system for typical spherical near-field rotator system (G. Hindman & A.C. Newell, 2004)

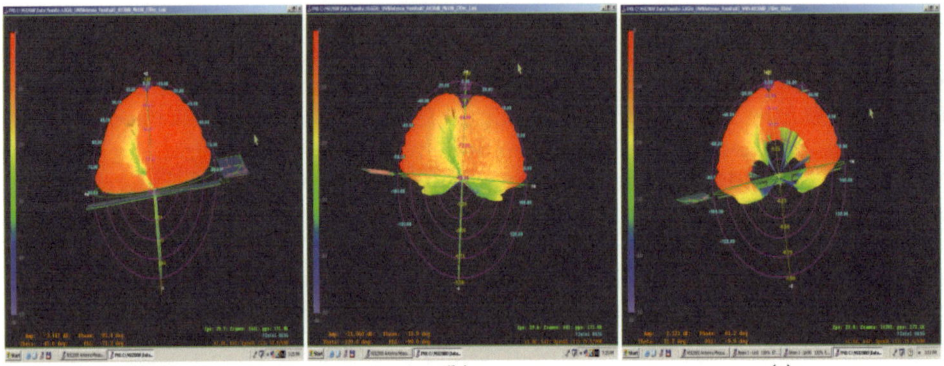

(a) (b) (c)

Fig. 11. Measured Radiation Pattern at (a) 4GHz, (b) 5.8GHz, (c)10.6 GHz

The elevation patterns for the antennas are simulated at the H-plane (φ = 0^0, yz-plane) and E-plane (φ = 90^0, xy-plane). The E-plane pattern is the radiation pattern measured in a plane containing feed, and the H-plane pattern is the radiation pattern in a plane orthogonal to the E-plane. The measured 3D radiation patterns of the antenna are shown in Figure 11 at frequencies 4 GHz, 5.8 GHz, and 10.6 GHz. The radiation patterns are nearly omni-directional.

4. Conclusion

In this chapter, various bandwidth enhancement techniques have been presented. The T slotted antenna has been designed and developed. Three bandwidth enhancement techniques were adopted in order to produce a small slotted UWB antenna. This proposed antenna uses two notches, T slot and a partial ground plane. An experimental prototype has been fabricated and tested. It shows that the measured return loss covering the UWB bandwidth requirements of 3.1 GHz - 10.6 GHz with respect to -10 dB. The measured radiation patterns of this prototype are also presented at frequencies 4, 5.8, and 10.6 GHz, respectively.

5. References

A. A. Eldek, (2006). Numerical analysis of a small ultra wideband microstrip-fed tap monopole antenna. *Progress In Electromagnetic Research*, PIER 65, pp.59-69.

A. Cai et al., (2005). Study of human head effects on UWB antenna. *in Proc. IEEE Intl. Workshop on Antenna Technology (iWAT)*. Singapore. Mar. 7–9, 2005. 310–313.

A. J. Kerkhoff et al., (2004). Design and analysis of planar monopole antennas using a genetic algorithm approach. *IEEE Transactions on Antennas and Propagation*. October, 2004. Vol. 52(10): 2709-2718.

A. J. Kerkhoff, (2001). The Use of Genetic Algorithm Approach in the Design of Ultra-Wide Band Antennas. *Proceedings of IEEE Radio and Wireless Conference (RAWCON) 2001*. Boston, MA. August 19-22, 2001.

C. Roblin et al., (2004). Antenna design, analysis and numerical modeling for impulse UWB. *International Symposium on Wireless Personal Multimedia Communication (WPMC) 2004 (Ultrawaves invited communication)*. Abano Terme, Italy. Sept. 12–15, 2004.

D. Valderas et al., (2006). Design of UWB folded-plate monopole antennas based on TLM. *IEEE Transactions on Antennas and Propagation*, Vol. 54, No. 6, pp. 1676-1687, June 2006.

E. Gueguen et al., (2005). A low cost UWB printed dipole antenna with high performance. *IEEE International Conference on Ultra Wideband (ICU)*, Zurich, 5-8th Sept, 2005.

Eva Antonino et al., (2004). Design of very wide-band linear-polarized antennas. Zeland Publication.

E. Antonio-Daviu et al., (2003). Wideband double-fed planar monopole antennas. *Electronics Letters*, Vol. 39, No. 23, pp. 1635-1636, November 2003.

E. Lee et al., (1999). Compact wide-band planar monopole antenna. *Electronics Letters*, Vol. 35, No. 25, pp. 2157-2158, December 1999.

Giuseppe R. & Max J. Ammann, (2006). A novel small wideband monopole antenna. *Loughborough Antennas & Propagation Conference (LAPC)*, Loughborough University, UK, 11-12th April 2006.

H. Ghannoum et al., (2006). Small-size UWB planar antenna and its behavior in WBAN/WPAN applications. *IET seminar on Ultra wideband System, Technologies and Applications*, April 2006.

H. Choo and H. Ling, (2003). Design of broadband and dual-band microstrip antennas on a high-dielectric substrate using a genetic algorithm. *IEE Proc. Microwave Antenna Propagation*. June, 2003. Vol. 150(3).

K. L. Wong, Chih Hsien Wu, and Saou Wen Su, (2005). Ultrawide-band square planar metal plate monopole antenna with trident-shaped feeding strip. *IEEE Transactions on Antennas and Propagation*, Vol. 53, No. 4, pp. 1262-1269, April 2005.

Liang Jianxin, (2006). *Antenna Study and Design for Ultra Wideband Communication Applications. PhD Thesis*. Queen Mary, University of London.

Pele I. et al., (2004). Antenna design with control of radiation pattern and frequency bandwidth. *Antennas and Propagation Society International Symposium*. IEEE.

Marta Cabedo Fabres(a) et al.,(2005). On the influence of the shape of planar monopole antennas in the impedance bandwidth performance. *International Union of Radio Science (URSI)*.

Marta Cabedo Fabres(b) et al., (2005). "On the influence of the shape of planar monopole antennas in the impedance bandwidth performance, "*Microwave and Optical Technology Letters*, Vol. 44, No. 3, Feb 2005.

M. J. Ammann and Z. N. Chen, (2004). An asymmetrical feed arrangement for improved impedance bandwidth of planar monopole antennas. *Microwave Optical Technology Letters*, Vol. 40, No. 2, pp. 156-158.

M. J. Ammann and Z. N. Chen, (2003). A wideband shorted planar monopole with bevel. *IEEE Trans. Antennas and Propagation*, Vol. 51(4), pp. 901-903.

M. J. Ammann, (2001). Control of the impedance bandwidth of wideband planar monopole antennas using a beveling technique. *Microwave. Opt. Tech. Letters*. July, 2001. Vol. 30(4): 229–232.

Nehdar Behdad and Kamal Sarabandi, (2005). A compact antenna for ultra wideband applications. *IEEE Transactions on Antennas and Propagation*, Vol. 53, No. 7, pp. 2185-2192, July 2005.

R. Holtzman et al., (2001). Ultra wideband antenna design using the Green's function method (GFM) ABC with genetic algorithm. *Antennas and Propagation Society International Symposium*. IEEE.

Serge Boris, Christophe Roblin, and Alan Sibille, (2005). Dual stripline fed metal sheet monopoles for UWB terminal applications. *ANTEM*, Saint Malo, France, 15-17th June 2005.

Seok H. Choi, et al., (2004). A new ultra-wideband antenna for UWB applications. *Microwave and Optical Technology Letters*, Vol. 40, No.5, pp. 399-401, March 5th 2004.

Shaqiu Xiao et al., (2003). Reconfigurable microstrip antenna design based on genetic algorithm. *Antennas and Propagation Society International Symposium*. IEEE.

T. Huynh and K. F. Lee, (1995). Single-layer single-patch wideband microstrip antenna. *Electronics Letters*. August 3, 1995. Vol. 31(16).

Xiao Ning Qiu, H. M. Chiu, and A. S. Mohan, (2005). Investigation on a class of modified planar monopole antennas for ultra-wideband performance. *9th Australian Symposium on Antennas*, Sydney, Australia, 16-17th Feb 2005.

Zhi Ning Chen[a] et al., (2006). Planar antennas. *IEEE Microwave Magazine*, Vol. 7, No. 6, Page(s): 63-73, December 2006.

Zhi Ning Chen[b], Terence S. P. See, and Xianming Qing, (2006). Small ground-independent planar UWB antenna. *IEEE Antennas and Propagation Society International Symposium*, pp. 1635-1638, 9-14th July 2006.

Zhi Ning Chen et al., (2004). Considerations for source pulses and antennas in UWB radio systems. *IEEE Transactions on Antennas and Propagation*. July, 2004. Vol. 52(7).

Z. N. Chen[a], M.Y.W. Chia, and M. J. Ammann, (2003). Optimization and comparison of broadband monopoles. *IEE Proceeding Microwave Antenna Propagation*, Vol. 150, No. 6, pp. 429-435, December 2003.

Z. N. Chen[b] et al., (2003). Circular annular planar monopoles with EM coupling. *Proc. Inst. Elect. Eng. Microw Antennas, Propagat.* Aug., 2003. Vol. 150(4): 269–273.